Warriors of God

Warriors of God

INSIDE HEZBOLLAH'S

THIRTY-YEAR STRUGGLE

AGAINST ISRAEL

NICHOLAS BLANFORD

RANDOM HOUSE

NEW YORK

Copyright © 2011 by Nicholas Blanford

Published in the United States by Random House,
an imprint of The Random House Publishing Group,
a division of Random House, Inc., New York.

Random House and colophon are registered
trademarks of Random House, Inc.

Library of Congress Cataloging-in-Publication Data
Blanford, Nicholas.
Warriors of god: inside Hezbollah's thirty-year struggle against Israel /
By Nicholas Blanford.—1st ed.
p.   cm.
Includes bibliographical references and index.
ISBN 978–1-4000–6836–4 (alk. paper)—ISBN 978–0-679–60516–4 (eBook)
1. Shi'ah—Lebanon—History.   2. Hezbollah (Lebanon)   3. Lebanon—
Military relations—Israel.   4. Israel—Military relations—Lebanon.   I. Title.
DS80.55.S54B53 2011
956.9204'5—dc22   2011012620

Printed in the United States of America on acid-free paper

www.atrandom.com

2 4 6 8 9 7 5 3 1

First Edition

Book design by Jo Anne Metsch

For Yasmine and Alexander

Contents

Introduction

CAMP SHAMROCK, Tibnine, south Lebanon—Like a stream of red ellipses, machine gun tracer rounds arched lazily across the inky night sky. Every few moments, a vivid white flash from an exploding artillery shell revealed for a microsecond the distant ridge line and the volcano-shaped silhouette of the outpost above Haddatha village, manned by Israeli-allied Lebanese militiamen and under attack by Hezbollah.

This was my first view of the fighting in south Lebanon and I was watching it with a cup of coffee alongside several Irish United Nations peacekeepers. The location of the Irish battalion's headquarters granted it a clear southward view across a shallow stony valley to the ridge that marked the edge of Israel's occupation zone.

To me, the battle unfolding a mile and a half away was a confusing kaleidoscope of colored lights and loud bangs. To the Irish officers, however, this was purely routine, an event they had witnessed many times. They sipped coffee, nonchalantly discussed where Hezbollah's mortars were probably located, and remarked on the improving accuracy of their bombardments.

This minor attack—recorded by the UN mission, known as UNIFIL, in one of many soon-forgotten "shoot reps"—came during a period in which Hezbollah was gradually shedding its Lebanese civil-war image as a shadowy band of kidnappers and suicide bombers, and emerging in the public eye as a resourceful guerrilla army recording a growing number of battlefield successes against the Israeli occupiers of southern Lebanon.

Hezbollah had surfaced twelve years earlier, in the wake of Israel's 1982 invasion of Lebanon. Few would have guessed at the time that this ragtag group of Shia militants, who drew guidance from Iran's Ayatollah Ruhollah Khomeini and inspiration from the martyrdom of the sect's founders fourteen centuries earlier, would survive the civil war—let alone become the dominant political and military force in Lebanon three decades later.

Indeed, it is extraordinary to contemplate that Lebanon, a country half the size of Connecticut, with no natural resources, fractious demographics, and an opaque sectarian political system, could give rise to an organization that has grown into the most powerful nonstate military group in the world.

In late 1996, when I began covering the conflict in south Lebanon for *The Daily Star*, Lebanon's English-language newspaper, Hezbollah's post-civil-war military evolution was fully underway. Back then, however, its weapons and tactics were comparatively rudimentary and appropriate for its guerrilla-style methods. It was a conflict largely overlooked by the rest of the world, which had lost interest in Lebanon once the last Western hostages were released in the early 1990s. But it was a fascinating conflict to observe nonetheless. I soon learned to navigate the potholed lanes winding through the steep stony hills of the frontline district, and gradually built up a network of contacts on the ground. I studied military manuals, absorbing data on the weapons systems used by both sides, and scrounged ever more detailed maps of southern Lebanon, marking with a red pen the front line and the locations of outposts manned by Israeli troops and their South Lebanon Army militia allies.

There was an element of the routine about Hezbollah's deadly roadside bomb attacks and the daily mortar barrages of Israeli and SLA outposts. Sometimes I would sit on the flat roof of the restored Crusader fortress in Tibnine and watch the puffs of smoke from mortar shells blossoming against distant SLA compounds and hear the metallic crack of exploding Israeli artillery rounds. It was easy to be lulled into a false sense of security by these daily tit-for-tat exchanges. But the conflict also had the ability to quickly spiral out of control and then south Lebanon became a very dangerous place indeed.

By the late 1990s, it was evident that Hezbollah had all but won its campaign of resistance. The Israeli military simply could not dent Hezbollah's attacks, and the steady flow of troop casualties helped turn the Israeli public against the occupation. When Israel finally abandoned the occupation zone in three desperate days in May 2000, it was a truly historic moment—the first time the Jewish state had been forced to yield occupied land by the force of Arab arms.

It was around that time that I began to mull a book tracing Hezbollah's military evolution from 1982 to its successful culmination in Israel's retreat from south Lebanon. Yet it soon transpired that that eighteen-year struggle was merely a precursor for what was to come next. The daily battles may have ended in May 2000 but the struggle continued, as Hezbollah in great secrecy morphed from an efficient guerrilla force using hit-and-run tactics into a crack infantry division capable of defending ground and defeating Israel's top-line battle tanks. The scale of the transformation between 2000 and the outbreak of war in 2006 dwarfed the military advances of the previous decade. That evolution continued after the 2006 war, as Hezbollah and Israel absorbed the lessons of that conflict and prepared for the next one. Some of the military hardware at Hezbollah's disposal today would not look out of place in the arsenal of a medium-sized European state.

And yet, Hezbollah's massive military expansion has inevitably brought it into conflict with non-Shia fellow Lebanese, who fear the party's ideological and material ties to Iran and its determination to keep its weapons at all costs to pursue the confrontation with Israel. Hezbollah's struggle against Israel since 2000 has been matched by an internal tussle against its domestic critics. Lebanon's complicated sectarian demography—with nineteen official sects squeezed into its cramped coastal cities, shadowed valleys, and soaring mountains—and recent history of communal strife has forced the Lebanese to embrace the gospel of consensus to maintain internal stability. Lebanon is a country that has been racked by civil conflict since long before the modern state was established in 1920. Although the Christian Maronites and the Muslim Sunnis and Shias are the three largest sects, none has sufficient weight to dominate all the others. As a result, Lebanon's feuding communal leaders traditionally look to external backing to grant them influence over their domestic rivals. By the same token, foreign powers, both regional and international, are drawn into supporting Lebanese proxies to gain greater leverage against their own rivals in a geostrategically significant slice of real estate on the eastern Mediterranean. This symbiotic relationship between domestic client and foreign patron was evident as long ago as the mid-nineteenth century when the British backed the Druze, the French sponsored the Maronites, and the Sunnis were championed by the Ottomans. The same dynamic continues to endure today with the West, chiefly the United States, France, and Saudi Arabia, backing a mainly Sunni and Christian coalition while Iran and Syria support Hezbollah and its allies.

To defend its resistance priority, Hezbollah has steadily immersed itself in Lebanon's political milieu since the end of the civil war in 1990. Each time it has faced a fresh challenge over its weapons, Hezbollah has taken another unwanted but necessary step into the unforgiving morass of Lebanese politics. Indeed, at the time of writing, Hezbollah effectively controls the levers of power in Lebanon, not only through the *force majeure* of its formidable military apparatus but also by wielding paramount influence over the government of Prime Minister Najib Mikati.

It is easy to imagine Sayyed Hassan Nasrallah, Hezbollah's charismatic leader, sometimes reflecting fondly on those heady days in the mid-1990s when his party had the broad backing of the Lebanese to pursue its resistance campaign and, parliamentary representation notwithstanding, did not have to sully itself too much with the sordid trade-offs and quid pro quos of daily Lebanese politics.

Instead, as I write this introduction, Hezbollah is facing some of the gravest challenges in its thirty-year existence: in June 2011, two senior Hezbollah figures were indicted by an international tribunal based in the Netherlands for their alleged involvement in the assassination of Rafik Hariri, an iconic former Lebanese prime minister. Hezbollah has disavowed the tribunal, accusing it of being a political tool of the West and Israel to defang the "resistance." There is some justification to such charges. The original UN investigation into Hariri's 2005 murder and the subsequent tribunal would not have existed without the support of the United States and France, both of which were at the time at odds with the Syrian regime, which was widely suspected of ordering Hariri's assassination. A UN-endorsed investigation into the murder was seen as a useful means of placing pressure on Damascus. Few doubt that if Israel had been the chief suspect, there never would have been an international investigation or tribunal. The fact that the investigation took an unexpected turn toward Hezbollah was an additional boon for the party's opponents, but it only reinforced the belief among Hezbollah's supporters that the judicial process was being manipulated by the party's Western enemies. It is most unlikely that the two Hezbollah officers will ever stand trial, yet regardless of the veracity of the charges against them, the party's carefully cultivated image as a successful resistance force against Israel has been irredeemably tarnished. Instead of lauding Hezbollah's resistance exploits, many Arab Sunnis now view the Shia party as a gang of contract killers in the pay of Syria and Iran.

Still, the impact of the Hariri investigation on Hezbollah pales in comparison to the more pressing dilemma posed by the unprecedented wave of street protests against the regime of Bashar al-Assad, the Syrian president, which broke out in March 2011 and threatens to bring an end to forty years of Assad dynasty rule.

The so-called "Arab Spring" protests began in January in Tunisia and soon spread like a wild contagion across north Africa into the Middle East. The first victim was Tunisia's President Zine El Abedine Ben Ali, quickly followed by Hosni Mubarak, the ossified Egyptian leader and one of the Arab world's grand old men. Libya collapsed into civil war as rebel forces battled Moammar Qaddafi's loyalists for control of the country. In Yemen, President Ali Abdullah Saleh was wounded in an explosion and fled to Saudi Arabia, leaving behind him a country reeling from anti-regime demonstrations, a strengthening al-Qaeda presence, a Shia revolt in the north, and civil unrest in the south. When demonstrations began in Bahrain, the Kingdom's desperate Sunni rulers turned to their Saudi neighbors for military assistance to put down the majority Shia protesters.

Syria, however, seemed to be the one country that would not succumb to the Arab Spring phenomenon. Assad appeared quite relaxed as he watched his counterparts fall and chaos engulf other countries. He even dispensed some advice to other leaders clinging to power, telling *The Wall Street Journal* in early February that Syria was immune from popular rage because his regime was "very closely linked to the beliefs of the people."

However, Assad's confidence was premature. In mid-March, demonstrations began in the southern town of Deraa and quickly spread. The regime sent in troops and security forces to crush the protests, but a rising death toll and countless reports of brutality and torture simply galvanized the opposition protest movement even more. As the weeks turned into months and the uprising showed no sign of diminishing, analysts began to ponder whether the Assad regime could possibly survive. Meanwhile, Iran and Hezbollah could only wring their hands and watch helplessly as the future of a strategic alliance—the so-called Axis of Resistance—that has endured for three decades suddenly was cast into doubt.

Syria is the vital geo-strategic lynchpin connecting Iran to Hezbollah. It grants Hezbollah strategic depth and political backing, and serves as a conduit for the transfer of heavy weapons across the rugged border with Lebanon. If Assad's Alawite-dominated regime falls and is replaced by an administration better reflecting the majority Sunni population, Hezbollah's stature in Lebanon inevitably will diminish, even if it remains the dominant political and military domestic actor.

In the five years since the last war between Hezbollah and Israel in 2006, a cautious calm has settled along the traditionally volatile Lebanon-Israel frontier. It is evident that both sides are acutely aware that the next confrontation will be of a magnitude unprecedented in the history of the Arab-Israeli conflict. Hezbollah's stockpile of weapons includes rockets with sufficient range to accurately strike all major urban centers in Israel, placing the Jewish state's heartland on the front line for the first time since the 1948 war. And if the reports that it has acquired Syrian Scud D missiles are confirmed, then nowhere in Israel is immune from Hezbollah's reach. By the same token, Israel promises to bring massive destruction onto Lebanon in the event of another war.

The "balance of terror" that has preserved a modicum of stability remains inherently unstable and still subject to miscalculation by either side. It has become customary since the 2006 war for pundits and politicians in Lebanon and Israel to begin speculating in late spring on whether the next war is imminent (tradition dictates that Arab-Israeli wars tend to be fought in the dry summer and fall months). So far Lebanon and Israel have survived five summers. But barring a major region-shaping development such as comprehensive Middle East peace or an entente between the U.S. and Iran, another war is all but inevitable.

In 2001, when I began to learn the scale of the military preparations being undertaken by Hezbollah in south Lebanon, I knew that a war was just a matter of time. The only questions were when and the catalyst. We found that out on July 12, 2006, when Hezbollah fighters abducted two Israeli soldiers.

The stakes this time around are far greater than in 2006, but none of the drivers that led to war five years ago have been resolved, and only the fragile "balance of terror" separates peace from disaster. Like my grim conclusion in 2001, I fear the next war is drawing ever closer, and only the timing and the trigger remain unknown.

Nicholas Blanford
Beirut, Lebanon
July 2011

Warriors of God

Prologue

NOVEMBER 5, 2009

Northern Israel—The old general's desk was bare except for a telephone, a stack of loose papers, and a yellow legal pad. He twisted off the cap of a pen and pulled the pad toward him. With the pen hovering above a clean sheet of paper, the general paused a moment to collect his thoughts. Then he began to write a letter to a man he had not seen in twenty-seven years.

"I hope you still remember me from our conversations at your home," he wrote.

The last time they had met was during the hot summer of 1982. The Israeli army had charged up from the south, encircled and then occupied west Beirut, forcing Yasser Arafat's Palestine Liberation Organization out of the Lebanese capital. It was a fleeting moment of triumph for the IDF and for Israel's ruthless and ambitious defense minister, Ariel Sharon.

In south Lebanon, Israeli soldiers openly walked the streets of Sidon and Tyre, shopping in the markets and watching movies in cinemas. Even some Israeli tourists and businessmen had come to admire the sights and explore possible commercial opportunities in the newly pacified region. The Shias of southern Lebanon had greeted the invading Israeli troops with handfuls of rice and cheers, thankful that the detested Palestinians had been forced out. The Israelis had basked in the goodwill.

But it soon became evident that the Israelis were in no hurry to leave. Temporary military positions were reinforced and began to take on a look of permanence. Gradually, the smiles of the southerners at their Israeli "liberators" grew less frequent.

One morning, the general had met a local Lebanese and heard some advice—and a warning that would stay with him for almost three decades.

"Thank you for kicking out the PLO, but go home quickly," the Lebanese man had told him. "If you stay, two things will happen. First, we will corrupt you because we know how to corrupt foreign invading armies. Second, we will create a guerrilla movement that will make you miss the Palestinians. Please, go home quickly."

The pen jerked rapidly across the yellow sheet as the general continued to write.

After that brief lull in late summer 1982, it had all started to go wrong. A local Shia resistance emerged in the villages around Tyre and steadily intensified. By 1985, the Israeli army had pulled back to a border strip and was facing a newly ferocious enemy of grim, bearded Shia militants who took their lead from Iran's Islamic revolutionaries and sought inspiration from the martyrdom of the sect's founders 1,400 years earlier. By the mid-1990s, Israel was fighting a losing battle against these determined guerrillas, and finally withdrew from Lebanon in 2000. But the conflict continued to simmer; in 2006 it exploded into a brutal monthlong war.

Even as the general was writing his letter, these two bitter foes were making preparations for another encounter that promised to be even more destructive than the last.

The general finished his letter and began to sign his name at the bottom, before scribbling it out and writing instead his old Arabic nom de guerre. He folded the sheet three times and inserted his business card into the crease.

Later, in south Lebanon, the recipient of the general's letter unfolded the yellow sheet and read, his eyes darting across the handwritten lines. He smiled thoughtfully.

"He should have listened to me back in 1982," he said, handing over the note.

The letter was short and reflective in tone, but one sentence stood out, a simple but rueful acknowledgment.

The general had written, "All your predictions were right."

ONE

The "Sleeping Giant"

The Lebanese Shia are as old as Lebanon itself. They have participated with the other communities in cultivating its plains and mountains, developing its land, and protecting its frontiers. The Shia have survived in Lebanon in prosperity and adversity. They have soaked its soil with the blood of their children, and have raised its banners of glory in its sky, for they have led most of the revolts.

—IMAM MUSA SADR

MARCH 17, 1974

BAALBEK, Bekaa Valley—They had waited for hours, a noisy, tumultuous throng jamming the narrow streets of this ancient town sprawling across the flatlands of the northern Bekaa Valley. From all the Shia territories in Lebanon they had come. From the cramped cinder block homes in the squalid slums of southern Beirut, from the banana plantations and citrus orchards of Tyre on the Mediterranean coast, from the olive groves and tobacco fields set among the steep stony hills of Bint Jbeil and Nabatiyah in the south, from the dusty villages clinging to the arid mountain slopes flanking the northern Bekaa Valley. Some had traveled for more than a day, filling buses and shared taxis and private vehicles as they navigated over the mountains separating the Bekaa from the coast and then bounced along the rutted roads that led toward Baalbek.

To the west, sinuous fingers of snow stroked the sepia peaks of

Mount Lebanon, fading remnants of the bitter winter months. A cool breeze wafted through Baalbek, rustling the branches of the poplar trees shading the shallow crystal waters of the Ras al-Ain spring.

It was a religious occasion, the fortieth day after Ashoura, marking the end of the traditional period of mourning for Imam Hussein, whose seventh-century martyrdom is the defining motif for the Shia faithful. But it was not the commemoration of Imam Hussein that had compelled such a multitude, perhaps seventy-five thousand people in all, to descend upon Baalbek this day. Nor was it Imam Hussein's sacrifice in the sands of Mesopotamia that had emboldened the men gathered in Baalbek to bring with them their weapons, bolt-action rifles passed from father to son or the more modern AK-47 assault rifle carried in hand or slung over shoulder. Instead, they had come to Baalbek to hear the words of one man—a tall, charismatic Iranian-born cleric whose soft smile and kindly eyes had won many admirers, Muslim and Christian alike, since he had arrived on Lebanese shores a decade and a half earlier. Known for his humility and the gentle timbre of his voice, Sayyed Musa Sadr, "Imam Musa" to his followers, had lately begun injecting steel into his oratory, preaching a bold new discourse of revolt and defiance. One month earlier, in the village of Bidnayil, a few miles south of Baalbek, Sadr had electrified his audience with an angry denunciation of the government's neglect of Lebanon's backwater regions and of the failure of the state to protect the southern Lebanese from Israel's destructive incursions. For too long, he proclaimed, the Shias of Lebanon had been marginalized and crushed, denigrated as "Mitwali."[1] Now was the time for "revolution and weapons."

"Starting from today," vowed Sadr in Bidnayil, "we will no longer complain nor cry. Our name is not Mitwali; our name is 'men of refusal,' 'men of vengeance,' 'men who revolt against tyranny' even though this costs us our blood and our lives."

On this fortieth day after Ashoura, the Shia faithful had chosen to answer Sadr's call by brandishing their weapons, a physical manifestation of their latent collective power and a stern warning to the Lebanese state that the Mitwali would be silent and submissive no more.

Sadr and his companions were making slow progress up the Bekaa

Valley toward Baalbek. As they passed through the Shia villages north of Shtaura, they found their route blocked by crowds bubbling with anticipation and excitement. Sadr was obliged to step out of his car, to greet the local dignitaries, to listen patiently to their warm welcomes and expressions of loyalty. Sheep were slaughtered on the road before him, a traditional gesture of respect for the honored visitor. Then, politely declining the entreaties of the villagers to linger a little longer, Sadr proceeded to the next village, where the same scene would be repeated.

As Sadr's entourage finally entered the southern outskirts of Baalbek, loudspeakers attached to the minarets of the town's mosques broadcast the news of the imam's arrival. As the word spread throughout the town, thousands of rifles were pointed skyward and the deafening clatter of gunfire erupted, almost drowning out the chants of "*Allah u-Akbar* (God is greater)." There were perhaps fifty thousand rifles firing all at once, a true Bekaa welcome for the venerated Sadr. The hail of falling bullets stripped leaves from trees. Ejected cartridge cases flew in through the open windows of the cars in Sadr's cortege.

As the imam climbed out of his vehicle, he was enveloped in a churning, unruly mob that bundled him toward the small platform where he would make his address. Outstretched hands snatched at his cloak, and his black turban was knocked off his head. It took twenty minutes for him to reach the podium, while the celebratory shooting continued unabated.

"I have words harsher than bullets, so spare your bullets," he exhorted the crowd, urging silence so that he could begin.

He castigated the government for its failure to meet the most basic needs of the people, noting that Baalbek itself, with a population of ten thousand, had only one government school, which dated back more than three decades to the French mandate era. He spoke of the south, battered by Israel, abused by the Palestinian armed factions that had taken root there, its people scorned, its waters plundered by the Lebanese authorities. The Shias, he thundered, were underrepresented in the civil service, industry, and academia. Thousands of Lebanese in the impoverished north and south were without identity cards, denying them basic state services as well as the right to vote.

He cited Imam Hussein's martyrdom, weaving together the religious imagery and symbolism of that earlier struggle against injustice with the plight of the contemporary Lebanese Shias. "Does Imam Hussein accept this for his children?" he asked rhetorically.

Referring to the weapons on display, Sadr declared that "armaments are the adornment of men," and he urged his followers to seize from the state what was rightfully due to them or to die in the attempt.

This was the language of "rage and revolution" that Sadr used to galvanize the Shia population of Lebanon, to stir the community from its apathy and slumber and instill within it a spirit of determination, pride, and a quest for justice.

Aql Hamiyah, at the time a student supporter of Sadr and who in the following decade would become the top military commander of the Shia Amal Movement, says, "There was a man and his name was Musa Sadr. It was Imam Sadr that woke up the sleeping giant that is the Shia of Lebanon."

The Partisans of Ali

No one knows for sure where the forebears of Lebanon's Shia population originated or why they chose to settle in the mountains and valleys of the Levant. The paucity of recorded Shia history in this region attests to the community's traditional dislocation from the affairs of its confessional neighbors, the Maronites, the Druze, and the Sunnis, whose political and social struggles form the backbone of Lebanon's historical narrative.

Shiism arose from the disputed succession from the Prophet Mohammed after his death in A.D. 632. Some of his followers believed that Mohammed's successor, the Caliph, should be chosen by consensus. Others argued that the succession should follow through Mohammed's family and that Ali, as the prophet's son-in-law, was the rightful heir. The title of Caliph was bestowed initially upon Abu Bakr, Mohammed's father-in-law and a close companion of the Prophet. Ali became the fourth Caliph, but for Ali's supporters—the Shiat al-Ali, or Partisans of

Ali—he was the first true Caliph, the beginning of a line of descendants known as Imams.

The "Twelver" Shia tradition holds that Ali was followed by eleven more Imams, the last of whom, Imam Mahdi, went into occultation to escape his oppressors. According to the Twelver Shias, the return of this last Imam, the "hidden Imam," will lead to the end of the world and to their salvation. The Twelvers comprise the majority of Shia Muslims—including those of Lebanon and Iran.

Jabal Amil, the hill country historically bordered by Sidon in the north, Mount Hermon in the east, upper Galilee in the south, and the Mediterranean in the west, where much of modern Lebanon's Shia population lives, fell under the sway of the Ottoman Empire in the early sixteenth century. Given its passive rural existence and its relative isolation from the centers of power, Jabal Amil attracted little direct attention from the region's rulers. Under a relatively benign system, the tradition of Shia scholarship quietly flourished in the hill villages of the area. By the sixteenth century, Jabal Amil had emerged as the main center of learning in the Shia world, with many newly licensed *alim*, or scholars, settling in Iran, Iraq, and Mecca.

When Shah Ismael I, the Safavid ruler of Iran, introduced Twelver Shiism as the state religion in the early sixteenth century, he turned to the scholars of Jabal Amil to help promulgate the new faith. Adopting Shiism was intended to stabilize the Shah's new empire through a sense of religious kinship and to sharpen the front line against the rival Sunni Ottomans to the west. Dozens of leading scholars from villages in Jabal Amil and the Bekaa Valley traveled to Iran, settling there, marrying, learning Persian, and involving themselves in the rivalries and intrigues of the Safavid court. Thus began a linkage of families and learning between the Shias of the Levant and Iran that endures today. Ironically, however, the very success of the Jabal Amil scholars in preaching Shiism in Safavid Iran shifted the center of the faith from the Arab world to the powerful Persian Empire. In the eyes of Arab Sunnis, Shiism, already deemed heretical, was further tainted with a Persian hue, and its adherents were considered potential agents for the non-Arab Persians. Indeed, Jabal Amil's gradual decline as a center of Shia learning was due not only to the ascension of the Safavids as a Shia power, but also to Ottoman suspicions that the Shias living within their domain were a potential source of collaboration with their Persian enemies. Such suspicions prevail today, with Hezbollah dogged by accusations from some Sunni Muslims that it is a Trojan horse carrying Iran's influence into the majority Sunni Arab Middle East.

Swift to Rebel

The conventional narrative of Shia history in Lebanon tends to dwell on the notion of the community's submissiveness, the passive assimilation of the browbeaten and hand-wringing "Mitwali" into a hostile Sunni environment. But the Shias were no mere timid subjects of Ottoman rule. Like other minorities dwelling in the fastness of the Levantine mountains, they possessed a tenaciously independent streak and were quick to rise to arms if provoked. Shia ferocity in battle was born of the realization that their villages among the hills of Jabal Amil and the plain of the northern Bekaa Valley represented their sole sanctuaries. To lose their territories meant potential annihilation, and they defended them with a determined belligerence that belied the more familiar Shia image of sullen acquiescence.

Furthermore, these Shia warriors possessed a cultural advantage over their enemies in their readiness to embrace martyrdom in battle. The paradigm of Shia martyrdom is Imam Hussein, Ali's second son, who perished in Karbala in A.D. 680 with a small band of followers against an army sent by Yazid, the Damascus-based Caliph. Hussein's readiness to sacrifice himself in battle against his oppressor helped crystallize the nascent sense of Shia identity, and it would become a source of emulation for future generations of Shia warriors.

"Life is the most precious thing that a human being has," says Hussein Sharafeddine, scion of a notable family of Lebanese Shias from Tyre in south Lebanon and brother-in-law of Musa Sadr. "But we Shia are willing to give up our life for God in emulation of Imam Hussein whose martyrdom was the pinnacle of sacrifice."

The Battle of Karbala continues to be commemorated in a passion play performed on Ashoura, the tenth day of the Muslim month of Muharram, in which the Shia faithful reenact Hussein's doomed struggle against Yazid's army. The most vivid example of the Ashoura ceremony in Lebanon is found in the southern market town of Nabatiyah. The passion play, usually lasting more than two hours, takes place in the dusty central square, where local residents don colorful uniforms and perform before an audience while a narrator mournfully relates the unfolding tragedy by loudspeaker. But the real spectacle occurs in the surrounding streets. Here, thousands of young Shias wearing white sheets cut their foreheads with razor blades and beat out the blood with the flat of their hands while jogging through the streets chanting "Haidar, Haidar," an honorific bestowed upon Ali. Senior Shia clerics in Lebanon oppose the bloodletting, which locals say was introduced by an Iranian doctor in the 1930s. Ayatollah Khomeini even issued a fatwa against it, which is why in Nabatiyah each year, Hezbollah's followers line up patiently outside Red Crescent tents, preferring to shed their blood via tubes into sterile plastic bags for the benefit of the infirm rather than to spill it wastefully onto the streets.

The sixteenth and seventeenth centuries were a period of rapid economic growth in Jabal Amil, owing mainly to the cultivation of cotton, cotton fabric then being highly prized in Europe and North Africa for the distinctive red dye that colored the cloth. To protect their prosperity from outsiders, the Shias of Jabal Amil built up a substantial military force in the 1760s of infantry and cavalry—"ten thousand horsemen, all resolute and formidable troops"[2]—and took over the old Crusader castles that dotted the limestone hills of the area. They forged an alliance with a rebellious Palestinian tribal chief, Dahir al-Omar, who had taken advantage of the tenuous Ottoman control to build a power base in Galilee and amass great wealth through the monopolization of the cotton trade. The alliance between Dahir and the Shias was based on mutual economic interests: cotton grown in Jabal Amil was exported through the port of Acre under Dahir's control.

Dahir's Shia troops fought with distinction against Ottoman forces at the battles of Hula in Galilee in 1771 and Ghaziyah, just south of

Sidon, a year later. Of the latter battle, Baron François de Tott, an eighteenth-century French soldier contracted by the Ottomans, wrote that the Shia chief Nassif Nasser led three thousand cavalry against forty thousand Druze and "put them to flight at the first onset," rendering "the name of the Mutualis [*sic*] formidable."[3]

Constantin-François Volney, a European traveler, recounted an incident in 1771 when a Druze army took advantage of the temporary absence of the Shia forces and "ravaged their country." When the returning Shias first learned of what had befallen their territory, "an advanced corps, of only five hundred men, were so enraged that they immediately rushed forward against the enemy, determined to perish in taking vengeance." But the "surprise and confusion" of the sudden attack fell in the favor of the Shias, and the twenty-five-thousand-strong Druze army was "completely overthrown."[4]

The Ottomans were reluctant to tangle with the defiant Shias and were generally content to grant them near autonomy so long as the imperative of tax collection was observed. In the words of one historian, the Ottomans before the 1760s regarded the Shias of Jabal Amil "simply as hard-working tillers of the soil, a fiercely independent mountain folk whom the central authorities were well advised to leave alone unless they wished to provoke the violent reaction that was certain to follow any interference in their affairs."[5]

But in 1775 with the empire reeling from defeat by Russia and with the Safavids raiding its eastern domains, the Ottomans took action to bring their errant Syrian territories, and Shia subjects, to heel. A ruthless Bosnian, Ahmad Pasha, was installed in Acre and authorized to use any means at his disposal to crush Dahir and his Shia allies and restore Ottoman authority to Syria.

After Dahir was killed in Acre that year, Pasha turned his attention to the Shias, launching punitive expeditions into Jabal Amil. Given the nickname "Jazzar," which means "butcher" in Arabic, and described by Baron de Tott as a "monster let loose upon mankind," Pasha was determined that the Shias would be taught through blood and fire the futility of resistance and struggle.[6] In 1781, he dispatched an army of three thousand against Nassif Nasser, the Shia chief who had defeated the

Ottomans at Sidon nine years earlier. They met at Yaroun, which today lies on Lebanon's southern border with Israel. Nasser was killed, along with a third of his army, which was outnumbered three to one. Pasha's troops seized all seven of the Shia village fortresses, strung along hilltops in Jabal Amil. Shia sheikhs and leaders fled to Mount Lebanon and the northern Bekaa Valley after the capture of the last of the fortresses, the stronghold known locally to this day as Shqif—the Crusader-era Beaufort Castle perched on a ravine overlooking the Litani River.

The swords, lances, and flintlock muskets wielded by Nasser's troops may have been replaced with automatic rifles, missiles, and roadside bombs, but the same fierce instinct that motivated Nasser's warriors to defend their land against external aggression would reappear in future generations of young Lebanese Shias who took up arms to confront the predations and humiliations of Israeli occupation. The sudden phenomenon of Shia militancy in late twentieth-century Lebanon initially took many foreign observers by surprise. Little attention had been devoted to the community before interest was kindled by the Islamic revolution in Iran in 1979, an event that shook the Middle East and helped radicalize the Shias of Lebanon. Yet, although the historical link should not be overstated, the tenacious guerrilla campaigns waged by Amal and then Hezbollah in south Lebanon beginning in the 1980s did not emerge from a vacuum but were drawn, in part, from the same cultural wellspring of defiance and dignity that had sustained Nassif Nasser's military adventures two hundred years earlier.

The "Belt of Misery"

Ahmad Pasha's campaign of suppression destroyed the primacy of Jabal Amil as a center of Shia teaching, a mauling from which it would never recover. It also ended the autonomy the Shia population had enjoyed under the former Ottoman administration, and in the following decades, Jabal Amil regressed into obscurity. Indeed, European travelers passing through the area in the latter half of the nineteenth century could barely hide their contempt for the squalor and poverty of the hill villages and for the apparent apathy and sullenness of the natives they found there. One wrote that "they are all in rags, except some of the Sheikhs, and all are mendicants. . . . The filth is revolting."[7]

Another English traveler, clearly unfamiliar with the Shias, observed that their abhorrence of other sects echoed that of the "Israelites" of Palestine and bizarrely concluded that "they may be an apostate body of Jews."[8]

The fortunes of the Shia community were not much improved by the transition from Ottoman colonial rule to the French mandatory authority at the end of World War I. The state of Greater Lebanon was established in 1920 and its borders delineated over the next three years. The residents of Jabal Amil had become Lebanese citizens, and their Arab neighbors to the south were now Palestinians under a British mandate, with a new frontier separating what had been a generally homogenous society.

Even after Lebanon gained independence from France in 1943, the Shia population, despite its size relative to that of other sects, found itself underrepresented in the new power-sharing system of government. Essentially a compromise between Sunnis and Maronites, the National Pact allocated positions based on a 1932 census—the last ever held in Lebanon—that was of questionable accuracy when conducted and was certainly out of date eleven years later. The Maronites, the largest sect at the time, gained most of the top political and security posts, including the presidency and the command of the Lebanese army.

In its early years of independence, Lebanon experienced a services-oriented boom period, profiting from its fortuitous geographic position between the West and the newly emerging oil-rich Gulf. But the nation's increasing prosperity during this period mainly benefited an oligarchy of powerful political families that monopolized the commercial and financial sectors and dominated the politics of the country. The revenues of the boom were spent mostly in Beirut and parts of Christian-dominated Mount Lebanon. The peripheral areas in the north, and the Shia-populated Bekaa Valley and south, were left to stagnate. In 1943, there was not a single hospital in south Lebanon.

The lure of booming Beirut—where earnings in the 1950s were five times higher than in the peripheral regions—encouraged tens of thousands of Shias to abandon their farms and villages and seek fresh opportunities in the city. Most of them settled in the southern quarters of Beirut, cramming into dense and unsanitary neighborhoods. Here they labored on building sites, helping construct the new concrete high-rise buildings that were rapidly changing Beirut's skyline. By 1971, nearly half of Lebanon's Shias were living in southern Beirut, a "Belt of Misery" that formed a third distinct area of Shia habitation along with the Bekaa and the south.

The Shias were poorly represented by their powerful landlords, who exerted a feudalistic hold on their subjects by dispensing ad hoc patronage in exchange for unquestioning loyalty at election time.

Given the lack of political representation and the poor social conditions, the teeming slums of southern Beirut proved a fertile ground for the growth of the leftist pan-Arab ideologies that shook the Middle East in the 1950s. Young Shias, raised in the feudal atmosphere of Jabal Amil and the impoverished Bekaa, found themselves drawn to the secular parties of the left, with their goals of disrupting the existing order and promoting social equality.

"It Was as If He Was Jesus Christ"

It was into this budding Shia social and political ferment that Musa Sadr arrived in 1959 at the age of thirty-one. Sadr had first visited Lebanon four years earlier as a guest of Sayyed Abdel Hussein Sharafeddine, a relative and the aged mufti of Tyre, the most eminent Shia authority in Lebanon at the time. Sharafeddine, who was much impressed with the tall, charming Iranian, overlooked Sadr's youth, inexperience, and lack of knowledge of Lebanon to nominate him as his chosen successor.

Based in Tyre, Sadr quickly integrated himself within the local community, preaching at the Abbas Sharafeddine mosque each Friday and meeting with leading figures in the city.

"At the beginning, nobody knew who he was," recalls Abdullah Yazbek, at the time a local businessman who later became an aide to Sadr. "I used to pray with other religious sayyeds,[9] but I thought the message was always the same. Then I began praying with Sayyed Sadr, and suddenly I was hearing new things about religion and economics and social reforms, things I had never heard before."

Helped by some state funds and access to religious donations, Sadr embarked upon a program of social activism. One of his first acts was to abolish begging in Tyre. He reorganized and expanded a small local charity and founded an institute for Islamic studies and several vocational centers in Tyre. His flagship project in those early years was the Jabal Amil Institute, located in Bourj Shemali, just outside Tyre. The institute continues to run today under the leadership of Sadr's sister, Rabab. In Beirut, he opened orphanages and a hospital.

With his Persian-accented Arabic, striking physical appearance, and enormous energy, Sadr soon attracted the interest and support of the Shia middle class. Sadr represented an alternative path to the ossified feudal barons and the alarming revolutionaries of the left, one that combined communal awareness, progress, and reform.

He worked hard to heighten a sense of communal identity among the geographically isolated Shias, traveling with unflagging energy from one end of the country to the other. Although the focus of his work was on the betterment of Lebanon's Shias, Sadr also reached out to other communities and—to the initial outrage of the more conservative members of the Shia clerical establishment, known as the *ulama*—regularly preached in churches. On one occasion, Sadr was due to deliver a sermon in Alma Shaab, a Maronite village on the Israeli border, but found the road blocked by the huge crowd that had arrived to hear him speak. He and his aide Abdullah Yazbek were forced to leave their car and walk through fields of tobacco to reach the church.

"We arrived at the church thirty minutes late and the people had grown anxious," Yazbek recalls. "But the moment he arrived and stood on the pulpit where all could see him, the people lost control. They were Christians, but they were yelling '*Allah u-Akbar*' like Muslims. The way people treated him, it was as if he was Jesus Christ. Christians used to tell me how lucky we were to have someone like this."

Sadr's popularity provoked the enmity of the entrenched feudal barons, who recognized that this dynamic cleric represented a threat to their stranglehold on the Shia community. Sadr sought to undermine their influence by lobbying for the creation of the Higher Shia Council, which was established in 1967 as the principal representative organ for Lebanese Shias. The following year, he formed the Harakat al-Mahrummin, the Movement of the Deprived, which would become his main vehicle for civil and social activism on behalf of the poorest members of society. Although it was formed as a nonsectarian organization—its deputy was a Christian bishop—for all practical purposes it was the first large-scale Shia political and social organization in Lebanon.

The Rise of the Fedayeen

In the second half of the 1960s, Sadr found that his efforts to politically and socially mobilize the Shia community were becoming complicated by the emergence of Palestinian militants in south Lebanon and with it the initial sparks of a cross-border conflict with Israel.

Lebanon, like Israel's other Arab neighbors, had reluctantly absorbed large numbers of Palestinian refugees during the Arab-Israeli war that followed the creation of the Jewish state in 1948. By the late 1950s, Palestinian factions espousing armed resistance against Israel were beginning to emerge. The most important of these early Palestinian factions was Fatah, led by a young engineer called Yasser Arafat. Fatah's initial military operations—the first from Lebanon was in June 1965—were low-key, sporadic, and often unsuccessful. But that changed in the wake of the June 1967 war, when Israel launched surprise attacks against Egypt, Syria, and Jordan. By the time a cease-fire was signed six days later, Israel had captured the Gaza Strip and Sinai peninsula from Egypt, the West Bank (including East Jerusalem) from Jordan, and the Golan Heights from Syria, tripling the size of the Jewish state in just six days.

Lebanon was spared direct involvement in the war, but Israel's swift seizure of the Golan Heights from Syria was to have future implications for Lebanese territorial sovereignty and regional security. While Israeli forces pushed eastward deeper into Syrian territory, their land grab in the northern Golan was checked by the border with Lebanon. However, the Israelis discovered that there was some ambiguity over exactly where Syria ended and Lebanon began, thanks to the laxity with which the French mandatory authorities had delineated the joint border.

One small hamlet called Ghajar, lying on a grassy plain between the Hasbani River and the jagged limestone foothills of Mount Hermon, was populated by members of the Alawite sect, an obscure offshoot of Shiism. The Israelis stopped just short of the village because, according to their maps, Ghajar was in Lebanon. But the residents of Ghajar considered themselves Syrian. One group of villagers approached the Israelis asking to be taken into Israel's newly seized territory, while another delegation asked the Lebanese authorities to formally incorporate their village. The Lebanese refused and, after some hesitation, the Israelis accepted the offer and troops deployed into Ghajar.

The Israelis faced similar territorial uncertainty just to the east of Ghajar, where the volcanic plateau of the Golan buckles and folds into the pale gray limestone foothills of Mount Hermon. Cutting through these hills is a deep brush-covered ravine called Wadi al-Aasal, the Valley of Honey. In 1967, the terrain on the northern side of the valley contained some fourteen farmsteads populated mainly by Lebanese residents of Shebaa and Kfar Shuba villages. The area today is collectively known as the Shebaa Farms and Kfar Shuba Heights. During the mild summer months, the villagers farmed the flatter reaches of the valley's upper slopes, growing wheat and lentils and grazing sheep, cattle, and goats. During the cold winters, most of the farmsteads were abandoned as their occupants descended to warmer climes in the valleys below.

Having seized Ghajar, the Israelis moved east into the adjacent hills, overrunning the farmsteads on the lower slopes of the Shebaa Farms area. The residents fled to Shebaa and Kfar Shuba or to other farms higher up the mountainside.

Fatahland

With the armies of the Arab world defeated and disgraced by Israel in the 1967 war, the nascent Palestinian armed movement gained traction.

In October 1968, fighters belonging to the Palestine Liberation Organization (PLO) began moving out of the refugee camps and establishing military bases in south Lebanon close to the border with Israel.

The Lebanese government watched this post-1967-war buildup with apprehension. Even before Palestinian raids from Lebanon had begun in earnest, Israel gave the Lebanese a foretaste of what they could expect if the Palestinians were not kept in check. On December 26, helicopter-borne Israeli commandos landed at Beirut airport and blew up thirteen aircraft, including eight airliners belonging to Middle East Airlines, Lebanon's flag carrier. The subsequent public protests in Lebanon forced the resignation of the government.

In April and October 1969, violent clashes erupted between the Lebanese army and the PLO in south Lebanon, quickly spreading to the streets of Lebanese cities. The actions of the Palestinians were seriously aggravating the strains of communal power sharing between the entrenched, predominantly Maronite ruling elite and the mainly Muslim and leftist groups. The former resented the growing power of the PLO and its potential to upset the status quo, while the latter viewed the Palestinians as useful allies in the struggle for greater representation.

A set of understandings known as the "Cairo Accords" was reached in October 1968 between the Lebanese state and the PLO, permitting the Palestinians the right to participate in the armed struggle against Israel "in accordance with the principles of the sovereignty and security of Lebanon." The fact that the interests of the Lebanese state were incompatible with the right of the Palestinians to armed struggle was left unaddressed.

The beginning of 1970 marked an increase in Palestinian attacks against Israel, which inevitably provoked harsh retaliation. In July, the Israelis moved to occupy the entire Shebaa Farms mountainside, from where Palestinian spotters had directed artillery bombardments against the plain of northern Galilee far below. Israeli engineers bulldozed supply roads into the hillside and built military outposts on the rocky bluffs overlooking Kfar Shuba and Shebaa. The last farmers and shepherds who had stubbornly resisted the harassment of Israeli troops were forced to leave. The new hilltop positions afforded the Israelis commanding views over much of southeast Lebanon.

By 1974, barely a day went by without south Lebanon's experiencing Israeli troop incursions, artillery shelling, or air strikes. The United Nations had, at Lebanon's request, established three observation posts along the border in 1972. But the unarmed UN observers could only log the transgressions of the Palestinians and Israelis and write post-facto reports on damages and casualties on the Lebanese side of the border; they had no mandate to intervene.

After a Palestinian cross-border commando raid in May, the Israeli government decided to seal off the Lebanon frontier by constructing a nine-foot-high electrified fence, fitted with motion detectors, alongside coils of razor wire and a parallel "smudge trail," a dirt track to record the footprints of infiltrators. Military observation posts were established at regular intervals along the border; undergrowth was cleared and mines planted on the Lebanese side of the fence. Searchlights and flares were used for nighttime detection. The Israelis also stepped up interdiction and observation patrols inside Lebanon. Tanks accompanied by troops during daylight hours crossed the border and took up positions with commanding views of the terrain to the north. The Lebanese government issued some formal complaints to the UN, but the army was instructed not to intervene.

Israel's policy of deliberately inflicting punishment on the southern Lebanese was intended to compel the Lebanese authorities to take action against the PLO themselves. But Lebanon was small, weak, and polarized between rival sectarian and ideological allegiances and social disparity. The Lebanese state could not reach consensus on what to do with the PLO, which left the southerners at the mercy of the martial whims of the Palestinians and Israelis.

The Lebanese Resistance Battalions

Musa Sadr urged the Lebanese state to redress the plight of the southern Lebanese, but to little effect. As an Iranian trying to make headway in an Arab environment, he found it expedient to publicly and repeatedly declare his antipathy toward Israel and his support for the right of the

Palestinians to win back their homeland. Yet despite his declarations and genuine feelings of sympathy for the Palestinians, Sadr could see that the actions of the PLO were bringing ruin and misery to his constituents in south Lebanon. He found it increasingly difficult to reconcile his sympathies for the stateless Palestinians with the reckless behavior of the PLO in the south.

In early 1974, Sadr lost patience with the apathy and impotence of the Lebanese government and took matters into his own hands, advocating, for the first time, armed struggle as a means of defending the southerners and advancing the rights of the dispossessed. It was an unlikely departure for the mild-mannered cleric who once confided to a colleague that until he arrived in Lebanon, he had never heard a shot fired in anger. But Sadr recognized that if he was to remain relevant, he would have to adopt a more muscular approach.

He set the tone at the mass rally in the Bekaa Valley village of Bidnayil in February, telling his followers that there was "no alternative for us except revolution and weapons." The Bidnayil speech was followed a month later by the huge event in Baalbek, where he controversially declared that "armaments are the adornment of men." It was here that Sadr told the Shia clans of the Bekaa to stop feuding and join a new force he would establish to defend the south against Israel. Baalbek was followed by another mass rally in Tyre. The rallies helped crystallize the Movement of the Deprived in the public consciousness. Although the movement had been founded some seven years earlier, it had not been particularly well organized and only became truly relevant beginning in 1974.

Following those rallies, Sadr began recruiting volunteer fighters for a new group that would operate as the military wing of the Movement of the Deprived, tasked with defending the south against the Israelis. He named it Afwaj Muqawama al-Lubnaniyya—the Lebanese Resistance Battalions—better known by its Arabic acronym, Amal, which means "hope."

"Imam Musa began visiting universities in 1974 and 1975 and asked students to join Amal," recalls Aql Hamiyah, who at the time was a student follower of Sadr. "The Shia intellectuals developed relations with

Imam Musa and he persuaded them to be part of the struggle with the Palestinians. It was not easy, however, because relations between the Shias and the Palestinians were bad at the time."

Sadr and Yasser Arafat agreed that Fatah would help train the recruits at newly established Amal camps in the eastern Bekaa, a move intended to enhance relations between the Shias and the Palestinians as much as to provide military instruction to the new Amal cadres. The formation of Amal and the training by Fatah were conducted in secrecy. Sadr, after all, had crafted an image of peace and tolerance, which stood to be discredited if it emerged that he, like other political bosses in Lebanon, was in the game of militia building.

Fate forced his hand, however. In April 1975 the communal tensions in Lebanon finally erupted into civil war. Three months later, at the beginning of July, a Fatah instructor accidentally detonated an antitank mine he was handling at an Amal training camp in Ain Boulay in the hills east of Baalbek. Nearly thirty Amal recruits were killed in the explosion and dozens more wounded. Sadr, who had just ended a well-publicized hunger strike in a Beirut mosque to protest the civil war, was compelled to admit that he had established a militia. Although he insisted that Amal's purpose was to defend the south against Israel, the revelation that he was now head of a Lebanese militia made his public fast against the civil war seem hypocritical. The episode marked the beginning of a decline in Sadr's status and influence, his social activism overwhelmed by the grim realities of war.

"We Were Pushed into Israel's Arms"

South Lebanon, meanwhile, had been spared the initial horrors of the civil war raging farther north. The bulk of the PLO had deployed to the north to fight on the front lines in Beirut. However, the tentacles of war extended southward in January 1976, when a split in the army saw units deserting to join militias or leaderless soldiers simply going home.

Despite his wariness at becoming sucked into Lebanon's fractious, complex, and treacherous political landscape, Yitzhak Rabin, the Israeli prime minister, gave his blessing to offering both humanitarian assistance to the Christians of southern border villages that found themselves besieged by the PLO and their Lebanese militia allies, and material support for the Christian militias farther north. Israel, Rabin explained, would help the Lebanese Christians help themselves.

A formal border crossing was constructed next to an Israeli army post on the western side of Metulla, Israel's most northerly town. A small open-air clinic was established in a nearby apple orchard, providing free medical aid to Lebanese. Soon Lebanese farmers began crossing the border to sell their produce to Israeli merchants, and others found work in factories, supermarkets, and hotels.

Shimon Peres, the Israeli defense minister, gave his full backing to the budding relations with the Christians of south Lebanon, formally announcing his "Good Fence" policy in June.

The southern Christians were under no illusions about the risks of cooperating with the Israelis, but besieged by the PLO and cut off from Beirut, they felt they had no choice. "Why do you think we would break down the wall and go to Israel?" asked Father Mansour Hokayem, the Maronite priest of Qlaya, the first village to build ties with Israel. "We had a thousand shells raining on us. We had many casualties and they had to go to Israel. There was no escape for us. . . . We were pushed into Israel's arms."

Inevitably, the cooperation soon moved from humanitarian relief to military support. The Israel Defense Forces (IDF) secretly lent assistance to the building of a local border militia centered on the redundant Lebanese army regulars and enlarged with local youths from Christian villages. Some of the newly recruited militiamen wore olive-green Israeli army uniforms (with the Hebrew patches scribbled over with ink) and carried Israeli rifles. The Israelis set up a liaison unit in Metulla and handed over to their new Lebanese allies some thirty World War II–vintage Sherman tanks, light mortars, heavy machine guns, radio equipment, and old Soviet armored personnel carriers (APCs)—each emblazoned with the militia's signature white cross. Israeli troops, who had maintained a presence just inside the Lebanese border for the previous two years, began patrolling deeper into Lebanon.

Neighboring Syria, meanwhile, was keeping a close eye on the burgeoning relationship between Israel and the Christians of Lebanon. Hafez al-Assad, the Syrian president, feared that Israel would intervene in Lebanon to protect the Christians if it appeared their militias were on the verge of defeat. An Israeli intervention would grant the Jewish state a toehold in Lebanon and represent a threat to Damascus's western flank, a development Assad was determined to thwart.

Assad's concerns appeared close to being realized in early 1976 as the Christian militias lost ground to the PLO and its Lebanese allies. When Kamal Jumblatt, the leader of the leftist National Movement, stubbornly refused Syria's request to ease his assault on the Christians, Assad abruptly switched sides and sent his army into Lebanon. The Israelis relished the irony of their Syrian enemies' smashing the PLO in Lebanon, but insisted that Syrian troops must not venture south of a "red line" that, although left undefined, effectively included all of south Lebanon.

By October, the Lebanese leftists and the PLO were defeated, leaving Syria holding the balance of power in Lebanon at the head of a thirty-thousand-strong Arab Deterrent Force sanctioned by the Arab League.

In an attempt to restore some order to the south, the Lebanese army command in Beirut instructed Major Saad Haddad, a resident of the southern town of Marjayoun, to bring the army remnants and Israeli-backed militia under his control. The loss of state authority in Lebanon placed the army in the awkward position of having to tacitly cooperate with the Israelis in controlling south Lebanon. The only safe route open to Haddad to reach his new command was by sea, on an Israeli missile boat from Jouniyah in the Christian heartland north of Beirut to Haifa in northern Israel. In the months ahead, Haddad found himself in the curious position of reporting to the Lebanese army command in Beirut and continuing to draw his army salary from the Lebanese government (as did other members of the Israeli-supported militia) while cooperating with, and taking orders from, the IDF.

In early 1977, at the prodding of his Israeli handlers, Haddad launched a halfhearted offensive to expand his area of control around

Marjayoun and Qlaya with the ultimate goal of uniting all the Christian village enclaves along the border to form a homogenous security belt. While the rest of Lebanon enjoyed a welcome period of calm under the Pax Syriana, a scrappy war developed in the south, with Haddad's militia attacking neighboring Shia villages and then more often than not being forced to retreat during counterattacks by the PLO and the leftists. Both sides shelled each other remorselessly, and the flow of civilian casualties kept the Israeli medics along the "Good Fence" busy.

A Dynamic Islam

Musa Sadr's campaigning may have been the most public attempt to mobilize Lebanon's dispossessed Shia population, but it was not the only dynamic effecting the community. Another, quieter form of religious activism emerged in Lebanon during the 1970s, the roots of which lay not in the rocky hills and valleys of south Lebanon, but far to the east in the blazing desert heat of southern Iraq.

The holy city of Najaf is the primary center of learning and theology for the Shia faithful and the seat of the leading *maraji'*, or Grand Ayatollahs. Hundreds of students arrive each year to enroll in religious seminaries, or *hawza*, tucked away in the warrenlike alleyways that surround the gold-domed mausoleum marking the burial place of Imam Ali ibn Abi Talib, the Prophet Mohammed's son-in-law and the first Caliph recognized by the Shias.

Najaf was the birthplace of Mohammed Hussein Fadlallah, the son of a respected ayatollah originally from south Lebanon. Fadlallah would later serve as a source of inspiration for the nascent Hezbollah and its leadership and would become the leading Shia authority in Lebanon. Born in 1935, the young Fadlallah was raised in the rarified atmosphere of Najaf and steeped in religion and piety from childhood. A gifted student, by the age of thirteen he was winning acclaim for his poetry and writings in numerous cultural magazines circulating in the Arab world.

As he continued his religious studies in his young adulthood, his worldview was shaped by the political turbulence that roiled Iraq in the late 1950s. Much as Musa Sadr had attempted in Lebanon to check the penetration of Shia society by secular Arab nationalist movements, Fadlallah and some of his clerical contemporaries in Najaf recognized the challenge to religious observance posed by the growing influence of the Communists and the Arab nationalist Baath Party in Iraq.

Beginning in 1958, Fadlallah became closely involved with the newly formed Hizb al-Dawa al-Islamiyya, the Party of the Islamic Call, which espoused a revolutionary Islamist agenda and whose leading activist was a close friend of Fadlallah, Sayyed Mohammed Baqr as-Sadr. The Dawa Party sought to promote Islam and Islamic values as a counterweight to secularism and leftist ideologies with the eventual goal of establishing an Islamic state in Iraq.

Although Fadlallah claimed never to have occupied a formal position in Dawa, he was a leading proponent of its beliefs, of what he dubbed a "dynamic Islam." He developed his ideas in the early 1960s, industriously writing monographs while continuing his studies and teaching.

In 1966, Fadlallah left Najaf for Lebanon, a country he had visited only a handful of times. Settling in the Nabaa district of east Beirut, a poor neighborhood populated by Shia emigrants from the south and Palestinian refugees, Fadlallah was invited by a local businessman to helm a social and cultural organization called Usrat al-Taakhi, the Family of Fraternity. He then opened a prayer hall and a *husseiniyah,* a religious meeting place for Shia men, and began lecturing and preaching to the young in an effort to dampen enthusiasm for the leftist creeds of the secular political parties then taking hold among Shia youth. Fadlallah additionally established Al-Mahad al-Sharia al-Islami, the Islamic Legal Institute, then a unique institution in Lebanon for advanced religious studies modeled on the seminaries of Najaf.

Fadlallah quickly built a reputation as a charismatic orator whose vision of a contemporary universal Islam won adherents not only among the ill-educated poor of Nabaa but also among students at secular universities. In 1966, Fadlallah founded Al-Ittihad al-Lubnani lil Talabah al-Muslimeen, the Lebanese Union of Muslim Students, as a vehicle to steer educated youths onto a path where they could practice a progressive Islam while still pursuing careers in the modern secular world. Future leaders of Hezbollah were among the early admirers of Fadlallah, among them Sheikh Ragheb Harb, a tough firebrand cleric who studied in Najaf before taking up the position of mosque imam in his home village of Jibsheet in south Lebanon.

During the late 1960s and early 1970s, Fadlallah and Imam Musa Sadr were the two most active and dynamic Shia religious figures in Lebanon. Both were brilliant orators and supported the Palestinian cause; but there the similarities ended. Musa Sadr was slim, tall, and charismatic, possessing star quality enlivened with boundless energy that saw him always on the move, holding meetings and giving lectures and sermons up and down the country. Fadlallah was short and portly, a scholarly figure who centered his activities on his Nabaa neighborhood. Sadr won followers by weaving into his discourse Shia imagery of Karbala and the examples of Imams Ali and Hussein. Fadlallah was more ecumenical in outlook, glossing over doctrinal differences between Shias and Sunnis and emphasizing the unity of all Muslims. Sadr's purview was essentially limited to the communal betterment of Shias in Lebanon within the Lebanese system, while Fadlallah advocated the creation of a modern Islamic state and espoused a universal Islam that shunned man-made frontiers. While Sadr came to regard Palestinian actions in south Lebanon with misgivings, Fadlallah displayed no such hesitancy, wholeheartedly embracing the Palestinian cause and regarding the eradication of the Zionist state as a moral and Islamic imperative.

Among those regularly attending Fadlallah's lectures at the Usrat al-Taakhi mosque in Nabaa in the mid-1970s was a slim, earnest-looking boy in his midteens. His name was Imad Mughniyah. In the years ahead, Mughniyah would achieve international notoriety as the elusive, cunning, and resolute military commander of Hezbollah and alleged architect of large-scale suicide bomb attacks against Western targets and kidnappings of foreigners in the war-ravaged Lebanon of the 1980s. Born in 1962, Mughniyah was raised in the slums of Beirut's southern suburbs, although his family was from Teir Dibna, a small village in the hills east of Tyre. Little is known of his childhood, but friends recall that he was a natural leader, devout from a young age and a devoted admirer of Fadlallah and supporter of the Palestinian cause. Friends and acquaintances variously described Mughniyah as "very smart," "always alert," someone who "never slept" and who possessed a good sense of humor and "joked a lot."

In 1976, he and a group of friends arrived at a small Fatah training camp near Damour, a Christian village on the coastal highway south of Beirut whose residents had been massacred and driven out by Palestinian and leftist militias that January. The camp was run by Anis Naqqash, by then a legendary figure within PLO circles. Today, his ginger hair and beard having turned steely gray, the affable fifty-nine-year-old looks more like a retired university professor than a onetime revolutionary. A Sunni Muslim from Beirut, Naqqash joined Fatah in 1968 and was a confederate of Ilich Ramirez Sanchez, better known as Carlos the Jackal. He was a member of the team that boldly kidnapped a group of OPEC oil ministers meeting in Vienna in 1975.

After Damour fell to the PLO, Naqqash set up a small military training camp to teach basic weapons skills and tactics over a twenty-day period to a diverse array of small factions and individuals. "Imad Mughniyah came up to me and said that he and his friends were an Islamist group that wanted to be trained militarily but did not want to join Fatah," Naqqash recalls. "Most of them were very young, just seventeen or eighteen years old. Imad stood out from the others because while everyone was looking forward to the end of the course when they would get to fire guns, Imad was more interested in learning about tactics. He was the only one, apart from a teacher and a Maoist, who wrote down notes during the course. He was not interested in shooting guns like the others."

Naqqash drilled into his militant students the necessity of strategic and tactical planning. For resistance to be effective, he argued, it could not be merely reactive to developments, but had to be proactive in order to retain the element of surprise and to stay one step ahead of the enemy. "I used to make speeches," he recalls, "about the need to think where we would be in a year, or two years or three years. What would be the enemy's movements by then? How would we be deployed? How would we be ready for whatever events might come? This is what I taught Imad from the beginning."

"People honor me by saying that I was Imad's teacher," Naqqash adds with a soft chuckle, "but all I did was to teach him the A's, B's, and C's. Imad later 'graduated' from a 'university of resistance' and then set up his own 'school of resistance' to teach others."

Thirsty for Learning

Another religious-minded youngster enamored by Fadlallah's sermons was Hassan Nasrallah. A shy, skinny boy with long, thick eyebrows and full lips who had yet to reach his tenth birthday when he began visiting the Usrat al-Taakhi mosque in Nabaa in the late 1960s, Nasrallah would later become the charismatic leader of Hezbollah and one of the most influential leaders in the Arab world, a figure adored by the party faithful and treated with wary respect by his enemies.

He was born in 1960, the eldest of nine siblings. His father, Abdel-Karim, was a greengrocer who sold fruit and vegetables from a street cart in the slum quarter of Karantina, near Nabaa. The young Hassan spent his time reading the Koran and studying religious tracts, and by his own account he was a fully observant Muslim by the age of nine.

With the beginning of the civil war in 1975, the Nasrallah family escaped Karantina just before it fell to Christian militias for the relative peace of Bazouriyah, their home village surrounded by dense orange orchards on the outskirts of Tyre in south Lebanon.

Bazouriyah was a Communist stronghold in the mid-1970s, and Nasrallah's political consciousness quickly developed as he set about organizing religious youths into a study group held at an Islamic library in the village. That same year, he joined Amal, and although only fifteen years old, he was appointed the group's representative for his village.

Yet, for the young Nasrallah, the seminaries of Najaf beckoned. With a letter of introduction from a cleric in Tyre, he traveled to Baghdad, then Najaf, hoping to meet Sayyed Mohammed Baqr as-Sadr, the Dawa party leader and Fadlallah's old friend. By the late 1970s, the Shia religious institutions were facing pressure from the Baathist regime in Baghdad. On arrival in Najaf, Nasrallah met with a friend from Lebanon, who warned him that being seen with Baqr as-Sadr could cause him problems with the Iraqi authorities. The friend said he would introduce Nasrallah to someone close to Baqr as-Sadr who would arrange a meeting. The intermediary's name was Abbas Mussawi.

"I met Sayyed Abbas Mussawi for the first time in the street while we were on our way to see him, and, maybe because of his dark skin, I thought he was an Iraqi at first," Nasrallah later recalled. "I had already spent two days in Baghdad and Najaf and had become accustomed to the Iraqi accent, so I started talking to Sayyed Abbas in an Iraqi-tinged Lebanese accent; but he laughed and said, 'I am Lebanese, not Iraqi, you can relax.'"[10]

It was the beginning of a long and fruitful relationship between the two young men. Originally from Nabi Sheet, a small village scattered over a barren mountainside in the eastern Bekaa, Mussawi was eight years Nasrallah's senior and had been studying in Najaf with Baqr as-Sadr since 1970. On meeting Nasrallah, Baqr as-Sadr instructed Mussawi to take the Lebanese youngster under his wing and serve as his mentor and tutor.

Nasrallah spent the next eighteen months immersed in studies alongside a handful of other students under the guidance of Mussawi, whom the future Hezbollah leader considered as "a father, an educator, a friend."

"Under Sayyed Abbas, our group broke all routines, never took time off, and never rested, because Sayyed Abbas converted us into an active beehive and made us thirsty for learning," Nasrallah said.[11]

But his studies were cut short in early 1978 when the Iraqi regime launched a crackdown on the Najaf seminaries, arresting and expelling Lebanese clerical students. Nasrallah slipped out of Iraq avoiding arrest and returned to Lebanon, where he enrolled in a new *hawza* established by Mussawi in Baalbek.

Territorial Integrity

Nasrallah's return to Lebanon in mid-1978 coincided with several pivotal developments that were to have a profound impact on Lebanon's Shia community.

On March 11, a dozen armed Fatah fighters infiltrated northern Israel by sea, hijacked a bus with its passengers, and embarked on a shooting spree along the highway toward Tel Aviv. By the time the fighting had ended, all but two of the Palestinians were dead, along with thirty-seven Israelis, twenty-five of whom burned to death when the Fatah fighters blew up the bus with hand grenades.

The Israelis had been looking for an excuse to move into south Lebanon to drive out the PLO and consolidate Saad Haddad's militia. Now they had one. On the night of March 14, the Israelis invaded south Lebanon, punching north along four main axes between the coastal road in the west and the mountainous Arkoub district in the east. The Israeli government said it had no intention of occupying the area, but General Mordechai Gur, the IDF chief of staff, said that the goal was to link up Haddad's militia-controlled Christian enclaves and establish a "security belt" along the length of the border. The PLO had been expecting a major operation by the Israelis after the bus hijacking, but they underestimated the scale of the attack and were driven northward.

On March 19, the UN Security Council adopted Resolution 425, which called for "strict respect" of Lebanon's "territorial integrity, sovereignty and political independence" and demanded of Israel "immediately to cease its military action" against Lebanon and "withdraw forthwith its forces from all Lebanese territory." It also agreed to establish a UN Interim Force in Lebanon (UNIFIL) to oversee the Israeli withdrawal and help the Lebanese government restore its authority over the area.

The Israelis agreed to a cease-fire on March 21, by which time the IDF had occupied much of the area between the border and the Litani River. On May 22, Israel announced that it would withdraw its forces from Lebanon by June 13. But on the scheduled day of withdrawal, the departing Israelis handed over the border strip to its ally Saad Haddad rather than to UNIFIL, a move that simultaneously prevented the peacekeeping force from deploying along the border and fulfilled General Gur's pledge to establish a "security zone" in the south.

The Israelis refused to implement Resolution 425, and there was a lack of international will to force Israel to comply. The peacekeepers of

UNIFIL suddenly found themselves uncomfortably sandwiched between two enemies—Haddad's militia to the south and the PLO factions to the north. As the stalemate hardened, the "Interim" of UNIFIL's name soon became ironic; by 2011, the peacekeeping force was more than double the size of the six thousand peacekeepers that originally deployed in south Lebanon thirty-three years earlier.

Hemmed in on both sides, it was not long before UNIFIL was coming under regular attack from PLO fighters attempting to infiltrate its area and from Haddad's militia, which routinely harassed the peacekeepers with artillery and heavy machine gun fire.

The Vanished Imam

Just over two months after Israel's purported withdrawal from Lebanon, Musa Sadr vanished, along with his two companions, while on a visit to Libya. The Libyan authorities said that Sadr had left the country on an Alitalia flight bound for Rome, but the cleric and his two colleagues failed to arrive in Italy, and they have never been seen since.

Most probably Colonel Moammar Qaddafi, Libya's leader, had Sadr killed, for any number of possible reasons, and the cleric's body lies buried somewhere in the Libyan desert. Yet many Shias openly cling to the hope that Sadr is still alive (although he was already fifty years old in 1978) and will one day return to resume his role as champion of the community.

Inevitably, his mysterious disappearance evoked comparisons to the "hidden Imam" who vanished in the ninth century and whose return, the Twelver Shias believe, will herald the end of the world, and their salvation. It was an appropriately ambiguous end for a cleric who had so skillfully exploited the Shia motifs of Karbala and the martyrdom of Imams Ali and Hussein to mobilize the Shias from their communal languor.

The leadership of Amal fell in 1980 to Nabih Berri, a lawyer who had recently returned from the United States and who would emerge as one of Lebanon's most enduring and wily political players. Under Berri,

Amal moved in a secular direction, to the dismay of the religious cadres. In response, several prominent Dawa activists joined Amal, including Hassan Nasrallah, in a covert attempt to subtly influence the group along radical Islamic lines. Nasrallah became an official for Amal in the Bekaa Valley, organizing seminars, cultural meetings, and lectures in *husseiniyah*s and mosques to raise Islamic awareness among the local population.

Nonetheless, for the bulk of Lebanese Shias, the disappearance of Musa Sadr left a gaping void at the level of the community's leadership that could not be filled by the relatively colorless Berri and the secretive activities of a handful of Islamic activists. The vanished imam left many Shias hungry for a new leader who would inspire them and in whom they could invest their hopes for the future.

Absolute Authority

That figurehead emerged within months of Sadr's disappearance in the form of Ruhollah Khomeini, an Iranian Grand Ayatollah who by 1978 was regarded by many Iranians as the spiritual and political leader of the opposition to Mohammed Reza Shah Pahlavi, the ruler of Iran.

Khomeini had been a persistent critic of the Shah for many years and was exiled in 1964 for his verbal attacks against the Pahlavi regime. He settled in Najaf the following year, where he became known to a wider audience of Shia students and clerics.

In early 1970, Khomeini gave a landmark series of lectures in which he outlined his theories of an Islamic government, known as the *wilayat al-faqih*—the guardianship of the jurisprudent. Khomeini postulated that the laws of a nation should be the laws of God, the Sharia, and therefore those holding power should possess a full knowledge and understanding of the holy laws. The ruler of an Islamic state should be the preeminent *faqih*, or jurist, who "surpasses all others in knowledge" and whose ordinances must be obeyed because "the law of Islam, divine command, has absolute authority over all individuals and the Islamic government."

His theory was not unique but was a distillation of ideas propounded by earlier prominent clerics. But it was controversial and many Shia clerics opposed it, believing that the clergy's role was to provide guidance and advice on religious and moral matters, not running the daily affairs of a state.

By the beginning of 1978, unrest against the Shah in Iran had erupted into street demonstrations drawing tens of thousands of protesters, which turned into revolution as the months progressed. In January 1979, the Shah fled Iran, and two weeks later Khomeini set foot on Iranian soil for the first time in fourteen years.

The establishment of a theocratic Shia state in Iran was greeted with silent dismay among most Arab states. Syria, however, was the first Arab nation to offer congratulations to Khomeini, followed by the PLO, Algeria, and Libya. Despite Khomeini's absorption with Iranian politics during his long years of exile, he was a committed supporter of the Palestinian cause. Since the early 1970s, Yasser Arafat's Fatah movement had provided military training in camps in Lebanon to Iranian anti-Shah revolutionaries, including one of Khomeini's sons. Arafat had craftily cultivated public displays of support for Khomeini (even putting up posters of the Iranian ayatollah in PLO-controlled areas of Beirut) in an attempt to soften the hostility of southern Lebanese Shias toward the Palestinians. Arafat was the first foreign official to travel to Iran following Khomeini's return, and he was rewarded with the newly vacated Israeli embassy in Tehran to house the Palestinian diplomatic mission.

For Lebanon's Shias, the Islamic revolution had an electrifying effect. Khomeini and his fellow revolutionaries had boldly demonstrated the benefits of organized religious action and given a new sense of empowerment and pride to Shias in general. Khomeini quickly became the new inspiration and leader for Lebanese Shias lamenting the vanished Musa Sadr and for those who considered the Islamic revolution an exemplar of action against one's oppressors and enemies.

Not only Shias were inspired by the Islamic revolution. Khomeini's ideas of an Islamic state were not rooted in exclusivist Shia dogma, but were a pan-Islamic concept to be embraced by all Muslims. Anis Naqqash, the Fatah guerilla commander who helped train Imad Mughniyah, was a Sunni but became an early convert to the Islamic revolution, which he hoped would help him construct a Lebanese anti-Israel resistance.

"After the Islamic revolution, we changed all our articles and speeches to support Khomeini," Naqqash recalls. He left Fatah following the 1978 Israeli invasion and established a small militant group called Harakat al-Lubnan al-Arabi, the Arab Lebanese Movement. The ALM consisted of some 150 recruits drawn from Fatah's Student Battalions as well as other factions.

The Lebanese Dawa activists also formed a network of secret armed cells, dubbed Qassam, that was based mainly in Beirut and clashed regularly with fighters from the Iraqi Baath Party, particularly after war broke out between Iran and Iraq in 1980. The Qassam militants also served as bodyguards to senior figures in the Lebanese Dawa, and its cadres would later play an important role in the Islamic Resistance, Hezbollah's military wing.

The success of the Islamic revolution inevitably aggravated the divergent viewpoints within Amal, distancing even further the besuited secularists of Nabih Berri from the turbaned Islamists such as Hassan Nasrallah. It was evident to the Iranians that Amal was not a suitable vehicle to carry the Islamic revolution into Lebanon. Khomeini was profoundly sympathetic to the Palestinian cause and lent support to PLO factions in Lebanon. But Amal's relations with the Palestinians deteriorated steadily from 1979 on, clashes between the two erupting with increasing regularity and ferocity. Furthermore, Iran enjoyed warm relations with Colonel Moammar Qaddafi of Libya, whom Amal's leadership continued to blame for Musa Sadr's disappearance. The Iranians effectively ignored Amal's entreaties to use their ties with Libya to discover Sadr's fate.

But Iran's disregard for Amal did not translate into immediate financial and logistical support for the pro-Khomeini Islamist elements in Lebanon. For the first two years after the revolution, Khomeini and his Islamic radicals were locked in competition with the Iranian leftist revolutionaries for control of the republic. Then, starting in 1980, Iran was embroiled in a debilitating war with neighboring Iraq. Both priorities sidetracked Iran from mobilizing the state's resources to promote the Islamic revolution in Lebanon. Sheikh Sobhi Tufayli, a gruff, dark-skinned cleric with piercing coal-black eyes from the Bekaa village of Brital, remembers that many discussions were held between Lebanese Islamists and the new leadership in Iran about the "ideas of Imam Khomeini on liberating Jerusalem from Lebanon."

"The only thing we lacked was financial support to lay the foundation of our resistance," he says.

Ariel Sharon's Grand Plan

In April 1979, Saad Haddad irrevocably split from the Lebanese state and confirmed his alliance with Israel by proclaiming his narrow border strip as "Independent Free Lebanon" and his militia as the "Army of Free Lebanon." The pugnacious major marked the announcement by bombarding the UNIFIL headquarters in the coastal village of Naqoura, which actually lay inside Haddad's area, using rockets, artillery, and heavy machine guns. Eight peacekeepers were wounded in the exchange and three UN helicopters damaged. The next day, the Lebanese government condemned Haddad as a traitor and officially dismissed him from the Lebanese army. Haddad and his Army of Free Lebanon militia were now wholly dependent on Israeli support.

The AFL was still essentially a Christian militia, but some Israeli commanders believed that recruitment should be broadened to other communities, especially the Shia, now that the border "security belt" had expanded. There had been some attempts before the 1978 invasion to win over those Shia villages adjacent to the Christian enclaves. Six villages were approached by the Israelis in early 1978 with promises of jobs in Israel and protection from the PLO if the residents agreed to be linked to the IDF Northern Command headquarters by radio and telephones. All six villages declined the offer.[12]

Further attempts to recruit Shias into Haddad's militia followed the 1978 invasion. "We organized Ashoura celebrations for them and allowed them to come into Israel to work," recalls Ephraim Sneh, the commander of the IDF's Lebanon Liaison Unit before 1982. On one occasion, he arranged for five thousand Shias to enter Israel to pray at the shrine of Nabi Yusha, which had been a popular place of pilgrimage before 1948. "It was risky," he says. "If just five of the five thousand had decided to stay in Israel and cause trouble, my head would have been chopped off."

In June 1981, the Likud government of Prime Minister Menachem Begin was reelected and Ariel Sharon was appointed defense minister. Sharon was a war hero in Israel, a barrel-chested warrior of the old school, a brilliant tactician who had played important roles in Israel's earlier conflicts. But he was also compulsive and politically ambitious, a bulldozing character who brooked no dissension.

A month after the Israeli election, the most serious fighting in years erupted between the Palestinians and Israel. The PLO's restraint against repeated Israeli air strikes in the spring of 1981 finally ended in early July, when it launched a sustained and unprecedented rocket barrage against northern Israel. Thousands of Israeli civilians fled Kiryat Shemona and other towns in the north, the first time rocket fire from Lebanon had spurred such an exodus. The Israelis hit back by bombing PLO centers in the densely populated Fakhani district in Beirut, killing scores of civilians. But the Israelis had no answer for the Katyusha rocket barrages, and after two weeks of fighting, they agreed to a U.S.-brokered cease-fire deal.

With the guns on both sides falling silent, Sharon concluded that the only solution to the Katyusha problem was to drive the PLO out of Lebanon altogether. In the following months, he devised a grand scheme that he believed not only would end the PLO scourge but would change the very shape of the region. Israel would mount an all-out invasion of Lebanon to oust the PLO and remove Syrian forces. The IDF would link up with its Christian militia allies, and Bashir Gemayel, the head of the Kataeb, the most powerful faction, would be installed as Lebanese president. Israel and Lebanon would then sign a peace treaty, and all would be well.

The full details of the plan Sharon kept to himself and his key lieutenants, but by the beginning of 1982 it was common knowledge that

Israel was looking to stage a second, larger incursion into Lebanon. As the months passed, Ariel Sharon was like a tethered pit bull terrier straining at the leash and desperately looking for an excuse to launch his grand plan. But the Palestinians knew what was coming and ignored Israel's repeated provocations in the spring of 1982, which included IDF troop surges in the Haddad enclave, jets flying over Syrian positions, and an air strike against PLO positions after an Israeli soldier was killed when he stepped on an old land mine in south Lebanon. Although an invasion was clearly imminent, the PLO was ill prepared to confront the Israelis. By 1982, the fighting strength of the PLO was around five thousand full-time Palestinian fighters and another eight or nine thousand part-timers and Lebanese volunteers marshaled into regular military structures from platoons to companies, battalions, and brigades.[13] But most units were well below strength, the fighters insufficiently trained, poorly organized, and lacking a military doctrine to successfully make the switch from small-unit guerrilla tactics with which most cadres were familiar. Furthermore, the PLO failed to draw up contingency plans in which the semi-organized military structure could be broken down into autonomous guerrilla units to harass the Israeli supply lines and attack troops to the rear. Indeed, General Rafael Eitan, the IDF chief of staff in 1982, had expressed satisfaction at the sight of the PLO "going regular," knowing that it would be easier to smash them as a weak conventional force than as bands of lightly armed and mobile guerrillas.[14]

In the end, the catalyst for the invasion did not occur along the Lebanon-Israel border, nor indeed in the Middle East, but four thousand miles away, in London. On June 3, Shlomo Argov, the Israeli ambassador, was shot and badly wounded by members of the radical Revolutionary Fatah Council of Abu Nidal, a sworn enemy of Yasser Arafat.

Although the assassination attempt was clearly the act of an agent provocateur, Israel launched retaliatory air raids against PLO offices and facilities in Beirut, killing more than two hundred people. General Eitan, who had recommended the option of air strikes to the Israeli cabinet, knew that the PLO had standing orders to automatically shell settlements in northern Israel in response to raids on its headquarters in Beirut, a fact he omitted to mention to the ministers.[15]

As Eitan expected, two hours after the air raids, the Palestinians opened fire on northern Israel for the first time since the July 1981 cease-fire.

Ariel Sharon at last had his excuse for war.

The "Shia Genie"

We are prepared to put our facilities and necessary training at the disposal
of all the Muslims who are prepared to fight against the Zionist regime.

—ALI KHAMENEI,
President of Iran, June 1982

JUNE 6, 1982

DAMASCUS, Syria—Sheikh Sobhi Tufayli was told the news while
waiting at Damascus airport for a flight to Tehran: Israel was bombing
PLO bases in Beirut and south Lebanon. Columns of Israeli troops and
tanks were massed along the border, and it was evident that the long-
anticipated invasion of Lebanon was about to begin. Tufayli and his
young colleague, Sheikh Ragheb Harb, the imam of Jibsheet village in
south Lebanon, were traveling to the Iranian capital to attend a conference
of Islamic liberation movements. But Israel's imminent invasion was
bound to overshadow the event. Normally dour and severe, Tufayli felt a
tremor of excitement as he contemplated what this would mean for the
goal of building an Islamic resistance against Israel. Although Tufayli and
other Lebanese Shia leaders had held many discussions with top Iranian
officials about how to build an anti-Israel resistance, nothing concrete
had emerged. But now, surely, with the Israelis poised to charge into
Lebanon, it would change everything, Tufayli thought.[1]

At nine o'clock that same Sunday morning, General William Callaghan, commander of UNIFIL, received a phone call from General

Eitan, the IDF chief of staff, requesting an urgent meeting. The border was only a five-minute drive from Callaghan's headquarters in Naqoura. The Irish general assumed the meeting was in connection with the impending invasion, which looked set to occur at any moment.

The meeting with Eitan was brief, and once it was over, Callaghan, seething at the short notice given him by the Israelis, telephoned UNIFIL headquarters from Israel and said tersely, "Rubicon"—the peacekeepers' code word that the invasion was on.

The first tanks crossed the border at 10:00 A.M., entering Lebanon at five main points along the frontier. The UNIFIL troops were impotent in the face of Israel's armored juggernaut. A unit of Dutch soldiers manning a checkpoint on the coast two miles north of Naqoura threw obstacles onto the road to block the advance. The lead tank, a British-built Centurion, struck the steel obstacles and was disabled, and the second Israeli tank lost a caterpillar track. After that, the six Dutch soldiers ran out of tank traps and stood by helplessly. One soldier fetched a camera and took pictures as the armored column rumbled past.

In Naqoura, Timur Goksel, a Turkish UNIFIL press officer who had joined the peacekeeping force three years earlier, watched the seemingly endless armored vehicles trundle by. "They were facing so little opposition that they did not bother with a combat formation," he recalled. "In Naqoura alone, we counted twelve hundred tanks and four thousand armored personnel carriers. God knows what else was pouring in. If a tank braked in Tyre, they were backed up all the way to Nahariya in Israel."

UNIFIL's helplessness irked Yasser Arafat, who had forlornly hoped that the moral authority of the UN might slow the advance. "At least you could have shot in the air, like when our people approach you," he later grumbled to a UN official.[2] But the PLO had done itself few favors in its lack of adequate defensive preparations to confront an invasion that had been expected for months. The main roads were unmined and the bridges left intact, the latter contrary to the expectations of even Israeli military commanders. With many PLO commanders fleeing north, the fighters simply dropped their weapons, shed their uniforms, and tried to escape the approaching Israelis.

The poor performance was redeemed somewhat by courageous individual stands. Among them were the handful of Palestinian defenders of Beaufort Castle who fought to the death against a unit of Golani Brigade commandos, the last one firing his machine gun from a concrete bunker until it was destroyed by a hurled satchel of explosives.

The stiffest defense mounted in south Lebanon was by the militias guarding the Palestinian refugee camps. The Palestinians, including children as young as thirteen or fourteen, blocked the narrow alleyways and fought the Israelis at close range with rocket-propelled grenades (RPGs). Even with air raids, it still took four days to subdue the Tyre camps. The fighting in the larger refugee camp of Ain al-Hilweh, on the outskirts of Sidon, was even fiercer. The Israelis razed the camp with artillery, air strikes, and tank fire after failing to persuade the residents to leave by dropping leaflets and broadcasting warnings over mosque loudspeakers.

While the Palestinians in the camps greeted the Israeli invaders with RPGs and grenades, the Lebanese Shias of the south, for the most part, welcomed them with handfuls of thrown rice. For the Shia population, the Israelis were liberators, driving the boorish and detested Palestinian gunmen from their villages and towns. Amal's leadership in the south instructed the fighters not to resist the Israelis, and even ordered them to hand over their weapons if required.

Syrian forces in the southern Bekaa Valley fought bravely against overwhelming odds. The Israeli Air Force first jammed and destroyed Syrian radar, then attacked the blinded surface-to-air missile (SAM) sites in the Bekaa. The Syrian Air Force was completely outmatched in the skies over southern Lebanon when some seventy Syrian MiGs took on about a hundred Israeli F-15s and F-16s, losing a total of sixty-four planes in two days' fighting. With Syria's air cover smashed, the IDF charged up the Bekaa Valley toward the Syrian positions. The Syrian ground forces fought stubbornly for every inch of ground gained by the IDF. An Israeli armored column was halted by Syrian tanks at the village of Sultan Yacoub and prevented from reaching the crucial Beirut–Damascus highway that bisected the Bekaa Valley.

The Israelis also met with fierce and unexpected resistance at Khalde at the southern approach to Beirut. Here a mixed bag of Syrian soldiers, Syrian-backed Palestinian fighters, Lebanese militiamen, Amal militants, and Khomeini-inspired Shia radicals checked the Israeli armored column as it pushed up the coastal road. Among them were Imad Mughniyah and his friends, who tied strips of cloth around their foreheads in emulation of Iranian fighters battling Iraqi troops and rushed out of the southern suburbs to confront the advancing Israelis. They fought with suicidal abandon, blasting Israeli tanks with RPGs at point-blank range. Ahmad Hallaq, a fearsome, bearded giant of a man who fought with the Syrian-backed As-Saiqa Palestinian faction, even captured an Israeli Centurion tank and rode it in triumph back to his headquarters in the Shatila refugee camp.

Meanwhile, in Tehran, Tufayli and Harb were busy arranging Iranian support for a new Shia resistance force to confront the Israelis. Even though Iran was focused on war with neighboring Iraq, its leaders recognized that the Israeli invasion of Lebanon was an opportunity to spread the Islamic revolution to the front lines of the Arab-Israeli conflict. It was an opportunity that had to be seized.

"I met with certain leaders and they recognized the need for support. Khomeini was very realistic about this," Tufayli recalls. "When the invasion happened it accelerated everything."

A military communiqué in Tehran said that Iranian troops and Revolutionary Guards were being dispatched to Lebanon "to engage in face-to-face battle against Israel, the primary enemy of Islam and the Muslims." Two days into the invasion, an Iranian delegation comprising the defense minister and top army commanders was in Damascus discussing terms of military assistance with the Syrians.

"To us, there is no difference between the fronts in the south of Iran [against Iraq] and in south Lebanon," said Ali Khamenei, then president of Iran. "We are prepared to put our facilities and necessary training at the disposal of all the Muslims who are prepared to fight against the Zionist regime."

Preaching Religion

Farhan Ali Ismael could have been no older than twenty when he died on November 16, 1983. The Iranian soldier's youthful face gazes with a wide-eyed and slightly nervous expression from a black-and-white photograph tucked into a small glass box filled with colorful plastic and silk flowers that sits on a stand above the gray marble slab marking his grave. Ismael is one of eight Iranian Revolutionary Guards buried in the "martyrs' cemetery" in a corner of Brital, a dusty, disheveled village scattered along either side of a shallow stream running down the rugged, barren mountains on the eastern flank of the Bekaa Valley. There are no Iranian soldiers stationed in Brital today, but it was here and in the surrounding Shia villages in 1982 that the Iranian Revolutionary Guards Corps (IRGC) began the process of mobilization, recruitment, religious education, and military training that provided the foundation for the emergence of Hezbollah.

The first Iranians to arrive in Syria in the wake of the Israeli invasion consisted of some five thousand Iranian Revolutionary Guards and religious officers who were expecting to deploy quickly into Lebanon and confront the IDF advance up the southern Bekaa Valley. But by the time they landed at Damascus airport, the fighting between the IDF and Syrian forces in the Bekaa Valley was over. The Israelis had halted a few miles south of the key Beirut–Damascus highway, well short of the Bekaa's Shia areas farther north. Assad had no desire to allow the IRGC into Lebanon to reignite a war that had proved so costly to Syria in equipment and manpower and could yet threaten his regime. But he did agree to a military accord with Tehran in which the Iranians would help build a Lebanese resistance force to do the fighting instead. In exchange for this Iranian toehold on Lebanese soil, Tehran agreed to supply Syria with 9 million tons of free oil a year.

Most of the Revolutionary Guards returned to Iran, but around fifteen hundred elements, mainly drawn from the IRGC's Office of the Islamic Liberation Movements, stayed behind to establish a base of operations in Syria on the outskirts of the resort town of Zabadani on the border with Lebanon.

The physical link between the new IRGC base at Zabadani and the nearest Shia villages in the Bekaa was an old smuggler's track that snaked through a narrow valley cutting through barren 4,500-foot-high mountains. The track terminated at the hamlet of Janta, a cluster of small stone houses beside a river, lined with poplar and walnut trees, that gushed and splashed through a steep valley of towering limestone crags before emerging into the Bekaa plain.

The first few hundred Revolutionary Guards used this track to move into the Bekaa, renting houses in Baalbek and then visiting the surrounding villages. They adopted a low-key and convivial approach. The IRGC wore khaki military uniforms, but they were unarmed. The mission initially was to raise the religious consciousness of the local people and to spread the teachings of Khomeini in preparation for resistance against Israel.

Among the Iranians arriving in the Bekaa was a diminutive engineer in his late twenties with narrow eyes, called Mahmoud Ahmadinejad. The future president of the Islamic Republic was one of a group of Iranians who set up a camp beside a copse of spindly poplar trees in a shallow valley called Hawsh Bay near the village of Taraya. Local residents still remember Ahmadinejad with affection and not a little pride at his later public role.

Before the civil war, Baalbek attracted coachloads of tourists who came to gape at the magnificent Roman temples beside the town and attend the world-renowned music festival each summer. But with the arrival of the Iranians, Baalbek and some of the nearby villages soon began to take on the trappings of a mini-Iran. Huge, eye-catching murals appeared on walls depicting Shia motifs and images—Imam Hussein in the blood-splattered sands of Karbala; Khomeini gazing with beetle-browed intensity at the Al-Aqsa mosque in Jerusalem, Islam's third holiest site. Iranian flags fluttered alongside banners hanging from electricity pylons or suspended across roads exhorting "Death to America." The main square in Baalbek was renamed after Khomeini. Women began to wear the full-length black chador. Alcohol was removed from the shelves in shops and hotels. IRGC clerics taught classes on the Koran and Khomeini's theories on Islam. Others visited *husseiniyahs* in villages to give lectures on the Iranian revolution and show films of the Iran-Iraq war.

It was a slow process, but the Iranians were methodical and patient.

"Most people were happy to see them, but others were suspicious," recalls Hussein Hamiyah, then a university student from the Bekaa village of Taraya. "Some thought that the Iranians should have fought the Israelis and couldn't understand why they were wasting their time preaching religion to us."

The Iranian campaign to persuade and recruit the Shias was aided by a split within the ranks of Amal a week into the Israeli invasion when Nabih Berri, the movement's leader, agreed to join a committee of "national salvation" under the leadership of President Elias Sarkis. Also included in the committee was Bashir Gemayel, leader of the Christian Kataeb militia, whom Ariel Sharon had earmarked as the next president of Lebanon. The Islamists within Amal were outraged that Berri would sit at the same table as an ally of Israel. Hussein Mussawi, the deputy leader of Amal, angrily denounced Berri as a collaborator and moved to the Bekaa with his followers to establish a new faction called Islamic Amal. In Tehran, Sayyed Ibrahim al-Amine, Amal's representative to the Iranian capital, publicly announced his split from the movement. Another defector from Amal was Hassan Nasrallah.

Gradually, shepherded by the IRGC, a loose coalition began to emerge in the Bekaa consisting of the Amal defectors, Mussawi's Islamic Amal, members of the Lebanese Union of Muslim Students, and adherents of the Lebanese Dawa party, as well as numerous tiny institutes and study groups that comprised the radical Shia milieu in Lebanon. Although they lacked an organizational framework, they shared common ideas and outlooks. The ranks were also augmented with those Shias who had fought with Palestinian factions and were looking for a new paymaster after the bulk of the PLO evacuated from Beirut at the end of August. Among them was Imad Mughniyah, who recognized that the new group coalescing in the Bekaa under Iranian stewardship was the right vehicle for him and his comrades. Mughniyah exploited his connections with Fatah and Anis Naqqash's Arab Lebanese Movement to persuade fresh recruits to join the new Iranian-directed resistance in the Bekaa.

The leaders were Lebanese clerics, mainly from the Bekaa, such as

Sheikh Sobhi Tufayli, Sayyed Abbas Mussawi, and Sheikh Mohammed Yazbek, all of whom had studied in Najaf under Sayyed Mohammed Baqr as-Sadr. They expressed commitment to Khomeini's leadership and sought to build an organization rooted in Islam that looked beyond Lebanon's parochial purview and was dedicated to the struggle against Israel.

"We wanted our own organization, which would be more pan-Islamic and supportive of the Palestinians [than Amal]," Tufayli recalls. "We wanted to lay the foundations of an institution that would be independent and not have specific influences on the Lebanese scene. We wanted it to be completely dependent on Islamic law and not influenced by nationalist ideologies. During that period there were many discussions and details worked out."

The result was the "Manifesto of the Nine," a synthesis of the new organization's ideas and goals. The three main tenets of the manifesto were, first, the recognition of Islam as the "comprehensive, complete and appropriate program for a better life" that would provide the "intellectual, religious, ideological and practical foundation" of the new organization; second, that resistance against Israel was the "ultimate confrontation priority," requiring the creation of a "jihad structure"; and third, recognition of the "legitimate leadership" of the *wali al-faqih,* whose "commands and proscriptions are enforceable."[3] Nine delegates were selected to represent the different elements within the new movement—three from the Bekaa, three from Islamic Amal, and three representing the other factions.

The new movement initially went unnamed, and it was not until the beginning of 1984 that the leadership settled on a quotation from the Koran to provide the name of the new organization: "Verily, the party of God shall be victorious."

" 'Hezbollah' is a Koranic term, and we used to see Iranian leaders address crowds, saying 'O Hezbollah,' and we chose that phrase as our new name," Tufayli recalls.

The nascent organization made its first move on November 21, 1982, the eve of Lebanon's independence day, when units of Mussawi's Islamic Amal stormed Baalbek, seizing the municipal offices and the Sheikh

Abdullah army barracks on a hill overlooking the town. The Lebanese troops in the barracks were expelled from Baalbek along a main road lined with armed and jeering Shia militants. The Sheikh Abdullah barracks became the new Bekaa headquarters for the Revolutionary Guards.

Amal's leadership watched with unease as the Revolutionary Guards mobilized the Shias of the Bekaa Valley. Although Amal dominated the south, it was evident that the movement was beginning to lose traction in the Bekaa.

"We tried talking to the Iranians, saying that we didn't want tensions," recalls Aql Hamiyah, by 1982 a top military commander in Amal. "Hezbollah became more stubborn in Baalbek and the villages around Baalbek. The Iranians told us that we could resist together, but on the ground things were going differently. The Iranians had their own agenda. The Iranians were working for something new."

"We Called Ourselves Al-Shabab al-Aamel"

In south Lebanon, meanwhile, the Israeli troops were enjoying a halcyon existence, having been seduced by the handfuls of thrown rice and the cheers that had greeted their armored columns into believing that the Shias cared only about the departure of the detested Palestinians and had no objection to the Israelis' filling the vacuum. In those early weeks of the occupation, Israeli troops frequented local shops, lounged in the sun atop armored vehicles, and visited movie theaters. Road signs in Hebrew were erected. Coachloads of Israeli tourists visited the Roman ruins in Tyre and looked for bargains in the Sidon souks. Israel's national flag carrier, El Al, opened an office in Sidon and in its first two weeks sold 350 tickets to Lebanese, Egyptians, Palestinians, Saudis, foreigners, and others.[4]

Instead of taking advantage of Amal's anti-PLO attitude to forge a new security arrangement for the south, the Israelis resorted to their Christian ally, Saad Haddad, allowing him to expand his area of operations from the narrow buffer strip along the border to include the entire south up to the Awali River just north of Sidon. By mid-July, Haddad's militia had recruited and armed hundreds of Shias and instituted a new tax regime that included levies on car registration, sand for building, and gasoline sales, which did little to endear the major from Marjayoun to the Shias.

The Israelis also established Al-Haras al-Watani li Qura al-Janoub, the National Guard for the Villages of the South, a mercenary force of locally recruited Shias that was supposed to operate independently of Haddad's Army of Free Lebanon militia. The units were given names such as the Partisans of the Army, the Forces of Karbala, or the Sons of the Cedars.

Those Shias who declined to accept the Israeli shekel risked falling afoul of the harsh security regime imposed by the IDF. Suspected militants or PLO sympathizers were rounded up, interrogated, and detained in one of several prison camps established in the south. The largest prison was a purpose-built internment camp constructed near the village of Ansar in the chalky hills midway between Sidon and Tyre.

The Israelis built new outposts, leveled ground for helicopter landing pads, consolidated their control of the main transport routes, and imposed a security regime on the south that looked set to stay. South Lebanon became known as the "North Bank" of the Jordan, an analogy with the West Bank captured by Israel in 1967 and subsequently colonized by Jewish settlers. The analogy was misleading—the Israelis were not intending to build settlements in south Lebanon. Yet although the southern Shias were glad to see the PLO gone, it was not long before they began to wonder whether they had simply exchanged one oppressor for another.

While the south simmered in the late summer of 1982, an organized resistance against the Israeli occupation was beginning to emerge farther north. Spearheaded by secular leftist groups, the National Resistance Movement was established in early September and was soon carrying out isolated attacks on Israeli troops in west Beirut and the mountains overlooking the capital. The resistance operations in and around Beirut caught the attention of those Shias in the south who were chafing at Amal's acquiescence toward the Israeli occupation. Among them was a skinny Amal recruit in his midteens from a small village near

Sidon, whom we shall call "the Kid." He went to his local Amal commander and told him that resistance was a "religious duty and we have to fight." His commander smiled benignly, congratulated him for his zeal, and told him to await orders. "Then I opened my eyes and saw that Amal was not willing to do anything. When I saw the operations [in Beirut] increasing, I decided to go ahead anyway."

The Kid's first operation was typical of the period. He and three other friends hid in an orange grove on the southern edge of Sidon and shot up a passing Israeli jeep with AK-47s. Word of the ambush quickly spread, and the next day he was visited by a stranger who called himself Abu Hussein and said he had learned the Kid wished to join the resistance.

"I said, 'Yes, we will do whatever you want.' He said, 'Okay, but our resistance is different. We are the followers of Imam Khomeini. We believe in the *wilayat al-faqih*.' I said, 'Of course! I am like this.' I believed in these things, but I didn't have a framework in which to practice this faith."

The Kid formally recruited his three comrades and became the cell's sole link to Abu Hussein for security reasons. Slowly, more young Shias were brought into the network. Initially, there were about eighty members and ten commanders. The Kid soon developed a deadly proficiency for killing collaborators. "It was easy at the time. The collaborators were well known. I killed many persons," the Kid says with a sheepish smile.

His first victim was a top agent for the Israelis. The Kid and a colleague slipped one evening into the collaborator's home but backed away when they heard the voices of his wife and children. The collaborator was marked for death, but there was no need to kill him in front of his family. Another opportunity soon arose when the Kid saw the collaborator walk into a shop.

"We opened the door and went inside the store. He was in front of me and I started firing at him. The bullets hit his body and shook him. Then my friend came in and also fired at him. He died straightaway. I was very professional at killing collaborators. I saw it as a duty. I never felt guilty."

For the Kid and his confederates, nothing mattered except the "holy cause" of resistance. Families and peacetime friendships were neglected. No thought was given to money or the enjoyments of life. "We didn't have salaries for years. We were paying from our own pockets. The first time they talked about salaries for us, I felt it was shameful. We all wanted to be martyrs. . . . We believed in the *wilayat al-faqih*. If [Abu Hussein] told me to do something, I would obey. If I didn't it would be like disobeying God. We called ourselves Al-Shabab al-Aamel [the Men of Work]. This was the very beginning."

"We Should Call It the Islamic Resistance"

The Shia followers of Khomeini were not the only Islamists in south Lebanon looking to launch resistance operations against the Israelis. In Sidon, a mainly Sunni city, militants belonging to the Muslim Brotherhood were pondering how to strike at the Israeli soldiers wandering carefree around the port city.

Abdullah Tiryaki, a prominent member of the Brotherhood, was eager to begin a resistance campaign, but the leadership in Sidon was hesitant. Tiring of the procrastination, Tiryaki and some of his friends split from the Brotherhood and began scavenging rubbish dumps for discarded weapons and old mortar shells they could turn into bombs. Like the Kid and the emerging Shia resistance network, the Sunni Islamists formed close-knit cells of three volunteers each. Their first military operation was in October 1982, detonating an old mortar shell they had found in the street against a passing Israeli patrol. Other attacks followed, but they evaded capture by the Israelis, partly by adopting bland secular names for their group—the Interior Forces, the Patriotic People's Party—so that the Israelis would not focus on the Islamists.

After one of their number was caught, Tiryaki and several colleagues escaped to Beirut, where they could train and organize themselves. They changed their name to Quwat al-Fajr, the Dawn Forces, and soon caught the attention of Sayyed Abbas Mussawi, then a key leader in the nascent Hezbollah resistance. Mussawi provided Quwat al-Fajr with logistical assistance and sent its cadres to the Sheikh Abdullah barracks in Baalbek for training. "Our relationship with Mussawi was very special, so we began working with the Shias and gaining from their presence," Tiryaki recalls.

Although Hezbollah is a Shia organization, throughout its existence it has actively sought to build ties with Sunnis with the goal of uniting the Muslim community of believers, the *umma*, in resistance against Israel. While Khomeini's doctrine of *wilayat al-faqih* is anathema to most Sunni Islamists, the Iranian leader's staunch and sustained support for the Palestinian cause helped blur the distinctions between Sunnis and Shias. In 1982, the Iranians helped set up the Tajammu al-Ulama al-Muslimeen, the Congregation of Muslim Ulama [Islamic scholars], which brought together Lebanese and Palestinian clerics, both Shias and Sunnis, with the aim of encouraging Islamic observance and smoothing over sectarian differences between the two Muslim sects. "The Islamic revolution in Iran made our dreams come true," says Sheikh Maher Hammoud, a prominent Sunni cleric from Sidon who was a founder of the Tajammu.

In Tripoli in north Lebanon, the Iranians cultivated close contacts with Saeed Shaaban, the head of Harakat Tawheed Islami, the Islamic Unification Movement, also a supporter of the Islamic revolution in Iran. Shaaban, who established an Islamic fief in Tripoli in the mid-1980s and fought against the Syrians, was among those attending the fateful Islamic conference in Tehran in June 1982 when Sheikh Sobhi Tufayli and Sheikh Ragheb Harb won support for the creation of an anti-Israel resistance. His son, Bilal, who heads the Tawheed today, still maintains the group's alliance with Hezbollah.

The Khomeini-inspired Shia resistance in south Lebanon had no formal organizational moniker in the first two years after the Israeli invasion. According to Abdullah Tiryaki, the future name of Hezbollah's military wing arose out of a series of conversations he held with Mussawi. "Mussawi liked our name Quwat al-Fajr because the Iranians were using the word *Fajr* [Dawn] as the code name for some of their offensives against Iraq," he recalls.

But Tiryaki told Mussawi that the name was "too small," and after a few meetings together, "I came up with the idea that we should call it the

Islamic Resistance." Mussawi consulted with his colleagues and a week later told Tiryaki that the name had been approved.

"Who Would Want to Blow Themselves Up?"

While the Iranians steadily mobilized the Shias of the Bekaa Valley and Lebanese members of freshly departed Palestinian groups pondered their options, some militants were impatient to begin the campaign of resistance against the Israelis.

"Imad Mughniyah came to me and said he had someone willing to blow himself up against the Israelis," recalls Bilal Sharara, then a prominent Lebanese member of Fatah. "He wanted some explosives and wondered whether I had some for him. I laughed and thought he was crazy. Who would want to blow themselves up? No one had done anything like that at the time. Mughniyah went to other people and asked for explosives, but they did not believe him either."

But one man did believe Mughniyah—Khalil Wazir, better known as Abu Jihad, Arafat's popular second in command. Abu Jihad provided the explosives for Mughniyah's planned operation, according to Sharara.

Mughniyah's volunteer suicide bomber was a childhood friend, Ahmad Qassir, a seventeen-year-old from Deir Qanoun an-Nahr near Tyre with thick, dark hair, soulful eyes, and a wispy adolescent moustache. Devout from an early age, Qassir passed messages between cells of fighters and transferred weapons in his pickup truck in the fall of 1982, as the Israelis were feeling the first pinpricks of resistance in the south.

In early November, he left home, telling his family he was going to Beirut, and that was the last they saw of him. Shortly before seven o'clock on the morning of November 11, Qassir drove a white Peugeot sedan packed with explosives into the entrance of a seven-story building on the edge of Tyre that served as the IDF headquarters. The massive blast ignited an ammunition storeroom, pancaking the building and killing 75 Israeli soldiers, border police, and intelligence personnel. Additionally, 15 Lebanese and Palestinians who were being detained for questioning were killed.

Mughniyah had planned the attack carefully, having personally re-connoitered the IDF headquarters in Tyre. The operation aimed to cause the maximum casualties by timing the bomb attack to coincide with the return to the headquarters of IDF night patrols, but before the morning patrols had departed. Also, the building was fuller than usual because Israeli troops had relocated to the headquarters after heavy rains had damaged their tents in a nearby encampment.

There were two telephoned claims of responsibility—one of them by a previously unknown group called Islamic Jihad, which claimed that it had infiltrated bombs set to a timer into the building. No mention was made of a suicide bomb attack. Days later, the Israelis announced that an investigation had concluded it was an accident caused by leaky gas bottles in the kitchen.

Among Qassir's final requests was that his identity as the perpetrator of the attack remain secret until after the withdrawal of the Israelis so that his family in Deir Qanoun would not face reprisals. Hezbollah honored his dying wish, and Qassir's role in the first ever suicide attack against the Israelis in Lebanon was not revealed until two and a half years later, on May 19, 1985, just after the Israelis had withdrawn from the Tyre district.

The suicide bombing of the IDF headquarters in Tyre was the first major attack against the Israelis since the invasion. The Israelis thought—or hoped—it was an isolated incident. But even as the bodies were being pulled from the rubble of the IDF headquarters in Tyre, the Iranian Revolutionary Guards in the Bekaa were planning to introduce military training programs alongside the religious lessons to build a new Shia resistance force whose cadres would soon be making their way to the front lines in Beirut and the south.

The first IRGC-run military camp was located in a valley near Janta village. The recruitment process was surprisingly slow and meticulous in the beginning. Volunteers were required to submit a written request to join the resistance, along with a reference from two Shia clerics. The wait could be as long as six months while the volunteer was vetted for security purposes.

Once an application had been approved, the recruit would be picked up, blindfolded, and transported with other volunteers to the Janta camp. Hezbollah expanded upon the camp's meager facilities by sinking several large tunnels into the side of the narrow 900-foot-deep valley. The tunnel roofs were around 18 feet high, and they were equipped with generators for light and electricity and running water. Antiaircraft guns were positioned on the craggy peaks surrounding the site.

The first intake consisted of 150 recruits, including Sayyed Abbas Mussawi, drawn from villages and towns in the Bekaa. Their training consisted of basic fitness, weapons handling, and religious instruction. They slept in tents fully clothed in uniforms and boots and were frequently tested for their reactions. "They would fire flares and antiaircraft guns into the air in the middle of the night to wake us up. If we didn't wake up, they would come to our tents and throw cold water over us," recalls Hussein Hamiyah, the university student who was among the third intake of volunteers at Janta.

The day would begin with fitness training, usually repeated runs up the steep, rocky slopes of the surrounding hills. After a breakfast of tea, bread, and yogurt, the recruits had half an hour to wash themselves in the small river running through Janta before beginning religious instruction, each class lasting around ninety minutes.

The recruits sat cross-legged on the earth floor of derelict, roofless farm buildings to listen to lectures given by Lebanese clerics, such as Tufayli and Abbas Mussawi, who wore military uniforms beneath their cloaks and turbans. The young Hassan Nasrallah, his face framed by a light beard, also taught classes; one volunteer at the time remembers the future Hezbollah leader as "skinny and shy," clearly knowledgeable about religion "but wouldn't look you in the eye when he talked."

The military training included learning how to operate basic weapons such as the AK-47 rifle, light machine guns, and rocket-propelled grenades. Recruits were given one hour of firing practice each week. They learned hand-to-hand combat, how to handle and plant land mines, the art of camouflage, and how to move stealthily through rugged terrain.

Iranian instructors ran the first two courses, but by the time of the third intake, Lebanese trainers oversaw the basic fitness work, leaving the Iranians in charge of teaching the more advanced skills. In the early stages, each training program lasted forty-five days, but the duration was later reduced to a month. Recruits who showed promise and a will to continue with the training were sent to Iran for three-month advanced courses.

The Sheikh from Jibsheet

Ariel Sharon's plan to install Bashir Gemayel as president of an Israel-friendly Lebanon collapsed on September 14, 1982, when the Christian militia commander was killed in a bomb blast in Beirut days after being elected head of state but before he formally took office. With Gemayel's death, Israel needed to find a new arrangement fast, especially as resistance operations were beginning to intensify in the Beirut area.

That sense of urgency was soon shared by the Americans. U.S. marines were deployed in southern Beirut by the airport as part of a four-nation multinational force (MNF) that had overseen the departure of the PLO in August 1982 and returned after the subsequent massacre of thousands of Palestinians in the Sabra/Shatila refugee camps by Israeli-allied Christian militiamen in the wake of Gemayel's assassination. By March 1983, the U.S. marines and other contingents in the MNF were facing shooting attacks from suspected Shia militants. Then, on April 18, a suicide bomber drove an explosives-laden pickup truck into the U.S. embassy on the seafront corniche in Beirut. The explosion flattened the center of the seven-story building, killing sixty-three people, including seventeen Americans. Of the seventeen, six were CIA officers, including the local chief and his deputy and Bob Ames, the top CIA officer for the Near East, who was attending a meeting in the embassy at the time.

American diplomats accelerated efforts to conclude a Lebanese-Israeli peace deal. In early May, the Israelis agreed to a U.S.-engineered treaty with Lebanon, which was formally signed on May 17. But Assad instructed his Lebanese allies to derail the treaty by stepping up attacks against the U.S.-supported regime of President Amine Gemayel, Bashir's brother, who was elected in his stead. Fighting erupted in the Chouf Mountains above southern Beirut between Druze militiamen and the Lebanese army and Christian militias with the Israelis caught uncomfortably in between. In early September 1983, the Israelis cut their losses and withdrew from the Chouf, leaving the Christians and Druze to slaughter each other in the vacuum.

The new Israeli front line ran some sixty miles, from the mouth of the Awali River just north of Sidon, eastward along yawning ravines of limestone cliffs up into the barren, snow-capped heights of the Barouk Mountains. The line was supposed to be strong enough to rebuff a conventional attack by Syrian forces and tight enough to prevent guerrillas from the north from slipping through to launch attacks. But the Israelis still failed to fully appreciate that their main enemy lay to the south, inside the occupied area, not to the north.

The public face of resistance in south Lebanon was Sheikh Ragheb Harb, the young imam of Jibsheet who had accompanied Sheikh Sobhi Tufayli to Tehran in June 1982. Harb's unflinching support for resistance challenged the prevailing orthodoxy of most Shia clerics in south Lebanon at the time, who hesitated to provoke the wrath of the powerful Israeli army. "Harb was very charismatic and well respected in the south," recalls Timur Goksel, the UNIFIL spokesman. "He was mobilizing cells of five or six young kids each. The cells were very tight and impossible to penetrate."

Harb's mosque and *husseiniyah* in Jibsheet, decorated with pictures of Khomeini and black flags and banners inscribed with Koranic quotations, became a hub of resistance activities. He refused to meet Israeli officers who asked to see him and famously declared that shaking hands with the enemy was an act of collaboration, while rebuffing them was an act of resistance. With his thick beard and strong dark eyebrows, white turban and gray cloak, Harb was a popular figure in Jibsheet and the surrounding villages. On March 18, 1983, Harb was arrested by the Israelis shortly before he was due to deliver a fatwa in his Friday sermon forbidding all contact with the Israeli occupiers. The Israelis had hoped to forestall the fatwa, but all they did was stir up a hornet's nest of protest. For the next two weeks, strikes and demonstrations were held and roads repeatedly blocked with burning tires. The Israelis gave in, and in early April, Harb returned to Jibsheet, where he unabashedly continued to encourage resistance. A few months later, he was summoned to Tehran, where he told the Iranians that his home in Lebanon was "the embassy of the Islamic Republic of Iran." Having impressed the Iranians with his commitment, Harb returned to Jibsheet to continue his mobilization efforts, knowing that he was unlikely to live much longer. Indeed, he frequently forecast his own death to his followers, predicting that the Israelis would "shed my blood."

The "Shia Genie"

Opposition against the Israelis had been building for months in south Lebanon, but the catalyst that turned hostility into rebellion came on October 16, 1983, during the Ashoura commemoration marking the martyrdom of Imam Hussein. As many as sixty thousand Shias had converged upon the southern market town of Nabatiyah for the ceremony when an Israeli patrol of jeeps and trucks made the mistake of barging through the throng. The Israeli soldiers probably had no idea of the significance of their blunder, although the patrol commander had been warned by his superiors to stay away from the town that day. But the enraged celebrants saw the Israeli intrusion on their holiest of days as sacrilege and reacted with fury. The crowd mobbed the vehicles and threw stones. Shots were fired at the patrol, and someone tossed a hand grenade at a jeep, the explosion setting it alight. The frightened Israelis opened fire on the crowd, killing one man and wounding up to ten.

IDF commanders realized immediately the seriousness of the incident and arrested the patrol commander. But the gesture was undermined when the next day Haddad's militiamen stormed Nabatiyah and conducted house-to-house searches for those who had attacked the Israeli convoy. The Shia clerics came off the fence and issued calls for confrontation and fatwas forbidding cooperation with the Israelis. The Shia recruits to the Israeli-controlled National Guard deserted and the militia collapsed.

Worse was to follow for the Israelis. On November 4, a green Chevrolet truck crashed through the main gate of an IDF headquarters housed in a school building on the coastal road south of Tyre. The Israeli guards fired a few shots, at least one round hitting the youthful-looking driver, but the truck continued moving and had almost reached the main building when it exploded. The blast, caused by an estimated 440 pounds of explosive, demolished the building, killing twenty-nine Israelis, mainly border security guards, as well as thirty-two Lebanese and Palestinian detainees.

The deadly attack not only echoed that of Ahmad Qassir against the previous IDF headquarters in Tyre almost a year before, but also mirrored a devastating simultaneous suicide truck bombing less than two weeks earlier against the U.S. marine barracks at Beirut airport and the French paratroop headquarters in southern Beirut on October 23 that killed 241 American servicemen and 58 French soldiers. The marine casualties were the highest in a single day for the corps since Iwo Jima in World War II. Once again, the mysterious Islamic Jihad claimed responsibility for both attacks as well as the latest bombing of the Tyre headquarters.

Hezbollah has always officially denied involvement in the bombing of the U.S. marine barracks and French paratroop headquarters, although its leaders publicly supported the attacks at the time. Hezbollah later described them as the "first punishment" of "our people" against the "imams of infidelity of America, France and Israel."[5]

Nearly a quarter of a century later, Tufayli, now no longer a member of the party he helped to found, admitted to me that Hezbollah was responsible for the U.S. marine barracks bombing.

"The marines were not civilians. I considered the Americans as an occupying force and I fought them," he said. While he remained "proud" of the attack, he confessed that he was not personally involved in the planning of the operation. "If I had anything to do with it I would say so because my relations with the Americans are not so good," he said with a chuckle.

When the United States declined to retaliate for the attack on the marines, Israel on November 16 struck the IRGC training camp at Janta, the first time it had staged an air raid against its new Shia foes. The jets swooped low over the valley dropping bombs for thirty minutes, killing nearly three dozen Hezbollah recruits and Iranian instructors, among them the youthful-looking Farhan Ali Ismael, who is buried in the "martyrs' cemetery" in nearby Brital.

For the Israelis, there was no escaping the fact that they had, as Yitzhak Rabin later put it, "let the Shia genie out of the bottle." Israel could have taken advantage of the early goodwill shown by the Shias of southern Lebanon to cultivate an amicable and mutually beneficial cross-border relationship. Instead, through a combination of ignorance, negligence, recklessness, and bad luck, Israel had created a ferocious and resolutely determined new enemy.

The Israeli author of a study on the post-1982 Israeli experience in Lebanon wrote, "The quick change in the south of Lebanon from a relatively hospitable territory to an extremely hostile one was among the greatest failures of national intelligence estimates that Israel had ever known. No one, not even the most persistent opponents of the war, had ever raised this possibility."[6]

The Military Genius

After the Nabatiyah incident, Amal could no longer ignore the sentiment of its constituents in the south, and at last they came off the fence and endorsed a campaign of active resistance. In the months ahead, the focus of the Amal resistance campaign centered on Marakeh and six other villages lying in the hills to the east of Tyre. Known as the "arc of resistance" or the "seven villages resistance," it was led by the unlikely figure of Mohammed Saad, an electronics teacher at the Jabal Amil Institute in Bourj Shemali and a prominent activist within the local Amal movement. With his narrow shoulders and skinny "childlike" physique, Saad hardly looked the part of an influential underground military leader. His thick mane of wavy black hair, thin mustache, and scraggly tuft of beard on his lower chin gave him the appearance of an American beat poet from the early 1960s instead of a charismatic guerrilla commander—Bob Dylan rather than Che Guevara.

Although the Amal leadership had instructed the cadres not to confront the Israeli invasion, Saad and his comrades around Tyre were certain that an active resistance was only a matter of time, and they began making preparations. They shaved off their beards, destroyed any documentation linking them to Amal, and collected and hid any weapons left by the Palestinians.

One of the main cell leaders in Tyre was Mohammed Zaghloul, then a lean, bespectacled twenty-nine-year-old who had joined Amal in 1978 and was close to Mohammed Saad. "Mohammed was very clever, a military genius, and he put the idea of resistance into people's heads, convincing those who thought it was hopeless to fight the Israelis," he recalls. "As young men at the time, we saw something special in him and we decided to follow him."

Saad's key lieutenant in Marakeh was Khalil Jerardi, a charismatic theology teacher at the Jabal Amil Institute. As Saad became more involved in directing resistance attacks, he disappeared from public view, and it was Jerardi, with his languid eyes and his beard, which grew longer and more pointed as the resistance progressed, who became the public face of the Amal resistance.

The first attacks consisted of roadside bombings and assassinations of collaborators. The Israeli military headquarters in Tyre was constantly monitored for Lebanese collaborators entering and leaving. "They would follow the suspects on motorcycles from the Israeli headquarters and then put on a hood and shoot them in the head, often in public, in a café in Tyre in front of everybody. Then they would drop leaflets saying 'This is the fate of all collaborators,'" recalls Hassan Siklawi, at the time a UNIFIL liaison officer with local Lebanese groups.

Cut off initially from a regular supply of weapons, ammunition, and funds in Beirut, the Amal fighters were forced to improvise. They constructed homemade bombs by mixing fertilizer, sugar, and sawdust in kitchen sinks and packing the explosive with nails into empty powdered milk tins. Gas cylinders were also turned into crude incendiary bombs.

The IEDs were usually planted along the coastal road near Tyre, the main route used by the IDF traveling between Israel and the front lines farther north. Initially, traditional lit fuses were used to detonate the charges. The resistance fighters learned through trial and error when to light the fuse so that the bomb would explode just as the IDF target passed by. Later they acquired electrical fuses and detonated the bombs using command wires that they would disguise by stringing them along telegraph pylons beside real telephone cables.

Israeli casualties began to increase in tandem with the rising rate of attacks. IDF bulldozers destroyed stone or cinder block walls along the coastal road and uprooted orange and lemon trees and banana groves to deprive the resistance men of cover to launch attacks. The Israelis attempted without success to revive anti-Palestinian feeling among the Shias by spreading rumors that Musa Sadr had been discovered as a prisoner of the PLO in the Rashidiyah Palestinian refugee camp south of Tyre. Israeli-allied militiamen or plainclothes Israeli security personnel were sent into villages to smash down front doors, search homes, and arrest "suspects," who could face interrogation in the IDF intelligence headquarters in Tyre or incarceration in the Ansar prison camp.

Looking for Mohammed Saad

To evade capture, the Amal men dug small chambers and tunnels beneath their homes with disguised entrances. Other hiding places included fake water tanks that were only half filled with water, the other half providing space for a man to hide. They made use of the natural caves that riddled the limestone valleys around the villages, employing children to cover the entrances with bushes and twigs. Resistance became a community effort. When the Israelis approached a village, the warning would be relayed from the loudspeaker attached to the minaret of the mosque or *husseiniyah,* alerting the residents. Women and children would gather in the street or clamber on the roofs of buildings to hurl stones and pans of boiling oil at the Israeli soldiers while the men in the village hurried to their hideouts.

On one occasion, the IDF learned that Mohammed Saad was in Kfar Sir and surrounded the village with troops. Saad ran into a house and without saying a word to the startled family climbed into a pair of pajamas he saw lying on a bed. When Israeli soldiers banged at the front door, Saad himself opened it. The soldiers said they were looking for Mohammed Saad. Saad turned to the family inside and said, "Mother, they're looking for someone called Mohammed Saad."

"Never heard of him," the mother replied, and the soldiers left.

The Amal resistance lived by secrecy and caution. Messages were sent between separate cells in simple yet inventive ways. One method was to write a message or press statement on cigarette papers, which the courier would crumple and leave in the ashtray of his car until he reached his destination. Sometimes two resistance men would identify themselves to each other by matching the two halves of a torn Lebanese one-lira note.

They developed ingenious methods of smuggling weapons and ammunition into the occupied area. One morning, Sheikh Najib Sweidan, the Shia mufti of Tyre, found a written death threat on his doorstep. The worried cleric met with Saad and showed him the letter. Saad told Sweidan that he must be careful and should no longer travel to Beirut alone in case he was ambushed along the way. A few days later, Sweidan contacted Saad and told him that he needed to go to Beirut the next day. Saad told the mufti that he would send a chauffeur to his home. The chauffeur turned out to be Saad himself, and he drove Sweidan to the capital and back again. They repeated the trips several times, although unknown to the mufti, Saad was packing the car with weapons and ammunition in Beirut before returning to Tyre. Saad calculated that the Israelis would never inspect too thoroughly the vehicle of such a prominent religious figure. However, one day Saad learned that the Israelis had grown suspicious of Sweidan and guessed that his vehicle might be carrying arms to the resistance in Tyre. On the next trip, Sweidan traveled alone to Beirut while Saad stayed at home. On the return journey, the infuriated mufti had his car searched at every IDF checkpoint. The Israelis, finding no weapons, allowed the fuming Sweidan to proceed. Later, when the mufti complained to Saad about his treatment at the hands of the Israelis, Saad broke into laughter and confessed that he had been using the mufti's car all along to smuggle weapons. What's more, he told the stunned cleric, it was Saad who had written the death threat that encouraged Sweidan to seek the protection of the wily resistance commander in the first place.

"Martyrdom Operations"

By the first half of 1983, Hezbollah's influence was seeping from the scattered villages in the plain of the northern Bekaa into the cramped slums of Beirut's southern suburbs, where the new party intended to consolidate a presence before projecting its influence more deeply into the south. The impoverished district was a melting pot of Shia families and clans from south Lebanon and the Bekaa, and Hezbollah faced little difficulty in attracting a loyal support base.

Slowly, Hezbollah's presence began to grow in the southern villages. Residents of Amal-dominated villages noticed the arrival of severe-looking young men with neatly trimmed pointed beards wearing long-sleeved shirts who constantly fingered prayer beads and spent most of their time in local mosques deep in prayer. The local Amal leadership paid the new Hezbollah arrivals little heed initially, thinking that all they were interested in was prayer and that they could not possibly pose a challenge to the well-entrenched movement.

With resistance activity heating up, the Israelis struck back. On the evening of February 16, 1984, Sheikh Ragheb Harb was gunned down by three Lebanese collaborators as he walked to his home in Jibsheet, fulfilling the cleric's prediction that he would die at the hands of the Israelis. His murder sparked a wave of demonstrations and strikes in south Lebanon and southern Beirut.

It also hastened the emergence of a new tactic of warfare into the south Lebanon theater. On April 12, 1984, Ali Safieddine drove his explosives-laden car between two Israeli armored personnel carriers near Deir Qanoun and blew himself up, killing six soldiers. Safieddine was Hezbollah's first official suicide bomber (Ahmad Qassir had not yet been identified as the perpetrator of the 1982 IDF headquarters blast), and his immolation was the organization's revenge for Harb's assassination.

Other bombers followed, and not only from Shia groups such as Amal and Hezbollah. Strikingly, the majority of suicide attacks against the Israelis and their Lebanese militia allies in the mid-1980s were carried out not by religious Shia militants drawing upon the sect's tradition of martyrdom, but by volunteers from secular political parties, notably the Syrian Social Nationalist Party (SSNP), which accounted for more suicide bombings in the 1980s than any other group. Indeed, during the peak of the suicide bombing phenomenon in 1985, of the nineteen attacks recorded, only one was by Hezbollah.[7]

Although the phenomenon of suicide bombing captured international headlines and underlined the determination of the Lebanese to rid their country of the Israelis, as a military tactic the results were mixed. Other than the carefully planned Hezbollah spectaculars against the IDF headquarters in 1982 and 1983, which accounted for a total of 136 fatalities, 104 of them Israelis, most attacks killed only a handful of soldiers or militiamen. Fifteen of the thirty-three attacks, including Amal's two operations, failed to kill anybody other than the bomber. As the number of suicide bombings increased, the tactic became a source of competition between the different factions, especially among the secular parties. For the SSNP and the Baathists in particular, suicide bombings were acts of prestige and patriotism, powerful declarations of commitment to the cause of liberating Lebanon. The results of the attacks in terms of enemy casualties were less important than the acts themselves and the propaganda value they accrued.

Hezbollah could justify sending suicide bombers against Israeli targets on religious grounds, as well as for "nationalist" reasons of liberating occupied territory, but it used the tactic sparingly, and generally each operation was planned with more care than those of its secular counterparts. Martyrdom for the sake of martyrdom was deemed wasteful and possibly *haram,* or forbidden by Islamic convention. Hezbollah, Nasrallah explained in 1996, does not carry out "indiscriminate martyrdom operations." Although he admitted coming under pressure every day from young men eager to carry out suicide missions that he could easily have authorized, he said, "If the operation is not productive and effective, and [doesn't] cause the enemy to bleed, we cannot legally, religiously, morally, or humanely justify giving an explosive device to our brothers and telling them, 'Go and become martyrs, no matter how'!"[8]

Suicide bombings began to tail off in the latter half of the 1980s as the influence of the secular groups began to wane and Hezbollah came to dominate the resistance.

The Iron Fist

By late 1984, Israel was in deep trouble in Lebanon. The U.S. marines had pulled out of Lebanon that February after west Beirut fell to the militias and the Lebanese army disintegrated for the second time in eight years. That same month, Saad Haddad, Israel's top ally in south Lebanon, died after a battle with cancer. Haddad could be petulant and bullheaded, but he had remained a dependable ally of Israel for eight years, and his loss was keenly felt by the IDF. Appointed in his place was Antoine Lahd, a retired brigadier general in the Lebanese army, who was not from the south and lacked the loyal base of support that the major from Marjayoun had built. Then Amine Gemayel, the Lebanese president, formally abrogated the ill-fated May 17 peace agreement with Israel under Syrian pressure.

The Israeli government also had to contend with a heated domestic debate over what was proving a highly controversial war. Menachem Begin was an early political casualty. His spirit crushed by the mounting casualty toll and domestic criticism of the war, Begin became a near-total recluse in his Jerusalem home before resigning from the premiership in September 1983.

Even IDF officers and soldiers were torn between those who supported their presence in Lebanon and those who just wanted to go home. This was Israel's first full war of choice in its four decades of existence, and many soldiers were deeply unhappy at having to risk their lives patrolling the roads of south Lebanon for what they considered an immoral and unsuccessful policy. Nearly 150 soldiers had been punished for refusing to serve in Lebanon. And each soldier killed by a roadside bomb or shot dead in an ambush by elusive Lebanese militants further sapped morale. Nervous Israeli soldiers conducted reconnaissance-by-fire, blasting away with machine guns mounted on armored personnel carriers into the banana groves and orange orchards flanking the roads they patrolled.

"You see the change first of all in the eyes of the soldiers," commented Zeev Schiff, the military correspondent for Israel's *Haaretz* newspaper, in comparing the deterioration of the IDF in Lebanon over an eighteen-month period from summer 1983 to early 1985. "It's a look that reminded me of the look in the eyes of the American soldiers I saw in the final stages of Vietnam. It is the look of soldiers and officers who know that their chances of winning in Lebanon are less than zero. In Lebanon you can see an army that has experienced firsthand how military might is rendered impotent."[9]

On January 14, 1985, Israeli announced a three-stage plan for a unilateral pullout from Lebanon. The plan was to withdraw to the old "Haddad enclave" along the border that had existed between 1978 and 1982. The strip would be patrolled by the Israeli-allied militia under the command of Antoine Lahd. Lahd's Army of Free Lebanon was renamed the South Lebanon Army (SLA) and reorganized along conventional military lines with brigades and battalions. The Israelis hoped to recruit some five thousand soldiers to the SLA, but they were unable to coerce or dragoon sufficient numbers, and the total strength of the militia never exceeded half that figure.

During the first phase of the withdrawal between January 15 and February 16, the IDF adopted a "velvet glove" approach, concentrating on dismantling its military infrastructure and trucking it southward. The Israelis seemed to hope that the declaration that it was leaving and the visible activity of the withdrawal from Sidon would persuade Amal, if not Hezbollah, to discontinue its attacks. But Amal echoed the official Lebanese stand, which was to demand a total Israeli troop withdrawal from Lebanese territory and the dismantling of the SLA. If the SLA was to remain in control of a security belt along the border, then Israel would still be considered an occupying force. The IDF had faced around fifty attacks a month in 1984, but in the first two months of 1985 the rate nearly doubled. Among the fatalities were two senior officers, a colonel, and a major, killed in separate attacks.

In response, the IDF implemented a new policy at the end of the first phase of withdrawal, exchanging the velvet glove for the iron fist. Movement in the occupied area was severely restricted with the imposition of a dusk-to-dawn curfew. Motorists were required to carry at least one passenger—a measure to curb suicide bombers, on the assumption that it was harder to find two people willing to blow themselves up at the same time. Motorcycles were banned, and parking was forbidden along main roads. The crossing points into the Israeli-occupied area were sealed, preventing the exchange of goods from Beirut and agricultural produce from the south. Prices of basic commodities steadily climbed in the occupation zone.

The crackdown was marked by a series of punitive raids against villages. The pattern was repeated throughout the zone: A mechanized battalion would surround and cordon off the targeted village, blocking all approach roads. Troops accompanied by sniffer dogs and plainclothes Shin Bet (Israeli Security Agency) officers would round up all males between the ages of fourteen and seventy and hold them for interrogations, while houses were searched for militants and weapons. The homes of suspected resistance fighters were bulldozed, and there were repeated incidents of deliberate vandalism. Troops took dogs into mosques and husseiniyahs knowing that it was a grave insult to Muslims. Copies of the Koran were torn up and the pages scattered on the ground for the dogs to walk over. Sacks of lentils, rice, and wheat were split open and mixed together, making the contents inedible.

Israeli troops made use of civilians as "human shields" to protect them when passing through hostile villages. On one occasion, the Israelis tied a young man to the front of an armored personnel carrier as they drove through Tyre. The Israelis denied the incident, but a photograph was taken showing the unfortunate man strapped to the APC.

Dozens of men were handcuffed, blindfolded, and taken away during the raids. Some were shot, their bodies left in the rubble of bulldozed homes or found later lying on the side of the road, victims of executions, according to the villagers. At least fifteen Lebanese were killed in the raids, all but one "shot while trying to escape," according to the Israelis.[10] In UNIFIL's area of operations, more than 773 Shias were detained and forty-nine houses were bulldozed.[11] French UNIFIL troops often attempted to block the IDF bulldozers from demolishing homes and made sure that at least they were present when the raids were conducted. Inevitably, tempers frayed, and after scuffles broke out in one village between French and IDF soldiers, Yitzhak Rabin, the Israeli defense minister, castigated the peacekeepers as "bastards."

It must have been evident to the IDF that its repressive "iron fist" measures would not crush the resistance but instead only harden its resolve and sow greater hatred for the Israeli occupiers among the Shia population of the south. Indeed, the gratuitous destruction, vandalism, and brutality meted out by the Israeli troops reflected their fear, resentment, and frustration. It was a cathartic lashing out against their unseen tormentors, the ghosts that flitted from wadi to wadi, orchard to orchard, silently plucking the lives of Israeli soldiers before disappearing once again.

On March 2, Marakeh became the target of the largest raid yet. As usual, Mohammed Saad, Khalil Jerardi, and the others slipped away to their hiding places when the Israeli armored column was spotted grinding up the hill toward the village. Around 800 IDF troops and Shin Bet agents took part in the operation backed by 50 armored vehicles and bulldozers. One man was shot while "trying to escape." Some 350 men were rounded up and questioned in the village school, with 17 of them taken away. The *husseiniyah* in the center of the village was ransacked, the troops climbing the outside staircase to search the second-floor offices where Saad and his lieutenants often met to plot their operations.

Two days later, Saad, Jerardi, and several other resistance figures met in a small back office on the first floor of the *husseiniyah*. The building had been thoroughly searched for explosives following the Israeli raid on the village, but nothing had been found. Unknown to the resistance commanders meeting in the first-floor office, however, their arrival at the *husseiniyah* had been noted by a collaborator who had been keeping watch on the building from the balcony of his home about a hundred yards away. When he saw the resistance leaders climbing the outside staircase of the *husseiniyah,* he raised a walkie-talkie to his mouth and quietly informed the Israelis.

Jerardi was sitting on the edge of the desk and speaking to the men assembled in the office. Saad was leaning against the open doorway and had been listening quietly when he suddenly interrupted his friend.

"Something is wrong," Saad told them. "We should leave immediately."

But the building was searched. *It's safe,* he was told.

"No, no," Saad insisted. "We need to leave right now."[12]

Just then, the twenty-five-pound bomb hidden beneath the desk on which Jerardi was sitting exploded, destroying the office and most of the second floor. It took several hours for the villagers and French UNIFIL soldiers to dig the casualties from the rubble. Saad was found first and rushed to the UNIFIL hospital in Naqoura while Jerardi was still lying under the rubble. But the two leaders were dead, along with ten other people, the biggest blow suffered by the Amal-led resistance of the "seven villages" since it began in 1982.

Israel denied involvement in the bombing; Uri Lubrani, Israel's Lebanon coordinator, claimed that it was the result of rising tensions between Amal and Hezbollah. But the Lebanese had no doubt that Israel was responsible. The collaborator who alerted the Israelis to the arrival of Saad and Jerardi at the *husseiniyah* was subsequently arrested by Amal and executed, his family expelled from Marakeh. Sheikh Mahdi Shamseddine, the deputy head of the Higher Shia Council, called for a "relentless jihad" against Israel as long as Israeli troops remained on Lebanese soil.

The Open Letter

With the death of Saad and Jerardi, Amal's contribution to the resistance against the Israeli occupation began to decline. Even before the Israelis completed the pullback to their new occupied belt along the border in June 1985, Amal, acting on the orders of Syria, had become embroiled in a savage war against Yasser Arafat's Fatah movement in the

Palestinian refugee camps of Beirut. The Syrians wanted to smash Arafat's influence in the camps of Beirut and the south once and for all, and they used Amal as their proxy to implement the policy. The "war of the camps" ran for three years before Arafat's men were finally defeated. But the conflict inflicted a costly toll on Amal's cadres, with some of its top commanders and combatants killed fighting the Palestinians. The "war of the camps" diverted Amal's attention from the continuing resistance against the Israelis and SLA in south Lebanon, which, along with the loss of charismatic leaders like Mohammed Saad, provided a point of entry for Hezbollah's influence to seep farther south and begin the long process of supplanting Amal as the dominant Shia force in the area.

A foretaste of Hezbollah's determination to expand its influence came on February 18, 1985, two days after the last Israeli troops pulled out of Sidon, when thousands of armed Hezbollah men drove from the southern suburbs of Beirut to hold a rally in the newly liberated port town.

Chanting *"Allah u-Akbar,"* and carrying banners describing Amine Gemayel as the "Shah of Lebanon," the Hezbollah men drove through the center of the town and ended the day by burning three bars and smashing bottles of whisky in the street.[13]

The rally, the most public manifestation yet of Hezbollah's growing strength, came as the party formally announced its existence in a press conference in a mosque in the southern Beirut quarter of Ouzai. The date chosen for Hezbollah's unveiling, February 16, was the first anniversary of the assassination of Sheikh Ragheb Harb. Hezbollah used the occasion to publish its political charter, the "Open Letter Addressed by Hezbollah to the Downtrodden in Lebanon and in the World," which articulated its political goals and ideology.

The forty-eight-page document, read out by Sayyed Ibrahim al-Amine, Hezbollah's spokesman, proclaimed that the party abided by the "orders of a single wise and just command" currently embodied by Khomeini, "the rightly-guided imam who combines the qualities of the total imam, who has detonated the Muslim's revolution, and who is bringing about the glorious Islamic renaissance."

It listed its objectives in Lebanon as driving Israel out of the country "as a prelude to its final obliteration from existence and the liberation of the venerable Jerusalem from the talons of occupation"; an end to American and French influence in Lebanon; and allowing the Lebanese to select a system of government of their own choosing. The Open Letter stated Hezbollah's preference for a system of Islamic rule in Lebanon, but carefully added that "we do not wish to impose Islam on anybody.... But we stress that we are convinced of Islam as a faith, system, thought, and rule, and we urge all to recognize it and to resort to its law."

This public introduction was Hezbollah's first move toward formally establishing itself as an entity within the Lebanese political arena. Before 1985, Hezbollah had existed as a secret underground movement, lacking a formal structure and invariably referred to by the Western press as "shadowy." By publishing its ideology, agenda, and ambitions in documentary format for the enlightenment of other Lebanese, both friends and foes, Hezbollah had conveyed its determination to remain an enduring presence in Lebanon, one that other factions and players could not ignore or dismiss as a fleeting aberration of the civil war.

Nonetheless, the tone and language used in the document reflected a certain arrogance of conviction, like an angry, self-righteous teenager brashly challenging the status quo of the older generation. Even in the years ahead, as developments in Lebanon and the region compelled Hezbollah to adopt greater pragmatism in pursuing its agenda, the fundamental aspirations set forth in the Open Letter—resistance against Israel, the destruction of the Jewish state, and the desire for an Islamic state in Lebanon—would remain the immutable ideological pillars upon which the party rested.

Hezbollah had emerged from the stygian murk of war, and in time it would become renowned for its martial exploits against Israeli troops occupying south Lebanon. But in those early years, Hezbollah's identity was irredeemably linked in the public mind to attacks against Western targets in Lebanon, particularly the kidnapping of foreigners.

Hezbollah's leaders have always denied involvement in any of the kidnappings of nearly a hundred foreigners that plagued Lebanon from 1982 until the release of the last hostages a decade later. While it is possible that some of the militant Shia kidnappers were operating independently of Hezbollah as an organization (the kidnappers generally operated in clan and family networks to preserve security), it is stretching the bounds of credibility to accept that the party was totally uninvolved. Some of the hostages are known to have been incarcerated in Hezbollah-controlled areas, including Beirut's southern suburbs and the Sheikh Abdullah barracks in Baalbek (which was a base for the IRGC at the time). The CIA believes that Nasrallah himself was involved in helping organize the kidnapping operations.[14] The demands of the kidnappers reflected the political objectives of Hezbollah: to rid Lebanon of Westerners and Western influence and to secure the release of Lebanese Shia detainees held by Israel. When Israel closed the Ansar prison camp in April 1985 during its phased pullback to the border, it released 752 detainees but transferred the remaining 1,167 to a new prison in Atlit in northern Israel.[15] It also opened a new SLA-run prison in the old French mandate barracks in the border village of Khiam to replace the facility at Ansar. The detainees transferred to Israel apparently were intended as bargaining chips to secure information on missing Israeli servicemen in Lebanon. Instead, it provoked Hezbollah into hijacking TWA Flight 847 in June 1985 and demanding the release of the Lebanese prisoners from Atlit. Imad Mughniyah himself allegedly ran the hijacking operation, which later earned him a U.S. federal indictment. The crisis lasted ten tense days and ended with Israel's agreeing to the staged release of 764 prisoners from Atlit over the following three months.

"The Hostages Were a Big Treasure for Iran"

The demands of the kidnappers in Beirut also reflected personal interests of some key figures linked to Hezbollah and Islamic Amal, namely, Imad Mughniyah and Hussein Mussawi. Mughniyah's brother-in-law, Mustafa Badreddine, who traveled on a fake Lebanese passport identifying him as a Christian named Elias Saab, and a cousin of Mussawi were among seventeen Shia militants convicted by a court in Kuwait for a string of attacks in the emirate, including bombings of the U.S. and French embassies, in December 1983.

French citizens were targeted for abduction in the mid-1980s in an attempt to secure the release of Anis Naqqash, Mughniyah's Lebanese friend and instructor from the late 1970s. Naqqash was languishing in a French prison for killing a policeman in Paris in a bungled assassination attempt against Shapour Bakhtiar, a former Iranian prime minister under the Shah who was a leader of the anti-Khomeinist opposition.

The responses of nations whose citizens were abducted in Lebanon varied from country to country. As part of the U.S. government's clandestine efforts to build covert counterterrorist groups in Lebanon, the CIA helped train a special unit of the Lebanese Forces, the Christian militia then headed by Elie Hobeika, whose militiamen had carried out the massacre of Palestinians and Lebanese in the Sabra/Shatila refugee camps in September 1982. According to a former member of the unit, Hobeika recognized early on that the emerging Hezbollah would become a major power in Lebanon and began working with the Americans and French against the nascent Shia organization.

The CIA also assembled and trained another unit, dubbed "Strike Force" and consisting of some fifty people drawn mainly from elite Lebanese army units. Trained by three or four CIA paramilitary operatives, Strike Force was created as a hostage rescue unit. But it never carried out any missions, despite obtaining actionable intelligence on at least one occasion on the location of several hostages.

"The Americans wanted guarantees of the mission's success and that none of the hostages would be killed," recalls a former Lebanese intelligence officer involved with Strike Force. "It was impossible to give such guarantees, so nothing happened. The Americans got cold feet."

On March 8, a massive car bomb ripped through the Bir al-Abed district of southern Beirut, killing more than ninety people. The target of the bomb attack was Sayyed Mohammed Hussein Fadlallah, who narrowly escaped injury as he was leaving his mosque. One of his bodyguards, Jihad Mughniyah, a brother of Imad, was killed in the explosion. Hezbollah strung a banner above the bomb site with the words "Made in the USA."

The CIA denied all knowledge of the attack, claiming that rogue elements from one of its secret counterterrorism units were responsible.

According to Lebanese intelligence veterans, the blame rests with the CIA's then Beirut station chief, who ran an unauthorized operation using CIA-trained personnel from the Mukafaha counterterrorism unit of Lebanese military intelligence to create a "balance of terror" with the Shia militants responsible for the U.S. marine barracks bombing and other attacks.

Given the hidden nature of Hezbollah's leadership at the time, the more visible Fadlallah was often cited as being either the head of the party, or at the very least its "spiritual leader." In fact, Fadlallah never had any organizational role in Hezbollah; even the term "spiritual leader" was inaccurate. Although he was revered by many Hezbollah members, Fadlallah always eschewed participation in a formal political organization.

Perhaps the most valuable cooperation between the United States and Lebanon in the hunt for the kidnap victims was the establishment of an electronic listening facility operated by Lebanese military intelligence and funded by the CIA. Following the abduction of William Buckley, the CIA station chief in Beirut, in 1984, the Americans sought the help of the Israelis, who had a listening post on the summit of Barouk Mountain, the highest point in southern Lebanon. But the Israelis, who resented the U.S. military involvement in Lebanon, refused to provide any assistance. The CIA turned to the Lebanese and under a "gentleman's agreement" helped fund and build a sophisticated multi-million-dollar signals intelligence (SIGINT) site near the frost-shattered summit of Mount Sannine, at eight thousand feet, Lebanon's third-highest mountain. The facility, run by the Signals Service of Lebanese military intelligence, was staffed with personnel fluent in Farsi, Hebrew, English, and French. The Sannine listening post could intercept radio communications throughout the Middle East as far as Iran to the east and southern Europe to the west. Intelligence gleaned by the facility was shared with the CIA. A former CIA field officer acknowledged that the listening post was the source of much valuable intelligence on the hostages and on the structure and activities of the nascent Hezbollah. The focus of the intelligence gathering was on Baalbek, a few dozen miles to the east in the Bekaa Valley and easily visible from Jabal Sannine on cloudless days. It was known that William Buckley was one of several Western hostages then held at the Sheikh Abdullah barracks.[16]

According to a former Lebanese Signals Service officer, the Sannine facility in 1986 intercepted a voice frequency sample of Imad Mughniyah, which was used to trace the Hezbollah militant to the luxurious Le Crillon hotel on the Champs Elysées in Paris. The DGSE, France's intelligence service, was alerted, and officers met with Mughniyah in his hotel room, according to the former officer. Mughniyah, who was traveling under a false name, was not arrested and was allowed to leave France. The secret meeting bolstered the belief that France eventually cut a deal with the kidnappers that led in 1990 to the release of Anis Naqqash along with four accomplices and the unfreezing of financial assets and military hardware for Iran.

The Russians resorted to more forceful measures when four of their diplomats were abducted in 1985 by Ali Deeb, also known as Abu Hassan Salameh, a top Hezbollah operative who had been a close colleague of Mughniyah since the 1970s and whose name the CIA had linked to the bombing of the U.S. embassy in Beirut in 1983.[17] Two days after the Russians were kidnapped, one of them was killed, and his body was thrown onto the street a few hundred yards from the Soviet embassy. In response, the KGB, assisted by the Druze militia of Walid Jumblatt (the son of the National Movement leader, Kamal), kidnapped and killed a relative of Deeb. The body was delivered to Hezbollah with a message that other leaders would be similarly disposed of unless the three surviving diplomats were released at once. The Russians were freed, promptly and unharmed, near the Soviet embassy.

Lingering questions over the kidnapping crisis of the 1980s continue to haunt Hezbollah's leadership to this day. Sheikh Sobhi Tufayli's home on a lonely road outside Baalbek is within clear view of the whitewashed walls and watchtowers of the Sheikh Abdullah barracks where so many of the hostages were held. But the former Hezbollah leader, who is at odds with the current party leadership, consistently maintains that the abductions of foreigners had "nothing to do with Hezbollah. Nothing at all." The kidnappings, he avers, were a "mistake" that "ruined the image of the resistance and the image of Islam."

But Tufayli has a curious story concerning his alleged attempts to end the hostage crisis when he was in telephone contact with the kidnappers in May 1986. The Syrians were urging Tufayli to conclude a deal to release the hostages. The Hezbollah chief reassured them that an agreement had been reached and he expected the release of the hostages within days. However, the arrangement collapsed, Tufayli claims, when just three days after securing the pledge from the kidnappers, Robert McFarlane, then the recently retired U.S. national security advisor, made his now infamous secret trip to Tehran accompanied by Colonel Oliver North as part of the arms-for-hostages affair known as Irangate. "We discovered then that the hostages were a big treasure for Iran," Tufayli recalls. "They wanted to sell the hostages piece for piece."

By the early 1990s, the kidnapping crisis was over. Mustafa Badreddine and the Dawa prisoners in Kuwait escaped from prison during Iraq's August 1990 invasion of the emirate; the radicals held in France had been released; the Iran-Iraq war had ended, and Tehran was looking for a new relationship with the West.

Commenting on the kidnapping crisis several years later, Nasrallah admitted, with some understatement, "I cannot, of course, say that the Islamic scene is a total stranger to the incident [abductions of Westerners] and that the kidnappers were Arab nationalists or communists."[18] He said that the Kuwait seventeen had friends and relatives in "Islamic circles," "but the fact remains that they were not members of Hezbollah and they acted on an individual basis." Ultimately, he argued, Hezbollah wanted to see the end of kidnappings "since its fallout ended up entirely on the party's shoulders."

"A World Stronger Than Flesh or Bone"

The Israelis completed the phased pullback to the border on schedule and by the end of June 1985 occupied a strip of territory varying in depth from three to twenty-two miles. The new occupation zone was an enlarged version of the old "Haddad enclave" and in several places over-lapped with the operational areas of some UNIFIL battalions. The new zone also included a fingerlike extension of territory that ran up to the Christian-populated mountain town of Jezzine, almost twenty miles north of the border.

Israel's pullback to the border area necessitated a change in the na-ture of resistance operations by Amal, Hezbollah, and the secular groups of the National Resistance Movement. Before 1985 the resistance orga-nizations had often operated from within the occupied areas, but now there was a defined and guarded front line separating the Israeli troops and their Lebanese allies from the resistance factions. The new situation imposed advantages and disadvantages for Hezbollah. Close-quarter at-tacks against Israeli troops now required the additional hazard of first penetrating the zone before bombs could be planted and ambushes mounted. On the other hand, the existence of a front line meant that the resistance groups were no longer surrounded by the enemy but had an area of operational and logistical security to the rear to regroup and plan, relatively safe from attack or arrest.

A major base of operations was established in an area known as Mlita on the rocky, forested slopes of Jabal Safi, which lies on the west-ern edge of the occupied Jezzine enclave. Hidden in the mottled shad-ows beneath the dense canopy of stubby oak trees and camouflage netting, Hezbollah fighters dug foxholes and small shelters from which they launched operations against Israeli and SLA outposts dotting the mountainous skyline on the other side of a gaping valley to the east.

Shortly after Hezbollah moved onto the hillside, the fighters began expanding upon a shallow cave that had been used as a shelter against periodic Israeli air strikes and shelling. Using picks and pneumatic drills, they methodically dug a tunnel with adjacent rooms and chambers that eventually stretched some six hundred feet into the mountain. It took three years to construct the bunker system, the first of a chain of under-ground strongholds built by Hezbollah in the remoter frontline dis-tricts. They lined the passageways and rooms with soldered steel plates. The estimated one thousand tons of rock spoil were carefully scattered around the hillside beneath the trees and bushes so as not to betray the digging activity to Israeli aircraft patrolling overhead. The bunker contained sleeping quarters, a bathroom and latrine, and an operations room where attacks were planned and the aftermaths assessed. Lighting was provided by fluorescent tubes hooked up to car batteries.

Sayyed Abbas Mussawi was a regular visitor to the Mlita base, trudging up the steep, rocky slopes, his portly frame swaddled in a camouflage uniform while still retaining his clerical turban. The leader of the Islamic Resistance would pray at a niche in the rocks, his sonorous, gravelly voice wafting through the bushes and trees a source of comfort to the fighters assembled there.

Abu Hadi, a short, wiry Hezbollah fighter with a thick jet-black beard and inquisitive eyes, was just fifteen years old when he was sent to the Mlita base in 1986 as a fresh recruit into the Islamic Resistance. "I used to be scared at first," he recalls. "I felt like I was entering a world stronger than flesh or bone."

One evening shortly after he arrived, he saw Mussawi praying and weeping at his customary alcove among the rocks. Abu Hadi wanted to ask why he was crying, but was too shy to approach the venerated Islamic Resistance commander. "I kept the question with me for three months and then I found myself sitting next to him one day, so I asked him," Abu Hadi says. "He said, 'Every time I come here I feel that much closer to God. I see the eyes of the sky and the maker of the world who rejects oppression and reminds me that whoever fights oppression fights with God.' I lost my fear at that moment. I felt armed by God and I grew stronger and stronger until I became a true resistance fighter and I still carry this identity with pride. I have five children today, yet I would gladly sacrifice them all for this holy cause."

A "Society of Resistance"

Once the Israelis had retreated into their border zone, Hezbollah began to organize itself for the first time in the newly liberated areas of the south. The region was split into four administrative enclaves facing the occupation zone: the Iqlim al-Touffah adjacent to the occupied Jezzine sector, Nabatiyah in the northern sector, Tibnine in the center, and Tyre in the west.[19] The enclaves were further subdivided into *qita'at*, or sectors, of around twelve villages each.

In addition to the full-time fighters in the military wing, Hezbollah formed the *tabbiyya*, or mobilization, essentially a village guard unit of part-time fighters. Among the duties of the *tabbiyya* was to help expand Hezbollah's influence in the villages through such activities as hanging up posters, banners, and flags and distributing Hezbollah's literature, including the weekly *Al-Ahad* newspaper. Twice a week, the *tabbiyya* organized prayer sessions at the local mosque, which would be followed by religious lessons. The village guards each received a month or two of military training to prepare them, mainly for fire support roles in attacks on Israeli and SLA compounds. They could be farmers, schoolteachers, or mechanics during the day only to exchange their plows, books, and wrenches for rifles, RPGs, and mortars at night. The village guard units also were responsible for the nighttime *haras*, or guardian, duties in their respective villages to protect against Israeli commando raids. Over the years, the village guard units gained considerable combat experience, regularly topped up with refresher training courses. Their effectiveness would be proven during the 2006 war, when they defended their villages against invading Israeli troops.

In each village, Hezbollah appointed a *raabet*, or link, a liaison officer who was responsible for the party's local activities. Each week, the village liaison officers would hold administrative meetings with the commander of the south. At the time, there was no administrative separation between the full-time Islamic Resistance combatants and the *tabbiyya:* Hezbollah's chief for the south was responsible for both elements.

Hezbollah, determined to be the dominant force fighting the Israelis, mounted a campaign of recruitment, intimidation, and violence against its potential rivals within the broader resistance movement. In 1986, during clashes between Hezbollah and the communists in Beirut, Nasrallah said, "Our strategy is to build a future for ourselves through confrontation with the Zionist enemy. Let [the communists] therefore leave us alone to fight Israel, for we have no ambitions in the liberated areas of the south; the border zone is a different matter and should be left to us."[20]

Hezbollah officials approached Amal fighters to persuade them to join their party and continue fighting the Israelis under the banner of the Islamic Resistance. Some accepted, drawn by the relatively sizable salaries that the well-funded Hezbollah could afford to offer. Others declined, preferring to remain with Amal or quit the resistance altogether.

Nasser Abu Khalil, an Amal cell commander and confederate of Mohammed Saad, recalls being paid a visit by Sayyed Abbas Mussawi. "He tried to recruit me, but I told him no," he says. "Hezbollah was very active in their recruiting. One minute an Amal leader was fighting with Amal, the next minute he was fighting with Hezbollah."

Hezbollah's effort to spread its influence throughout the south was underpinned by an extensive multi-million-dollar social welfare program to alleviate the poverty and lack of state utilities in Shia-populated areas. It began in the wake of the 1982 invasion as the first IRGC trainers entered the Bekaa Valley, when the Khomeini Support Committee was established to bring aid, such as food, clothing, and monthly stipends, to impoverished families and a twenty-four-bed Imam Khomeini Hospital was opened in Baalbek. That same year, the Martyrs' Foundation was created to support the families of dead resistance fighters through the provision of pensions, and free health and education for children.

When Hezbollah's influence reached the teeming slums of southern Beirut, trucks were purchased and volunteers hired to remove the mountains of garbage that had remained uncollected for years. Hezbollah launched a construction organ in 1985, Jihad al-Bina, the Holy Struggle for Construction, that initially rebuilt war-damaged homes and buildings. One of its first tasks was to repair the damage caused by the massive car bomb that came close to killing Fadlallah in March 1985. Jihad al-Bina also established infrastructure for sewage disposal and delivered drinking water to households by truck. Over the years, the organization has expanded its services around the country, building and rehabilitating dozens of schools, hospitals, clinics, mosques, homes, and shops. It offers agricultural assistance to farmers, digging wells and providing financial credit and advice on land reclamation and crop cultivation.

In the aftermath of Israeli offensives against southern Lebanon in the 1990s, Jihad al-Bina's teams of volunteers quickly and efficiently surveyed damaged properties and began reconstruction plans even as politicians squabbled over how to spend foreign relief aid. Even during routine periods of daily conflict in the south, homes that had been struck by shellfire or machine gun rounds were speedily patched up by Jihad al-Bina.

Hezbollah's social welfare network astutely filled the void left by a neglectful Lebanese state, deliberately creating a culture of dependency that bonded Lebanon's Shias to the organization. It was the bedrock upon which Hezbollah could build its "society of resistance," an all-inclusive vision of a steadfast and resolute community existing in a constant state of war readiness to confront the enduring threat posed by Israel. Although Hezbollah's leaders have never disguised its goal of creating a "society of resistance," it is only in recent years, as the debate over Hezbollah's arms has come to dominate the political agenda in Lebanon, that the concept has been articulated more clearly on a public level.

In 2007, Sheikh Naim Qassem, the diminutive gray-bearded deputy leader of Hezbollah who often expounds upon the party's ideology, described resistance as "a societal vision in all its dimensions, for it is a military, cultural, political, and media resistance."[21] Hezbollah, he said, had always sought to build a "society of resistance" rather than limit it to a "group of resistance," meaning a military organization operating independently of the society in which it exists. In Hezbollah's concept of the "society of resistance" lie echoes of Mao Tse-tung's famous principle of guerrilla warfare in which he likened guerrillas to "fish" swimming in the "sea" of the peasantry—the sea sustains and supports the fish in the same way that the peasantry sustains and supports the guerrillas. But Hezbollah takes the idea further than merely rallying the local population behind the guerrillas. For Hezbollah, the local population—Mao's peasantry—are also the guerrillas, both directly as combatants and indirectly in support roles.

"The resistance community is an integration of the people, whereby everyone gives, with each member of this society living their own normal life, of going to school, attending universities, working in factories, businesses, and the like, but should a confrontation arise requiring his involvement, his participation will be according to the confrontation requirements," Qassem explained.[22] Those requirements could involve frontline fighting, providing logistical support, defending rear areas, speaking in support of the cause to the media, or simply enduring the privations and sacrifices of warfare with stoicism and steadfastness. Hezbollah's social welfare networks help sustain the community's will to embrace resistance. If your house is blown up by Israeli jets, never mind, Hezbollah will build you a new one. If your husband is killed fighting the Israelis, he will be honored and memorialized as a martyr, and you and your children will be provided for. "Thus the whole society becomes a resistance society; it provides what is required of it, then goes back to the normalcy of daily life," Qassem adds. "Hence a resistance society is not one in which arms are randomly distributed to all the people, but such a community governs energies and capacities into an integrated process of confrontation."

Building a community committed to an all-encompassing concept of resistance—resistance as a way of life—does not occur overnight. The resistance organization must inculcate this idea into the populace through the gentle arts of persuasion and emulation, immersing the community in a culture of resistance that begins in childhood and continues uninterrupted into young adulthood and beyond. The culture of resistance has been sustained through lectures, meetings, study groups, media propaganda—Hezbollah's *Al-Ahad* weekly newspaper began publication in 1984, and two years later its Al-Nour radio station began broadcasting.

The process of cultivating the "society of resistance" was intended as an enduring enterprise, one spanning generations, testifying to Hezbollah's patience and willingness to forgo short-term benefits for long-term sustainability.

"Becoming More Radical"

The process of building the "society of resistance" has grown more intensive and sophisticated over the years as Hezbollah has gained influence and experience. Initially, however, its methods were crude and clumsy. The Hezbollah men from Beirut and the Bekaa who infiltrated the villages of the south imposed on the generally laid-back residents a stringent moral regimen. Alcohol was banished from shops and restaurants; card and board games, including the ubiquitous backgammon, were banned. Women were required to wear headscarves, and the playing of music was frowned upon.

The UNIFIL peacekeepers watched with some unease as the area and people with which they had grown familiar over the previous eight years became steadily radicalized. "We noticed the increasing Islamization of the locals," recalls Commandant John Hamill, who served five tours with the Irish UNIFIL battalion, two of them during the 1980s. "In 1978, there were few headscarves in our area, but by the late 1980s, they were becoming more radical."

Some of the older southerners were ill at ease with the arrival of the zealous Hezbollah cadres, but many of the younger men were inspired by the party's religious rhetoric, which filled a void in their lives that the more secular Amal had ignored.

One veteran Hezbollah combatant says his eagerness to embrace the party was shaped by an upbringing in a south Lebanon border village that blended religious observance with violence, occupation, and eviction:

> Being evicted from my village and having my village occupied left a strong impression upon me. It made me very angry. I wanted to do something about it. I was very young then. All the factors of anger and youth were polished by an Islamic upbringing. I was motivated to read—especially the Koran. I watched events unfold between 1979 and 1982 like the Islamic revolution in Iran, which meant a great deal to me because it was related to my religious beliefs. I wanted to be a resistance fighter anyway, but when Hezbollah appeared on the scene I was naturally drawn to it because of its culture and ideology.

Besides the intrusive moral code it imposed on southern villages, Hezbollah quickly gained attention for its bold attacks against the Israelis and the SLA. By mid-1985, Hezbollah was accounting for the majority of attacks against the occupation forces. UNIFIL recorded 248 attacks in its area of operations alone in the period between May and September 1985. In the second half of 1986, Hezbollah began launching "human wave" assaults against Israeli and SLA outposts dotting the front line of the occupation zone. The SLA's outposts were usually circular fortifications with walls of bulldozed earth and cement-filled oil barrels supplemented by a layer of old car tires, ringed by minefields and located on hills with dominant views of the terrain to the north of the zone. The positions had something of a medieval aspect, dominating, as many of them did, villages on the edge of the zone like feudal castles of old.

On January 2, 1987, Hezbollah launched an assault against the SLA outpost on a hill overlooking the village of Braasheet in what was the first concerted attempt to storm and overrun a militia position. The attack was headed by the Kid, the shy young man who had earned his spurs executing collaborators in the Sidon area as a member of al-Shabab al-Aamel. By 1987, he was a well-respected combatant and a sector commander responsible for part of the western edge of the occupation zone.

Prior to the nighttime attack, the unit spearheading the assault, consisting of about twelve fighters, walked beneath a Koran held aloft by Sayyed Abbas Mussawi as a blessing. Then the assault unit made its way through the darkness up the hill toward the SLA outpost. The Kid split his team into two columns for the final approach. There was another unit held in reserve and a fire support unit armed with mortars to the rear. They cut a path through the barbed wire and reached the wall of the compound, close enough to see the glow of a cigarette being smoked by a militiaman on the ramparts above. Once the attack began, several fighters equipped with RPGs quickly knocked out the SLA machine gun nests.

"One of the Lahd militiamen (SLA) was going berserk with his machine gun, firing wildly all over the place. One of our RPGs destroyed his position. There was a big explosion and he was killed," the Kid recalls. The attackers scrambled over the parapets and down into the center of the compound. The militiamen ducked into concrete bunkers and bolted the steel doors from the inside, leaving the Kid and his men roaming around the position. The Hezbollah men blew up an old Sherman tank and captured an armored personnel carrier, which they drove out of the occupation zone. The APC was driven all the way to Beirut with the Kid riding in triumph on the vehicle and Mussawi following behind in his car.

There was never any intention to hold on to captured SLA outposts. This was a campaign of hit-and-run assaults. Hezbollah's strategy in those early days, as articulated by Sayyed Mohammed Hussein Fadlallah at the funeral of the two fighters killed in Braasheet, was to "terrorize" and "exhaust" the SLA. If the SLA were to fall apart, Israel's hold on the south Lebanon "security zone" would inevitably weaken, requiring the Israelis either to reinforce the zone with their own troops, thus risking further casualties, or to pull out altogether.

While Hezbollah's strategy may have been sound, the tactics employed generally were counterproductive. The "human wave" assaults, some of which saw as many as two hundred fighters charging the well-defended SLA outposts in broad daylight, exacted a costly toll among the resistance cadres. In April 1987, about a third of the attacking force of sixty Hezbollah fighters were killed during a single assault on an SLA outpost.

Many of the Hezbollah men moving into the south were from the Bekaa and Beirut and were unfamiliar with the peacekeeping troops deployed with UNIFIL. While the local residents had come to appreciate the presence of UNIFIL in their villages, and Amal especially had cordial relations with the peacekeepers, to Hezbollah, the UN troops were just another foreign army on Lebanese soil whose checkpoints and patrols hampered the ability of the Islamic Resistance to confront the Israeli occupation forces. In August 1986, Hezbollah began attacking UNIFIL troops, mainly French soldiers. In early September, a roadside bomb killed three French soldiers on a morning run, and days later another French soldier died in a bomb attack against his patrol. The sudden slew of attacks led to the French pulling the bulk of its troops from UNIFIL.

Daily Harassment

The Irish battalion also faced its own problems with local militants, specifically members of a radical offshoot from Amal that later allied with Hezbollah: the Believers' Resistance, led by Mustafa Dirani. A young Irish lieutenant, Aonghus Murphy, was killed by a roadside bomb in August 1986 while leading a mine-clearing patrol along a dirt track near At-Tiri village. The attack deliberately targeted the patrol and was orchestrated, the Irish believe, by Jawad Kaspi, a local official with the Believers' Resistance, who had grown irritated at the peacekeepers' ability to uncover his IEDs. Irish soldiers nearby apprehended two teenagers who had detonated the bomb and turned them over to the local police, whereupon they vanished. More than two years later, when the Believers' Resistance was operationally dormant, Israeli troops abducted Kaspi in the hope that he had information on the fate of Ron Arad, an Israeli Air Force navigator, who had been captured by Amal militants in 1986 after bailing out of his Phantom F-4 jet when a faulty bomb exploded beneath it. The Believers' Resistance suspected that the Israelis were aided by the Irish peacekeepers in revenge for Murphy's death. Irish posts came under attack and three Irish soldiers were briefly abducted. A few months later, three Irish soldiers were killed when a large mine blew up a truck. It is still unclear whether the explosion was a deliberate attack or an accident; however, following the deadly incident tensions began to ease in the Irish area.

UNIFIL not only had to put up with threats from newly radicalized militants, it continued to face daily harassment from the IDF and SLA. SLA militiamen routinely fired heavy machine guns and mortar rounds in the general direction of UNIFIL outposts, sometimes with the deliberate intention of causing casualties, more often out of frustration at Hezbollah's attacks.

Given the attacks and harassment they faced from both sides, UNIFIL performed its duties with admirable restraint, despite the urge felt by many peacekeepers over the years to shoot back. In the early 1980s, the Dutch peacekeepers monitoring a stretch of the coastal littoral just north of the occupation zone were routinely harassed by a local SLA commander. The Dutch battalion was replaced in 1985 by troops from Fiji. The Fijians, while gentle giants most of the time, had little patience for the SLA commander's routine provocations. One day, a Fijian officer spotted the militia officer at a checkpoint more than four hundred yards away. Undeterred by the distance, the Fijian officer raised his M-16 rifle and shot the militiaman through the throat. The SLA officer survived, but the Fijian area suddenly became very quiet.

Hezbollah's harassment of UNIFIL further exacerbated tensions with Amal, the latter already unhappy with the emergence of a robust Shia rival in its traditional stomping ground. By early 1988, it became obvious that a battle between Hezbollah and Amal for control of the south was imminent. Indeed, the catalyst for what would prove to be the first round in a bloody fratricidal war was Hezbollah's abduction of Lieutenant Colonel William Higgins, the head of the 76-man Observer Group Lebanon (OGL), the unarmed UN observer force that had patrolled the Lebanon-Israel border since 1949.

On February 17, 1988, Higgins held a routine liaison meeting in Tyre with Daoud Daoud, the top Amal leader in the south after Mohammed Saad's death. After the meeting, Higgins was returning to UNIFIL headquarters in Naqoura when his white UN-marked Jeep Wagoneer was intercepted on the potholed coastal road south of Tyre by a brown Volvo. Armed men dragged Higgins out of his car and into the Volvo, which then disappeared into the narrow lanes cutting though the coastal belt of orange orchards.

Two days later, a group called the Organization of the Oppressed on Earth issued a statement declaring it had snatched Higgins, "the criminal agent of the satanic CIA." The kidnappers demanded the withdrawal of Israeli forces from south Lebanon; the release of all Lebanese detainees held in Khiam prison and all Palestinian prisoners in Israeli jails; the end of U.S. influence in Lebanon; and the closure of all American diplomatic missions in the Middle East.

Although Hezbollah denied responsibility for kidnapping Higgins, it is common knowledge in south Lebanon that the operation was carried out by local Hezbollah men familiar with the area. According to several well-placed sources in south Lebanon, Hezbollah bribed a local Amal security officer to ensure safe passage for the kidnappers through territory controlled by the movement. According to the sources, Higgins was initially held in the *husseiniyah* of Siddiqine village, a few minutes drive from the scene of the abduction, before being transferred elsewhere.

More than a year later, in July 1989, Israeli helicopter-borne commandos kidnapped Sheikh Abdel-Karim Obeid, who had replaced Sheikh Ragheb Harb as imam of Jibsheet village following the latter's murder in 1984. The Israelis justified the kidnapping on the basis that Obeid had information on the whereabouts of Ron Arad, the missing Israeli Air Force navigator, and two Israeli soldiers abducted by Hezbollah from the occupation zone in 1986. Furious at the abduction of Obeid, the kidnappers warned that they would execute Higgins unless the Lebanese cleric was freed. When the Israelis ignored the ultimatum, a videotape was released showing Higgins's lifeless body swinging from a makeshift gallows.

Higgins's remains were recovered in 1991, and a forensic examination confirmed that the videotaped execution had been a fake. The marine colonel had been tortured to death earlier and his body preserved. The United States offered a reward of $4 million for information leading to the arrest of Higgins's kidnappers. No American has served with OGL since.

In a twist to the story, in 2003, Zvi Rish, Sheikh Obeid's Israeli lawyer, claimed that the abduction of the Lebanese cleric had nothing to do with Arad and other missing Israelis but was a jointly planned operation by the United States and Israel to allow American investigators to question Obeid about the fate of Higgins and use him as a bargaining chip for the colonel's release. It was suspected that Higgins had been held in Jibsheet at one point and that a relative of Obeid had been involved in the snatch.

"It didn't sound good to admit that we kidnapped Obeid for the sake of Colonel Higgins," Rish said. "It sounded better to say we did it for Ron Arad. It was a cynical exploitation of Arad's plight, because he had become a national myth by then."

"The Shia Community Is Committing Mass Suicide"

Higgins's kidnapping embarrassed and angered Nabih Berri and the Amal leadership in the south and brought the rivalry with Hezbollah to a breaking point. For Amal and its Syrian patrons, Hezbollah had gone too far. The Syrians already were unhappy at the extent to which its Iranian ally had penetrated Lebanon's Shia community. Furthermore, Hezbollah had cheekily assisted Fatah in its "war of the camps" with Amal by sending weapons and ammunition to the besieged Palestinians. The support was due partly to a moral sympathy for the Palestinian cause but also to a desire to further emasculate its Shia rival in a costly conflict. Hezbollah had even clashed with Syrian troops in early 1987, when Damascus sent its forces into west Beirut to smash the rule of the militias and restore some semblance of order. When Hezbollah refused to turn over a barracks in the Basta neighborhood of Beirut, Syrian soldiers killed twenty-three Hezbollah militants. Hezbollah leaders denounced the killings, and some fifty thousand supporters took to the streets in protest. Hezbollah militants even attempted to assassinate Colonel Ghazi Kanaan, the head of Syrian military intelligence in Lebanon, by firing rocket-propelled grenades at his car.

With the backing of Damascus, Amal launched a massive manhunt in cooperation with UNIFIL to locate Higgins, and in the process they cracked down on their Hezbollah rival. Fighting quickly spread throughout the south in what Hezbollah dubbed the "war for domination." Hezbollah lost ground, and its cadres retreated to its mountain redoubts in the villages of the Iqlim al-Touffah heights east of Sidon.

Fresh fighting erupted in Beirut's southern suburbs a month later. This time, Hezbollah had the upper hand against an Amal that was weakened by poor leadership and undermined by Islamists within its ranks who secretly cooperated with Hezbollah. In one of the more bizarre tactical alliances that emerged during Lebanon's civil war, Samir Geagea's Lebanese Forces militia, Israel's ally in 1982 and an enemy of Damascus, began sending weapons from Christian east Beirut to Hezbollah's cadres in the southern suburbs. In desperation, Nabih Berri appealed for a Syrian military intervention to crush his Islamist rivals. Hafez al-Assad decided instead to meet with a small delegation of senior Hezbollah officials at his summer palace in Latakia to hear their views directly. In his first meeting with Hezbollah representatives, Assad was told that the party did not seek to supplant Amal, but was primarily a resistance force against the Israeli occupation.

As Nasrallah explained a few months later, "we do not seek power and do not wish to compete with anyone over state positions; our political movement is based on the premise of fighting Israel. . . . For us, safeguarding the Islamic Resistance is what really matters."[23]

Hezbollah was learning the logic of survival through pragmatism and compromise to defend its resistance priority. The cold reality facing Hezbollah and its sponsors in Iran was that the party faced annihilation if Assad chose to send his troops against it. A compromise was arranged at the end of May in which Syrian troops were allowed to deploy into the southern suburbs, while Hezbollah was permitted to keep its arms and resume limited operations against the Israelis in the south.

Despite the presence of Syrian troops in the southern suburbs, intermittent street battles broke out during the summer months between Hezbollah and Amal. In September, three top Amal officials, including Daoud Daoud, were killed in an ambush mounted by Hezbollah. Two months later, several Hezbollah leaders, including Nasrallah, Tufayli, and Mussawi, narrowly escaped injury when a bomb exploded beside their ten-car motorcade in the Bekaa Valley.

The worst clashes occurred in January 1989, when Hezbollah launched an offensive from its bases in the Iqlim al-Touffah heights against Amal-controlled villages to the west. Hezbollah quickly overran the villages, killing their Shia rivals in their homes and barracks. Amal rallied and launched a counteroffensive, slowly driving the Hezbollah cadres back into their strongholds of Jbaa and Ain Boussoir, villages that tower over the landscape to the west. Using old Soviet T-54 tanks, RPGs, and even axes and knives, the Shia combatants, many of them high on Valium and hashish, butchered one another with a ferocity scarcely matched at any other time during the civil war. Corpses with heads chopped off or throats slit littered the bloody streets. "Alas, the Shia community is committing mass suicide," wailed Sheikh Abdel-Amir Qabalan, a senior Amal cleric.

An agreement was reached at the end of January 1989 between Iran and Syria and their two quarrelsome proxies that strengthened the un-written deal of May 1988. But fighting waxed and waned over the fol-lowing months, flaring in December 1989 and again in July 1990 as a handful of Hezbollah fighters endured a three-month siege in their bases in the Iqlim al-Touffah. Among them was Hassan Nasrallah, who had intended only to visit the Hezbollah cadres but found himself trapped in the mountain pocket when Amal tightened its grip. Nasrallah had never played a direct military role in Hezbollah; his forte was logis-tics and organization. He had moved to Beirut in 1984 to work ostensi-bly as an assistant to Sayyed Ibrahim al-Amine, the party's spokesman, but was promoted three years later to the newly formed post of chief executive officer and a member of the Consultative Council. Although only twenty-nine years old when he was trapped with the hardened Hezbollah combatants in the Iqlim al-Touffah, Nasrallah was clearly a rising star within the party. The hardships and dangers of the "hundred-day siege," during which he exchanged his black turban and cloak for combat fatigues, added to his stock and earned him the respect of the fighters. One Hezbollah fighter from the 1980s recalls his col-leagues referring to Nasrallah as a "beacon" who would one day lead the party.

Iran and Syria hammered out a second "Damascus Agreement" in November 1990 to bring the internecine fighting to an end once and for all. This time, the arrangement held, and the fighting between the two Shia groups ended.

The Moderates Prevail

The end of the Hezbollah-Amal conflicts also marked the resolution of Lebanon's civil war, after sixteen long years. The momentum toward finding a lasting political solution to end the war had picked up a year earlier, when Lebanon's aging parliamentarians were flown to Saudi Arabia and corralled in a hotel in the resort of Taif to negotiate a compromise agreement. After twenty-two days of argument, the parliamentarians reached consensus on a National Reconciliation Accord, more commonly known as the Taif Agreement. The agreement essentially permitted a more balanced distribution of power among the sects and provided for the gradual abolishment of the sectarian system, although no time frame was given. Syria's influence in Lebanon was formally enshrined by the accord, granting Damascus a role in helping establish and preserve security in the country. It also demanded the dismantling of all militias within six months of the agreement's adoption by parliament.

For Hezbollah, the Taif Agreement was wholly unsatisfactory. Not only did it fail to produce the sweeping constitutional reforms that Hezbollah sought, such as the immediate abolition of the sectarian political system, but the clause calling for the dismantling of all militias threatened the party's resistance priority.

Despite its misgivings about Taif, however, Hezbollah was compelled to accept the agreement due to dramatic domestic and regional changes that required the party to modify its position.

First, the Taif Agreement and the end of the civil war established Syria as the preeminent power in Lebanon, one that could not be ignored by Hezbollah despite their recent history of animosity and distrust. Following Iraq's invasion of Kuwait in August 1990, Syria sided with the U.S.-led coalition against Saddam Hussein, a move that permitted Damascus to finalize its control over Lebanon, with tacit American blessing, and also to secure a seat at the subsequent Madrid peace conference in September 1991. If Hezbollah was to maintain its ability to pursue resistance against Israel, it would have to accept the reality of the Pax Syriana and operate within whatever parameters Damascus wished to set.

Second, there was new leadership in Iran. Ayatollah Khomeini had died in June 1989 and been replaced by Ayatollah Ali Khamenei, who, as supreme leader of the Islamic Republic of Iran, was also Hezbollah's new source of authority. Khamenei was adamant that Hezbollah must maintain resistance against Israel, but Iran also was emerging from a crippling eight-year war with Iraq and was seeking an understanding with the West. The argument in Iran over accommodation with the West was reflected in a fervent internal debate within Hezbollah over how, or indeed whether, the party should shape its policies to reflect the new realities in Lebanon and the region. Sheikh Sobhi Tufayli, who had been formally elected Hezbollah's first secretary general in 1989, believed that Hezbollah should maintain its distance from Lebanese politics and concentrate on the broader goal of confronting Israel. Tufayli, a disciple of Khomeini, had little respect for Khamenei, who would be dogged by suspicions that his religious credentials were insufficient for the position of *wali al-faqih* and supreme leader of the Islamic Republic. Lebanon's political system with its inequities, self-serving alliances, and trade-offs was anathema to a rigid ideologue like Tufayli.

But other leaders, such as Mussawi and Nasrallah, argued that if Hezbollah was to survive the post–civil war era, it would have to accommodate itself to the new situation. The dogmatic Islamist rhetoric and demands for an Islamic state would have to be softened, in public at least. Syria's paramount role in Lebanon must be recognized. Railing against the new realities was futile and possibly self-destructive.

The split within Hezbollah over its future direction was profound. Tufayli had watched with some dismay as his hold on the party he had helped establish began to weaken, his role as secretary general notwithstanding. The ranks of the emerging leadership were drawn from south Lebanon, and they were more open to the path of pragmatism than the dour and obdurate clerics from the Bekaa like Tufayli, or dogmatists like Hussein Mussawi, the leader of Islamic Amal. The differences were personal as well as doctrinal. In 1989, Nasrallah left Lebanon for the holy city of Qom in Iran, where he intended to pursue his studies having decided he could no longer work with Tufayli. Although he intended to remain in Iran for five years, he was persuaded to return and resume his duties after a few months when the situation with Amal deteriorated once more.

With the backing of Khamenei, the moderate line within Hezbollah prevailed. Tufayli's term as secretary general ended in May 1991 and he was replaced by Mussawi, a transition that symbolized the end of the unflinching zealotry of Hezbollah's early years. Certainly, the core ideological pillars upon which Hezbollah was founded had not changed: driving Israeli forces from south Lebanon as a precursor to the destruction of Israel and the liberation of Jerusalem, adherence to the *wilayat al-faqih,* the abolition of political sectarianism, and the establishment of an Islamic state in Lebanon. But Lebanon was stepping into a new era of Syrian-policed stability, central government control and the rule of law, and the beginning of the Madrid peace process, which promised a settlement of the Arab-Israeli conflict. These presented a new set of challenges for Hezbollah that would have to be met with caution, guile, and tact.

Under Mussawi, Hezbollah began moderating its public image. The last of the Western hostages was released, and the Islamic Resistance allowed the Lebanese army to deploy into their strongholds in the Iqlim al-Touffah. A press information office was established where polite multilingual men sporting neatly trimmed beards and dark suits would offer bemused journalists glasses of sweet tea and smile benignly as they answered questions.

Hezbollah's newfound pragmatism was rewarded by Syria's sparing the Islamic Resistance the fate of wartime militias eligible for termination under the Taif Agreement. Instead, Hezbollah was classified as an officially sanctioned resistance against the Israeli occupation, in accordance with Taif's stipulation that the state must take "all necessary measures to liberate all Lebanese territory."

The Madrid peace process notwithstanding, Syria was not inclined to abandon a potentially valuable bargaining chip prior to what were likely to be protracted and difficult negotiations with Israel. Hafez al-Assad may have had little liking for the Iran-backed radicals of Hezbollah, but he recognized that the ability of the Islamic Resistance to bleed Israeli troops in south Lebanon even as his representatives debated peace at the negotiating table would win him valuable leverage against Israel.

For Hezbollah, the path ahead was clear. The immediate threat to its resistance priority was over, and with Iran's religious blessing and continued material support as well as Syria's political backing, Hezbollah could concentrate on the task for which it was born: confronting the Israeli occupation.

THREE

The "Gate of the Mujahideen"

Paradise has a gate called the Gate of the Mujahideen, which when they approach they will find open, their swords they will bear and all shall stand to receive them and the angels shall welcome them.

—AL-KITAB AL-KAFI

FEBRUARY 16, 1992

TOUFFAHTA, south Lebanon—Mohammed Jeziyah heard the helicopters before he saw them. Stepping outside his small whitewashed house on the edge of Touffahta village, the fifty-nine-year-old farmer saw the black, insectlike lines of two Apache AH-64 helicopters hanging in the air just to the east, the heavy beat of their rotor blades reverberating through the deep blue late afternoon sky. One of the helicopters unleashed a missile, a dart of light that streaked toward the ground at a sharp angle. The Hellfire missile struck the gas tank of the black Mercedes passing down a narrow lane toward Touffahta. The vehicle exploded in a ball of fire, sending a thick cloud of black smoke billowing skyward as more of the laser-guided missiles homed in on the two Range Rovers following just behind.

Jeziyah instantly knew who was inside the burning Mercedes. He had returned minutes earlier from Jibsheet, a small hill village a few miles to the south, where Sayyed Abbas Mussawi, Hezbollah's secretary general, had led a commemoration marking the eighth anniversary of the assassination of Sheikh Ragheb Harb. But there had been an air of unease rippling through the crowd in Jibsheet, felt particularly by the body-guards of the Hezbollah chief. The whine of Israeli reconnaissance drones and the rumble of jets had been heard above the village all day. By afternoon, Israeli helicopter gunships were also present in the skies near Jibsheet. Residents of the area were accustomed to hearing war-planes and helicopters—Jibsheet was less than five miles from the clos-est Israeli outposts on the hills overlooking the market town of Nabatiyah. But the unusually high level of Israeli air activity coinciding with Mussawi's visit to Jibsheet was unnerving.

Mussawi conducted prayers at Harb's tomb in the cemetery before leading the crowd up the hill to the mosque in the center of the village. Three Israeli helicopters could be seen hovering in the distance.

Residents urged Mussawi not to leave the village. It was too danger-ous, they said. But Mussawi simply replied, "What's the matter? You think I am afraid of dying?"

His bodyguards insisted that he at least switch cars for the drive back to Beirut. But the Hezbollah leader refused and climbed into the black Mercedes along with his wife, Siham, and five-year-old son, Hussein.

The two Apaches above Touffahta pummeled the burning vehicles and the road on either side with bursts from the 30 mm cannons slung beneath the nose of the helicopters, creating a perimeter of fire that pre-vented rescuers from reaching the stricken convoy. The surviving body-guards shot back at the helicopters with automatic rifles in a courageous but futile act. Five of them were killed in the attack.

The Israeli helicopters eventually departed, having stayed long enough to ensure that Mussawi was dead. His wife and child were killed alongside him. For several days afterward, the fire-blackened hulk of the Mercedes was kept under close guard in Touffahta until Shia clerics and Hezbollah officials were satisfied that every last scrap of flesh belonging to Mussawi and his family had been collected from the wreck.[1]

Mussawi's death was a pivotal moment for Hezbollah, serving as a catalyst for several key precedents that would help shape the conflict with Israel over the next decade.

On March 17, a month and a day after Mussawi's assassination, a suicide bomber detonated his explosives-laden car beside the four-story

Israeli embassy in Buenos Aires, killing twenty-nine people and wounding more than two hundred. Islamic Jihad claimed responsibility for the suicide bombing, naming Abu Yasser, an Argentine convert to Islam, as the perpetrator and dedicating it to the "martyr infant Hussein," Mussawi's five-year-old son.

It was a sobering moment for the Israelis, especially as Mussawi's assassination apparently was an unplanned tactical "target of opportunity" strike rather than the outcome of a strategic decision to kill the Hezbollah chief. A former Israeli intelligence officer revealed to me that the original intention was to abduct Mussawi from Jibsheet and exchange him for Ron Arad, the missing Israeli air force navigator. However, when the snatch squad assessed that it was too dangerous to touch down and grab Mussawi, the order was given to kill him instead, using the Apache helicopter gunships that were monitoring the Hezbollah leader's movements on the ground.

"The order was given by a relatively junior officer who was not in a position to make such a decision. It was not intended to be an assassination," the former intelligence officer said.

Although Hezbollah officially absolved itself of involvement in the Buenos Aires bombing, the message was clear: the organization had the means and will to retaliate on a global basis to Israeli assassinations of its leadership cadre. It was a lesson that the Israelis evidently absorbed; although top resistance commanders were subsequently targeted when opportunities arose, no further assassination attempts were made against senior party leaders for the next sixteen years.

The second key repercussion of Mussawi's death was the decision by Hezbollah to fire, for the first time, Katyusha rockets at population centers in northern Israel. Hezbollah had used Katyusha rockets to attack Israeli and SLA positions inside the occupation zone in south Lebanon, but as a policy the party had refrained from firing them into Israel. The first barrage of two dozen 122 mm rockets was launched before dawn on February 17, some twelve hours after the helicopter attack on Mussawi's motorcade. Some of the rockets exploded in and around Kiryat Shemona in northern Galilee and in areas of western Galilee. The Israeli army immediately ordered the shocked residents of Kiryat Shemona into the town's bomb shelters. Kiryat Shemona had been a regular target of PLO artillery before the 1982 invasion, but since then there had been almost no rocket attacks against the town. Israeli troops, punching north of the occupation zone to destroy the Katyusha launchers, clashed with Hezbollah. By the time the fighting ended three days later, more than a hundred Katyusha rockets had been launched, with about a third of them striking Israel.

But the rocket fire was greeted with some apprehension in Lebanon, even by supporters of the resistance. Cross-border rocket fire was reminiscent of the bleak era when the south had been the PLO's stronghold. The PLO's random Katyusha attacks into Israel invariably triggered heavy Israeli retaliation, with Lebanese civilians tending to bear the brunt. No one wanted a return to those grim days.

"Now that the enemy has been defeated and forced to retreat, there is no need to resume the firing of Katyusha rockets," said Sayyed Mohammed Hussein Fadlallah, the influential Shia cleric. Omar Karami, the Lebanese prime minister, also said that firing rockets into Israel could not be classified as resistance.

Even Nasrallah played down the party's role in launching the rockets. Asked if he knew who fired them, Nasrallah replied, "We have no information in this regard and cannot point a finger at anyone."[2]

But he did articulate a new tactic that would turn the 122 mm Katyusha rocket into a strategic asset that would impose future restraints on the IDF's freedom to act. The resistance, Nasrallah said, should work toward "creating a situation in which the enemy is subject to our conditions."

"We should tell him: 'If you attack us, we will use our Katyushas; if you do not attack us, we will not use our Katyushas.' . . . We have to turn the situation around," he said.[3]

The third major consequence of Mussawi's assassination was the election of Nasrallah as his successor. It had been clear for some years that Nasrallah's star was in the ascendant. His charisma and organizational skills had won him many admirers in the party. One veteran

Hezbollah member recalls that even when Mussawi was elected secretary general in 1991, it was his protégé, Nasrallah, who drew the eyes of the rank and file.

Hezbollah's consultative council met the day after Mussawi's death and unanimously elected the thirty-two-year-old Nasrallah. He was expected to follow Mussawi's realist line in which the dogmatic extremism of the 1980s would give way to greater pragmatism in dealings with the Lebanese state. But on Israel and the resistance, there would be no softening. Speaking before some forty thousand mourners at Mussawi's funeral in Nabi Sheet a day after his election, Nasrallah vowed to follow his predecessor's path.

"America will remain the nation's chief enemy and the greatest Satan of all," he said. "Israel will always be for us a cancerous growth that needs to be eradicated, and an artificial entity that should be removed.... The Islamic Resistance will remain our only option, our constant response, the path we shall not relinquish, and the battle we will pursue even if the entire world surrenders."

"A State of Resistance"

Nasrallah's ascension to the party leadership heralded a fresh beginning for Hezbollah. In line with the increased focus on armed activities in south Lebanon, Hezbollah began moderating its public image, shedding the aura of the war-torn 1980s when wild-eyed and bearded gunmen imposed an austere ad hoc Islamic rule on the areas under its control. The most visible shift in public attitude was the heated internal debate over whether to run candidates in the parliamentary election, the first for twenty years, scheduled for August and September 1992. While Nasrallah supported participating in the election, he faced stiff opposition from party hard-liners led by Sheikh Sobhi Tufayli. Tufayli argued that it was impermissible for Hezbollah to participate in, and give legitimacy to, a form of government that was non-Islamic. The legacy of Khomeini must be preserved, he said, and Hezbollah should not waver from its path simply because of changed circumstances in Lebanon.

"We would have been much stronger," Tufayli told me many years later when asked how Hezbollah could have survived into the 1990s without adapting to the new political environment. "This point was discussed thoroughly at the time. [Our] view was that Hezbollah could continue as a strong force with all the other players orbiting us instead of us chasing after them. It was Iran that stepped in and said we had to run candidates in the elections."

The debate might have been fervent within the leadership circle, but ultimately the party had little option. A special internal consultative council of twelve delegates voted 10 to 2 in favor of electoral participation. Khamenei pronounced that it was legitimate for Hezbollah to contest the elections and approved the council's vote. The supreme leader had spoken, and for Hezbollah the matter was settled. Although Hezbollah was obliged by the Syrians to form an electoral alliance with Amal, the party fared well, gaining eight seats, which, along with four allies, gave it the largest bloc in the 128-seat parliament.

Following the elections, Hezbollah underwent an internal reorganization, adding new bodies to handle its ever-expanding activities— the political council, the jihad council to oversee military affairs, the judicial council, and the "Loyalty to the Resistance" parliamentary bloc.

Rafik Hariri, a billionaire construction tycoon with close ties to the Saudis, was appointed prime minister, and he began implementing an ambitious multi-billion-dollar reconstruction program to repair the damage of the civil war years and restore Lebanon as the financial and commercial hub of the Middle East.

Hezbollah was not offered, nor did it apparently seek, a seat in Hariri's first government, instead opting for an opposition role, using its parliamentary foothold to rail against the government's spending excesses, which focused on Beirut and neglected Hezbollah's strongholds in the Bekaa and the south. Hariri's reconstruction policies were based on a massive gamble. He would use his international contacts and credibility to amass billions of dollars in grants and loans to help pay for the rehabilitation of Lebanon's infrastructure on the premise that comprehensive Middle East peace would be realized by 1996. The new era of peace and consequent international investment in the region, Hariri assumed, would allow Lebanon to pay back its debts, or, better still, have them written off as part of the peace dividend. But Hezbollah, which vehemently opposed the peace process, was less than impressed. Mohammed Raad, one of the eight Hezbollah MPs elected in 1992, told me that the party was at odds with Hariri's "continual optimism" about achieving peace and considered his ambitions for the country "unrealistic."

Relations between Hezbollah and Hariri's governments in the 1990s were marked by tension and rooted in mutual irritation and mistrust. In September 1993, nine Hezbollah supporters were shot dead by Lebanese soldiers during a peaceful demonstration against the signing of the Oslo Accords between Israel and Yasser Arafat's PLO. The killings provoked angry public protests until Hariri attempted to mollify Hezbollah by officially declaring the dead to be "martyrs," thus making their families eligible for government compensation.

Hariri was obliged to pay lip service to Hezbollah's resistance campaign in the south because it was sanctioned by Syria, but it was evident that he considered it a nuisance that continually threatened to disrupt his reconstruction agenda. The paradox of resistance and reconstruction would plague his governments in the years ahead.

The policy of pragmatism pursued by Hezbollah from 1992 on did not represent an ideological softening, but was intended first and foremost to sustain the armed struggle in the south. The resistance was to be protected and insulated through layers of political influence in parliament, by the expansion of popular support among Lebanese Shias, and by fostering a public dialogue with all shades of Lebanese society to mollify, appease, reassure, and persuade. But Hezbollah's resistance priority, its beating heart, would remain paramount.

"In reality, we were, and will always be, the party of the resistance that [operates] from Lebanon in reaction to occupation and daily aggression," Nasrallah said days after the 1992 elections. "Our participation in the elections and entry into the [parliament] do not alter the fact that we are a resistance party; we shall, in fact, work to turn the whole of Lebanon into a country of resistance, and the state into a state of resistance."[4]

"An Atmosphere of Religion and Faithfulness"

The process of joining Hezbollah has evolved as the organization has grown in size and become more institutionalized and entrenched within Shia society. In the initial stages following Israel's 1982 invasion, personnel were recruited in the Bekaa Valley through a process of mass mobilization along family and clan lines, which helped preserve internal security as well as facilitate the enrollment of hundreds of volunteer fighters. In south Lebanon, devout young Shias needed little incentive to join the nascent resistance, given that it was their homes and land that bore the brunt of Israeli occupation.

Today, however, the motivations for joining Hezbollah are more multidimensional, blending religious observance, hostility toward Israel, and the Shia commitment to justice and dignity. On a more prosaic level, many young Shias naturally gravitate toward an organization that has helped empower their community in Lebanon and has earned respect for its martial exploits over the years.

"Our fighters are driven by complex motives—patriotism and Islamic motives," Sheikh Khodr Noureddine told me in 1996, when he was Hezbollah's political chief in south Lebanon. "Our Islamic beliefs makes these young men refuse to accept injustice. They will do anything to resist Israel. I know the West does not understand, but our youth cannot live with Israel."

Recruits drawn from the south who have grown up with an inherent distrust of Israel will dwell more on the aspect of defending their border communities against the perceived perpetual threat of the Jewish state.

"It's an honor to serve," said one veteran Hezbollah fighter, explaining in 2009 why he still served with the Islamic Resistance even though Israel had withdrawn from Lebanon almost a decade earlier. "It's like this. If you have a house or a villa and someone powerful takes it over, you have a long struggle and after a while he gives you a room. You struggle a bit longer and then he gives up and hands back the house to you. You might think the struggle is over, but then he parks his car in your parking spot outside the house. Do you accept this? We are in the south because Israel is like this powerful usurper and there is no government to protect us, and the UN can't protect us either. That's why we need the resistance."

Given Hezbollah's long-term strategic perspective and commitment to building a "society of resistance," the process of mobilization and radicalization of its potential recruits begins at an early age. Children as young as six or seven are encouraged to participate in Hezbollah's youth movement, a first step on the long path to becoming a resistance fighter. Activities include lectures, plays, and sporting events through which the youthful participants are immersed in Hezbollah's moral, religious, political, and cultural milieu. Hezbollah-affiliated cultural associations and publishing houses churn out books and pamphlets and hold seminars and conferences to spread the creed of resistance. Among them are the Islamic Maaref Cultural Association, the Imam al-Mahdi Institute, and the Imam Khomeini Cultural Center, all of which promote the teachings of Ayatollah Khomeini. Other institutes produce material that ranges from explaining Hezbollah's concept of jihad and promoting hostility toward Israel to treatises on the role of women in Islamic society and the importance of a healthy lifestyle. Some of the material is intended for a youthful audience, with cartoon books telling stories of resistance fighters or fairy tales featuring villainous Israelis and heroic Palestinian and Lebanese children.

During the summer holiday months, a common sight in the southern suburbs of Beirut is rows of wide-eyed children sitting patiently at desks in outdoor classes being taught the way of Hezbollah. They are raised in a heavily militarized environment in which the youngsters are encouraged to venerate and emulate the fighters of the Islamic Resistance. During the Ashoura commemoration or the annual Jerusalem Day parades, small children march alongside regular combatants, all of them dressed in camouflage uniforms and carrying plastic toy rifles, wearing headbands inscribed with slogans such as "O Jerusalem, we are coming."

The process continues in the Hezbollah-affiliated nationwide network of Mustafa schools, where pupils study religion and pray for Islamic Resistance fighters. Hundreds of youngsters each year pass through the dozens of summer camps held by the Hezbollah-run Imam

Mahdi Scouts in valleys and hills in southern Lebanon and the northern Bekaa, where they are imbued with a sense of military brotherhood and discipline replete with uniforms, parades, and martial bands.

Hezbollah generally does not accept combatants into the Islamic Resistance below the age of eighteen, but basic military training and familiarization with weapons does begin at a much younger age. A tall, rangy Hezbollah fighter in his midthirties, whom we shall call "the Chief," once showed me video footage shot on his cell phone of more than fifty children aged between six and nine dressed in camouflage uniforms marching through rugged mountains and woodland in a south Lebanon valley. The children were the sons of "martyrs"—Hezbollah fighters killed in action—and they were participating in a military-style training exercise. Uniformed adult instructors walked alongside the children, helping them plunge across a narrow river and scramble up steep, rocky slopes. They smeared their faces with dirt, and some even fired a few rounds from an AK-47 rifle, each one aiming at rocks in the river with a kneeling instructor helping prop up the heavy weapon.

"The next generation of mujahideen," said the Chief with a smile of paternal pride.

In addition to the childhood induction process, Hezbollah deploys recruiters in every village and neighborhood where the party wields influence to look out for likely prospects among the local young men and women. The recruiter is looking for pious, disciplined, modest, intelligent, healthy, well-behaved individuals who could fit into Hezbollah's way of life. Young men who listen to music, drink alcohol, drive fast cars, and flirt with girls stand little chance.

"The idea is to meet potential recruits and cultivate a friendship. You don't hit him at the same moment with an offer to join. You make him love Hezbollah first. You sell the idea, then he can choose whether to join or not," explained the Chief, himself a recruiter.

After observing a potential recruit for a period of months, even years, the recruiter will make his move, inquiring whether he or she would consider joining Hezbollah. If the person accepts there follows an intensive initial phase known as *tahdirat*, or "preparation," lasting up to a year, in which recruits are taught the ideological foundations of

Hezbollah. "At this stage, we give them Islamic lessons, ethical, political [and] social lessons, as a preparation, as part of the resistance. He will live in an atmosphere of religion and faithfulness," says Sheikh Naim Qassem, Hezbollah's deputy leader.

"Our Life Dictates Our Death"

The new recruits absorb the principles of the Islamic revolution in Iran, obedience to the *wali al-faqih,* and enmity toward Israel. They are taught the Islamic texts according to the interpretation of Hezbollah's clerics, and learn to pursue the "greater jihad" of spiritual transformation to bring them closer to God. "The religious lessons are first," says the Chief. "Religion first, before you even see a gun."

A recruit can have different reasons for joining the party in the first place—a desire to resist occupation, religious commitment, or simply peer pressure—but realizing the importance of jihad as it is taught by Hezbollah is critical to understanding what drives the fully trained and committed Islamic Resistance fighter.

Sheikh Naim Qassem describes the world as a "perishable home," a transient "place of test and tribulation for man," and how a person chooses to live his life will dictate his fate in the hereafter.[5] The "greater jihad" is the daily spiritual struggle within the carnal soul to resist and overcome the temptations and vices of the human condition in order to achieve divine knowledge, love, and spiritual harmony. According to Hezbollah, success on the "greater jihad"—the inner spiritual struggle— is a necessary precondition to undertaking the "lesser jihad"—the outer, material struggle. The "lesser jihad," or "military jihad," falls into two categories. The first is "offensive jihad," in which Muslims are permitted to invade other countries or wage war against other societies on the basis that Islam is the one true religion. However, "offensive jihad," according to the interpretation of Hezbollah's clerics, is not considered applicable until the return of the "awaited imam." The second category is "defensive jihad," which confers not just the right but the obligation of Muslims to defend their lands and communities from aggression and occupation. For Hezbollah, the call for "defensive jihad" can be made only by the *wali al-faqih*. Hezbollah's campaign of resistance against Israeli occupation in south Lebanon and its post-2000 military confrontation with Israel were conducted under the rubric of "defensive jihad" sanctioned by Khomeini in his role as *wali al-faqih*, and later endorsed by his successor Khamenei. Accordingly, Hezbollah fighters are taught that when they confront Israeli troops in the stony hills and valleys of south Lebanon, they are not merely resisting occupation but also fulfilling the deeper religious obligation of pursuing jihad.

Central to Hezbollah's observance of the "lesser jihad" is the culture of martyrdom. For the Shias, the paradigm of jihad, resistance, and sacrifice is Imam Hussein, whose death at Karbala against the numerically superior forces of Yazid epitomizes the struggle against oppression and injustice and serves as a powerful inspiration and exemplar for new generations of Shia warriors serving with Hezbollah. Hezbollah teaches that Imam Hussein actively sought martyrdom at Karbala, rather than choosing to engage with Yazid's army knowing that despite the odds there was a faint possibility of survival.

A Hezbollah fighter who has advanced in the "greater jihad" will have spiritually moved beyond the human fear of death, instead welcoming it as a sacrifice in God's name during the fulfillment of the "lesser jihad." Unlike suicide, which is forbidden by Islam, Hezbollah considers the act of self-sacrifice as a paramount demonstration of faith in God, far removed from earthly, corporeal concerns. The motifs of martyrdom are inescapable in Hezbollah's strongholds, where streets and roads are lined with the portraits of "martyrs"—fighters who have died in battle—and billboards with paintings of fallen fighters entering garish representations of paradise with richly colored landscapes of green hills, wildflowers, and flowing rivers bathed in bright sunlight. The annual Martyrs' Day commemoration held each November 11 (the anniversary of Ahmad Qassir's suicide bombing of the IDF headquarters in Tyre in 1982) is one of the most important events in Hezbollah's calendar. Each Hezbollah fighter is photographed for an official "martyr's" portrait on joining the Islamic Resistance. His picture will adorn his neighborhood's lampposts should he be killed in the course of duty, and each year he updates a "martyr's letter," containing his final thoughts and wishes.

Conversations with committed Hezbollah fighters on the subject of martyrdom hold a certain surreal quality. When I met Maher, commander of a sector in south Lebanon, in May 2000, he mentioned that two of his friends had been killed days earlier in an operation inside the occupation zone. Normally, one would offer a polite commiseration, but Maher forestalled any expression of condolence with a raised hand. "Do not be sorry for them, be happy for them," he said with a wistful smile. "God chose them to be martyrs, and, God willing, one day I, too, will be martyred fighting the Israelis."

Maher had light brown crew-cut hair and a neatly trimmed beard, and his pale blue eyes shone with unquestioning confidence in the certainty of his convictions. At thirty-three years of age, Maher was a combat veteran, having joined the resistance in 1983. He was in charge of four units, two assault and two fire support. But he was also married and a father; when I met him, his wife was pregnant with their fourth child. If he were to die in combat, Hezbollah would provide for his family—a house, free education for his children, medical care, and a pension of around $350 a month. Yet how could he relish the prospect of death when he would leave behind him a widow and four fatherless children? Maher smiled again, nodding sympathetically.

"It is difficult for you to understand because you are not a Muslim. My wife will feel great joy and pride if I am martyred," he said. "Martyrdom is a religious and philosophical concept. Islam is the same as Christianity and Judaism in the sense that if you follow God you will go to Heaven. But in Islam, it's explained differently. We are born to get acquainted with God. Our goal of living is to reach God. To reach God we have to move from the living world to the next world. This is done by death. We are all going to die, but each person has a choice of how to die. The way we lead our life dictates our death. According to Islam, the best way to die is to die for God."

Hezbollah fighters can volunteer to join the Martyrdom (Istishadiyun) Unit, which means that they could be selected for specific suicide attacks or particularly perilous missions where chances of survival are low. Although Hezbollah has always been associated in the public mind with suicide bombings, it conducted only eleven such operations in Lebanon during the years of Israeli occupation between 1982 and 2000. Of the eleven, only four were carried out during the 1990s.

"Martyrdom is a personal initiative," says Maher. "A potential martyr makes his decision, then tells his religious leader [*marja'*]. The religious leader decides whether the candidate is suitable or not. Sayyed Nasrallah is the only one who can decide these things in Lebanon. He makes the decision according to priorities. He assesses whether the result is worthy of the act, then decides. It also depends on the situation on the ground. An act of martyrdom is like a military operation."

This type of martyrdom is an alien concept in Western philosophy, which emphasizes the sanctity of life, but for many Hezbollah combatants, seeking death is a desirable outcome, one that is nurtured and constantly reinforced by the religious and cultural environment in which he lives. For unlike a member of a political party in the West, the Hezbollah recruit is submitting to a way of life that will dictate almost every aspect of his or her future: choice of friends, employment, social amenities, and often even marriage.

"In one home you could have a brother who is a communist, another who is with Amal, and a third who is with Hezbollah," explains the Chief. "They are all brothers in the same family, but for the Hezbollah man, Hezbollah is his family. He breathes Hezbollah, eats Hezbollah, everything is Hezbollah. . . . None of our fighters join because they want a job. Many of us are educated people—university graduates, teachers, doctors. We are like everyone else. We want to live in peace, but we also want to live in dignity and without having our rights trampled upon."

After a recruit has passed through the initial *tahdirat* phase, he will enter the second stage of induction, known as *intizam*, or commitment, which also lasts around a year, during which the rigors of party discipline are instilled along with basic military training. "Afterward, it depends on his improvements, he can undergo other courses with higher levels that enable him to hold positions within the organization," Qassem says. "Some are gradual and some are specialized. You can say it's like a university."

Paradoxically, despite the cultish aspects of the indoctrination and educational process, Hezbollah is not interested in churning out an army of mindless drones blindly sacrificing themselves. A degree of self-reliance and autonomy is encouraged, so long as the parameters of party discipline are not breached. Even within Hezbollah, there are those who practice their religious observance more deeply than others. Speaking in the context of the resistance against the Israeli occupation in the late 1990s, Nasrallah admitted that there were two categories of fighters in the Islamic Resistance: "Fighters and officers whose objective is eventually to go back home, and those whose objective is martyrdom, pure and simple. The latter have a far higher morale on the battlefield, and regardless of the kind of weapons they carry, their faith and spirit makes them strong and steadfast and allows them to deal the enemy a severe blow."

The lengthy and intense process of religious instruction attempts to inculcate within the recruit the moral and religious rectitude of the second category to which Nasrallah refers. Maher, for example, fitted into this category. Raised in an austere and violent environment in south Lebanon and devout from childhood, he had known nothing but resistance and jihad throughout his young adult life. Maher was a single-minded combatant for whom the act of resisting Israel was considered a religious obligation that even took precedence over his human desire to end Israel's occupation of his natal village.

The Chief, on the other hand, although pious, had not reached the same level of religious intensity as that attained by Maher. He admitted to me that his principal motivation was a desire to protect Lebanon from Israel. The Chief's upbringing was generally secular, and he had been a talented athlete before joining Hezbollah. His easygoing, friendly nature made him a popular figure in his neighborhood, which is why Hezbollah appointed him a recruiter and placed dozens of fighters under his charge. The Chief was an organizer and a team leader rather than a resolute seeker of martyrdom.

"A Matter of Conviction"

Still, despite the arduous induction process, there is no compulsion to join Hezbollah. The party seeks only those who are unreservedly committed to its ideology and willing to follow the doctrine of *wilayat al-faqih,* which is an unconditional prerequisite for membership. Recruits who remain unconvinced after weeks of educational courses are free to leave.

"The *wali al-faqih* is the leader as far as we are concerned," Qassem says. "His status in Islam is a religious one. If we are to be reassured that our applications of the teaching of our religion are correct, we need to know the restrictions and the rules that the religion endorses. He gives us these rules and our general political performance. He does not interfere in details."

As an example, Qassem said that the resistance campaign against Israel in Lebanon from 1982 was religiously sanctioned by the *wali al-faqih,* Khomeini at the time. But the *wali al-faqih* did not bother with the tactical details of how Hezbollah waged its resistance campaign. Similarly, the *wali al-faqih,* this time Khamenei, was the ultimate arbiter of Hezbollah's decision to enter parliamentary politics in 1992. But Hezbollah's parliamentary policies are left up to the party and do not individually require approval by the *wali al-faqih.*

"During this period, the [recruit] will have a vision forming through information. If he becomes convinced . . . he will become a member. If he doesn't believe in it, he will leave us. It's a matter of conviction," Qassem explained to me. "Hezbollah has a doctrinal intellectual Islamic code of law. It regards the *wilayat al-faqih* as part of its system. We believe in the leadership of the *wali al-faqih.* This is a religious issue as far as we are concerned. All those who want to be a part of Hezbollah have to commit themselves to its intellectual code of law, and the *wilayat al-faqih* is part of this."

Many recruits receive little or no pay from Hezbollah for the first two or three years, and most will find day jobs to provide an income. Later they will receive monthly salaries and financial support for housing, education of children, and medical needs.

After the 2006 war with Israel, Nasrallah authorized a onetime payment of $100 to each Hezbollah fighter and members of his immediate family in a simple gesture of appreciation. The sum was deliberately kept small. "If we gave them all Range Rovers, they wouldn't want to fight anymore," noted one Hezbollah official.

Hezbollah fights for God, not Mammon, but the party's leadership knows from the experiences of others the temptations that arise when an organization is awash with funds and practices lax accounting. The lure of cash can easily dull the sharp edge of commitment to the cause. In the 1970s, Hezbollah's future leaders had watched the PLO leadership become corrupt and lazy when it was the recipient of substantial funds from foreign donor countries. The Amal movement today is inefficient and bloated by graft, corrupted by access to state funds to sustain its patronage networks—a grubby legacy to the integrity of Musa Sadr's original vision.

Recruits into Hezbollah are expected to be financially honest and reliable in accordance with Islamic tenets. Anis Naqqash, the early tutor of the young Imad Mughniyah, recalls sharing a taxi from Damascus to Beirut with a young Hezbollah fighter who had just returned from a training session in Iran. Naqqash offered to pay the fighter's $15 taxi fare, but the youngster insisted on paying for himself. Naqqash took offense and told him, "Shame on you. I am like your father. I am a businessman and you are a student." But the youngster would not yield. Later, Naqqash discussed the incident with a friend in Hezbollah.

"Yes, this is normal," the Hezbollah man said. "We would have given him the fifteen dollars for the taxi fare. It was impossible for him to keep the money for himself."

Although salaries may be limited, the Hezbollah member knows that his needs will be met by the party, which acts as a vast social welfare network in a country where state social support is almost nonexistent. If a Hezbollah fighter has an accident and requires hospitalization but lacks insurance or the funds to be admitted for treatment, the party will step in and provide the financial coverage and handle the paperwork. I heard of one young Hezbollah man who fought bravely on the front lines in south Lebanon during the 2006 war who was rewarded afterward with a grant of $40,000, allowing him to marry and purchase a home.

Self-discipline and obedience are integral characteristics of Hezbollah. Hezbollah fighters are expected to obey all orders promptly and fully when they are given. They are also expected to behave correctly toward each other as well as toward people outside the party, a natural outcome of successfully pursuing the "greater jihad." Transgressors face being fined, having pay docked, or spending time in Hezbollah's own prison in the southern suburbs of Beirut.

During the preparatory phase, each recruit is subjected to a rigorous background security check by Hezbollah's internal security apparatus. Anyone who has lived abroad for a lengthy period of time, for example, will be treated as a potential security risk and face great difficulty in joining. The security assessment is constantly updated during the recruit's subsequent life within Hezbollah. Hezbollah has managed to maintain a high level of internal security over the years due to each recruit's learning self-discipline and developing a sense of security. Nevertheless, individual Hezbollah fighters feel the tug of human emotion— anger, jealousy, humor—just like anyone else. Many of the Hezbollah fighters who spoke to me for this book were not authorized to do so, but some of them had become friends over the years, and others were willing to talk on the assurances of mutual acquaintances.

Hezbollah men tend to be wary of strangers and are required to report any contact with a foreigner to their superiors. Foreigners appearing in Hezbollah-controlled areas are sometimes stopped and questioned and occasionally followed. Every now and then one hears stories of unsuspecting foreign tourists swooped upon by vigilant Hezbollah men while innocently snapping photographs in Beirut's southern suburbs. A newcomer to Lebanon doubtless will be unsettled, to say the least, when apprehended by burly Hezbollah men or tailed by a militant riding an off-road motorcycle while driving through southern villages. But Hezbollah personnel are generally disciplined and polite, albeit firm, when quizzing a visitor. Over the years I have run the gamut of Hezbollah security procedures, from the mild (being stopped and politely questioned for a few minutes) to the mildly annoying (being stopped, politely questioned, and having a roll of film confiscated) to the disconcerting (being stopped, politely questioned, and photographed, face-on and profile, mug-shot-style, by a Hezbollah security officer) to the thoroughly vexing (being stopped, detained, interrogated, accused of being a spy, handed over to Lebanese military intelligence, and thrown in jail for the night).

Walking in the Path of Ahl al-Bayt

Khodr was not even born when Israel invaded Lebanon in 1982, but the soft-spoken university student knew from childhood that he would join Hezbollah one day and serve in the ranks of the resistance just as his father had done. Raised in a pious environment in the southern suburbs of Beirut, Khodr was twelve when he joined Hezbollah's youth program in 1998.

His stocky physique and thickly muscled arms are testament to the hours he spends pumping iron in a local gym. But while he mixes with his neighborhood Shia friends even though they do not share his beliefs, Khodr has no appetite for listening to music, going to parties, or generally enjoying the indolence of youth. "I look at my friends and see them chasing girls and drinking, but in the end I am laughing and they are crying," he says. "Everything I do is with the Prophet Mohammed and the Ahl al-Bayt [the Prophet's family line through Imam Ali] in mind. I am walking the same path."

Each recruit undergoes an initial military training program lasting thirty-three days, during which the rudiments of guerrilla warfare are taught and basic fitness attained. During the 1980s and early 1990s, much of the training was carried out at established camps in the barren valleys of the Anti-Lebanon Mountains on the eastern flank of the Bekaa Valley beside the border with Syria. There was no ground cover to mask Hezbollah's activities from Israeli jets and drones, and the recruits usually slept in tents, caves, and huts. Hezbollah assumed that the presence of air defense systems—its own rudimentary weapons and Syria's more advanced missiles on the other side of the adjacent border—were sufficient to deter the Israeli Air Force from attacking the training sites.

However, on the night of June 2, 1994, Israeli jets and Apache helicopter gunships swooped on the Ain Dardara camp east of Baalbek, where some 150 recruits were sleeping in their tents. The jets dropped bombs on the camp and the helicopter gunships mopped up, using thermal imaging to locate fleeing militants and tear them to shreds with bursts of fire from their 30 mm guns. More than forty recruits were killed in the raid, the deepest into Lebanon in seven years. Hezbollah and Lebanese army antiaircraft units shot blindly into the night sky without hitting any Israeli aircraft, and the Syrian SAM batteries remained quiet. It was Hezbollah's largest loss of life in a single incident, and party leaders were quick to vow revenge. "We are preparing an operation that will surprise the world," Hajj Hassan Huballah, a top official, warned.[6]

Six weeks later, on July 13, a suicide bomber blew up a van packed with more than six hundred pounds of explosive beside the seven-story building of the Mutual Israeli Association of Argentina, an umbrella group of Jewish charities in Buenos Aires. The blast killed 85 people, wounded another 300, and completely demolished the building. Hezbollah denied responsibility, but for Israel, the bombing again demonstrated Hezbollah's ability and will to exact revenge on a global scale for extraordinary actions undertaken by the Israeli military. Whether Israel would have repeated the Ain Dardara air strike in view of the blowback in Argentina is unclear, although Hezbollah would not give them the opportunity.

"We Could Hear the Sizz of the Fuse"

Following the Ain Dardara raid, Hezbollah changed its training procedures in the Bekaa Valley, switching to the more wooded western flanks of the valley, which provided better ground cover from Israeli aircraft. The training, while as intensive and rigorous as ever, was conducted on a more ad hoc level, with recruits no longer sleeping in fixed locations on a regular basis.

Basic military training begins with the recruit receiving instructions to be at a certain rendezvous point at a given time. The recruit brings nothing with him apart from a change of underwear and toiletries. He is picked up by a minibus with windows masked by black cotton sheets, and along with some fifteen other recruits begins the journey to a training area in the Bekaa Valley. Although it normally takes only about ninety minutes to reach the nearest Hezbollah training areas from Beirut's southern suburbs, the journey for the recruits is usually considerably longer, as the minibus driver deliberately follows a meandering route, doubling back more than once to thoroughly disorient his passengers. When close to the training area, the recruits leave the minibus, and for the final stage of the journey along rough dirt tracks, they sit hidden beneath canvas awnings in the back of pickup trucks or large SUVs. By the time they are deposited on a mountainside along with perhaps two more groups of recruits from elsewhere in Lebanon, none of them will have any idea where they are.

The emphasis of the first thirty-three-day training period is to build fitness and endurance. The recruits, in batches of around fifty and dressed in camouflage uniforms, are sent on punishing marches across the rocky limestone mountains weighed down with rifles and backpacks filled with stones. Sometimes they carry cement-filled ammunition tubes for the B-10 82 mm recoilless rifle. They are given one canteen of water a day, which they use for drinking and for washing before prayers. Their instructors are experienced combat veterans, usually in their midthirties or older, who maintain steady pressure on their youthful charges. The marches are augmented by uphill sprints and seemingly endless push-ups.

"They wore me out," recalls Khodr of his initial training session. "I had to do fifty push-ups, but I could only do thirty, so they made me run back up the hill. One time, they told us to take off our boots and socks and climb a mountain while they shot at us. You should see how we suffered. I spent nights when I couldn't sleep because of the pain from blisters and sore muscles."

Training occurs throughout the year, regardless of weather. In the winter months, Hezbollah takes advantage of the snowy conditions in the mountains to teach alpine warfare techniques. Alpine training is not as incongruous as it might at first seem. The peaks of Mount Hermon between Lebanon, Syria, and the Israeli-occupied Golan Heights, the scene of fierce confrontations in the 1973 Arab-Israeli war, are topped with snow for about five months of the year. The IDF's Unit Alpinistim is deployed on Mount Hermon to protect the signals intelligence (SIG-INT) station on one of the lower peaks.

"When it's very cold, I stay away from water," Khodr says. "The first time I washed in water in winter I couldn't breathe. We spent one night in an open field without tents or sleeping bags. I spent all night awake shivering and trying to get a little warmer. One guy sleeping beside me was so cold that he stood up and cursed and cursed and cursed and then fell back down and went to sleep."

At night, each recruit does at least one hour of guard duty, fighting off fatigue and trying to remain alert in case the instructors decide to spring another surprise. "One hour on guard duty can seem like one year. The trees seem to be walking in the darkness. We see wild boar, hyenas, and in the summer we have big problems with snakes," Khodr says.

The recruits also have to endure a "toughness day" when they are forced to crawl on thorns or jump from heights. The instructors keep the recruits on edge with "shock tactics," such as ambushing them by firing live rounds at their feet and RPGs above their heads. "On my first session, we were lined up in rows and the instructors planted blocks of C-4 explosive among us attached to fuses. We could hear the sizz of the fuse but we had to stand still," Khodr says.

He recalls one occasion when he and some fifty other recruits had marched for several hours and were passing through a narrow valley when they were ambushed by a group of instructors hidden in the rocks above. "They set off a roadside bomb close to us. Some of the recruits were in shock. The guys in the middle of the column ducked down while the guys at either end charged up the hillside to flank the instructors who were shooting past us with live ammunition."

In addition to fitness and stamina, the recruits are taught how to use the basic weaponry standard to the Hezbollah fighter—the AK-47 and M-16 assault rifles, the PKM 7.62 mm light machine gun, the .50 caliber heavy machine gun, the RPG-7—until they can strip, reassemble, and load each weapon blindfolded. They practice firing during the day and at night using tracer rounds. Each recruit is handed a limited amount of ammunition and told the importance of conserving rounds. Fire aimed single rounds, they are told, and avoid switching the rifle to automatic: you lose accuracy and waste ammunition.

The recruits learn how to plant roadside bombs and land mines. They study the different types of armored vehicles used by the Israeli army and how to fire RPGs at their more vulnerable spots.

The instructors ram home the need to maintain constant vigilance no matter how tired the recruits. Rifles must be kept in hand at all times, including when sleeping, eating, or praying. Recruits are taught to be fully awake and combat ready within five seconds of being woken in the middle of the night. Radio communications must be answered at once. Failure to comply with these basic rules results in punishment, such as being forced into stress positions for a prolonged period.

They learn the art of camouflage and stealth, various kinds of crawl, and the ability to lie in position on observation duty without moving for hours on end. The recruits are taught navigation using map and compass and GPS instruments before embarking upon five-day orienteering treks across the mountains. They learn how to find their direction from a simple sundial consisting of a stick planted in the ground, or determining north using a wristwatch. Occasionally, one group of recruits will be ordered to launch a sneak raid against another group camped a few miles away in the mountains or to keep them under observation without being spotted.

The "Rebellion Against Fear"

Military training is obligatory for every Hezbollah recruit even if he does not intend to serve in the ranks of the Islamic Resistance afterward.

Still, not all recruits aspiring to become combatants pass the military training program. Those who cannot cope with the punishing schedule but still believe in the cause can drop out and are allotted jobs in Hezbollah's administrative apparatus.

Every Hezbollah fighter is trained in medical support and carries a first aid pack into combat. In an average-sized combat unit of five fighters, two will be medics. Hezbollah places great importance on battlefield medical treatment, partly to ensure that months of training are not wasted and that combatants live to fight another day, and partly for purposes of morale—a Hezbollah fighter may ultimately seek martyrdom in battle, but no one welcomes a lingering death in the mud of some frontline valley because his comrades lack either the kit or the knowledge to cope with wounds. Furthermore, any corpse left on the battlefield could be retrieved by Israeli troops and become a card in Israel's hands during any future prisoner swap negotiations.

Hezbollah even provides a nuclear, biological, and chemical warfare training course, in which fighters learn how to cope with the difficulties of combat in thick protective suits, boots, and gloves and with vision obscured by gas masks.

Nor is it all physical work; the recruits undertake written and practical exams in the field under the watchful eyes of their trainers.

Although the training areas are located in dense undergrowth and under cover of trees, "sky watchers" constantly look out for approaching Israeli jets or Unmanned Aerial Vehicles (UAVs). Each training area is protected by air defense units armed with antiaircraft guns and shoulder-fired missiles.

The initial training phase is only the first of many in the course of a combatant's career. As a university student—Hezbollah pays some of the tuition fees—Khodr can choose when to attend fitness training sessions and refresher courses in the Bekaa Valley even after opting for specialized training in antiarmor weapons.

By the time the recruit has completed the initial stages of religious instruction and military training to the satisfaction of his superiors, he will have earned a greater level of trust and can then join specific units or pursue certain advanced military disciplines such as sniping, antitank missiles, communications, or explosives. While there is flexibility in allowing recruits to select their area of specialization, Hezbollah commanders will sometimes steer them toward units that are experiencing a manpower shortage, or will encourage them to follow certain disciplines in keeping with the recruit's education and character.

"We have a gradual training course. It's variegated according to specialization," says Maher, the sector commander in the Islamic Resistance. "We study each of the recruits' strengths, physically and mentally. If he's good at physics, then he will study trajectories [for artillery]. If he's good at chemistry, then he will study explosives. In line with their basic training, they also receive training in their skills."

The military training program undertaken by each recruit in the Islamic Resistance not only prepares them for future combat operations but also helps build esprit de corps, an important asset on the battlefield aside from deep commitment to the Islamic faith. Hezbollah's military successes, especially during the 1990s, helped convey among the cadres a sense of fraternal and communal pride, achievement, and empowerment, sentiments that also inspire new generations of volunteers to join the party.

Specialized training usually takes place in Iran, or sometimes Syria. The Bekaa Valley is too small and too easily accessed by Israeli reconnaissance aircraft for training on larger-scale weapons systems such as artillery rockets and air defense systems. Those undergoing training in Iran usually travel to Damascus, then board flights to Tehran before being bused to one of several training camps run by the Quds Force of the Iranian Revolutionary Guard near Karaj, Isfahan, Qom, or Tehran. Fighters can attend multiple courses in Iran lasting several weeks each. The trainers are full-time Hezbollah instructors, veterans who have proven themselves in combat in south Lebanon and share the same cultural background and Arabic language as the recruits.

Recruits into Hezbollah's Special Forces unit, the top combat element in the Islamic Resistance, endure an intensive three-month course split into two forty-five-day programs with a five-day break in between. While most Hezbollah combatants are part-timers holding down day jobs or attending college, the Special Forces cadres are full-time combatants who train relentlessly. Not only are they highly motivated combat fighters, they are also the embodiment of the religious and cultural values that make up the way of Hezbollah. Even within the generally homogeneous ranks of the Islamic Resistance, Special Forces fighters tend to stand out. In person, they are usually polite and modest with a quiet sense of humor while maintaining a level of reserve and distance before strangers.

Hezbollah believes that the unremitting religious and ideological instruction creates a combatant far superior to his opposite number in the Israeli army and helps overcome the organization's material shortcomings in technology, weapons, and funds compared with Israel. Never mind that Israel has Merkava tanks, F-16 fighter-bombers, and Apache helicopter gunships; the Islamic Resistance fighter is taught that God is on his side, an unrivaled affirmation of the sanctity of the cause and the supreme guarantor of eventual triumph over one's enemy. Furthermore, Hezbollah believes that its culture of martyrdom—this "rebellion against fear," as Sayyed Mohammed Hussein Fadlallah once put it—bestows upon the individual fighter an unmatched level of bravery, at least in the secular sense of the word.[7] After all, how can you defeat an army of fighters who believe their struggle is sanctioned by God and none of whom are afraid of dying in battle?

Hezbollah's leaders maintain that it is the psychological dimension of the individual fighter, rather than the equipment and arms at his disposal, that lies at the heart of the party's battlefield triumphs. "This group of fighters does not go to war in order to flex their military muscles, score a publicity coup or to achieve material advantages; they fight and do jihad with serious intent and a deep conviction that the only way to regain their usurped territory is by waging war on the enemy," Nasrallah explained.[8]

While other Islamist militant organizations operating around the world also draw direction from the Koran and pursue jihad, Sheikh Naim Qassem insists that it is the quality of the resistance fighter's faith that is the foundation for Hezbollah's "exceptional particularity."

"First, [it is] faith in Islam and what this means in connection with God, the exalted, and attaining a moral state that gives one self-confidence, strength, hope for the future, readiness to sacrifice [one-self] ... development, and self-improvement. This is something essential that we have," he told me.

The second component, Qassem continues, is "readiness for martyrdom" and an understanding that "martyrdom neither shortens nor prolongs life because the timing of death is predestined by God. ... Since the outcome of this martyrdom is a divine reward in Heaven, this is something quite important when it comes to mobilization, especially that we have historic leaders who have presented this example, such as the Prophet Mohammed, Imam Ali, and Imam Hussein and others."

The third advantage is the quality and integrity of Hezbollah's leadership, Qassem adds, citing the martyrdom of Sayyed Abbas Mussawi in 1992 and of Nasrallah's eldest son, Hadi, in combat in 1997 as examples of the leadership's willingness to stand in the same trench as the rank-and-file fighter.

The combination of these three assets—faith in Islam, readiness for martyrdom, and "honest, confident ... enlightened" leadership—ensures that the "limited [material] capabilities or potentials [of a non-state actor] become of value."

"Imagine the single machine gun with a faith in God and readiness for martyrdom and a faith in, and interaction with, the leadership, and then you have a person of great power who does not fear death," Qassem explains. "This differs from the enemy on the other side that does many calculations [to protect itself]. Then our machine gun becomes more powerful than their artillery. This moral issue is quite essential."

"The Enemy's Main Point of Weakness"

Of course, it takes more than a well-trained and motivated fighter to wage a successful campaign of resistance. By 1992, with Hezbollah's resistance priority assured, the Islamic Resistance commanders drew up a more focused campaign against the Israeli occupation. They understood the need to develop flexible tactics to fulfill a fixed strategy: namely, to expel Israeli forces from south Lebanon through force of arms—no negotiated settlement, no compromises, no conditions. Israel was to be humiliated and chased out of Lebanon by the Islamic Resistance.

To achieve that goal, Hezbollah would apply the tactics of attrition, capitalizing on the IDF's Achilles' heel: the Israeli public's aversion to casualties. All the Islamic Resistance had to do was to remain patient, stay one step ahead of the IDF's offensive and defensive measures, and keep sending Israeli soldiers back across the border in body bags. "We organized ourselves to serve that foremost priority, which is to resist the enemy and expel the troops of the occupation from Lebanon," Nasrallah told me in 2003. "We focused on striking at the enemy's main point of weakness, which is his inability to bear extensive human losses."[9]

A document captured by Israeli troops, entitled "The Principles of Warfare," reportedly compiled by Khalil Harb, from 1995 the head of military operations in the western sector of south Lebanon, illustrates Hezbollah's understanding of the elements of asymmetrical warfare:

1. Avoid the strong, attack the weak—attack and withdraw!
2. Protecting our fighters is more important than causing enemy casualties!
3. Strike only when success is assured!
4. Surprise is essential to success. If you are spotted, you've failed!
5. Don't get into a set-piece battle. Slip away like smoke, before the enemy can drive home his advantage!
6. Attaining the goal demands patience, in order to discover the enemy's weak points!
7. Keep moving, avoid formation of a front line!
8. Keep the enemy on constant alert, at the front and in the rear!
9. The road to the great victory passes through thousands of small victories!
10. Keep up the morale of the fighters, avoid notions of the enemy's superiority!
11. The media has innumerable guns, whose hits are like bullets. Use them in the battle!
12. The population is a treasure—nurture it!
13. Hurt the enemy, and then stop before he abandons restraint![10]

Gone were the costly human wave operations of the 1980s, when dozens of fighters bravely but recklessly charged well-defended hilltop outposts. Instead, Hezbollah operated in small units, staging hit-and-run raids against Israeli and SLA patrols. Field security was tightened, and a much greater emphasis was placed on intelligence gathering, both through observation and reconnaissance and by establishing spy cells among the civilian population of the occupation zone—and even by penetrating the ranks of the SLA.

The military wing was separated from the main body of the organization, with the secretary general, as nominal head of the Islamic Resistance, providing the only link between the two. The *tabbiyya,* the part-time combatants in the village guard units, were also split from the Islamic Resistance. Separation served the dual purpose of compartmentalizing the Islamic Resistance for security considerations, and also granting greater autonomy to the military commanders in directing the reinvigorated resistance campaign.

Nasrallah admitted to me in a 2003 interview that he played an indirect role in military affairs, with operational decisions left in the hands of the Islamic Resistance commanders, including Imad Mughniyah, who became Hezbollah's chief of staff sometime around 1993 or 1994. "The one who is in charge of all the resistance is the secretary general of Hezbollah. And under his command are a number of officials who assume different responsibilities," he explained. "Therefore, there are not one, two or three [but many]. Of course, our experience teaches us that we cannot centralize our actions within one person, because this is a very sensitive and dangerous issue and we are confronting the Israelis in a real battle."

As for his own leadership, Nasrallah said his role was one of "politics and guidance." He continued,

> The real credit in the development of the resistance is for its military cadres, and these people had their experiences under constant development. When I became secretary general in 1992, that was ten years after the launching of the resistance, and those cadres had become more experienced and their knowledge was greater. My job

was to strengthen the ties between these brothers. . . . It was quite natural for the improvement in the resistance and had nothing to do with me.

"Killing Israelis Is a Duty, Not a Joy"

There was no tangible barrier marking the front line of Israel's occupation zone. The roads leading into the zone were sealed with earth berms and land mines except for five crossing points guarded by SLA checkpoints. The approximate perimeter of the zone followed the forward positions of the IDF and SLA. The compounds for the most part were separated by an inhospitable terrain of deep wadis smothered in a thick undergrowth of stubby Mediterranean oak trees and thorn bushes, which could only be traversed by foot and even then with difficulty. The rugged terrain and absence of barriers and defending troops allowed Hezbollah fighters to slip between the outposts into the enclave with relative ease, often to a considerable depth, to meet with agents inside the zone, stash weapons, plant IEDs, or carry out lengthy reconnaissance missions.

Usually, three or four fighters at a time would carry out reconnaissance, creeping close to IDF and SLA outposts, often using darkness or poor weather conditions to mask their approach. They set up small surveillance posts, usually hidden in bushes camouflaged with netting. Using binoculars, SLR cameras, and, by the mid-1990s, video cameras and military-grade night vision goggles, they would monitor the positions, looking for routine and assessing troop numbers, armaments, and potential avenues of approach for bomb-laying missions on the supply routes. All information was diligently written down in notebooks. It was dangerous and uncomfortable duty, and often very boring. Fighters tucked copies of the Koran and other religious books into their backpacks so that they could continue their studies in the field. They had to contend with the blazing heat of summer and the bitter cold of winter nights, especially at the higher altitudes in the northern sector of the zone. One valley was known as "the wadi of the snakes" because of the large number of poisonous vipers; each fighter carried antivenom shots in his first aid kit.

"It takes a very special person, very religious and strong to stay there a month with the wild animals in the bush," says Abu Khalil, a tall, shaven-headed unit commander who organized reconnaissance missions. "Observation was a very big weapon for us against the Israelis."

Hezbollah fighters like to recount a tale from the 1980s about a colleague who had spent days monitoring an SLA-defended outpost on a rocky mountain in the northern sector. After his food and water ran out, he sneaked up to the outpost and scrambled over the ramparts. Seeing no one around, he dodged into a kitchen area and began helping himself to eggs, tins of tuna and sardines, and mugs of water. As he ate, an SLA militiaman walked into the kitchen and in a surprised voice asked him who he was. The quick-thinking Hezbollah fighter said he was part of an SLA intelligence unit visiting the outpost. Furthermore, the fighter added, what the hell was the militiaman doing wandering around the kitchen when he should be watching out for Hezbollah fighters? The chastened militiaman apologized and walked away.

"The *mujahid* returned to his observation position with a full stomach and a big smile on his face," said the fighter who told me the story.

The in-depth reconnaissance, which often saw several teams deployed in the enclave at any one time, provided a wealth of tactical intelligence that fed into operational planning. "The information we collected would be relayed to the military command and they would use it to draw up appropriate plans to achieve the best results with the minimum casualties," says Maher, the sector commander.

The infiltration trails winding through the undergrowth were also used by Hezbollah teams to penetrate the zone for combat missions, perhaps laying roadside bombs or staging ambushes. Each fighter in a combat unit carried a minimum of forty pounds of equipment and sometimes as much as sixty or seventy, depending on the mission. By the early 1990s, the Hezbollah combatant was wearing full military camouflage fatigues, boots, and helmet rather than the ad hoc 1980s "militia look" of jeans and T-shirt overlaid with webbing and ammunition pouches. The helmets usually were old IDF-issue ones that had fallen into Hezbollah's hands over the years. The combatants carried a choice of AK-47 or M-16 assault rifles. Some preferred the AK-47 for its robust reliability, others the M-16 for its greater accuracy and higher rate of fire on those rare occasions when they might flip the fire selector switch to fully automatic. Another important consideration was the weight of the ammunition. The M-16 fires a 5.56 mm round, compared with the AK-47's larger 7.62 mm round, giving the M-16 operator a weight-to-round advantage.

Other than ammunition, the rest of the standard gear included hand grenades, water, first aid kit, and walkie-talkies, plus food if the mission was to last a day or more. Additional equipment could include night vision binoculars; metal detectors and wooden probes to navigate through minefields; homemade Bangalore torpedoes to blast through barbed wire obstacles and to detonate land mines during assaults on SLA compounds; light machine guns and ammunition; antitank missiles; rocket-propelled grenades and launchers; and IEDs. Some IEDs weighed twenty pounds or more, consisting of casing, explosive, shrapnel of hundreds of steel ball bearings, detonating cord, and antipersonnel mines to plant separately or rig up to the main IED charge.

Unlike the 1980s, when the arrival of large numbers of fighters in a frontline village told everyone that an attack was imminent, military operations from the early 1990s were planned in great secrecy, with units being briefed on the mission only after the fighters had gathered at assembly points.

"Hezbollah took advantage of the fact that the IDF is a regular armed force that is large and heavy while the Hezbollah is a small organization whose method is guerrilla and terror," recalls Colonel Noam Ben-Zvi, a brigade commander in south Lebanon between 1996 and 2000. "He watched and learned the routine of our lives and he tried to hurt us where we were vulnerable. It's not possible to compare the means between the forces, so they had to be very careful, smart, and quick, otherwise they had no chance of succeeding in engagements."

The hazardous edges of the enclave, where Hezbollah fighters often clashed with Israeli troops, was known to the Islamic Resistance as the "yellow zone." Although Hezbollah fighters were fit, well trained, and highly motivated, it was not easy overcoming feelings of stress and tension when weighed down with weapons and equipment, maneuvering across inhospitable terrain and knowing that a firefight could erupt at any moment. "We reach a point where we can no longer tolerate the burden," Maher explains. "Then we begin to think of the relatives in the occupied villages. We begin to think that if we execute the operation successfully, God will reward us."

Hezbollah tended to avoid prolonged direct clashes with IDF troops on the ground. If a Hezbollah unit was staging a typical ambush of IED followed by small arms fire, it would withdraw from the scene within minutes, before the ambushed IDF troops could rally and to avoid Israeli air and artillery support. The sight of fleeing Hezbollah men on the battlefield was sometimes interpreted by IDF field commanders as a sign of weakness. But the tactic was in keeping with the "thirteen principles": once the element of surprise was gone, the IDF could begin utilizing its technological advantage.

"It is hard to describe the feeling when we open fire," Maher says.

> It gets very tranquil and everything becomes clear in my mind. I get a monumental strength and think of nothing but the battle. . . . I have two feelings when I kill an Israeli soldier and an SLA militiaman. According to Islam, killing is disturbing. The Koran says killing might be forced upon you, but it's not something you should like. When I kill an Israeli, I think of what they have done, the shelling, destroying villages. . . . I kill them to stop them [from] doing more of the same. Killing Israelis is a duty, not a joy.

Deadly Rocks

Hezbollah's deadliest weapon against the IDF and SLA was the roadside bomb, which accounted for the majority of fatalities. The bombs were usually simple homemade Claymore-style directional IEDs, which discharged hundreds of steel ball bearings when detonated. The average-sized bomb had a frontal killing range of up to fifty yards and a rear killing range of about fifteen yards.

From 1991 on, a technological war of wits began to emerge between Hezbollah's bomb-making engineers and the IDF. IDF trackers accompanied by sniffer dogs had become too adept at discovering the bombs and the telltale command wires used to trigger them. Hezbollah began hiding the IEDs inside fiberglass "rocks" painted to match the limestone geology of south Lebanon. The rock disguises were simple and effective. UNIFIL dubbed them Debbas bombs, after a store in Beirut that sold the rocks as garden ornaments. The fiberglass shells were packed with insulation foam into which the bomb was fitted. Once the device was placed on the ground, it was almost indistinguishable from a real rock.

Beginning in August 1991, Hezbollah began regularly detonating bombs by remote radio control, precluding the need for a detectable command wire. The IDF attempted to counter the remote control detonation by sweeping a wide spectrum of radio frequencies from its listening bases on the mountain peaks of Mount Hermon in order to explode the bombs prematurely. The Israelis then flew C-47 aircraft modified for multispectral sensing and electronic reconnaissance above south Lebanon.

Hezbollah returned to command-wire and pressure-mat detonation for a while before introducing a new coded remote control system in mid-1993. The bombs were fitted with two receivers and scramblers, initially defeating Israeli attempts to reproduce the detonating signals. Hezbollah's engineers then refined the bombs further by incorporating small jammers and detonating them by computerized multifrequency transmissions.[11]

By 1995, Hezbollah was equipping its IEDs with cellular phone receivers to trigger the firing switches. In turn, Israel jammed cell phone frequencies from aircraft flying high above southern Lebanon. As the technology improved and grew smaller, the IDF fitted cell phone jammers into armored personnel carriers and vehicles. Eventually, foot soldiers could carry the equipment in a backpack.

One of the roadside IED tactics used by Hezbollah was the "seven minute" bomb. The first IED would explode against the target—an IDF patrol, for example—and also trigger a timer on a second device hidden nearby. The second bomb would explode seven minutes later, just as the troops were recovering from the shock of the first blast and beginning to treat the wounded. Another version of the tactic involved planting a roadside bomb in such a way that it could be spotted by an IDF or SLA patrol. While the bomb was being defused, a second, better hidden IED would explode.

Some roadside bomb ambushes displayed deadly cunning in their execution. On March 21, 1994, SLA militiamen heard the sound of shooting coming from the Litani River valley west of Marjayoun. Fares Abi Samra, the head of the SLA's 20th battalion in the eastern sector, assembled a patrol to investigate the source of the shooting. A Maronite from Qlaya who had served with the militia since 1976, Abi Samra was a tough, compulsive officer who, against the better judgment of his militia comrades and the IDF, insisted on being among the first to investigate incidents in his area of responsibility. Slipping a flak jacket over his olive-green uniform and strapping a helmet on his head, Abi Samra clambered aboard one of two armored personnel carriers. The convoy of APCs and two Mercedes cars ground out of the 20th battalion headquarters just north of the border and headed to the location of the shooting in the Litani valley. On arrival, the militiamen spread out into the adjacent meadows to see if any militants were still in the area. A few feet from the road, they discovered spilled blood and an abandoned AK-47 rifle and ammunition pouch. The rifle and ammunition were placed in the back of one of the two Mercedes. Finding nothing else, Abi Samra took off his flak jacket and helmet and climbed into one of the Mercedes for the return journey. The convoy had traveled only a few hundred yards when a powerful IED blasted Abi Samra's car, killing the SLA commander instantly and wounding two other militiamen. In the wake of the explosion, a suspicious militiaman snatched the AK-47 rifle out of the back of the car to inspect it. But when he cocked the rifle, it blew up in his face, killing him and wounding two militiamen standing nearby.

The IED ambush was in fact an elaborate trap. Hezbollah knew that

Abi Samra had a dangerous tendency to rush to scenes of trouble. A team of Hezbollah fighters had penetrated the zone and planted the IED and booby-trapped AK-47. Chicken blood was splattered on the ground and a few rounds fired into the air to attract attention. The team had watched the arrival of the SLA patrol but only recognized Abi Samra when he removed his helmet.

The IDF also employed IEDs against Hezbollah fighters, copying the fiberglass rocks and planting them along Hezbollah's infiltration trails. One IDF roadside bomb discovered in south Lebanon by a demining company in 2001 consisted of a block of explosive weighing twenty-two pounds and shaped like a solid wheel with the rim studded with ball bearings. The IED was fitted with an antitampering device and was connected by "cordtex" (an explosive cable) to nineteen buried antipersonnel mines radiating outward like the spokes of a wheel. The bomb would have been lethal in all directions for up to a hundred yards.

Balance of Terror

In keeping with the "thirteen principles," Hezbollah further diversified its tactics, often acting on real-time tactical intelligence obtained through field observation and from agents living inside the zone. The effect was to keep the IDF and SLA constantly on edge and forced into a reactive role, responding to Hezbollah-initiated operations. On any given day, mortar shells could batter SLA outposts in the western sector, while Hezbollah Special Forces teams were laying IEDs in the mountainous northern tip of the enclave. The next day, the situation could be reversed.

"Their patience was unbelievable," recalls UNIFIL's Timur Goksel. "They attacked targets of opportunity. They would fill the spaces [between quality operations] by firing mortars at the SLA. That wasn't really resistance, but it kept the pot boiling."

Coordination was greatly tightened between separate squads, allowing the Islamic Resistance to launch complex fire-and-movement operations using multiple units. The first coordinated mass attack against

IDF and SLA compounds was on September 29, 1992, when at least eleven positions running the length of the zone were targeted by heavy mortar and rocket fire. The operation was significant not only for demonstrating an improved coordination between separate units, but also because it was the first time Hezbollah used AT-3 Sagger antitank missiles in south Lebanon. The AT-3 Sagger is a wire-guided antiarmor missile first introduced in the 1960s by the Soviet Union. Although it was considered obsolete by the early 1990s, Hezbollah's acquisition of the Sagger required the IDF to improve the defenses of its armored vehicles, particularly the relatively thin-skinned M-113 armored personnel carriers widely used by the SLA.

In November 1991, Hezbollah fired for the first time a shoulder-launched SAM-7 antiaircraft missile at an Israeli C-47 aircraft on an electronic warfare mission above south Lebanon. It locked on to the target, but the C-47 was flying above the missile's maximum range. The Israelis temporarily ceased C-47 flights in Lebanese airspace after that incident, but Hezbollah never brought down an Israeli aircraft with one of its SAM-7s.

The introduction of the Sagger and SAM-7 into the Lebanon theater was not a game changer for Israel, but it did represent a worrying improvement in Hezbollah's arsenal, suggesting that it was only a matter of time before the Lebanese group obtained weapons that would pose a real threat to the IDF. Certainly, the size of Hezbollah's arsenal was increasing rapidly, thanks to Iranian generosity. Iran Air Boeing 747s adapted to carry freight were flying in to Damascus airport between one and four times a month in the early 1990s. Each flight carried large quantities of ammunition and weapons, including Saggers and Katyusha rockets. The Syrians made little attempt to disguise the purpose of the shipments, and American and European diplomats in Damascus could monitor the flights with relative ease.

Although Hezbollah was beginning to acquire more sophisticated arms to attack the occupation forces in south Lebanon, the judicious use of the relatively unsophisticated 122 mm Katyusha rocket came to plague successive Israeli governments more than any other weapon. Hezbollah had fired Katyushas into Israel for the first time in February

1992 in response to Mussawi's assassination. Those opening salvos had been a spontaneous reaction of anger toward the death of the Hezbollah leader rather than the calculated launch of a new tactic.

But over the next two years, a clear pattern of reciprocity began to emerge. Whenever Israel or its SLA allies caused civilian casualties, Hezbollah would fire rockets across the border. The tactic imposed constraints upon an IDF that was already struggling to check Hezbollah's intensifying resistance campaign. The stated reason for the IDF's presence in south Lebanon was to protect the residents of northern Israel from attack. But from now on, the IDF understood that if it acted rashly against Hezbollah in south Lebanon and civilians were harmed, it could incur rockets falling into northern Israel, thus defeating the purpose of the Israeli presence in south Lebanon in the first place.

Nasrallah publicly confirmed the Katyusha policy for the first time in March 1995, when Hezbollah fired a salvo of rockets into Israel following the helicopter assassination of a senior resistance commander. The Hezbollah leader justified the rocket barrage as a reaction, not to the assassination, but to a list of complaints in which Israel since the beginning of the year had killed 16 civilians, wounded another 60, and bombed 75 villages, leaving 212 houses destroyed or damaged. "There is no safety for anyone if our people are not safe," he said. "Zionist settlers in northern Israel should know that their racist and aggressive government, their settlements and the residents inside, will not be in a better condition than our towns and their residents."

With the Katyusha taking on a greater importance in the resistance campaign, Hezbollah's artillery unit was reorganized and given intensified training. Speed of firing and accuracy were the key requirements, according to Abu Khalil, the unit commander. Fighters passed through four levels of instruction, much of it classwork followed by practice rocket-firing in the field watched closely by instructors.

A standard Katyusha launch usually involved two separate groups. The first was the full-time artillery unit specialists who set up the launchers in olive groves and valleys facing the occupation zone. Engineers would ensure that the launch tubes were correctly elevated and aimed, checking targeting data on laminated range cards. The first group would then disappear, and a second group would carry out the actual launch mission.

Although the IDF had no defensive system that could intercept the Katyushas in flight, its counterbattery radars could pinpoint the origin of a rocket firing within seconds, allowing artillery gunners to retaliate with a bombardment of the area. To avoid being caught in a retaliatory shelling, Hezbollah sometimes fitted simple wristwatch and battery timers to Katyushas, enabling the fighters to be gone long before the rockets were fired.

A Huge Psychological Effect

The IED may have been the deadliest tactical weapon in Hezbollah's arsenal, but arguably the most effective strategic weapon was the camera. From 1991, Hezbollah fighters wielding simple handheld video cameras filmed many of their attacks inside the occupation zone with the footage later broadcast on the organization's flagship Al-Manar (the Beacon) television station.

Typical combat footage would show uniformed Hezbollah fighters saluting a party flag planted on the ramparts of a seized hilltop outpost, or an antitank missile streaking across open countryside and exploding against an IDF armored vehicle, or a patrol of Israeli soldiers blasted by a roadside bomb. Sometimes the footage was broadcast on television before the IDF had notified the families of soldiers killed in the video-taped attack. Hezbollah had managed radio stations and published a weekly newspaper since the 1980s, but it expanded its propaganda machine significantly in 1991 with the launch of Al-Manar. With initial annual running costs of about $1 million, Al-Manar broadcast a combination of political talk shows, Arab soap operas, children's programs, religious programs, and heavily censored (for sexual content rather than violence) Hollywood movies. But it was the combat videos that captured the imagination of the viewers both in Lebanon and around the region. Al-Manar, after all, was not intended as a purveyor of impartial journalism, but as a tool to spread the message of jihad and resistance and rally support for Hezbollah's struggle to liberate south Lebanon. "Al-Manar is an important weapon for us," Nayyaf Krayyem, the chairman of Al-Manar, told me in 2001. "It's a political weapon, social weapon, and cultural weapon."

Hezbollah had an acute understanding of the critical role played by information operations—or psychological warfare—in its guerrilla campaign against the Israeli occupation. It tailored its campaign to its three targets—the home front, Israel, and the international community. Domestically, Hezbollah sought to allay the suspicions of non-Shia communities by downplaying its broader ideological goals of an Islamic state and its ties to Iran, presenting itself as a national resistance movement serving the interests of all Lebanese by opposing the Israeli occupation. It fostered hostility toward Israel by broadcasting on Al-Manar horrific footage of Lebanese civilian casualties and then bolstering a sense of pride and determination with its combat videos.

On the international front, Hezbollah opened a foreign press office in the early 1990s and readily granted interviews to the Western media. Hezbollah's spokesmen promoted the notion that Israel's occupation of Lebanon was illegal, brutal, and unjustified and that Hezbollah was simply resisting an occupation, just like any other national liberation movement, a right enshrined in international law. Its spokesmen often used as an analogy for a Western audience the French resistance to the Nazi occupation of France in World War II.

As for the enemy, Hezbollah relentlessly hammered home the message that Israel's determination to stay in south Lebanon was futile. The longer Israeli troops stayed in Lebanon, the more of them Hezbollah would kill. After some moral agonizing, Israeli television stations began broadcasting Hezbollah's combat videos, allowing an Israeli audience frontline views of a war that the IDF had deliberately tried to obscure from the public. "Riveted, Israelis watched them with a mixture of horror and fascination," wrote the author of a report on Hezbollah's psychological warfare campaign. "The cumulative psychological effect of these images was great, inducing, among other things, a persuasive belief in Hezbollah's military prowess."[12]

Such was the importance attached to information operations that

Hezbollah's entire resistance campaign could be termed "a guerrilla war psychologically waged," meaning that the pace and variety of military operations were dictated more by the propaganda accrued than by purely military gains.[13] Certainly, a bland Hezbollah press statement announcing a deadly roadside bomb attack against IDF troops could not produce the same impact as actually watching the operation on television that evening and seeing a squad of soldiers disappearing into a cloud of flame, smoke, and dust. Hezbollah's storming assaults on SLA frontline outposts carried no real military value in themselves, but the images of fighters weaving through minefields, shrugging off mortar explosions, and pouring machine gun fire over the sandbagged ramparts into SLA compounds had a great impact on the psychological front. Although often blurred and shaky, the footage of combat operations, along with a steady diet of slick propaganda videos depicting resolute resistance fighters marching across landscapes resembling south Lebanon and montages of past attacks set to stirring martial tunes, had an incalculable effect in boosting popular support in Lebanon and the Arab world for Hezbollah's military campaign.

To further its penetration of the Israeli home front, Hezbollah began in 1996 to air propaganda clips in Hebrew, directly addressing Israeli soldiers and civilians and warning them of the dangers of remaining in south Lebanon. The clips are prepared by the Hebrew Observation Department, a special section within Al-Manar that monitors Israeli television and radio broadcasts and scans news websites 24 hours a day. The clips are distributed to Al-Manar's news departments for inclusion in news bulletins, and also used in propaganda messages.

Most of the staff in the Hebrew Observation Department are former detainees who learned the language while in Israeli prisons. One of them, Ahmad Ammar, was captured in 1986 with two comrades while planting roadside bombs in the occupation zone. He was sentenced by an Israeli court to seven years in jail. His term was subsequently extended on the basis that he continued to represent a threat to Israel. He and his fellow Hezbollah inmates began learning Hebrew as a means of communicating with their guards. Arabic and Hebrew share many linguistic similarities, and it took Ahmad only six months to become conversant. "We found it a great opportunity to learn about the enemy, their culture, who they are. Hebrew was our link to them," he said. "According to the Prophet Mohammed, whoever learns the language of a new nation avoids its evil."

The department's work is not limited to providing material for propaganda and news segments. While Hezbollah's field reconnaissance and network of agents in the zone provided useful tactical intelligence, the department's Hebrew speakers probed deeper, amassing detailed information on Israeli politics, economy, and society. The information is carefully analyzed and helps Hezbollah build a comprehensive and incisive portrait of its enemy. Hezbollah believes that in order to defeat and destroy its Israeli enemies, it must understand them first.

"We know their priorities, their economy, their political structure, their institutions, and the variety of opinions and thoughts they hold," said Hassan Ezzieddine, in 2001 the head of Hezbollah's media relations department. "The more we know about them, the more we know their weak points. This makes it easier for us to confront them."

Moonlight Meetings with the Mujahideen

One of the key—but still largely undisclosed—factors behind Hezbollah's emerging battlefield successes in the early 1990s was the extensive intelligence penetration of the occupation zone by the Islamic Resistance and the military intelligence services of Lebanon and Syria. The intelligence network was not limited to Shia residents of the zone or press-ganged Shia conscripts in the SLA who might have sympathy for Hezbollah. It included senior Maronite and Druze civilians and officers in the SLA from villages like Qlaya, the militia's heartland, who had earned the trust of the IDF over many years of collaboration and loyal service. It was a hugely effective strategy: by the end of the decade, the SLA had been so thoroughly penetrated at all levels that the IDF could no longer trust its Lebanese ally.

"Hassan" was one of Hezbollah's most effective agents operating in the western sector of the occupation zone in the 1990s. Tall and power-fully built with a big bony face, hollow cheeks, and thick black beard, Hassan was a member of a prominent family in a Shia village in the western sector of the occupation zone. He joined Hezbollah in 1987 and soon began working from his village, providing information on IDF and SLA movements in the western sector and liaising with fighters pene-trating the zone. "I met the mujahideen at night in open areas and re-ceived from them weapons and ammunition," Hassan says.

The equipment included large quantities of explosives for IEDs, antitank missiles, rocket-propelled grenades, antipersonnel mines, bombs specially designed to be fitted to vehicles, and M-16 and AK-47 assault rifles. "It would take several trips over consecutive nights to pick up all the weapons and I'd hide them in prearranged locations," he says. "When I received a call from the resistance, I would collect all the weapons by car and distribute them to locations for collection by the mujahideen."

He worked alone and in total secrecy to the extent that even his wife was long unaware that he was an agent with Hezbollah. "When she found out, she was very happy," Hassan recalls.

Hassan's village was known as a bastion of support for Hezbollah, and it was often subject to punitive measures by the SLA, such as expul-sions of residents, house searches, arrests, interrogations, and beatings. In July 1999, Hassan helped carry out an IED assassination attempt against the local head of the SLA's Unit 504 intelligence wing. The SLA officer survived the bomb attack and launched a crackdown, conduct-ing house-to-house searches and preventing anyone from leaving the zone. The SLA came for Hassan one night, smashing down his front door and taking him to Khiam prison, where he was severely tortured. He was stripped naked and repeatedly submerged in a tank of water, his head held down by the boot of the interrogator. Electrodes were placed in the water and kept there until he passed out. Other forms of torture included electrodes attached to his tongue, earlobes, and penis; buckets of hot and cold water thrown over him; suspension by his wrists from a pole with his legs pulled apart by chains; and being repeatedly punched and kicked about the body and face. The interrogators made sure that his clothes and mattress were always soaking wet, despite the cold winter weather. He spent a total of fifty-two days in solitary confinement. One of the cells measured only six square feet.

Hassan was freed when the prison was liberated in May 2000 during the IDF withdrawal. After an audience with Nasrallah in Beirut, he returned to his home village, where he continues to work with the Islamic Resistance. The secrecy of his affiliation with Hezbollah, however, has long gone: the interior walls of his small home are plastered with posters of Nasrallah, Hezbollah "martyrs," and pictures of resistance fighters.

The "Button Pushers"

The Shia residents of the zone were naturally treated with suspicion by the IDF and SLA, even those Shia conscripts serving with the militia. But much of the intelligence work inside the zone was carried out by Christians, who, by virtue of their religion, were held in greater trust by the IDF and had better access to the SLA. One of the top agents for Lebanese military intelligence was a Maronite who was recruited in 1989 and whom we shall call "the Postman."

"I knew one day that the Israelis would leave, and I love my country," the Postman recalls. "It was an easy choice to make."

At first, the Postman relayed snippets of information via a contact who lived in the zone but traveled regularly to Beirut. Later, when Lebanon's cell phone network was installed, he directly contacted his handlers in the offices of military intelligence in Sidon. Although he was not formally in the SLA, he was friends with all the top leadership and was a trusted figure. Often invited to meetings with SLA commanders, the Postman would dial a number and leave the line open so that his handlers could listen in on the conversation.

He built up his network of agents slowly, both Christians and Muslims, militiamen and civilians. "I recruited about twenty people inside the SLA, Christians and Muslims, including senior officers. I would select certain people I could trust. I would watch them for some time and then assess that even if they refused to work with me, they would not turn me in," he says.

It required a strong sense of judgment and steely nerves to attempt recruiting SLA officers. If he miscalculated, the Postman could find himself thrown into Khiam prison, or, worse, shot in the head and dumped in a ditch. It was a twisted world of conflicting loyalties, paranoia, treachery, greed, fear, suspicion, and violent death.

The IEDs were usually planted by Hezbollah specialists who would set up the devices sometimes weeks, or even months, ahead of time. These bombs were often detonated by specially selected "button pushers" living inside the zone, whose identities were undisclosed even to other agents in the zone.

One of the more sensational intelligence coups involved Raja Ward, a tough Druze from Hasbayya who was deputy chief of SLA intelligence in the eastern sector. Ward was persuaded to defect from the SLA after he fell in love with a young woman whose family was closely connected to the Syrian Social Nationalist Party. One day in June 1998, he turned himself in at a Lebanese army checkpoint just north of the occupation zone. In a deal to protect himself from judicial retribution, he handed over a notebook containing the names of dozens of agents working for Israeli intelligence. Ward's defection caused an uproar when it was discovered that the formerly trusted SLA officer had just broken open one of Israel's biggest intelligence rings in Lebanon. The following month, a Lebanese court indicted seventy-seven people on charges of spying for Israel.

However, of all the Lebanese spies operating in the treacherous shadows of the occupation zone, none achieved greater success and notoriety than Ramzi Nohra. His remarkable career as an intelligence agent helped Hezbollah inflict some of its deadliest blows against Israel, both during and after the occupation.

The Unflappable Ramzi Nohra

When I met Ramzi for the first time in 2001, it was clear that he knew he was a marked man. The windows set in the thick stone walls of his os-

tentatious stone mansion in Ibl es-Saqi village near Marjayoun were fitted with tinted panes of bulletproof glass. Electronically controlled steel
shutters provided additional protection against would-be assassins.
Cameras were mounted on all sides of the building, covering every
square inch of Ramzi's property as well as the approaches along the
main road outside.

Ramzi was short and slim, with a mop of dark hair neatly parted in
the middle and a scar on one cheek symbolizing his violent past. His
stooped shoulders and intense, calculating gaze gave him a certain vul-
turine quality.

In a small, cozy reception room, a large television was tuned to
Hezbollah's Al-Manar station. On a shelf above the television were three
smaller monitors, each screen split into four separate wide-angle
black-and-white views of the outside of his mansion. As Ramzi talked,
his eyes kept straying instinctively to the twelve tiny screens. An AK-47
rifle protruded carelessly from beneath a sofa, and a 9 mm automatic
pistol was tucked into the side of his armchair.

Over the course of two decades, Ramzi had amassed considerable
wealth through smuggling drugs from Lebanon into Israel, an activity
that was tacitly facilitated during the years of occupation by the Israeli
authorities, who recruited him as an informer and turned a blind eye to
his illicit pursuits. However, his lucrative and relatively peaceful existence came to an end in the mid-1990s when he was tapped to carry out
an audacious kidnapping inside the occupation zone, the first of several
key secret operations that would turn Ramzi into a legend in the intelligence services of Lebanon, Israel, and Syria.

The target of the abduction was Ahmad Hallaq, the same ferocious
militiaman who had captured an Israeli tank in 1982 during the fierce
fighting at Khalde at the southern end of Beirut. A towering man of
imposing physique and sporting a thick bushy black beard, Hallaq was
ruthless and fearless in equal measure, earning the respect of his enemies and the dread of his subordinates. As a member of As-Saiqa, the
Syrian-backed Palestinian faction, he gained notoriety in the civil war
for wedging his captured enemies inside columns of car tires doused in
gasoline and setting them alight.

"Hallaq didn't know what fear was. He was an unbelievable person, utterly ruthless, a real killer. No one messed with him," recalls one of Hallaq's former lieutenants.

At the end of the civil war in 1990, a bored Hallaq was approached by men claiming to be with the CIA, who offered him money to trace American hostages in Lebanon. He later learned that his handlers were in fact from Mossad and he was now an agent on behalf of his former enemy.

In 1994, Hallaq was asked to make contact with Fuad Mughniyah, Imad's brother, a midlevel Hezbollah security chief who owned a tile and plumbing business in Beirut's southern suburbs. Mughniyah had served in As-Saiqa before 1982, and he and Hallaq had known each other for years. After realizing that Mughniyah was immune to recruitment and difficult to kidnap, the Israelis instructed Hallaq to assassinate him instead. On December 21, Hallaq parked a gray Volkswagen van packed with 120 pounds of explosive outside Mughniyah's warehouse in the southern suburbs of Beirut. He walked inside the building to ensure Mughniyah was present and found his intended victim sitting behind a desk. After a moment's pleasantries, Hallaq stepped outside, moved to a safe distance, and detonated the bomb. The blast ripped apart the front of the shop, instantly killing Mughniyah and three passersby.

Hallaq departed Beirut immediately and crossed into the occupation zone the following day. However, his wife, Hanan, was arrested along with two other confederates. It turned out that one of Mughniyah's colleagues who survived the blast told investigators that Hallaq had been in the shop moments before the bomb exploded.

After a few months in the Far East, Hallaq returned to Israel and begged for his old job back. The Israelis agreed and put him through an intensive training program to increase his physical fitness and shooting skills. He even served on a couple of missions with Mossad. One of them, according to Palestinian and former Lebanese intelligence sources, was the assassination of Fathi Shiqaqi, the head of Palestinian Islamic Jihad (PIJ), who was gunned down by hit men in Malta in October 1995.

Mossad gave him a new identity, Michel Kheir Amine, and a bodyguard, Mohammed al-Gharamti, better known as Abu Arida, a notorious collaborator who had run the Sidon port in the early years of the Israeli occupation before fleeing the city with his men in 1985. In November 1995, Hallaq and Abu Arida moved to Qlaya village in the occupation zone.

"Hezbollah Will Use Chain Saws on Me"

Lebanese and Syrian military intelligence soon learned that the newly arrived Michel Kheir Amine was in fact Ahmad Hallaq, Mughniyah's assassin, and they hatched a plot to have him kidnapped from the occupation zone and brought to Beirut. They tapped Ramzi Nohra and his brother Mufid for the job.

Ramzi knew that his relationship with Israel was a death sentence once the occupation was over, so he agreed to work with the Lebanese and Syrians as a double agent. He befriended Hallaq, inviting him to his house regularly to drink whisky and discuss means of jointly smuggling drugs into Israel. "I repeated these evenings several times," Ramzi recalls. "Hallaq thought I was with Israeli intelligence. Hallaq told the Israelis that he trusted me."

Ramzi and Mufid assembled a team that included Bassem Hasbani, a local agent for Lebanese military intelligence, Maher Touma, and Fadi Qassar, a taxi driver who regularly plied the route between the occupation zone and Beirut.

On the morning of February 20, 1996, Ramzi drove to Qlaya and invited Hallaq to lunch at his home in Ibl es-Saqi. Back at Ramzi's house, they were joined by Maher Touma, one of the other conspirators. The three men settled into their chairs, and Hallaq began drinking whisky, which Ramzi and Mufid had laced with valium pills crushed to powder. Mufid and Fadi, the taxi driver, were hiding in a nearby room armed with silenced Ingram machine pistols. Once Hallaq was befuddled by the whisky and pills, Mufid decided to spring the trap. Bursting into the room, machine gun cocked, he yelled dramatically, "Lebanese resistance! Nobody move!" An astonished Hallaq reached for his pistol, but Mufid smashed his gun on Hallaq's head, gashing it open.

"Hallaq looked at me for help, still thinking I was an agent for Israeli intelligence," Ramzi says. "But I told him 'I know who you are. You are Ahmad Hallaq. I am not with the Israelis. You are very wrong.' When he heard me say that, Hallaq seemed to crumple."

It took all four conspirators to subdue the burly ex-militiaman. They bound him with duct tape and injected him with more sedatives. The desperate Hallaq, his eyes wide with fear, begged his captors to kill him there and then. "Hezbollah will use chain saws on me for what I did to Mughniyah," he wailed.

Having swaddled Hallaq with the tape, they dumped him unconscious into the trunk of a Mercedes taxi and drove in two cars to the crossing point in Jezzine. They were prepared to shoot their way through the SLA checkpoint at Jezzine, but drastic measures were unnecessary. Maher Touma's brother was a senior SLA officer in Jezzine and well known to the guards at the crossing. As Ramzi, Mufid, and Touma returned to Ibl es-Saqi, Hallaq was driven by Fadi Qassar through the two-mile no-man's-land to the first Lebanese army checkpoint, where intelligence agents were waiting to arrest him.

Toward the end of the next day, the Israelis realized that Hallaq was missing, and suspicion fell on the Nohra brothers. In the following days, the entire cell, apart from Mufid Nohra and Fadi Qassar, was rounded up and imprisoned in Israel. Mufid hid in a safe house before slipping out of the zone through the rugged ravines near Shebaa village.

The hapless Hallaq was subsequently convicted of murder in a military court in Beirut and sentenced to death. Shortly before dawn on September 21, 1996, the onetime militia chief and assassin was led from his cell into the courtyard of the Roumiyah prison in the hills east of Beirut and executed by firing squad.

After the success of the Hallaq abduction, the Lebanese authorities asked Mufid Nohra to prepare a plan to kidnap Abdel-Karim as-Saadi, also known as Abu Mohjen, the leader of the al Qaeda–linked Esbat al-Ansar group in the Ain al-Hilweh Palestinian refugee camp. Mufid drew up a scheme in which two dozen soldiers would charge into the densely populated camp and kill or capture Abu Mohjen. The Lebanese authorities were unimpressed and dropped the plan. Mufid also was asked by Lebanese and Syrian military intelligence for the name of another senior collaborator with Israel who could be targeted for abduction. Mufid suggested Etienne Saqr, the leader of the ultranationalist Guardians of the Cedars militia, who had lived in Jezzine since the end of the civil war. That plan was also dropped, after the Syrians surmised that such an operation would upset Cardinal Nasrallah Sfeir, the Maronite patriarch.

As for Ramzi, he faced an array of charges in Israel, including kidnapping, supplying information to an enemy state, and even an old drug conviction. But protracted plea bargaining on the sidelines saw his sentence gradually reduced from ten years to four. Ramzi was led from the court and placed in solitary confinement in an Israeli prison. But his days as an agent for Lebanese intelligence were far from over.

"It Took Us Too Long to Adjust"

By the mid-1990s, the reinvigorated resistance campaign in south Lebanon was exacting an increasing toll of Israeli and SLA casualties. Thirteen IDF soldiers were killed in 1992, twelve in 1993, and twenty-one in 1994. More significantly, the IDF–Hezbollah fatality ratio was narrowing in the latter's favor. In 1990, five Hezbollah fighters were killed for every IDF fatality, but by 1991, the figure had dropped to two Hezbollah dead for every Israeli soldier killed. A year later it had narrowed further, to 1.7 to 1, and it remained at around 1.5 to 1 for the rest of the decade.[14]

The rate of attacks was steadily increasing as well. UNIFIL recorded a total of eighty attacks for 1991 in its area of operations, which excluded those conducted in the northern sector above the Litani River. By 1994, the number of attacks in the UNIFIL area had risen to 146. An unofficial tally recorded by UNIFIL for all attacks against the IDF and SLA recorded the much larger figure of 644 operations for 1994, increasing to 908 for 1995.

Israel was conducting peace negotiations with Syria and Lebanon during this period, and the conflict in south Lebanon was initially seen as the last fling of die-hard militants from the war-torn 1980s. But it gradually became evident to IDF commanders that what they were facing in south Lebanon was a full-fledged insurgency by an enemy trained and armed by Iran, politically protected by Syria, and implementing ever more effective and deadly tactics.

"We felt that the resistance had ended with the end of the civil war," recalls Major General Moshe Kaplinsky, who was head of the IDF's Golani Brigade from 1993 to 1997. "Then it started with an attack here and there, but we didn't change our attitude. We were too conservative. We slowly realized between 1990 and 1993 that we were facing a guerrilla war. It took us too long to adjust our behavior."

In a series of deadly assaults in July 1993, seven Israeli soldiers were killed and a barrage of Katyusha rockets struck northern Israel in response to IDF artillery shelling against Lebanese villages lying north of the zone. The IDF found itself caught in a trap largely of its own making: Hezbollah would kill Israeli soldiers in the zone, but when Israel's inevitable retaliatory artillery shelling or air strikes caused civilian casualties or damage, rockets would be fired into northern Israel. The problem for the IDF was that it had yet to figure out a way of striking back effectively at Hezbollah without risking Lebanese casualties and thus provoking the Katyusha salvos into the north. The IDF's main weapons in south Lebanon—artillery and air power—were too clumsy for the challenge it faced. It was like trying to swat a mosquito with a baseball bat in a china shop.

With seven soldiers killed in three weeks, a frustrated IDF lashed back, deliberately directing its firepower against civilian targets in south Lebanon in a week-long air and artillery offensive to inflict mass punishment on the Lebanese. There was no attempt to disguise the purpose of the operation; Israeli officials readily admitted that the aim was to batter south Lebanon and force the Lebanese government to curb Hezbollah. "We want Lebanese villagers to flee and we want to damage all those who were parties to Hezbollah's activities," Israeli prime minister Yitzhak Rabin told the Israeli Knesset.

Even the name for the offensive, Operation Accountability, left no room for doubt that this was a campaign of punishment and retribution. But the Israeli government was profoundly mistaken if it thought that bombing south Lebanon would improve the IDF's position in the occupation zone. Syria was the true authority in Lebanon, and the suffering of civilians in south Lebanon was not going to persuade Hafez al-Assad to alter his policy of using Hezbollah to further his negotiating position in peace talks with Israel.

By the time a cease-fire went into effect on July 31, 1993, after seven days of fighting, almost 130 Lebanese civilians had died, with another 500 wounded. Around three hundred thousand civilians were temporarily displaced, and damage to Lebanon was estimated at $28.8 million. Hezbollah had fired some three hundred Katyusha rockets into the occupation zone and northern Israel, killing two Israeli civilians and wounding about twenty-four.

Operation Accountability ended with a secret unwritten agreement brokered by Warren Christopher, the U.S. secretary of state, in which both sides agreed not to target civilians. It meant that Israel could no longer shell and bomb Lebanese villages and Hezbollah could not fire rockets into northern Israel, but both sides could continue to kill each other's combatants in the occupation zone.

The test of the cease-fire's durability came almost three weeks after Operation Accountability ended, when, on August 19, nine Israeli soldiers were killed in two roadside bomb attacks. The IDF, however, refrained from shelling areas facing the scene of the attack, opting instead for selective air strikes against a Hezbollah-operated radio station in the northern Bekaa Valley and the training area south of Janta village near the border with Syria.

The agreement had held—no Lebanese civilians were hurt, and no Katyusha rockets were fired into Israel. Yet the IDF still faced the same problem: how to blunt Hezbollah's deadly resistance campaign.

"A Learning Organization"

By late 1994, Israel had signed the Oslo Accords with the PLO that were supposed to lead to the gradual emergence of a Palestinian state, and had struck a peace deal with Jordan. But a breakthrough with Syria, which would lead to a treaty with Lebanon and an end to the occupation of south Lebanon, remained elusive.

By now, it was evident to IDF commanders that a different approach was required in dealing with an enemy that was showing distinct and constant improvements on the battlefield. The structure of the occupation zone was too static, the troop deployment too cumbersome. Hilltop outposts were magnets for Hezbollah's mortars, rockets, and missiles. Routine foot patrols along roads and dirt tracks were desperately vulnerable to Hezbollah's increasingly sophisticated and powerful roadside bombs. The terrain of south Lebanon, with its rocky, steep-sided hills and narrow valley floors, relegated Israel's fleet of tanks to little more than mobile artillery platforms. At dusk, tanks would maneuver into forward positions overlooking the front line, using their thermal imaging sights to scan for intruders, before slinking back to better protected compounds at dawn.

"We were a strong army, but we didn't have the right capabilities for [combating] guerrilla warfare," Kaplinsky, the Golani Brigade commander, told me. "Hezbollah is a learning organization. They would debrief after every operation. They had very good intelligence capabilities. We were playing into their hands in those days. We were operating in a heavy and high-intensity tactical manner, and they were studying us."

In February 1995, Lieutenant General Amnon Lipkin-Shahak, the IDF chief of staff, asked Kaplinsky to put together a new counterguerrilla unit under the command of the Golani Brigade in the Northern Command. The new unit was called Egoz, the Hebrew acronym for Anti-Guerrilla Micro-Warfare. While there were several other elite special forces units in the Israeli army, some of them regularly deployed in south Lebanon, Egoz was the only unit to be trained specifically in guerrilla warfare tactics to fight Hezbollah. "Shahak called me and said, 'You've got three months to build a special unit,'" Kaplinsky recalls. "We took soldiers from all infantry units with good commanders, people with open minds. We trained them in completely new tactics and in areas that resembled south Lebanon."

The Egoz volunteers, based at Kiryat Tivon near Haifa, were given weeks of clandestine training to prepare them for combat in the dense undergrowth and steep mountains and hills of southern Lebanon. The first recruits were drawn mainly from other special forces units, such as Sayeret Matkal, the Paratroop Reconnaissance Battalion, and Shayetet 13, the Israeli equivalent of the U.S. Navy SEALs or the Royal Navy's Special Boat Service. Already schooled in special operations, the first intake of Egoz recruits were ready for action in a relatively short period of time. Today, Egoz recruits undergo a fourteen-month training period that includes specialized courses in parachuting, airborne insertions, and navigation, with an emphasis on camouflage and fieldcraft.

"A Matter of Statistics"

The top secret company-sized unit became operational in July 1995 and was soon engaged in missions in the zone and beyond. But the IDF fatality count continued to rise. In 1995, twenty-three soldiers were killed in south Lebanon, two more than in the previous year, and another ninety-nine were wounded. Morale was sinking among troops serving in the zone, reminiscent of the fears experienced by an earlier generation of Israeli soldiers in south Lebanon before the 1985 pullback to the border zone. In early 1995, an Israeli paratrooper unit was disbanded after several of its soldiers asked their commander for an alternative mission on learning that they were to be sent to Lebanon for one last tour of duty before ending their compulsory service in the IDF. The furious commander told the soldiers that they were "not worth the spit of a dead monkey" and split up the unit.[15]

By fall 1995, the Israeli-Syrian peace track had reached an impasse. On November 4, Yitzhak Rabin was shot dead by a Jewish extremist as he emerged from a peace rally in Tel Aviv. Rabin was replaced by Shimon Peres, and the peace negotiations with Syria resumed the following month. Peres hoped that a deal could be reached with Syria before the next general election in Israel, scheduled for October 1996. The looming election was regarded as an opportunity for Israel to decide whether it wished to continue pursuing regional peace under Peres or opt for a more cautious and less yielding approach under Peres's rival, Benjamin Netanyahu, leader of the Likud Party.

The ruling Labor Party was riding high in the polls, buoyed by sympathy over Rabin's assassination, but Peres, a career politician who was more comfortable with negotiation, dialogue, and deal making than striking military poses, was keenly aware that the Israeli public was uncertain whether he was sufficiently robust on national security. After a top Hamas bomb maker was assassinated in January 1996, Israel was rocked by four deadly suicide bomb attacks in eight days that left almost sixty Israelis dead and many more wounded. The Labor Party's lead in the polls began to slip as a furious and frightened electorate blamed Peres for failing to stop the bombings. To compound Peres's woes, the ever-cautious Assad clearly was not going to be hurried into a peace deal with Israel just to save the Israeli premier's electoral skin. While Assad was willing to keep the talks going with the Israelis, he spurned a request by Peres for a summit between the two leaders. In umbrage, Peres brought forward the date of the election to May and postponed further peace moves with Syria until after the polls.

The embattled Israeli premier was also facing serious difficulties in south Lebanon. Hezbollah stepped up operations in mid-February and March, with UNIFIL recording more than two hundred attacks for the first three months of the year, including two simultaneous assaults against multiple IDF and SLA positions. IDF casualties climbed significantly in March in a series of ambushes. On March 4, four Israeli soldiers were killed and nine wounded while chasing a squad of Hezbollah fighters across the central sector of the zone. The Hezbollah team had ambushed the IDF patrol near the border. The Israelis gave chase, but the fleeing Hezbollah men led the soldiers into a cluster of roadside bombs detonated by another squad lying in wait.

Another soldier died and twelve more were wounded in separate IED ambushes in the following days. In mid-March, Ali Asmar, a fresh-faced Hezbollah fighter, accompanied by two comrades, slipped into the central sector of the zone and worked his way to the edge of Rubb Thalatheen village near the border. Asmar climbed into a well to hide while his two colleagues retreated out of the zone. Three days later,

Asmar, known within Hezbollah circles as Al-Shaheed al-Ammar, the Martyr of the Moon, for his round, youthful face, emerged from the well and blew himself up beside a passing IDF convoy, killing an officer.

On March 30, the IDF fired an antitank missile at three Lebanese workers repairing a water tower in the village of Yater, killing two of them. Hezbollah responded by firing more than twenty rockets into Israel. Peres admitted the next day that the IDF action had been a "mistake," but the damage was done, and it was evident from the surge in IDF casualties that Hezbollah and the Israelis were heading for another showdown.

"It was always a matter of statistics for me," recalls Timur Goksel, UNIFIL's veteran senior adviser, who had been watching developments in south Lebanon with growing unease. "Whenever there was an unusually heavy number of [IDF] casualties that attracted attention to Israel or the Israeli presence in Lebanon, and these casualties occurred in a short period of time, there was always the possibility that the Israelis would react very heavily. . . . Too many casualties in a short period of time meant big trouble."

FOUR

The Scent of Orange Blossom in the Spring

I look outside and see the spring flowers and remember that the last time I saw them, my family were all here and alive.

—Hameeda Deeb,
Qana massacre survivor, April 3, 1997

APRIL 9, 1996

BRAASHEET, south Lebanon—It was early evening, and a chill wind ruffled sixteen-year-old Mazen Farhat's sandy-colored hair as he trudged up the narrow, winding lane behind his parents' house.

Mazen's seven-year-old brother, Ibrahim, and his cousin Mohammed, down from Beirut for the spring holidays, followed a few paces behind. There were few people about, just a handful of farmers planting tobacco seedlings in the stony chocolate-colored soil. A compound defended by SLA militiamen was perched on a steep hill south of Braasheet, dominating the village like a scruffy medieval castle.

As the youngsters passed alongside a low stone wall, Mazen noticed a pale gray rock lying beside the road. He knew the lane intimately, and he was certain that the rock hadn't been there a few days ago.

Despite his youth, Mazen, like all residents of frontline villages, was well aware of "rock bombs"—those cunningly disguised IEDs used by both Hezbollah and the Israelis in which the explosive charge was hidden inside a fiberglass shell spray-painted to match the local geology.

Mohammed stood beside the road and urinated lazily against the stone wall as his cousin bent over to take a closer look at the rock.

Suddenly, Mazen realized what he was looking at. "Oh, mother," he wailed. And the bomb exploded.

Mazen's heavily pregnant mother, Amal, was chatting with friends in the living room of her house, less than two hundred yards from where the three boys had stopped to examine the strange rock. When Amal heard the blast, she was filled with an awful premonition that her children were involved. She ran screaming from the house and followed a crowd of people to the scene of the explosion.

The blast had killed Mazen instantly and thrown his body several feet into the adjacent field, far enough that it took several minutes for the villagers to find him. Ibrahim, who had been standing just a yard or two behind his older brother, was knocked unconscious by the explosion. His clothes were shredded, his body soaked in blood, and his flesh peppered with shrapnel.

"He looked like a sieve," his mother later recalled.

Mohammed was also seriously injured. The explosion tore open the seven-year-old boy's stomach, spilling his intestines onto the ground.

The local residents had no doubt who was responsible for the bombing. Some farmers who had been working in their fields at the southern edge of the village when the bomb exploded said they had heard the faint sound of cheering coming from the SLA position on the hill outside Braasheet. The militiamen in the compound were hidden from the bomb site by a ridge and could not have seen what happened. Nonetheless, it seemed they knew what the sound of the blast entailed.

Ordnance officers from the Irish UNIFIL battalion discovered that the explosion was in fact caused by four bombs, not one—serially linked explosive charges packed with steel ball bearings and fitted with anti-tampering mechanisms, hidden beneath fiberglass "rocks."[1] The bombs were typical antipersonnel charges employed by both Hezbollah and the Israeli army.

The Israelis denied responsibility for the bombing. A Hezbollah "explosives specialist" appeared on the group's Al-Manar television channel the next day, displaying fragments of the four bombs. He said that the wiring, the Israeli-manufactured battery, and parts of an antenna proved the bomb was the handiwork of the Israelis.

Shortly after seven o'clock the next morning, Hezbollah fired twenty-five Katyusha rockets across the border, striking the town of Kiryat Shemona. Seven Israeli civilians were wounded, one of them seriously. Hours later, an Israeli soldier was killed and three others wounded when Hezbollah fighters pounded an IDF compound with mortar shells.

"It's Time to Stop All the Blah Blah"

With northern Israel struck by Hezbollah rockets twice in two weeks, Peres's attempts to boost his security credentials in the run-up to the Israeli election slated for the end of May were looking increasingly frail. The rival Likud Party seized upon his apparent inability to stem the cross-border rocket fire, hammering home the fact that the dovish prime minister was weak on security.

"It's time to stop all the blah blah," said Yitzhak Mordechai, the former head of the IDF's Northern Command who was running as a Likud candidate in the election. "Peres has no message for the Israelis in the north who have to hide in their bomb shelters."

Hezbollah insisted that if Israel would only abide by the July 1993 understanding, there would be no need for rocket attacks on northern Israel. "The civilians on both sides must be considered neutral," Nasrallah said in an interview on Hezbollah's Al-Manar television channel hours after Mazen Farhat's death. "Not once did we start anything against civilians in north Palestine [Israel]. We were always on the defensive and reacting to what the [Israelis] have done against the civilians of south Lebanon and western Bekaa."

While Hezbollah's cross-border rocket barrages were deliberately aimed at civilians and were guaranteed to generate headlines, Israel's daily military activities were responsible for far more breaches of the July 1993 agreement to refrain from firing on civilians. According to a researcher with Amnesty International, between 1993 and 1996, the agreement was breached thirteen times by Hezbollah and 231 times by Israel.[2]

With the general election in Israel only six weeks away, Peres was initially hesitant to take drastic measures in Lebanon. But urged on by frustrated military commanders and feeling a compulsion to prove his martial resolve to a skeptical public, Peres gave the order for a massive air and artillery assault, the largest military operation against Lebanon since the 1982 invasion.

Destroying Infrastructure

At around 10:15 A.M. on April 11, four Apache helicopter gunships unleashed a volley of missiles toward two Hezbollah buildings in the Haret Hreik district of southern Beirut. The sudden clap of thunder from the exploding missiles shook west Beirut, startling Lebanese into scanning the brilliant blue sky for indications of inclement weather. The blast was followed seconds later by the earsplitting clatter of heavy machine gun fire as Lebanese troops shot at the insectlike helicopters flying high above the city. People scurried for cover, ducking into shops while panicked motorists sounded the horn as their cars jerked through the dense morning traffic.

The helicopter attack was the first Israeli air raid on the Lebanese capital since 1982, but it was not the only target that bright sunny morning.

Israeli warplanes flew up the Bekaa Valley and struck a Hezbollah weapons depot near Baalbek before swinging south and bombing frontline villages in the Iqlim al-Touffah hills east of Sidon. A Lebanese army tank was destroyed on the coastal road south of Beirut when its crew vainly opened fire at low-flying jets. The electricity plant at Jiyah on the coast midway between Beirut and Sidon was attacked by helicopters. Several civilians were killed and wounded when missiles smashed into a car and a crowded roadside café beside the electricity plant.

Farther south, Israeli artillery gunners opened up along the entire front line, pounding areas facing the occupation zone, striking villages and remoter areas from which Hezbollah launched assaults on the occupation zone. Israeli gunboats imposed a blockade on Lebanon's seaports, preventing docked ships from leaving and warning approaching vessels not to draw closer than fifteen miles from the coast.

Hezbollah launched its counteroffensive shortly after 9:30 A.M. the next day, April 12, firing more than two dozen Katyusha rockets at Kiryat Shemona and at western Galilee in what the group said was just a "preliminary response."

The SLA-run Voice of the South radio station began issuing direct threats against towns and villages, initially warning residents of villages close to the sources of Katyusha fire that they had four hours to leave. By April 13, some ninety towns and villages, including Tyre and villages north of the Litani River, had been placed under threat.

Hezbollah responded in similar fashion days later, broadcasting on its radio station in Arabic and Hebrew its own warnings to the Israelis to leave their homes in northern Israel or "face the consequences."

The SLA's radioed warnings and Israeli bombardments spurred some four hundred thousand Lebanese civilians to flee their homes in the south for the relative safety of Beirut and other areas to the north. The coastal road north of Tyre, cutting through banana groves and orange orchards fragrant with spring blossom, was clogged with northbound traffic. Battered old Mercedes and rusting Volvos sagged on their suspensions beneath the weight of entire families squashed inside, roofs piled high with bundled household goods, suitcases, and bags. Some stopped in Sidon, midway between Beirut and Tyre, fanning out in the city, filling schools and empty houses.

Yet many residents chose to remain in the south, either having nowhere else to go or refusing to flee the Israeli offensive. Thousands of people simply headed to the nearest UNIFIL position, hoping that the pale blue UN flag would afford them protection from the artillery shells and aerial bombs striking their villages. By the end of the first week of the so-called "Grapes of Wrath" offensive, UNIFIL was hosting some nine thousand civilians.

Israeli jets and helicopters returned to Beirut for five days, bombing targets in the southern suburbs. The jets floated high above the city, sunlight glinting off their silver wings. On the seafront corniche, an armored personnel carrier raced up and down, its crew of soldiers taking turns to blast away with a heavy machine gun at helicopters hanging above the southern suburbs. A crowd of curious onlookers stood silently watching the scene as if it was nothing more threatening than street theater. The helicopters released some flares and disappeared into the blue sky.

On day four, Israeli jets bombed the electricity switching station at Jamhour in the hills above Beirut. The next day, a power station in Bsalim, north of the capital, was struck, a dense black cloud of smoke casting a pall in the deep blue evening sky. The attacks on the power stations marked a qualitatively new step in Israeli actions against Lebanon. Grapes of Wrath initially appeared to be a rerun, albeit on a larger scale, of Operation Accountability three years earlier. But it was evident that destroying infrastructure was a key component of the 1996 operation. Dozens of roads and bridges were targeted throughout the south. The targeting of infrastructure sent a clear message to the Lebanese government: it could either resist or rebuild, but it could not do both.

Running the Gauntlet

On April 17, day six, the Israelis tightened their blockade on the south when navy gunboats stationed off Sidon began shelling the coastal road at the northern approach to the port town. The coastal road was the main route connecting the south to Beirut, used by northbound refugees to escape the fighting and by southbound emergency relief columns. While vehicles traveling north were generally left unmolested, the Israelis began firing at traffic moving south. Some motorists decided to risk the half-mile dash along the exposed stretch of road that ran alongside the sandy beach—the Israelis generally fired only one aimed round before the targeted vehicle reached the safety of the bridge over the Awali River at the entrance to Sidon.

Running the gauntlet for the first time was a stomach-tightening experience. A Lebanese soldier at a checkpoint on the coastal road north of Sidon warned us that the Israelis were shelling the road ahead and that we would be proceeding at our own risk. We gingerly drove to an abandoned Syrian army checkpoint at the beginning of the open road. Three Israeli gunboats were clearly visible riding the swell a few miles offshore. A dilapidated red Mercedes taxi roared past, the driver's body hunched over the steering wheel, a look of grim determination on his face. As the Mercedes rounded a wide bend and vanished from sight, a puff of black smoke blossomed from one of the gunboats squatting on the horizon. Moments later, we heard an explosion and saw a column of smoke rising beyond the corner where the taxi disappeared. There was no immediate way of knowing whether the driver had escaped unharmed.

We decided to take our chances; the story, after all, lay ahead, not behind us. Gunning the engine of the Range Rover, the driver stamped down hard on the accelerator. Again we saw that silent, harmless-looking puff of smoke billow from a gunboat, and we stiffened for the arrival of the shell. I had counted to five when the shell exploded a few yards behind us on the side of the road, throwing up dust and stones, the sound of the blast muted by the racing engine of the Range Rover. A crowd of spectators awaited us at the Awali bridge, some sitting on plastic seats, munching on sandwiches or sipping tiny plastic cups of coffee, watching the drama along the seafront. A television crew filmed our approach. The crowd cheered and yelled thanks to God for our safety.

"A Limited Operation"

Every type of combat aircraft possessed by the Israeli Air Force (IAF) was employed during the operation, from F-16s to Apache helicopter gunships. UAVs hunted for sources of Katyusha fire, and F-16s, fitted with up to three external fuel tanks for lengthy loitering, circled in Lebanese skies awaiting intelligence on freshly discovered targets.

The IAF enjoyed unhindered dominance of Lebanese airspace. Hezbollah's limited numbers of SA-7 shoulder-fired antiaircraft missiles posed little threat to Israel's well-protected, flare-spewing helicopters and jets. Indeed, for the Israeli aircrews, Grapes of Wrath represented a useful opportunity to gain combat experience at almost no risk. "As this was not a real war but a limited operation, we used all types of aircraft to give the younger pilots the chance to get some combat experience," Major General Herzl Bodinger, the head of the IAF, said. The large number of sorties flown around the clock meant "most pilots have had the chance to drop ordnance."[3]

During the operation, the IAF carried out some 2,350 air sorties, including 600 raids, and artillery units fired around 25,000 shells into Lebanon, killing some 160 people and causing up to $700 million in direct damages. Yet, as in 1993, Israel underestimated the tolerance of the Lebanese for hardship and suffering, and failed to foresee that bombing villages and infrastructure and uprooting half a million people from their homes would turn the Lebanese against Israel, not Hezbollah. Indeed, Hezbollah's popularity was never higher than during those two hot, bloody weeks. Even Christians, who tended to regard Hezbollah with unease, volunteered to help care for Shia refugees from the south in schools in east Beirut and openly donated money to the "resistance."

Hezbollah's objective during Grapes of Wrath was to maintain a barrage of Katyushas into Israel regardless of Israeli efforts to counter the rocket attacks and to be ready for a possible ground invasion. The damage caused by the rocket salvos was limited, certainly in comparison to the devastation wreaked on Lebanon by the Israeli military. But the Israelis had stated that their goal was to end the cross-border rocket attacks; therefore, each Katyusha that struck a town in northern Israel helped create an impression that the operation was not succeeding. Hezbollah had learned from the experience of Operation Accountability three years earlier and was better prepared to deal with Israel's latest offensive.

"In fact, July 1993 was a very good lesson for us as far as confronting this kind of aggression is concerned," Sayyed Hassan Nasrallah said, "because we pinpointed our strengths and weaknesses at the beginning of the war, and were therefore ready when the confrontation began."[4] The Israelis estimated that Hezbollah fired 746 Katyushas during the sixteen-day operation, around 80 percent of them striking northern Israel.

"Too Soon to Negotiate"

It was evident as the campaign progressed that the Israelis had once again woefully overestimated the ability of the Lebanese government to intercede against Hezbollah. Rafik Hariri, the prime minister, would have welcomed at the very least a respite in the bitter guerrilla war in the south that constantly threatened his reconstruction efforts. In a signal of their annoyance with Iran, Hariri and Fares Boueiz, the foreign minister, pointedly refused to meet Mohammed Kazem al-Khonsari, Iran's deputy foreign minister, when he visited Beirut during the offensive.

Yet, grumbling and diplomatic snubs aside, Hariri and his government were beholden to Damascus, the true authority in Lebanon, and were powerless to curb Hezbollah. Hariri could do little more than embark upon a diplomatic campaign, touring regional and foreign capitals to seek their support for bringing Israel's assault to an end as soon as possible. And Assad, sitting in the safety of Damascus and quietly watching Israel's punishing campaign unfold, had no intention of helping the Israelis by instructing Hezbollah to back down. Assad, perhaps more than the Israelis themselves, understood the limits of force, realizing that Israel's offensive would founder if the Lebanese refused to succumb to Israeli bombs and diplomatic démarches from the Americans.

In the opening week of Grapes of Wrath, the Israelis and the United States showed little inclination to reach a diplomatic solution. The Lebanese government said it was willing to return to the secret understandings of 1993. But Ehud Barak, the Israeli foreign minister, said negotiations could begin only if Beirut made it "impossible" for Katyushas to be fired into Israel.

The French proposed formalizing the July 1993 understanding by putting it into writing. Beirut and Damascus were sympathetic to the idea, but the Israelis were dismissive—Peres said, "it's too soon to negotiate."

The United States pitched a more ambitious initiative in which a cease-fire would herald a nine-month period of calm during which Hezbollah would be disarmed. If there were no attacks during the nine-month time frame, then negotiations would begin on an Israeli pullout from south Lebanon. However, the U.S. proposal was totally unacceptable to Syria, which relied on Hezbollah's resistance campaign to gain leverage against the Israelis in the peace process. Assad chose to play for time and see what might yet unfold on the ground in south Lebanon.

He would not have long to wait. For the turning point in the Grapes of Wrath campaign came in the early afternoon of day eight, Thursday, April 18.

1:50 P.M. APRIL 18, 1996

Three Apache helicopter gunships were strung out in a line south of the Tyre peninsula, facing inland and hovering just below the thick gray mantle of cloud. The beat of their rotor blades was barely audible above the breeze as the helicopters hung motionless in the air, like patient yet malevolent insects awaiting prey.

I was hoping to hitch a ride with the next UNIFIL relief convoy to visit the bombed villages south and east of the port town. While waiting for the latest convoy to return to base in Tyre, I passed the time by strolling over to the southern edge of the town, gazing southward along the coastline toward the gentle hills on the horizon that mark the border with Israel.

There was a faint scent of orange blossom on the breeze from the coastal orchards south of Tyre. The Grapes of Wrath operation coincided with the last days of the spring blooming. The tiny cream-colored flowers perfumed the coastal road that cut through the belt of orchards between Sidon and Tyre, momentarily diverting our attention from the fraught drive. Since then, the scent of orange blossom in the spring has become, in my mind, indelibly linked to April 1996, the aroma wafting from the orchards triggering an olfactory memory of the violence and carnage of Israel's onslaught against Lebanon that month.

A tiny high-pitched whine from far above, like a distant scooter struggling up a hill, pierced the sigh of the sea breeze. It was an Israeli UAV, a reconnaissance drone, an ineluctable and sinister presence in the skies over south Lebanon. Generally, drones flew too high to be spotted with the naked eye, but this one was clearly visible, its wide wingspan lending it the appearance of a crucifix silhouetted against the cloud. It buzzed purposefully over Tyre's high-rises and the Roman hippodrome and toward the low-lying hills to the southeast.

Two Apache helicopters hovering south of the peninsula slowly ascended until they disappeared into the cloud. The third and closest Apache began describing large, lazy circles that brought it even closer to Tyre. It turned 90 degrees until it faced the peninsula. We eyeballed each other across a one-mile expanse of steel-gray sea before it, too, slowly rose and was enveloped by the cloud.

As the last helicopter vanished from view, the soft crump of distant exploding artillery rounds rumbled across the silent city. To the southeast, tall columns of black smoke climbed into the sky from the foothills outside Tyre. The explosions appeared to be emanating from somewhere near Qana.

The headquarters of UNIFIL's Fijian battalion lay in the center of Qana village, a cluster of whitewashed one- and two-story buildings, some of them inscribed with "UN" painted in large black letters. The base had been there since UNIFIL's arrival in 1978. Residents from nearby villages had begun to arrive in Qana on the first day of Grapes of Wrath, seeking the protection of the UN against the shelling of their homes. By day eight, some eight hundred refugees were crammed inside the base, most of them housed in the Fijian officers' mess, a flimsy building consisting of a wooden frame and corrugated tin sheets, and the conference room, another simple prefabricated portacabin-style structure. The Fijian peacekeepers, tough soldiers but also gentle giants deeply committed to their Presbyterian faith, helped house and feed the refugees and played soccer with the children.

The shelling in the distant hills continued as I walked back to the

UNIFIL logistics base in Tyre. The UNIFIL convoy arrived minutes later, the heavy white-painted six-wheeled Finnish-built APCs lurching to a stop beside the gates. There was a sudden commotion as the peacekeepers, encased in light blue flak jackets and helmets, clambered out of the vehicles. Mike Lindvall, UNIFIL's Swedish press spokesman, hurriedly briefed a throng of reporters. The Fijian headquarters had been struck by Israeli shells, he told us, and an emergency armored convoy was leaving immediately for Qana. There was no room for us on the APCs, so most reporters ran to their cars and tagged on to the rear of the convoy for protection. The APCs charged through the abandoned city before heading inland, following the road that wound through the chalky hills. The news had spread that something terrible had happened in Qana. Cars carrying civilians raced alongside us. One Mercedes almost collided head-on with an ambulance hurtling in the opposite direction. The ambulance's windshield was smeared with the red earth of the south to prevent the sun from glinting on the glass and betraying its presence to Israeli jets and helicopters watching from the skies above.

Hameeda Deeb, twenty-eight, arrived in Qana from Rishkananiyah village on the fourth day of Grapes of Wrath. In the early afternoon of April 18, she was sheltering in the Fijian conference room along with her sister Sukaina, thirty-four, her sister-in-law Sadiyah, twenty-seven, her nephews Mohammed, seven, and Hamzi, six, and her niece Fatmeh, eight months, as well as five other relatives aged between five and twenty years.

"On that day in the early afternoon," she recalls, "we were eating lunch in our building [the conference room]. It was very crowded, with maybe a hundred people inside. I remember feeling that something was wrong. The weather was dry but gloomy, and everyone was quieter than usual. It seemed as if something bad was going to happen but we did not want to admit it to each other."[5]

Shortly before two in the afternoon, the Fijians heard the hollow thump of outgoing mortar rounds fired from near the compound. The Fijians were among the most combat-experienced of all the battalions serving with UNIFIL, and they knew that an Israeli counterbombard-ment would arrive within minutes. They pushed as many refugees as they could fit into the bomb shelters and instructed other civilians to return to their rooms.

As the UNIFIL convoy thundered into the narrow streets of Qana, a dense column of roiling black smoke marked the location of the Fijian battalion headquarters in the center of the village. Several headscarfed women stood on the side of the street, crying and wailing hysterically, their arms outstretched toward the passing UNIFIL vehicles.

We halted behind an APC that was blocking the entrance to the Fijian camp. Reporters, UNIFIL soldiers, and civilians squeezed past the APC and hurried into the base. As I climbed out of the car, I momen-tarily stopped dead in astonishment. The air was thick with the musty reek of freshly spilled blood. It smelled like a butcher's yard.

"My family were all around me, my sons were sitting in a row in front of me," recalls Saadallah Balhas, fifty-six, a tobacco farmer from neighboring Siddiqine village who was sheltering in Qana with twenty-two members of his extended family.

I remember a shell exploding in the room no more than a meter from where I was sitting. My children were all blown to pieces, but because they were between me and the explosion, they saved my life. I was hit in the eye by a piece of shrapnel and my eardrums burst from the sound. I brushed my face to wipe away the blood and my eye fell out. My brother had been standing beside me but I could not find him; there was nothing left but meat. I could not even identify my children because there was nothing left of them.

Fatmeh Balhas, twenty-five, a thin, sallow-faced mother of three children, was in line for food when the shell warning was announced. She returned to the officers' mess—the same building that housed Saadallah Balhas and his family. Fatmeh sat down holding her sons, Hussein, three, and Hassan, two, while Qassem, her husband, cradled the infant Mohammed, who was only seventeen days old.

"When the first shell landed, everybody started screaming and panicking," she recalls. "Then the second shell exploded and for a moment there was silence. The room was full of smoke and I could see nothing. I was dazed and numbed from the impact. It was only minutes later that I realized my children were dead and my husband as well. I was on my own."

A naked severed leg lay on the ground, ripped off at the hip and blasted out of the ruins of the officers' mess. The sheets of corrugated iron that comprised the walls and roof of the building had been blown away and lay on the ground, warped and twisted like autumn leaves. Only a knee-high cement wall and the wooden frame of the one-room building remained standing. The air was filled with the urgent shouts of rescue workers and the terrible screams of anguish and shock from the survivors frantically searching for their loved ones.

"Oh God! Oh God! Oh God!" wailed one man staring into the officers' mess, his hands gripping the sides of his head.

Mounira Taqi, forty-two, a tall woman with tired, melancholy eyes, was sitting beside the entrance of the officers' mess when the shelling began. Standing next to Mounira were her husband, Ibrahim, forty-three, and her two daughters, Dunia, eight, and Lina, seven. In her arms she held her seven-month-old baby boy, Ali.

"I was sitting next to the door with my husband, Ibrahim, when the second explosion occurred. A piece of shrapnel from the explosion slashed his throat open, and the last sound I heard him make was the rush of air emptying from his lungs as he collapsed. I also had Ali in my arms, but God helped him survive. I could not see my daughter [Dunia] because of the smoke. But as the smoke cleared, I was only able to recognize her from a piece of her pajamas. She had been blown to pieces and there was nothing else left."

. . .

The body of Ibrahim Taqi was lying at the entrance of the ruined officers' mess. His corpse was partially hidden by a woolen blanket thrown over him by one of the Fijian soldiers. A flap of flesh at the back of his neck was all that connected his head to his torso. His head was stretched back at an absurd angle, exposing the ghastly wound.

The officers' mess was a charnel house. The Fijian soldiers tried to lend the dead some dignity by covering the torn corpses with blankets. But the shrouds could not hide the horror. There were dozens of bodies, wrapped, embraced, and coiled together in the cold intimacy of death. They covered the entire floor of the officers' mess. Some had been blown into the corner, like a pile of swept leaves. Bewildered Fijian soldiers stood silently, wide-eyed with shock, staring at the corpses, momentarily unsure what to do next. Many of the corpses had lost heads, arms, and legs. Pieces of human meat had been blasted onto the low surrounding wall and the wooden support columns. Thick gouts of dark red blood smeared the floor and soaked the blankets. There was so much blood, streams of the stuff ran down the cement steps and collected in dark congealing pools in the dust. It stuck to our shoes. I later noticed that I had minced human flesh wedged into the rubber treads of my boots. Stunned camera crews and photographers raised the corners of blankets and gazed fearfully at what lay beneath, some of them openly sobbing as they mechanically recorded the horror in relentless and clinical detail.

A Fijian soldier, wearing rubber gloves and grasping a black trash bag, muttered prayers to himself as he stooped to pick up scraps of flesh from the ground outside the building.

A civil defense worker wearing a helmet and flak jacket raised the corpse of a tiny child. The top of the infant's head was gone. Its tiny arms and legs flopped lifelessly like a rag doll's as the civil defense worker, his face stricken, held the child aloft in front of the cameras. The infant was seventeen-day-old Mohammed Balhas, Fatmeh's youngest son.

· · ·

Hameeda Deeb, who had felt a sense of impending doom all day, was beside the Fijian battalion's conference room when the first shells struck.

> I heard no warning and the shelling came as a surprise. Everybody was panicking and looking for somewhere safe. Then I ran back inside the building [the conference room] and hugged Hamzi and Mohammed [her nephews]. There was an explosion and that was when I lost my arm and leg, although I didn't know they had gone at the time. Both Hamzi and Mohammed, who were in my arms, were killed. I felt no pain; I was in shock. My eyes were open but I was not aware of what was happening around me. The building was on fire and the flames were less than a meter away. But I could not move. I felt my back begin to burn and I looked around for my sister. She was lying next to me, but I was not sure if it was her at first because her face had disappeared. Someone, I don't know who, came into the room and saw that I was still alive. He dragged me . . . out of the flames. I hardly remember being taken to the hospital. I was in a car and my head was hanging out of the door and my hair was brushing the road. I could hear the screams of injured people in the car with me, so I knew I was not alone.

Three Fijian peacekeepers directed a feeble trickle of water over the smoldering remains of the conference room. Pools of pink diluted blood collected at their feet. The shell that tore the flimsy structure apart also turned it into an inferno. The mangled remains of the conference room contained a congealed, smoking, stinking mass of incinerated plastic chairs, tables, clothing, blankets, tinned food, and—as the eyes adjusted to the amorphous shapes—corpses, burned and blackened beyond any semblance of human form. Lying beside the conference room were yet more bodies dragged from the flames. One carbonized corpse was so hot when it was dragged out of the blaze that it had charred the blanket in which it was wrapped.

Nearby, a woman wailed over the dismembered corpse of her brother. With her arms raised and her face frozen with shock, she babbled a near-incoherent stream of grief. She tugged on her brother's lifeless arm. His other arm was missing, as were his legs. The shrapnel had cut him in half at the waist. A blanket covered the lower half of his body to conceal the terrible wounds. The brother's blood-smeared face wore an expression of placid indifference as his sister keened over him.

The clatter of approaching helicopters drew nervous glances skyward, but it was UNIFIL's Italian air wing arriving to evacuate the wounded. Even as the dead were gathered and the wounded taken away, Israel continued its relentless artillery barrage of the area, with shells exploding less than a mile away.

Amid the horror and shock, there was rage. Three young men ran into the compound. One of them screamed abuse at a cameraman and drew a pistol from beneath his shirt. His two colleagues restrained him. Another man knocked a camera aside and threatened to kill anyone who took more pictures. Gradually, the Fijians began to restore some order, marshaling themselves into a line clutching their M-16 rifles to block access to the bloody interior of their headquarters.

One shocked Fijian soldier told me, "Hezbollah fired some mortars near the camp and then the Israelis shelled us."

Another, staring blankly into the distance, simply said, "I can't speak. I'm too moved. They just have to find peace now."

"I Thought, My God, This Is Not an Accident"

To this day, no one knows exactly how many people died in the slaughter at the Fijian headquarters on April 18, 1996. Estimates vary between 102 and 109, with more than two hundred others wounded.

The massacre in Qana received instant and worldwide condemnation. In an abrupt reversal of his earlier indifference toward the fighting, Clinton called for an "immediate cease-fire" and dispatched Warren Christopher, the secretary of state, to the region. Boutros Boutros-Ghali, the UN secretary general, said he was "shocked and outraged" by the massacre and sent to Lebanon Major General Franklin van Kappen, his Dutch military adviser, to launch an investigation.

Israel's initial response was defiant. Peres blamed Hezbollah for launching rockets and mortars close to the Fijian battalion headquarters and said that the offensive would continue.

In Beirut, Hezbollah issued a statement denying it had fired from near the Fijian base. But as the UN's van Kappen subsequently revealed in his report, fifteen minutes before the Israeli shelling, Hezbollah had fired between five and eight 120 mm mortar rounds from beside a cemetery two hundred yards southwest of the Fijian base.[6] A unit of the still-classified Egoz commandos had been spotted by Hezbollah planting IEDs just north of the occupation zone. The first mortar rounds fell about a hundred yards from the commandos, then they inched closer, guided onto target by Hezbollah's forward observers. The Israelis said they initiated a rescue fire mission by shelling the location of the Hezbollah mortar. Some of the shells had overshot their target, the Israelis told van Kappen, and "regrettably" had hit the Fijian base.

But van Kappen's team was unconvinced. From an examination of the ground, they found evidence of thirty-six shell impacts and discerned that the rounds fell into two distinct concentrations. One was centered on a group of buildings close to the cemetery where the Hezbollah mortar team was located. The second impact site was in the middle of the Fijian headquarters. Witnesses said that there had been a perceptible shift in the weight of fire during the seventeen-minute bombardment, from the first location to the UNIFIL base. In other words, at some point during the shelling, the Israeli gunners had switched targets from near the cemetery to the Fijian base itself.

When van Kappen was dispatched to Lebanon, he initially believed that the slaughter was caused by a technical or operational error. A tragic accident, but an accident nonetheless.

"When I arrived in Lebanon at the Fijian headquarters, the first thing I did was stand on the roof of the main building and look at the fall of shot, and then I got an uncanny feeling . . . I thought, my God, this is not an accident," van Kappen recalls.

"We Got Five or Six of the Bastards"

Van Kappen's team also discovered that the majority of the shells that struck the Fijian headquarters were fitted with proximity fuses, designed to explode a few feet above the ground to maximize the shrapnel spray. Shells fitted with proximity fuses are typically employed against troop formations and soft-skinned vehicles rather than hardened positions such as buildings.

The Israeli explanation for the bombardment of Qana was looking increasingly suspect as van Kappen and his team probed deeper. The Israelis claimed that they were unaware that Lebanese civilians had been sheltering at the Fijian headquarters. However, UNIFIL had informed Israel that some nine thousand civilians were staying in UN facilities, a statistic that had also been widely reported in the media.

Then there was the discrepancy over the presence of helicopters and a drone above Qana. The Israelis repeatedly told van Kappen they had had no aerial assets over Qana "before, during, or after the shelling."

But the Dutch general had evidence from thirty-five eyewitnesses including UNIFIL peacekeepers, Lebanese soldiers, and civilians, all of whom testified to seeing a UAV and helicopters in the vicinity of Qana at the time of the shelling. Additionally, he had in his possession a videotape shot by a Norwegian UNIFIL soldier on a hilltop opposite Qana that clearly showed a drone flying above the village during the bombardment.

Israeli officials also claimed that the Hezbollah mortar team had sought protection from the shelling by running into the Fijian base. The allegation raised the obvious question of how the Israelis could have known that Hezbollah men were fleeing into the base unless they had a drone overhead relaying real-time video footage to Israel. Van Kappen suspected that the Israeli artillery gunners switched from targeting the mortar site to the Fijian headquarters because footage from the passing drone had shown Hezbollah men entering the camp. Indeed, Brigadier General Amiram Levine, the fiery-tempered head of the IDF Northern Command, inadvertently admitted as much to van Kappen. In a meeting between the two, Levine angrily denounced the investigation, accusing the UN of bias against Israel and blaming Hezbollah for consistently firing rockets and mortars from near the Fijian battalion headquarters.

"Then he said, 'But we got five or six of the bastards that fled into the camp.' I said, 'How do you know?' Then he realized he had made a mistake and tried to gloss it over.... That, for me, was a clear indication that Levine knew what had happened."

"It Was a War Crime"

While Israeli officials had responded to the massacre with somber-toned expressions of sorrow and regret, there were no such indications of remorse and soul-searching from the gunners who had fired the shells into Qana. In an extraordinary article published by the Israeli *Kol Ha'ir* weekly newspaper, several of the soldiers openly expressed indifference about the slaughter. According to one member of the artillery battery, the captain commanding the unit told his soldiers minutes after the fatal shelling that "It was war. 'Come on, the bastards fire at you, what can you do?' He told us that we were firing well and we should keep it up, and that Arabs, you know, there are millions of them."

Another soldier said, "No one spoke about it as if it was a mistake. We did our job and we are at peace with that. Even S [the captain] told us that we were great and that they were just Arabushes." *Arabushes* is Hebrew slang for "Arab rats."

Van Kappen met with the same artillery unit during his probe. The officers and soldiers were "extremely nervous . . . and very careful in what they said to me," he says. "Also, they had this attitude of 'What the hell are you doing here? We are in a war. Who are these peace doves and what is all this humanitarian crap?'"

The hostility toward van Kappen and his team was not confined to a few scowling Israeli soldiers. Despite coordinating with the IDF, the convoy carrying the UN investigation team along the coastal highway from Beirut to Naqoura came under repeated shell fire from Israeli navy ships. Even during his investigation on the ground, which occurred while Grapes of Wrath was still in progress, van Kappen and his team were dogged by near misses from artillery guns and air strikes.

On May 5, Israel concluded its own investigation into the shelling and shared its findings with van Kappen. The probe was headed by Brigadier General Dan Harel, the commander of the Israeli army's artillery section, which one UNIFIL officer later told me was like "asking a murderer to investigate his own crime." Harel said that the Fijian compound had been marked with a pin on a map that erroneously placed the base a hundred meters farther north than its actual position. His explanation earned guffaws of derision from UNIFIL headquarters.

The "pin-in-the-map" excuse was the "biggest, sickest joke I have heard in my life," Goksel said. The Israelis had extensive, highly detailed maps and aerial photographs covering all of south Lebanon. The idea that the Israelis had misplaced by a hundred meters a clearly visible, well-known UN compound of whitewashed buildings emblazoned with "UN" in large black letters that had been there for eighteen years was inconceivable, as far as UNIFIL officers were concerned.

The Israeli excuse that a map error had caused the tragedy in Qana also left van Kappen unpersuaded. Indeed, the accumulated evidence uncovered by van Kappen's team was damning, compounded by Israel's contradictory and unconvincing explanations. Van Kappen's findings were verified by artillery specialists attached to the UN. Back in New York, he showed his evidence to serving U.S. army officers for a second opinion. "They came back to me and said 'We can't officially support you, but you are absolutely right. Just don't quote us.'"

Van Kappen was left with a troubling conclusion: the cold, stark evidence suggested strongly that, even if the motivation was unclear, the Israelis had deliberately shelled the Fijian base. "While the possibility cannot be ruled out completely," van Kappen wrote in a carefully phrased conclusion to his report, "it is unlikely that the shelling of the United Nations compound was the result of gross technical and/or procedural errors."

Yet there were powerful political interests that had no desire to see such disturbing findings released to the public. The Dutch general came under pressure from numerous officials both inside and outside the UN to tone down his report. He was told that accusing Israel of shelling the Fijian camp would be detrimental to Peres's election campaign and would embarrass the Clinton administration in a presidential election year. Boutros Boutros-Ghali, the UN secretary general, was also urged to quash the report. Madeleine Albright, the U.S. ambassador to the UN, warned Boutros-Ghali that its publication would complicate Middle East peace efforts. She allegedly told him that it would open deep wounds in Israeli society, to which the UN chief bitingly retorted that Israel's artillery shells had opened even deeper wounds among the refugees in Qana.[7]

"Madeleine Albright didn't like the report at all," van Kappen says. "She told me several times that I had no proof, etcetera. I said that you don't need to be a rocket scientist to count holes in the ground."

The option of a cover-up was dashed, however, when some of the key findings were leaked to *Foreign Report,* a British publication specializing in international security and intelligence matters. UN headquarters in New York never discovered the source of the leak. However, I learned, it was released on the personal initiative of a UN official who was incensed by the massacre in Qana and worried that Boutros-Ghali would buckle under the pressure to quash the report. The leak was quickly picked up by the news wires, and once the story was in the public domain, there could be no question of suppressing van Kappen's findings. The report was published in full on May 8, to the irritation of Washington and the outrage of Israel.

Almost a decade and a half later, van Kappen's analysis of the circumstances behind the Qana massacre has not changed. "I think it was a deliberate act. It was a war crime," he says. "That is what I believe, although I refused to believe it for a long time. The evidence was so strong that there was no other way, as a professional soldier, you could come to any other conclusion."

In his view, the UAV above Qana relayed pictures of Hezbollah men running into the compound, and "somewhere in the line of command, somebody decided they had had enough of Hezbollah. . . . Someone in the chain of command broke the [moral] code and did it. When I look at all the evidence, this is the most logical [explanation]."

Snubbing Warren Christopher

The Qana massacre sealed the lid on Israel's Grapes of Wrath campaign. The United States realized that the fighting was spinning out of control and turning into a fiasco for its Israeli ally. Instead of neutralizing Hezbollah, Israel's disproportionate use of military muscle was deepening Arab sympathy for the Lebanese resistance and threatening to further undermine Washington's credibility as the neutral referee of the Middle East peace process.

Warren Christopher arrived in the region two days after the massacre and met with Hafez al-Assad in Damascus. Not for the first time, fortune had favored Assad's cool patience as the world turned once more to Damascus. Assad endorsed the French proposal, telling Christopher that he recommended a written reaffirmation of the July 1993 understanding that would safeguard civilians on both sides of the border but permit Hezbollah to continue resisting the occupation.

The Israelis insisted they wanted the United States, not France, to broker a deal, but Christopher found that he had little choice but to adopt the French proposal. Even then, Assad gave little ground, boldly refusing to meet the hapless American secretary of state on April 23, his third visit to Damascus in four days.

Shimon Peres, too, realized that his margin for maneuver had narrowed significantly since the attack on Qana. Christopher's earlier goal of reaching a detailed agreement signed by Lebanon, Syria, and Israel was scaled back to a simple one-page unsigned memorandum. The document was drafted and shown to Assad, who carefully scrutinized "every line, every word, every comma," according to a U.S. official accompanying Christopher.

On April 26, it was announced that an understanding had been reached to end the fighting. Hezbollah was prohibited from carrying out any attacks against northern Israel; Israel could not attack civilians or civilian targets; and both sides undertook not to launch attacks from populated areas or other civilian sites.

"Without violating this understanding, nothing herein shall preclude any party from exercising their right to self-defense," the memorandum said.

The understanding came into effect at 4:00 A.M. on April 27.

The "April Understanding," as it came to be known, additionally established a monitoring group consisting of delegates from Lebanon, Syria, France, Israel, and the United States to watch for any breaches. The group agreed that the UNIFIL headquarters in Naqoura would serve as the venue for their meetings. The American and French delegates would alternately chair the group, rotating every six months.

Peres had launched the Grapes of Wrath campaign in part to add muscle to his security credentials, always his weak point, in order to help maintain his slim lead in the polls during the closely fought electoral battle with Netanyahu. But it was to no avail. Four weeks after the operation ended, Peres narrowly lost the election to his Likud opponent, Benjamin Netanyahu, and the peace process between Israel and Syria went into deep freeze for the next three years.

The Grapes of Wrath operation was a military, political, and diplomatic failure for Israel. The disproportionate use of military firepower, culminating in the Qana slaughter, further blackened Israel's reputation internationally and embarrassed the United States, which had to intervene diplomatically to extricate its ally from a mess of Israel's own making. Despite Israel's wielding some of the most powerful and sophisticated weapons of war then available, only fourteen Hezbollah fighters were killed during the sixteen-day offensive, and the damage inflicted upon Hezbollah's military infrastructure—mainly the bombing of offices in the south and in southern Beirut—was negligible. Nawaf Mussawi, a member of Hezbollah's political council, said that the Israeli campaign had inflicted not "a scratch" on the group's capabilities.[8]

Israel was also unable to halt Hezbollah's daily barrage of Katyusha rockets. Fighter-bombers, UAVs, precision-guided missiles, and radar-directed artillery had shown their limitations against the mobile Hezbollah teams firing simple 122 mm Katyusha rockets from the hilly terrain of south Lebanon.

Grapes of Wrath was the last major military operation waged by Israel during the occupation of south Lebanon to try to alter the status quo on the ground in its favor. After sixteen days, it was evident that there was no realistic military solution for defeating Hezbollah, especially while Israel remained, in the eyes of the world, an illegal occupier of Lebanese territory. Neither Operation Grapes of Wrath nor Operation Accountability three years earlier had dented Hezbollah's resistance campaign nor turned the Lebanese population against the antioccupation struggle. On the contrary, Hezbollah emerged from the Grapes of Wrath campaign at the peak of its popularity, having won the consensus of the Lebanese to continue its resistance against the Israeli occupation. Syria had no intention of reining in Hezbollah, and the Lebanese government was in no position to object.

The April Understanding itself changed little on the ground. Indeed, far from curbing Hezbollah's resistance attacks and disarming the party, as the Americans and Israelis had originally intended, the Understanding enshrined for the first time Hezbollah's status as a resistance organization. How could anyone continue to describe Hezbollah's military operations against the Israelis in south Lebanon as acts of "terrorism" when the United States and Israel had tacitly recognized, in writing, Hezbollah's right to resist the occupation?

"It Feels Horrible to Still Be Alive"

Yet Grapes of Wrath was fundamentally a terrible human tragedy. More than 160 Lebanese civilians perished during those two dreadful weeks. And for those survivors of the Qana massacre who lost entire families to Israel's artillery shells, their experiences had scarred them physically and mentally for the rest of their lives.

Fatmeh Balhas's husband, brother, and three children, including baby Mohammed, were cut to pieces as they sat around her on the floor of the Fijian officers' mess. Shortly before the first anniversary of the massacre, she recounted her ordeal to me while flicking through a photo album containing dog-eared pictures of her dead family. Some of the pictures showed her baby sons, Hussein and Hassan, playing in the courtyard of her home. But there were no photographs of seventeen-day-old Mohammed.

Mounira Taqi, whose husband was almost decapitated by shrapnel as he stood beside her in the officers' mess, devoted most of her time caring for her daughter, Lina, who was six years old in 1996. Mounira had initially believed Lina died in the shelling. It was only five days later that the little girl was discovered by family friends in a hospital. Although alive, she had suffered brain damage from her head wounds and was partially paralyzed and unable to talk. It took several years of therapy before Lina was able to speak clearly again.

Hameeda Deeb lost a leg and an arm when shrapnel slashed through the conference room of the Fijian battalion headquarters. She lost nine members of her family. A year later, she was still struggling to learn to use crutches and artificial limbs. A bleak future lay ahead of her. Unmarried and childless, she had resigned herself to living the rest of her days with relatives and admitted that life held little value for her. "I look outside and see the spring flowers and remember that the last time I saw them my family were all here and alive," she says. "It feels horrible to still be alive now. But it is God's will."

Saadallah Balhas, a stocky man with a ruddy weather-beaten face framed by a shock of thick white hair and a white beard, lost his wife and nine children at Qana, from thirty-year-old Ghaleb to four-month-old Hassan. In all, thirty-two members of his extended family perished. The blast that killed his children also claimed his right eye. He plugged the empty socket with a glass substitute that gave him a permanent countenance of forlorn melancholy. Saadallah wore a pendant around his neck containing tiny photographs of his dead family. Hassan was represented by a bird, as there were no portrait photographs of the baby.

The first anniversary of the massacre in 1997 was marked with speeches, martial processions, brass bands, and the usual pomp and ceremony, ending, perhaps inevitably, in a fistfight between rival Hezbollah and Amal partisans outside the entrance to the cemetery.

Yet with each passing year, the massacre was slowly forgotten, the tributes and commemorations dwindling in size, until just a few survivors made the annual pilgrimage to the cemetery beside the abandoned buildings of the former Fijian battalion headquarters to pay their respects to their loved ones.

The cemetery itself fell into a pitiful, shameful state of disrepair. The long rows of marble-topped tombs were chipped and cracked, weeds grew between the tiles on the ground, cinder blocks and building materials lay scattered untidily around the site. The officers' mess, where more than half the victims died, lies a few yards from the cemetery. It was left untouched, probably more from indifference than design, and it is still possible to see the rusting tin cans from which some of the victims would have eaten their last meal minutes before the bombardment began.

I last saw Saadallah in April 2006, shortly before the tenth anniversary of the massacre. He was planting tobacco seedlings in the stony soil of a hilltop field. The noon sun was merciless, and Saadallah wiped his wrinkled brow with a thick, calloused hand. He looked frail and tired, his stockiness had gone, and he appeared a decade older than his sixty-six years. "My sons tried to marry me off again, but I refused," he says. "No one can replace my wife, my partner in life."

Saadallah lived through the July 2006 war—and yet another massacre in Qana—only to die in June 2008. A black banner was slung across the road outside his home in Siddiqine, paying tribute to the "living martyr." In accordance with his dying wishes, Saadallah was interred alongside his family in the Qana cemetery.

Today, beside the cemetery is a building that was supposed to be a museum, built with Syrian funds and opened in 2000. It is locked most of the time, not that there was much to see inside. The few exhibits consist of a handful of posters and gruesome photographs of the carnage wrought by the Israeli artillery shells.

But more haunting than all the images of butchered and burned corpses is one particular snapshot taken a few minutes before Israel unleashed its seventeen-minute bombardment. Men, women, and children were caught by the photographer chatting and laughing together, sitting on the floor of the Fijian officers' mess, unaware that they had but a few minutes left to live. And there, to one side of the picture, is Saadallah Balhas, a smile playing on his grizzled face as he hugs his infant son, Hassan, for what must have been the last time.

"Lebanon Pursues Us Like a Curse"

After a brief lull following the end of Grapes of Wrath, Hezbollah resumed military operations with an evident determination to demonstrate that it had not been cowed by Israel's offensive nor by the April Understanding. On May 9, two SLA militiamen were wounded by a roadside bomb explosion, the first attack since the understanding took effect. On May 30, as Israel was absorbing Netanyahu's electoral victory, Hezbollah detonated two roadside bombs against a convoy of Israeli jeeps in Marjayoun, killing four soldiers and wounding another three.

Just ten days later, Hezbollah fighters ambushed a squad of Israeli soldiers returning from a night patrol. Five soldiers were killed and another six were wounded.

In the weeks after Grapes of Wrath, planeloads of fresh arms were flown into Damascus airport from Tehran and then trucked across the border into Lebanon to replenish Hezbollah's arsenal. In August, Israeli officials claimed that Hezbollah had amassed a stockpile of a thousand Katyusha rockets, including about thirty of the larger 240 mm variety, capable of reaching Haifa, Israel's third-largest city.

Trying to ascertain exactly what weapons Hezbollah possessed was a permanent preoccupation of observers and journalists watching the war in south Lebanon. Hezbollah characteristically—if frustratingly—adopted a noncommittal policy, preferring to keep their Israeli foe guessing.

I had many interviews over the years with Sheikh Nabil Qawq, Hezbollah's southern commander, a tall, soft-spoken cleric whose amiability and strong sense of humor were at odds with his public image as a hard-liner. Qawq grew to tolerate my repeated questioning of Hezbollah's military assets, giving me a sympathetic smile every time I asked him to confirm whether the party had acquired this or that missile before declining to discuss the issue.

"It is true that if the enemy knows the size or effectiveness of your armaments it can create fear," he once explained to me. "But ignorance creates more fear. The enemy is always living with this uncertainty as to the strength of Hezbollah and we do not mind at all that they are uneasy about this."

The annual Israeli casualty toll continued to climb. In 1996, twenty-seven soldiers were killed, the highest toll in a single year since 1985, when the border zone was created.

On February 4, 1997, seventy-three Israeli soldiers died when two CH-53 troop transport helicopters collided over northern Galilee while en route to south Lebanon. It was Israel's worst aerial disaster and provoked more anguish about what to do with Israel's "little Vietnam" in south Lebanon.

"Lebanon pursues us like a curse," wrote Israeli commentator Yoel Marcus in *Haaretz*. "Lebanon has become Moloch [the Canaanite idol to whom children were sacrificed as burnt offerings], claiming casualties systematically and cruelly."

Nasrallah and other senior Hezbollah leaders were attending a Ramadan fast-breaking *iftar* meal in Nabatiyah in south Lebanon, raising speculation that the helicopters were carrying special forces troops to kill or capture the Hezbollah leader. Hezbollah said that "divine intervention" had spared the Lebanese many casualties.

Despite the huge loss of lives, Israeli military officials said that ferrying soldiers to south Lebanon by helicopter still remained the safest means of transport. "There is no other way," an Israeli officer said bleakly. "The alternative [by ground] is worse and more dangerous."[9]

The helicopter disaster spurred the mothers of four soldiers who died in the accident to create a new movement calling for a withdrawal from south Lebanon. The "Four Mothers" group would play an increasingly vocal role in the months ahead as the domestic debate about Israel's involvement in Lebanon deepened.

Aggressive use of the special forces suited the temperament of the Israeli commanders then overseeing Lebanon operations as well as of Prime Minister Netanyahu, himself a former member of the elite Sayeret Matkal unit. Before 1996, Israeli commando raids north of the zone were relatively rare. One exception occurred on May 21, 1994, when helicopter-borne commandos stormed the Bekaa Valley home of Mustafa Dirani, the leader of the Believers' Resistance and former top security chief of Amal. Dirani was kidnapped by the Israeli troops and flown to Israel for questioning over the fate of Ron Arad, the missing Israeli aviator who at one time was in his care. Along with Sheikh Abdel-Karim Obeid, who had been languishing in an Israeli jail since 1989, Dirani became the most celebrated Lebanese detainee held by Israel.

The presence of highly trained and motivated Egoz commandos and other Israeli special forces units staking out infiltration trails on the edges of the border strip hampered Hezbollah's ability to penetrate the zone and plant roadside bombs. In the first half of 1997, Hezbollah gradually fell back and resorted to long-range shelling of Israeli and SLA outposts. While the rate of attacks increased in the first six months of the year, the number of close-quarter operations dwindled.

Encouraged by the successes, Israeli commando units began infiltrating even farther into Lebanon to hit Hezbollah militants in their home villages, areas generally considered safe.

On the night of August 3, an Israeli Blackhawk helicopter skimmed above olive groves, hugging the hilly terrain before descending into a valley a few miles northwest of Nabatiyah. Soldiers from the Golani Brigade's Reconnaissance Battalion dismounted, split into two teams, and slipped through the undergrowth toward the nearby village of Kfour. One team crept through olive trees until they reached a stone wall running alongside a narrow lane. On the other side of the lane were several houses, one of them the home of Hussein Qassir, a district commander of the Islamic Resistance. The Israelis buried three roadside bombs packed with steel ball bearings, each one a yard apart, in the stone wall opposite Qassir's home before retreating through the olive grove. But before the Israelis reached the helicopter, they were spotted by Hezbollah fighters on night watch duty, and a firefight broke out. Israeli jets and helicopters flying cover for the Golani troops came under antiaircraft fire from Hezbollah and the Lebanese army. The shooting ended at three in the morning as the Blackhawk took off with all the Israeli troops safely on board.

As dawn broke two hours later, armed Hezbollah men swept the village, checking for booby-trapped explosive devices and making sure that all the Israelis had departed. The atmosphere was still tense from the unexpected raid and from the presence high above of an Israeli UAV, invisible against the watery blue sky but audible from its motorcycle whine. Among the fighters was Hussein Qassir, who was accompanied by another senior officer, Sheikh Taysir Badran, the Islamic Resistance commander in Nabatiyah, and three more combatants. As they passed the stone wall opposite Qassir's house, the three bombs exploded simultaneously, apparently detonated by a radio signal transmitted from the circling drone above. All five Hezbollah men were killed instantly. Qassir's severed head was later found seventy-five feet from his front door.

The next day, three of the dead, including Qassir, were buried in Kfour in a ceremony attended by some two thousand mourners, many of whom crammed into the small pine tree–shaded cemetery. The bodies, wrapped in plastic bags, were lifted out of the coffins and lowered into their graves. Hezbollah fighters wept as a sheikh clambered down to deliver a final prayer. Then the corpses, shrouded with Hezbollah flags, were entombed beneath stone slabs.

"We will create funerals for the occupation troops and our retaliation will be so hard that pain for the Israeli troops will head the next stage [of the conflict]," vowed Sheikh Nabil Qawq during a visit to Kfour.

The Israelis had reassessed their tactics months earlier, choosing to adopt a more confrontational policy using special forces units to wage roadside bomb attacks and deep penetration raids to keep Hezbollah on the defensive. Now it was Hezbollah's turn to reexamine its operational choices and devise new means of staying a step ahead of the Israelis.

"The Bombs Have Killed My Friends"

In June, Hezbollah switched its attention from the Israeli-controlled border zone to the Jezzine panhandle, the northern tip of the zone, which was patrolled by a three-hundred-strong garrison of SLA militiamen. The absence of Israeli troops and the rugged landscape of mountains and pine forests that surrounded the salient allowed Hezbollah to infiltrate the Jezzine area with relative ease to plant and detonate IEDs. A spate of attacks from mid-June on claimed the lives of several militiamen and civilians. Hezbollah took responsibility for the SLA fatalities, but the civilian deaths went unclaimed. As the casualty toll mounted, traffic along the bomb-laced mountain roads around Jezzine almost stopped, and many families fled to Beirut.

It was easy to understand the fear that gripped the population of Jezzine in the summer of 1997. The threat of roadside bombs made even a routine shopping trip in Jezzine a daunting prospect. Even the topography of the salient, with its tall, jagged peaks and forested slopes looming over the town and the neighboring villages, helped create a sense of isolation from the rest of the country and a paranoid feeling that one was being watched all the time by silent and unseen observers hidden in the surrounding mountains.

Most SLA officials attempted to convey an impression of confidence, but there was no doubt that their morale was sinking with each fresh bomb attack. "The bombs have killed my friends," said a thin, pale-faced SLA officer who chain-smoked as we chatted in his flat-roofed one-story home outside Jezzine. "They died in front of their families. I'm scared for my family and I'm scared to leave the house. I don't use my car anymore. I walk everywhere."

His wife, in her midtwenties but looking much older with her dyed yellow hair and gray skin, nervously twisted her wedding ring around her finger as she talked. "I can't sleep at night with worry," she said. "As women, it's as if we are in prison here. Our husbands are in the Army of the South [SLA] and we cannot leave the area. There are government agents here in Jezzine and they know everything about us."

During the hot summer months of 1997, tempers flared in tandem with civilian casualties—victims of roadside bombs in Jezzine or increasingly reckless Israeli and SLA shelling. On August 18, another roadside bomb killed Jean and Rima Nasr, a teenage brother and sister who were driving on a road south of Jezzine. Again, there was no claim of responsibility. Instead, Hezbollah and the Israeli army blamed each other for the attack. The victims were the children of Assad Nasr, an SLA security officer from the Christian village of Aishiyah, a few miles south of Jezzine, who had been killed a year earlier. Two of Assad Nasr's brothers had also died fighting with the SLA, and the fourth sibling, Emile, was the commander of the SLA's Jezzine battalion in 1997.

Enraged at the sight of his dead nephew and niece lying in the morgue of the Jezzine government hospital, Emile Nasr instructed SLA artillery gunners to open fire on Sidon. Over the next hour, around half a dozen 155 mm shells slammed into the center of the bustling port town, killing seven people and wounding nearly forty more.

Hezbollah launched as many as eighty Katyusha rockets into northern Israel. It was the first cross-border barrage since Grapes of Wrath sixteen months earlier, but both sides quickly moved to de-escalate the crisis. Still, Hezbollah had served notice that the pre–Grapes of Wrath equation of cross-border rockets for Lebanese civilian casualties would continue to hold regardless of the April Understanding and the possibility of censure by the monitoring group.

A week later, Emile Nasr stood at an SLA checkpoint on the Dahr al-Ramleh road outside Jezzine, where many of Hezbollah's roadside bombs had been planted. Several militiamen milled around a T-55 tank, the barrel of which pointed at oncoming traffic.

Dressed in a faded olive-green Israeli army uniform with bleached Hebrew markings on his breast pocket, his thumbs hooked nonchalantly into his belt loops, Nasr denied ordering the shelling of Sidon. The order, he said, had come from Antoine Lahd, the SLA commander. "We hit Sidon because it's more important than hitting the villages. It was a message to the Lebanese government for them to stop the roadside bombs," he said.

But Nasr now topped Hezbollah's hit list of SLA officers. Given the fate of his siblings, did he not fear assassination?

"It is in the hands of God," he replied simply.

New Tactics

Tensions began to ease in Jezzine toward the end of August as Hezbollah's attention returned to the Israeli-manned sectors of the occupation zone.

Following the Kfour commando raid, security was tightened in the villages north of the occupation zone to counter further Israeli airborne assaults. The *haras,* or guardian, units responsible for nighttime observation duties around southern villages increased their patrols, staking out potential helicopter landing spots or infiltration passages from the zone or by sea. IEDs were planted along potential access routes, tracks and roads alike. Key points around the villages, on hilltops, and in valleys, were observed each night by armed fighters equipped with walkie-talkies. "We realized after Kfour that the Israelis were trying new tactics against us, therefore, we planned new tactics to fight back," Sheikh Nabil Qawq told me at the end of September.

The turnaround began on August 23, when Hezbollah fighters staged a nighttime ambush against an Israeli army unit in a deep brush-covered ravine in the western sector, the first such raid in many weeks. At the end of the month, six Israeli soldiers burned to death during combat with Amal fighters in a deep frontline wadi when Israeli artillery guns fired phosphorus rounds into the tinder-dry undergrowth that covered the steep slopes. Four Amal fighters were killed in the clash, but several Israeli soldiers found themselves cut off and desperately climbed up the side of the valley to escape the blaze. But the hill was too steep and the flames too fast. The rings of white ash marking the impact site of each phosphorus shell on the blackened hillside were visible for weeks afterward, until they were finally washed away by the winter rains.

By the end of August, eighteen Israeli soldiers had been killed in south Lebanon, excluding the seventy-three soldiers who died in the helicopter collision, suggesting that 1997 might exceed the previous year's toll of twenty-seven, setting a new record in combat fatalities.

But worse was to come for Israel. For at the beginning of September, Hezbollah was putting in place the final touches for an operation to ensnare some of Israel's finest special forces troops in an elaborate and deadly trap. The outcome of the operation would force Israel to reassess once again its tactics in south Lebanon, and it would later be ranked by Hezbollah as one of its most successful missions ever.

FIVE

The "Deluxe Laboratory Without Settlers"

For the first time in the Jewish entity's history . . . the crème de la crème of the Israeli naval commandos cross over to carry out an operation in the south—not in Tunis, Entebbe, the depths of Beirut, or the capitals of Europe, but in the south, only a few kilometers away from their own country—and then are soundly defeated, outmaneuvred, destroyed, and humiliated by our God, who sent us a victory as the token of his esteem and generosity.

—Sayyed Hassan Nasrallah,
September 5, 1997

SEPTEMBER 4, 1997

ANSARIYAH, south Lebanon—For ten days, Ghalib Farhat, a citrus farmer, had been bothered by the near-constant whine of an Israeli reconnaissance drone circling invisibly high above the orange groves that surrounded his small home on the northern outskirts of Ansariyah. A small village of square whitewashed houses on a headland overlooking the cobalt-blue Mediterranean midway between Sidon and Tyre, Ansariyah was far from Israel's front line. Adding to Farhat's unease was the strange Hezbollah activity in the village, which had begun about the same time that the UAV had appeared. Each night around ten o'clock, a car drove slowly past his home, the headlights switched off, along a lane lined with pine trees. Four or five people would climb out of the car and slip into the orange groves on either side of the road. Farhat assumed that the fighters stayed there all night; but there was never any sign of them by daybreak. That evening, he had seen them enter the orange groves as usual.

While Farhat and his wife, Kholoud, watched television that night and their four children slept in the next room, a mile to the west, sixteen black-clad figures silently emerged from the sea onto a rocky beach near an abandoned two-story building. They were members of Israel's Shayetet 13 naval commando unit. All were dressed in matte black clothing with soft rubber boots. Most of them carried AK-47 rifles, favored by the naval commandos for their rugged dependability. At least one of them was weighed down by explosives for IEDs. The stretch of coastline where they had come ashore was the only place where there were no inhabited buildings. But it was still risky. The coastal road was separated from the narrow beach by a few yards of bamboo thickets, and cars continued to pass despite the late hour. The team hurried across the road one at a time while their comrades spread out to cover them. Once across, they began the hard uphill slog toward the northern end of Ansariyah.

Ahmad, a slim, hollow-cheeked nineteen-year-old Amal fighter, crouched among bushes on the edge of an orange grove at the northern end of Ansariyah. Somewhere in the blackness near him were three more of his Amal comrades, all of them armed with AK-47 rifles and rocket-propelled grenades. They were part of a backup unit deployed around the village to support the Hezbollah fighters hidden among the orange trees a few hundred yards to the north of his position. The Hezbollah ambush squad, all of them with extensive combat experience in the south, was split into three sections—two of six combatants each and one of eight. Their commander was "Abu Shamran," who lived in Ansariyah.[1]

Ansariyah and the surrounding villages were traditional Amal strongholds where Hezbollah had only a light presence. A few days earlier, Hezbollah men had met with local Amal commanders and informed them that resistance fighters were on operational duty each night on the northern perimeter of the village. The Amal commanders were given few details, for security reasons, but the Hezbollah men told them that if they were to hear shooting and explosions, they would know what was happening. *Be careful*, the Hezbollah men said, *that you don't shoot us in the confusion. Our men will be out there, too.*

Local Amal units were rotated each night to provide assistance to the Hezbollah professionals. On this night it was the turn of Ahmad and his comrades. Ahmad was glad of the opportunity to participate in an operation alongside Hezbollah. He and his comrades often grumbled that it was always Hezbollah that grabbed the headlines for its resistance exploits, rarely Amal. *At least we are getting a share of the action this time,* he thought.

The naval commandos struggled through the dense undergrowth on the steep climb leading to the northern edge of the village. As they reached the brow of the hill, they moved onto a dirt track running beside an orange grove and a windbreak of scrawny pine trees. The team cautiously approached a lane on the northern edge of Ansariyah.

Hidden among the orange trees were Abu Shamran, the Hezbollah commander, and another fighter crouching barely four yards from the Israelis.[2] Abu Shamran could hear the soldiers talking to each other in Hebrew and felt they were close enough to touch. But he waited for the right moment before springing the trap.

That moment came as the naval commandos bunched up on reaching an iron gate beside the lane. Abu Shamran silently gave the order to attack and the first roadside bomb exploded in a deafening thunderclap, blasting the assembled soldiers with steel ball bearings and knocking them all to the ground. As they were recovering from the shock of the blast, the team was hit by a second bomb, which exploded in a large bubble of orange flame. Then the Hezbollah men hidden in the orchard opened fire with machine guns and rocket-propelled grenades. One bullet struck the commander of the Israeli team in the head, killing him instantly.

At the sound of the first explosion, Amina Farhat, Ghalib's mother, sat bolt upright in bed. *Could Amal and Hezbollah be fighting each other again?*, she wondered. Her son, Ghalib, a former fighter with the Communist Party, immediately recognized that the explosions and rate of fire signaled something far more serious than another clash between the rival Shia groups.

"Get the children up," Ghalib Farhat ordered Kholoud, his wife. The firefight was just two hundred yards up the road, and Ghalib figured that his mother's two-story house next door would provide better protection than his simple bungalow. The terrified family ran outside and barged in through the back door of his mother's home. As they took cover beneath the stairway, Ghalib noticed the flash and heard the report of a third explosion among the orange trees.

The third blast was caused by a bullet detonating explosives carried by Sergeant Itamar Ilya, the Israeli unit's sapper. The explosives were intended for roadside bombs that the team planned to set up around Ansariyah. The blast tore Ilya into bloody fragments and killed more members of the team. Eleven of the sixteen naval commandos were now dead, with at least another four wounded.

As the firefight raged among the orange trees and the surviving Israeli commandos desperately radioed for support and evacuation, Hussein Younis, a baker from the nearby village of Msaylah, drove his BMW toward Ansariyah, completely unaware of the fighting ahead of him. In the backseat was Samira, a young married woman with whom he was having an affair. As Hussein approached the scene of the ambush, he noticed black shapes moving on either side of the road just ahead and then saw bright flashes as the Israeli soldiers opened fire on his vehicle. The bullets punched holes through the windshield, showering Hussein with glass chips as he ducked down onto the passenger seat. The car's momentum propelled the vehicle forward into the firefight as bullets shredded the chassis and tore into Hussein. One gave him a glancing blow to the skull, another hit an arm, another a shoulder. The car rolled off the road and stopped against an irrigation pipe. Still the Israelis blasted the car at almost point-blank range. Hussein saw the dashboard above his head explode into splinters of wood, plastic, and glass. The shooting stopped, and Hussein eased himself out of the passenger door onto the road.

"Get out of the car," he whispered to Samira. He could hear her whimpering faintly and see she was not moving. There was nothing he could do for her. Hussein crawled into an overgrown ditch and hid.

The thud of helicopter rotor blades alerted the surviving Israeli commandos that help was at hand. Cobra helicopter gunships unleashed TOW antitank missiles into the orange trees and blasted the area with their 20 mm chain guns slung beneath the aircraft, creating a perimeter of fire to allow CH-53 rescue helicopters to land. Abu Shamran and his team, two of them slightly wounded, pulled back from the ambush site and slipped away unseen. Ahmad and his Amal comrades opened fire with their rifles and rocket-propelled grenades in the direction of the Israelis before pulling back themselves. It was twenty minutes since the first explosion had decimated the naval commandos.

Under the cover of fire from the Cobra helicopters, two CH-53 helicopters touched down in open fields. Reinforcements from the elite Sayeret Matkal unit and the Israeli Air Force's aeromedical evacuation force dismounted from the CH-53 helicopters about a hundred yards from the ambush site and split into two groups. The commandos formed a defensive perimeter while the medics began ferrying survivors and bodies into the stationary helicopters.

The medics had a terrible task to perform. Some of the commandos had been blown to pieces, but the medics were obliged to observe Jewish custom and recover the entire remains of each individual. The rescuers were certain that two bodies were missing, but despite scouring the darkness with their night vision goggles, they could find no trace of them. What they failed to realize at the time was that the remains of one of the missing commandos were already on board a helicopter. The body parts of the other commando, Sergeant Ilya, whose explosives had been detonated by a bullet, were lying scattered over the battlefield. Hezbollah's close-quarter machine gun fire had stopped, but the Israeli rescuers faced a new threat as mortar rounds began falling around them. The shelling claimed a final victim. A doctor from the rescuing force was killed when a mortar round exploded beside him. Nearby Lebanese army antiaircraft units blindly pumped rounds into the night sky, hoping to hit the helicopters and jets flying overhead. They also fired illumination shells to light up the ambush site. An F-16 jet fired a missile at an antiaircraft position. Israeli missile boats offshore fired a few rounds toward the village to silence the mortar fire. Several houses were damaged and two civilians wounded.

When news of the enormity of the disaster unfolding in south Lebanon reached the Israeli government, urgent contacts were made to the Americans to pass a message to Syria. Israel would respond with massive force if Hezbollah prevented the rescue mission from proceeding, the Israelis warned. The Americans contacted Damascus, and the message was then relayed to the Lebanese. Hezbollah pulled back, and Lebanese troops began moving into the area. One Amal fighter with an RPG on his shoulder who was running to join in the battle was seen being picked up by a hulking Lebanese army sergeant and thrown into the back of a jeep.

Shortly before dawn, more than four hours after the battle began, the last CH-53 lifted off and headed south.

Hussein Younis was still conscious as the Israelis departed. After hours of noise and commotion, the sudden silence was unnerving. He listened to the sound of the morning breeze blowing dust and garbage across the road. Ignoring the pain from his torn and bruised muscles, he inched toward the car and climbed inside. Samira was lying facedown on the backseat. It was obvious she was dead.

Hearing voices, Hussein looked through the shattered windshield to see two men walking toward the ambush site. He called out to them, but the men froze and turned away. He called to them again, and one of the men paused and spoke to his companion. Then they turned toward Hussein's car. For the first time since he had driven his Mercedes into the middle of the firefight, Hussein Younis thought he might survive after all.

A row of pine trees beside the lane was on fire, the branches crackling with orange flames and thin tendrils of smoke spiraling into the pale blue dawn sky. The branches of trees lay smashed and torn on the ground covered in rubbish from a nearby garbage dump. Civilians and a few local Amal fighters clutching AK-47s and wearing T-shirts and jeans milled around the site, collecting trophies of the battle—weapons, ammunition, clothing, wet suits, helmets, and flippers abandoned by the Israelis. The Hezbollah fighters had departed the battleground long before, ensuring they were well away before the media arrived with their cameras. Lebanese soldiers cordoned off part of the scene to search for booby-trapped explosive devices left by the retreating Israelis. A UAV circling above caused some anxiety. Everyone remembered the Kfour incident a month earlier, when five Hezbollah men had been killed by bombs detonated by a drone after the Israeli assault force had departed.

On the edge of the orange orchard beside the dirt track where the Israeli commandos were ambushed, two small holes beside a metal water pipe marked the spot where the roadside bombs had exploded. Several flattened ball bearings were fused to the metal pipe by the heat of the explosion.

Mingled with the fragrant smell of burning pine wood was the reek of fresh blood. Scattered amid the debris were pieces of human flesh—a jawbone with a set of teeth, white blobs of brain matter. Someone had ripped a piece of cardboard from a box and used it as a tray for a grue-some collection of small body parts, including individual fingers, two fingers joined at the knuckle, an elbow, and several pieces of unidentifi-able flesh. There were more body parts hanging from trees, including what was left of the head of Sergeant Ilya, the Israeli sapper whose ex-plosives had been detonated by a bullet. In a gesture that captured the horror of the battle, a grinning Amal fighter lifted the shattered head by an ear and held it aloft in triumph.

"We Feel We Had a Leak"

The bungled naval commando raid on Ansariyah resulted in the death of twelve elite troops, including eleven of the sixteen-man Shayetet 13 team. It was the worst single-day casualty toll for the Israeli military in south Lebanon since 1985. To add to the blow, the disastrous raid came just hours after three Hamas suicide bombers blew themselves up in a crowded street in Jerusalem, killing seven civilians and wounding nearly a hundred others.

Netanyahu, himself a former Sayeret Matkal soldier, described the raid as "one of the worst tragedies that has ever occurred to us." "We lost some of our best soldiers, and that's not an exaggeration," he said. "There have been several tragedies in the past, but I've never seen this type of tragedy."

It was a staggering success for Hezbollah, yet many questions remained unanswered. What were the naval commandos doing in Ansariyah? Did Hezbollah have prior knowledge of the raid and set up the ambush?

In October, an Israeli commission of inquiry concluded that the naval commandos had fallen into a chance ambush by Lebanese guerrillas. The casualties were caused by two roadside bombs and the detonation of explosives carried by Sergeant Ilya. Most important, the investigation claimed there had been no breach of intelligence that could have forewarned Hezbollah. Not everyone was convinced, however. Two more army inquiries were held over the next eighteen months, as well as a separate investigation by the Israeli Knesset. All produced inconclusive results. "We feel we had a leak, but we can't prove it," Major General Moshe Kaplinsky admitted to me a decade later.

While the Israelis pondered what had gone wrong, Hezbollah quickly offered an explanation. Nasrallah told reporters later on the day of the ambush that the Islamic Resistance had tightened its defenses and nighttime *haras* units around southern villages to prevent any repetitions of the Kfour raid. His explanation dovetailed with the subsequent findings of the first Israeli inquiry.

Yet rumors persisted that Hezbollah had concocted an elaborate trap for the Israeli commandos, perhaps by turning a spy and giving him information to deliver to his Israeli handlers about a meeting of top Islamic Resistance commanders, with names and dates, in Ansariyah. Although Hezbollah refused to address such speculation, as the years passed, it began offering a different version of events.

In September 1998, on the first anniversary of the ambush, Nasrallah admitted on Lebanese television that Hezbollah had had foreknowledge of the Israeli raid, setting in motion a tantalizing psychological campaign that would keep everyone guessing for another twelve years.

"All I can say now is that we knew beforehand that there was going to be an operation," he said. "Now the question is: If the resistance knew, who told them? But we can't disclose that, because that won't be in the Resistance's best interest."[3]

The truth was finally revealed by Nasrallah in August 2010 during a lengthy press conference. It turned out that Hezbollah had discovered in the mid-1990s how to intercept Israeli UAV video transmissions. The video footage captured by Israeli drones was unencrypted at the time, which allowed Hezbollah technicians to download the intercepted data and watch it on television screens.

Nasrallah said that they noticed the Israelis were showing an unusual amount of interest in Ansariyah, particularly the northern entrance of the village. Hezbollah surmised that the Israelis were planning another Kfour-style operation, and set up an ambush.

Yet it still remains unclear what the Israelis were doing in Ansariyah. Nasrallah admitted in his press conference that the purpose of the mission was still a mystery to Hezbollah.

Local residents claimed that a senior Hezbollah official used to spend some nights in the village. Could the Israelis have intended to kidnap or kill him? That possibility was lent some support by Amiram Levine, the former head of the IDF's Northern Command, who told me that the intended target was a Hezbollah military commander.

There may yet be more to the Ansariyah story that Hezbollah prefers to keep under wraps. But Hezbollah's official view is that the Israelis had no particular target in mind, contrary to speculation at the time. Instead, the Israeli assault fell within the prevailing policy of deep-penetration commando raids, similar to the one at Kfour, to kill resistance fighters and to signal to Hezbollah's leadership that Israel could operate where it pleased.

"The Israelis were trying to spread panic in the souls of the resistance fighters," Sheikh Naim Qassem told me in July 2009. "The number of killed Hezbollah fighters and their individual status within the organization was not as important as the fact that the Israelis could say they had infiltrated into the depths of the resistance.

"They had a plan to do [IED] set-up operations in several places," Qassem added. "After Ansariyah, the whole project just collapsed."

"How Can One Man Have Five Legs?"

Not only was the Ansariyah ambush a military success, but Hezbollah also reaped a propaganda coup over Israel's mix-up of body parts belonging to the slain naval commandos.

In July 1998, after months of negotiations brokered by a German intelligence officer, a deal was concluded in which Ilya's remains were exchanged for the bodies of forty resistance fighters and sixty Lebanese detainees. Among the freed prisoners was Ramzi Nohra. The wily double agent returned to Ibl es-Saqi for a few days before being dragged from his home by SLA intelligence agents and expelled from the occupation zone.

Sergeant Ilya's remains were conveyed to Israel via the International Committee for the Red Cross, and here the story could have ended. But Hezbollah had another trick up its sleeve.

Questions were posed on its website, addressed to the Israeli public. The first queried the findings of the two Israeli inquiries into the Ansariyah debacle. Hezbollah's teasing questions about how the group could have known the commandos were coming led to public pressure on the Israeli government to convene a third commission of inquiry. Then Hezbollah raised questions about the body parts it had returned to Israel. Hezbollah had always said that the remains included body parts from two soldiers apart from Ilya, adding that they had DNA evidence. But the Israeli authorities had kept that gruesome fact quiet, creating the impression to the Israeli public and the grieving relatives of the dead commandos that the only missing soldier from Ansariyah was Ilya and that the other eleven soldiers had been buried intact.

Hezbollah then posted on the website grisly photographs of the body parts, which included five feet. "How can one man have five legs?" taunted the caption. "Your army is concealing the facts. They not only disrespect your sons when they are alive by sending them to certain death, they also disrespect them after they are dead. The bodies of your sons are incomplete and mixed up with pieces of others."

The propaganda ploy sparked an uproar in Israel, as a deeply embarrassed IDF was forced to admit that it had opened up the graves of two soldiers killed at Ansariyah to add the new body parts recovered in the swap.

Suddenly, families of the dead soldiers were demanding autopsies and DNA tests to check that the remains in the graves were really their relatives and not a mishmash of different bodies.

The Ansariyah episode encapsulated Hezbollah's increasingly multidimensional and skillful approach to the conflict with Israel. Through a combination of resourceful intelligence work, battlefield prowess, and deft propaganda, Hezbollah had produced a highly effective result that forced Israel to readjust its tactics once more. Although Israel continued to employ special forces units inside the zone and along its edges until its troop withdrawal in 2000, the Ansariyah raid was the last deep-penetration operation into Lebanon.

Ending "the Myth of the Merkava"

The fall of 1997 was a miserable period for the Israelis in south Lebanon. Even apparent achievements fell flat. On September 12, exactly one week after Ansariyah, Hadi Nasrallah, the eighteen-year-old eldest son of the Hezbollah leader, was killed along with two comrades in a clash with an Egoz unit on the edge of the zone. His corpse was recovered from the field and brought to Israeli headquarters in Marjayoun, where local reporters filmed it lying in a corridor as grinning SLA militiamen stood by.

But the outpouring of public sympathy in Lebanon for Nasrallah boosted his credibility even further. Rafik Hariri, who had also lost a son, was deeply moved by Hadi Nasrallah's death. "Rafik Hariri used to tell me that all the political leaders in Lebanon usually provide their kids nice cars, send them to the best universities, and prepare them to inherit their political roles. And only Hassan Nasrallah sends his son to be a martyr. He said he had never met anyone like that before. 'Nasrallah is a man I can trust,' he used to say," recalls Mustafa Nasr, Hariri's interlocutor with Hezbollah.

Nasrallah refused to accept condolences, instead telling supporters to congratulate him on Hadi's "martyrdom." At a ceremony a week later, Nasrallah announced that Hezbollah was forming a new resistance unit, the Saraya Muqawama al-Lubnaniyya, or Lebanese Resistance Brigades, open to all volunteers regardless of religion. The unit was a response to the number of Lebanese clamoring to join the resistance, Nasrallah said. The new recruits would be trained and guided by regular Hezbollah cadres, he added, after which they would carry out operations against the Israelis in the south. Phone numbers were printed in Lebanese newspapers that hopeful recruits could call for instructions on how to join.

To demonstrate that it remained unbowed by Hadi Nasrallah's death, Hezbollah upped the tempo in the following week. On September 14, a pair of Israeli soldiers were killed by a large roadside bomb, and four days later, Hezbollah launched a simultaneous multipronged dawn attack against twenty-five Israeli and SLA outposts stretching the length of the occupation zone. The assault, involving almost two hundred fighters, began at 7:00 A.M. precisely when Hezbollah mortar and rocket batteries opened fire toward Israeli and SLA positions stretching from the Mediterranean to the hills west of Mount Hermon. As the fighting raged along the front line, a fighter squinted through the rubber-lined optic sight of an AT-4 Spigot antitank missile, an improved version of the AT-3 Sagger, and took careful aim at the rectangular lines of a Merkava Mark 2 tank nestled near an Israeli outpost in Rihan village. On firing, the missile streaked toward its target while the operator kept the sight aimed steadily at the side of the tank. The wire-guided missile slammed into the side of the Merkava, the shaped-charge warhead burning through the armor plating and spraying its molten copper plasma jet inside, killing the tank's commander.

It was the first time that Hezbollah had successfully penetrated the armor of a Merkava tank with an antitank missile. The Merkava's Israeli manufacturers marketed the tank as the safest in the world, thanks to a dense layer of reactive armor designed to explode antitank warheads before the missiles could reach the steel skin. Hezbollah's newfound ability to blast missiles through the tank's armor sent the Merkava's designers hurrying back to the drawing board to check for the "weak point" that Nasrallah boasted his fighters had found.

The destruction of the Merkava was the result of a steady improvement in Hezbollah's antitank skills. Hezbollah received the Spigot missile from Iran in 1995. Although the warhead was smaller than that of the AT-3, its velocity was greater, and, crucially, its guidance system allowed for much greater accuracy. The introduction of the AT-4 into south Lebanon forced the Israelis to improve the armor of some tanks and replace others with the top-of-the-line Merkava.

Hezbollah built a team specialized in antiarmor skills, sending them to training camps in Syria and Iran for intensive courses in which they improved their accuracy against life-sized mock-ups of Merkava tanks. They were taught to aim for the same point on a tank using two or more missiles in succession. The idea was to blast off the layers of reactive armor, exposing the steel skin to follow-up missiles. The technique was refined over the years as Hezbollah learned to "swarm" Israeli armored vehicles with missiles.

In the weeks that followed the fatal strike against the Merkava in Rihan in September, two more Merkava Mark 2 tanks were destroyed by Hezbollah's antitank missiles. "Our fighters transformed the Merkava tank into scrap metal. We know all the tank's secrets, and it is now an easy target," said Qawq, Hezbollah's southern commander, boasting that the resistance had "ended the myth of the Merkava."

The AT-4 Spigot was not the only second-generation antitank missile employed by Hezbollah. It was also using the U.S.-made TOW missile, which, ironically, had been delivered by Israel to Iran as part of the arms-for-hostages affair during the 1980s. The Iranians had transferred the TOWs to Hezbollah, and the missiles were now being returned to the Israelis on the battlefields of southern Lebanon.

The disabling attacks against the Merkavas in 1997 could not have been more ill-timed for Israel. The Israeli government was attempting to sell to Turkey a fleet of Merkava Mark 3s as part of a multi-billion-dollar arms deal. Although the tanks hit by Hezbollah were the earlier, Mark 2 version, the Mark 3, which had entered service in 1990, differed from its predecessor only in the size of engine, the caliber of the main gun, and the fire control system. Both tanks shared the same armor protection.[4]

Tiring of Lebanon

To compound Israel's misery in south Lebanon, Hezbollah's intelligence penetration of the SLA was reaping deadly rewards. In mid-October, Hezbollah fighters slipped into the zone and reached within a hundred yards of the border. There they detonated a roadside bomb against a convoy of three armor-plated Mercedes carrying senior IDF officers who were on their way to a meeting with SLA commanders at the militia's 70th battalion headquarters outside Markaba village. The ambush was followed by another attack in the same area against more Israeli officers in civilian cars, this time using a combination of roadside bombs, rocket-propelled grenades, and machine guns. Two Israelis were killed and six wounded in the attacks.

It was a well-planned ambush, but more worrying for the Israelis was that Hezbollah had clearly gained prior intelligence about the meeting between the Israeli and SLA officers. The Israelis were traveling in civilian cars, but the Hezbollah team was still able to identify them and knew what time they were crossing the border.

Lieutenant General Amnon Shahak, the IDF chief of staff, admitted a month later that the Israeli army had a "serious intelligence problem" in infiltrating Hezbollah. Senior IDF commanders became hunted figures as Hezbollah used intelligence gathered in the zone to trace their movements and plot attacks against them. "I became a very desirable target of the organization," recalls Colonel Noam Ben-Zvi, a brigade commander between 1996 and 2000 and the last commander of the western sector of the zone. "They followed me on my tours to SLA posts, also on trips to visit civilians. They tried to hit me with mortar fire to the posts I visited, roadside bombs that were waiting for me personally."

On one occasion, Israeli military intelligence learned of a specific assassination plot against Ben-Zvi being prepared by a Hezbollah operative who owned a metal workshop in Bint Jbeil. When Israeli troops raided the workshop, they found a photograph of Ben-Zvi that Hezbollah had grabbed from Israeli television footage. "Also, we found written instructions on how to do the preparations and the exact way to recognize me and my car," Ben-Zvi says.

Israel's hold on the occupation zone was unraveling. In the three-month period from August through October 1997, twenty-seven Israeli soldiers had been killed, more than the total for 1996. Hezbollah had learned how to destroy Israeli tanks and stage elaborate ambushes just yards from the border fence. Its intelligence-gathering capabilities had steadily improved. The morale of the SLA was sinking, and the militia was riddled with agents reporting to Hezbollah or Lebanese military intelligence.

The total of thirty-seven Israeli troop fatalities in south Lebanon in 1997 was the highest since 1985, but in strictly military terms it was easily sustainable, indeed negligible. But Hezbollah was acutely aware of Israel's sensitivity to casualties. "The more Israelis we kill the more disputes we'll be sowing among them," Sheikh Nabil Qawq crowed at the end of October.

Certainly, Hezbollah's successes were having an impact in Israel. The Israeli public was fast tiring of Lebanon. How much longer would they have to endure the deaths of their brothers, husbands, and sons in the dust and mud of south Lebanon? The Four Mothers group in Israel staged regular demonstrations outside the Israeli Ministry of Defense and distributed leaflets at road junctions to further their goal of ending Israel's involvement in Lebanon.

A poll in September, after the Ansariyah raid, found that 52 percent of Israelis now favored a troop pullout from south Lebanon, so long as it was accompanied by security guarantees. Even Ariel Sharon, the architect of the 1982 invasion of Lebanon and an advocate of expanding the zone to twenty-five miles from the border, now conceded that a unilateral withdrawal was an option for consideration.

But a military review in November found that the IDF had no choice but to remain in south Lebanon, pending a peace deal with Syria. Instead, troop numbers would be increased in the occupation zone, more aggressive tactics would be introduced, and armored vehicles and Israeli outposts would receive greater protection.

Yet the new tactics were little more than a holding action, an attempt to stave off the collapse of the zone while the politicians sought to find a means of exiting Lebanon with some reassurances for the postwithdrawal security of northern Israel.

A "Deluxe Laboratory Without Settlers"

The Israeli government could not commit to an unconditional withdrawal, despite the rising Israeli public discontent over the Lebanon imbroglio. A unilateral withdrawal from Lebanon would convey the impression of defeat, the idea that the IDF had been chased out by a band of Shia zealots, which would have unwelcome ramifications for Israel's policy of deterrence against the Palestinians and other Arab foes.

Brigadier General Erez Gerstein, who as head of the IDF's Lebanon Liaison Unit was the top Israeli commander in south Lebanon, was a strong supporter of a continued military presence in Lebanon and an outspoken critic of the peaceniks in Israel. "They are certainly a threat to [Israeli] soldiers," he fumed in the summer of 1998. "Firstly, by encouraging the local population to cooperate with Hezbollah, because we are on our way out of their territory, and secondly, by boosting the morale of the terrorists who feel this is a sign of the IDF's weakness."

The IDF's general staff, unwilling to abandon the occupation zone, encouraged the government to stand fast. But their reasons went beyond concern over a loss of prestige and a weakening of Israel's deterrence power. After all, for a relatively small price—in military terms at least—of an average of twenty soldiers killed each year, the army controlled what was in effect a free military training ground, a "deluxe laboratory without settlers," the Israeli *Haaretz* newspaper once wrote. What better place for the IDF to develop doctrine, test new weapons, provide combat experience to troops and aircrews, and subcontract a proxy militia to do the bulk of the frontline fighting while demanding and receiving a substantial slice of the annual government budget?

Furthermore, the conflict was conducted out of sight of the Israeli media—journalists were banned from the zone except under rare and controlled circumstances, allowing the military to manipulate the flow of information to the public. And new battlefield skills and tactics could be honed. Egoz, the Israeli army's elite antiguerrilla warfare unit, owed its existence to the conflict in south Lebanon. Hezbollah's ability to destroy Merkava tanks in 1997 with AT-4 and TOW antitank missiles helped shape the design of the Merkava Mark 4, the latest version, which entered service in 2002. As a consequence of that experience in south Lebanon in the 1990s, the Merkava Mark 4, one of the most heavily armored tanks in the world, coped remarkably well against Hezbollah's third-generation antitank missiles in its first proper combat action during the July 2006 war.

Artillery crews used south Lebanon as a firing range beyond the requirements of combating Hezbollah attacks. Outdated stocks of ammunition were routinely fired into south Lebanon, according to senior UNIFIL officers, a more cost effective means of disposing of old ammunition than transporting it to the Negev desert in southern Israel for destruction.

"A Slap on the Face of the Zionists"

One spring morning in 1999, while I was driving through a small frontline village called Jabal Botm, the sudden roar of an Israeli F-16 swooping over the village and a tall column of smoke and dust blooming above a hill warned that yet another air raid was in progress. In the center of the village, a cluster of small stone and cement houses on a steep hill, a Hezbollah man in combat trousers and a black baseball cap held a walkie-talkie to his face and watched the raid. An old woman sat on a rug nearby, enjoying the morning sunshine as she sorted through a pile of freshly picked thyme and peppery arugula leaves. Hezbollah had shelled a nearby Israeli outpost about half an hour earlier, and the air raid was Israel's response.

The two jets, like flecks of silver, floated lazily across the sky in sweeping circles, taking turns to drop, nose first, into a graceful dive, release a bomb, and then rise again, leaving a trail of antimissile flares in their wake. The unperturbed Hezbollah man counted into his walkie-talkie each bomb dropped into the nearby wadi, while the old woman smiled contentedly as she picked through her herbs, completely ignoring the air raid. The measured pace of the bombing runs and the calm indifference of the woman and the Hezbollah man made the air raid seem soporific and banal.

Air combat patrols increased beginning in 1998, when Israeli troops spent more time hunkered down in newly hardened hilltop outposts. That year, Israel staged almost 150 air raids (compared to just 21 in 1990), but the vast bulk of them consisted of dropping aerial bombs into wadis vacated earlier by Hezbollah's "shoot and scoot" teams. "Crushing rocks" was the cynical term used by UNIFIL officers for these air strikes. But the combat air patrols speeded up the response time to Hezbollah attacks in the zone and also granted the crews useful experience, operating in a war scenario and flying over hostile territory.

Other than the routine combat patrols, the Israelis employed helicopter gunships for pinpoint strikes and assassinations and UAVs for reconnaissance and remote control IED detonation. The war in south Lebanon helped Israel become one of the world's leading pioneers in UAV technology, second only to the United States.

In October 1999, a pair of Cobra helicopters staged a missile strike against a house on the edge of Qabrikha, which overlooked the rolling grassland of the zone's central sector. I was in the village at the time, chatting with residents, when our conversation was interrupted by the sound of approaching helicopters. A loud explosion shook the village, then we saw two Cobras, painted in drab olive brown, emerge from a backdrop of dun-colored hills. Shedding antimissile flares in their wake, the helicopters wheeled and turned a few hundred yards east of the village before heading toward the low hills on the horizon that marked the border. Two cars, horns blaring, raced down the lane. In the backseat of the rear car, a man had his face buried in his hands. The explosion was caused by a missile fired from one of the helicopters that struck a half-built home of cinder block walls. A crowd had gathered in the center of the village: women with anxious faces, old men kneading worry beads. Grim-faced Hezbollah members cordoned off the targeted house while their comrades sifted through the rubble. Fragments of the missile lay scattered in the garden, some of the components still too hot to touch. A UAV, which had been circling the village all morning, continued to whine overhead, filming the aftermath of the helicopter strike.

In mid-August 1999, a UAV was employed to kill a senior Hezbollah military commander, one of Israel's most successful assassinations in Lebanon. Ali Deeb, also known as Khodr "Abu Hassan" Salameh, the same operative who had kidnapped four Russian diplomats in 1985, was the head of Hezbollah's special operations unit for south Lebanon in the late 1990s. Deeb was killed while driving his old BMW in a Sidon suburb when two bombs exploded beside his vehicle, detonated by a UAV overhead. Although the Israelis denied involvement in the assassination at the time, it was a significant intelligence coup to locate and kill a Hezbollah commander of such stature and experience.

The Israelis almost repeated that success six months later in a helicopter assassination attempt against Ibrahim Aql, a close aide to Imad Mughniyah and a top military commander. Four Apache helicopters sped across the zone and tailed a red Mercedes carrying Aql and one other person. One of the Apaches fired a missile at his car. It missed and struck an adjacent building. Alerted by the explosion, Aql leaped out of the car just before a second missile struck the vehicle. A third missile hit the road beside him but failed to explode. Aql jumped to his feet and ran into a building as the helicopters abandoned the attack and returned to Israel.

Aql was a top resistance leader, so his narrow escape received little comment from Hezbollah. But a similar incident a few days earlier was given the full propaganda treatment. A four-man Hezbollah squad had penetrated the zone's central sector and clashed with an SLA patrol near the village of Markaba. One of the Hezbollah men told his comrades he would provide covering fire for them to slip out of the zone. Now on his own, the fighter was spotted by an Israeli UAV, which tracked him as he ran past a house, across a field, and down a street in Markaba. He entered an empty house and moments later jumped out the back just before a helicopter fired a missile into the building. The UAV continued to track the lone fighter as he ran through more fields. An F-16, one of several jets circling overhead, fired a missile at the fighter, and there was a large explosion. It appeared to be a job well done, and in a rare move, the Israeli Air Force handed a copy of the UAV video footage to Israeli television stations. The previous day, three officers from the Paratroop Reconnaissance Battalion had been killed in a Hezbollah ambush. The release of the dramatic UAV tape appeared to be an attempt to show the Israeli public that despite setbacks, the IDF was also achieving successes in Lebanon.

But two days later, the star of the UAV tape showed up alive and only moderately wounded in a hospital in Sidon. He said that the missile fired by the F-16 had landed just feet away, and that he was struck by shrapnel and lost his hearing briefly. Once he recovered his senses, he continued running until he reached safe territory and reported back to his unit.

"What will they field next against the holy fighters?" crowed a commentary on Hezbollah radio. "They have tried electronic sensors, drones, infrared cameras, jets, helicopters. . . . What a slap on the face of the Zionists who aired this footage to give the impression of great success to their impotent army."

Crucially for a casualty-conscious Israel, despite the variety of aerial tactics used in Lebanon—air combat patrols, UAV surveillance, helicopter gunship assassinations—the risk of losing Israeli air crews to Hezbollah ground fire was almost nonexistent. Hezbollah's rudimentary air defense systems—23 mm and 57 mm cannons and shoulder-fired SAM-7 missiles—represented little threat to Israeli jets. Low-flying helicopters were more vulnerable to these weapons, especially when Hezbollah's antiaircraft guns began playing a more prominent role in 1998 in response to Israel's increased use of airpower in Lebanon. But the Israeli helicopter crews soon developed countermeasures against the menace of Hezbollah ground fire. UNIFIL peacekeepers reported witnessing on several occasions Israeli helicopter gunships deliberately hovering just out of range to draw Hezbollah fire while other helicopters attacked the antiaircraft positions at low level. No Israeli jets were downed over Lebanon in the 1990s, and only one helicopter, a Cobra, fell victim to ground fire when its tail rotor was struck and damaged by a 23 mm gun in June 1999 and it crash-landed inside the zone.

Given the relative safety of air combat missions and the enormous experience gained, it is small wonder that Israeli air commanders were loath to abandon the occupation zone. After the loss of the vast expanse of the Sinai peninsula following the peace treaty with Egypt in 1979, Lebanon became the main training ground for the air force and a "paradise" for its combat pilots, wrote Gal Luft, a former IDF battalion commander in south Lebanon.[5] "More: for over fifteen years, Israeli pilots gained the experience of launching pinpoint air strikes against real targets with live munitions. As a result, Israeli pilots have been among the most well-trained pilots in the world."

"Combat Proven"

Besides providing military training and combat experience, south Lebanon represented a free testing range for Israel's flourishing arms industry to try out new weapons and equipment. It came with the added bonus that new military gear could be marked as "combat proven," a valuable marketing asset and one that many competitors could not share.

"South Lebanon was a free laboratory," says Timur Goksel. "It was an arms manufacturing man's dream to have a laboratory like this one. The Israeli military industry always had an advantage over rivals because they could always claim that their weapons had been combat proven, from tanks to radio sets."

One of Israel's combat-proven weapons, thought to have been developed and tested in secret in south Lebanon, was the Spike-ER (Extended Range) antitank missile, designed by Israel's state-owned Rafael armaments company.

In early 1998, rumors began to surface in south Lebanon of the existence of a new "mini–cruise missile" that could dodge trees and skirt hills before hitting its target. The first recorded sighting of this mysterious missile was in late February, when Finnish UNIFIL peacekeepers saw a projectile fired from a hilltop Israeli position. The missile exploded beside a civilian car on the edge of a frontline village about five miles away.

In the middle of May, two identical missiles were fired from the same Israeli position at a squad of Amal fighters attempting to infiltrate the occupation zone. Finnish UNIFIL soldiers reported that the missiles sounded like a "jet plane" as they flew through the air. The first missile veered off course and exploded harmlessly. The second exploded beside the startled Amal fighters. "It came as a complete surprise to us," one of the Amal guerrillas later grumbled to me. "We were more angry at having been spotted than at being wounded."

Twelve days later, Hussein Moqalled, twenty, and his seventeen-year-old brother Mohammed were walking through a valley on the edge of the zone beside Arab Salim village when a missile flew up the length of the valley, swung toward them at the last moment, and exploded. Mohammed took the brunt of the blast and died instantly. His brother was badly burned on the back but survived.

In early July, a Norwegian UNIFIL soldier manning a checkpoint in the eastern sector of the zone saw a missile fired from an Israeli position. The missile left a long trail of white smoke, "had an unstable course and moved with a loud whizzing sound," according to an internal UNIFIL report. The missile crashed into a hillside. The Israeli army admitted to UNIFIL that the missile had gone out of control, and they instructed the peacekeepers to stay away from the crash site. Israeli troops later collected the vital components, leaving a few scraps of twisted metal for the curious peacekeepers to examine.

It was known at the time in arms industry circles that Rafael was developing a long-range antitank missile then code-named the NTD Dandy, or Long Spike, the daddy of a family of antitank missiles that included the short-range Gill and the medium-range Spike. Of the three, only the Gill had been declassified and supplied to Israeli troops deployed in south Lebanon. But the Gill's range was only a mile and a half, too short to have been responsible for the attacks and sightings in south Lebanon.

In early August 1998, after several months of investigation, I wrote a story for *The Daily Star* claiming that the mystery missile spotted in south Lebanon was almost certainly the NTD Dandy. It was against Lebanese law for *The Daily Star* to contact the Israel-based Rafael directly for comment, but a wire agency that picked up the story was told by a spokesman for the arms company that no such missile existed. The only antitank missile being manufactured by Rafael was the Gill, the spokesman said.

Yet it was public knowledge that Rafael had signed in October 1997—ten months before the *Daily Star* story—an $800 million contract with the Polish government to upgrade the Polish army's Huzar helicopters and fit them with NTD missiles. In other words, Rafael had sold to Poland a missile that the company's spokesman almost a year later denied even existed.

In November 1999, NTD Dandy was declassified and renamed Spike-ER, with a range of almost five miles, by which time it was thought responsible for the death of one Lebanese civilian and the wounding of at least four more. A year earlier, Rafael had formed the EuroSpike consortium with the German companies STN Atlas, Diehl, and Rheinmetall to produce, market, and sell the Spike family of antitank missiles to foreign governments. By 2011, EuroSpike had sold its missiles to numerous countries worldwide, including NATO members—the Netherlands, Poland, Italy, Spain, Romania, the Czech Republic, and Finland, the latter sale somewhat ironic, given that it was Finnish UNIFIL soldiers who first spotted the missile in south Lebanon more than a decade earlier.

"The Great Terrain Robbery"

Yet not all aspects of Israel's control of the south were as exploitative as training air crews or as sinister as test-firing secret missiles.

Early one morning in late October 1998, a Norwegian UNIFIL soldier chauffeured me to his battalion headquarters outside Ibl es-Saqi in the eastern sector of the occupation zone. As the UN jeep headed north out of the Lebanese border village of Kfar Kila, the driver gestured to the flat, fertile plain lying below us and asked, "Do you see those holes down there?"

One hundred yards north of the border fence separating Lebanon from the square red-roofed houses of Metulla, Israel's most northerly town, were several deep pits dug into the soft chocolate-colored soil. Bulldozers and trucks were parked nearby. "The Israelis are stealing the topsoil and taking it across the border," the driver said.

Seriously?

"Yes. They're building agricultural terraces. You can see them near the border. I'll show you on the way out."

On the return journey that afternoon, the Norwegian driver paused briefly to allow me to snap a couple of photographs of the excavation site. Minutes later, while driving up the hill beside the border south of Kfar Kila, he indicated a large, newly built terrace of familiar rich brown earth supporting rows of recently planted apple tree saplings. The terraces were inside Israel, just a hundred yards from the border fence.

UNIFIL headquarters said it was unaware of the theft of topsoil but would check. Phone calls to contacts living inside the occupation zone confirmed that the Israelis had been trucking soil across the border for two weeks.

The story was bereft of details, but a short article ran on the front page of *The Daily Star* the next day, accompanied by a photo of the excavation site. "The Israelis may not be able to stay in southern Lebanon forever, but it appears that they have decided to take part of it home with them," it began.

As expected, there was no reaction the next day to this mini-scoop. *The Daily Star* was not widely read in Lebanon, and a small tale of soil theft could easily pass unnoticed. The story clearly needed a little promotional shove. Jamil Mroue, *The Daily Star*'s publisher, was consulted, and he agreed that the paper should approach Nabih Berri, the parliamentary speaker, with an offer to write a letter on his behalf protesting the theft of the topsoil. The letter could then be sent to the Beirut embassies of the five permanent members of the UN Security Council, the European Union, and the Arab League. Once Berri's permission had been secured by *The Daily Star*'s parliamentary correspondent, we wrote, in his name, a communiqué denouncing Israel's "appallingly cynical policy" of stealing Lebanese soil.

A copy was printed and duly dispatched to Berri's office, where it was translated into Arabic and in turn delivered to the top embassies in Beirut and circulated to the Lebanese media.

With the release of Berri's statement, the story quickly gained momentum. The energetic Lebanese media, sniffing a good yarn, gave it extensive coverage, in some cases exaggerating the scale of the theft as well as misidentifying the location. Lebanese MPs showered the press with condemnatory statements, calls for international pressure against Israel, and increased resistance operations.

Not to be outdone by Berri, Fares Boueiz, the foreign minister, issued his own letter of complaint to the UN and the European Union, warning that the soil theft threatened an "ecological disaster."

By now the Israeli media was picking up on this bizarre story, spurring a denial from Uri Lubrani, Israel's Lebanon coordinator. "I wonder where all that came from," he said. "We are used to such accusations as Israel bringing the Litani River to Lake Kinneret [the Sea of Galilee]. Now it is soil. Tomorrow they will say we are stealing their air."

But ten days after the original story broke, UNIFIL confirmed that Israeli civilians were indeed excavating and trucking Lebanese soil across the border to build agricultural terraces. Lebanese officials hollered in triumphant vindication, while Israeli officials backpedaled furiously. Tzvi Mazel, the Israeli ambassador to Cairo, cornered by Egyptian journalists, said in some desperation, "No, no, no, we don't take this accusation from Lebanon. But we discovered yesterday and the day before yesterday that there are private sector contractors who are working with the Lebanese and they take the soil, not fertile or anything, but soil for building purposes."

Of course, the Israeli army was aware of the theft, as the site was located in a clearly visible location in view of Israeli military positions on both sides of the border. Furthermore, the trucks carting the soil away had to pass through border gates manned by Israeli troops.

By now, the story had gone international: THE GREAT TERRAIN ROBBERY, quipped a headline in *The Economist.* With UNIFIL and the Israelis confirming the soil theft, the United States was stirred into action and asked Israel to halt the operation.

The soil was never returned. The excavation pits were left untouched—ponds in winter, dusty holes in summer—while two miles to the southwest, a small piece of Lebanon continues to provide a firm foundation for a flourishing apple orchard in northern Israel.

"It's Just Like the Real Thing"

Following the disastrous second half of 1997, Israeli troops spent more time in their hilltop compounds, which had been newly fortified with large quantities of reinforced concrete to protect against Hezbollah rocket and mortar barrages. Open areas within the compounds were roofed over, and soldiers were ordered to wear flak jackets and helmets at all times. All infantry troops preparing to deploy for duty in Lebanon were now required to pass a three-week course at a guerrilla warfare training school.

Yet the number of resistance attacks increased steadily, almost all of them by Hezbollah. In May 1998, 150 separate assaults were recorded, the highest tally in a single month since 1985. In November, the figure rose to 160, and the total for the year reached nearly 1,500, almost double the 855 attacks recorded in 1997.

Despite the soaring rate of attacks, the defensive measures undertaken by the Israelis helped to lower the rate of troop casualties. Twenty-three soldiers were killed in 1998 compared to 39 the previous year. However, SLA casualties nearly doubled, totaling 45 killed in action in 1998 compared to around 23 in 1997. The increase was due to the militia shouldering more of the frontline duties as their Israeli allies hunkered down in fortified compounds. In an attempt to stem the SLA's declining morale, the militiamen were given a pay raise of $75, bringing the basic salary to \$575 a month, while time on duty was cut from fifteen to twelve hours a month.

On March 14, 1998, the newly formed multifaith Lebanese Resistance Brigades, the Saraya, staged its first attack, six months after Nasrallah had announced that Hezbollah would create, train, and direct a new resistance force composed of Lebanese volunteers from all sects. The date for the Saraya's first operation—a few mortar rounds lobbed into three SLA outposts—commemorated the twentieth anniversary of Israel's first invasion of Lebanon. In the months that followed, the Saraya kept up a steady trickle of attacks, all of them long-range mortar bombardments. Skeptics questioned whether the attacks really were carried out by the multifaith volunteers or by Hezbollah's regulars, with the media department simply attributing credit to the Saraya.

Nasrallah responded to the speculation, saying that the group was new and its fighters relatively inexperienced. "I can't assign them operations deep in the occupied area. I will be risking their lives," he said. "Some say there are no martyrs for the Saraya. Am I supposed to send a group of fighters and get them killed just to say there are martyrs in the Saraya?"[6]

Perhaps in an attempt to scuttle such rumors, Hezbollah in November 1999 arranged a one-time press trip to a Saraya training session in the barren ochre-hued mountains east of Baalbek. Jolting up a dirt track in a minibus with the windows covered by tightly drawn black curtains, the reporters were dropped off in a rocky valley. A short walk deeper into the mountains revealed twenty-four Saraya fighters squatting on the ground. They were dressed in plain green combat uniforms and helmets, their faces smeared in thick green and black camouflage paint that made them all but unrecognizable.

Carefully observed by seasoned Hezbollah instructors wearing camouflage uniforms and forage caps, the fighters took turns obliterating cardboard targets at the end of a makeshift firing range with an assortment of small arms, including AK-47s and light machine guns. Others fired rocket-propelled grenades at targets farther up the hillside: a loud blast, a tiny ball of light flitting up the rocky slope, a puff of gray smoke marking the impact, and an instant later the report of the exploding warhead echoing from the surrounding crags.

Tires were set alight and the fighters ran through dense clouds of black smoke and crawled beneath barbed wire as instructors fired live rounds above their heads.

"We have people from all over Lebanon: Sunnis, Christians, Shias, Druze, even Armenians," said Mohammed, a burly veteran Hezbollah fighter accompanying the reporters.

One of the Saraya militants, whose ponytail dangled incongruously from beneath his helmet, said he was a twenty-three-year-old university student who had participated in ten operations. Asked his religion, he paused.

"I'm Lebanese," he said.

An even unlikelier figure was a forty-four-year-old Maronite surgeon who admitted that his family had no idea he spent weekends in south Lebanon fighting Israelis. "I tell them I'm going to France on business when I'm called up for service," he said.

The climax of the military display was a simulated ambush of an Israeli patrol. Four cardboard cutout figures were placed to one side of a track at the foot of a steep hill. Hezbollah men buried a roadside bomb beside the cardboard patrol while the Saraya fighters moved into position. To the rear, a pair of jeeps fitted with 106 mm recoilless rifles provided fire support.

When the order to attack was given, the IED exploded in a huge sheet of flame, the heat sweeping over us seventy yards away. As the din of the explosion died away, the fighters opened up with machine guns and RPGs, shredding the cardboard soldiers in seconds.

"It's just like the real thing," Mohammed beamed.

The fire support team behind us sent recoilless rifle rounds zipping across the wadi while the hills rumbled to the rhythmic staccato beat of the heavy machine guns.

"A Contest of Technology"

With the bulk of Israeli soldiers lying low in their fortified compounds, Hezbollah was able to penetrate deep into the zone more frequently to plant IEDs and stage ambushes. More worrying for the Israelis, it became evident by mid-1998 that Hezbollah had developed a new, more powerful roadside bomb incorporating a more sophisticated means of detonation.

For much of the 1990s, Hezbollah had relied on antipersonnel Claymore-style directional IEDs packed with steel ball bearings. But in 1998, Hezbollah introduced a new shaped-charge IED—an explosively formed projectile (EFP)—that could cut through the sides of armored vehicles like a knife through soft butter. The concept had been around for decades and had been exploited by the Provisional Irish Republican Army in Northern Ireland since the early 1970s. The EFP works on the same principle as an antitank warhead. The bomb consists of a tube packed with explosive with a concave metal (usually copper) plate fitted at one end. When the bomb is detonated, the explosive force turns the copper plate into a molten slug traveling at a speed of more than seven miles per second, which can punch through 120 mm of tank armor. The EFP is a direct-fire device—more like a missile than an area weapon like the Claymore—and can be detonated as far as two hundred yards from the targeted vehicle. Given the distances involved and the need for split-second timing, EFPs are usually fitted with passive infrared firing switches to achieve accurate detonation. When the target approaches the IED, the operator switches on the invisible infrared beam, similar to those found on elevator doors, by remote control or a command wire. The beam shoots across to a receptor on the other side of the path traveled by the targeted vehicle. When the beam is broken, the bomb explodes. The method allowed for a far more precise detonation than an operator watching the ambush site from a distance of three hundred or four hundred yards with his finger on a button. Hezbollah fitted the bombs inside their battle-proven fiberglass rocks filled with insulation foam, leaving holes for the infrared beam, and often planted them in stone walls or on cuttings at head height beside the road.

Hezbollah employed IEDs fitted with infrared firing switches in Jezzine in the summer of 1997. But the first use of antiarmor EFPs occurred in the latter half of 1998, when Hezbollah stepped up the number and variety of roadside bomb ambushes with lethal results.

On October 5, a convoy of Israeli Humvees and armored vehicles was ambushed in a double roadside bomb blast in the Druze town of Hasbaya. The blasts killed two soldiers and wounded six more. The Israeli media referred to the bombs as having been "hollow charge," the first indication that Hezbollah was using something new.

On November 16, seven soldiers from the Golani Brigade left their outpost on the border at Sheikh Abbad hill and wandered casually down the road toward a firing range for a routine testing of weapons. The Sheikh Abbad compound, distinctive because of its two tall red-and-white-striped radio masts, straddled the border and was deemed relatively safe. Certainly, the seven soldiers were not expecting trouble; they walked bunched together in a group, rather than in patrol formation with spacing between each person. They had reached some thirty-five yards from the front gate of the Sheikh Abbad compound when they were hit by a large roadside bomb packed with steel ball bearings. Three soldiers were killed and four wounded, the highest casualty toll in a single incident since Ansariyah more than a year earlier. The ambush was filmed by a Hezbollah combat cameraman, and the tape was whisked out of the zone and broadcast on Al-Manar television just a few hours later, before the Israelis had even notified the families of the dead soldiers. A subsequent Israeli military investigation found that the Golani unit in the Sheikh Abbad post had walked the same route on twenty consecutive occasions without varying the routine. Hezbollah had probably noticed the pattern and set the ambush accordingly, the investigation concluded. The bomb, although not a shaped-charge device, was thought to have been triggered by an infrared beam.

Yet how was it possible that Hezbollah fighters had reached within yards of the border and beside the entrance to one of the biggest Israeli outposts in south Lebanon to plant a large IED without being spotted? "It's not impossible, but it is complicated and demands a high level of training, and that is apparently what happened in this instance," said Brigadier General Erez Gerstein, the top Israeli commander in south Lebanon.

But it was not a fluke. On November 25, Hezbollah repeated the attack by detonating another large roadside bomb in almost exactly the same location as the previous ambush nine days earlier. This time, two soldiers were killed. More soldiers died the very next day from a double roadside bomb attack just four hundred yards from the border fence in the western sector of the zone. That ambush was a Hezbollah classic. The first bomb disabled two APCs without causing casualties, but the second bomb targeted the rescue force, killing two soldiers and wounding another two.

With seven soldiers dead in just ten days, Netanyahu cut short a visit to Europe to deal with the deterioration in south Lebanon. The mood in Israel was extremely tense, and the prospect of another air and artillery blitz on Lebanon was high. "The Israeli army came very close to launching a second Grapes of Wrath," Timur Goksel recalls.

But instead of another air and artillery blitz against south Lebanon, Israel mounted an air offensive of a different kind. For several days in early December 1998, Israeli jets streaked at low altitude above Beirut and other cities and towns, causing earsplitting sonic booms. But the muscle-flexing aerial sorties drew the scorn of the war-hardened Lebanese and were treated as evidence of Israel's impotence against Hezbollah's attacks. "The only way they found to deal with holy fighters is terrorize the people in hospitals and children in schools," Nasrallah jeered.

Roadside bombs accounted for roughly half of Israel's casualty figures in south Lebanon in the late 1990s; in 1998, 60 IED attacks claimed 16 of the IDF's 24 fatalities for the year.[7] Finding a means of detecting and neutralizing them was a priority. Following the Ansariyah ambush, Israel lobbied the five-nation group monitoring the April Understanding to have IEDs prohibited, a move that had little chance of succeeding. Hezbollah certainly was not going to abandon its most effective weapon.

Driving along the roads of the occupation zone became a nerve-racking experience for IDF commanders, who were forced to adopt shifting procedures to stay one step ahead of Hezbollah's bombs. "I traveled to a lot of the SLA posts and villages [and] it was very dangerous," recalls Colonel Noam Ben-Zvi, who served in south Lebanon as a brigade commander between 1996 and 2000. "We were in armored vehicles, usually Mercedes, that over the years, with the development of [roadside] charges, no longer protected the passengers. Fear accompanied us on all such tours.... We joked about the danger using black humor."

Various safety precautions were instituted, such as traveling at night, changing routines, and avoiding known or suspected ambush sites. IDF and SLA patrols learned literally to count the number of rocks on the sides of roads during daily foot patrols to see if any new "rocks" had materialized overnight. Israeli D-9 armored bulldozers routinely uprooted trees and scraped away vegetation and topsoil for a distance of twenty or thirty yards on either side of main roads to remove cover for Hezbollah's bombs and destroy any IEDs already in place. Remote control video cameras with long-range infrared sensors were placed beside outposts, along tracks and roads, and even in the rough terrain of wadis to trace potential Hezbollah infiltrators. But Hezbollah fighters were equipped with their own night vision goggles, and they sometimes wore camouflaged neoprene diving suits to mask their heat signature from Israeli thermal-imaging equipment. To infiltrate close to Israeli positions, the wet-suit-clad Hezbollah man would crawl on all fours with his equipment strapped to his chest, appearing on Israeli sensors as nothing more threatening than a wild boar rooting in the undergrowth.

By the end of 1999, the Israeli army was claiming that it and the SLA were discovering and neutralizing 90 percent of roadside bombs planted in the zone.

"Hezbollah is constantly trying to improve and increase the destructive powers of the devices," said Brigadier General Amos Malka, the head of Israeli Military Intelligence in November 1998. "There is a constant improvement on their part and an improvement in our countermeasures. There is a contest of technology and a contest of brain power."[8]

The threat of roadside bombs in early 1999 prompted the Israeli military to provide additional training to SLA militiamen so that they could replace Israeli soldiers manning the vulnerable frontline outposts. No wonder Hezbollah mocked the SLA as Israel's "sandbags." The IED threat also required IDF soldiers to serve especially lengthy tours in the zone without leave because of their vulnerability during troop rotations. Sometimes, troops were ferried in and out of the zone by helicopter at night. Some were even transported in civilian vans.

"Stop! The Border Is in Front of You"

In January 1999, the struggle between Hezbollah and Israel over the roadside bomb cast the spotlight on the small, isolated village of Arnoun, three miles east of Nabatiyah on the edge of the zone, where only 250 people continued to live, most of them elderly.

By a quirk of the zone's configuration, the eastern half of Arnoun was incorporated inside Israeli-controlled territory, while the western half fell into an uneasy no-man's-land where the Lebanese state had no jurisdiction. A rusty metal swing gate marked the boundary in the center of the village.

Dominating the village on a bluff to the east was Beaufort Castle, the Crusader-era fortress where a handful of PLO fighters had fought to the death during the 1982 invasion. The Israelis had bolstered Beaufort's crumbling, weed-encrusted walls with reinforced concrete bunkers, accommodation blocks, machine gun nests, and bomb shelters. Concrete T-walls and ragged sheets of camouflage netting lined the upper reaches of the road winding down the hill from the castle to the village, intended to hide Israeli patrols from Hezbollah's missiles and bomb ambushes.

The imposing castle garrisoned by army troops and the huddled village lying in its shadow conjured irresistible images of feudal eras past. On the grassy slopes below the castle walls, now stealthily traversed by Hezbollah fighters on bomb-laying missions, Salah Eddine, the great Muslim warrior, once bound and tortured Reynaud of Sidon in an unsuccessful attempt to persuade the Frankish occupants to surrender. The Templars had owned the castle for eight years in the thirteenth century before it was stormed and captured by the Mamluke Sultan Baibars. Ahmad Pasha al-Jazzar had destroyed much of Beaufort's upper fortifications when he seized it along with the other forts strung throughout south Lebanon during his bloody purges against the rebellious Shias of Jabal Amil in the late eighteenth century. What centuries of war and neglect left intact was largely destroyed by Israeli F-16 jets in 1982 before Israeli commandos wrested the castle from its Palestinian defenders. Where Crusader pennants and Islamic banners once adorned the castle ramparts, the blue and white Star of David flag now defiantly snapped in the breeze, an ineluctable reminder to the villagers below of the identity of their latest conqueror.

The rise and lethality of roadside bomb attacks in the Beaufort Castle area in 1998 led the Israelis and the SLA to impose harsher measures on the residents of Arnoun. On December 27, hours after Hezbollah fighters detonated a roadside bomb beneath the castle wall, Israeli troops demolished seven houses close to where the bomb was planted. Ten days later, the Israelis bulldozed sixteen uninhabited houses after another roadside bomb attack in the same location wounded an Israeli soldier, the first casualty of 1999. The Monitoring Group ruled that the house demolitions were a violation of the 1996 April Understanding, but the Israelis were past caring.

On February 17, Israeli and SLA forces marched into Arnoun and annexed the unoccupied half of the village into the zone. The few dozen residents awoke the next morning to find themselves separated from the rest of Lebanon by new barricades of bulldozed earth and coils of barbed wire. Dangling from the wire were yellow metal signs warning of land mines, helpfully inscribed in Arabic, English, and Hebrew. On the reverse side was a message written in Arabic: "Stop! The border is in front of you."

The IDF said that the measures in Arnoun were designed to "protect its residents" from attacks by Hezbollah. But it was the Israelis in Beaufort Castle that needed protecting from Hezbollah's roadside bombs, not the hapless residents.

"We don't want to live here any longer, not if the wire is going to stay in place. The whole village wants to leave now," said Khadija Khawaja, a forty-year-old mother, one of several residents who stood on that first morning in a disconsolate huddle behind the wire facing a crowd of reporters and relatives.

Over the following days, relatives and friends traveled to the edge of the barricaded village to exchange news and hurl bags of bananas, oranges, and flat unleavened bread to the residents. The Lebanese government wrung its hands and fired off volleys of formal, and futile, complaints to the Monitoring Group and the UN Security Council.

Nine days after Israel sealed off Arnoun, some thousand students from a Communist youth group were bused from Beirut to the outskirts of the village. They carried Lebanese flags and sang patriotic songs, observed from the other side of the fence by a handful of anxious residents. As the crowd grew more boisterous, some of them began tugging at the metal stakes tying down the barbed wire. By now it was well known that the yellow land mine warning signs attached to the wire barricades were fake—the Israelis had not planted any mines when they annexed the village. Someone produced some wire cutters, and with a roar of triumph, the students pulled aside the severed barbed wire and surged into the village. The word quickly spread through mosque loudspeakers in nearby villages and radios and television. As hundreds of people converged on Arnoun, the astonished Israelis could do nothing but watch from the ramparts of Beaufort Castle. The swing gate in the center of the village was shoved open and the students began advancing along the road, past the recently demolished houses, up the hill toward the castle. The Israelis fired warning shots with a machine gun to keep the crowd at bay, but they were powerless to reverse this unexpected development.

That weekend, Arnoun turned into a circus with thousands of people flocking to celebrate the liberation of the village. Politicians, many of whom had probably never heard of Arnoun a month earlier, hurried to the village to bask in the glow of camera lights and to deliver banal statements.

The government quickly stepped in, bulldozing away the earth ramparts and barbed wire, asphalting a new road, mending the electricity cables, and digging trenches for water pipes. Prime Minister Salim Hoss also visited the village, promising that the government's facilities were at the disposal of this "dear part of Lebanon."

Suddenly, it seemed, everyone loved Arnoun.

Crowds of enthusiastic young men played a game of dare with the Israelis in Beaufort Castle, marching up the road to see how close they could get. The dare ended each time with the vicious whip-crack of bullets fired from Israeli machine guns over the heads of the protesters, prompting a swift retreat back to the center of the village.

Inevitably, after a day of baiting the Israelis in this fashion, a group of youngsters ignored the initial warning shots and continued their progress toward the castle; and, with equal inevitability, the Israeli soldiers, tiring of the sport, lowered their aim and shot and wounded a teenager.

The storming of Arnoun was not preplanned. But it was a stark demonstration of the power of mass action by unarmed civilians marching against troops whose weapons suddenly were rendered impotent. The lesson was not lost on the Israelis.

"Can you imagine what would happen if ten thousand [Lebanese] residents came and simply marched up to the Beaufort? What would we do? Shoot them?" asked an unidentified Israeli army officer of *Haaretz*. The officer noted that the Palestinian intifada a few years earlier had succeeded because of the mobilization of the masses. "As soon as the intifada is employed in the Lebanese context, we're going to have an even more difficult problem."[9]

The officer could not have known at the time just how prescient were his remarks. In a little over a year, a spontaneous march by a crowd of civilians would bring the occupation to a swift and surprising conclusion.

"Now We Are Finished"

In the days that followed the liberation of Arnoun, the crowds began to dwindle, and slowly a semblance of normality returned to the village. The Israelis had no intention of accepting the status quo, however.

After the SLA allegedly discovered six more IEDs inside an empty house on the still-occupied eastern half of the village, Israel issued a complaint to the Monitoring Group that Hezbollah was using "populated areas to launch terror operations." It was evident that Israel was preparing the ground for retaking the village.

The new sense of despondency pervading Arnoun matched the bleak weather one Sunday in late March as a cold wind moaned through the newly strung electric cables and icy rain spattered the pristine black asphalt roads laid in the wake of the village's liberation. Up the hill toward Beaufort Castle, Israeli engineers worked in the rain to erect more concrete T-walls along the exposed road. Nearby, bulldozers wheeled to and fro, building a new road to bypass the bomb alley in Arnoun.

A patrol of Israeli soldiers, backed by two armored personnel carriers, inched cautiously down the road from the castle toward the center of the village, each soldier separated from his neighbor by several yards. A bomb-sniffing dog and his handler led the way while the other soldiers followed, moving with catlike stealth, rifles raised, their heads constantly turning, eyes sweeping the sides of the road. Hussein Marouni, an elderly man hunched over a brazier of burning twigs outside his stable, stiffened as the soldiers approached the swing gate just ten yards away, fearful that they might cross into "liberated" Arnoun. As the soldiers reached the gate, one of them squatted on his haunches and slowly aimed his rifle at us, blinking away the rain and squinting through his telescopic sight. After a few seconds, he rose to his feet, and without saying a word, the patrol slowly moved on until they disappeared into a dip in the road.

In early April, after a hiatus of two months, Hezbollah staged two roadside bomb ambushes along the Beaufort–Arnoun road in the space of one week. The second bomb, which killed a soldier, was placed just yards from the entrance to the castle. The next day, two more bombs were detonated against SLA militiamen patrolling near Beaufort.

Arnoun's short-lived freedom ended on the night of April 15. Israeli troops and armored vehicles moved into the village to seal it off once and for all with rows of coiled razor wire thirty yards deep. The road, which had been constructed and asphalted with such haste following Arnoun's liberation six weeks earlier, was destroyed. At least two trenches three feet deep were dug across the road, severing the newly installed water pipes.

Guarding access to Arnoun was a new outpost of bulldozed earth rammed up against the first house in the village. From behind the earth ramparts the silhouettes of Israeli soldiers were clearly visible against the rising sun the following morning. Some individuals abandoned the village, walking along a narrow dirt path through the coils of razor wire, carrying suitcases or bundles of clothing tied up with belts or cord. Among them was Saed Alawiyah, who claimed to be a hundred years old. Bent double with age and helped along by his wife, Kemli, the frail couple struggled across the uneven path before being defeated by one of the trenches. The pathetic sight of the old man feebly trying to climb out of the trench stirred one reporter to raise his hands in the air for the benefit of the watching soldiers and walk forward to help.

In a tremulous voice, Alawiyah said, "We built Arnoun, we have always lived here, but now we are finished."

Using a bullhorn, a soldier told the throng of reporters, in Arabic, to leave the area, and a handful of smoke grenades were hurled across the barricades to encourage our departure. But the billowing clouds of white smoke proved an attractive sight to capture on film and failed to disperse the journalists.

"Go to your cars. Get out now," the soldier yelled. Rifle shots rang out and we ran for cover as bullets cracked past us, striking cars and flicking the dust on the road. Qassem Dergham, a sound engineer for Abu Dhabi television and a veteran of Lebanon's wars, was hit in the back—fortunately, by a plastic bullet rather than a live round, and he was not seriously hurt.

The SLA warned that anyone approaching the village from then on would be shot. But if the Israelis hoped that seizing Arnoun would ease the pressure on Beaufort, they were mistaken. Over the following month, Hezbollah concentrated its efforts on the castle, finding little difficulty in penetrating the new defenses around Arnoun to plant further roadside bombs. On May 4, three Israeli soldiers were wounded when Hezbollah mortar teams dropped rounds with impressive accuracy right on top of the Israeli fortifications inside the castle.

"It's All a Matter of Luck"

The highlight of Hezbollah's roadside bomb campaign came at the end of February 1999. Brigadier General Erez Gerstein, the top Israeli commander in Lebanon, had driven to Shebaa on the eastern tip of the occupation zone to pay condolences to the family of a local SLA intelligence chief murdered two months earlier in a dispute over the sharing of proceeds in the lucrative cross-border smuggling trade into Syria, which lay a short donkey ride over the mountain passes of Mount Hermon northeast of the village. Shortly before midday, Gerstein left Shebaa in his armor-plated Mercedes, accompanied by three other civilian vehicles. Traveling with the general in his car were two soldiers and a reporter from Israel Radio.

The convoy had just passed an Indian UNIFIL position near the village of Kawkaba when the Mercedes carrying Gerstein broke an infrared beam and detonated a shaped-charge IED that blasted the vehicle off the road, sending it tumbling down the side of a valley in a ball of fire. The car was completely destroyed and all four occupants killed. A second bomb exploded twenty-five minutes later against an SLA vehicle, wounding two militiamen.

This was the second attempt by Hezbollah to kill Gerstein, and it was planned well in advance. The bombs had been planted a month earlier by a Hezbollah Special Forces team that infiltrated the zone from the north and crept through the rugged hills near Kawkaba to the stretch of road selected for the ambush. A second Hezbollah unit even slipped back into the zone after a couple of weeks to exchange the battery on the main IED for a fully charged replacement. But the batteries on three other IEDs were not replaced, an oversight that spared the Israelis further casualties in the minutes after Gerstein's Mercedes was blasted off the road.

In the days that followed, Israeli and SLA forces imposed a clampdown on neighboring villages, suspecting Hezbollah had inside assistance for the assassination. Although the culprits were never found, several Lebanese intelligence sources confirmed that the information on Gerstein's condolence trip to Shebaa was leaked to Syrian military intelligence by a network of agents under the control of Ramzi Nohra. After his expulsion from the zone in July 1998 following his release from prison in Israel, Ramzi had continued his clandestine activities from Beirut. His network covered much of the northern sector, the corridor running from his home village of Ibl es-Saqi to Jezzine at the northern tip of the zone.

Gerstein's assassination was a spectacular success for Hezbollah. He was the most senior Israeli commander to be assassinated in Lebanon since Israel's military involvement with its northern neighbor began in the mid-1970s. A few months before his death, Gerstein had been asked by a reporter if he believed that his armored Mercedes could withstand a roadside bomb attack. "It's all a matter of luck," Gerstein had replied.

Sheikh Nabil Qawq would later tell me that Gerstein's killing ranked alongside the 1997 Ansariyah ambush and Ahmad Qassir's suicide bombing of the Israeli headquarters in Tyre in 1982 as the top three operations carried out by Hezbollah during the years of occupation.

The loss of the IDF's top commander in Lebanon had a profound impact on Israeli public opinion. This was not a junior-ranking soldier serving in dangerous frontline positions or on ambush duty in Wadi Salouqi. Gerstein was the tough, no-nonsense combat commander who believed in the value of the "security zone" and viewed Hezbollah as "third-rate terrorists."[10] His death underlined the stark fact that no Israeli soldier in south Lebanon was immune to Hezbollah's bombs and missiles, that the Shia group seemingly could pick off whomever it wanted whenever it wanted.

"Reality has thrown us a slap in the face. Of all people, Erez was a guy who was wholeheartedly in favor of staying in Lebanon and taking a tough stance, a fellow who always belittled the Hezbollah," said an anonymous senior Israeli army officer in an extraordinary and frank monologue published by Israel's *Haaretz* newspaper, entitled "Time to Go."[11]

> The time has come to stop mincing words: we have no business staying in Lebanon. . . . Have you been to south Lebanon recently? Have you seen what kind of outposts we've built there in the last year? We are sitting in these huge armored fortresses, which of course invite enemy shelling, and we make convoys leading to them into easy targets. Little by little we're becoming Crusaders who primarily guard only ourselves.

Ehud Barak, then the leader of the opposition Labor Party, sensed the declining public support for continued Israeli involvement in Lebanon and announced the day after Gerstein was killed that if he won the elections that May, he would "bring the boys home" from Lebanon within a year.

"A Strategic Weapon in Lebanese Hands"

While Hezbollah's roadside bombs provided the main tactical challenge to Israeli troops and SLA militiamen in the zone in the late 1990s, the Netanyahu government found itself confounded by the strategic threat posed by the Katyusha rocket.

Since the Grapes of Wrath operation, Hezbollah had further refined its Katyusha tactic. When Israel or the SLA caused an insufficient number of Lebanese civilian casualties to warrant a full-scale cross-border rocket attack, Hezbollah would send a "limited" warning by pounding IDF positions straddling the border, allowing a few stray rounds to fly over the frontier to explode harmlessly in Israel.

One August morning in 1998, two Israeli Apache helicopter gunships killed Hussam Amine, a longtime Amal member who served on Nabih Berri's bodyguard detail. Amine was driving along a lane through orange orchards near the coast south of Tyre when the helicopters struck. The first missile missed Amine's blue Mercedes and burrowed deep into the sun-softened asphalt of the road before exploding. The second hit the vehicle, knocking it off the road and blowing Amine to pieces. Thick gouts of blood pooled on the seats of the fire-blackened car. Strips of red meat hung like grotesque fruit from the branches of an orange tree as youngsters scampered through the undergrowth retrieving wreckage from the car and the scattered remains of the dead Amal man.

That evening, Hezbollah fired forty-seven Katyusha rockets into northern Israel, slightly wounding seventeen civilians. The gut instinct of the Israeli government and army was to lash back at Hezbollah to avenge the rocket attack as well as the deaths of three Israeli soldiers in separate attacks that week. But the Israeli government knew that a retaliation in Lebanon risked triggering more Katyusha rocket salvos. The dilemma facing the Israelis was that Hezbollah's rocket barrage had nothing to do with Amine's death. While the Apache helicopters were firing missiles at Amine's car, Hezbollah guerrillas farther north killed an SLA militiaman in the Jezzine district. The SLA retaliated by shelling Mashghara, a mixed Christian and Shia village adjacent to the Jezzine enclave, wounding six civilians, setting a car on fire, and damaging houses. Hezbollah had cautioned just two days earlier that the rate of Lebanese civilian casualties was increasing and that it could force a Katyusha rocket response against Israel. Hezbollah fulfilled its warning and rocketed Israel, and the Israeli government, tacitly acknowledging that Hezbollah had played within the rules of the game, was stuck for a counterresponse.

"In the past, anyone who launched rockets into Israel could count on a counterstrike by the Israel Defense Forces; nowadays, Hezbollah has the last word," wrote Zvi Barel, an Israeli commentator in *Haaretz*. "The primitive Katyusha rocket has become, in the Israeli-Lebanese arena, a strategic weapon in Lebanese hands."

"This Time We Will Respond"

The Netanyahu government found itself stuck, once again, for a retaliatory option when Hezbollah fired a volley of rockets into Israel four months later in response to the deaths of seven members of a family during an Israeli air strike against a Hezbollah radio antenna in the Bekaa Valley. Israel was at fault for the civilian deaths, and Hezbollah had retaliated according to the unwritten rules of the game.

Netanyahu, who had been criticized for not retaliating for the Katyusha attack the previous August, told reporters during a tour of rocket damage in Kiryat Shemona, "This time we will respond." But he didn't.

Two months later, on February 28, 1999, hours after General Gerstein was killed, Netanyahu, Major General Shaul Mofaz, the IDF chief of staff, and Moshe Arens, the defense minister, stood before the television cameras and announced the launch of a new offensive against Hezbollah. The Israelis were understandably incensed over Gerstein's assassination as well as the deaths five days earlier of three officers, including a major, when a unit from the Paratroop Reconnaissance Battalion stumbled into a Hezbollah ambush. But the roadside bomb attack against Gerstein and the ambush against the paratroops fell within the April Understanding and could not be used to justify a punishing counterstrike. So the Israeli government seized upon a pair of Katyusha rockets fired across the border hours before Gerstein was killed as the excuse for launching the offensive, even though Hezbollah had denied firing any rockets and UNIFIL said it had seen nothing. As Israeli jets flew up the Bekaa Valley to bomb a building near Baalbek as well as other targets along the edges of the zone, a stern-faced Mofaz told reporters assembled in the ministry of defense, "The offensive action will continue also on the ground, from the air and the sea. The army will fight Hezbollah."

In an apparent gesture of Israeli resolve, a convoy of armored personnel carriers and self-propelled artillery guns drove through the streets of Kiryat Shemona, slowly enough to be filmed by eager television crews, conveying the impression that the Israeli army was preparing to smash Hezbollah.

UNIFIL went on red alert, anticipating another Grapes of Wrath operation. Civilians in northern Israel hurried into their air-conditioned underground bomb shelters and civilians in southern Lebanon closed their front doors, lit cigarettes, and awaited Israel's latest punishment.

But after the initial half dozen air raids that night, nothing more happened.

As I stood the next morning on the rooftop ramparts of the Crusader castle in Tibnine with its panoramic views over the hills and ridges of the western and central sectors of the zone, nothing stirred. Not a bullet, shell, or bomb interrupted the pastoral calm.

Netanyahu's fist-shaking threats and vows of retaliation were becoming King Lear–like in their emptiness. Israeli columnist Alex Fishman cuttingly wrote of the one-night offensive, "It wasn't a lion that roared. It was a mouse crying before it wriggled back into its hole."[12]

The beleaguered Israeli prime minister was loath to undertake any action that risked more rockets on northern Israel and more unfavorable press headlines. He was fighting a tough electoral battle against

Ehud Barak, whose pledge to pull the troops out of Lebanon within a year of taking office had won broad public support.

Barak subsequently trounced his Likud rival in the general election in mid-May 1999. He had won a broad mandate to pursue peace with Syria, but the clock was ticking. He had promised the electorate that Israel would be out of Lebanon within a year. But the collapsing morale of the SLA militia in the Jezzine salient at the northern tip of the zone suggested that a major reconfiguration of the occupation zone was imminent and would not await diplomatic developments between Israel and Syria.

"The Lebanese Valley of the Dead"

This is one war we have lost. If we are fated to leave anyway—
let's do it now.

—YOEL MARCUS,
Haaretz, *February 11, 2000*

JUNE 1, 1999

JEZZINE, south Lebanon—The thunderclap of an explosion burst along the broad main street and echoed off the steep limestone mountains that flanked the town. A column of black smoke coiled swiftly into the air from behind pale gray stone houses on the northern edge of Jezzine, just around the corner from where we were chatting with a group of SLA militiamen. Hezbollah fighters hidden in the rocky slopes of Niha Mountain, which towered over Jezzine to the east, had detonated a roadside bomb. Militiamen in the stark gray cinder block fortress that housed the SLA's Jezzine battalion headquarters opened fire with heavy machine guns, raking the imposing slopes of the adjacent mountains in a hopeless attempt to hit the perpetrators of the bombing. Hezbollah mortar rounds pummeled an SLA outpost on a hill to the southwest of the town, each round sending up blossoms of yellow dust and gray smoke.

The roadside bomb had targeted a car driven by one of the SLA militiamen deployed at the checkpoint at the northern entrance of the town. The blast killed the militiaman and knocked his car off the road onto the roof of a house in the valley below. Hezbollah had apparently earmarked the militiaman for assassination. A subsequent videotape of the bomb attack broadcast on Al-Manar showed a civilian car passing the hidden bomb. The audio just caught the faint voice of a Hezbollah man saying "No, no, no," telling a colleague that it was not the correct target. Moments later the hapless militiaman's vehicle came into view and then disappeared in a puff of gray smoke as the bomb exploded.

"Are you coming?" a Lebanese reporter called to me, holding the door of his car open as other journalists crammed inside. I squeezed into the back and we tore down the road toward the scene of the bombing. But militiamen on the embankment above us fired their rifles in the air and yelled at us to go back. An M-113 armored personnel carrier clattered down the high street at high speed, swerving violently. A wild-eyed militiaman stood through the hatch and screamed at reporters not to take photographs. "*Mamnoua! Mamnoua!* (Forbidden! Forbidden!)" he yelled.

It was the second day of the SLA's pullout from the mountainous Jezzine salient, and it was not going well.

"Jesus, Save Me!"

The SLA battalion in Jezzine had all but lost control of the enclave in the first few months of 1999, and it was clear that the militia could not hold on for another year while Ehud Barak tentatively explored the diplomatic track with Syria. At the beginning of January, seventeen men abruptly announced they were quitting the militia and requested asylum from the Lebanese government. In February, Hezbollah staged an unprecedented assault on the headquarters of the SLA in the center of Jezzine, pinning down SLA reinforcements in nearby hilltop outposts with accurate mortar fire while destroying armored vehicles and buildings inside the compound.

Emile Nasr had been replaced as commander of the SLA's Jezzine battalion the previous August after he suffered a nervous breakdown brought on by the threat of assassination by Hezbollah. According to sources connected to Lebanese military intelligence as well as former SLA double agents, shortly before Nasr returned to his home village of Aishiyah, a few miles south of Jezzine, he brokered a deal through Ramzi Nohra in which he offered to provide intelligence from inside the zone in exchange for his life. The offer was accepted, and Nasr lived the last months of the occupation in peace. Nasr slipped out of the zone in May 2000, just days before the Israelis withdrew, and turned himself over to the Lebanese army.

Nasr's replacement, Joseph Karam, nicknamed "Alloush," was critically wounded in an IED ambush in April, the third to target the SLA commander since he took over the Jezzine battalion. His driver was killed, and Karam was flown to Israel for treatment.

The Israelis struggled to find a replacement for Karam, but no one wanted a job that was little more than a suicide mission. Mouna Touma, the brother of Maher who had assisted Ramzi Nohra in the abduction of Ahmad Hallaq, was appointed acting SLA commander pending a full-time replacement. According to former intelligence sources, Hezbollah had warned Maher Touma that it was about to begin targeting senior SLA commanders and he should tell his brother to quit the militia before it was too late. If he stayed, he could end up dead. But Mouna Touma did not heed the advice. Two weeks after the IED ambush that ended Karam's tenure in Jezzine, Touma was killed in another roadside bomb ambush staged in almost exactly the same location.

SLA militiamen from farther south were deployed to the salient to help reinforce the dwindling battalion, which now numbered fewer than two hundred militiamen, most of whom stayed at home and refused to travel along the bomb-lined roads. Armed Hezbollah fighters began roaming the district in broad daylight, twice setting up checkpoints on main roads and abducting militiamen. "Collaborators! Watch and learn what your fate will be if you don't repent," Al-Manar television said in a commentary accompanying one of the filmed abductions.

Two weeks after Touma's death, Antoine Lahd, the SLA chief, finally gave up. He informed the IDF that the situation in Jezzine was no longer tenable and that the militia would have to be withdrawn from the salient.

The pullout began on May 27 when families of SLA militiamen living in Jezzine packed their belongings into cars and drove south toward Marjayoun. Three days later, the SLA abandoned outposts to the west of Jezzine and pulled back to the mountain town. A convoy of T-55 tanks and armored personnel carriers transported militiamen and equipment from Jezzine along a winding mountain road toward the new frontline positions nearly six miles to the south. Hezbollah was waiting for them, however. An hour after the convoy departed, a series of flashes lit up the night sky to the south, followed seconds later by the thump of explosions as Hezbollah fighters, hidden in the hills flanking the road, detonated a string of IEDs. One militiaman was killed and another wounded in the attacks, which bogged down the retreat and left several bomb-damaged vehicles abandoned on the side of the road. A nervous militiaman in Jezzine fired a burst from his .50 caliber machine gun into the mountains to the east where Hezbollah had its hidden observation posts overlooking the town. A T-55 tank parked on the edge of the town fired a few shells into the hills, orange bubbles of flame from each exploding round pricking the blackness of the night.

The next morning, bored militiamen sat in the shade beside the high street waiting for the order to pull out. A T-55 tank, a towed artillery cannon, and two trucks laden with household goods were parked nearby. One teenage militiaman, called Manny, dressed in an olive-green Israeli uniform, said he had been forced to join the SLA only four months earlier. "I keep asking them if I can leave, but they won't let me," Manny said quietly so his comrades could not overhear.

Why didn't he simply defect?

"If they catch me they would put me in the trunk of the car and drive me to Khiam," he said, referring to the SLA-run prison.

Another veteran militiaman observed sourly, "We're leaving because the people don't want us here anymore. Many of them are collaborators with Hezbollah."

Another nodded in agreement. "You see someone in the street and you say 'hi.' He says 'hi' and then he goes around a corner and plants a bomb," he said.

In a newly abandoned SLA outpost in the Christian village of Roum, west of Jezzine, children collected ammunition boxes and brass cartridge cases as other residents wandered around the empty bunkers and offices. The outpost overlooked the coastal hills to the west all the way to Sidon and the silvery sun-speckled Mediterranean.

On a wall at the rear of the outpost, an SLA militiaman had written in English the heartfelt plea, "Jesus, save me!"

"The Fighting in Sojod Is a Good War"

That night, the SLA prepared to pull out of its last remaining positions in Jezzine and withdraw to the new front line just south of Kfar Houne village. The SLA expelled reporters from the town as they prepared for the southbound retreat. We congregated at Jezzine's western entrance, where an M-113 armored personnel carrier, painted pale green and covered in scratches and rust spots, blocked the road beneath the town's landmark statue of the Virgin Mary. The crew of the APC was tasked with bringing up the rear of the last SLA column to leave Jezzine that night. They knew there was a strong chance that they would be hit by roadside bombs on the journey.

"The worst thing that can happen to us is that we get killed," said Johnny, the thick-set and unshaven APC commander, with war-weary bravado as he swigged from a bottle of whisky. Johnny and his comrade Nimr, a skinny militiaman with unkempt hair and a straggly beard, were both former Lebanese Forces militiamen and veterans of the civil war. They had joined the SLA in 1990 at the war's end and had served in frontline positions such as Sojod in the northern sector, one of Hezbollah's favorite targets.

"The fighting in Sojod is a good war," Johnny observed as he fed a belt of ammunition into his .50 caliber machine gun mounted on top of the APC. "Hezbollah come up the hill to us and we kill them. But here in Jezzine, they are like cats. We never see them."

Manny, the young SLA recruit who wanted to leave, was clearly unnerved at what Hezbollah might have in store for them in a few hours' time. He fiddled with the strap of his AK-47 rifle and tried to smile for the cameras. He personified the predicament facing many SLA militiamen: he wanted to quit, but feared the prospect of arrest and imprisonment by the Lebanese authorities or the wrath of the SLA if caught deserting. Staying in the militia, however, he risked injury or death in combat with Hezbollah and an uncertain future if, or when, Israel withdrew from Lebanon.

Just before 2:00 A.M., two Mercedes cars pulled up beside the checkpoint and Johnny was ordered to pull out. Nimr handed us tiny pictures of the Virgin Mary and Saint Charbel with short prayers inscribed on the back. Manny's face was frozen in a rictus of fear as he hauled himself through the rear hatch of the APC. Nimr followed him and gave us a brief, fleeting smile and wave before slamming the steel door.

A somber-looking Johnny politely shook our hands and thanked us for keeping him and his crew company that evening. The bluster and fiery rhetoric were gone, dampened by whisky and trepidation for the journey ahead.

"Our fate is now in the hands of God," he said quietly as he climbed in through the rooftop hatch of the APC. Taking a final slug of whisky and a deep drag on his cigarette, Johnny gunned the engine, and without a backward glance he steered the APC into the darkness of the road leading south from Jezzine.

After the SLA vehicles disappeared into the night, we waited quietly and listened for any sound of fighting that would indicate the militiamen had run into trouble. But the only explosions heard that night came from an abandoned SLA position on a hill above the town where the militia had dynamited the munitions they had chosen to leave behind.

"We were telling each other earlier that if God wills it, these will be the last explosions we will hear," said an elderly resident standing on the balcony of his home at the southern end of Jezzine as he watched the orange glow from the fires raging in the SLA outpost in the darkness above the town.

"The People Here Never Stop Worrying"

Johnny and his companions survived the retreat from Jezzine. I found him three weeks later in Marjayoun, sitting in the smoke-filled, sparsely furnished living room of a small stone house in the center of the town. He said they had discovered twelve roadside bombs and had been attacked with antitank missiles during the tense drive. "We were the last to leave Jezzine, but I was at the head of the column that entered Marjayoun the next day," he said proudly.

Jocelyne, his wife, sat quietly beside him nursing her baby. Her skin was gray and she looked very tired. On Johnny's biceps was a tattoo of a skull smoking a pipe with a dagger rammed through it. "It's a dead man smoking hashish," he said with a grin.

Manny, I learned, had been sent by the SLA on a medical course which would keep him away from the frontline fighting. But the future for Johnny was much bleaker. He had fought with the Lebanese forces in the civil war and had been arrested and beaten by Syrian and Lebanese intelligence officers in 1990 when the conflict ended. He had no desire to live in a Lebanon dominated by Syria, but the idea of moving to Israel held little appeal, either. Johnny tried to remain cheerful, but it was clear that he knew the occupation was entering its final stages. "What can I do? I do as I'm told. I will carry on driving my tank," he said, referring to his APC. "That's all I know and all I can do."

It was impossible to disguise the mood of apprehension and uncertainty within the ranks of the SLA. You could see it in the tired, cheerless demeanor of the militiamen on duty at checkpoints or in their tense expressions as they huddled over tiny cups of coffee at the cafés near the SLA headquarters in Marjayoun. Despite some confident bluster, the war was being lost in south Lebanon, and the SLA knew it.

"They long ago entered a tunnel that is now very hard to come out of," said Monsignor Antoine Hayek, the head of the Greek Catholic community in Marjayoun, sitting in the cool splendor of his residence beside the Church of Saint Peter. Pictures of Hayek with Pope John Paul II vied for space on the walls with oil-painted triptychs of the

Virgin Mary. We walked out onto a balcony overlooking the neighboring church. The dying sun warmed the pastel yellow paint of the church's dome. The square red-tiled roofs of Marjayoun's traditional stone houses spilled down the hillside below us. Far to the east, the distant foothills of Mount Hermon turned golden in the evening light.

"You know, there's no real joy of life in the area," Hayek said, gazing at the view. "We celebrate holidays and feasts, but there's always firing going on. The people here never stop worrying."

Israel's occupation zone was a claustrophobic world of oppression, fear, and paranoia. The daily bouts of violence and the privations of occupation—a mix of arbitrary arrests, restricted movements, routine shelling, and the dreadful uncertainty of roadside bombs—fostered feelings of impotence and despair. Suspected as collaborators by a largely unsympathetic Lebanese government, and treated by the Israeli occupiers as pawns whose welfare was subordinate to the security interests of the Jewish state, no one living here, whether a Shia farmer in a hardscrabble frontline village or a Christian SLA officer from relatively prosperous Marjayoun, could escape the unremitting anxiety and sense of isolation that pervaded the zone.

From the winding road heading out of the coastal village of Naqoura, the location of UNIFIL's headquarters, up into the low stony hills of the occupied border district, the tall buildings of Tyre could be seen a dozen miles to the north crowding the city's peninsula jutting into the shimmering blue Mediterranean. Tyre lay beyond the volatile frontline districts. Its easygoing inhabitants could be lying on the sandy beaches, eating fried fish washed down with icy cold bottles of local Almaza beer, the fishermen in the port mending torn nets or playing backgammon in the shade of a quayside café. But the border road east from Naqoura took one far from such languid pleasures. Gazing at the far-off serenity of Tyre was like looking through the bars of a bleak prison cell at distant green meadows and a blue sky, comforting in its familiarity and beautiful to behold, yet beyond reach.

"This Is the Road to Vietnam"

To witness the real misery of the zone, one had to visit the handful of Shia villages that had the misfortune to lie on the front line—places like At-Tiri, where around eighty aging residents clung to their homes, having nowhere else to go. There were no cars in At-Tiri and no telephones. Transport was provided by one taxi, which every Thursday braved the IED-laced road to ferry three or four passengers at a time to the market in Bint Jbeil. Many of the houses were destroyed in the 1978 invasion two decades earlier, the shattered walls, rusted reinforcing rods, and weed-ridden interiors emblematic of past violence and current neglect. No children had lived in At-Tiri since 1985. But there was the incongruous spectacle of a pristine school building, its classrooms filled with neat rows of wooden desks and chairs and spotless blackboards. The village school was given an overhaul in 1994 in a brief optimistic expectation of an imminent Middle East peace. The peace never came, of course, and so the children never returned, and the plate glass windows lining one side of the building were gradually shot out by bored militiamen in nearby compounds.

A wizened seventy-year-old woman engulfed in a voluminous black shawl opened a door leading into a gloomy room furnished with a few tatty armchairs. Several pigeons exploded out through a broken window as we entered, and the room smelled of their droppings. She rocked slowly back and forth in an armchair and spoke in a thin, tremulous voice of her health problems and of her children, who lived in Beirut. She grew wistful when describing At-Tiri before the Israelis came. "It was the most beautiful village," she says. "There were many people here. You could sit outside all day in front of your house and just watch people pass by."

The small, disheveled village of Rihan, tucked into mountains north of the Litani River, had the misfortune of hosting two compounds in the center of the village, one for the IDF and the other for the SLA.

When I visited Rihan in June 1999, dusk was descending upon south Lebanon. The Israelis had built a new road connecting the headquarters in Marjayoun to the northern sector on the other side of the Litani. The

Antoine Lahd Bridge, named after the SLA commander, crossed the shallow waters of the river, and the Israeli road climbed into the steep pine-forested hills and jagged mountain peaks of the zone's northern sector. It was here that one gained a very real sense of driving into a war zone. The fingerlike salient was flanked by steep mountains to the east and west where Hezbollah fighters had hidden bases and observation positions and from where they infiltrated the enclave to ambush IDF troops or attack SLA compounds. The sides of the road were stripped bare of all vegetation for at least sixty feet to prevent the planting of bombs. There were no other vehicles on the road, no houses, and no people to be seen.

At the old farmstead of Jarmaq, where the SLA had an outpost, suspicious militiamen trained their heavy machine guns on our car as we passed by. Several gray-painted T-55 tanks and armored personnel carriers jammed the entrance of the position. The sleek lines of an IDF Merkava tank, all but hidden behind a wall of sandbags, flashed into view.

Each corner of this meandering mountain road had to be approached with caution. Dusk was when the Israelis drove their tanks to reach their nighttime positions. Concrete T-walls and camouflage netting flapping loosely in the evening breeze lined sections of the road to mask Israeli troop movements from prying eyes in the surrounding mountains.

By 1999, Rihan was the most northerly deployment of the IDF in south Lebanon. The road that ran through the village had been reduced to a rutted dirt track, churned by tank caterpillar treads into a muddy morass in winter and choking dust in summer.

A handful of old men sat in silence outside a store. An out-of-uniform militiaman leaning on the balcony of his house spoke into his walkie-talkie as we climbed out of the car. The evening tranquility was broken by the roar of a tank engine from inside the Israeli compound. Thick black exhaust smoke billowed above the ramparts as Israeli soldiers prepared the tank for its nighttime duty.

From the center of the village a narrow, potholed lane led southeast to Sojod, a small village that was totally destroyed in 1985. The outpost at Sojod, manned by the SLA and sometimes reinforced with IDF troops, was one of the most heavily hit compounds in the entire zone. "This is the road to Vietnam," a young Shia militiaman joked bleakly, indicating the lane to Sojod.

The militiaman said he had been press-ganged four years earlier, "and I'm still objecting." Small and wiry, with cropped hair and several days' stubble on his hollow cheeks, he had a weary, fatalistic disdain, all too aware that he stood a more than reasonable chance of being killed or wounded by his fellow Shias in Hezbollah. "It could be a roadside bomb or bullets. Who knows?" he said with a shrug.

A dust-coated Mercedes pulled up. Inside were two very fat, unsmiling men with AK-47 rifles cradled in their laps. Both wore tight-fitting grubby jeans and denim shirts and both wore their black hair long, greasy, and slicked back. They were like grotesque cartoon characters—Tweedledum and Tweedledee with guns.

The young militiaman with us shuffled his feet uncomfortably and backed away from the SLA security officers. One of them removed the cigarette from his mouth, examined the burning tip, and asked who we were and what we were doing in Rihan. His obese colleague stared at himself in the rearview mirror and smoothed back his hair with fingers the size of bratwursts, choked by several clunky gold rings. After a few minutes of questioning, the two men drove away.

It was getting dark, and Rihan was not a place in which to linger. As we departed, I noticed the young militiaman standing alone in the center of the dusty street, staring after us, on his face an expression of utter despair.

"Remaining Silent"

As summer turned into fall in 1999, the Israelis, Syrians, and Americans maneuvered and bargained behind the scenes in a preliminary diplomatic dance to hasten the resumption of peace talks. During this period of expectation, the most common question put to Hezbollah officials in interviews was what the party would do in the event of regional peace. The answer was always the same: a frustrating "wait and see." "We think

that remaining silent . . . and not talking in detail about our role following the settlement . . . gives Lebanon and Syria strength as they continue
on the tracks they believe in," Nasrallah said in July 1999.

In August, Bashar al-Assad, the son of the Syrian president, who was
being groomed to succeed his father, hinted in a newspaper interview
that Hezbollah would lay down its weapons once the Israeli occupation
of south Lebanon was ended. "When the causes that led to the resistance
are gone, I believe its members will go back to normal life and will
choose other ways to serve their country after achieving their long-
cherished victory," he said.

For many observers, that was the clearest expression yet of Hezbollah's
likely fate following a peace deal between Syria and Israel. There were
other teasing indications, too, that Syria might be planning for a future
of peace with Israel. They included reports that Damascus had advised
Hezbollah and pro-Syrian Palestinian groups that they should prepare
for disarming once peace had been achieved with Israel. There were reports that the Syrians were holding up Iranian arms shipments for
Hezbollah at Damascus airport. The Iranians, instead, reportedly began
airlifting arms directly to Hezbollah via Beirut airport, a move that must
have had the tacit approval of Syria, even as it was sending subtle messages to Israel that it could rein in the Lebanese group if Barak fulfilled
Syria's peace demands.

After all, if Syria won back the Golan Heights in its entirety and no
longer had a territorial grievance with Israel, Hezbollah's utility as a bargaining chip for Damascus was at an end. Clearly, the Israelis would not
agree to a peace deal with Syria in which all the Golan was returned unless it received ironclad guarantees that the Islamic Resistance would be
dismantled and the Lebanon-Israel border pacified.

Meanwhile, the IDF General Command were gritting their teeth at
the prospect of losing their fiefdom in south Lebanon, especially if Barak
ordered a unilateral withdrawal should the prospective negotiations
with Syria go nowhere. Not only would it bring Hezbollah to Israel's
northern border, it would also signal to the Palestinians and other Arab
enemies that the Jewish state would surrender to determined armed resistance. "This message will be a beacon to all the anti-peace forces in

the Arab world, especially Islamic fundamentalists," wrote Clinton Bailey, a former adviser at the Israeli foreign ministry.[1]

While some IDF commanders supported leaving Lebanon, others had difficulty hiding their bitterness toward those lobbying for a troop withdrawal, deducing that Israeli society had gone dangerously soft if it could no longer tolerate the deaths of soldiers defending the state. In early 2000, Colonel Shmuel Zakai, the commander of the Golani Brigade, referred to the "Four Mothers" as the "four worthless rags." He made the remark to a group of soldiers who were about to deploy into south Lebanon. Unfortunately for Zakai, the mothers of some of the soldiers were members of the Four Mothers, and his comment made it into the press, earning the colonel a rebuke from his superiors.

The "Unlikely" Seven Villages

The Lebanese government recognized that it played a secondary role to the Syrian-Israeli track in the pre-negotiations phase. Once Syria's demands were satisfied, then Damascus would allow Lebanon to press its own case in talks with Israel. So low was Lebanon's importance that even when President Clinton announced on December 8 that peace talks would begin the following week with a preliminary meeting in Washington between Ehud Barak and Syrian foreign minister Farouq al-Sharaa, Beirut was left in the dark.

"The prime minister saw the announcement on CNN like everyone else, and now he's gone to bed," an aide to Salim Hoss told me when I telephoned the prime minister's home for a reaction. Amid all the smiles, back-slapping, and congratulatory rhetoric, nobody, apparently, had thought to let the Lebanese know prior to the formal announcement that the Israeli-Syrian peace track had been revived.

A week earlier, Lebanon had presented its list of seven demands that would have to be met before peace could be agreed with Israel. Among them was the return of all Lebanese territory annexed by Israel, including the Seven Villages and the Shebaa Farms. The "Seven Villages" referred to a handful of villages populated by Shias that had ended up inside Palestine when the Lebanon-Palestine boundary was formally ratified in 1924, even though the residents had been handed Lebanese citizenship four years earlier. The Shias of the Seven Villages became Palestinian citizens and were expelled or fled their homes during the 1948 Arab-Israeli war, joining the Palestinian refugees streaming into Lebanon.

Lebanon's demand for the Seven Villages was clearly unacceptable to Israel, and it was hard to imagine that the Lebanese were serious about the claim. After all, it would effectively entail nonrecognition of the border between Lebanon and Israel, paving the way for the Jewish state to claim its own amendments to a frontier with which it had never been satisfied. If the path of the border was open to dispute, then UN Resolution 425—which called for an Israeli troop withdrawal to Lebanon's internationally recognized boundaries—would become meaningless.

Shortly after the Lebanese government issued its seven-point list, I contacted Salim Hoss to question him on the inconsistencies of the Seven Villages demand.

Hoss was a veteran politician and three-time former prime minister whose lugubrious composure and reputation for honesty stood at odds with some of his more flamboyant and less scrupulous colleagues. Yes, he agreed, "The villages were never part of Lebanon as they were incorporated into Palestine." Pressed further, Hoss said it was "unlikely" that the demand would remain on the list.

The Daily Star ran Hoss's comments on the front page of the next day's edition. That evening, on returning to the *Daily Star* office from south Lebanon, I was told by a flustered receptionist that Hoss had been trying to reach me all day. When I called the prime minister, he said in a tired voice that while the Seven Villages were not covered by Resolution 425, the claim was not being dropped from the government's list of demands after all, and would we please print a statement in *The Daily Star* to that effect. Someone whose ear was close to Syria, it seemed, had taken exception to the prime minister's unilateral amendment of the seven-point list and had advised him to retract.

Hezbollah reacted to the resumption of Israeli-Syrian peace talks by launching a simultaneous attack against twenty Israeli and SLA outposts. The coordinated assault, which included a Special Forces team storming the Sojod compound in the northern sector, came just hours ahead of the Barak-Sharaa meeting in Washington. Days later, a Hezbollah car bomber blew himself up beside a convoy of Israeli army vehicles in Marjayoun, the first such attack in nearly four years, although only one soldier was slightly wounded.

Nonetheless, it was evident that Hezbollah was facing difficulties in the south. The IED ambushes were not meeting with the same level of success as in the past, partly because there were relatively few targets available—Israeli troops were barely seen anymore, spending all their time in reinforced concrete bunkers. Barak had pledged to have the soldiers back home by July, and no one wanted to be the last to die in the dust of south Lebanon.

"We didn't like the announcement of a withdrawal," recalls Brigadier General Moshe Kaplinsky, then the head of the Israeli army's Galilee Division. "It put us as commanders in the field in a troubling situation. How could we convince troops in the field to fight when they knew they were going home?"

On the other hand, no Israeli soldiers had been killed in south Lebanon since August, but Hezbollah fatalities had spiked in the last two months of 1999. In November, an attack on the Sojod compound to plant a flag on the ramparts had cost the lives of seven Hezbollah men, the highest single fatality toll for the party since the mid-1980s.

On January 19, Major General Shaul Mofaz, the IDF chief of staff, held an upbeat news conference during which he announced that 1999 had been a comparatively good year, with only thirteen soldiers killed in south Lebanon, half the toll for 1998.

Hezbollah replied in a statement that the lower casualties were due to resistance operations having led to a reduction in the number of troops in the zone. Furthermore, Hezbollah added, the soldiers who remained in the zone "are in fact paralyzed and captive in their fortified positions."

As of January 20, the day after Mofaz's news conference, Hezbollah significantly stepped up operations, launching fifteen or more attacks a day, detonating roadside bombs, and battering Israeli and SLA outposts with large quantities of AT-3 Sagger antitank missiles, mortar rounds, and shells from an old towed 122 mm artillery cannon, one of two it had acquired a year earlier.

The fresh offensive came days after the first major round of peace talks between the Israelis and Syrians at Shepherdstown, Virginia, had come to an inconclusive end. Farouq al-Sharaa had surprised the American mediators by showing behind closed doors an uncharacteristic flexibility and an evident desire to push the talks forward, despite maintaining a hostile stance in public. Barak, however, failed to reciprocate. To the anger of the Syrians and the irritation of the Americans, Barak hedged, fearful of weakening his political position back home by being seen as too eager to grant concessions to the Syrians. The Syrian delegation returned home assuming that Barak was not serious about peace.

Now the Israelis were going to pay the price in south Lebanon.

The Chink in Israel's Armor

The brilliant sunshine on the morning of Sunday, January 30, failed to warm the chilly air in the rocky hills around the Christian village of Dibil in the zone's western sector. Aql Hashem, the stocky, self-confident SLA commander of the zone's western sector, drove to a small farmhouse he owned about half a mile outside the village to prepare a barbecue for a group of farmers whom he had invited to discuss the season's tobacco harvest. Hashem was a tough militia veteran, respected by his men and highly regarded by the Israelis, who saw him as a potential future commander of the SLA.

When Hashem arrived at the farm, he found his son waiting for him. They chatted for a few minutes, unaware that they were being watched and filmed by Hezbollah Special Forces operatives hidden on a small hillock just two hundred yards to the north.

Hashem strode over to a log pile to gather fuel for the wood-burning stove in the farmhouse. As he bent down to pick up the logs, at least three IEDs exploded simultaneously beside him. Hashem died instantly.

Hezbollah had been planning to kill Hashem for months, knowing that his death would deal a mortal blow to the militia. Hashem had been placed under close observation, his movements and habits carefully studied. The assassination plan was set in motion when Hezbollah was tipped off about Hashem's scheduled meeting with the tobacco farmers. The Hezbollah hit team infiltrated the zone three days earlier, planting the bombs and then settling into a camouflaged observation post nearby.

The dismay in Israel over Hashem's death was palpable. "He was one of my best friends. We had many days and nights together all over the western [sector], hours of talking about everything," recalls Colonel Noam Ben-Zvi, the IDF commander of Hashem's area. "We knew that it would happen. We warned him that it would happen, and even warned him that it would happen at the place where he died. But he had a lot of confidence and after so many years became careless about his security."

But Hashem's assassination was only the beginning. The following morning, a team from Hezbollah's antitank unit fired a TOW missile toward the Ezziyah compound on a hill high above the Litani River where it squeezed through a narrow gorge. The position was rarely attacked and was regarded by the Israelis as one of the safest postings in the occupation zone. Its relative safety and proximity to the border—less than ten minutes' drive from Metulla in northern Galilee—made it a popular viewing point for Israeli politicians visiting the zone. The TOW missile streaked across the six-hundred-foot Litani ravine and straight through the slit window of a concrete observation bunker. The blast from the missile killed three soldiers and wounded another four.

Hezbollah had achieved a similar feat six days earlier, shooting an antitank missile through the viewing slit in another frontline IDF outpost, killing the first Israeli soldier since the previous August. With this second penetration of a fortified bunker, it was evident that Hezbollah had found a chink in the IDF's protective armor.

In response, Barak threatened to break off peace talks with Syria until Damascus reined in Hezbollah. The Israelis sought revenge by attempting to kill top resistance leader Ibrahim Aql in a bungled helicopter gunship attack. Barak was furious at Aql's narrow escape, while Ephraim Sneh, the Israeli deputy defense minister, ruefully observed that the Hezbollah commander had a "gentile's luck."

"The Lebanese Valley of the Dead"

Two days later, on February 6, a Hezbollah Special Forces unit ambushed an Israeli patrol six hundred yards from the border, on a track near the prominent Jabal Blat outpost in the western sector. A bomb-sniffing dog accompanying the patrol detected the IED just before it detonated. The dog disappeared in the blast, but the last-second warning ensured that only three soldiers were wounded. As the casualties were being treated on the spot, the Hezbollah fighters observing from nearby directed accurate mortar and rocket fire onto the patrol. One soldier was killed and another four wounded as rockets and mortar rounds fell among them. The intense fire prevented helicopters from touching down to evacuate the casualties, forcing medics to treat them on the main road beside the border with Israel. At that moment, cameramen from two Israeli television channels arrived and filmed through the border fence the screaming, blood-soaked soldiers being treated just a few yards away. The grim reality of the south Lebanon quagmire was broadcast into Israeli homes that night to a stunned audience. It was the first time that the Israeli public had been presented with such shocking and graphic footage of the war in Lebanon.

PICTURES FROM HELL, ran a banner headline in Israel's *Maariv* newspaper the next morning. "The Lebanese valley of the dead penetrated the living room of Mr. Israel after 18 years of avoidance."

Barak was caught in a dilemma. He knew that a heavy retaliation to the spate of military fatalities in south Lebanon could jeopardize prospects of further talks with Syria. But the upsetting television images of the wounded soldiers and the inability to stop Hezbollah's deadly missile attacks could not be ignored. With his top military commanders screaming for action, Barak gave the order for air strikes against Lebanese infrastructure targets. That night, three electricity plants were bombed, including the Jamhour electricity switching station in the hills above Beirut, the third time the facility had been blown up in four years. Seventeen civilians were wounded in the air raids.

In south Lebanon, the Katyusha rockets were on the launchers hidden in wadis and olive groves and the Hezbollah operators were waiting for the order to fire. But the order never came. Hezbollah stayed its hand, choosing instead to respond in the most appropriate manner possible.

At 2:50 P.M. the next day, thirteen hours after the Israeli jets finished smashing the electricity plants, a Hezbollah antitank squad shot yet another TOW missile into an Israeli outpost, killing one more soldier.

Israel had expected Hezbollah to retaliate with a Katyusha barrage on Galilee and was prepared to counterrespond with an even more damaging bombing campaign against Lebanese infrastructure. But Hezbollah did not take the bait. How much influence Syria had in the decision to refrain from launching rockets is unclear, but either way it was a smart move. The mere threat to retaliate with Katyushas was sufficient to achieve paralysis in northern Israel. Barak ordered a 48-hour state of emergency in the north, forcing some three hundred thousand people to flee or sit in bomb shelters. Around 80 percent of the population of Kiryat Shemona abandoned the town. Economic losses ran at $2.4 million per day. All that without a single Katyusha rocket crossing the border.

Israeli officials accused Hezbollah of breaching the April Understanding by firing its TOW missiles from populated areas. But that was untrue. Hezbollah had fired from open areas and aimed at military targets. It was Israel that had broken the rules by attacking Lebanese infrastructure. Now, with this latest death of a soldier in south Lebanon, Barak knew he could not justify a second night of air strikes against civilian targets in Lebanon. He had exhausted his political capital with the first round of raids.

On February 11, the delegates to the Monitoring Group arrived in Naqoura to address a flurry of protests filed by both sides. But the session was in trouble from the start. The Israeli delegation refused to leave its room despite coaxing by the American and French representatives. Then, an hour and a half after the meeting was supposed to start, Hezbollah struck again. This time the target of the antitank missile was an observation turret on the ramparts of Beaufort Castle. Another Israeli soldier was killed—the seventh in three weeks. When the news of the latest fatality reached Naqoura, the Israeli delegation stormed out. It was the last time the Monitoring Group convened.

In the days that followed, the Israeli government sanctioned the creation of a three-man committee empowered to order immediate raids into Lebanon without having to seek prior cabinet approval. David Levy, the hawkish foreign minister, delivered a series of bloodcurdling threats redolent of the Old Testament in which he warned that if Hezbollah rocketed northern Israel, Lebanon would pay "soul for soul, blood for blood, child for child." On the ground, the IDF belatedly began erecting steel mesh antimissile fences around its outposts to protect the vulnerable observation bunkers.

Hezbollah's propaganda machine took full advantage of the escalation, with Al-Manar broadcasting a clip showing portraits of each of the seven dead soldiers, one after the other. The clip ended with a blank box containing a question mark and a message in Hebrew asking who would be the next victim.

Hezbollah had scored more impressive single achievements, such as the Ansariyah ambush and General Gerstein's assassination, and it was the sustained and deadly IED campaign that sapped Israel's resolve to stay in Lebanon; but the three-week escalation in January and February 2000 was perhaps the pinnacle of Hezbollah's resistance campaign against the Israeli occupation. It blended thoughtful intelligence work to discover the weak spots in the Israeli outposts; skillful battlefield exploitation of the TOW missiles; and tactical foresight by playing within the rules of the April Understanding.

In three short weeks, Hezbollah had turned the tables on Mofaz's confident declaration that the Israeli army had gained the upper hand in south Lebanon. The spate of military casualties and the television footage of wounded soldiers deepened Israeli public opposition to the occupation in Lebanon. In March, a Gallup poll for *Maariv* newspaper found that 61 percent of respondents wanted an immediate withdrawal from Lebanon, even without an agreement with Lebanon and Syria.

"This is one war we have lost," opined Yoel Marcus in *Haaretz*. "If we are fated to leave anyway—let's do it now."

Failure in Geneva

On March 5, the Israeli government announced that it would pull the troops out of Lebanon by July 2000, hopefully within the framework of an agreement. If no agreement was forthcoming, "the government will convene at an appropriate time to discuss the method of implementation of the above-mentioned decision," promised the Israeli cabinet communiqué.

There was no going back now; the countdown to withdrawal had begun.

The Israeli army drew up two plans of withdrawal. The first, dubbed "New Horizon," envisioned a pullback to the international border in conformity with Resolution 425. The second, "Morning Twilight," was an option in the event of a unilateral withdrawal. The one significant difference was that Morning Twilight envisaged a redeployment to the Purple Line, Israel's military border where the fence had been pushed deeper into Lebanon in certain places over the years to seize the high ground. This plan would leave under Israeli control eight outposts either straddling the border or fully inside Lebanese territory on the annexed pockets of land. The Israeli army assessed that if a withdrawal was conducted without an agreement with Syria, Hezbollah would continue to launch attacks against Israel. Therefore, if fighting was unavoidable, Israel might as well retain the tactical advantages offered by the Purple Line deployment.

Yet the Lebanese would consider the adoption of the Morning Twilight plan to be a redeployment, not a full withdrawal, thus making the Israeli army's prediction of continued fighting a self-fulfilling prophecy. Hezbollah consistently declared that it would continue to attack Israeli forces as long as "one inch" of Lebanese land remained under occupation.

The Israeli-Syrian talks had gone into limbo following the failure of the Shepherdstown meeting in January. But by late March, the Clinton administration had extracted some bottom-line concessions from Barak over the extent of the withdrawal from the Golan Heights, and the U.S. president prepared to sell the package to Assad. The two met at a summit in Geneva on March 26. The sight of the visibly frail Assad wearing a wool overcoat and flat cap making the effort to meet Clinton in the icy cold Swiss city suggested that the peace deal was all but done.

But it was not to be. According to Dennis Ross, the American Middle East peace coordinator who attended the summit meeting, Assad simply showed no interest as Clinton carefully read out Barak's concessions.[2] Ross concluded that Assad's priorities had shifted to ensuring a smooth transition to the presidency for his son, Bashar, rather than achieving peace with Israel. Assad had been angered by Barak's foot-dragging in Shepherdstown, which may have dampened his enthusiasm for a deal.

But the Syrians have a contrary explanation for the summit's failure. According to Abdel-Halim Khaddam, then Syria's vice president, Assad had wanted to conclude a peace deal with Israel before his death because he believed it would smooth the succession of Bashar to the presidency. Despite his ill health, Assad undertook the trip to Geneva because he had been told by Sharaa that Barak was willing to withdraw to the June 4, 1967, line, thus satisfying the Syrian president's long-standing demand. He had also been reassured by Clinton, who telephoned Assad prior to the Geneva summit to say that he was bringing some new and serious proposals from the Israeli prime minister.

"I think if he had known the position did not include the withdrawal of all the territory prior to 1967, he would not have even accepted to go to Geneva," Khaddam told me. "Of course, he was disappointed. He thought he was tricked by the Americans."

Clinton and Barak initially blamed Assad for the failure at Geneva. Since then, however, even Israeli negotiators acknowledge that the primary responsibility rested with Barak, who dithered at the crucial moment in Shepherdstown when the Syrians were clearly eager for a deal.[3] Even Clinton subsequently wrote in his memoirs that he believed Assad was serious about peace and that Barak had gotten "cold feet."[4]

The collapse of the Israel-Syria track in March 2000 set in motion a series of events that have helped shape the current political landscape in Lebanon, Syria, and Israel. If a peace deal had been concluded in the spring of 2000, Israel, Lebanon, and Syria probably would have enjoyed calm and stability along their respective borders for the past decade.

Lebanon would have followed Syria's lead and signed a deal with Israel, Hezbollah would have been disarmed under Syrian fiat, and quiet would have prevailed along Israel's northern border. There would have been no Shebaa Farms campaign, no military buildup by Hezbollah in south Lebanon from 2000 on, and no war in 2006, nor would the Lebanese and Israelis continue to be living under the unremitting threat of a fresh conflict that promises to be even more destructive than the last.

"A Worthless Piece of Land"

After Geneva, Barak abandoned hopes of achieving a withdrawal from Lebanon within the framework of an agreement with Syria and began preparing for a unilateral pullout. Initially, on the advice of his military staff, Barak leaned toward implementing Morning Twilight's partial withdrawal option, but he changed his mind when warned by the UN that the Security Council would recognize only a full pullout to the international border.

The Lebanese and Syrian authorities, meanwhile, appeared to be in denial about the impending troop withdrawal, a denial that slowly evolved into panic. Lebanese officials believed—or hoped—that the promise of an Israeli pullout was just a bluff and that Barak would not have the courage to take a plunge into the unknown. Nabih Berri told Terje Roed Larsen, the UN Middle East peace coordinator, that he would "eat his hat and dance with you in the street" if the withdrawal actually went ahead.

After the Israeli government formally declared that the IDF would leave Lebanon by July, Farouq al-Sharaa said Israel would be committing "suicide" to withdraw without making a deal with Syria first. "They will bear the consequences and should never use this possibility as a means of pressure against us," he said.[5]

The evident unease that Barak's pledged withdrawal evoked in Damascus and Beirut was a paradox that did not go unnoticed in the Arab world. "It was as though he [Sharaa] were urging Israel not to withdraw but to remain in south Lebanon, thus contradicting Arab and indeed

Syrian policy, which demands day and night that Israel should withdraw unilaterally," wrote columnist Abdel Bari-Atwan in *Al-Quds al-Arabi*. "If such a withdrawal were indeed tantamount to 'suicide' for Israel, then let it go ahead and commit suicide and do us all a favor."[6]

The Syrians stood to lose an important means of leverage against Israel if the unilateral withdrawal went ahead as planned. If there were no longer any Israeli soldiers for Hezbollah to kill in south Lebanon, how could Syria exert pressure on Israel to yield to Damascus's peace demands? With an end to the occupation of south Lebanon, any future attacks across the border into Israel would be deemed acts of aggression against a sovereign state, not legitimate resistance against illegal occupiers. Hezbollah faced the same dilemma. How could it continue to justify bearing arms if there was no occupation to resist?

There was, however, one possibility: a small, remote, almost uninhabited mountainside of weathered limestone, dense thickets of evergreen oak, and a few long-abandoned stone hovels, known collectively as the Shebaa Farms.

Ever since the Israelis had seized the lower slopes of the Shebaa Farms mountain in the June 1967 war and secured the upper reaches over the following three years, the occupation of the area had lingered only in the memory of a handful of aging residents living in the adjacent villages of Shebaa and Kfar Shuba. Although the place name was familiar to most Lebanese and cited as one of the enduring examples of Israeli aggression against Lebanese sovereignty, few knew where it was located, let alone what it contained.

In early May, the Lebanese government told Terje Roed Larsen that the Shebaa Farms was sovereign Lebanese territory and demanded that Israel withdraw from the mountainside along with the rest of the south. Larsen was told that the territory had been transferred to Lebanon in an oral agreement with Syria in 1964, but the border had not been formally re-delineated and demarcated on the ground.

As far as the UN was concerned, however, the Shebaa Farms area was inside Syria. Maps submitted by Syria and Israel to the UN in 1974 during the process of establishing a UN-patrolled buffer zone on the Golan Heights clearly marked the Shebaa Farms as Syrian territory. On that basis, the Shebaa Farms was not included within the UNIFIL zone in 1978, and twenty-two years later, Israel was not required to pull out of the area to satisfy UN Resolution 425. If the area was Lebanese, the UN noted, why had the Lebanese government in 1978 not protested the exclusion of the Shebaa Farms when 425 was adopted and UNIFIL's mandate determined?

It was true, however, that the exiled farmers who once tilled the stony soil of the Shebaa Farms were Lebanese, not Syrian, citizens. Even though they had been evicted three decades earlier from their mountain farms, they still possessed their property deeds as proof of ownership.

The haziness of who bore rightful sovereignty over the area provided sufficient excuse for the Lebanese—prodded, as ever, by the Syrians—to argue to the UN that if Israel failed to withdraw from the Shebaa Farms, then Beirut would consider Israel still an occupying power, leaving open the option for continued resistance operations.

"My Lebanese and Syrian counterparts did not want a full withdrawal," Larsen recalls. "That was why the Shebaa Farms [issue] was raised. I went to see the Shebaa Farms and saw it was a worthless piece of land. I very quickly realized that this was what they would construct in order to say that this was not an end to the occupation and use it as a justification for having Hezbollah as a resistance."

"It's Occupied Arab Land"

The UN studied more than eighty maps from sources in Damascus, Moscow, Paris, and London, among other locations, to determine the sovereignty of the Shebaa Farms. All of them portrayed the Farms as lying inside Syria. But the ham-fisted attempts by the Lebanese and Syrians to persuade the UN that the territory belonged to Lebanon at times verged on farce.

Just as Lebanon's case for the Farms was looking increasingly flimsy, Larsen was summoned to a meeting at the presidential palace with Emile Lahoud and Jamil Sayyed, the powerful head of the General Security department. Lahoud triumphantly presented the UN envoy with a

Lebanese map dating from 1966 that clearly marked the Shebaa Farms as being inside Lebanon. Larsen took the map back to New York, where it was examined by UN cartographic experts.

"Yes, indeed, the map was from 1966," Larsen says, "but the ink was not dry on the line drawn on the map. It was two weeks old."

Larsen returned to Beirut and confronted Lahoud and Sayyed, telling them that the map was of "questionable authenticity" and that if he ever heard about this map again, he would go public with the forgery. "Of course they were completely mad at me, but I never heard again a word about that map," Larsen says.

Nabih Berri had his own brush with cartographic ignominy in early May, when, before assembled television cameras, he proudly unveiled an "American" military map that he said marked the Farms inside Lebanon. Berri said he had received the map within the past week and that it refuted a recent claim by Ehud Barak that Lebanon possessed no documents showing the Farms as Lebanese territory. "I'm presenting this map today to Arab and international public opinion through the Lebanese media in response to Barak's claims," he said, jabbing a finger in the general direction of Shebaa on the map.

The map brandished by Berri was prepared by the Defense Mapping Agency Topographic Center, a former division of the U.S. Department of Defense. It was, in fact, the standard map used at the time by UNIFIL in south Lebanon. Indeed, I had a copy of that very same map on the wall of my study. There was a problem, though. The map clearly portrayed the Shebaa Farms inside Syria, not Lebanon. Presumably, someone had a quiet word with Berri after his press conference, for no more was heard about the "American map."

The farce continued into 2001, when someone noticed that the two-inch-high map of Lebanon on the thousand-lira bill placed the Shebaa Farms inside Syria. The revelation sparked a scandal, with a writer, Naji Zeidan, filing a lawsuit against the currency designers. The thousand-lira bill was first issued in 1988 during the term of President Amine Gemayel, a onetime ally of Israel, which only deepened the conspiracy theories. Zeidan's lawyer said that his client claimed the thousand-lira bill was helping the Israelis "because they can say that all

Lebanese are walking around with maps that show the Shebaa Farms are not part of Lebanon."

The Lebanese were not alone in tripping over their own feet in attempting to convince the UN that the Shebaa Farms rightfully belonged to Lebanon. The Syrians were also in a bind over the sovereignty of the mountainside. Damascus wanted the Shebaa Farms to serve as the new casus belli that would validate Hezbollah's keeping its weapons and continuing to attack Israeli troops after Israel had withdrawn from the rest of south Lebanon. But they could not bring themselves to state to the UN in clear and simple terms that the territory was Lebanese, not Syrian. Syria, even before the advent of the Baathist regime, had never really accepted the notion of Lebanese independence. Lebanon, the Syrians averred, was an aberration, ripped from the motherland at the behest of separatist Maronites and the indulgence of their French colonial patrons.

When the Shebaa Farms issue arose, Larsen traveled to Damascus and met with Bashar al-Assad and Farouq al-Sharaa to hear Syria's view on the sovereignty of the area. In his meeting with Sharaa, Larsen asked the foreign minister, "Is it [the Shebaa Farms] Lebanese or Syrian? I want a straight answer."

"It's occupied Arab land," Sharaa said.

"That's not my question. Is it Syrian or Lebanese occupied land?" Larsen asked again.

Sharaa looked hard at Larsen. "It's occupied Arab land," he repeated.

"That was the best answer I got [from Damascus] at the time," Larsen recalls.

Sharaa subsequently informed Kofi Annan by telephone that Damascus supported Lebanon's demands for the restoration of all its occupied land, including the Shebaa Farms. But it would take more than a vague assurance over the phone to persuade the UN of the validity of Lebanon's argument for the Farms.

On May 22, Kofi Annan released a report on the implementation of Resolution 425 in which he stated that Israel would be required to withdraw to a line "conforming to the internationally recognized boundaries of Lebanon." But the Lebanese, unsurprisingly, lost the argument for the

Shebaa Farms, leaving its fate subject to future peace negotiations between Israel and Syria.

Keeping Up the Pressure

Meanwhile, in the south, the Israeli withdrawal had already begun. Trucks crossed the border bringing fresh supplies to Israeli outposts but returned to Israel filled with equipment. By mid-May, several Israeli outposts had been handed over to the SLA. Only some 120 Israeli soldiers were estimated still to be in Lebanon by May 19, half of them in frontline bases and the rest in positions on the border. The Israelis intended that by July 7, the stated deadline for the withdrawal, there would be only a skeleton crew of soldiers left in Lebanon manning positions all but stripped of equipment. The Lebanese would wake up one morning and discover that the last Israelis had slipped away overnight, and that would be that.

The Israeli preparations were evidently under way when I toured the zone's western sector with UN observers in mid-May. From the UN observation post on the border near Markaba village, we watched Israeli engineers reinforcing an outpost just inside Israel with bulldozed earth and concrete T-walls. The huge Israeli position on top of Sheikh Abbad Hill, recognizable by its distinctive twin radio masts, was being dismantled. The outpost straddled the border, and the Israelis were dragging equipment from the Lebanese half and rebuilding the position on the Israeli side of the line. Far below us in a deep wadi, Israeli soldiers milled around a self-propelled 155 mm cannon, one of five established as a temporary artillery post. Some of the soldiers sunbathed on armored personnel carriers, others lounged in the grass outside a row of canvas tents.

However, Hezbollah was not allowing the construction activity to proceed unhindered. As we drove along the border road close to the Israeli position on Sheikh Abbad Hill, a terse alert was broadcast over the UN radio: "Warning, warning, warning. Operational activity is taking place in Irishbatt."

Several mortar rounds exploded against the Sheikh Abbad outpost, sending plumes of dust and smoke into the sky. We pulled over in a nearby village to sit out the attack. Moments later came the thunderclap of outgoing Israeli artillery fire from a position a few hundred yards away on the other side of the border. "This is typical of what's going on here," said Major Brendan O'Shea, the Irish operations officer for the UN observers. "They [Hezbollah] are keeping up the pressure."

Indeed, Hezbollah was determined that Israel would leave under fire. In late April, Hezbollah fighters mounted an audacious operation against the SLA outpost on the edge of Aramta village in the mountainous northern tip of the occupation zone. Shortly after dawn, a Hezbollah man, accompanied by several comrades riding trail bikes, drove a car packed with explosives down the road from Jezzine to Aramta. As the group approached the village, the trail bikers hung back and the car continued up to the outpost. Simultaneously, Hezbollah mortar teams began shelling the outpost and SLA compounds on surrounding mountaintops. With shells exploding nearby, the Hezbollah man, pretending to be a civilian, asked the SLA if he could enter the compound with his car to escape the barrage. The militiamen agreed, and he drove his vehicle in through the front gate. Parking the vehicle, he slipped out the gate, seconds before the car bomb blew up. The huge blast killed three militiamen, wounded another four, and almost completely destroyed the outpost. The SLA abandoned the position and withdrew two miles farther south to Rihan.

Hezbollah stepped up its psychological warfare campaign against the SLA, exploiting their insecurities with bloodcurdling threats. Nasrallah said no mercy should be shown the SLA, who must either "leave with the Jews, turn themselves in, or be killed."

On May 18, I headed back into the occupation zone for what, as it turned out, would be my last trip there. I was driven to Jezzine, just north of the zone, by Abed Taqqoush, a jovial Beiruti who was one of a breed of taxi drivers who made a living chauffeuring foreign journalists around Lebanon during the civil war years. He was the favorite driver of visiting BBC correspondents, having worked for the British broadcaster for twenty-five years, and had ferried one of my colleagues from *The*

Times of London around Lebanon a few months earlier. He scarcely stopped chatting all the way from Beirut to Jezzine. He was looking forward to the Israelis' leaving, as that meant the BBC and other foreign television crews would be arriving in Lebanon to cover the big story. For Abed, the love of the story was even greater than the promise of lucrative work. Abed dropped me off in Jezzine, where I was to catch a ride with a taxi driver from Marjayoun. Our trip was delayed an hour or so, as Hezbollah had spent the night battering Israeli and SLA positions in Rihan, the frontline village ten miles to the south.

Guns or Toys?

The shelling sputtered out midmorning, and we took advantage of the lull to head south toward Rihan along the same winding road down which Johnny, the SLA militiaman, and his two comrades, Nimr and the terrified Manny, had ridden the last armored personnel carrier from Jezzine almost a year earlier. One of my three fellow passengers in the cab had brought a small round drum with him. He tapped out a rhythm and sang to calm our nerves; Hezbollah's shelling could have resumed at any moment. On the northern edge of Rihan, we lined up to hand our papers to a plainclothes SLA officer who checked off our names in a ledger. As I waited, a militiaman staggered toward me. He looked shell-shocked. His bloodshot eyes bulged from their sockets as he pawed at my shirt and gabbled in broken English, stumbling over the unfamiliar words. His faded olive-green Israeli army uniform fit him like a second skin. He had scribbled a cross in blue ballpoint on his snug but tatty flak jacket, God's protection augmenting man-made Kevlar. Short and squat with an unkempt beard, tangled curly hair, and grimy creases around his eyes, he looked like a militiaman of many years' standing.

But he had had enough. He had spent the night in his outpost in Rihan sheltering while Hezbollah had pounded his compound and the neighboring Israeli position, dropping mortar shells with merciless accuracy onto the reinforced concrete roofs of the bunkers. The stocky militiaman babbled incessantly. He held my arm and tugged it for emphasis, imploring me to do something to help him. I was British, yes? Couldn't I ask the British embassy to get him a passport? Was there much work in London? His plainclothes colleague writing our names in the ledger smirked but said nothing. My fellow passengers from the taxi looked embarrassed and turned away.

Gradually his tone changed, his desperation turning into a jumbled stream of bitterness and despair. Why wouldn't the Lebanese government grant amnesty to the SLA? All they were doing was protecting themselves, their families and homes. The SLA were patriots, so why were they being treated like traitors? At last he fell silent and let go of my arm. With his AK-47 rifle dangling loosely from his hand, the broken militiaman wandered away up the road.

His despair was emblematic of the disintegration of morale and manpower afflicting the SLA. Hezbollah's threats, the Lebanese government's refusal to offer amnesty, and Israel's silence on its plans to protect the SLA had further aggravated the already deep-rooted paranoia that existed within the militia.

By early 2000, Shia militiamen were deserting their positions, slipping out of the zone to hand themselves over to the Lebanese army. Hezbollah had begun snatching militiamen from inside the zone, echoing the tactic of a year earlier in the weeks before the SLA withdrawal from Jezzine. Some Christian villagers had already left south Lebanon, and many others were making plans to flee. The exodus of nervous residents had sparked a lucrative spin-off business in some Christian villages. Elias, a resident of Qlaya who had left the SLA a few months earlier, said he had paid $2,000 for a fake Lebanese passport. His service in the SLA prevented him from obtaining a genuine passport. Another $1,000 secured his airfare from Israel to Canada. If the forged travel documents were discovered on arrival in Canada, he would plead political asylum.

Elias articulated a widely held belief in the zone: that Hezbollah men would steal into their homes at night and slaughter them in their beds after the Israelis had gone. His wife muttered darkly that she had heard many of the SLA men who surrendered the previous year during the pullout from Jezzine had been secretly executed in prison. "But they have hushed it up," she whispered.

While some militiamen were packing their bags and making plans to be well away by the time Israel withdrew, others struck a tone of defiance, proclaiming their determination to continue defending their villages and homes against the "outsiders" of Hezbollah.

A month earlier, Antoine Lahd, the SLA commander who spent much of his time in Paris, vowed to continue fighting Hezbollah after the Israelis had gone. "We will prefer to commit suicide as in Masada, rather than become refugees," he said, referring to the Jewish Zealots defending the Masada fortress in A.D. 70 who chose to die by their own hand rather than surrender to the Roman legions.

Such bravado was echoed by several SLA intelligence officers sipping tiny cups of Turkish coffee in a café in Qlaya. "We will fight until the end," said one, to mutters of approval from his comrades. "If Hezbollah attacks civilians, we will shoot all over the south. They fire one rocket at civilians and we will fire twenty rockets at them."

These men were among the originals, former Lebanese soldiers who returned to their homes in Qlaya in 1975 when the army split apart, and formed the nucleus of Saad Haddad's Army of Free Lebanon (later the SLA). Now gray-haired and paunchy, they were contemplating a return to the past, reviving the old Haddad enclave of the late 1970s and resurrecting the village militias in Christian- and Druze-populated areas of the border district. Already new SLA checkpoints were sprouting up on the edges of Christian villages. Civilians were buying up weapons including rifles, heavy machine guns, and rocket-propelled grenades and were being taught how to fire them at the SLA's training camp in Majidiyah at the foot of the Shebaa Farms and in woods near the Druze town of Hasbaya.

"We have relied on our brothers, fathers, uncles, and cousins in the SLA to defend us, but now the time has come where we have to defend ourselves," said Bassam, a civilian from Qlaya in his midthirties. Displaying his recent purchases on the floor of his small home, Bassam said that he had spent $430 on an M-16 fitted with an M-203 grenade launcher and another $220 on ammunition for the rifle, flares, a helmet, and a backpack with magazine pouches. "I asked myself, should I spend the money on toys for my children, food for my family, or to buy guns?" he said. "I decided to buy guns so that I can defend my family."

The contradictory fear and defiance of the militiamen underlined the stark fact that as this vicious little war finally drew to a close, the real losers were the SLA. True, the Israelis would suffer a certain amount of humiliation at being chased out of Lebanon by the Shia warriors of Hezbollah; but the prospects facing the SLA were bleak. They could escape Lebanon for an uncertain future of exile in Israel or elsewhere, banished from their homeland possibly forever; die fighting Hezbollah in a futile and bloody last gesture of defiance; or surrender themselves to the authorities in Beirut and pray for leniency.

Through necessity rather than design, they had entered an uneasy alliance with Israel a quarter century earlier to confront the menace of the Palestinian militants then threatening their villages. But as the years passed, they had found themselves sucked ever deeper into a vortex of collaboration, their fate becoming shackled to Israel's fortunes in Lebanon. They were the unwitting victims of tragic circumstance, but now they were about to pay the inevitable price.

The Collapse

The end came just three days after my last trip into the zone. A small crowd of mourners had gathered in the frontline village of Ghandouriyah to mark the seventh day since the death of an elderly woman. The woman and the mourners were exiled residents of Qantara, a small hilltop village lying just inside the occupation zone a mile east of Ghandouriyah. Despite the solemn ocassion, the crowd was bubbling with excitement. Days earlier, the SLA had pulled out of its position in Qantara and withdrawn closer to the border, a move that effectively left a large swath of the zone's central sector no longer under the control of the Israelis. Two men had sneaked into Qantara for a look and then had used their cell phones to pass the message that the village was free of the

SLA and it was safe for people to enter. Suddenly the only obstacle preventing the crowd from returning to their former homes in Qantara was a swing gate manned by some increasingly uneasy Finnish UNIFIL soldiers. The peacekeepers tried to warn the crowd that it was dangerous to proceed, but to no avail. They stood back as the swing gate was forced open and the crowd surged down the narrow, potholed lane that descended into Wadi Hojeir before climbing the steep eastern slopes of the valley into Qantara.

Nazih Mansour, an MP with Hezbollah, was among the first to enter the village. He stopped at one of the first homes. "I entered the house and saw an old man and a woman," Mansour recalled. "I recognized the man as Abdo Saghir. He used to take me to school. He was scared and didn't recognize me. I told him who I was and he yelled and burst into tears. I began crying, too, and we hugged each other."

Mansour and the crowd pressed on, driven by the momentum of the hundreds of people converging on Qantara as news of its liberation rapidly spread throughout the south. They pushed through another Finnish-manned gate and surged through the villages of Qsair and Deir Sirian before entering the outskirts of Taibe, the largest village in the area. "The scene in Taibe was indescribable," Mansour said. "People were running out of their houses barefoot to greet us. It was truly a historic moment."

The SLA militiamen in a large fortified outpost on a hill above the village fired a few desultory warning shots but were unable to quell the triumphant advance. Using a bullhorn, Mansour called on the militiamen to surrender. Around sixteen of them did so. The others began abandoning the position and streaming eastward toward Addaysah village, a little over a mile to the east of Taibe and adjacent to the border itself.

By early evening, the Israelis were scrambling to check the headlong civilian advance. A bulldozed earth barricade blocked the entrance to Addaysah on the Taibe road, and tanks maneuvered into position on the outskirts of the village.

The civilian push into the northern part of the central sector came close to severing the zone in half. By nightfall, only a narrow strip of territory at Addaysah, between the dizzying depths of the Litani River gorge and the border with Israel, linked the eastern sector to the central and western sectors.

It was a remarkable development that threatened to upset Israel's plans for an orderly withdrawal. Hezbollah's leadership was as surprised as everyone else at the day's turn of events. "Hezbollah had plans for the withdrawal and we were almost ready," Mansour said. "But no one expected it to end like this. The popular movement changed all our programs."

Instead of mounting a final offensive against the departing Israelis, Hezbollah decided to take advantage of the momentum created by the civilian marches. As night fell, Hezbollah fighters went on full alert throughout the south as local commanders turned their attention to another occupied village lying some five miles south of Qantara: Houla.

SEVEN

The "Spider's Web"

I tell you: the Israel that owns nuclear weapons and has the strongest air force in the region is weaker than the spider's web.

—SAYYED HASSAN NASRALLAH

May 26, 2000

MAY 22, 2000

SHAQRA, south Lebanon—A densely packed convoy of cars, motorcycles, minibuses, and pickup trucks jammed the narrow, potholed lane snaking down the steep western slope of Wadi Salouqi, a valley that a few hours earlier had marked the front line of Israel's occupation zone. Now the front line was on the move, retreating almost by the minute toward the Israeli frontier three miles to the east, as thousands of civilians streamed into the zone through this narrow breach.

Hezbollah had moved quickly to capitalize on the extraordinary events of the day before, selecting Shaqra village as the rallying point for a march on occupied Houla, lying on the eastern side of Wadi Salouqi. If the civilians could seize Houla, there was nothing to stop them from reaching the border with Israel itself, effectively severing the occupation zone in two.

Hezbollah commanders contacted some former residents of Houla and urged them to spread the word to assemble beside the Irish UNIFIL checkpoint on the eastern outskirts of Shaqra, ready for a dawn march across Wadi Salouqi. The exiled villagers needed little encouragement. Many of them had not set foot in their home village for at least fifteen years.

By the time the dawn sun inched over the eastern skyline, several hundred people had gathered in Shaqra beside a swing gate, guarded by Irish UNIFIL soldiers, that barred access to Wadi Salouqi and a road that no civilian had driven along since 1985. The Irish soldiers vainly tried to persuade the crowd not to proceed, but they had no more luck than their Finnish colleagues a day earlier. Israeli artillery guns shelled the tinder-dry slopes of Wadi Salouqi, starting small brush fires, in an attempt to intimidate the crowd from proceeding toward Houla. But the crowd was not to be put off, neither by Israeli shelling nor by the entreaties of Irish peacekeepers. At 9:00 A.M., Hezbollah men, dressed in civilian clothes, made the decision to force open the gate. The helpless Irish soldiers stood back as the gate swung open and the crowd surged through.

In a final attempt to stop the crowd from reaching Houla, an Israeli jet dropped an aerial bomb onto the road two hundred yards short of the village. The blast sent a towering column of gray smoke and dust into the air. But the bomb cratered only two thirds of the road, leaving enough space for cars to inch past and enter Houla. There was nothing more the Israelis could do but watch in frustration and alarm. "We discussed whether to stop them, but that would have meant killing civilians. And we were leaving the area anyway," recalls Major General Moshe Kaplinsky, then commander of the Galilee Division, part of the IDF's Northern Command.

Residents of Houla came running down the road to greet the motorcade, withered old women hurling handfuls of rice in welcome and stooped old men wearing keffiyahs hobbling along with the support of walking sticks. The traffic ground to a halt as entire families burst out of their vehicles on seeing loved ones or reaching their original homes.

Sixty-five-year-old Sikni Said hugged a bearded man in his thirties who had a huge grin on his face. "My son, my son," she said softly as tears coursed down her wrinkled cheeks.

"I have not seen my parents for thirteen years," sobbed Abdullah

Mustafa as he greeted his elderly mother and father. "I am feeling a great happiness that cannot be described. This is our land and we have come back."

The chaotic scenes of jubilation and greeting on the streets of the village were tempered by the throng of stern-looking Hezbollah and Amal men who also entered the village. One suspected collaborator was pushed into the back of a Mercedes by a group of men carrying automatic pistols. Some residents tried to intervene, insisting he was a civilian. An aggrieved resident snatched a pistol and fired several shots into the air before being calmed by friends. The Mercedes with the suspected collaborator inside sped out of the village on a side road as scuffles broke out between the rival Hezbollah and Amal men.

"This Is Palestine!"

The crowd, buoyed by their success in "liberating" Houla, turned their attention to Markaba, the neighboring village just to the north. A long burst of heavy machine gun fire erupted from the SLA's outpost in Markaba as the last defenders loosed off warning rounds before fleeing.

The vanguard of the motorcade inched through Houla's tight, winding streets. On reaching the border road, some vehicles turned south toward the village of Meiss al-Jabal, others north toward Markaba and Addaysah.

It was an extraordinary moment. Enthusiastic Hezbollah supporters carrying yellow party flags surged up the road just a few yards from the border fence and in full view of Israeli army positions. The road followed a two-thousand-foot ridge that afforded impressive views to the east—the flat irrigated farmland of northern Galilee lying far below, and beyond that the gently rising grassy slopes of the Golan Heights, and to the north the imposing massif of Mount Hermon barely visible through the early summer haze.

"This is Palestine," said an awestruck man to his friend, gesturing expansively at the sight before them.

With Hezbollah flags fluttering from car windows, the first vehicles passed directly beneath Israeli troops in their border outposts and entered Markaba to receive another rapturous welcome from the residents hurling fistfuls of rice that stung our faces, caught in our hair, and beat against car windshields like tiny hail. A group of Hezbollah fighters raced into the SLA's now-abandoned outpost on the edge of the village, reappearing minutes later with a victor's booty of grenades, helmets, flak jackets, and belts of ammunition which they packed into their car.

The occupation zone was now split in two, the civilian marchers having established a narrow bridgehead on the border between Markaba and Houla. Israeli commanders knew that it was impossible to reverse the situation, but they agreed that it must be contained as long as possible to prevent a general collapse of the SLA and give time for the Israeli troops to retreat across the border. For there would be no waiting until the self-imposed July deadline for the final pullout. The IDF knew that this was the end; the only concern now was to withdraw their soldiers as swiftly and as safely as possible.

The SLA regrouped in Addaysah, two miles north of Markaba. Addaysah lay in a narrow bottleneck between the Litani River and the border with Israel with only one road cutting through. It was a natural choke point, and the SLA, backed by Israeli firepower, seemed determined to make a stand there.

Five Apache helicopter gunships hovered with undisguised menace high above the jubilant civilian crowds racing up and down the short stretch of border road. Two teenagers on scooters shot past me, heading north. One of the Apaches opened fire at the road just ahead of them, its 30 mm chain gun flaying the asphalt, whipping up small fountains of dust and stones as the rotor blades spun the gun smoke into spirals. Both teenagers fell off their scooters in surprise, then hurriedly remounted and raced back to Houla. A pair of Merkava tanks emerged on the edge of the Israeli outpost at Misgav Am on a hill overlooking Addaysah, their barrels pointed ominously at the border road. Another tank sidled into position beside the large Israeli compound on Sheikh Abbad Hill. Israeli artillery units began a widespread bombardment of areas facing the western and central sectors, the dirty gray puffs of smoke visible from the border road striking the outskirts of what were just a day earlier the frontline villages of Majdal Silm and Shaqra. The Taibe outpost, abandoned by the SLA the previous day, was destroyed in a large explosion that sent a huge column of smoke and dust rising into the air. Like the mainsail of a vast Spanish galleon, the cloud of dust drifted on the breeze eastward across the border into Israel before gradually dissipating. Hezbollah men had set charges around the old position and blown it up, as they would other abandoned Israeli and SLA outposts in the coming days.

Under Fire

Israeli tanks prevented a southbound advance along the border road from Houla by firing at any vehicle attempting to do so. Two civilians were killed about a mile farther down the road in separate incidents when their vehicles were struck by tank shells. On the southern outskirts of Houla, orange flames darted from the hatch of a burning T-55 tank that had been abandoned by its SLA crew after it broke down earlier in the morning. An Israeli helicopter had fired a missile into the tank to prevent its falling into the hands of Hezbollah. A crowd gathered two hundred yards from the burning tank, watching the blaze and wondering whether to risk proceeding. Steven Wallace, an American photographer, and I walked farther down the road to a teenager holding a yellow Hezbollah flag. He said he intended to plant the flag on the tank once the fire had burned itself out. He would not get the chance, however. Moments after a pickup truck raced past carrying the bodies of the two civilians killed earlier, a tank round exploded on the other side of the road, just five yards from us. The crowd up the road behind us scattered for cover around a bend, followed at a speedy pace by Steve, the teenager, and me as machine gun bullets cracked past our heads. As we reached the corner, a missile shrieked and exploded just behind us in a thick cloud of brilliant white smoke.

Israeli firepower halted the civilian advance from spreading along the border road beyond Houla and Markaba, but farther west, the occupation zone was collapsing. Some forty SLA militiamen left their positions in the frontline village of Beit Yahoun and surrendered to the Lebanese army. Other frontline positions were abandoned by the SLA during the afternoon, the desperate militiamen forced to choose between exile in Israel and turning themselves in to the Lebanese army or Hezbollah.

A battered Volvo accelerated up the lane from the tiny hamlet of Srobbine, the back doors swinging open as tank rounds exploded in quick succession in the hillside above. The car halted beside a UNIFIL checkpoint, and wide-eyed Hezbollah men pulled two badly wounded people from the blood-soaked backseat. More tank rounds exploded nearby, sending onlookers scurrying for cover in doorways. The crackle of automatic weapons rose from the folds of the deep wadis near Srobbine as Hezbollah men advanced on the neighboring village of Beit Leif.

That night, the IDF's western sector headquarters at Saff al-Hawa on the edge of Bint Jbeil was vacated and hundreds of SLA militiamen and their families stampeded across the border into Israel. In Tyre that evening, we watched the flashes of explosions and brief orange bubbles of fire light up the area around Biyyada village on the coast to the south as Israeli artillery and naval gunboats shelled the edges of the zone to provide cover for the retreating SLA.

While the Shia residents of the rapidly collapsing zone celebrated their liberation, nervous residents of Christian villages gathered in churches wondering what the next day would hold for them.

"Fear of the Unknown"

UNIFIL soldiers were no longer bothering to try to stop the mass of civilian traffic from entering the zone. Just after dawn on Tuesday, May 23, at the Hamra crossing point on the coastal road, Fijian peacekeepers stood back and watched as a motley collection of disheveled Mercedes sedans, pickup trucks, vans, and motorcycles passed an abandoned SLA outpost that a day earlier had marked the beginning of Israel's jurisdiction.

At the newly abandoned SLA position outside Teir Harfa village, a bearded Amal militant dressed in a black uniform stepped on some strands of coiled razor wire, allowing two of his colleagues to hurry across a fifty-yard patch of rock and grass to reach the compound, apparently oblivious or unconcerned that they were traversing a minefield. Minutes later, the two Amal men reappeared laden with ammunition belts, green tin boxes of ammunition, and a .50 caliber machine gun. The looting of the SLA and Israeli outposts had begun in earnest.

The roads heading away from the coast into the heart of the western sector were almost empty. It was still unclear whether the SLA and the Israelis had completely abandoned the area. Steve Wallace and I drove gingerly along the main border road, no other vehicles in sight. An abandoned T-55 tank lay on the side of the road beside the turning to Dibil, the Christian village that was home to Aql Hashem, the recently deceased SLA commander of the western sector. The tank was draped in camouflage netting, its barrel spray-painted in greens and blacks. A .50 caliber machine gun was still fixed to the turret. We approached cautiously, wary of booby traps. A car raced up to us from the opposite direction, the first we had seen in more than half an hour. Young men sat on the vehicle's windowsills brandishing green Amal flags. The car braked to a halt and two teenagers jumped out and ran toward the tank, showing none of the caution of the two foreign journalists. One of them grabbed a belt of ammunition, slung it around his neck, and posed for Steve's photographs, while the second leaped onto the tank. As he did so, we were surprised by a loud bang. I felt tiny chips hit me in the face and thought for a split second that the boy had triggered a booby-trapped hand grenade. But the two teenagers were unhurt and pelted back to their car like startled rabbits, whooping with excitement and festooned with looted booty from the tank. An ashen-faced but grinning Steve told me that the boy had used the grip of the .50 caliber machine gun to haul himself up onto the turret of the tank. But there was still one round chambered in the gun, and he had accidentally fired it. The round had struck the road by my feet and chipped the asphalt.

In Dibil, the shops were closed and villagers milled uncertainly in the narrow streets. They had thrown in their lot with the Israelis since 1976, and now their benefactors had gone, leaving them to ponder their fate at the hands of Hezbollah.

One resident claimed in a sonorous voice that an eighty-year-old woman had died that very morning, "from fear of the unknown."

"I hope UNIFIL comes here soon. If it takes them two weeks, Hezbollah will kill us all," said a middle-aged man, drawing a finger across his throat in emphasis.

Most of the SLA from the village had fled into Israel, but at least one opted to remain behind. Najib Attiyah, a veteran of thirteen years, sat quietly in his small stone house near the church waiting for the Lebanese authorities to arrive. "I have a wife and seven children," he said. "Where am I going to go?"

In Rmeish, a group of heavily armed Hezbollah guerrillas swarmed over a T-55 tank. Belching a thick cloud of exhaust smoke, the tank lurched down the high street with Hezbollah fighters clinging to the turret, giving victory salutes to the stony-faced audience of elderly Christian residents.

Abed Taqqoush

Bint Jbeil, the largest Shia town in the western sector, was rapidly filling with traffic streaming in from the main road leading north. Most of the vehicles were festooned with Hezbollah and Amal flags and some were plastered with pictures of Nasrallah, a colorful cavalcade that jammed the town's narrow streets and filled the air with car horns sounding off in celebration.

In Aittaroun village, east of Bint Jbeil, a procession of captured SLA armored vehicles ground slowly down the main road, forcing civilian traffic to move out of the way. The driver of a jeep crammed with armed Hezbollah fighters motioned people aside as he tried to weave through the throng. Behind the jeep lurched a T-55 tank driven by a Hezbollah man whose bearded head poked through the front hatch, his face scowling in concentration as he steered the unwieldy vehicle. Several of his comrades, some wearing plain green military uniforms and webbing, sat on top of the tank waving yellow and red party flags.

I heard a voice calling my name and saw a familiar figure hurrying out of a shop carrying several cans of soda. It was Abed Taqqoush, the taxi driver who a week earlier had driven me to Jezzine for my last trip into the occupation zone. Abed's face was lit up with a magnificent smile, his eyes bulging with excitement. He slapped me on the back and offered me a Pepsi.

We were joined by Jeremy Bowen, a veteran Middle East correspondent for the BBC, and his Lebanese cameraman, Malek Kanaan. Abed was their driver. After a few minutes of chatting, the BBC team moved on.

The crowds began to thin as the border road gradually turned from east to north as we entered the central sector. I pulled over to make a call to *The Times*. As I spoke to one of the editors, we heard an explosion in the near distance, the report loud enough to travel down the phone line to Wapping in east London. A thin column of smoke rose gently into the sky ahead of us. As we drew closer to the smoke a few minutes later, a car speeding toward us from the other direction slowed and the passenger waved at us to stop.

"The Israelis are shooting at cars on the road. They have just killed a journalist," he warned. "No, it wasn't a journalist. It's a Lebanese," the driver corrected him.

I should have made the connection instantly, but for some reason I did not, and it was only a little later that I learned that the "Lebanese" was Abed Taqqoush. The BBC crew had stopped on a corner opposite the Israeli settlement of Manara, the squat European-looking houses visible through a screen of pine trees on a ridge a few hundred yards away. Bowen and Kanaan left the car and walked a hundred yards back down the road to set up the camera and record a piece using as background Manara and the wreckage of a Mercedes in which a civilian had been killed by Israeli tank fire the day before. Bowen, who was wearing a distinctly unmilitary pink shirt, saw what looked like an observation position at Manara and waved to indicate his friendly intentions. Abed remained in the car chatting on the phone to his twenty-one-year-old son, Mohammed.

Days later, Mohammed recalled his father telling him, "You should see it down here. A settlement is right next to me, and it looks beautiful."[1]

Those were the last words Abed ever uttered. An Israeli tank positioned on the border beside Manara fired a single round into his Mercedes, striking the gas tank and engulfing the car in a ball of fire. Bowen was speaking to the camera when the blast occurred; wreckage from Abed's car flew into the background of Kanaan's camera shot. The horrified pair ducked behind a wall. After a few minutes, Bowen ventured out into the road to check on Abed, but he immediately came under machine gun fire, forcing him to seek cover again. He contacted the Israeli army's media office by cell phone to alert them to their predicament and halt the shooting. For an hour, Bowen and Kanaan were pinned down by the Israeli machine gunner while the flames stripped Abed's car to a metal skeleton. It was not until four hours later that a Lebanese civil defense team was able to remove Abed's body.

The IDF subsequently claimed that the tank crew at Manara had suspected Bowen and Kanaan of being "members of a Lebanese group preparing to fire an antitank missile against Israel Defense Forces tanks and vehicles."[2] Pink shirts are not the customary garb of Hezbollah fighters, nor do their antitank teams fire from the middle of roads in broad daylight within clear view of their target and begin the operation by giving a cheery wave to their intended victims. If they thought Kanaan's camera was an antitank missile, why did the Israelis fire at Abed's car a hundred yards away?

Abed was not the only civilian victim of Israeli tank fire during the withdrawal, but he had the tragic distinction of being the very last Lebanese civilian killed during Israel's occupation of Lebanon.

The Storming of Lebanon's "Bastille"

With the western half of the zone liberated, the mainly Christian and Druze eastern sector began to disintegrate. Druze militiamen from Hasbaya fled northward to turn themselves in at Lebanese army positions on the edge of the zone. Israeli artillery gunners pounded areas facing the northern and eastern sectors in preparation for the final pullout.

During the afternoon, Israeli commanders delivered a blunt ultimatum to their SLA counterparts: Israel was leaving and the border would be sealed the moment the last soldier exited Lebanon. Any militiaman failing to cross the border by then would have to meet his fate in Lebanon.

Panicked militia commanders hurried home, packed their bags, bundled their families into cars, and dashed headlong for the border. There would be no defiant last stand after all. The bravado exhibited by the SLA leadership in recent weeks—the talk of a return to the "Haddad enclave," Antoine Lahd's promise that the SLA would commit collective suicide rather than live as refugees in Israel—had been nothing more than bluster.

Tensions ran high at the Fatima Gate crossing as huge queues formed of SLA men and their families desperate to enter Israel before it was too late. The Israelis instructed them to leave weapons behind and to abandon their vehicles at the border crossing. The surging crowd attempting to squeeze through the crossing panicked some Israeli soldiers who were trying to maintain order. The soldiers fired shots into the crowd, killing at least two people and wounding several others, a shabby and shameful end to twenty-five years of sacrifice by Israel's Lebanese allies. Once inside Israel, the new refugees were bused to a temporary camp near Tiberias on the Sea of Galilee.

"Barak gave them [the SLA] the illusion that we would not leave them, but we did in a very cynical way," recalls Ephraim Sneh, the deputy defense minister and an ardent champion of Israel's Lebanese allies in the SLA. "What we did to them was unforgivable, unpardonable.... It was one of the most immoral things Israel has ever done."

In Khiam, in the eastern sector of the zone, the Shia residents, aware of what had happened in the previous two days in the western and central sectors, assembled at a mosque and began a march on the SLA-run prison at the southern end of the town. As the crowd approached the stone walls of the prison, SLA jailers began shooting in the air as a warning.

When the inmates, all 160 of them, heard the gunshots and distant cries of "*Allah u-Akbar* (God is greater)" from the crowd of marchers, many of them thought the SLA was massacring the prisoners before fleeing. The inmates began chanting *"Allah u-Akbar"* as well as they awaited their fate.

The SLA guards knew they were in an untenable position. A deal was struck allowing the jailers to leave unharmed in exchange for not opposing the liberation of the prison. With the departure of the guards, the crowd surged through the open gate into the prison compound. The locks were smashed from the cells, and the prisoners were hugged and kissed by their liberators.

"I thought we were all going to be taken to Israel," recalls Riad Kalakish, who had been incarcerated in Khiam prison since 1985. "I was not expecting to be released. It was only when I walked outside that I understood we were free. I felt as though I had been born again."

That night, under the cover of artillery fire, the last Israeli troops pulled out of Lebanon, blowing up their compounds in the northern sector and creeping in armored columns along the winding mountain road to the safety of the border at Metulla.

The soldiers broke into relieved smiles and hugged one another as they crossed into Israel. It had been a retreat, but not under fire, and they had incurred no casualties. Hezbollah could have harried the departing Israelis, but wisely took the decision to let them leave unmolested. The hasty manner of the Israeli withdrawal was triumph enough.

"People were flocking to the villages and the Israelis were pulling out under heavy covering fire," said Nazih Mansour, the Hezbollah MP. "If civilians were killed needlessly, then we would have lost the flavor of victory. I'm not going to risk my people just to shoot a bullet at the Israelis."

At 6:42 A.M., as dawn broke on May 24, 2000, an Israeli officer snapped the padlock on the metal swing gate in the border fence, a simple gesture that symbolized the end of the occupation after twenty-two long years.

"C'est Fini"

The thump of exploding munitions echoed through the eastern sector that morning as an ammunition dump set alight hours earlier by the departing Israelis continued to burn, cooking off an assortment of missiles, flares, and artillery and mortar shells. The ammunition had been stockpiled beside the main road between several houses just south of Qlaya. The explosions had blown out all the glass from the sides of houses facing the dump. For Ghada Khoury, a twenty-four-year-old mother of two infants, it had been a terrifying night.

"They never even told us to leave. They left us sleeping in our beds," she said, her voice shaking with hysteria and her face caked in dried blood. "There were bombs exploding all the time. My little daughter is in shock. She can't speak. She's only a year old and she's not accepting her milk."

She led us through her small home to inspect the damage, her feet crunching on the shattered glass. "We spent the night in the bathroom because it has no windows," Khoury said. "My baby was screaming and I was crying and my husband didn't know what to do."

The ground outside her home was littered with shiny aluminum missile fragments and steel shrapnel. The burning munitions sent clouds of smoke billowing into the blue sky. A blazing flare shot skyward, cartwheeling through the air before tumbling into the main road. Across the road from Khoury's home, local residents prayed in the church as others swept up broken glass.

In Marjayoun, a mile to the north, at the headquarters of the now-defunct SLA, a bearded gunman booted open the door of a room and fired a few rounds from his AK-47 rifle into the dark interior. He stepped inside and emerged moments later laden with military clothing. To the victors, the spoils. And there was plenty to choose from in the abandoned headquarters. Dozens of gunmen, mainly Amal militants, ransacked the barracks, bursting into offices and grabbing what they could. Others attempted to start up a fleet of T-55 tanks, armored personnel carriers, trucks, military jeeps, and a few World War II–vintage half-track vehicles parked in a mechanics depot. Black smoke billowed out a window where someone had started a small fire. A hand grenade exploded in another burning room. Hundreds of civilians mingled with the militants. A headscarfed teenage girl, one of a class of students from Nabatiyah, less than five miles to the west, gazed eastward across the flat

Marj Valley to the hilltop town of Khiam and beyond to the mountainous skyline where the Shebaa Farms hills melded into the soaring heights of Mount Hermon. The distant mountains were a washed-out pale gray in the early morning sunlight. "What a wonderful country," she exclaimed. "I had no idea that it was so beautiful here."

Aloof from the mayhem around him, a young Hezbollah fighter dressed in black uniform stood by with his rifle, eyeing the looting and pointless gunplay with an expression of disdain. He said that he and his comrades were under orders not to harass Christian residents of the border district. "Our people said, 'Don't show your guns. Don't let them say you came in with your guns,'" he said quietly. "We have instructions not to enter Christian villages."

Hezbollah's leadership had deliberately issued the order to prove wrong those who had predicted that bloody chaos and revenge killings would follow in the wake of the Israeli withdrawal. The leaders knew that the eyes of the world were upon them in their moment of triumph and were careful to ensure that their cadres maintained discipline.

In Qlaya, the mood among the few remaining Maronite residents grew more resentful as the day progressed with no letup to the triumphalism of the mainly Shia crowds. Most of the population of Qlaya, the cradle of the SLA, had fled across the border, accounting for nearly two-thirds of the six thousand militiamen and their families who left for Israel. Another fifteen hundred militiamen turned themselves in to the Lebanese authorities.

Bassam, who a week earlier had proudly displayed his $650 worth of weapons, ammunition, and equipment on his living room floor and proclaimed his intention to stay and fight, was gone, along with his family. The front door of his home was not even locked, such had been his haste in departing.

Inevitably, rumors soon circulated that houses belonging to fleeing SLA militiamen were being looted and roadside shrines to the Virgin Mary desecrated. But Sheikh Nabil Qawq promised that the Christians and other residents of the zone would be treated well.

"From tomorrow morning you will not see any weapons being carried here. We will provide protection for everyone, including the Christians," the white-turbaned cleric told me when we bumped into each other at the entrance to Khiam prison. Qawq had just toured the prison's cramped, fetid cells and interrogation rooms, which reeked of stale sweat, urine, and unwashed bodies. Among the visitors wandering the narrow corridors of the detention blocks were former detainees, some released the previous day, others freed long ago, who could not resist returning to a place where they had experienced such hardship and misery.

"This place proves for sure that Israel is the number one terrorist state in the world," Qawq said.

As Hezbollah's southern commander, Qawq had played a key role in the resistance campaign against Israel. It was evident that he was elated with the outcome, but even in that moment of victory, the tall cleric cast his brown eyes toward the sepia-tinted Shebaa Farms hills to the east of Khiam.

"Our feeling is one of great happiness and victory. It's a big holiday," he said. "We look forward to many more victories, hopefully the Shebaa Farms, and, having seen Khiam prison, hopefully the rest of our detainees will come home soon."

The late afternoon light bathed southern Lebanon in a pale gold as I drove up the steep lane from Arnoun to Beaufort Castle, fulfilling a personal ambition to visit the Crusader fortress the day the Israelis left. I steered through the open swing gate that had marked the edge of the occupation zone, where an Israeli soldier once had leveled his rifle at my companions and me in the pouring rain, past the rubble of the homes bulldozed by Israeli troops eighteen months earlier when the lane had been a "roadside bomb alley," past the spot the crowds had reached in their game of dare with Israeli machine gunners in the wake of Arnoun's brief liberation. The Israelis had dynamited their concrete bunkers, machine gun posts, and accommodation blocks beside the castle the previous night. Some Lebanese assumed the distant explosions meant that the castle itself was being destroyed. But Beaufort's eight-hundred-year-old walls remained standing, although the open area between its western wall and a bulldozed earth rampart was filled with smashed cinder blocks, broken chunks of reinforced concrete, cracked green-painted cement slabs, and collapsed T-walls, the air caustic with cement dust and chemical residues from the explosions. An acrid pile of rubble was all that remained of Israel's presence at the castle.

A few dozen curious sightseers climbed the ramparts, following walkways guarded by metal railings that wound over the castle's overgrown ruins. Someone had already hoisted a yellow Hezbollah flag atop one of the turrets where 24 hours earlier the blue and white Star of David had fluttered. From the parapets, the whole of southern Lebanon was laid out below like an aerial photograph. Far to the west, across the rolling, hazy hills, the silver Mediterranean shimmered as the sun sank ever lower in the sky. The castle's eastern ramparts were perched on the edge of the six-hundred-foot precipice of the Litani gorge, the river itself fleetingly visible far below as it gushed and frothed beneath the shadows of the dense undergrowth that lined its banks. On ridges farther east lay the red-roofed houses of Marjayoun, and beyond that Khiam. In the far distance the Shebaa Farms hills and Mount Hermon gradually turned crimson in the face of the setting sun. Metulla, with its neat rows of houses, and the flat plain of northern Galilee could be seen to the southeast; no wonder the Israelis once called Beaufort "the Scourge of Galilee" when Palestinians had manned its lofty parapets. With its latest defenders gone, the tired ruins of Beaufort were back in the hands of the Lebanese state for the first time since the 1960s.

That night, far to the south of Beaufort Castle, in a refugee camp on the shores of the Sea of Galilee, angry and bitter SLA militiamen and their families dwelled on their new status as exiles in a foreign land.

One unwelcome visitor to the SLA refugee camp near Tiberias that first bleak night was Antoine Lahd, who arrived in Israel from his home in Paris only after the withdrawal was over. The Lebanese refugees angrily accused Lahd and Israel of betrayal. What had happened to all the promises from Barak that the SLA would be protected? What did their future hold now that they had been forced to abandon their homes and flee their country? Lahd yelled back at his former comrades-in-arms and then stormed out of the camp. As he climbed into his car, the ex-militia leader was heard to mutter, "C'est fini."

The Blue Line

Two days after the last Israeli soldier departed Lebanon, Hezbollah held a huge victory rally in Bint Jbeil. Some hundred thousand people descended on the border town to hear Nasrallah speak on his first visit to the former occupation zone. It was a moment for the Hezbollah leader to savor, the culmination of eighteen long years in which the Islamic Resistance was born, nurtured, shaped, and developed until it had achieved a feat of arms unprecedented in the history of the Arab-Israeli conflict. Neither the armies of Jordan, Egypt, nor Syria had been able to drive Israeli forces from occupied Arab land. But a relatively small yet resolute band of Shia warriors from Lebanon had achieved just that. Nasrallah stood on a podium inscribed with the figure 1,276, the number of Hezbollah "martyrs" since 1982, and gazed out at the sea of supporters before him. Significantly, a Lebanese national flag hung behind the Hezbollah leader; Nasrallah wanted to convey the message that this was a day of victory for all Lebanese, not just one party.

But he also served warning that the struggle against Israel was not over just because Israeli troops had left Lebanon. The confrontation would continue. The resistance, he said, was determined to win the freedom of the remaining Lebanese detainees in Israel and secure the return of the Shebaa Farms.

The most significant part of Nasrallah's address was directed toward the Palestinians. Hezbollah's victory over the Israelis in Lebanon, he said, represented a model of resistance that could be adopted and adapted by other subjugated people:

> [W]e offer this lofty Lebanese example to our people in Palestine. You do not need tanks, strategic balance, rockets, or cannons to liberate your land; all you need are the martyrs who shook and struck fear into this angry Zionist entity. You can regain your land, you oppressed, helpless, and besieged people of Palestine. . . . The choice is yours, and the example is clear before your eyes. A genuine and serious resistance can lead you to the dawn of freedom. . . . I tell

you: the Israel that owns nuclear weapons and has the strongest air force in the region is weaker than the spider's web.

It was a powerful and compelling message, and it was sown on fertile ground. For unrest was building in the Palestinian territories of the West Bank and Gaza Strip even as the Clinton administration was preparing a fresh push at striking a deal between Ehud Barak and Yasser Arafat. For decades, the Arabs had viewed the small but potent state of Israel with a mixture of hostility, awe, and trepidation. But Nasrallah was telling them that there was no need to fear Israel, because for all its military might and international influence, it could be defeated, as proven by Hezbollah's successful resistance in Lebanon. Israel's "threats and menaces," he said, "do not scare us anymore."

Nasrallah's defiance clearly hit a nerve among the Palestinian leadership, which found itself caught between its commitment to the peace process and the growing impatience of the Palestinian street. At the end of June, Yasser Abed Rabbo, an adviser to Arafat, told Ephraim Sneh, the Israeli deputy defense minister: "With you Israelis, one should only speak in 'Lebanese.' It's the only language you understand."[3]

In the days that followed the liberation of the south, crowds continued to roam the former occupation zone, gathering at several places along the border such as at the former Fatima Gate crossing and on top of Sheikh Abbad Hill to hurl stones and abuse across the fence at increasingly irate Israeli soldiers. UNIFIL began armored patrols of the border district, but the Lebanese government refused to permit a full deployment of army troops and UN peacekeepers into the border area until the process of verifying Israel's withdrawal was completed.

In early 2000, when it became clear that Israel was planning to leave Lebanon, the UN had begun to focus attention on Lebanon's long-neglected border with Israel. Clearly, the exact path traced by the boundary would have to be identified on the ground in order to confirm that Israel had fulfilled Resolution 425 and pulled out of all Lebanese territory. But Lebanon's southern border, first delineated in 1920, demarcated three years later, and reaffirmed as the Armistice Demarcation Line in 1949 at the end of the first Arab-Israeli war, had not been surveyed properly for decades. Israel had altered the shape of the border with its Purple Line incursions; the original whitewashed stone cairns had long ago disappeared, and what existing boundary markers remained often fell in the middle of the chain of minefields planted by Israel stretching almost the entire length of the frontier.

At a two-day seminar in April in New York attended by diplomats and cartographic experts from the UN and the U.S. State Department, it quickly became evident that attempting to re-delineate Lebanon's southern border was impractical. Instead, Miklos Pinther, the UN's chief cartographer, suggested devising a line, matching the border as much as possible, that could be used to gauge the extent of Israel's compliance with Resolution 425. To forestall endless bickering between the Lebanese and Israeli governments, the line of withdrawal—which later became known as the Blue Line—was a temporary measure without prejudice to any future alterations to the international border agreed upon by Lebanon and Israel.

The path of the Blue Line left the Shebaa Farms under Israeli control, but it bisected the village of Ghajar, which had been occupied by Israel since the June 1967 Arab-Israeli war when the adjacent Golan Heights was seized. The village's Alawite residents had accepted Israeli citizenship in 1981, when the Syrian territories occupied fourteen years earlier were formally annexed by Israel. Since then, what had been an impoverished and isolated farming community had grown relatively prosperous. Residents found steady work in Israel, while others earned a lucrative income from smuggling drugs from Lebanon, helping transform Ghajar into a village of whitewashed and pastel-tinted houses and streets lined with lush purple bougainvillea. But the Blue Line threatened to disrupt that peaceful existence.

"Just Juggled Things Around"

While the Israelis objected to the partition of Ghajar, the Lebanese also had reservations over the path of the Blue Line. One complaint was a curious anomaly beside the kibbutz of Misgav Am, which abuts Lebanese territory. During the years of Israeli occupation, the kibbutz had expanded across the original border onto Lebanese soil. The UN cartographers finessed the problem by bending the Blue Line around the kibbutz, thus sparing the Israelis from evacuating their homes. They justified the decision on a misleading description of the Lebanon-Israel border from a fifty-year-old UN report, even though it clearly deviated the Blue Line from the original boundary.

Another Lebanese complaint was over a three-mile stretch of the border southeast of Metulla, where the UN placed the Blue Line a hundred meters north of the true frontier. The UN team appeared to have misread the original 1923 Anglo-French boundary agreement, a point Miklos Pinther subsequently conceded to me when I raised it in an interview in July 2000. The delineation of the Blue Line at this point was "murky," he said, due to conflicting sets of data, and he and his team "just juggled things around." The result, however, was that Israel was not required to pull back another hundred meters along this stretch of the frontier, which allowed it to keep one military outpost intact and saved Israeli farmers from losing some apple orchards.

More significantly, minor deviations in the path of the Blue Line additionally spared the Israelis from having to pull back their forward outposts on the mountain peaks of the Shebaa Farms. The most common delineation of the border in this area places the boundary along the watershed, running from mountaintop to mountaintop. But if the Blue Line had followed this exact path, it would have shaved off the edges of three IDF outposts, requiring the Israelis to dismantle the positions. Instead, the Blue Line follows the border but loops around each IDF compound.

"The UN saw that the border cut right in front of our positions, so they gave us a few tens of meters in front of each one," Giora Eiland, in 2000 the head of the IDF's Operations Branch, confirmed to me nine years later.

The UN also had to contend with more arcane challenges. One of them concerned the sovereignty of the tomb on the summit of Sheikh Abbad Hill near Houla village. The local Lebanese insisted that the tomb belonged to the eponymous Sheikh Abbad, a hermit who lived in the area some five hundred years ago and achieved local renown for the quality of the reed mats he and his followers made and sold by the Sea of Galilee. The Israelis, however, claimed that the tomb belonged to Rabbi Ashi, the fifth-century editor of the Babylonian Talmud, an interpretation of Jewish oral law. When the Israelis constructed their compound on Sheikh Abbad Hill after 1978, a new tomb containing the remains of the Lebanese cleric, or the rabbi, was erected on a platform in the center of the compound along with an archway and an inscription in Hebrew.

The Lebanese government insisted that Sheikh Abbad's final resting place remain inside Lebanon; rabbinical authorities in Israel were equally insistent that the Barak government retain Rabbi Ashi's tomb inside the Jewish state. The dilemma facing the UN was that the tomb lay within the five- or six-yard GPS margin of error of boundary pillar 33 on the original 1923 border, which the Blue Line was supposed to follow.

The solution was provided by Brigadier General Jim Sreenan, UNIFIL's deputy commander, who headed the UN team tasked with verifying Israel's withdrawal on the ground. Sreenan, a burly no-nonsense Irishman, suggested a Solomonic compromise in which the Blue Line would pass down the middle of the tomb, allowing access from both sides. The eastern half would fall inside Israel and could be acclaimed as Rabbi Ashi's resting place, while the western half would lie inside Lebanon and could be recognized as that of Sheikh Abbad.

Dancing on Sheikh Abbad's Tomb

The UNIFIL and Lebanese border inspection teams in early June jointly began the process of formally verifying Israel's withdrawal from Lebanon in compliance with UN Resolution 425. But it quickly became evident that an exercise that should have been completed within a few days, was going to take much longer owing to the dawdling of the Lebanese team and repeated petty border violations by the Israelis.

The process grew increasingly rancorous as the weeks trickled by.

One morning, a hidden Israeli sniper fired shots at the border inspectors and the small band of reporters following them when we tried to cross through an old gate some hundred yards north of the Blue Line. Several bullets ricocheted off the road just a few feet from Sreenan and General Amin Hoteit, the head of the Lebanese border team. A furious Hoteit ordered an immediate halt to the operation for the day.

At Manara, the Blue Line actually ran alongside the road running around the western edge of the Israeli settlement. The Lebanese even complained that the streetlights were an Israeli "violation" because they now fell on the Lebanese side of the line. In a bizarre scene emblematic of the process, Israeli soldiers standing on the road in Israel chatted amiably with Ghanaian UNIFIL peacekeepers standing on the curb in Lebanon, the two groups separated by nothing more than fresh splotches of blue paint marking the path of the Blue Line. Astonished Israeli motorists slowed down and gaped at the UN soldiers and the small crowd of Lebanese reporters filming them on the side of the road. Other Israeli residents of Manara wandered up to see what was going on. Like shy teenagers at a school dance, they stared at the Lebanese, who stared back at them in mutual awed silence.

In early July, Terje Roed Larsen, the UN peace coordinator, negotiated a written agreement with President Lahoud in which Lebanon would accept and honor the Blue Line, "with reservations." The Israelis provided a similar document, and on July 24, two months to the day after the last Israeli tank crossed the border, UNIFIL finally was able to confirm that Israel had departed Lebanon in conformity with Resolution 425.

In early August 2000, UNIFIL began moving to new positions along the Blue Line, followed days later by the first Lebanese troops to deploy in the border district in a quarter century. The soldiers were met with tears and handfuls of thrown rice in Qlaya and Marjayoun. Lebanese politicians and UN officials spoke of a new dawn for southern Lebanon, a "welcome exercise of sovereignty," and the restoration of state control in compliance with Resolution 425. However, the deployment was a chimera. Only a thousand personnel moved into the former occupation zone, a joint task force of five hundred military police and five hundred paramilitary Internal Security officers. Ghazi Zeaiter, the Lebanese defense minister, said that the force would not deploy along the Blue Line as "border guards" for Israel.

During that long, hot summer, a cautious calm settled over southern Lebanon as all parties adjusted to the new realities on the ground. Within days of the withdrawal, Hezbollah began to quietly deploy militarily along the Blue Line. Fighters took over several former Israeli outposts close to the border. The former SLA training camp at Majidiyah at the foot of the Shebaa Farms hills became Hezbollah's logistical headquarters for the eastern sector. Small observation positions were established along the Blue Line, initially consisting of a little more than a tent or hut, some camouflage netting, and seats. One observation post was located beside the Israeli security fence near an outpost on the edge of the Shebaa Farms. Unknown to the hospitable Hezbollah men who offered us small glasses of tea freshly brewed over an open fire, they had crossed the unmarked Blue Line and were about two hundred yards into the Israeli-controlled Farms. The militants were unarmed, wearing civilian clothes and carrying only walkie-talkies and binoculars. *The daily clashes may have ended,* ran the unspoken message, *but Hezbollah is still here.*

Although Hezbollah refrained from direct military action against Israel, it quietly encouraged the phenomenon of stone throwing at some key locations along the border, chiefly the Fatima Gate crossing in Kfar Kila and on the summit of Sheikh Abbad Hill. On weekends, large crowds congregated to lob stones and other missiles across the border fence at Israeli soldiers hidden in fortified observation posts fitted with bulletproof glass. While stones may have been preferable to bullets, the Israelis leveled constant complaints to the UN that UNIFIL was not doing enough to prevent disturbances along the border. By late August, Israel had lodged 348 complaints with the UN over Lebanese civilians hurling stones, metal rods, bottles of boiling oil, fireworks, and firebombs across the border fence at Israeli soldier and civilians. Sheikh Naim Qassem described the stone throwing as a "form of freedom"; UNIFIL refused to become involved in what it said was a policing duty.

Despite the tensions generated by the stone-throwing, Fatima Gate

and Sheikh Abbad Hill often exuded a carnival-like atmosphere, especially on weekends when hundreds of sightseers flocked to the border.
Visitors could take a break from lobbing stones over the fence and buy
Hezbollah kitsch at a stall beside the crossing, such as flags, bumper
stickers, T-shirts, key chains, watches with portraits of Nasrallah on the
face, tapes of martial songs, propaganda videos, and books. Other stalls
sold grilled corn on the cob or Arabic coffee.

On Sheikh Abbad Hill, Lebanese civilians could stand as close as
three feet from stern-faced Israeli soldiers, separated only by the tomb
of the sheikh (or rabbi). One day a group of grinning Lebanese men
stood on the tomb, arms locked, and danced the *dabke*, Lebanon's national dance, before two very unhappy-looking Israeli soldiers. After
that incident, the Israelis placed a stiff wire fence lengthwise along the
tomb. Undaunted by the new obstacle, a Lebanese youth one morning
taunted Israeli soldiers by dangling a yellow Hezbollah flag on the end
of a stick over the top of the fence. The youth's friends laughed as the
flag bobbed just inches above the head of a visibly irritated soldier. Losing his patience, the soldier made a grab for the flag, but the Lebanese
youth was too quick and flicked it out of reach. The soldier scowled and
stroked the trigger of his rifle as the Lebanese mocked him with raucous
laughter.

Dreaming of Hezbollah

Yet the Israeli army had more troubling concerns about the future stability of the Lebanon-Israel border than the odd stone flying over the
fence. Since the withdrawal in May, there had been a near-ceaseless barrage of warnings from Israeli military officials that Hezbollah was preparing for a renewed military struggle. Specifically, the Israelis expected
Hezbollah to carry out kidnappings of soldiers or civilians, in Israel or
abroad, and also to exploit the Shebaa Farms as a new theater of military
operations.

Hezbollah took every opportunity to flex its military muscles rhetorically and remind Israel that there was unfinished business between the two of them, namely, the occupation of the Shebaa Farms and the continued detention of Lebanese prisoners in Israel. In July, Israel extended the administrative detention of Sheikh Abdel-Karim Obeid and Mustafa Dirani, prolonging their indefinite incarceration as bargaining chips for the return of missing Israeli servicemen. Dirani, the onetime leader of the Believers' Resistance, had just begun his seventh year behind bars in Israel, and Obeid had been a detainee for eleven years. Hezbollah vowed to secure the release of Obeid, Dirani, and the remaining Lebanese prisoners. "We will never rest until we see them free; we will work with all means to secure the release of Sheikh Obeid, Dirani, and all the hostages," a statement from the party said.

The pledge was not mere rhetoric. Nasrallah had warned Kofi Annan when the two met in Beirut in June that he would allow only a few months for diplomacy to secure the release of the detainees. If diplomacy failed, Nasrallah told the UN chief, he would seek more drastic methods to bring the detainees home. And by late summer, despite the semblance of calm along the border, Israel's gloomy predictions had proved entirely accurate: Hezbollah was preparing the next stage in its military campaign against Israel.

Ideologically, Hezbollah's conflict with Israel had always been much bigger than simply ending the occupation of south Lebanon. There was a moral and religious obligation to confront the Zionist state all the way to the liberation of Jerusalem. Yet that ideological objective was necessarily tempered by the realities of the political environment within which Hezbollah operated. In the months before the collapse of the Israel-Syria peace talks at Geneva in March 2000, when expectations of a breakthrough were high, Hezbollah was forced to digest the possibility that the armed struggle against Israel might soon come to an end. But the failure of Geneva, and the subsequent abandoning of the Syria track by Israel and the United States, forestalled any further need for internal mulling of the party's future options if a regional peace deal had been concluded.

The end of the peace process provided the opportunity, while Israel's occupation of the Shebaa Farms and its refusal to release the last Lebanese detainees granted Hezbollah and the Lebanese government public justification, endorsed by the new leadership in Damascus.

Hafez al-Assad had died on June 10, just seventeen days after the last Israeli soldier had departed from Lebanon. His son Bashar, who had been groomed to inherit the presidency since the death of his older brother, Basil, six years earlier, was elected head of state the following month. Hafez al-Assad had always viewed Hezbollah as a useful tool that not only helped cement Syria's relationship with Iran but also could be exploited to extract concessions from Israel during peace negotiations. Bashar al-Assad, however, did not share his father's cold realism, and viewed Hezbollah's martial accomplishments with admiration. Unlike his father, who only met with Nasrallah twice, Bashar was well acquainted with the Hezbollah chief and appeared to hold him in high regard.

While the collapse of the peace process was greeted with satisfaction by Iran and Hezbollah, it made for an inopportune moment to become the new leader of Syria. The Americans and Ehud Barak had abandoned Syria to pursue a last-minute deal with the Palestinians before President Clinton's term in office expired. Israel had withdrawn from south Lebanon, removing Syria's main means of leverage against the Jewish state as well as principal justification for maintaining its military presence in Lebanon. For Syria, a new limited conflict on the Shebaa Farms front would serve the dual purpose of renewing pressure on Israel and reminding the United States that Damascus could not be ignored if stability was to be maintained between Lebanon and Israel.

The Return of Ramzi Nohra

Hezbollah's military leadership settled on a kidnapping operation as the best means of launching its new campaign against Israel and the most effective option to secure the release of the detainees. The Shebaa Farms was selected as the venue for the abduction operation, rather than the Lebanon-Israel border, in order to confirm the occupied mountainside as the new theater of conflict and bolster the notion of legitimacy, at least in the eyes of the Arab and Islamic worlds if not the West.

"The operation in Shebaa had a double meaning," Nasrallah said later.[4] "One, to remind that Shebaa is Lebanese-occupied land and it is only our natural right to fight to recover it. Second, the operation has a humanitarian goal, that of releasing the Lebanese hostages and prisoners held in Israel. I think choosing this place will enjoy national consent since we fought on occupied land and took Israeli soldiers from occupied Lebanese land."

Imad Mughniyah was placed in overall charge of the planning, and he enlisted some of Hezbollah's top combat commanders to head the operation on the ground. They settled on a gate in the border fence, about a mile south of Shebaa village, for the location of the kidnapping. It was the obvious choice, as the gate lay beside a road that allowed the abduction team swift egress either to Shebaa or to Kfar Shuba. Although Israeli troops routinely inspected the padlock on the gate, the Hezbollah planners needed to find a way to guarantee the presence of soldiers at a prearranged time to ensure the success of an operation that required split-second timing and coordination between multiple units. They turned once again to Ramzi Nohra.

Following the Israeli withdrawal, Nohra had returned to his home in Ibl es-Saqi and reestablished his cross-border links to Israeli drug smugglers. Hezbollah harnessed Nohra's access to Israel for intelligence purposes. Despite its opposition to drugs on moral and religious grounds, Hezbollah was not averse to using narcotics as a weapon of war against Israel. According to Lebanese sources with intimate knowledge of the operation, Nohra told his Israeli contacts that he had a package of drugs for them and could arrange a transaction across the Blue Line in the rugged Shebaa Farms area. His Israeli interlocutors approached relatives in the Israeli army who were deployed on the Shebaa Farms front to pick up the package.

In the weeks leading to the abduction, Indian peacekeepers saw Israeli soldiers and what they took to be Hezbollah men talking to one another through the fence at the Shebaa pond gate.[5]

By the end of September, preparations for the abduction were in place; all that remained to be decided was the timing. Ironically, the person who started the countdown for the kidnapping was none other than Ariel Sharon. On September 28, Sharon, the opposition leader, escorted by a thousand policemen and bodyguards, went for an early morning stroll around the Temple Mount compound in Jerusalem, which houses the Al-Aqsa mosque, the third-holiest shrine in Islam. Sharon claimed he was simply making the point that Israel was in charge of the compound and that Jews had the right to visit the Temple Mount. But the hundreds of Palestinians who were praying at the site that morning saw Sharon's visit as a deliberate act of provocation. The worshippers rioted and threw stones at the police and Sharon's entourage. The Al-Aqsa intifada had begun.

The Abduction

Nine days later, on Saturday, October 7, four UN observers from the Observer Group Lebanon (OGL), call sign "Team Sierra," departed their post at the southern end of Khiam in their white UN-marked SUV for a routine patrol of the Blue Line in their sector of southeast Lebanon. The route took them past a Hezbollah observation post on a small hill overlooking the divided village of Ghajar. They noticed that the position was empty. Driving down the hill into Wazzani, a small village on the western bank of the Hasbani River opposite Ghajar, the observers were surprised to see that the Hezbollah position there was also vacant.

Team Sierra drove on to the Majidiyah estate, since May, Hezbollah's logistical base for the eastern sector sitting at the foot of the Shebaa Farms hills. But that morning, the base was empty. All the Hezbollah personnel had gone. Team Sierra contacted the OGL headquarters in Naqoura and informed them of the abandoned Hezbollah positions, concluding that "something was up."

Around midmorning, several busloads of Palestinians from refugee camps in Beirut arrived near Marwahine, a Sunni border village in the western sector. They had been mobilized by the Popular Front for the Liberation of Palestine–General Command (PFLP–GC) an ally of Hezbollah, and transported to the border to stage a demonstration in support of the intifada. On their arrival, waiting Hezbollah operatives marshaled the few hundred Palestinians toward an old crossing point facing the Israeli town of Zarit. Several ambulances were already parked at the scene. The Palestinians unfurled flags and banners and began throwing stones across the fence. Israeli troops materialized and fanned out on the opposite side of the fence, warily watching the crowd of protesters.

At around 11:30 A.M., Team Sierra swung by an Indian UNIFIL position on a hillock overlooking the Shebaa gate. From the observation tower, the UN team could see the Hezbollah post four hundred yards away at the bottom of the hill. Unlike the other Hezbollah positions they had passed that morning, this one was still occupied by unarmed plainclothes fighters. At least three vehicles were parked nearby. Three or four Hezbollah men were busy erecting a wooden sign displaying the party logo, a rifle clutched in a fist, on a steep slope about forty yards from the gate.

By midday, the Palestinian protest at Marwahine had grown more heated. Tires were set ablaze, and the crowd hurled Molotov cocktails over the fence. When several youths attempted to scramble over the fence, Israeli soldiers opened fire with live ammunition. Three Palestinians were shot dead and another fifteen were wounded. Despite Team Sierra's radioed observation about the empty Hezbollah positions in the eastern sector, it was the Palestinian demonstration in the western sector that held UNIFIL's attention. Then, shortly after the shooting at Marwahine, UNIFIL headquarters began receiving reports that Hezbollah men were leaving their posts all along the Blue Line.

At 12:40 P.M., the Hezbollah abduction team caught sight of the target vehicle coming around the bend to the south and heading down the hill toward the Shebaa gate. The vehicle was a soft-skinned military jeep carrying three soldiers. All armored jeeps had been withdrawn from the Shebaa Farms sector just a week earlier and sent to the West Bank and Gaza, where the intifada was raging.

The jeep drove slowly past the gate, then made a U-turn and pulled off the road. Two soldiers climbed out of the car and approached the gate. As they did so, two roadside bombs exploded simultaneously on the dirt bank forty yards away where, a little over an hour earlier, the Hezbollah men had planted the wooden sign.

As the blast echoed from the surrounding hills and the gate itself was shrouded in a dense fog of dust and smoke, the exultant Hezbollah fighters cried out "*Ya sahib as-zamen!*"—a triumphant exhortation to the Hidden Imam.

The brief five-month interlude of calm in south Lebanon was over; the new phase in Hezbollah's struggle against Israel had begun.

Hezbollah fire support teams laid down a swift and heavy mortar and rocket barrage against Israeli outposts in the Shebaa Farms. Hidden in a rocky bluff behind the Hezbollah post, the first of eight AT-3 Sagger antitank missiles was fired toward an IDF position, barely visible a mile and a half to the southwest. A dark blue Range Rover bounced along the dirt track toward the gate, the passenger door held open. Before it reached the gate, two Hezbollah fighters burst out of the vehicle. One of them sprinted to the gate and fitted a small explosive charge to the heavy padlock. The second fighter provided covering fire from a few paces behind, his bullets kicking up dust near the Israeli jeep. The fighter by the gate turned and ran back toward some large concrete blocks nearby, ducking behind one as the charge blew the padlock off. Several Hezbollah men, wearing plain clothes and black bulletproof vests, raced through the gate, followed by the Range Rover. The three Israeli soldiers were bundled into the rear of the Hezbollah vehicle, which then accelerated back through the gate with the rest of the team running behind. It was the most sophisticated military operation ever undertaken by the Islamic Resistance; and it was over in less than three and a half minutes.

"The Silence Has Been Driving Me Crazy!"

As the abduction squad raced away to the north, the fire support teams continued pounding the Israeli outposts for another forty minutes, firing a total of 313 mortar rounds, missiles, and rockets, by UNIFIL's count. Several soldiers were wounded by the shelling, and, amid the chaos and shock, it was at least thirty minutes before the Israelis realized that three of their men were unaccounted for. By the time Israeli soldiers reached the scene of the kidnapping, the Hezbollah team and their hostages were long gone. Bloodstains from all three soldiers were discovered at the site, but the extent of their injuries was unknown.

I was later able to piece together what had happened during the kidnapping from the equipment abandoned by the Hezbollah squad. Hidden among rocks about 150 yards from the gate was a small white canvas tent containing clothes, sleeping bags, pots, pans, even a radio set. A table and chair stood in front of the tent. On the table were a telephone and two remote control units, the triggers for the roadside bombs. Thick cables ran from the units toward the Blue Line and ended among a pile of fractured rock and burned earth where the roadside bombs had been placed. The wooden screen, set up by the Hezbollah men and noticed by the OGL observers from the nearby UNIFIL position an hour before the kidnapping, was used to mask the planting of the two bombs. Barely visible on the ground were numerous trails of fine wire, all running in roughly the same direction. They were the guidance wires for the Sagger antitank missiles fired at the IDF outpost. The wires were draped over the border fence, but following the thin strands in the opposite direction revealed the launching site of the missiles. Eight launchers in two separate batteries lurked in a rocky outcrop above the Hezbollah camp. The Soviet-era missiles were launched electronically from collapsible runners attached to the weapons' packing cases.

Helicopter gunships and jets penetrated Lebanese airspace for the first time since May in a bid to intercept the kidnappers. The helicopters clattered above Shebaa and Kfar Shuba villages, blasting the approach roads with their 30 mm guns to prevent any vehicles from leaving. A convoy of civilian cars was shot at on a mountain road between the two villages. The panicked motorists abandoned their cars and fled on foot. At the entrance to Shebaa, at least twenty civilians were wounded when their cars were attacked by helicopters. When ambulances tried to ferry the casualties away, they, too, were hit with missiles.

Two hours after the kidnapping, the helicopters still hung stationary above Shebaa and Kfar Shuba. A crowd of residents in Kfar Shuba watched puffs of dirty gray smoke from Israeli artillery shells explode intermittently against the brush-covered hillsides below one of the IDF's forward outposts on the edge of the Shebaa Farms. A column of black smoke billowed from another outpost farther down the mountainside. Phosphorus shells had set fire to a large section of the hill and a thick pall of smoke slowly enveloped the Shebaa Farms front. The shelling, the smoke, the helicopters—for a moment, it was if the Israelis had never left. On seeing me, a friend from Marjayoun who had lived his entire life in the south broke away from the small crowd and, bursting into delighted laughter, hurried toward me with a big grin on his face. "*Habibi*, Nick, I am so happy, so happy," he said, grabbing my shoulder, as another explosion echoed across the hillside.

"It's the shelling, the shelling," he explained on seeing my puzzled expression. "For thirty years I have been listening to the sounds of war: explosions, shooting, bombs. But the silence in the south over the past five months since the Israelis left has been driving me crazy!"

Few others seemed to share my war-happy friend's elation. The rest of the crowd appeared stunned by the sudden violence that had engulfed their village. "It's the first time I have seen anything like this," said a young girl. "Hezbollah are saying they have captured three Israeli soldiers." She shook her head in wonder. "This is a great achievement."

Barak warned that Israel would take "decisive action" against Lebanon, and rumors circulated that Israel was threatening to bomb Beirut if the three soldiers were not returned within four hours. Hezbollah was prepared for a stiff Israeli response. The backup teams were in position in the hills facing the Shebaa Farms, and explosive charges had been laid in bomb pits dug beneath roads beside the border. Leaning against the twelfth-century stone wall of Beaufort Castle was a SAM-7 antiaircraft missile launcher. A pair of Hezbollah fighters crouched nearby, heads raised, scanning the blue skies above.

Senior Israeli army officers urged Barak to hit back quickly, concerned that a failure to do so would only embolden Hezbollah to strike again. "We were sure it was only the beginning," recalls Major General Moshe Kaplinsky, then commander of the Israeli army's Galilee Division. "We demanded to retaliate strongly straight away. I told [Barak] personally we have to create new rules on the ground."

But Barak stayed his hand. Despite his threats to respond forcefully to any Hezbollah attack along Israel's northern border, Barak had no wish to ignite a second front with Hezbollah while he was busy handling the Palestinian intifada. In the sixteen months he had been in office, the Lebanon withdrawal had been his boldest political decision. But the long-term implications of the move were still uncertain—not enough time had elapsed to judge whether the troop pullout would ultimately be beneficial to Israel. Forceful action by Israel in response to the kidnapping was certain to elicit Hezbollah rocket attacks on northern Israel, leaving Barak vulnerable to his critics who had argued against leaving Lebanon in the first place.

Additionally, Barak felt there was little sense in risking a war along the border when much of the blame for the kidnapping had to lie with the Israeli army. Since June, Israeli military officials had warned repeatedly of kidnapping attempts by Hezbollah. Indeed, it appears that the scale of the Hezbollah operation—in which dozens of fighters were involved at one level or another—was picked up by the Israelis and provided the foundation for the public warnings. Kaplinsky admitted to me that the abduction was a "tactical surprise" but not a "strategic surprise." Given the expectations of an attack in the Shebaa Farms, how was it possible that an unarmored jeep—of a variety normally used along Israel's quieter borders with Jordan and Egypt—could be permitted to patrol the Blue Line unaccompanied?

Zeev Schiff, the veteran military correspondent for *Haaretz*, wrote that October 7, 2000, would be remembered as a "black day" for the IDF, which he found "guilty of blatant nonvigilance."

"A Privilege to Attack Israel"

That evening, UNIFIL discovered two abandoned cars, engines still running, on a road near Kfar Hamam village, three miles east of the Shebaa gate. One of the vehicles, a white Nissan Pathfinder, had been in an accident. The other car was the dark blue Range Rover used in the abduction. Both vehicles had been abandoned in a hurry. Discovered in the back of the Range Rover were bloodstains. At first, the amount of blood found was not made public, but a month later, a senior UNIFIL officer, who had seen both vehicles, told me that "there was very heavy blood loss" in the rear of the Range Rover.

"If it was all from one person, then he would almost certainly have been dead within thirty minutes unless he was treated," the officer said. In his estimation, even if the blood had been from two people, the wounds would still have been life-threatening.

In fact, the three soldiers were killed in the ambush or died from their wounds shortly afterward. But in the subsequent lengthy negotiations brokered by Ernst Uhrlau, the coordinator of the German secret service, to exchange the three soldiers for Lebanese and Arab detainees in Israel, Nasrallah consistently refused to divulge the condition of his captives. If the Israelis had known the soldiers were dead, they assuredly would have hardened their negotiating position. Other than being a trick of psychological warfare to maximize the pressure on the Israelis, the decision to remain silent on the well-being of the captives also set a precedent for future abductions. If the three soldiers had been kidnapped alive and Nasrallah had provided evidence, he might have obtained a better deal from the Israelis. But it would also have meant that in any future abduction, the Israelis would expect similar proof of life. Without it, they would conclude that the captives were dead and negotiate on that basis. The grim reality, therefore, is that because Nasrallah does not exploit the well-being of the captives to gain additional leverage in the negotiations, it makes no difference whether the hostages are alive. Indeed, a kidnapping is easier if the abductors do not have to worry about snatching the hostage alive—a fact that does not bode well for future victims of Hezbollah abductions.

In the weeks following the kidnapping, rumors emerged in Israel that the three soldiers might have been involved in a drug deal when they were snatched. The Israeli army repeatedly denied the allegations, but the rumors persisted. In April 2001, the German edition of the *Fi-*

nancial Times revealed Ramzi Nohra's involvement in the kidnapping.[6] I visited Nohra in his fortified stone mansion in Ibl es-Saqi a few days after the *Financial Times* report was published and asked him to comment. He regarded me with his lazy smile and said, "It's laughable. . . . I deny having anything to do with this. [But] if I was involved, it would have been a privilege to attack Israel."

Sheikh Nabil Qawq, Hezbollah's southern commander, was similarly noncommittal, saying the abduction was "a security-military operation and confidential within the framework of Hezbollah operations."

But the abduction of the three soldiers was not the only kidnapping undertaken by Hezbollah. Eight days after the Shebaa Farms operation, as Nasrallah delivered an address at a conference of Arab and Islamist groups in support of the Palestinian intifada, he stunned his audience by declaring that Hezbollah had captured an Israeli officer in an elaborate sting operation. "With God's help, I am honored to inform you gladly that the Islamic Resistance performed a qualitative and complex security operation, capturing an Israeli colonel, who works for an Israeli security apparatus," he said.

Even before he had finished speaking, the audience erupted into applause and chants of *"Allah u-Akbar."* Amid the euphoria, Nasrallah noticed the look of glum resignation on the face of Salim Hoss, the outgoing prime minister, whose final days in office before yielding to Rafik Hariri had been occupied with handling the diplomatic fallout from the kidnapping of the three Israeli soldiers. On seeing Hoss's gloomy expression, the Hezbollah chief smiled mischievously and joked, "God will help the prime minister for the many phone calls he will get from [U.S. secretary of state Madeleine] Albright."

The captured Israeli officer was Elhanan Tannenbaum, a fifty-four-year-old businessman and reservist colonel in the Israeli army. Nasrallah claimed that Tannenbaum was working for Mossad and had been attempting to recruit a senior Hezbollah official when he was lured from Switzerland to Beirut, where he was seized. It later emerged that Tannenbaum was kidnapped during the course of arranging a massive shipment of heroin and cocaine from Lebanon into Israel.

As an unexpected bonus for Hezbollah, it was revealed, to the understandable consternation of Israeli military officials, that Tannenbaum had attended a top secret military exercise just five days before his capture.[7] The exercise, code-named Northern Forest, was a drill simulation of a war with Syria and involved some of Israel's best-guarded secrets. Tannenbaum had also helped develop a secret weapons program in which Israel was collaborating with the United States. The program was subsequently scrapped on the assumption that the kidnapped colonel had revealed its details to his Hezbollah interrogators.

EIGHT

The "Fence Around the Homeland"

"It will come, but I don't know when."
"Only God knows that."
—HEZBOLLAH FIGHTERS,
Discussing the potential for war with Israel,
March 29, 2002

NOVEMBER 27, 2000

BASTARA, Shebaa Farms—Qassem Zohra and the other ten members of his family were the last remaining inhabitants of the Shebaa Farms. They lived in two single-room stone hovels at Bastara, one of the fourteen original farms, which lay on a bluff overlooking a vast swath of southeast Lebanon. For more than three decades the Zohras had clung to their farm, existing in conditions of extreme poverty and privation. There was no electricity or running water. The only natural light filtering into the gloomy interior of their home came from the open door and a small glassless window. There was no chimney for the crackling fire in the corner, leaving the room filled with dense acrid smoke and the ceiling of tin sheets black with soot. Swarms of flies and wasps surrounded the entrance, attracted by piles of fresh goat dung. The family slept each night on the rough earthen floor beside black plastic bags containing their clothes and sacks of lentils, rice, salt, and wheat.

Provisions had to be brought from Kfar Shuba village, a five-mile drive, for the most part along a rutted dirt track. Part of the route followed the old Israeli military patrol road, affording visitors to Bastara the bizarre experience of driving along an Israeli-built road with signs in Hebrew while peering through the nine-foot-high chain-link fence into south Lebanon. It was easy to forget that the road was on Lebanese territory.

Although the Israelis had permitted the family to stay in Bastara during the occupation, the Zohras faced routine harassment, such as the destruction of olive trees, restricted movements, even the theft of goats. "They kicked us out of my old home in Mazraat Qafwa [another of the Shebaa Farms] and blew up the buildings when they invaded in 1967," Mohammed Zohra, the family's elderly patriarch, told me. "I owned the land here in Bastara, so I brought my family here. I was not going to move out again."

But by October 2000, the Zohra family's austere but peaceful existence came to an abrupt end as they suddenly found themselves in the middle of a new war zone.

Six weeks after the abduction of the three Israeli soldiers, Hezbollah detonated two roadside bombs against Israeli army jeeps on the edge of the Shebaa Farms. Two soldiers were slightly hurt. Ten days later, another roadside bomb was detonated against a motorized patrol, wounding two more soldiers. It was now obvious that the abduction of the soldiers was not an isolated operation but marked the beginning of a new campaign against the Israelis in the Shebaa Farms. The Israeli army ordered Hezbollah's old foe, the Egoz commando unit, back to the northern border, a deployment that did not go unnoticed. In a commentary on Al-Manar television, viewers were reminded how the Egoz was "torn apart" during the years of occupation by the Islamic Resistance. "In any case," the commentary concluded, "we can't but tell the Egoz unit, welcome to hell once again."

A day after the second IED attack, Qassem Zohra, Mohammed's nephew, who ran the family, struck a tone of defiance. "We have lived like this for thirty years and we will continue to live here until all our land is liberated," he said, sitting on a log beside an open fire outside his home. "We all support the resistance and are ready to fight with them."

It took one glass of tea and three cigarettes before Qassem displayed his true feelings. "Finally, we were liberated," he said, staring at the ground and shaking his thick, shaggy black hair, "but now we are worse off than before. We sometimes take our flocks into the hills, but the Israelis shoot at us and we never know if we will come back alive. If there is fighting here, we're stuck in the middle. Doesn't the army want to come here to the border to calm things down?"

But the plight of one impoverished family was of no consequence to the powers that sanctioned the Shebaa Farms campaign. In December, two of Qassem's children were nearly killed when Israeli mortar shells exploded near them as they tended their goats. In early January 2001, Israeli shelling in response to an unclaimed mortar attack slaughtered more than sixty goats in Bastara. The family fled, but returned days later, complaining that they had been unable to find alternative grazing. At the end of January, three PFLP-GC fighters on reconnaissance patrol near Bastara were spotted by the Israelis and attacked by helicopters and tanks. Two of the Palestinians were killed. The clash was the final straw for the beleaguered Zohra family. "We could hear the shrapnel [from exploding shells] hitting the roof," Qassem told me. "The children hid under the mattresses because they were so scared." Once more they packed their bags, and this time they left for good.

A pattern soon emerged for this new conflict. Hezbollah struck at Israeli forces in the Shebaa Farms on a periodic basis in a finely tuned "balance of terror" designed to keep the Israelis on edge but without triggering a full-scale war. "When we took the decision to continue the resistance, we took into account all possibilities," Sheikh Nabil Qawq told me in an interview days after the second IED attack. "If Israel stages a large-scale attack, it will not be to their benefit. Our aim is not to have a wide-scale war. Our aim is to liberate our land and free our detainees."

Yet the Shebaa Farms campaign stripped Hezbollah of the internationally recognized legitimacy it had earned battling Israeli occupation forces in south Lebanon, validated by the 1996 April Understanding. Then, Israel had been an illegal occupier of Lebanese sovereign territory; and while its occupation of the Shebaa Farms was also judged illegal, according to UN Security Council resolutions, because it was regarded as Syrian land, Israel had officially withdrawn from Lebanese soil, thus making Hezbollah's attacks across the Blue Line impermissible.

Hezbollah also faced a domestic challenge to its arms. The Israeli withdrawal inevitably ended the national consensus on Hezbollah's right to resist Israel. With the Israelis gone, Hezbollah's critics argued, only the Lebanese state should bear arms in defense of the nation and decide matters of war and peace, not a movement drawn from just one sect that owed its ideological allegiance to the leader of another country. Furthermore, the rate of one attack every month or so was insufficient to compel Israel to cede the territory. Instead, the sporadic campaign needlessly antagonized a powerful enemy and was nothing but a cynical ploy to defer Hezbollah's disarmament. But Hezbollah made no apology for the limited pace of attacks, noting that the strategic concept for the Shebaa Farms campaign was very different from the effort to liberate the occupied south.

"We estimated that the Shebaa Farms did not require more from the resistance than reminder operations separate in time because we are not a regular army that attacks, takes positions, and defends positions. If we had fired on a regular basis, it would have been a useless exchange of fire," Sheikh Naim Qassem told me.

A Shift of Resistance

The abduction of the three Israeli soldiers and Elhanan Tannenbaum heralded not only Hezbollah's campaign to liberate the Shebaa Farms but also its new military strategy for the postwithdrawal phase. Israel's withdrawal from south Lebanon necessitated a change in Hezbollah's strategic and tactical behavior to take into consideration the new circumstances on the ground and the evolving geopolitical climate in the Middle East.

During the previous two decades, Hezbollah's objective had been to drive Israel out of Lebanon through force of arms. To achieve that goal, it had waged a classic guerrilla-style war of attrition to liberate occupied territory, using deadly hit-and-run tactics to outwit and kill Israeli troops combined with a persuasive propaganda program to grind down the will of the Israeli domestic front to support the occupation.

Israel, as the occupier, adopted a static defensive strategy to retain its hold on captured territory—building fortified hilltop compounds to dominate the ground, employing a local proxy militia, establishing an array of human, aerial, and ground surveillance and early warning systems. Although the Israelis occasionally used offensive measures, such as the air and artillery blitzes of July 1993 and April 1996, commando raids, and helicopter gunship assassinations north of the zone, these were generally tactical reactions to developments on the ground. Hezbollah, as the resistance force, was the principal initiator, choosing where and when to strike, leaving the Israelis primarily in a reactive role.

After May 2000, the strategic situation changed. Hezbollah was no longer confronting an occupier of sovereign Lebanese territory (the Shebaa Farms anomaly gave Hezbollah public justification to retain the Islamic Resistance, but its postwithdrawal military concept was not predicated solely on ousting the Israelis from the mountainside). Instead, Hezbollah's new strategic profile was principally one of defense. The next major confrontation between Hezbollah and Israel would likely involve a ground incursion by Israeli troops into south Lebanon with Hezbollah this time in the role of defender, a reversal of the situation that had prevailed during the previous two decades.

When confronted with the same situation before 1982, Yasser Arafat's PLO had built a third-rate conventional army to defend against the IDF. But Hezbollah's planners opted for a more unorthodox approach, one that combined elements of low-signature guerrilla-style warfare with the technology and sophisticated armaments of a conventional army. Resistance from now on was intended to defend the homeland rather than expel an occupier. This new concept, Nasrallah explained in 2008, "needs close examination." "I do not think this is paralleled in the world or in history," he said. "Resistance liberates land, but resistance to prevent an aggression against a country is something new."

Hezbollah's concept of defensive resistance—the blending of guerrilla and conventional tactics and weaponry—was regarded as the most practical means of confronting Israel militarily after 2000, but it also served as an additional justification to skeptical Lebanese who questioned the need for Hezbollah to keep its weapons. It was not enough to expel Israel from Lebanese soil, Hezbollah argued. Now the "resistance" had to ensure the Israelis would not come back.

The Lebanese army, with its bloated officer corps and arsenal of obsolete and diverse U.S. and Soviet-era armaments, was incapable of defending the homeland against the most powerful army in the Middle East, Hezbollah's leaders averred. On the other hand, the resistance had demonstrated its strengths by driving Israel out of south Lebanon and proven its deterrence capabilities through the evident reluctance of Israel to mount a powerful retaliation to Hezbollah's attacks in the Shebaa Farms. As Nasrallah explained to me in 2003,

> The best means of defending Lebanon in the face of a potential Israeli aggression is the presence of a popular resistance in south Lebanon. Any regular army that may exist in south Lebanon will be dealt a severe blow if the Israelis launch an overall aggression. The regular army has tanks and armored vehicles all above ground and Lebanon does not have air defenses, which means that the Israeli Air Force can destroy regular forces within a few hours. What the Israeli Air Force cannot destroy is the popular resistance, which exists in every mountain, every hilltop, every wadi, every house, and every street. And its members come from the villages themselves. The real equation right now is that the presence of Hezbollah in south Lebanon is a defensive necessity to defend Lebanon, not just the south but also Beirut. Any disarming of Hezbollah or removing it from the south will mean that the [Lebanese] arena will be left open for the Israelis to do whatever they want.

Significantly, Hezbollah's new case for preserving its arms effectively ended any assumption that the resolution of tangible outstanding disputes between Lebanon and Israel, such as the release of the last Lebanese detainees and the withdrawal of Israeli forces from the Shebaa Farms, would result in a quid pro quo disarming of the Islamic Resistance.

Indeed, Ali Ammar, a Hezbollah MP, made it abundantly clear in June 2006 that "the resistance will go on; the extent of the resistance is not the Shebaa Farms . . . nor the return of the prisoners [from Israel], but its extent is when it becomes impossible for Israel to violate Lebanon's sovereignty even with a paper kite."

Still, Hezbollah was careful not to publicly disparage the Lebanese army, an institution that is broadly respected in Lebanon and seen as the principal guarantor of internal stability. Hezbollah's leadership carefully articulated the notion that the army could play a collaborative role with the Islamic Resistance to form what Nasrallah called in 2004 "a fence around the homeland."[1]

In reality, however, such declarations were for public consumption only. The Lebanese army was irrelevant to Hezbollah's battle plans, and the Shia organization, in coordination with the Iranians and with the blessing of the Syrians, continued to pursue its military agenda.

The argument that the Islamic Resistance was necessary for Lebanon's national defense was contrived, and it merely confirmed in the eyes of many that Hezbollah was determined to pursue its struggle against Israel irrespective of Lebanon's national interests. Hezbollah's leadership understood that its somewhat strained argument for keeping its weapons would not convince everyone, but it also knew that its armed status was guaranteed while Lebanon stayed in Syria's shadow and the Middle East peace process remained deadlocked.

Hitting the Syrians

Hezbollah's war of attrition against Israel along the Blue Line soon began to evolve along the same lines that had shaped the larger conflict in south Lebanon over the previous decade and a half, in which each group struggled to outwit the other. Hezbollah's first two attacks in the Shebaa Farms in November 2000 were roadside bomb ambushes, with fighters infiltrating the Israeli side of the Blue Line to plant the IEDs. But as the Israelis tightened security, Hezbollah began launching assaults from the Lebanese side, firing wire-guided TOW antitank missiles at Israeli armored vehicles in sporadic attacks in the first six months of 2001. The Israelis ringed outposts in the Shebaa Farms with antimissile fencing and strengthened bunkers with reinforced concrete. They built new supply roads hidden from the Lebanese side of the Blue Line, thus denying Hezbollah targets with their line-of-sight missiles. From June 2001, Hezbollah's attacks reverted to mortar, rocket, and antitank missile barrages against the seven outposts in the Shebaa Farms.[2] In one attack in October 2001, Hezbollah fired thirty-three AT-3 Sagger antitank missiles at one Israeli compound, a large number for a single operation.

The Shebaa Farms was treated as a free-fire zone by Hezbollah and the Israelis, and was the most visible source of friction between the two enemies. Yet despite the efforts of foreign diplomats to devise creative solutions to resolve the conflict, paradoxically the mountainside became a useful pressure valve, allowing both sides to let off steam and thus mitigating the possibility of a broader conflict erupting along the border. The area was remote and unpopulated and the risk of civilian casualties, especially on the Israeli side, was minimal.

The renewal of hostilities once more placed Hezbollah at odds with Rafik Hariri, who returned to the premiership in November 2000 after an absence of two years. Hariri had hoped that the Israeli withdrawal would end the violence in south Lebanon that constantly threatened to undermine his efforts to attract foreign investment and rebuild the economy. But unhappily for him, his return to the premiership coincided with the advent of Hezbollah's new military campaign.

Hariri's worries were not helped by the arrival in February 2001 of a new Israeli government headed by none other than Ariel Sharon, the architect of the 1982 invasion. Many Lebanese feared that the pugnacious old general would not hesitate to respond harshly to Hezbollah's attacks in the Shebaa Farms. But Hezbollah's leadership remained confident that the "balance of terror" between the Islamic Resistance and Israel would continue to hold regardless of who held the premiership in Israel. "The coming of Sharon does not change the reality that northern Israel is still within range of our rockets. Sharon will return to his natural size when confronting Hezbollah and will swallow his threats," Qawq told me.

But Lieutenant General Shaul Mofaz, the IDF chief of staff, and other top officers were pushing Sharon's government to establish new rules along Israel's northern border. Mofaz and others argued that each unanswered attack in the Shebaa Farms was eroding Israel's deterrence, and that Syria, as the instigator of the violence along the Lebanese-Israeli border, should no longer be spared reprisals. The test came on April 14, when Hezbollah fighters hit a Merkava tank with an antitank missile, killing the radio operator. The next day, Israeli jets bombed a Syrian radar position at Dahr al-Baydar, the lofty pass in the mountains separating Beirut from the Bekaa Valley. Three Syrian soldiers were killed and the radar facility was destroyed in what was the first Israeli attack against a Syrian post since the Grapes of Wrath operation in 1996.

At the end of June, Hezbollah fired a volley of antitank missiles at an Israeli patrol on the edge of the Shebaa Farms. Again Israel hit back against the Syrians, bombing an antiaircraft site in the Bekaa Valley. This time, however, Hezbollah counterretaliated almost immediately with a heavy mortar bombardment of Israeli outposts in the Shebaa Farms. Hezbollah's leadership recognized that it could not afford to let Israel set a new precedent of destroying Syrian positions every time the Islamic Resistance launched an operation in the Farms. The mortar shelling focused on the "Radar" outpost on a sharp mountain peak opposite Shebaa village. It was the first time that the compound, which actually lay just north of the Shebaa Farms area, was struck, and it was deliberately selected because of its equivalence to the bombed Syrian position in the Bekaa Valley. RADAR FOR RADAR ran a headline in Lebanon's *Al-Mustaqbal* newspaper a day after the attacks. The Israelis refrained from further retaliation. The "balance of terror" had held.

While the attacks and retaliation centered on the Shebaa Farms were the most obvious examples of friction between Hezbollah and Israel, a more subtle conflict was waged almost every day along the Blue Line. Hezbollah erected billboards and dummy Katyusha rocket launchers visible to Israelis on the other side of the border as part of its psychological warfare effort. The most conspicuous example was a billboard placed directly opposite the Israeli compound on the summit of Sheikh Abbad Hill displaying photographs of dead and injured Israeli soldiers, including what was left of the head of Sergeant Itamar Ilya, the Shayetet 13 naval commando who was blown to pieces in the Ansariyah ambush. Written in Arabic and Hebrew beneath the gruesome pictures was the caption "Sharon: your soldiers are still in Lebanon."

When the wind was favorable, Hezbollah supporters would release dozens of balloons carrying anti-Israel messages or pictures of Nasrallah across the border into northern Israel. Hezbollah took to tapping the Israeli security fence along the border with sticks, triggering the alarm system, then timing how long it took Israeli soldiers to reach the scene to check if there had been a breach. "We are in a state of war with them, and psychological warfare is one of the arenas of war," Sheikh Nabil Qawq explained.

Israeli soldiers were not averse to unilaterally goading their opponents on the other side of the fence, either. In January 2002, a Hezbollah militant manning an observation post was temporarily blinded when Israeli soldiers directed a tank's laser range finder at him. Hezbollah fighters lasered Israeli soldiers in kind.

In another incident, soldiers from the Golani Brigade took to dashing across the border and snatching Hezbollah and Amal flags on a dare, an act apparently blessed by the unit's commanding officer. In retaliation, Hezbollah booby-trapped the flags, and the cross-border forays stopped.

Sometimes, however, Hezbollah's psychological needling of the Israelis went dangerously close to snapping the fragile "balance of terror." In March 2002, Hezbollah engineered an audacious—and risky—operation in which two Islamic Jihad volunteers were dispatched across the border to carry out a deadly ambush near the kibbutz of Metsuva. Wearing IDF uniforms and carrying army issue M-16 rifles, the two gunmen opened fire on passing vehicles. By the time Israeli troops rushed to the scene of the ambush and shot the two gunmen dead, five civilians, including a shepherd, two truck drivers, a woman, and her daughter, had been killed.

Although the Israelis were initially unsure whether the gunmen had originated from Lebanon or the West Bank, soldiers tracking the militants found a ladder hidden in brush beside the border fence, which the IDF said was as of "special design." The Israelis concluded that Hezbollah was responsible for the attack.

Hezbollah responded coyly. Nasrallah maintained his usual ambiguity, saying, "Whatever the Israelis are accusing us of, be it realistic or not, is a great honor for us."

Still, Hezbollah's fingerprints were all over the operation. The area of the border on the Lebanese side where the militants had crossed into Israel was under Hezbollah control. The location of the ambush site lay within sight of a Hezbollah observation post on an escarpment from which fighters enjoyed unhindered views of the western Galilee coastline to Haifa, twenty-five miles to the south. The actual attack was even filmed from the Hezbollah post and broadcast live on Al-Manar television.

Although the attack crossed the red line in the evolving "balance of terror" between Hezbollah and Israel, the Israeli government again chose to stay its hand.

The Green Light Turns to Red

In March 2002, rising violence in Israel claimed the lives of 135 Israelis, the highest monthly toll during the Al-Aqsa intifada. During the same period, more than 230 Palestinians died at the hands of the Israeli army, many of them during a major two-week incursion into the West Bank in the first half of the month.

At the end of March, Beirut hosted the annual Arab League summit, during which Crown Prince Abdullah of Saudi Arabia unveiled a proposal to achieve comprehensive peace in the Middle East. In essence, his plan, subsequently known as the Arab Peace Initiative, offered full normalization and security in exchange for an Israeli withdrawal from all Arab territory occupied since 1967, the creation of a Palestinian state, and the return of Palestinian refugees to their original homes. Although Syria endorsed the plan on March 29, along with the twenty-one other members of the Arab League, it did so with reluctance. Syria had consistently refused to discuss normalizing ties with Israel before receiving a guarantee that Israel would fully withdraw from the Golan Heights. In Syrian eyes, the Saudi initiative weakened its negotiating position in future peace talks.

Hours after the vote in Beirut, a Hamas suicide bomber blew himself up in a hotel in Netanya on the eve of the Jewish Passover holiday, killing thirty Israelis. Sharon ignored the Arab Peace Initiative and sent his army back into the West Bank in a massive punitive offensive.

As Israel launched its "Defensive Shield" operation against the Palestinians, Hezbollah, Syria, and Iran sensed an opportunity to squeeze Israel from the north. Nasrallah reportedly ordered the Islamic Resistance to prepare for stepped-up operations in the Shebaa Farms and then met with Bashar al-Assad to secure a green light. Nasrallah is said to have told Assad that Hezbollah could not stand idly by while the Palestinians were being slaughtered in the West Bank and recommended a controlled escalation along the Blue Line. Such a meeting would have been unthinkable during the presidency of Hafez al-Assad, which only underlined how the relationship between Syria and Hezbollah under Bashar al-Assad was evolving from one of client and proxy to a more balanced partnership. For Syria, fuming over the Arab Peace Initiative, a controlled escalation along the Blue Line could be useful.

The Islamic Resistance launched its offensive on March 30, hitting Israeli outposts on the occupied mountainside with an estimated fifty AT-3 Sagger antitank missiles and one hundred mortar rounds. While a symbolic gesture of support by Hezbollah for the Palestinians had been widely expected, the events of the next few days caught most observers by surprise. Hezbollah was soon battering Israeli outposts in the Shebaa Farms on a daily basis, with ever-increasing ferocity. After two weeks of clashes, UNIFIL estimated that Hezbollah had fired 1,160 mortar rounds, 205 antitank missiles, and Katyusha rockets as well as several SAM-7 antiaircraft missiles, the first recorded use of SAMs since before 2000. The attacks peaked on April 10, when all outposts in the Shebaa Farms came under what UNIFIL said in an internal memo was probably the heaviest artillery barrage by the Islamic Resistance since 1992. According to one report, an estimated $800,000 worth of ordnance was expended.[3] At least four hundred mortar rounds were fired in the attack, some of them 120 mm "bunker-busters" fitted with delayed-action fuses designed to penetrate the thick reinforced concrete roofs of outposts before exploding, the first time Hezbollah had employed such munitions. The barrage provided cover for a "publicity raid," in which a squad of Hezbollah fighters approached an IDF forward base on the edge of the Shebaa Farms to plant a yellow party flag on the ramparts.

Within two or three days, Hezbollah's bombardments settled into a routine. Most of the attacks occurred in the late afternoon when the setting sun shone directly into the west-facing Israeli outposts. The offensive was tailor-made for the media. Camera crews obediently lined up each afternoon beside an Indian UNIFIL observation post facing an IDF outpost less than a mile away, ready to capture the next attack on film.

While Hezbollah was preoccupied with the Shebaa Farms, a more worrying development emerged when unidentified militants began staging attacks across the Blue Line directly into Israel. They were scrappy and amateurish for the most part: a handful of rocket-propelled grenades fired at an IDF border post or a pair of old 107 mm rockets sailing across the border. Several Palestinians—"disorganized individuals," a Lebanese army officer told me—were caught in possession of rockets.

Yet by the second week, it appeared that what had begun as a controlled escalation was slipping out of control, to Hezbollah's apparent discomfort. When militants attacked an IDF border post one afternoon, an eyewitness told me he saw several startled Hezbollah men leave their own observation post, jump into a car, and chase the fleeing attackers down a valley.

Even Yasser Arafat sent a message to President Emile Lahoud grumbling that the fighting along Israel's northern border was drawing international attention away from the beleaguered Palestinians in the West Bank.

Sensing that the situation was growing unpredictable, Nasrallah chose to ease tensions by announcing that widening the conflict with Israel "all the way from the [Mediterranean] sea to Mount Hermon" would not take place at this time. That option, he said, was being held in reserve in the event that Israel expelled the Palestinians from the occupied territories.

After two weeks, the offensive had played its course, and all sides began to de-escalate.

Although the April offensive came close to upsetting the "balance of terror," the outcome was more than satisfying for Hezbollah and Syria. Hezbollah had flexed its resistance muscles and burnished its reputation as the spearhead of the struggle against Israel, while Syria had demonstrated once again that it remained essential to stability along Israel's northern border. The violence along the Lebanon-Israel border successfully diverted some international attention from the West Bank to Damascus. Dick Cheney, the U.S. vice president, had held a "polite and courteous" phone conversation with Assad, and the fighting had forced Colin Powell, the U.S. secretary of state, to readjust his schedule for a planned trip to the Middle East to include Beirut and Damascus on his itinerary.[4]

Significantly, the outcome hardened the view within Hezbollah and in Damascus that Israel had gone soft, that it was no longer the feisty, belligerent nation of soldier-settlers that had crushed and humiliated the Arabs, smashing their armies and seizing their land. Now the average young Israeli looked for a lucrative career in finance or technology rather than serving in the military or living the ascetic life of a kibbutznik. Even Ariel Sharon, that old Jewish warrior, had chosen to overrule his own cabinet when midway through the crisis it had voted by a margin of one for forceful military action against Lebanon. Sharon, who himself had voted in favor of heavy retaliation, decided that a one-vote majority was insufficient to launch reprisals that risked developing into a war with Syria.

Hezbollah took encouragement and satisfaction from what it perceived was the crumbling morale of the Israeli people as the Al-Aqsa intifada raged on. Israel's frail economy, the slump in the number of tourists, and the growing polarization between Israelis calling for a withdrawal from the occupied territories and those demanding harsher action against the Palestinians merely strengthened Hezbollah's conviction that the Jewish state could be defeated through resistance and jihad.

"Israel is exploding from inside," Sheikh Nabil Qawq told me in February 2002. "Tel Aviv is turning into a city of ghosts. The Israelis have lost confidence in their leaders and their army. . . . The only and lasting way for the Arab people is the path of resistance."

Subversive Activities

While the attacks in the Shebaa Farms captured the headlines and provoked speculation on the possibilities of a new front opening, Hezbollah also waged a more insidious and covert war across the Blue Line. Even before the May 2000 Israeli withdrawal, Hezbollah had begun making contacts with Israeli Arab communities in Galilee in order to build a network of intelligence-gathering cells. The program accelerated following the Israeli withdrawal when Hezbollah deployed into the border district and co-opted some of the cross-border drug smuggling networks. Hezbollah's intelligence penetration of Israel was well planned, multitiered, and conducted with a high degree of professionalism, ruefully acknowledged by Western and Israeli intelligence officials.

In exchange for cash and narcotics, such as Lebanese hashish, or cocaine and heroin refined in secret laboratories in the northern Bekaa Valley, the Israeli Arab agents provided Hezbollah with valuable intelligence on Israel's northern border, including details of IDF outposts, the number of troops deployed, ambush locations along the border fence, surveillance and reconnaissance measures, personal details about IDF officers, and maps and photographs of military installations. The tactical intelligence was fed into potential plans for cross-border penetrations, abductions, and localized attacks.

Hezbollah also gathered detailed operational intelligence on facilities, military and civilian, throughout Israel to be included in a target bank for potential rocket strikes or bomb attacks in a future war. These facilities included IDF bases, government institutions, and industrial centers as well as major road junctions, towns, and cities.

On a strategic level, Hezbollah sought intelligence about Israeli politics, economy, and society. Some of Hezbollah's agents were tasked with gathering seemingly mundane information, such as statistical annuals, telephone directories, reference books, and periodicals. Along with the activities of the party's Hebrew speakers in the Hebrew Observation Department at Al-Manar television who trawl Israeli newspapers, television, and radio each day, the information provided by the network of agents inside Israel helped Hezbollah build a more comprehensive and thorough picture of how Israel works in order to better analyze future moves by Israel as well as to predict potential Israeli reactions to attacks.

In tandem with the direct intelligence-gathering operations using the cross-border drug smuggling connections, trained Hezbollah intelligence officers traveled abroad seeking to recruit university-educated Israeli Arabs attending conferences and even the annual pilgrimage, or Hajj, when the Muslim faithful travel to Mecca in Saudi Arabia.

The favorite location for exchanging drugs, information, and cash was in the northern—Lebanese—two-thirds of Ghajar, which remained unfenced from the southern one-third of the village under Israeli control. Ghajar, described by one Israeli army officer as Israel's "soft underbelly," was a persistent worry on account of its vulnerability to penetration from the Lebanese side and the doubtful loyalties of its residents.

Initially, access to Ghajar from Lebanon was blocked because of the presence of a UNIFIL position beside a gate in the old Israeli security fence that encircled the northern tip of the village. But in August 2001, UNIFIL relocated its observation post to a new site a hundred yards farther south. Suddenly, anyone could drive through the gate and follow the dilapidated former Israeli patrol road on the southern side of the fence straight into the northern end of Ghajar. To the alarm of the Israelis and the Alawite residents, the first visitors were from Hezbollah. A dozen or so fighters erected a white tent on the outskirts of the village and turned an old bomb shelter built from blocks of black basalt into a command post. The new Hezbollah position beside the village renewed speculation that the Israelis would divide Ghajar with a security fence, a move vigorously opposed by the residents. Apart from Hezbollah mili-

tants, the only other visitors to the village were curious Lebanese reporters. Neither group was made particularly welcome by the villagers.

"Israel is making it very difficult for us because of you coming here,"
said Bassem Khatib to a group of us who wandered into the village one
August morning. "When the Israeli soldiers see someone coming into
Ghajar they close the gate at the [southern] entrance to the village and
we are stuck here. It doesn't matter if someone is sick, they won't open
the gate to let them out."

Most residents studiously ignored us. A young girl hurried past.
Would she stop and talk for a moment? "Talk? About what?" she replied,
with a nervous smile and an apologetic half shrug.

A convoy of cars drove slowly past, kicking up a cloud of white dust.
Stony-faced men, some with shaved heads and wearing black wrap-
around sunglasses, scowled at us through the windows.

"Israeli *mukhabarat,*" whispered one of the Lebanese journalists.

A car drove up from the southern end of the village and a cameraman and his colleague climbed out. "Hi, we're from Channel Two," said
the cameraman cheerfully, referring to Israel's leading television station.
He shouldered his camera and began filming. The Lebanese reporters
accompanying me glanced at each other uneasily as they realized that
their faces would be splashed all over Israeli television that evening. It is
illegal for Lebanese to have any contact with Israel.

"How did you get into the village?" the cameraman asked, apparently unaware that he had crossed the Blue Line and was standing on
Lebanese soil. The Israeli and Lebanese cameramen stood two yards
apart and filmed each other filming each other in part of a village that
lay inside Lebanon but whose residents considered themselves Syrian
nationals even though they held Israeli citizenship. Such was the unusual position in which Ghajar found itself.

The encounter with the Israeli camera crew underlined just how easy
it was to smuggle goods or information from Lebanon into Israel
through Ghajar. Before long, the Hezbollah fighters began barring visitors from entering the village. Their command post in the old bomb
shelter was festooned with yellow Hezbollah flags and camouflage netting slung over the entrance.

A Hezbollah man accompanied me on a stroll down the side of the village to the new security fence along the Blue Line. Little stirred in Ghajar. A few children played in a street, and a couple of elderly residents stared blankly at us. No one attempted to strike up a conversation. Across the hot, grassy plain a few hundred yards to the southeast lay a large Israeli compound, a line of Merkava tanks and armored personnel carriers baking in the scorching sun.

Did the Hezbollah fighter and his comrades have any contact with the residents of Ghajar?

"No," he said. "It's forbidden."

By whom?

"Orders," he replied.

"The Alliance of Blood Is Coming Apart"

That was not exactly true. In September 2002, the Israeli authorities broke up the biggest spy ring yet. Altogether, eleven Israeli Arabs were detained, six of them serving with the Israeli army, including the leader of the ring, Omar Hayeb, a lieutenant colonel. Ironically, Hayeb had lost an eye to a Hezbollah roadside bomb in 1996. The lure of cash and hard drugs evidently overcame any lingering resentment Hayeb might have felt toward his former adversaries. He was recruited in late 2000 by Ramzi Nohra's brother, Kamil. According to a Lebanese intelligence source, Ramzi ran the cell in coordination with a Hezbollah intelligence officer, while Kamil was the link man to Hayeb.

In exchange for cash and drugs, Hayeb fulfilled requests for items and information, such as large-scale maps of the Shebaa Farms and northern Golan Heights and details of Israeli army compounds along the border, including surveillance equipment used on the bases. Hezbollah even attempted to obtain and crack the Israeli army's radio encryption code, dubbed Otiyot, Hebrew for "letters."[5]

The exposure of the Hayeb spy ring stunned the Israeli army and sent a tremor of unease throughout Israeli society. "When a high-ranking officer, a scion of a loyal and well-rooted community, one of the system's darlings, one of the most senior signatories to the alliance of blood between us [Jews] and those [Arabs] who live among us, forsakes IDF soldiers with such ease to the graces of Hezbollah—that is a sign that something fundamental has gone awry. The alliance of blood is coming apart at the seams," wrote the Israeli columnist Ben Caspit in the *Maariv* daily.[6]

With the discovery of the Omar Hayeb espionage cell in September 2002, Israel's patience with Ramzi Nohra appears to have run out. During the eight years he had cooperated with Hezbollah and the military intelligence services of Syria and Lebanon, Ramzi had played roles in some of the most sophisticated and successful operations waged against Israel—the capture of Ahmad Hallaq in 1996, the assassination of General Erez Gerstein in 1999, the abduction of the three Israeli soldiers from the Shebaa Farms in 2000, and the handling of drugs-for-intelligence spy rings in Israel following the Israeli withdrawal from Lebanon. The Israelis decided it was time to settle accounts.

On the morning of December 6, 2002, Ramzi, accompanied by his thirty-year-old nephew Elie Issa, drove his Mercedes out of Ibl es-Saqi village and turned right onto the main road heading north. He had driven barely two miles from his home when a rock-disguised IED exploded beside his vehicle. Both Ramzi and Issa were killed instantly.

As soon as the news of the assassination broke, a team from Hezbollah hurriedly drove to Ramzi's home and locked one of the rooms in his villa, according to a Lebanese intelligence source. What was in the room remains unknown, but Ramzi held many secrets that Hezbollah and others would prefer stay hidden.

Nasrallah, attending Issa's funeral in the Bekaa Valley, vowed to "cut off the criminal terrorist hand that reached this martyr and the martyr Ramzi." And revenge was swift in coming. Two days after Ramzi's death, a powerful roadside bomb exploded beside the border fence in the western sector as an Israeli army Humvee passed by. The two soldiers in the vehicle were badly wounded; one of them lost both his legs in the blast. A statement claiming responsibility was released in Beirut by the "Ramzi

Nohra Martyr Group." Hezbollah denied any knowledge, although no one doubted that the party had perpetrated the attack, just as it was obvious that Israel was responsible for killing Ramzi.

Even though Israel remained silent about Ramzi's death, Hezbollah and others who closely followed the cycle of violence in south Lebanon recognized an implicit claim of responsibility in the location the assassins selected for the roadside bomb attack. For Ramzi Nohra died in exactly the same place as the IED explosion nearly four years earlier that had killed General Gerstein.

Water Wars

Israel's own actions along the border sometimes played into Hezbollah's hands, helping the organization make its case for retaining its arms. The most intrusive example was the near daily overflights in Lebanese airspace, which had resumed following the abduction of the three soldiers in October 2000. Israel's sensitivity over its water resources also created a series of unnecessary crises between 2001 and 2002, swiftly seized by Hezbollah as evidence of Israel's ill intentions toward Lebanon.

In March 2001, the Lebanese government installed a small pump and a pipe to supply drinking water to the tiny village of Wazzani from the nearby spring that bubbles up into the Hasbani River. The Hasbani flows into Israel two miles south of the spring, where it forms one of three tributaries of the Jordan River, which runs into the Sea of Galilee, Israel's largest source of fresh water.

Although Israel had been informed of the pumping project a month earlier, the Israeli government issued a flurry of warnings against Lebanese attempts to divert water and threatened to destroy the new pumping station. The fuss died down when the UN pointed out to the Israelis that the pipe was only four inches in diameter. But three months later, Hussein Abdullah, a local landowner, inadvertently roiled the waters when he began installing a six-inch-diameter pipe to irrigate his farmland. The Israelis cried foul once more and warned that continued pumping from the Hasbani River could trigger a confrontation between Lebanon and Israel.

In the blinding heat of summer, the only source of water for the Hasbani River was the Wazzani spring, a tranquil pool of shallow water some twenty yards across, strewn with black basalt boulders and shaded by oleander and eucalyptus trees. Years earlier, the Israelis had installed two small pumps at the spring to provide drinking water for Ghajar, which lies adjacent on the eastern bank of the Hasbani. The Lebanese authorities had allowed the pumping to continue after the Israeli withdrawal, presumably because the recipients of the water were Syrian Alawites rather than Jewish Israelis.

When Lebanon announced in the summer of 2002 that it was expanding the project by installing a larger pipe to convey water to some sixty villages, Ariel Sharon called it a casus belli and warned that the pumping station could be destroyed if the project went ahead.

Such inflammatory rhetoric was a godsend for Hezbollah. Nasrallah cautioned Israel that it would fall into an "unrelenting death mill . . . from village to village, house to house and canyon to canyon" if it proceeded with its plans to attack the pumping site.[7]

The UN and the United States were dragged into the dispute and attempted to mediate a solution. Ultimately, Lebanon was within its rights to draw off some of the water, and there was nothing Israel could do about it. What should have been a minor infrastructure project was inflated into a national celebration when the pumping facility was formally inaugurated in September 2002. Before a crowd of thousands, President Emile Lahoud turned on the tap, washed his hands, and drank some of the water as hundreds of balloons were released and carried by the gentle evening breeze toward the grassy slopes of the Golan Heights.

"The Battle Is Open with Israel"

While the Shebaa Farms was the designated "hot" zone for combat operations, Hezbollah constantly devised new tactics to keep the Israelis on edge elsewhere along the border. These tactics were sufficiently subtle and low-key to stay within the rules of the game and prevent an unwanted escalation while at the same time robust enough to reinforce Hezbollah's deterrence posture and preserve the "balance of terror." The tactics were steadily refined between 2000 and 2006 as the rules of the game evolved.

"The battle is open with Israel," Sheikh Naim Qassem explained to me in 2004. "We are not supposed to make them comfortable. It is a basic rule of combat to make the enemy nervous. And we try to achieve this with whatever tool we have at our disposal, be it political or military. Israel must understand that the resistance is present and watching and can reach them at any time."

In response to Israel's near-daily breaches of Lebanese airspace with jets and UAVs, Hezbollah in January 2002 began firing 57 mm antiaircraft shells across the border. The foot-long shells were not aimed at the jets; instead, they exploded with a loud bang high above Israeli border settlements, spattering whatever lay below with light shrapnel. The new tactic had been in development for some months as Hezbollah mulled a way of confronting Israel's aerial reconnaissance flights. Initially, Hezbollah considered firing modified RPG-7 rocket-propelled grenades or small-caliber Katyusha rockets across the border, as "noisemakers" rather than to score casualties or damage. But after test-firing them in a deep valley near the border and launching them out to sea, they soon found that the RPGs lacked range and the Katyushas were unsuitable, so they settled on the 57 mm cannons.

Hezbollah eventually installed up to twenty antiaircraft cannons covering the length of the border, some close to the Blue Line. I stumbled across the location of one by chance in 2002. Driving along a back road near the border early one afternoon, I pulled over for a moment to have a look at an old SLA outpost near the village of Talloussa. As I parked, a bearded man dressed in a camouflage uniform emerged from the entrance riding a small scooter. His jaw dropped as he saw a foreigner climb out of the car. The fighter spoke into his walkie-talkie to summon his comrades, and they, too, emerged from the compound. They searched my car and took my bag with my notebook and camera along with my wristwatch and wallet. They allowed me to call Hezbollah's press office in Beirut on my mobile phone. I handed the phone to one of the Hezbollah men, and the press assistant Hussein Naboulsi vouched for me. But it would be some time before I was released.

The Hezbollah men told me to drive to nearby Markaba and park beside the mosque, where someone would meet me. When I arrived at the mosque a few minutes later, a bearded and demure young man ushered me into an empty room at the back and offered me tea. It took three hours for the requisite checks to be made; the local military commanders had apparently been in a lengthy meeting and could not be disturbed until it was over. A Hezbollah man eventually arrived at the mosque, carrying my belongings in a plastic bag. He insisted that I check that everything was there before leaving. As I stepped outside, the early evening stillness was broken by the thump of antiaircraft rounds. Looking to the southeast I could just make out the tip of the barrel of the gun in the old Talloussa outpost and see dust and smoke rising from the position. The 57 mm rounds exploded over the border in white cottonball puffs of smoke against a Prussian-blue evening sky.

As the months ticked by, Hezbollah began to lower its aim, sending the shells deeper into Israel and increasing the risk of civilian casualties. In August 2003, a sixteen-year-old boy was killed by falling shrapnel in the border settlement of Shelomi, the first Israeli civilian to die since the withdrawal from Lebanon three years earlier. Israel ended its restraint and sent jets into Lebanon to bomb the antiaircraft battery that had fired the fatal rounds. In the following months, Israel struck twice more against Hezbollah positions in response to bursts of cross-border antiaircraft fire. The Israelis had called Hezbollah's bluff, and the tactic came to an end.

But Hezbollah soon came up with another trick. At the end of October 2004, Nasrallah said that Hezbollah was planning "a new equation" to confront the aerial violations. That "new equation" was unveiled eight days later when Hezbollah launched a UAV fitted with a video camera (dubbed Mirsad-1, Arabic for "observer") and sent it on a short reconnaissance flight over northern Israel. Hezbollah claimed to have manufactured the UAV itself, but according to Israel, Mirsad-1 was Hezbollah's name for the Iranian Ababil-T, a pneumatically launched attack and reconnaissance drone. The Mirsad-1 flew a second mission six months later.

Dispatching UAVs across the border was a crafty response to Israel's continued overflights. Not only did it embarrass the IDF, which failed to detect the UAV intrusions, it exposed the vulnerability of Israel's northern border to airborne attack (the drone could have been fitted with a bomb weighing dozens of pounds). Furthermore, it frustrated Israel's retaliatory options. Under the rules of the game, Israel would have been hard-pressed to justify bombing more Hezbollah positions, given that flying the drone over northern Israel was a benign response to Israel's repeated overflights in Lebanese airspace.

A Carefully Planned Setup

As this complex game of mild attrition was played out along the Blue Line, it was easy to imagine seasoned Hezbollah veterans sitting around a table, brows furrowed in concentration as they brainstormed ever more elaborate and cunning ploys to alarm and infuriate the Israelis. One tactic used between November 2003 and May 2004 was the planting of several IED clusters along the length of the Blue Line. The bombs were generally hidden beneath hollow fiberglass "rocks" but not so well disguised that they could not be spotted by vigilant Israeli soldiers patrolling the border fence. The intention was to keep the Israeli troops on edge, never quite sure whether one of the bombs would suddenly explode as they drove by in a Humvee. Although the bombs were planted on the Lebanese side of Israel's security fence, they were often on the Israeli side of the Blue Line. Israel's border fence does not exactly follow the Blue Line but deviates by as much as a hundred yards or more into Israeli territory, depending on the topography and security requirements. The anomaly allowed the Israelis to cut through the fence and remove the bomb clusters without transgressing the Lebanese side of the Blue Line.

One January morning in 2004, an Israeli D-9 armored bulldozer crossed the fence to clear several IEDs planted just inside Israeli territory. Unknown to the Israeli troops monitoring the operation, the bulldozer was under close observation by Hezbollah. At some point, the bulldozer accidentally strayed across the Blue Line while removing the bombs. It was the moment the watching Hezbollah men had been waiting for. Later the same day, the bulldozer was struck by an antitank missile and the driver killed. Hezbollah defended its action, saying that the bulldozer had transgressed the Blue Line, in just one of sixty-five land, sea, and air violations of Lebanese territory recorded that month alone.[8] It was a disingenuous excuse—the missile was fired several hours after the bulldozer edged over the Blue Line—but Hezbollah was playing by the same uncompromising rules as the Israelis. Three months earlier, Egoz soldiers on ambush duty on the border had shot dead two Lebanese hunters who had accidentally strayed over the Blue Line by a few yards. Israeli troops were under standing orders to shoot any armed person who crossed the line, even a hunter carrying only a shotgun. Hezbollah was ruthlessly applying the same measure.

Four months later, Hezbollah took the tactic one step further. At dawn one May morning, Israeli soldiers in a compound on the Shebaa Farms front line spotted a group of five Hezbollah fighters carrying equipment through the rocky terrain on the Lebanese side of the Blue Line. The Israelis opened fire, and the Hezbollah men vanished from sight. Puzzled at the unusual sighting of Islamic Resistance fighters close to an Israeli outpost, IDF commanders dispatched a unit of Egoz commandos to scout the area early the next morning. In the course of the patrol, the Egoz squad crossed the Blue Line and discovered hidden among rocks a roadside bomb inside a backpack, sleeping bags, warm weather clothing, a stretcher, and a camouflage net. The patrol concluded that it had foiled an attempt to kidnap Israeli troops and returned to base. However, as the commandos reached the entrance of their compound, several IEDs exploded beside them, as Hezbollah fire support teams simultaneously shelled Israeli positions throughout the Shebaa Farms. One soldier was killed and another five wounded. Again, Hezbollah publicly billed the ambush as a successful effort to thwart an IDF incursion onto Lebanese territory. In fact, it was a carefully planned setup. The unusual sighting of fighters was intended to lure Israeli troops across the Blue Line as a pretext for launching a deadly assault with roadside bombs. It came as an unpleasant surprise to the Israelis that for all their defensive measures in the Shebaa Farms, Hezbollah fighters had still been able to infiltrate undetected right up to the entrance of an outpost to plant the IEDs, echoing similar feats in the occupation zone in the late 1990s.

"Respond to Any Israeli Violation"

Besides initiating various ploys to needle the Israelis, Hezbollah also used the Blue Line as a locus of retaliation in which eye-for-an-eye tactics were developed as a response to Israeli actions in Lebanon and further afield.

When Ramzi Nohra was killed by an IED in December 2002, Hezbollah responded with a roadside bomb attack that wounded two Israeli soldiers.

In August 2003, Ali Saleh, a top Hezbollah operative, was killed in a car bomb blast in the southern suburbs of Beirut in what appeared to be a rare penetration by Israel of Hezbollah's usually airtight security. Six days later, Hezbollah pounded outposts in the Shebaa Farms in an attack dedicated to the slain militant.

The Shebaa Farms was shelled again in March 2004 in honor of Sheikh Ahmad Yassin, the blind, paraplegic spiritual leader of Hamas, less than twelve hours after missile-firing Israeli helicopters killed him as he was wheeled out of a prayer session in Gaza.

When Israeli jets bombed a Palestinian training camp near Damascus in October 2003, the retaliation came not from the Syrians or Palestinians, but from a Hezbollah sniper who the following day shot and killed a Golani Brigade soldier on ambush duty beside the border fence.

On July 20, 2004, two Israeli soldiers clambered onto the roof of a border compound opposite Aitta Shaab village in the western sector to fix an antenna. They had just begun their work when both were shot dead by a Hezbollah sniper in a camouflaged observation post in dense brush about five hundred yards to the east. The sniper achieved two head shots and one to the chest. Israeli tank fire blasted the sniper's location, killing him, while helicopter gunships fired missiles into a nearby Hezbollah outpost. The shooting had come hours after another top Hezbollah operative, Ghaleb Awali, was killed in a car bomb explosion in the southern suburbs, an attack that, for Hezbollah, bore alarming similarities to the assassination of Saleh almost a year earlier.

Months before, Hezbollah's leadership had instructed its cadres in the south to automatically retaliate to breaches of the Blue Line, whether by ground, air, or sea, including assassinations. "[W]e have given an authorization to the brother mujahideen on the front lines to act. We told them: respond to any Israeli violation of the border with Lebanon by opening fire directly without referring to the political leadership," Nasrallah said in October 2004.

With Awali's death in Beirut, the Islamic Resistance went on alert along the Blue Line looking for targets of opportunity. The retaliation could have come in the form of a roadside bomb detonated beside the fence or an antitank missile strike. The Israeli army imposed a security alert along the northern border with troop movements severely restricted. But an officer in the outpost opposite Aitta Shaab made a mistake in ordering the two soldiers onto the roof of the compound to fix a broken antenna. The soldiers were not even wearing body armor. The Hezbollah sniper on watch in his observation post saw the two soldiers climb onto the roof and immediately took advantage of the Israeli error and shot them dead.

"The resistance movement will always be ready and on alert in order to consolidate the equation: security for security and economy for economy and aggression for aggression. . . . In other words, deterrence for the enemy," said Sayyed Hisham Safieddine, the head of Hezbollah's Executive Council, a week after Awali's assassination.

The Israeli media in the two days following the killing of the soldiers was filled with quotes from anonymous army officers warning that "the region is a powder keg," stressing the importance of sending a "tough warning," and asserting that the sniping had "definitely crossed a red line." But other than the retaliatory air strikes in the south, Israel settled for a muscle-flexing low-level sonic boom sortie over Beirut, a response that the Lebanese had long ago learned to associate with Israeli frustration.

"The deterrence is in the other direction," said an editorial in Israel's *Hatzofe* newspaper. "The IDF and the Israeli government fear Hezbollah's response, and therefore, after every murder or attempt at murder by the Hezbollah bums, the IDF carries out some sort of tepid act for show in order not to annoy, God forbid, Sheikh Nasrallah."[9]

NINE

Spoonfuls of Cement

We are confident enough in our capabilities to make any Israeli adventure very expensive, so high that they cannot tolerate the burden.

—SHEIKH NABIL QAWQ,
June 14, 2006

MARCH 25, 2007

ALMA SHAAB, south Lebanon—The dirt track wound through blossom-scented orange orchards before entering a narrow valley flanked by an impenetrable-looking mantle of bushes and small trees. Lizards and snakes slithered from under our feet, but we kept a wary eye open for unexploded cluster bombs left over from repeated Israeli artillery strikes on the western end of the valley during the monthlong war between Hezbollah and Israel seven months earlier.

Every few seconds I glanced at the electronic arrow on my handheld global-positioning system that was directing us toward what I hoped would be the entrance to one of Hezbollah's secret wartime underground bunkers. Since the end of the war, finding and exploring a Hezbollah bunker had become a near obsession, ever since I had been given a tantalizing hint shortly after the August cease-fire at what Hezbollah had covertly and skillfully constructed between 2000 and 2006.

Before the war, no one had imagined that Hezbollah was installing such an extravagant military infrastructure in the border district. Their visible activities generally consisted of establishing between twenty-five and thirty observation posts along the Blue Line, stretching from the chalk cliffs of Ras Naqoura on the coast in the west to the lofty limestone mountains of the Shebaa Farms in the east. Hezbollah also placed off-limits several stretches of rugged hills and valleys in the border district. The entrances were guarded by armed and uniformed fighters. Local farmers and even UNIFIL peacekeepers were denied access to some of these "security pockets." One valley, a deep ravine of limestone cliffs and caves that slashed through the western sector like a giant ax stroke, was marked as a no-fly zone on the maps used by UNIFIL's Italian air wing.

In August 2002, Hezbollah took over a hillside overlooking the coast outside Naqoura, the location of UNIFIL's headquarters. A narrow lane wound up the hill, ending at a small UNIFIL observation post at the long-disappeared farmstead of Labboune. It was a popular spot for tourists, as the ridge granted a grandstand view of western Galilee down the coast to Haifa and Mount Carmel, twenty-five miles to the south. After Hezbollah seized the Labboune hillside for its own purposes, only UNIFIL was allowed to use the lane to reach its observation post. Shortly after the hillside was sealed off, I drove up the lane to see what would happen. About halfway up I spotted several fighters in the dense brush crouched beside a large object smothered in camouflage netting, possibly an antiaircraft gun. They scowled at me as I passed by and evidently alerted some of their colleagues by radio, as there was a small reception committee waiting for me beside the road as I returned to Naqoura. "This is a military zone. You can't come here anymore," one of them chided me.

Two months later, a convoy of American diplomats from the U.S. embassy in Beirut ran into a similar problem when they were intercepted by armed Hezbollah men while en route to the Labboune viewing point, unaware that the hillside was no longer accessible. With the Hezbollah men refusing to allow the diplomatic convoy to proceed, the embassy's security team called off the planned tour of the Blue Line and headed back to Beirut. As the motorcade drove north out of Naqoura along the coastal road, they were joined by two carloads of armed

Hezbollah men, who wove between the convoy vehicles. The U.S. embassy and the State Department lodged formal complaints with the Lebanese government, but it was the last time diplomats attempted to peer into Israel from Labboune.

It was unclear to us exactly what Hezbollah was up to inside these security pockets, although clues hinting at clandestine activity emerged from time to time. In early June 2002, residents of two small villages at the foot of the Shebaa Farms hills were kept awake at night by the sound of dynamite explosions emanating from a remote wadi near an abandoned farmstead. The peak of Hezbollah's construction activities appears to have been in 2003, when UNIFIL was recording "sustained explosions" numbering as many as twenty-five at a time, all in remote wadis and hillsides.

But it was only following the August 14 cease-fire ending the monthlong war in 2006 that the astonishing scale of Hezbollah's underground network of bunkers and firing positions in the southern border district came to light.

For example, the Labboune hillside, which was covered in thick brush and small evergreen oaks, was the source of almost constant rocket fire by Hezbollah throughout the war, from the first day until shortly before the 8:00 A.M. cease-fire on August 14. The Israeli military attempted to stanch the flow of rockets with air strikes, cluster bombs, and artillery shells packed with phosphorus, but the Katyusha fire was relentless. After the cease-fire, Israeli soldiers deployed onto the hill and discovered an elaborate bunker and artillery-firing system sunk into solid rock some 120 feet deep and spread over an area three-quarters of a square mile. The bunkers included firing positions, ammunition storage facilities, operations rooms, dormitories, medical facilities, lighting and ventilation, and kitchens and bathrooms with latrines and hot and cold running water—sufficient to allow dozens of fighters to live underground for weeks without need for resupply. A day after the bunker was dynamited by the Israelis, I visited the site with Lorenzo Cremonesi, a correspondent for Italy's Corriere della Sera newspaper. We gingerly followed a caterpillar track into the old minefield running on the Lebanese side of the border fence. All that remained of the bunker was a field of churned earth and slabs of yard-thick reinforced concrete poking out of the ground like broken teeth. Yet the most extraordinary discovery was not that Hezbollah had built the bunker beneath a minefield, but that the bunker began just a hundred yards from, and within full view of, the UNIFIL observation post on the border. It was only fifty yards from the lane used by UNIFIL traffic each day. The bunker was also in full view of an Israeli border position some four hundred yards to the west on the other side of the fence. How was it possible for Hezbollah to construct such a large facility with neither UNIFIL nor the Israelis having any idea of its existence?

"We never saw them build anything," a UNIFIL officer told me. "They must have brought the cement in by the spoonful."

Spiders and Claustrophobia

The sight of the dynamited ruins at Labboune inspired me to find an intact bunker. Although the border district was littered with newly abandoned bunkers, finding them was difficult and hazardous given their remote locations, the presence of unexploded munitions, and the superbly camouflaged entrances, some of them covered by hollow fiber- glass "rocks" similar to those used to hide IEDs. After several false leads, I acquired a set of map coordinates marking the locations of Hezbollah bunkers and rocket-firing posts near the village of Alma Shaab. Punch- ing the coordinates into a handheld GPS device, I headed into a former Hezbollah security pocket accompanied by Ghaith Abdul-Ahad, an in- trepid war correspondent for *The Guardian* and a photographer for the Getty agency.

We had walked along the track at the bottom of the valley for about ten minutes when the arrow on the GPS began to rotate to the right. We left the track and, once beneath the canopy of dense foliage, noticed numerous thin trails made by Hezbollah militants crisscrossing the hill- side. Steps of rock-hard sandbags helped overcome the steeper sections. We scanned the footpath carefully, not only for cluster bombs but also for possible booby traps. Hezbollah had rigged some simple IEDs consisting of trip wires attached to blocks of TNT around some of their old positions to deter snoopers.

After a five-minute climb, my GPS informed us that we had reached our destination. But there was no bunker entrance to be seen, just outcrops of rock, thickets of thorn bushes, scrub oak, and tree roots snaking across the bedrock beneath a carpet of dead leaves and dried twigs. Thinking the GPS must be off by a few feet, I moved away to examine the surrounding area for the entrance. But it was Ghaith who found it. He was tapping the ground with a stick when he struck something metallic and hollow-sounding. Together we brushed away the leaves and twigs to reveal a square matte black metal lid with two handles. Dragging the heavy lid to one side exposed a narrow steel-lined shaft that dropped vertically about fifteen feet into the bedrock. Dank, musty air rose from the gloom. It had taken seven months to finally discover one of Hezbollah's war bunkers; but any exhilaration was dampened by the dread of claustrophobia. "If we have to crawl when we're down there, I can't do it," Ghaith said.

Wearing a headlamp and using metal footholds welded onto the side of the shaft, I climbed down into the shadows below and saw with some relief that the tunnel extending into the hillside at the bottom was taller than we had feared. We would have to crouch, but not crawl. It was still a tight squeeze as we inched cautiously along the damp, silent passageway, which ran for about seven yards before turning left and descending in a gradual slant. The rock sides of the tunnel were lined with a mesh of steel bars and girders painted white. Huge motionless brown spiders clung to the walls, watching the human intruders impassively. A side tunnel reinforced with walls and ceiling of glossy white-painted steel plates and girders led into a small steel-lined chamber. The room, which was bare apart from two empty five-gallon water containers, must have been at least ninety feet underground and probably could have withstood a direct hit by one of Israel's massive aerial bombs—assuming the Israelis had known where to drop it. An electric cable ran along the walls linking several bare bulbs. A black plastic bag hanging from a hook contained the remains of what seven months earlier could have been fresh oranges or apples. A second entrance lower down the hill had been blocked with rocks and cement. It was not a large bunker, probably home to several fighters who manned the Katyusha firing positions nearby.

Weeks later, I had an opportunity to explore a much larger command bunker near Rshaf village in the western sector. I had to crawl over a pile of rocks partially blocking the narrow square access shaft, which was sunk horizontally into the side of a valley. After a couple of yards, the passageway opened up, allowing me to stand. The passage was little more than shoulder-width, and I had to stoop slightly to avoid hitting the ceiling with my head. For the first ten yards, the walls and ceiling were reinforced with steel plates and girders painted matte black to prevent stray reflections of sunlight from giving away the concealed entrance. Around a corner, the steel plates were painted glossy white to better reflect the electric lighting. Electric cables ran through white plastic tubes fixed to the walls leading to switches and glass-encased light sockets. A blue plastic hose running along the top of the wall carried the bunker's water supply. There was a small bathroom complete with an Arab-style latrine, a shower, a basin with taps, and a hot water boiler. A drainage system had even been constructed beneath the concrete floor. In two places along the main passage—which must have been more than forty yards long—were vertical ventilation shafts covered by metal grilles, ensuring a steady flow of fresh air. There was a kitchen with storage shelves and an aluminum sink with taps, its white metal walls mottled with brown rust. Every ten yards or so along the passage was a heavy steel blast door that could be bolted from the inside. I switched off my headlamp for a minute and the silent chilly subterranean blackness closed in around me. What must it have been like for the fighters living here in the war, waiting for the advancing Israeli troops?

At the far end of the bunker, the narrow steel-lined passage broadened out into a rock cavern. In a niche to one side were four metal water tanks with "*fidai,*" Arabic for "sacrifice," painted across them. A twist of a tap at the bottom of one tank and icy water gushed out. Several steep steps cut into the rock at the end of the cavern led to an access shaft about fifteen feet high with rungs welded onto the lining of black metal plates. This exit emerged into a thicket of stubby oak trees about forty yards from the entrance and farther up the hill.

The effort that went into building it was extraordinary, and yet it, like the bunkers at Labboune and Alma Shaab, was constructed in complete secrecy, remaining undetected by satellite surveillance, Israeli aerial reconnaissance, intelligence assets on the ground, and UNIFIL peacekeepers, let alone nosy journalists. Every piece of equipment, including the steel plates, girders, and doors, had had to be carried by hand up the side of the valley and fitted into place inside the bunker. The hundreds of tons of quarried rock were removed, also in secrecy, from the site of each tunnel and bunker, presumably to be scattered carefully beneath the trees of the surrounding hillside—the same technique Hezbollah had used when constructing the prototype tunnels in Mlita on the mountainous edge of the Israeli-occupied Jezzine enclave in the mid-1980s. Certainly, there were no fantails or spoil for patrolling Israeli jets and drones to detect.

This small wadi near Rshaf was home to at least seven other bunkers and rocket-firing positions. A larger valley system a few miles to the east contained more than thirty different positions consisting of at least one command bunker similar to the one I explored near Rshaf, Katyusha-firing positions, one- or two-room huts of cinder block walls draped in camouflage netting, bivouacs, checkpoints at the entrances, observation posts, and expanded natural caves. In all there may have been more than a thousand positions of one type or another covering the southern border district.

Once again, Hezbollah had absorbed and improved upon the earlier experiences of the Palestinians in south Lebanon. Ahmad Jibril, the head of the PFLP-GC and a onetime military engineer, had built in the late 1970s several tunnels sunk into mountainsides in the southern half of Lebanon, large enough to accommodate trucks and tons of armaments. There was nothing discreet about the construction of the tunnels; everyone knew where they were, and the engineers and laborers who built them were regularly subjected to Israeli air raids. While the tunnels were the PFLP-GC's trademark, other Palestinian groups had

eschewed underground fortifications, believing them vulnerable to Israeli commando assaults and preferring instead the low-signature mobility of guerrilla warfare.

Hezbollah, however, had developed a tactic that selected the best elements from both schools. It used the bunker-and-tunnel system to
strengthen its defensive posture in the border district in the event of an
Israeli ground invasion, while constructing the facilities in total secrecy
and limiting their size to retain the element of surprise.

"Truck[load] After Truckload" of Weapons

A visitor to the southern border district in those early months of 2000
following Israel's withdrawal and the onset of Hezbollah's campaign in
the Shebaa Farms would likely have witnessed pastoral routine rather
than a war zone. Even as Hezbollah was quietly sealing off tracts of land
and drawing up blueprints for its underground bunker networks, farmers continued to plant, nurture, and harvest their fields of bright green
tobacco and golden wheat in the stony valleys. In the early fall, families
moved slowly through olive groves, picking the fruit and sorting it on
wool blankets spread on the ground. Wrinkled old ladies smothered in
thick, colorful cotton dresses and headscarves sold seasonal fruit from
roadside stalls—shiny strawberries in the spring, green or purple figs
bursting with sweetness in the late summer heat, crisp apples and water-
melons in the fall. Wiry mahogany-skinned goatherds tossed stones at
errant members of their flock while rangy dogs slumbered in the shade
of oak trees. In the dusty villages, children played in the potholed lanes
that passed for roads in south Lebanon. New villas and mansions built
of stone and marble and surrounded by verdant watered lawns—
ostentatious flauntings of Africa-generated wealth—sprouted on
once-barren hillsides to accommodate long-absent residents during the
summer holiday months.

It was easy to be lulled into a feeling that the military confrontation
between Hezbollah and Israel was relatively straightforward and lim-

ited. If Israel reacted disproportionately to an attack in the Shebaa Farms, then yes, it could expect Hezbollah to unleash salvos of Katyusha rockets from the olive groves of south Lebanon into Galilee. But there was no obvious reason to assume that the balance was fundamentally different from that of the 1990s.

But by the second half of 2001, it was dawning on me that out of sight, something of far greater scale and significance was taking place in the remoter wadis and hilltop villages of south Lebanon. One of my sources referred to "truck[load] after truckload" of weapons arriving in the border district between May 2000 and December 2001. Another source told me that Hezbollah had "more weapons now than they know what to do with." Hezbollah fighters boasted of their psychological readiness to confront Israel and the training that continued despite the Israeli withdrawal. Gradually, the information gleaned from my sources in south Lebanon, observations in the field, interviews with Hezbollah officials, and conversations with fighters left only one conclusion to be drawn—Hezbollah was not contenting itself by simply needling Israel along the Blue Line from time to time, but was engaged in a massive, wide-ranging military buildup in preparation for a possible war with Israel—a war it had every intention of winning.

The arms floodgate to Hezbollah opened after Bashar al-Assad became president of Syria. His father, Hafez, had imposed controls on the quantity and variety of arms he allowed Iran to send to Hezbollah via Damascus airport. Hafez al-Assad preferred to maintain a tactical alliance with Hezbollah and permitted a sufficient flow of arms to the Shia group to resist the Israelis in south Lebanon, but he drew the line at delivering game-changing weapons that could destabilize the Lebanon-Israel theater, possibly at Syria's expense. Under Bashar al-Assad, however, the relationship grew more strategic, with greater quantities of weapons and more advanced systems dispatched across the border into Hezbollah's arms depots. Significantly, Syria for the first time became a major supplier of weaponry to Hezbollah. The Syrians delivered large quantities of 220 mm Uragan rockets, with a forty-two-mile range, and B-302 rockets, which are a Syrian version of a Chinese multiple-launch

rocket system. Some of the rockets were fitted with antipersonnel warheads that spray hundreds of ball bearings on detonation. A few rockets
were filled with Chinese cluster submunitions.

Syria also was the chief supplier of Hezbollah's most advanced antitank missiles after 2000, acquiring from Russia and transferring to its
Shia ally the AT-13 Metis-M, which has a tandem warhead and a range
of just under a mile, and the third generation AT-14 Kornet-E, which
has a laser-beam-riding guidance system and a range of more than three
miles. The AT-14, one of the most advanced missiles in the world, can be
fitted with antiarmor or bunker-busting thermobaric warheads and includes thermal-imaging capability for use at night. Hezbollah's acquisition of the AT-14 significantly raised the level of threat to Israel's fleet of
tanks and armored vehicles.

Hezbollah was thought to have acquired a handful of 240 mm artillery rockets in the late 1990s, although the largest-caliber Katyusha ever
fired into Israel before the IDF withdrawal was the standard 122 mm
with a range of twelve miles. But from 2000 on, in addition to the Syrian
rockets, Hezbollah received the Iranian Fajr family of rockets, with
ranges from twenty-five to fifty miles, and the Falaq system of large-
caliber but short-range rockets. Around 2002, Iran began delivering 610
mm Zelzal-1 and Zelzal-2 sub-ballistic rockets, which can carry an
eleven-hundred-pound payload and travel up to 75 miles and 126 miles
respectively.

In 2003, Israeli military intelligence learned that Hezbollah might
have acquired a weapons system previously unseen in the south Lebanon theater: a shore-to-ship cruise missile. A warning was passed on to
the Israeli navy, but when nothing more was heard, the initial reports
were no longer taken seriously—an oversight that would have deadly
consequences three years later during the July 2006 war. As was subsequently learned, Hezbollah had received a consignment of Iranian Noor
antiship missiles, a reverse-engineered version of the Chinese C-802, a
fifteen-hundred-pound radar-guided cruise missile with a range of
seventy-two miles.

The acquisition of new longer-range rocket systems did not go unnoticed by the Israelis. Even before the Israeli withdrawal in 2000, Israeli

officials, military and civilian, regularly fed the media with assessments of Hezbollah's arms buildup. The number of rockets in Hezbollah's arsenal was estimated at eight thousand in 2000, a figure that two years later had risen to ten thousand. In May 2006, Major General Amos Gilad, a senior defense ministry official, claimed that Hezbollah had acquired thirteen to fourteen thousand rockets.

Typically, Hezbollah would deflect repeated inquiries about its rocket arsenal, maintaining its preference for ambiguity. But Hezbollah's leaders often alluded in speeches to the existence of long-range rockets, teasing the Israelis with vague hints rather than hard facts. "We have the power to destroy important and sensitive targets in northern occupied Palestine," Nasrallah said in a May 2006 speech marking the sixth anniversary of the Israeli troop withdrawal from south Lebanon. "The resistance now has over thirteen thousand rockets. All of north occupied Palestine is within our firing range. This is the minimum range. As for the range beyond the north . . . it is best to be silent."

"The Launcher Rose Out of the Ground"

The same level of creativity that went into the bunker networks could also be found in the construction and deployment of Hezbollah's fixed firing platforms for its arsenal of 122 mm Katyusha rockets. The rocket posts were placed in dense undergrowth on reverse (north-facing) slopes of valleys to make them more difficult targets for Israeli artillery guns firing from the south. The 122 mm rockets, standard and upgraded, which between them have ranges of twelve to thirty miles, covered a belt adjacent to Israel to a depth of about six miles from the border. Some positions were simple shelters of cinder block walls and concrete roof open at opposite ends, protected by sandbags and rock-filled Hesco blast protection barriers and disguised by camouflage netting and foliage. Thermal blankets were thrown over the launchers immediately after firing to mask the heat signature from patrolling Israeli aircraft overhead. One typical position I found was a firing pit about four meters deep, the walls lined with concrete. The top of the southern wall was angled 45 degrees to facilitate the launching of the rocket. At the back of the pit was a short tunnel that doglegged into a small chamber where the rockets were kept. In the one I explored, a house-proud Hezbollah militant had decorated the walls of the chamber with panels from the wooden crates in which the rockets were packed.

Some rocket launchers were fixed to platforms that could be raised or lowered electronically from holes in the ground. Abu Mahdi, a veteran Hezbollah fighter, told me after the 2006 war that a comrade of his was taken to a mountaintop and told that that he was in charge of a Katyusha rocket launcher. "My friend looked around him and asked, 'Where is it?' The other man pressed a button and the launcher rose out of the ground next to him," he said.

Residents of a village in south Lebanon, about thirteen miles north of the border, remember on July 28, 2006, midway through the war, a group of Hezbollah men arriving in the village carrying laptop computers. The men entered an orchard and began tapping at a keyboard. A launcher emerged from the ground among the trees and a single large-caliber rocket was fired. The rocket, carrying a 220-pound warhead, hit the Israeli town of Afula in what was then the deepest strike into Israel of the war.

Perhaps the most ingenious rocket launcher was a homemade contraption consisting of ten 122 mm Katyusha launching tubes arrayed in two rows of five encased in a block of cement. The cement blocks, hinged at one end, were laid horizontally into shallow pits prealigned in the direction of the targeted town or kibbutz. The blocks were then covered by a steel plate and camouflaged by a roll of turf. To launch them, the Hezbollah team would roll back the turf, remove the steel plate, and electronically raise the concrete block to a predesignated firing angle. Once the rockets were fired, the block was lowered back into its pit, the steel plate replaced, and the turf unfurled, and the militants would take cover in a nearby cave or bunker long before Israeli artillery initiated a counterbombardment.

Beyond a belt extending roughly six miles north of the border, Hezbollah built emplacements for its stock of larger-caliber rockets, some of them fired from multibarreled launchers on the back of Mercedes-Benz trucks. The trucks were hidden in ground-floor garages of buildings and houses, generally lying on the outskirts of towns or villages. In a time of war, the trucks would emerge from the buildings, unleash a salvo of rockets, and then return to cover inside.

Due to their longer range and larger size—which makes them more difficult to conceal—the Zelzal rockets were positioned farther north. According to Western intelligence sources, the Zelzals are launched from specially adapted shipping containers carried on trucks. The roof of the shipping container is hinged and flips open at the touch of a button, allowing the rocket to be elevated on a launch rail and fired.

"I Am 103 and Abu Mohammed Is 121"

Arguably the most significant improvement to the capabilities of the Islamic Resistance from 2000 on was the introduction of a new and more advanced communications and signals intelligence (SIGINT) infrastructure.

Originally, in the late 1980s, Hezbollah communicated by walkie-talkie and hand-cranked cable-linked military field telephones that connected the secret bases in the Jabal Safi Mountains on the western edge of the Jezzine enclave. The field telephones were apparently introduced after Israel was able to intercept Hezbollah's radio chatter and track and target the fighters. Even Nasrallah is rumored never to have used a cell phone, for that same reason.

In the 1990s, Hezbollah installed an internal telephone network using copper lines that initially linked command nodes and senior officials and officers. The network was expanded during that decade until it connected Hezbollah's main operational areas in southern Beirut, the south, and the southern Bekaa Valley. The cables were buried alongside government communications lines, allowing Hezbollah to take advantage of existing infrastructure and affording a level of security for its network. After 2000, the lines were extended into the border district, and some of the copper lines were replaced with fiber optic cables. In

2003, UNIFIL peacekeepers often saw Hezbollah engineers laying the inch-thick black fiber optic cables in trenches alongside roads in the south. Not only does a fiber optic cable transmit substantially more information than a traditional copper line (one fiber optic cable can carry about the same amount of data as a thousand copper lines), it provides greater security and is less prone to interception and tapping. In addition to voice communications, the network allowed Hezbollah to send images and to communicate by instant messaging and emails.

Hezbollah knew that in the event of war, the Israeli military would seek to impose a "jamming blanket" in southern Lebanon to block radio and cell phone signals. Each electronic jammer covers a relatively small geographic area, making it impossible for the Israelis to cover south Lebanon in its entirety. But Hezbollah anticipated that the frontline areas would be affected, requiring combat units to use the fiber optic network, which cannot be jammed electronically, to communicate with command posts farther north. Indeed, during the 2006 war, cell phones continued to operate in Tyre even when Israeli troops advanced to within eight miles of the town. But in Bint Jbeil, scene of one of the fiercest confrontations, neither cell phones nor satellite phones used by reporters worked due to Israeli jamming.

Still, Hezbollah had another trick up its sleeve to allow it to continue using radios even in jammed combat zones. Communications personnel carried military-grade portable spectrum analyzers, the size of a laptop computer, to discover which frequencies were being blocked. That allowed the fighters to switch to clear frequencies to maintain radio communications with one another even while operating in a jammed environment.

For wireless communications, Hezbollah fighters carry Icom V8, V82, and V85 handheld radios. The range of the radio signals are boosted by hundred-watt transmitter antennae, enabling conversations by walkie-talkie as far apart as Beirut to Tyre, a distance of forty-three miles.

Although the radio sets are not encrypted, secure communications are ensured through a regularly updated vocal code system using letters and numbers. "We have codes for everything, references to martyrs, casualties, locations, fighters, weapons, radio frequencies, tactics," explains one Hezbollah fighter. "We change them regularly, at least once a month, sometimes every day."

Hezbollah's communications unit devises the codes, which are printed on laminated cards and distributed to unit commanders, who then pass them on to the fighters. Other than a universal code for the organization, separate codes are issued for different *qita'at,* or sectors, all the way down to a subsector of two or three villages. At the subsector level, fighters will augment the official coding system with an ad hoc code based on their intimate knowledge of the local terrain and of each other. Two veteran Hezbollah fighters in the southern village of Srifa gave a demonstration of how the code worked during the 2006 war. Hajj Rabieh, a schoolteacher in normal times, pulled from his pocket a small laminated card listing Hezbollah's code numbers for positions in the area and for each fighter. "I am 103 and Abu Mohammed is 121," he said, referring to his comrade squatting nearby. Abu Mohammed said, "Hajj Rabieh once loved a woman in the village. I could call him [on the walkie-talkie] and say 'let's meet at the house of the woman who melted your heart.' How can the Israeli enemy understand that?"

During the 2006 war, each Hezbollah fighter went by the generic name Fallah but was identified by a following code number. In demonstrating how it worked, Hajj Rabieh picked up his walkie-talkie and spoke into it: "Fallah 47, 47, 47." When a voice answered, he said in greeting, "God give you strength," then "Go, go, go." He tapped at the walkie-talkie, switching to a preselected frequency to continue the conversation.

"What did you have for lunch?" Hajj Rabieh asked.

"Rice and potatoes," came the tinny answer.

Since the mid-1990s, Hezbollah had used scanners to record conversations on Israeli cell phones for translation by the party's Hebrew speakers. This technique allowed Hezbollah to glean valuable intelligence from garrulous soldiers deployed in south Lebanon or in positions along the border.

From 2000 on, technicians from the Iranian Revolutionary Guard Corps–Quds Force instructed a special Hezbollah intelligence-gathering unit in the use of the latest Iranian electronic interception devices and jamming equipment to monitor and block Israeli military communications. The high-tech Iranian equipment even overcame the complex frequency-hopping techniques used by the Israelis to avoid jamming and interception, according to U.S. and Israeli intelligence officials as well as Hezbollah sources. Hezbollah's SIGINT personnel were required to be fluent Hebrew speakers, and many were conversant in two or three more languages. Surveillance centers were established in apartments and houses in villages near the border, often within view of the security fence and adjacent Israeli army compounds. Here, the SIGINT personnel carefully monitored and recorded Israeli communications traffic, sending the data via fiber optic links to Beirut, where it was translated into Arabic. Even the individual cell phones of Israeli military commanders were tapped by the SIGINT specialists, thanks to Hezbollah's network of spies in northern Israel passing on lists of the phone numbers. The buried fiber optic network also ensured that in a time of war critical data collected by the SIGINT unit could be translated immediately by the intelligence operators and distributed directly to commanders in the field.

Hezbollah's SIGINT capabilities also benefited from the military partnership between Iran and Syria. In November 2005, Iran and Syria signed and ratified a joint strategic defense cooperation agreement that in part called for the establishment of four SIGINT stations covering Syria's border regions. The highly secret and compartmentalized listening stations are staffed by Syrian and Iranian intelligence officers, technicians, and electronic warfare experts as well as Hebrew-, English-, and Turkish-speaking translators. Two of the four stations were reportedly up and running by the outbreak of war in July 2006. One of the two was located on the Golan Heights and reportedly passed on intelligence data to Hezbollah commanders in Lebanon via dedicated fiber optic links, which were impervious to Israeli electronic countermeasures.[1]

Hezbollah's electronic intelligence gathering was supplemented by a visual reconnaissance infrastructure along the Blue Line. CCTV cameras and long-range thermal vision cameras capable of detecting humans at night at a distance of six miles were installed in Hezbollah observation posts and other points along the Blue Line. In addition to the static observation posts, fighters reconnoitered the border from temporary camouflaged positions beside the security fence or even inside the Shebaa Farms, echoing the surveillance missions conducted by Hezbollah in the occupation zone in the 1990s.

In June 2005, Israeli troops stumbled across a three-man Hezbollah Special Forces squad that had established a camouflaged observation point in dense brush inside the Shebaa Farms, about three hundred yards from the Blue Line. In the ensuing firefight, one member of the squad was killed and his body left at the scene. Hezbollah fire support teams shelled Israeli outposts to cover the extraction of the two surviving squad members, killing one Israeli soldier and wounding three others. Israeli troops recovered equipment abandoned by the Hezbollah unit, including expensive digital SLR cameras with an array of lenses, video cameras, GPS devices, and night vision goggles.

The SIGINT and communications personnel are among the most highly trained and secretive operators within the Islamic Resistance. Each recruit undergoes a far more extensive vetting process than a normal newcomer into Hezbollah. Even after being accepted, they are kept under continual close scrutiny by security officers.

The information gleaned from SIGINT, spy rings in Israel, surveillance cameras, and reconnaissance patrols along the Blue Line was carefully collated and disseminated to unit commanders. In November 2009, Israel's *Yedioth Ahronoth* newspaper revealed that the Israeli army had obtained a 150-page book stamped "Top Secret" in which Hezbollah gave a highly detailed and accurate analysis of Israel's security infrastructure along the border.[2] The table of contents alone was four pages long. It included detailed descriptions of the ground radar, surveillance cameras, and UAVs used by the IDF to monitor the border and the area just to the north. It contained photographs of Israel's northern border taken from inside Israel as well as details of Israeli patrolling procedures, protection for maintenance crews operating along the border fence, security for border settlements, operational procedures of the IDF's tracking unit, and even techniques for fooling the trackers and their sniffer dogs.

"It is hard to believe, but the Hezbollah intelligence sources who wrote the document seem to have copied from internal documents belonging to the Northern Command," wrote Ronen Bergman, the *Yedioth* correspondent.

Deployment

Following Israel's troop withdrawal in 2000, Hezbollah reconfigured its administrative division of south Lebanon to include the newly liberated areas in the border district. The Islamic Resistance was divided into four territorial commands covering the south, southern Beirut, the Bekaa Valley, and the Mediterranean coastline.

The Nasr Unit (Wahadiyah Nasr) was positioned between the Blue Line and the Litani River and formed the operational core of the Islamic Resistance. Its total strength was estimated at a few thousand, of which some eight hundred to one thousand were Special Forces operatives and full-time regulars deployed in the rural "security pockets" and the rest, perhaps three thousand, were members of the *tabbiyya,* the "village guard" reservists.

The area under the command of the Nasr Unit was split into at least five *qita'at,* or sectors, of around twelve to fifteen villages each, the same system that Hezbollah introduced in 1985 following Israel's pullback to the occupation zone. The sectors were further divided into smaller components of two to three villages each. The headquarters of each sector was responsible for the military preparations within its area, from the construction of bunkers and the deployment of rocket-firing positions to the disposition of weapons arsenals and the organization of individual combat units.

Houses and apartments in villages were purchased or rented from landlords, after a vetting process by local Hezbollah security personnel, and used as storage facilities for arms and other items such as medical supplies, food, and water. Basic ammunition stocks such as Katyusha rockets, mortar rounds, and small arms ammunition were kept separately from more advanced weapons systems including antiarmor and antiaircraft missiles. Hezbollah constructed houses specifically to store weapons and ammunition. In February 2004, a two-story building used as an ammunition dump near Shehabiyah village blew up when a lightning storm caused a short circuit. The arms dump was packed with mortar rounds and rocket-propelled grenades.

The mission of the Nasr Unit was to pound Israel with a steady barrage of short- and medium-range rockets to pressure the Israeli civilian population (and, by extension, the Israeli government) and to vigorously confront any ground invasion by Israeli troops. Maintaining the flow of rockets into Israel was critical to Hezbollah's strategic thinking, which is why so much effort went into the deployment and camouflaging of the rocket-firing posts to make them as hard as possible to detect and destroy. If Israeli forces were on the ground in sizable numbers and met with limited opposition, they would soon neutralize the rocket-firing positions, denying Hezbollah its main leverage to influence the outcome of the war. Therefore, Hezbollah had to mount a far more robust defense of the border district than the fleeting hit-and-run tactics of classical guerrilla warfare, a requirement that led to the construction of the secret and extensive underground fortifications and static-firing points where ground could be defended.

Targets in northern Israel, both civilian and military, were carefully selected. Some of the targeting data was provided by agents in northern Israel through military maps and photographs. Hezbollah may have been able to acquire satellite photographs of northern Israel from commercial companies. The introduction of the Google Earth global satellite imagery program in 2005 may have also helped facilitate the collation of targeting data. Most of northern Israel is covered by satellite images with a resolution of two meters, clearly showing useful military sites such as the air traffic control base on Mount Meron, six miles south of the border.

The Nasr Unit's artillery section prepared ranging cards for each rocket-firing position listing the target number, the target name, and aiming data such as range and angle of elevation. Meticulously detailed battle plans were drawn up in which each combat unit (*al-tashkeel al-qutali*), numbering from five to a dozen fighters each, depending on the task, was given precise instructions on their respective missions, whether laying IEDs and antitank mines, manning antiaircraft defenses, providing fire support, or preparing ambushes. The orders also analyzed potential actions by the Israelis and listed the required responses by the combat units. Battle plans were coded in conformity with Hezbollah's communications security. UNIFIL peacekeepers overheard conversations between fighters during the 2006 war, when Hezbollah sometimes broke in to UNIFIL's radio frequencies to communicate. "They say, 'This is Brother 13. We are going to carry out operation seven. Hope you are all safe,'" a senior UNIFIL officer in Naqoura told me at the time.

"Hunter-Killer" Teams and Frogmen

The topography of south Lebanon, with its steep hills and ravines, is not suited to armored warfare, as the Israelis had discovered during two decades of occupation. The Islamic Resistance took advantage of the terrain to form tank "hunter-killer" teams of around five fighters each, armed with half a dozen missiles seeking targets of opportunity as well as laying ambushes at natural choke points. The numerous munitions bunkers dotting the landscape ensured that the antitank teams could maintain mobility without worrying about straying too far from sources of resupply. Fighting bunkers and firing points were also constructed specifically along axes of anticipated Israeli advance. The generally east-west orientation of the road network between the border and the Litani River limited the number of possible northbound routes for advancing Israeli forces, allowing Hezbollah's battle planners to narrow down the best locations to construct fortified permanent ambush sites. One of them was the Wadi Salouqi–Wadi Hojeir valley system, the occupation zone's front line between 1985 and 2000. The valley begins near Bint Jbeil beside the border and runs north for eleven miles before joining the Litani River, a convenient axis of northbound advance for Israeli armored columns. Hezbollah constructed numerous firing posts and ambush positions in the dense undergrowth on the side of the valley and its tributaries to which fighters could quickly deploy if Israeli forces entered the valley system.

A dedicated sniper unit was created after 2000 with marksmen equipped with Russian semiautomatic 7.62 mm Dragunov rifles and possibly Austrian Steyr HS50 12.7 mm rifles, eight hundred of which were sold to Iran in 2004. The sniper teams are among the most heavily trained members of the Islamic Resistance. Not only must they develop expert marksmanship skills, they have to learn the arts of camouflage, stealth, and patience when lying prone for long periods of time in search of targets.

Other than missiles, antiarmor tactics included preparing "explosive pits" dug beneath roads near the border, at intersections, and along main north-south axes. The pits were each packed with three hundred to six hundred pounds of TNT, to be detonated by remote control beneath armored vehicles, especially tanks, such as the Merkava Mark 4, one of the most heavily protected tanks in the world in 2006 but still vulnerable to such a large explosive charge.

In June 2002, a shepherd accidentally stumbled across one of Hezbollah's explosive pits while guiding his flock along a lane near the Shebaa gate, scene of the abduction of the three Israeli soldiers in October 2000. Thinking he had found an Israeli bomb, he alerted the local police. Initial reports, encouraged by Hezbollah officials irritated at the discovery of the pit, claimed the bomb consisted of three explosive charges weighing about two pounds each and may have been an Israeli assassination attempt against Sheikh Nabil Qawq, who was hosting an Iranian delegation on a tour of the border district the same day. But a local source who saw the bomb told me that it consisted of four hundred pounds of TNT split into sixteen separate blocks.

The region north of the Litani River, which included the Nabatiyah district, the southern Bekaa Valley, and the mountains lying between the two, was the domain of the Badr Unit, the operational rear of the Islamic Resistance. The Badr Unit's principal role was to launch longer-range rockets into Israel, provide reinforcements if necessary to the Nasr Unit, and confront any Israeli penetration north of the Litani.

A coastal defense command operating alongside the Nasr and Badr units was responsible for maritime surveillance and oversaw the activities of Hezbollah's amphibious warfare unit. The coastal surveillance included radar-fitted observation posts to monitor for Israeli naval commando infiltrations and shipping movements. The amphibious warfare unit was established in the 1990s, but details of its activities are scarce. Although its cadres fought in south Lebanon during the 1990s as regular combatants, according to Hezbollah sources, the party leadership has never formally mentioned the existence of the unit. Recruits receive training in Iran, probably at the IRGC underwater combat school in Bandar Abbas, as well as learning basic frogman skills in a camp near the Assi River in the northern Bekaa Valley. Training is thought to include beach landings and underwater demolition skills.

The logistical command was located in the northern Bekaa and was principally responsible for training and the storage of armaments arriving from Syria. Tunnels sunk into the sides of sealed-off valleys near Janta in the jagged and barren limestone peaks close to the Syrian border were the initial repositories for Hezbollah's smuggled rockets. The logistical unit then organized the transfer of the rockets to arms warehouses and bunkers farther south.

The command and control center of the Islamic Resistance was based in the "security quarter" in Beirut's southern suburbs. Before the 2006 war, armed guards wearing black uniforms and berets controlled heavy steel sliding gates that barred access into Hezbollah's nerve center and home to the leadership, an otherwise nondescript cluster of drab concrete apartment buildings looking much like any other part of the city. Secondary locations, known as "the points," were selected and equipped for almost all Hezbollah's offices and facilities in the southern suburbs, including a fully functioning mirror facility for the Al-Manar television channel. In the event of war, if the southern suburbs came under attack, Hezbollah personnel could abandon their normal offices and relocate to the safety of the points, allowing them to continue with their tasks. "We are now highly prepared to face Israel. We are more highly prepared than at any previous time," Sheikh Naim Qassem told me in August 2004.

What We Should Do for the Intifada

While Hezbollah's main focus between 2000 and 2006 was on building its military capabilities in Lebanon and waging its campaign of brinkmanship along the Blue Line, the organization also played a support role in the Palestinian Al-Aqsa intifada. The destruction of Israel and the liberation of Jerusalem remain core ideological goals for Hezbollah. But the party tempers such ambitions by declaring that although it is willing to lend assistance when possible, the Palestinians must take the lead in securing their own emancipation from Israel.

As the Al-Aqsa intifada gained momentum, Hezbollah established a unit to expedite assistance to the Palestinians on behalf of Iran. The unit oversaw the creation of cells and networks in the occupied Palestinian territories as well as in Israel, trained Palestinian militants at camps in the Bekaa Valley, or sent them on to Iran for advanced training.

Hezbollah also facilitated the smuggling of arms and ammunition by sea directly to Gaza or Egypt and then by tunnels dug under the Gaza-Egypt border. The most ambitious known smuggling operation was the fifty tons of Iranian-supplied weapons worth $15 million carried on board the *Karine-A* cargo ship, which was intercepted by Israeli commandos in January 2002 in the Red Sea about three hundred miles south of Eilat. Following the seizure of the *Karine-A*, Hezbollah abandoned attempts to smuggle weapons into the Palestinian territories, finding it more expedient to provide funds with which the Palestinians could procure arms themselves. "In principle, we don't have anything against assisting them in arms, but for practical and technical reasons providing money is easier. When they get the money they can obtain the weapons they want from within occupied Palestine," Nasrallah told me in 2003.

The Internet was used to send instructions and transfer funds into accounts held with Arab banks that had branches in the West Bank and Gaza. Technical data, such as bomb-building techniques and rocket design, was passed on by couriers or cell phone text messages. That expertise was manifested in dramatic fashion in February 2002 when Fatah militants blew up a Merkava Mark 3 in the Gaza Strip with a 110-pound "belly charge," killing three of its four-man crew. Not even Hezbollah had totally destroyed a Merkava tank before.

Hezbollah also mobilized its media resources to aid the intifada, particularly Al-Manar television, which devoted about 70 percent of its airtime to the Palestinian struggle and became the leading weapon in the propaganda war against Israel. By the beginning of 2001, it was broadcasting via satellite 24 hours a day, covering the globe except for Australia and Southeast Asia. "President Bush can watch Al-Manar in the White House if he wants," joked Nayyaf Krayyem, the station's chairman. By 2001, Al-Manar's budget had risen to $10 million a year, a tenfold increase since its inception a decade earlier.

Transmission antennae were set up along the border to beam Al-Manar into Israel. Through propaganda clips, nonstop updated news developments relayed by Palestinian reporters on the ground, interviews, and discussion panels, Hezbollah relentlessly hammered home its message that resistance was the only path for the Palestinians to regain their homeland. And the Palestinians were listening.

By the first anniversary of the Al-Aqsa intifada in September 2001, Hezbollah's yellow flag, with its distinctive emblem of a fist clutching a Kalashnikov rifle, fluttered alongside banners of mainstream Palestinian groups at funerals and demonstrations in the occupied territories. Cassette tapes of Nasrallah's speeches were listened to avidly. Occasionally, the Hezbollah leader addressed Palestinian audiences from Beirut, more than 130 miles to the north, his words relayed to the crowd by cell phone and loudspeaker.

A "Terrible Deed"

Hezbollah had just begun implementing its military plans in south Lebanon and the Palestinian territories when nineteen young Arab men hijacked four airliners and flew three of them into the World Trade Center in New York and the Pentagon on September 11, 2001. The scale of the devastating attacks and the horrifying, mesmerizing images of the Twin Towers crumbling into dust stunned Hezbollah as much as the rest of the world. Until then, Hezbollah had stood accused of killing more Americans than any other militant group. Now, the party found itself elbowed off the top of the list by al-Qaeda, but still very much in the crosshairs of President George W. Bush's newly declared "war on terrorism." With smoke still rising from the rubble of the Twin Towers, Bush warned that the war would begin with al-Qaeda, "but it does not end there. It will not end until every terrorist group with global reach has been found, stopped, and defeated."

Syria, recognizing that it, too, was uncomfortably close to being listed among Washington's enemies, opted initially to cooperate with the United States, sharing intelligence with the CIA and allowing FBI investigators to question Islamist nationals suspected of having contacts with al-Qaeda.

Sayyed Mohammed Hussein Fadlallah, the leading Shia cleric in Lebanon, was swift to condemn 9/11, describing it as a "terrible deed" and "impermissible and disapproved by all religions." Nasrallah struck a more confrontational tone in his first public comments on the attacks, saying that while Hezbollah condemned "all killings of innocent civilians all over the world," the party would remain true to its agenda regardless of the U.S. war on terrorism. "September 11 might change the whole world, but it will not change our way at all," he said.

But the United States was determined to apply pressure on Syria and Lebanon to curb Hezbollah's activities. The Bush administration's ideologues, the so-called neoconservatives, saw the war on terrorism as an opportunity to mold the Middle East to benefit the strategic interests of the United States, which would include the elimination of Hezbollah as an enduring threat. Some U.S. officials who had served in the earlier administrations of Ronald Reagan and George H. W. Bush had personal grudges against Hezbollah, associating the organization with the traumas and bloody setbacks of Washington's Lebanon policies in the 1980s. In 2002, Richard Armitage, the deputy secretary of state who had served at the Pentagon at the time of the U.S. marine barracks bombing in 1983, famously described Hezbollah as the "A-team of terrorists," relegating the perpetrators of the 9/11 attacks to the B-team.

Still, there were at least two alleged attempts by the United States to buy off Hezbollah with hundreds of millions of dollars in exchange for the party's renouncing its struggle against Israel and dismantling the Islamic Resistance. The proposals were rejected by Nasrallah, who described one of the offers as a "political hand grenade intended to finish us off."[3]

The 9/11 attacks inevitably reawakened interest in the whereabouts and activities of the ever-elusive Imad Mughniyah, of whom little had been heard in the previous decade. The only pictures of Mughniyah publicly available were a few grainy black-and-white snapshots from the 1980s, portraying a serious, sallow-faced young man with a pointed black beard.

Mughniyah, Nasrallah, Fadlallah, and Sheikh Sobhi Tufayli were listed by the U.S. Treasury Department as Specially Designated Terrorists. A month after 9/11, Mughniyah appeared on an FBI list of the top twenty-two most wanted terrorists, alongside Ali Atwi and Hassan Ezzieddine, both of whom were also wanted, along with Mughniyah, for the hijacking of TWA Flight 847 in June 1985.

Weeks after 9/11, a rumor surfaced in Lebanon that Jawad Noureddine, the unknown but newly elected head of Hezbollah's military council in the seven-man Shura Council, was none other than Mughniyah himself.

For Hezbollah officials, Mughniyah became a tiresome subject brought up by journalists during interviews. Some denied he had anything to do with Hezbollah; most simply declined to talk about him at all.

Two weeks after 9/11, I interviewed Anis Naqqash, the former Fatah member who had overseen Mughniyah's initial military training in the 1970s. With the rubble of the Twin Towers still smoking, Naqqash chose to deny ever having known Mughniyah.

I once asked Sheikh Sobhi Tufayli if Mughniyah was responsible for the U.S. marine barracks bombing. Tufayli scowled at the floor and said, "He had nothing to do with it." Then, lifting his head and fixing me with a stern gaze, he added in his typically gruff manner, "Besides, if he did, do you think I would tell you?"

"The Kid," the former Hezbollah assassin and unit commander from the 1980s, smiled and shook his head pityingly when I brought up the subject of Mughniyah over a cup of coffee one morning. "Who is Imad Mughniyah?" he asked rhetorically. "No one in Hezbollah knows who is Imad Mughniyah. Seriously. In Hezbollah, there are different names for different people. Anyone can give themselves a different name. I know people in the Hezbollah leadership who have different names. Some people know him by one name and somebody else by another. You would think they are two different people, but they are the same person. You get me? No one at all in Hezbollah can tell you who is Imad Mughniyah."

The most candid comment I received on Mughniyah was from Nasrallah himself. When I asked if Jawad Noureddine was the nom de guerre of Imad Mughniyah, Nasrallah said, "No. I heard the rumor and I laughed at it. . . . [Noureddine] is a real person, and he has worked in the ranks of the resistance and has assumed many responsibilities in the resistance. The officials in the resistance are not media personalities. . . . When the battle is over, or these people become old men, then it is possible that we could present them through the media."

But does Mughniyah have any connections with Hezbollah?

"Hajj Imad Mughniyah is among the best freedom fighters in the Lebanese arena," Nasrallah replied. "He had an important role in resisting the occupation, but [as for] his relations with Hezbollah, or whether he has a position in Hezbollah, we observe the tradition of not providing lists of names of cadres or those that cooperate with us."

Mughniyah was rumored to have had plastic surgery—twice—to alter his appearance. He was supposed to be living in Tehran and traveling under an Iranian diplomatic passport on unscheduled flights. In fact, Mughniyah spent most of his time in Beirut, playing soccer with children in the southern suburbs or shopping in the western half of the city with his wife. As chief of staff of the Islamic Resistance, he often visited his fighters in their frontline positions, traveling alone along the highway between Beirut and the south, his bulky frame perched on a tiny Vespa scooter. The Kid's explanation, as it later turned out, was entirely correct. Mughniyah never had plastic surgery. He simply operated under many different names, and almost no one knew his real identity.

"He didn't believe in bodyguards," recalls one of Mughniyah's friends. "He didn't need them. Sometimes he would arrive for a meeting with resistance people and the guard at the entrance wouldn't know him and would refuse to let him enter. Most Lebanese politicians would get upset and say something like 'Don't you know who I am?' But Imad would say nothing, and then someone would tell the guard, 'No, it's okay. He's with me. He can come in.'"

"Some May Not Sit Idly By"

In the context of the war on terrorism, the United States perceived Hezbollah as a terrorist organization with global reach. It was Hezbollah's potential to attack U.S. interests worldwide, rather than the threat it posed to Israel from south Lebanon, that earned it such a high ranking on the Bush administration's hit list.

Hezbollah's influence extends to wherever there are sizable communities of the Lebanese Shia diaspora, which includes most regions of the world: the Arab Gulf, West and Central Africa, Latin America, Australia, the Far East, Europe, Canada, and the United States. The diaspora represents a fertile source of fundraising, which appears to be the principal purpose driving the establishment of Hezbollah's global network. The fundraising apparatus is extensive and ranges from legitimate commercial enterprises in which the profits are delivered to Hezbollah and religious donations, known as *zakat*, to illegal transnational activities such as bank frauds, currency counterfeiting, drug trafficking, the manufacture and sale of fake goods, intellectual property piracy, and the trade in African "blood diamonds."

Still, illicit activities aside, Hezbollah's reputation for piety and financial integrity has encouraged expatriate Shia bourgeoisie to send religious tithes to the party. These donations alone evidently constitute a substantial source of income. In December 2003, a Union Transport Africaine flight bound for Beirut from Cotonou in the West African state of Benin crashed on takeoff. According to Lebanese press reports, among the dead was a Hezbollah courier carrying $2 million in cash contributions from wealthy supporters in West Africa.

Since the end of Lebanon's civil war in 1990, allegations of Hezbollah involvement in anti-American attacks around the world have declined. The last major anti-American attack in which Hezbollah is alleged to have participated was in June 1996, when a militant from the Shia "Saudi Hezbollah" group suicide-car-bombed the Khobar Towers U.S. air force dormitory in Saudi Arabia, leaving nineteen American servicemen dead. According to the indictment, Hezbollah is alleged to have provided the car bomb.

From 2003, a number of Hezbollah operatives are alleged to have assisted the Quds Force unit of the Iranian Revolutionary Guards Corps in helping train Iraqi Shia insurgents, members of the so-called Special Groups, which include small but potent factions such as the Hezbollah Brigades and the League of the Righteous. According to U.S. defense officials and transcripts of interrogations from captured Iraqi fighters, Hezbollah personnel train insurgents mainly at Quds Force–run camps in Iran, although a few recruits receive training at Hezbollah facilities in Lebanon.[4]

Hezbollah also is alleged to have played an organizational and logistical role in Iraq itself under the direction of the Iranians, helping form and direct cells within the Special Groups. In March 2007, U.S. troops in Iraq captured Ali Musa Daqduq, a Hezbollah operative since 1983 who was responsible for liaison between the Special Groups and the Quds Force. Daqduq pretended to be a deaf-mute for several weeks to not betray his Lebanese accent to interrogators.

Hezbollah's external operations—such as assisting the Palestinians during the Al-Aqsa intifada and helping organize and train Shia militants in Iraq—are carried out under the direction and coordination of Iran rather than being unilateral decisions of the party leadership. These moonlighting activities away from the main Lebanon-Israel front add grist to Hezbollah's critics who charge that the organization is a tool of Iranian foreign policy—the Lebanese branch of the IRGC, if you will.

There is substance to these accusations. While supporting the Palestinian intifada was a moral and ideological duty, Hezbollah would not have intervened without the orders and logistical assistance of Iran. Hezbollah's role in Iraq, albeit limited, testifies even more strongly to Iranian influence over the party. As a Lebanese resistance against Israel, Hezbollah had little motive to step into the Iraqi morass from 2003. Indeed, at the time of the U.S.-led invasion in March 2003, Hezbollah's cadres were under strict instructions not to join the flow of volunteer militants streaming into Iraq to fight the American invaders. But the Iranians clearly had a use for Hezbollah operatives in training and organizing Iran-guided factions, and Hezbollah was obliged to obey.

Hezbollah does not share the disorganized nihilism of al-Qaeda, but operates according to a carefully assessed, rationally applied long-term strategy that is principally directed toward the struggle against Israel. Gratuitous attacks against American or other Western targets around the world have no practical value for Hezbollah, as they would only serve to raise the ire of the international community and threaten to disrupt the flow of funds into the party's coffers. But Hezbollah's "global reach" is not only a useful mechanism for generating funds. It also furnishes the party with a tool of deterrence against its enemies. If Hezbollah were to come under serious attack, such as the assassination of a top leader, or to face an existential threat, it has an international infrastructure in situ to facilitate reprisal operations.

In the immediate aftermath of the U.S.-led invasion of Iraq, it was speculated that Hezbollah could be the target of the next phase in the war on terrorism. When I met Nasrallah in his headquarters in Beirut's southern suburbs in July 2003, it was evident that he and his advisers had been mulling that possibility.

"Let's talk a little bit about the past," Nasrallah said. "Can anyone come up with one example where Hezbollah targeted American interests in the world, civilian or military, diplomatic or economic? Such a thing never happened."

What about the 1983 bombings of the U.S. marine barracks and U.S. embassy? The kidnapping of American citizens in the late 1980s?

"Those events took place in the civil war . . . and at that time Hezbollah did not even exist," Nasrallah replied. "If Hezbollah has not targeted American interests until now despite the fact that Hezbollah's existence has been very difficult [for] twenty years, especially [because of] Israel . . . [then where] is the justification for such accusations? If Hezbollah has the assumed ability [to strike globally] but has not used it, despite twenty years of war, when is it going to use it?"

What if Israel or the United States launched a war against Hezbollah that threatened the organization's very existence? Would it retaliate globally?

"In such a case, everyone has a right to defend its rights, its existence, its people, and its country by any means, and at any time and in any place," Nasrallah replied. "In addition to this fact, there are many people who love Hezbollah and support Hezbollah throughout the world. Some may not sit idly by [if Hezbollah comes under attack]."

The point Nasrallah wanted to make was in that final sentence, of course. His denial of "external branches" notwithstanding, Nasrallah was implying that Hezbollah had the potential to stage attacks globally and might do so if it felt sufficiently threatened.

"Two Great Arab *Zaim*"

When I met Nasrallah in 2003, the Hezbollah leader was at the apex of his popularity, hailed by friends and acknowledged by enemies as one of the most credible leaders in the Middle East and beyond compare with any other Islamist leader in the region.

He lived in Hezbollah's security quarter—the sealed-off quadrant of bland concrete high-rise buildings in the heart of Beirut's southern suburbs. Although security surrounding the Hezbollah leader was tight, he still appeared in public and attended meetings with politicians. When my interview request was granted, all I had to do was drive my car up to the entrance of the security quarter, where a guard in a black uniform with an AK-47 slung over his shoulder checked my press ID and then slid open the heavy steel gate, allowing me through. My car was not searched, to my surprise, and I was told to park in the ground-floor garage of a tall apartment building. Security measures were limited to

passing through an airport-style metal detector and having to briefly
surrender my watch, wallet, notebook, pens, and tape recorder. Accompanied by security staff, I ascended in a small elevator to an apartment
on the fourth floor and was ushered into a cozy living room fitted with
thick velvet drapes over the windows and Louis XV–style armchairs and
sofas. Nasrallah joined us minutes later.

Just short of his forty-forth birthday, the Hezbollah leader exuded a
calm confidence, having long ago overcome an initial awkwardness in
dealing with the media when he was elected secretary general in 1992. In
conversation, he was polite, good-humored, soft-spoken, and quick to
smile, his lisp further softening his image. He was dressed in his customary brown cloak and black turban, the color denoting his status as a
sayyed, or descendant of the Prophet. His full beard had expanded in
size over the previous decade and was turning a steely gray, a sign of
aging that Nasrallah probably welcomed, as it conferred upon him a
certain gravitas that his youth, and his chubby face, otherwise belied.

Nasrallah saved the passionate outbursts for his public performances,
whipping up sentiment among Hezbollah's cadres and the party's supporters with powerful speeches that he invariably laced with quips and
bons mots to balance his thunder and fiery rhetoric. Not only his audiences hung on his every word. Analysts closely studied his speeches and
interviews, parsing his comments for insights and hints as to Hezbollah's
intentions.

He developed a reputation among Israelis as someone whose word
could be trusted and whose promises would be kept, which did not always bode well for Israel. Senior Israeli army officers admitted to a
grudging admiration for Nasrallah, an enemy to be treated with wary
respect. "I must say that the way in which he leads his organization fas-
cinates me," said Major General Amos Malka, the IDF's military intelligence chief in 2001. "He combines strategic thinking, perfect control,
tactical work, and use of the psychological element. He is definitely a
fascinating figure for any intelligence agent."[5]

In mid-2004, Nasrallah struck up a secret and close relationship with
Rafik Hariri, who was then caught in a bitter rivalry with President Lahoud and whose relations with the Syrian regime were deteriorating.

Politically, Nasrallah and Hariri were poles apart. The former was committed to an unrelenting struggle against Israel and obedience to the *wali al-faqih*. The latter was a businessman-philanthropist of boundless ambition who regarded the Arab-Israeli conflict as a distraction to the goal of rebuilding Lebanon and reviving its pre–civil war role as the financial and services center for the Middle East. Yet the two men possessed many similarities. Both were devout Muslims from south Lebanon who shared a strong sense of humor, who had suffered the tragedy of losing a son, and whose achievements had cast them far above the ranks of their political contemporaries in Lebanon.

They met at night at least twice a week at different secure locations in Hezbollah's "security quarter" in the southern suburbs of Beirut. The meetings would begin at eleven o'clock or midnight and continue often until the early hours of the morning, and the conversations included regional issues such as the unfolding chaos in Iraq, worsening Sunni-Shia tensions, and the plight of the Palestinians. "They didn't talk to each other like one was a Lebanese prime minister and the other a Lebanese party leader. They used to talk to each other in the manner of two great Arab *zaim*[6] whose responsibilities covered the region," recalls Mustafa Nasr, Hariri's go-between with Hezbollah, who, along with Hussein Khalil, Nasrallah's top political adviser, was the only other person to attend the meetings.

They found they had much in common, and, according to Mustafa Nasser and other advisers to Hariri, a close personal relationship blossomed between the two leaders. "Rafik Hariri trusted Hassan Nasrallah and liked him. Nasrallah similarly liked and respected him. This talk expressed itself in the secrets they used to tell each other. Rafik Hariri used to say to me, 'I don't trust Lebanese political leaders except for Hassan Nasrallah,'" Nasr recalls.

Their conversations occurred during a period of political turbulence in Lebanon as opposition steadily grew against Syria's viselike grip over its smaller neighbor. At the beginning of September 2004, ignoring the wishes of the Lebanese opposition and international warnings, Syria forced the Lebanese parliament to vote for an amendment to the constitution allowing a three-year extension of Lahoud's six-year presidential mandate, which was due to expire the following month. On September 2, a day before the parliamentary vote, the UN Security Council adopted Resolution 1559, which called for a "free and fair" presidential election; for "all remaining foreign forces to withdraw from Lebanon," a reference to the fifteen thousand Syrian troops still on Lebanese soil; for the "extension of the control of the government of Lebanon over all Lebanese territory," which chiefly meant the deployment of Lebanese troops up to the Blue Line; and for "the disbanding of all Lebanese and non-Lebanese militias." The last clause referred to Hezbollah and Palestinian armed groups.

Despite initial intelligence cooperation in the wake of 9/11, U.S.-Syrian relations had steadily declined since then, especially during and after the U.S.-led invasion of Iraq that began in March 2003. Syria had turned a blind eye toward the flow of volunteer Arab fighters slipping across its border with Iraq, and also continued to host and support militant Palestinian groups in Damascus and to provide backing for Hezbollah in Lebanon.

In an attempt to ameliorate growing international pressure, Bashar al-Assad had shown some flexibility in a resumption of peace talks with Israel. In December 2003, he said in an interview with *The New York Times* that he was willing to restart peace talks with Israel immediately. In the following ten months, he repeated the same message at least five times, in public and through intermediaries. In Israel, even senior military officers began advocating a renewed peace process with Syria. In August 2004, Lieutenant General Moshe Yaalon, then the IDF chief of staff, dropped a bombshell by declaring that Israel was strong enough militarily that it could hand the Golan Heights back to Syria. Israel had long argued that the retention of the strategic heights was vital for the defense of the north.

Sharon, however, ruled out negotiations with Syria, insisting that Damascus would have to end its support for radical Palestinian groups and Hezbollah before he would consider sitting at the same table with the Syrians. In fact, Sharon was more than happy with the status quo in which Israel faced no pressure to yield the Golan Heights to the beleaguered regime in Damascus. One of Sharon's top advisers related to me an incident in a cabinet meeting in 2004 when Silvan Shalom, then the foreign minister, suggested that the time was opportune to launch operations to destabilize Syria and bring down the Assad regime. "Sharon replied, 'No way,' " recalls the Israeli adviser. "He said that 'this is the best situation for us. If we get rid of Assad, one of two things will happen. Either the [Sunni Islamist] Muslim Brotherhood will take over, or Syria will become a democracy—and then we will have to make peace with it.' "

In Lebanon, Resolution 1559 helped deepen the political rift between supporters and opponents of the Syrian-backed regime and complicated Hariri's hope that the relationship with Damascus could be modified from one of dominance and subordination to a mutually respectful partnership. Resolution 1559's clauses relating to Hezbollah's arms and freedom of action in the south put the party on the defensive even as Hariri attempted to persuade Nasrallah of the necessity in redefining relations between Lebanon and Syria. Hariri allegedly reassured Nasrallah that despite his objections to Hezbollah's continued armed status, he would not seek to disarm the group by force. "My two hands cannot sign a decision by the Lebanese government for a war against Hezbollah," Hariri told Nasrallah, according to Mustafa Nasr. Instead, Hariri would convince international opinion to allow the Lebanese to resolve the issue of Hezbollah's arms, irrespective of the demands of Resolution 1559.

Nasrallah must have recognized that Hariri's preference for compromise over confrontation was an asset that could be exploited to Hezbollah's benefit. Hariri was respected internationally; his views were received sympathetically and carried weight. In January 2005, Hariri used his influence with Jacques Chirac, the French president and a close friend, to keep Hezbollah's name off a European list of terrorist organizations. Nasrallah appreciated Hariri's intervention with Chirac and reciprocated by promising to broker a secret meeting in Damascus between himself, Hariri, and Bashar al-Assad to resolve their differences. A senior Hezbollah figure was in Damascus making the arrangements on the morning of February 14, 2005, the day that Rafik Hariri died, along with twenty-one other people, when a massive truck bomb ripped through his motorcade on the seafront corniche in downtown Beirut.

"Beirut on Fire"

With Syria instantly blamed for Hariri's murder, tens of thousands of Lebanese protesters gathered in central Beirut for a series of demonstrations to demand an end to Syrian domination. In less than two months, international pressure and the extraordinary "independence intifada" rallies in Beirut, which peaked on March 14 when some one million people gathered in Martyrs' Square, had brought down the pro-Syrian government and forced Damascus to withdraw its troops from Lebanese soil.

Syria's disengagement from Lebanon also deprived Hezbollah of the political cover it had enjoyed since 1990. With Syria no longer directly pulling the strings in Lebanon, Hezbollah had little choice but to become more politically engaged to safeguard its own interests. It was the continuation of a process that had begun fifteen years earlier, when Hezbollah's leadership understood that with the end of the civil war and the advent of the Pax Syriana, the party could no longer pursue its anti-Israel agenda in isolation from its environment. With the Syrians gone, Hezbollah was compelled to take another step into the morass of Lebanese politics. It consolidated an alliance with the Amal movement, its erstwhile rival for the Shia vote, and in February 2006 signed a memorandum of understanding with Michel Aoun, a once-vociferous anti-Syrian Christian leader who spent the 1990s in exile in Paris before returning to Lebanon in the wake of the Hariri assassination. Aoun, who had his eyes on the presidency, was shunned by the newly formed March 14 coalition, named after the date of the anti-Syrian rally in Beirut, but he calculated that allying with Hezbollah could bolster his presidential hopes. Following the May-June 2005 general election, which was dominated by the March 14 bloc, Mohammed Fneish became Hezbollah's first cabinet minister when he was handed the electricity portfolio in the new government headed by Fouad Siniora, Rafik Hariri's long-serving finance minister.

It was a profoundly unsettling period for Hezbollah, and especially for Syria's staunch allies in Lebanon, who kept low profiles in the aftermath of the Beirut Spring and the onset of a UN investigation into Hariri's murder. But in the south, the Islamic Resistance diligently pursued its war preparations irrespective of the seismic political shift in Beirut.

Hezbollah and Israel had conducted a prisoner swap in January 2004 in which Elhanan Tannenbaum, the Israeli reservist colonel and would-be drug smuggler, along with the bodies of the three soldiers abducted from the Shebaa Farms in October 2000, were exchanged for twenty-three Lebanese detainees, four hundred Palestinian prisoners, and twelve other Arabs. Among the detainees were Mustafa Dirani and Sheikh Abdel-Karim Obeid. Israel also agreed to repatriate the bodies of fifty-nine Lebanese resistance fighters, provide information on twenty-four Lebanese who went missing during Israel's 1982 invasion, and hand over maps of land mines planted in south Lebanon during the years of occupation.

The swap deal included a follow-up component in which Hezbollah promised to try to find definitive proof of the whereabouts of Ron Arad, the missing Israeli aviator. In exchange for concrete information, Israel would release the last Lebanese detainees, including Samir Kuntar, a Druze who was serving a 542-year jail sentence for killing an Israeli policeman and three members of a family during a commando raid on northern Israel in 1979.

Whether Hezbollah knows what happened to Arad or genuinely lost track of him in 1988 remains unclear. By April 2005, fifteen months after the prisoner exchange, no progress had been made in concluding the second part of the deal. Nasrallah then declared that it was unacceptable for Kuntar and the other Lebanese detainees to remain in jail just because Hezbollah had so far been unable to discover Arad's whereabouts. "If we fail in the negotiations, the result of which, no matter what, will be known very soon . . . we will have only one option," he said, referring to kidnapping more Israeli soldiers.

Hezbollah exercised that option seven months later. In the early afternoon of November 21, the Islamic Resistance launched a coordinated
multipronged assault against Israeli positions in Ghajar village and the
adjacent Shebaa Farms in what was the largest and most complex operation since the October 2000 abduction of the three soldiers. Under
cover of a heavy mortar and rocket barrage against Israeli outposts,
some twenty members of Hezbollah's Special Forces unit traveling in
jeeps, all-terrain vehicles, and a motorcycle penetrated the Israel-
controlled southern neighborhood of Ghajar. But the Israelis had received intelligence of an impending kidnapping operation and had
redeployed the troops in Ghajar. An Israeli corporal armed with a sniper's rifle, who was fortuitously placed along the route used by the
Hezbollah men to infiltrate the village, shot and killed four of the attackers, foiling the raid. The operation was notable for being the first
time that Hezbollah employed the tandem warhead RPG-29, the more
modern version of the ubiquitous RPG-7, which it fired in large numbers at Merkava tanks and armored personnel carriers at a compound
just east of Ghajar. One Merkava was struck seven times by antitank
missiles and RPGs, but the crew survived unscathed. After the assault
team pulled out of Ghajar, Israeli troops entered the northern third of
the village and blew up the old bomb shelter that Hezbollah had used as
a command post. Israeli Air Force jets bombed around thirteen Hezbollah positions in the southern border district, the largest air strikes
since May 2000.

A few months earlier, Major General Alain Pellegrini, a short,
moon-faced French officer who commanded UNIFIL, had attended a
meeting in Jerusalem with senior Israeli military staff at which the
subject of a possible Hezbollah kidnapping along the Blue Line was
brought up. Pellegrini was told that if there was another abduction,
Israel would set "Beirut on fire." "This was a real red line for Israel,"
Pellegrini told me.

The UNIFIL commander passed the warning on to the Lebanese
government, but he was unaware whether it reached Hezbollah. If it
had, it is unlikely that Hezbollah would have paid much attention.
Hezbollah believed that the "balance of terror" along the Blue Line

would continue to hold even if more Israeli soldiers were abducted. For all the headaches Hezbollah caused the Israeli government, there was little appetite in Israel for a war. In the aftermath of the raid on Ghajar, Major General Aharam Zeevi-Farkash, the IDF military intelligence chief, met with Ariel Sharon and told the premier that Nasrallah was trying to drag Israel into a war. "You worry too much," Sharon replied to Farkash. "I know what they are trying to do."

"It's Up to God"

On January 4, 2006, Sharon suffered a stroke and fell into a coma. He was replaced by his deputy, Ehud Olmert, who went on to narrowly win a general election two months later. The key defense portfolio was conferred upon Amir Peretz, a former trade union leader who, like Olmert, a former mayor of Jerusalem, had no military background.

All the pieces were in place for a disaster. A hubristic Hezbollah was determined to kidnap more Israeli soldiers, confident in its powers of deterrence against an Israel that time and time again since 2000 had demonstrated no appetite for a major confrontation. And in Israel there was a raw, untested government whose top security ministers lacked any military experience. Adding to the brew was Lieutenant General Dan Halutz, the IDF chief of staff since 2005. A former head of the Israeli Air Force, Halutz strongly opposed the IDF withdrawal from Lebanon, supported the continued overflights in Lebanese airspace despite international protestations, and, according to Timur Goksel, the veteran UNIFIL official, believed that "every problem can be solved with a suitable application of firepower from his F-16s or Apache assault helicopters."[7]

On the morning of May 26, Mohammed and Nidal Majzoub, two brothers who were top officials in Palestinian Islamic Jihad, died when their booby-trapped car blew up on a busy street in Sidon. Mohammed Majzoub was PIJ's liaison officer with Hezbollah, and until recently he and his brother had lived under Hezbollah's protection in its "security quarter" in the southern suburbs of Beirut. According to a senior Hezbollah official, their fate was sealed when their wives grew bored

with being cloistered in the "security quarter" and badgered their husbands into moving to Sidon, where Hezbollah could not provide the
same level of security.

In keeping with the tit-for-tat brinkmanship along the Blue Line, a
retaliation was expected for the deaths of the Majzoub brothers. It came
two days later, when eight Katyusha rockets were fired from close to the
border fence south of the village of Aittaroun in the western sector. The
surprising choice of target was the Israeli air control base on Mount
Meron, six miles south of the border. Seven of the eight Katyushas struck
the facility in what was at the time the deepest penetration into Israel by
Hezbollah's rockets. Hezbollah denied responsibility, but no other group
in Lebanon had the capacity for such accurate rocket fire or the tactical
bravado in selecting such a pertinent target.

The Israelis initially preferred to blame the PFLP-GC, the usual address for messages involving rockets crossing the border. Israeli jets
bombed PFLP-GC bases in the Bekaa Valley and south of Beirut. But
after an unidentified gunman shot and wounded an Israeli soldier along
the border hours later, the jets returned to Lebanese skies and staged
more than sixty air strikes against Hezbollah positions in the border
district. Hezbollah responded by mortaring Israeli border outposts, and
by midafternoon, the biggest confrontation in five years was under way
all along the Blue Line. The Israelis took advantage of the fighting to
destroy most of Hezbollah's observation posts along the border. Tanks
blasted lookout towers and smashed walls and fortifications following
what was clearly a pre-prepared plan. Only one Hezbollah fighter was
killed in the clashes, however; all Hezbollah men had vacated the visible
positions before the fighting began, in accordance with normal procedure.

UNIFIL helped broker a cease-fire in the late afternoon, and both
sides retired to assess the outcome. The following day, I drove along a
narrow lane that wound up the side of a steep hill overlooking the border village of Kfar Kila. Hezbollah had a position on the summit of the
hill that had apparently been heavily damaged by Israeli air strikes during the fighting the previous day. I was not expecting to reach the top of
the hill, but it was sometimes worth blithely driving into Hezbollah's

security pockets to see what would happen. A steel chain suspended between two concrete blocks marked the end of the road for me. A Hezbollah man, dressed in a green camouflage uniform and floppy bush hat and with an AK-47 slung over his shoulder, stepped into the center of the road and raised his hand.

Explaining that I was a journalist and flashing my Lebanese government-issued press card, I told him I had heard there had been an air raid on the hill and I was here to have a look. The fighter spoke into his walkie-talkie and instructed me to switch off the car engine and wait, as this would take some time, an hour, perhaps longer. The warm spring breeze carried the scent of wild thyme and ruffled the fluffy heads of purple thistles lining the road.

Initially taciturn, the Hezbollah fighter grew friendlier as the minutes passed. He had joined the resistance ten years earlier and fought during the occupation and afterward in the Shebaa Farms. He denied that the Israelis had bombed the hilltop outpost the previous day, saying that the bulldozer grinding to and fro, out of sight but clearly audible to both of us, was simply destroying an old Israeli outpost. "The Israelis started the fighting by killing the two Islamic Jihad men in Sidon," he said. "The Israelis are always making wars against their neighbors—Lebanon, the Palestinians, Syria, Jordan, Egypt. When the Israelis occupied Lebanon it was natural for me to join the resistance and fight. Now we are defending Lebanon."

So when would the next battle with the Israelis be?

The fighter smiled and said, "It's up to God."

A black Range Rover without license plates—the mark of a Hezbollah security vehicle—pulled up beside us. A small, thin man with a wispy beard and dressed in civilian clothes and a baseball cap scrutinized my press card. He pulled from his pocket a small digital camera and sheepishly asked me to stand beside my car. *Does one give a friendly smile or stare with a scowl for a Hezbollah mug shot?*, I thought, as the photographer took the picture. Then, looking even more embarrassed and apologizing profusely, he asked me to turn sideways so that he could snap a shot of my profile. I was released shortly afterward, with more apologies for having been detained for so long.

The following week, I met with Sheikh Nabil Qawq in Hezbollah's press office in the southern suburbs of Beirut. The tall white-turbaned cleric strode into the room and we shook hands and greeted each other. He sat down in an armchair and leaned forward.

"I liked your pictures," he said with an amused smile.

Qawq was Hezbollah's top man in southern Lebanon, and it was natural that the mug shots of a foreign snooper would have been passed on to him. I could imagine him shaking his head in exasperation as he flicked through the photos. *Blanford up to mischief again.*

He was in good spirits, though, and a lively conversation ensued. We discussed the latest round of fighting. The Israelis had struck a self-congratulatory tone, believing that the swift use of heavy firepower against the Hezbollah positions had given the party a bloody nose.

"We hope the message from our response was understood correctly by the other side," said Brigadier General Gal Hirsch, commander of the IDF's Galilee Division. "If the message was not internalized and violence recurs, we will know how to retaliate even stronger."[8]

Amos Harel, the defense correspondent of Israel's *Haaretz* newspaper, wrote that Nasrallah had fallen into an "ambush" by firing rockets at the Mount Meron air control base, thus giving Israel an excuse to smash its military infrastructure along the border. "When a guerrilla organization builds permanent positions, it provides its enemy with a range of easy targets," he wrote.

Yet unknown to everyone outside the circles of the Islamic Resistance was the fact that Hezbollah's real positions—the steel-lined tunnels, bunkers, and camouflaged rocket-firing positions buried deep in the sides of south Lebanon's hills—remained undiscovered and untouched. No wonder Qawq was dismissive of the Israeli claims.

"We were not surprised by the Israeli escalation," he said. "We knew it was likely . . . so we took precautions. Our positions were all empty. These positions are not real positions anyway. . . . [The Israelis] have an inferiority complex. They hit empty positions and then talk about an imaginary success."

Israel had ended the latest bout with restored confidence in its ability to confront Hezbollah and deal the organization a blow of sufficient strength for Hezbollah's leadership to think twice before embarking on any more escapades along the border. And Hezbollah had emerged unimpressed with Israel's boasts of military strength, remaining convinced that its own powers of deterrence still held. Both sides, blinded by hubris, had taken another step closer to the brink of disaster.

"We are confident enough in our capabilities to make any Israeli adventure very expensive, so high that they cannot tolerate the burden," Qawq said. "In fact they will have more damage than Lebanon."

In less than one month, that boast would be put to the test.

TEN

"Birth Pangs"

You wanted an open war, an open war is what you will get. It will be a full-scale war. To Haifa and—believe me—beyond Haifa and beyond beyond Haifa.

—SAYYED HASSAN NASRALLAH,
July 14, 2006

JULY 22, 2006

SIDDIQINE, south Lebanon—The white minibus had coasted to a halt beside a metal garbage container on the side of the road overlooking a steep valley. The missile had struck the center of the tin roof, punching a gaping, jagged hole before exploding inside.

A man slouched to one side in his seat as if the drive had lulled him to sleep. But the top of his head was gone, leaving an empty skull and thick gouts of blood and brain matter dribbling down what was left of his face. His yellowing hand dangled nonchalantly out the glassless window. A dead woman sat beside him slumped over the seat in front, the back of her pale blue dress drenched in blood, scorched from the explosion, and pockmarked by shrapnel. The interior of the vehicle looked as though someone had flung in buckets of scarlet paint. Beside the dead man and covered in the contents of his skull, a woman sat upright staring blankly ahead, lost in shock. Her black dress was sodden with blood, her face a gory mask.

"Can you stand?" asked a Red Cross medic. The woman—I later discovered her name was Ibtissam Shayto—moved her mouth slightly, but her words were unintelligible. Two of the medics clambered onto the roof of the minibus, struggling under the weight of their cumbersome orange flak jackets and white helmets. They carefully hauled Ibtissam through the hole in the roof, tied a bandage around her head, and gently lowered her into the waiting arms of their colleagues.

A few yards away, the other passengers lay on the ground, the more serious casualties groaning and writhing as medics tended to them. The driver of the minibus, a thin man with an unkempt beard, lay on his back, his hands over his eyes, crying out in anguish, "*Ya Allah! Ya Allah!* (Oh God! Oh God!)"

There were nineteen passengers, all of them from the village of At-Tiri near Bint Jbeil. They had squeezed themselves inside the minibus in a desperate attempt to escape the killing zone that south Lebanon had become over the past week. Ali Shayto, a pudgy twelve-year-old boy whose naked torso was speckled in blood, said that they had been instructed by the Israelis over the radio to leave the village. "Someone came for us and we drove with our cars out of the village," he said. "We were trying to keep up with the others when we were hit."

Like so many other civilian vehicles fleeing the south, they had trailed white sheets from the windows to signal to Israeli helicopters and drones that they were noncombatants. It had made no difference. The missile, probably fired from a drone, struck the minibus as it approached the village of Siddiqine. It was a miracle that only three people were killed in the densely packed vehicle; among them were Ibtissam's mother and brother-in-law. All the other passengers were wounded to varying degrees of severity. Ali's brother, Abbas, sobbed beside his supine mother, whose bandaged left arm was streaked with blood. She silently raised her right hand and held her son's arm in a consoling gesture.

This was our first trip out of the relative safety of Tyre since arriving in the port town five days earlier. We had planned to reach Tibnine and had shadowed an ambulance, hoping that the Red Cross emblem on the roof would provide some protection from the prowling missile-firing pilotless drones that had turned the narrow roads meandering through valleys and steep chalky hills east of Tyre into places of terror and death.

The journey to Tibnine was abandoned, however, when we came across the minibus just minutes after it was hit. The ambulance loaded as many casualties as it could hold, and we hurtled back to Tyre. A car was burning furiously on the road outside the Najem hospital on Tyre's outskirts, the result of yet another missile strike. The three occupants had managed to escape just before the vehicle was engulfed in orange flames.

"This is getting worse and worse by the day," said Qassem Shaalan, a young Lebanese Red Cross volunteer. His unit had made twenty trips into the Tyre hinterland that morning alone to recover casualties. By midday, he told me, ten cars, including an ambulance belonging to a local charity, had been attacked in the vicinity of Tyre. That night, Shaalan was almost killed when a pair of missiles, believed fired from an Israeli drone, slammed into two parked ambulances in Qana during a transfer of wounded civilians.

At the Jabal Amil hospital in Tyre, the casualties continued to arrive along with more reports of targeted cars—two from At-Tiri, including the minibus, one from Qlayly, one from Aytit, and two from Jmayjme.

A UNIFIL officer told me that the Israelis had promised the peace-keeping force they would not hinder vehicles traveling north on the main roads. But the evidence suggested that cars were being attacked regardless of their occupants and the direction in which they were headed.

"They have been hitting civilian cars all over the place," Peter Bouckart of Human Rights Watch told me. "I have been in many war zones, but this one is one of the most dangerous places I have ever seen."

"Yes, Our Fighters Are in Action"

It had begun eleven days earlier on a bright sunny morning. I was scanning Lebanese and Israeli news websites as part of my morning routine when, shortly after 9:00 A.M., a one-line news flash popped up on the *Haaretz* ticker. Rockets fired from Lebanon had just struck the area of Shelomi in western Galilee. This was not an unusual occurrence. Every few months, anonymous groups or individuals launched short-range 107 mm rockets across the Blue Line into Israel, but rarely causing damage or casualties. I telephoned Hussein Naboulsi, Hezbollah's foreign media spokesman, to try to find out what was happening. I expected him to say that Hezbollah had no information. Since May 2000, the only operations claimed by Hezbollah had all occurred in the Shebaa Farms, the tacitly accepted theater of conflict between the Islamic Resistance and the Israeli army. The Shebaa Farms was occupied Arab territory, which helped legitimize Hezbollah's military actions, but attacks across the border into Israel would be considered acts of war.

When Hussein picked up the phone, I jokingly asked if his "boys" were up to anything along the border. His reply made me sit up. "Yes, our fighters are in action," Hussein said, "but I don't have any further details."

If Hezbollah was admitting that it had launched an operation along the border with Israel, then it could only be something significant.

"Hussein, has Hezbollah kidnapped an Israeli soldier?"

Hussein hesitated before responding.

"I don't know," he said. "The military people haven't told me anything yet."

In fact, Hezbollah had abducted not one but two soldiers, snatching them from an army Humvee seconds after attacking it with rifle fire and rocket-propelled grenades. The Humvee was one of two on a routine patrol of the border fence facing the western sector, close to the Hezbollah bastion of Aitta Shaab. The rear Humvee, traveling about a hundred yards behind the lead vehicle, was disabled by machine gun fire and RPGs, the three soldiers inside shot dead. Two of the four soldiers in the lead vehicle were wounded but escaped and hid in bushes. The remaining two, Sergeant Udi Goldwasser, the patrol's commander, and Eldad Regev, were grabbed by the Hezbollah fighters and driven away in civilian jeeps along a dirt track in the direction of Aitta Shaab.

The ambush site was well chosen. It fell into a "dead zone," out of sight of nearby IDF compounds, at the bottom of a wadi between the Israeli border settlements of Zarit and Shetula. The IDF had planned to erect a surveillance camera in the wadi the following week. As the kidnappers raced away, Hezbollah fire support teams staged a diversionary bombardment with mortars and Katyusha rockets against nearby Israeli outposts and the settlements of Zarit and Shetula. Hezbollah snipers shot out surveillance cameras along the border fence.

Some forty minutes later, the Israelis confirmed that two of their soldiers were missing. A Merkava tank and a platoon of troops in armored personnel carriers crossed the border in hot pursuit of the Hezbollah abductors. But the tank struck one of Hezbollah's belly charges, a massive IED consisting of an estimated five hundred pounds of explosive, one of many planted at potential breach points along the border. The huge blast tore the tank to pieces, killing all four crew members. Another soldier was killed in clashes with local Hezbollah men lying in wait. That brought the number of Israeli soldiers killed that morning to eight, the highest single day fatality toll for Israeli troops in Lebanon since the Ansariyah disaster in September 1997.

I was well on the way to south Lebanon by the time it was publicly confirmed that two Israeli soldiers had been kidnapped. The clashes around Aitta Shaab had spread. The Israelis were bombing bridges in a forlorn attempt to prevent the kidnappers from taking the two hostages farther north. The bridge spanning the limpid green waters of the Litani River on the coastal road just north of Tyre had already been destroyed by Israeli jets by the time I arrived there. A Lebanese soldier and two civilians were killed in the air strike. Soldiers blocked the road at a checkpoint a mile from the collapsed bridge and yelled at southbound motorists to turn around. I headed east through rolling chalky hills toward Nabatiyah, trying to find another way across the river. In the dusty hilltop villages, convoys of cars with yellow Hezbollah flags streaming in the wind drove through the streets honking horns at the news of the capture of the two soldiers. Hezbollah supporters stood in the center of roads handing out sweets to passing motorists in celebration.

From Marjayoun, the crump of artillery fire echoed across the valley to the east as round after round exploded at the foot of the Shebaa Farms. The roar of a low-flying jet signaled an air strike was about to commence. A loud blast was followed moments later by a tall column of dust and smoke that climbed into the deep blue sky beyond Khiam.

Within minutes of Hezbollah commanders learning of the success of the kidnapping operation, the call went out to hundreds of fighters living in the south to move to frontline positions in expectation of an Israeli counterattack. Among those receiving call-up orders was Abu Khalil, the veteran Hezbollah fighter who used to load Katyusha rockets for launching in the 1990s. He was at home when he received a call instructing him to report to a position in the Marjayoun area. Abu Khalil left his mobile phone behind, said farewell to his family without telling them where he was going, and rendezvoused with a Renault van that carried him to his destination. There were two other passengers in the vehicle besides the driver. None of them spoke. They listened to Koranic verses playing on the Renault's CD player and contemplated what lay ahead. Abu Khalil thought of his two young daughters and his wife and parents and wondered if God would make him a martyr in the coming conflict. By midday, he was in position near Marjayoun, listening intently to his orders from a Hezbollah commander.

Another fighter, Hajj Ali, a slightly built, gaunt-faced fifty-year-old veteran of more than two decades' service with Hezbollah who today trains new recruits at camps in Iran, was sent to the southern Bekaa Valley at the start of the war to join a crew firing long-range rockets into Israel. "In 2000, when the Israelis withdrew from Lebanon many people [in Hezbollah] were upset because the line we follow is jihad and it had ended," he said. "Don't misunderstand me—we don't like war. We don't treat it as a hobby. But when war came in 2006, many of us smiled because it was chance for us to once more follow the path of jihad."

"Lebanon Is Not Gaza"

Nasrallah gave a press conference at 5:00 A.M. that was covered live on television. I watched it in a café in Marjayoun as I wrote my first dispatch for the day. The Hezbollah chief said that the Israeli soldiers were abducted to secure the release of the last remaining detainees in Israel, especially Samir Kuntar. And the only way the soldiers would return home was through indirect negotiations. "Any military operation," he said, "will not result in rescuing these prisoners."

Even as he spoke, the Israelis had taken out two more bridges across the Litani River and were dropping aerial bombs on main roads, rendering them impassable. Hezbollah observation posts and security pockets were coming under air attack and shell fire.

Nasrallah was not looking for a serious confrontation with Israel. He was gambling that a new, untested, and civilian-heavy Israeli cabinet would balk at launching a war against Hezbollah and instead would opt for prisoner swap negotiations as previous governments had done. Yet was there just a sense of unease in his voice as he warned Israel about the folly of overreacting to the abductions? Did Nasrallah, the master tactician, at that moment begin to wonder if he had miscalculated how the Israelis might react?

"We do not want to escalate things in the south," he said. "We do not want to push Israel into war. We do not want to push the region into war."

Senior Israeli military officials were already threatening that the "period of quiet is over" and that if the abducted soldiers were not released "we'll turn Lebanon's clock back twenty years."

Responding to the threats, Nasrallah cautioned that the Lebanon of today was "different from the Lebanon of twenty years ago. If they choose confrontation, then they should expect surprises."

The ministers belonging to the Western-backed March 14 parliamentary bloc in Lebanon's coalition government were furious at the kidnapping operation, especially as Nasrallah had previously provided assurances that Hezbollah would not embark upon any military adventures during the summer months that could jeopardize the lucrative tourist season.

Saudi Arabia, which backed Prime Minister Fouad Siniora's government, released an unusually frank statement, tacitly blaming Hezbollah and Iran for "irresponsible actions" and "uncalculated adventures."

Siniora learned of the kidnapping operation while meeting with Emile Lahoud, the Lebanese president. On returning to his office, he summoned

Hussein Khalil, Nasrallah's top adviser, and asked him why Hezbollah had mounted such an operation, and outside the Shebaa Farms.

"He replied, 'We got the chance,'" Siniora later recalled. "I asked him, 'What will the Israelis do?' He answered, 'Nothing.'"[1]

But Siniora was worried that Israel would unleash the same anger on Lebanon as it had on Gaza just three weeks earlier, when Palestinian militants from three separate groups had tunneled their way out of the Gaza Strip, infiltrated an IDF outpost, and snatched a soldier, Gilad Shalit. Israel launched a major offensive against northern Gaza to punish militant groups.

Siniora reminded Khalil of the heavy Israeli response to the kidnapping in Gaza, but the unruffled Hezbollah official told Siniora, "Lebanon is not Gaza."

"This Is the First Surprise"

But Israel at that moment was making plans that would lead to war. Lieutenant General Dan Halutz, the IDF chief of staff and a former head of the air force, recommended using air power to punish and cow Hezbollah in a series of surgical strikes. One operation would target facilities suspected of containing Hezbollah's arsenal of Iranian Fajr rockets and their launchers. Another would hit the runways of Beirut's Rafik Hariri International Airport, the border crossings with Syria, and a selection of infrastructure targets. The operations were approved by the Israeli cabinet on the evening of July 12. Most Israeli ministers assumed that the aerial offensive would be over in a couple of days and that Hezbollah, stunned by the ferocity of the Israeli response and suitably chastened, would sue for a cease-fire. The offensive would change the "rules of the game" in south Lebanon. Israeli deterrence would be restored and the international community would be well positioned to press for the fulfillment of UN Security Council Resolution 1559, which demanded Hezbollah's disarming. In the early stages of the war, some Israeli officials were looking to replace UNIFIL's two thousand armed observers deployed along the Blue Line with a robust NATO force. A UNIFIL official who was on leave in Israel on July 12 recalls meeting with top military staff and urging them to take advantage of the kidnapping to pursue a diplomatic path and not to resort to a punishing military campaign. But the Israelis told him, "No. The Americans and French can put their troops where their mouths are."

The Israelis claim the operation to knock out the Fajr rockets in the early hours of July 13 took just thirty-four minutes, during which fifty-nine targets throughout south Lebanon were bombed, including private homes where launchers were allegedly stored. The Israelis hailed the operation as a "singular achievement" and the result of years of patient intelligence collection and analysis.

Halutz would later claim that 90 percent of Hezbollah's long-range rocket arsenal was destroyed during the war. That may be an overly optimistic assessment. Indeed, in Lebanon there was a certain amount of skepticism about the claimed success of the Fajr operation. Hezbollah was known to have built decoy launchers and rockets to fool the Israelis. Years earlier, Hezbollah had constructed a fake rocket from several oil drums soldered together with a cone fixed to one end. The rocket was placed on the back of a trailer, loosely covered with a tarpaulin sheet, and driven around the south, allowing it to be detected by Israeli reconnaissance drones or jets.

Ehud Olmert and the Israeli government, buoyed by the apparent success of the Fajr operation, wanted more. The decision was made to escalate the reprisals by bombing Hezbollah's stronghold in the southern suburbs of Beirut. The attacks began that evening. Multistory buildings, the homes and offices of Hezbollah's leadership, including the building where I had interviewed Nasrallah three years earlier, pancaked into rubble and dust, each missile exploding in a huge percussive blast that shook the entire city. Hezbollah's security center in the heart of the southern suburbs was turned into a wasteland of smashed concrete.

It was only when the Israelis dropped leaflets warning residents of the southern suburbs to flee prior to the attack that the magnitude of the Israeli retaliation seemed to dawn on Hezbollah's leadership. Until then, it was business as usual for Hezbollah staff at offices in Beirut and elsewhere. With the Israeli leaflet drop, the cadres received orders to re-locate to "the points," the secret wartime locations for the leadership, administrative, and media branches. The building housing the Al-Manar television channel was destroyed, but broadcasts were barely interrupted as the channel continued operating from its alternative location.

Hezbollah responded with a heavy barrage of rockets, targeting for the first time Haifa, twenty-five miles south of the border. On the eve-ning of July 14, Nasrallah gave a live speech on Al-Manar by telephone from his underground bunker deep below the southern suburbs. After praising the Islamic Resistance fighters, he directly addressed the Israe-lis, accusing them of "changing the rules of the game." "You wanted an open war, an open war is what you will get. It will be a full-scale war. To Haifa and—believe me—beyond Haifa and beyond beyond Haifa."

At that moment, unseen by the listening audience, Nasrallah was handed a note by an assistant. Continuing with his speech, the Hezbollah leader recalled that he had promised surprises in this war. "This is the first surprise," he said, urging people in Beirut to stare out to sea. "Right now, the Israeli warship at sea—look at it now, it's burning."

In the inky blackness of the night there was a distinct orange glow and showers of sparks. It was a stunning piece of theatrics. Cheers and applause could be heard emanating from balconies throughout west Beirut facing the Mediterranean. Nasrallah had promised surprises, and he had delivered.

The stricken vessel was the INS *Hanit,* a Saar-5 missile boat. Hezbollah had launched at least three of its Iranian Noor radar-guided antiship missiles from the port of Ouzai at the southern end of Beirut. The first missile overshot the ship and continued flying out to sea before homing in on an Egyptian-crewed Cambodian merchant vessel, striking and sinking it more than forty miles offshore. The second Noor missile hit the *Hanit,* which was lying six miles off the Lebanese coast, killing four sailors and disabling the vessel. It turned out that the outcome of the attack could have been much worse. According to a diplomat briefed on the Israeli investigation into the *Hanit* attack, the third missile struck a section of the vessel's superstructure at the last instant, deflecting it into the sea, where it exploded harmlessly. If the missile had maintained its original trajectory, the *Hanit* would have sustained much greater damage and could have sunk.

A subsequent investigation by the Israeli navy claimed that the *Hanit*'s defense systems had been placed on "standby" mode instead of "high alert combat readiness" because the Israeli navy did not believe that Hezbollah had acquired a system that could threaten its vessels. However, there is a lingering suspicion within Western intelligence circles that rather than human error by the Israelis, Hezbollah actively jammed the *Hanit*'s radar, allowing the Noor missiles to speed toward the ship undetected. The claim remains unconfirmed—Hezbollah maintains its usual ambiguous silence on the matter. But Israel had good reason to pin the blame on the carelessness of an electronic warfare systems officer on board the *Hanit* rather than reveal a potential weakness of its Barak antimissile defense system. Israel was in intense negotiations with India at the time for a $300 million contract to co-develop the next generation of the Barak missile—a deal that could have collapsed if it was shown that the Barak was vulnerable to jamming.

"This Is Israeli Terror, but We Will Resist"

In the southern villages, the exodus had begun in earnest, with hundreds of thousands of civilians fleeing the onslaught. The Israelis told UNIFIL that Israel intended to establish a "special security zone" including twenty-one villages along the Blue Line and that any vehicle seen entering the zone would be fired upon. The Israelis attempted to empty the border district of its population by issuing ultimatums via leaflet drops and radio broadcasts on the same frequency once used by the SLA-run "Voice of the South" station, which had closed in 2000. Even bullhorns were used for those villages close enough to the border fence to hear Israel's instructions to leave. On July 16, the Sunni inhabitants of Marwahine, a tiny village close to the border, were informed by bullhorn that they had two hours to leave their homes. A pickup truck and a Mercedes, carrying among them thirty-three men, women, and children, drove out of the village and headed west toward the coast. The pickup truck broke down, however, close to the chalk cliffs at Biyyada and within view of an Israeli navy gunboat. The driver frantically tried to restart his vehicle while some of the passengers climbed out of the two vehicles, hoping that the Israelis could see they were civilians. But within minutes both vehicles were attacked by a drone firing missiles and a helicopter gunship blasting the burning vehicles and initial survivors with its 30 mm machine gun. In all, twenty-three people were killed, including fourteen children and seven women, two of whom were pregnant. The next day, a UNIFIL relief column attempting to rescue the remaining beleaguered residents of Marwahine came under Israeli shell fire. As a dozen 155 mm rounds exploded nearby, the body-armored peacekeepers flung themselves on top of civilians to protect them from flying shrapnel.

On July 17, I headed toward Nabatiyah, planning to spend the night in the area. The bridges across the Litani had all been destroyed, cutting off a large part of southwest Lebanon, including Tyre. Israeli navy ships were imposing a blockade along the coast and had threatened to target any southbound vehicles driving along the coastal highway, echoing the tactic of the Grapes of Wrath operation in 1996.

I joined three carloads of other reporters and we drove south along the empty highway out of Beirut. With the coastal route off-limits, we headed up into the Chouf Mountains and wound along the sides of yawning, densely forested valleys. Near Mukhtara, the ancestral seat of Walid Jumblatt, the paramount Druze leader, the road became clogged with the familiar sight of northbound refugees who had escaped their homes in the Shia areas south of the Chouf. There were hundreds of cars crammed with people—bearded fathers hunched over steering wheels, mothers with babies on their laps, grandparents squeezed into the back with cousins, aunts, and uncles. Black trash bags full of clothing and household goods were tied to the roofs along with the ubiquitous foam mattresses. Children sat in open car trunks and dangled their legs above the road. This was the first major evacuation from the south since April 1996, and these children were fulfilling what had become a tragic rite of passage for generations of southern Lebanese fleeing violence.

In Nabatiyah, we were told that there was a route across the Litani after all, a small causeway of bulldozed earth over cement pipes to allow the water to flow through. The causeway lay just over a mile from the coast and was the only route to the beleaguered Tyre district. It was an unpleasantly tense drive along the empty roads leading down into the Litani River valley. We could see explosions emanating from villages south of the river, and when we paused to check directions, we could hear the ineluctable rumble of jets and whine of drones. Once across the causeway, it was a mere ten-minute dash along the coastal road to reach the outskirts of Tyre.

We found the town in a state of panic. The beachfront Rest House hotel, a popular weekend destination in normal times, was filled with refugees from nearby villages. Many of them were expatriate Lebanese, citizens of the United States, Canada, Australia, and European countries who had returned to their ancestral homes for the summer holidays. Talking to them gave us the first idea of what conditions were like in the villages along the border. Ali Hijazi said that his village of Aittaroun, just east of Bint Jbeil, had run out of basic food and there was almost no drinking water left. At least twenty villagers had been killed when their homes were demolished in Israeli air strikes, he said. The residents of Aittaroun and Bint Jbeil were ordered by the Israelis to leave their homes by 3:00 P.M. on July 18.

"We left immediately when we heard the warning, not stopping to pack or even bring money," Ali said. "We saw people in Bint Jbeil and other places pleading at us to stop and take them, but we had no room. There was nothing we could do for them."

Three loud blasts close to the Rest House sent panicked refugees scurrying for cover, ducking behind chairs and shoving one another to get away from the vulnerable plate glass windows. The blasts were not Israeli bombs but Hezbollah's latest salvo of rockets, fired from hidden launchers among the orange groves outside Tyre, thin wavy trails of smoke marking their southbound trajectory. Shortly afterward, the refugees in the hotel watched the Arabic satellite television channels report that Haifa, thirty-seven miles south of Tyre, had been hit by rockets again.

"Let them suffer as we are suffering," said one man to mutters of agreement from his companions.

In the Jabal Amil hospital, Walid Abu Zeidi, thirteen, trembling with shock, writhed on his hospital bed, his small body daubed with bright red iodine and his arm wrapped in a bandage. He and his friends had been swimming in a culvert beside the Litani River five miles north of Tyre when a missile dropped by a jet exploded nearby. "I saw the flash of the missile, then I was thrown down," he said.

The corridor in the basement of the hospital was filled with people sitting on the floor, wide-eyed with shock and apprehension. Children sat with their mothers and sisters on foam mattresses as doctors, nurses, and relatives of the wounded hurried past. "This is Israeli terror," a headscarfed teenage girl whispered, "but we will resist."

In the hush of the intensive care unit lay Alia Alieddine, a thirty-year-old woman, one of only two casualties to make it to the hospital from the hill village of Srifa, ten miles east of Tyre. Israeli aircraft had flattened several neighborhoods in the village the previous night. Ten bodies had been recovered, but it was feared that many more remained under the rubble. Connected to breathing tubes and drips, her head heavily bandaged, Alieddine's bruised, half-closed eyes stared sightlessly at the ceiling. "She suffered major wounds, her arm is broken, and she has lost a lot of blood," Dr. Abdullah Abbas said quietly. "Her chances are not good. It is in God's hands."

A steady stream of casualties trickled into the hospital, ferried from outlying villages by the exceptionally brave young men and women volunteers of the Lebanese Red Cross. By the end of the second week of the war, the medics were reporting that starving dogs had begun to eat the dead. The unrelenting pressure to bring aid to the stranded villagers was beginning to take a psychological toll on the fifty medics in Tyre. Terrified civilians constantly called in to the Red Cross center begging for help, but there was little the medics could do. Even the distinctive white ambulances emblazoned with the Red Cross symbol and lit up at night with rotating blue lights and spotlights were coming under attack, with bombs dropped perilously close to them, apparently on purpose. "I don't know what the Israelis are thinking when they do this. They certainly can see us," said Sami Yazbek, the Red Cross chief in Tyre.

"Half of Them Have No Heads, No Hands"

Some 80 percent of Tyre's population of a hundred thousand had fled by the end of the first week. Even the twenty thousand refugees who had descended on Tyre from neighboring villages had mostly departed, either evacuated by sea or driven to the Litani River, where they waded across the shallow river to be picked up by relatives or taxis charging exorbitant fees for the perilous drive to Sidon and Beirut.

Television journalists replaced the refugees at the Rest House hotel. The hotel had panoramic views to the south and east, and a bank of cameras was set up beside the swimming pool to capture images of explosions and rocket launches. The print media took over the Al-Fanar hotel on the seafront in the picturesque Christian quarter on Tyre's promontory. We began eating communal meals in the evening, simple dishes of rice, lentils, and salads as the hotel's food stocks began to run out. There were always mountains of fresh fish, sold to the hotel by enterprising youths who tossed hand grenades into the sea outside the Fanar. The hotel regularly shook to the reverberations of these underwater explosions.

The hotel's proprietor, the silver-haired and baggy-eyed Raymond, was a permanent lugubrious presence, sitting at a small table in the reception area smoking a water pipe and flicking through piles of bills and receipts. At least someone was making money from this disaster.

Our Christian neighbors left en masse one afternoon after Israeli aircraft dropped warning leaflets over Tyre, a plastic barrel bursting open in the air and the yellow paper fluttering in a cloud of confetti onto the narrow streets and small stone houses of the quarter.

Lebanese troops, loaded with webbing and ammunition, deployed along Tyre's streets, preparing to repel a possible Israeli invasion. One soldier, a stocky Maronite Christian from Bsharre in north Lebanon, lounged in the shade of the Rest House hotel, ruminating on what was to come. He would do his duty, he said, if Israel invaded, but then after a moment's pause he asked, "Do you see any signs of hope? I have only been married two weeks."

After many years driving around south Lebanon, I knew my way around well. But I found that my geographical knowledge of the south was almost meaningless during the war because the roads were so heavily bombed we had to find alternative routes, tiny back lanes and even farm tracks through orange groves and banana plantations.

On my initial trip out of Tyre, I followed a Red Cross ambulance that wove around the first gaping crater on the outskirts of the town then detoured around the second by following a track through an orange orchard. Houses and shops destroyed in air strikes spilled untidily onto the road. The burned-out wrecks of vehicles littered the sides of the road, some having slammed into metal telegraph poles or into buildings, driven perhaps by motorists who lost control in their panic to escape the area. Some vehicles clearly had been struck by missiles, transforming the cars into twisted heaps of fire-scorched metal.

Siddiqine was under shell fire. We had to take back lanes through the village as the main road was blocked by the rubble of bombed buildings. We could hear the shells ripping through the air above us and see them exploding in dirty gray puffs of smoke and dust some three hundred yards away. I gritted my teeth as the tires of my rented BMW crunched over the jagged glass shards and shattered cinder blocks that carpeted the road. This was not a place to change a flat tire. We later learned that Layal Najib, a twenty-three-year-old photographer for Agence France Presse, was killed in Siddiqine that morning during the same artillery bombardment.

By the end of the first full week of the war, the morgue in Tyre's government hospital was full. A refrigerator truck that had been driven to Tyre from Tripoli in north Lebanon on the first day of the conflict in anticipation of a heavy toll of dead had carried the overspill. But the truck was filled to capacity, and the feeble generator that blew cold air over the corpses could not compete with the blistering summer heat. Local residents were beginning to complain about the smell, and a decision was made to bury the victims in a mass grave.

Stacked inside on shelves of wooden slats, wrapped in sheets and plastic bags, were the remains of 115 people, most of them children. "Half of them have no heads, no hands. There's a baby inside that was burned like a piece of coal," said Hala Hijazi, a nurse at the government hospital, her tired eyes and haggard expression momentarily betraying the horror of what she had witnessed in the past week.

The bodies were lowered from the back of the truck into simple pine coffins doused with chemical spray to mask, with little success, the cloying odor of putrefaction. A carpenter continued to hammer together planks of wood for another coffin to join the pile of more than a hundred already assembled and ready to receive bodies.

A crowd of wide-eyed Palestinian children from the surrounding refugee camp scrambled up a wall beside the hospital to stare in morbid fascination at the gruesome scene in the courtyard. Grieving relatives of the dead sat on plastic chairs in a row, sobbing quietly and holding one another's hands. Some of the bags placed in coffins were pitifully small; other coffins were filled with more than one bag, grim evidence of the destructive firepower Israel had unleashed on south Lebanon. By the time the third body had been lifted from the truck, the green canvas stretcher on which they were carried to the coffins was streaked with black blood that had oozed from the plastic and cloth bindings. Each body was inscribed with the victim's name, which someone would read out to a soldier who would tick a list on a clipboard. I recognized the name of one victim whose wrapped corpse was squeezed into a narrow coffin: Alia Alieddine, the same woman I had seen struggling to live in the intensive care unit of Jabal Amil hospital just two days earlier.

"We Expected a Tent and Three Kalashnikovs"

By the end of the first week of fighting, Ehud Olmert was brimming with confidence, buoyed by 78 percent approval ratings and glowing coverage in the Israeli press.

A UN delegation appeared to have won some concessions from the Lebanese government regarding a possible cease-fire, including Hezbollah potentially agreeing to hand over the captured Israeli soldiers to the jurisdiction of the state. But Olmert was uninterested in mulling an exit strategy when he believed he had Hezbollah on the ropes. General Halutz, the IDF chief of staff, was confident that Hezbollah could be smashed using airpower alone with some limited ground incursions along the border.

Israel had prepared two contingency plans in the event of a conflict with Hezbollah. The first was an air-only bombing campaign lasting 48 to 72 hours. The second was a ground invasion to push Hezbollah north of the Litani River.[2] Both operations were intended to run in tandem. However, Halutz abandoned the ground invasion plan and instead chose an expanded version of the air campaign. He recommended a gradual escalation of air attacks, including against major Lebanese infrastructure facilities. The Americans worried that bombing infrastructure could undermine the Siniora government and leaned on Olmert to concentrate on Hezbollah targets instead.

After five days of fighting, Israel could have secured a favorable cease-fire deal, but instead, on July 17, Olmert addressed the Israeli Knesset and delivered a set of wholly unrealistic conditions to end the conflict. They included the return of the hostages, a complete cease-fire, deployment of the Lebanese army throughout south Lebanon up to the Blue Line, the expulsion of Hezbollah from the border district, and the party's disarming under UN Security Council Resolution 1559. "We will continue to operate in full force until we achieve this," he thundered.

Olmert's maximalist position quashed any chance of achieving a swift and favorable cease-fire deal for Israel and inadvertently played into Hezbollah's hands. Hezbollah may have been surprised by the initial onslaught, but its fighting capabilities remained essentially intact, and, contrary to Halutz's assessment, it knew it could withstand many more weeks of Israeli aerial punishment.

The same day that Olmert delivered his ultimatums, units of IDF special forces troops staged the first serious incursion into Lebanon, advancing on the village of Maroun er-Ras, a mile north of the border. Capturing the hilltop village would grant the Israelis a toehold inside Lebanon with dominating views overlooking Bint Jbeil to the northwest. But the IDF troops found themselves ambushed by Hezbollah men fighting from well-prepared defensive positions. Far from hitting the Israelis and then disappearing in the usual guerrilla fashion, the Hezbollah fighters held their ground and within hours the soldiers had taken casualties and were surrounded. The IDF threw more forces into the battle. But the Hezbollah men refused to yield the ground and fought with a determination that stunned the Israelis. Soldiers spoke of Hezbollah men popping out of the ground to loose a rocket-propelled grenade before disappearing again. "We expected a tent and three Kalashnikovs—that was the intelligence we were given," a special forces soldier later said. "Instead, we found a hydraulic steel door leading to a well-equipped network of tunnels."[3]

Several Israeli soldiers were killed and more than a dozen and a half wounded in fierce close-quarters battles before Israel declared on July 23, after seven days of fighting, that it had captured Maroun er-Ras. Yet the Israeli forces in the village continued to come under attack in the following days and took more casualties.

"We Never Received Orders to Fire the SAMs"

With Maroun er-Ras more or less under Israeli control, IDF commanders turned their attention to Bint Jbeil, which sprawled across the hilly landscape directly below the new IDF positions.

Nasrallah had chosen Bint Jbeil to deliver his victory speech in May 2000, two days after the Israelis pulled out of Lebanon, in which he described Israel as weak as a "spider's web." Mindful of that insult, Israeli commanders dubbed the operation to attack Bint Jbeil "Web of Steel." Yet the decision to strike at Hezbollah's presence in the town was informed by hubris rather than tactical need. The center of Bint Jbeil was a warrenlike network of narrow lanes and alleyways, too tight to use armor effectively and well prepared in advance by Hezbollah. Hezbollah commanders could see the IDF Merkava tanks sliding into position on the Maroun er-Ras hill and knew that Bint Jbeil would be next. The attack on Bint Jbeil began on July 24, following two days of softening up with artillery and air strikes. But it was a scrappy, unconvincing assault, muddled by bickering IDF generals who could not agree on how to proceed and consisting of a series of hard-fought skirmishes between separate Israeli units and Hezbollah fighters. After four days, the Israelis pulled back, leaving the ruined town in Hezbollah's hands.

The Israelis were discovering the hard way Hezbollah's new military doctrine of "defensive resistance." Not only were the Hezbollah combatants tenaciously defending the ground from their fortified positions, they were also maneuvering across ground, or under it, to fill gaps, encircle Israeli troops, or confront additional IDF thrusts. "It's not a huge force," one UNIFIL officer told me, estimating Hezbollah's frontline combat strength at around eight hundred to a thousand fighters, "but they are mobile, very well prepared, and devoted. They're willing to act. There's heavy shelling and air strikes, but they are not sitting scared in their bunkers."

The Hezbollah men knew what they had to do: hold ground to protect the rocket launchers and kill as many Israeli soldiers as possible to weaken their morale and embarrass the Israeli military and political leadership. But within that general strategy, there was much tactical flexibility given to commanders on the ground. Hezbollah sometimes allowed the Israelis to enter Lebanon unopposed, especially in open terrain, choosing to attack them once they had advanced into urban areas where the Israeli advantage of air and armored power was diminished.

"It is beneficial for us to allow them to advance to the entrances of the villages. This is our goal," Nasrallah explained in a televised statement on August 3. "Our goal is to inflict maximum casualties and damage to the capabilities of the enemy, and we are succeeding."

The Hezbollah units maintained contact with command bases as much as possible using the fiber optic landline network. Intelligence picked up by Hezbollah's Hebrew-speaking electronic warfare technicians was dispatched to commanders who could then relay instructions to the cadres on the ground. But once squads were on the move, they had to rely on walkie-talkies to communicate, which carried risks of jamming or detection. Hezbollah's technicians working their spectrum analyzers could inform fighters which frequencies were jammed, allowing communications to continue using unblocked frequencies. Sometimes the fighters intercepted Israeli radio traffic and listened to the chatter between combat units. "We used to play mind games with them. We would interrupt them and say things like 'we're waiting for you' or 'we're just around the corner,'" one Hezbollah veteran of the war recalled.

Another fighter who was deployed on the edges of Bint Jbeil said his unit broke in to radio communications of Israeli troops who had just been ambushed and were calling for backup.

"One of the brothers spoke to them in Hebrew on the radio, saying that we knew where they were and we were about to drop a bomb on their heads. The Israeli cursed Sayyed Nasrallah and the Prophet Mohammed," he said, chuckling at the memory.

It soon became evident that unlike other Israeli military campaigns in Lebanon since the early 1990s, the Israelis for the first time were limiting the use of their helicopter gunships in Lebanese airspace, relying instead on low-signature missile-firing pilotless drones. The only helicopters I saw during the war were off the coast of Tyre, usually flying far out to sea and at high altitude. The Israelis believed Hezbollah had acquired SA-18 "Grouse" shoulder-fired surface-to-air missiles, even though none were known to have been fired during the war and the only antiaircraft missiles recovered by Israeli troops were the older SA-7 and SA-14 models.

Nonetheless, a former senior Israeli military intelligence official insisted to me in 2008 that the Israeli Air Force was not acting with excessive caution in reducing the number of helicopters above Lebanon. "We knew they had the missiles, so we adjusted our tactics," the official said. That assertion is supported by the comments of some Hezbollah fighters who told me that the SAMs were deliberately held in reserve as an additional "surprise" if necessary. "We never received orders to fire the SAMs because there were no helicopters to threaten us, and the bombing by jets didn't have much impact on us. If the jets had been a problem, we would have used the SAMs," recalls one Hezbollah recruit who fought on the front lines.

The New "Beyond Haifa" Stage

Far from being cowed by Israel's air attacks on Beirut and the south as the Israeli government had anticipated, Hezbollah steadily increased the number of rockets fired into Israel. The rate of fire for the first ten days averaged from 150 to 180 rockets per day, with as many as 47 being fired in a single salvo. The rate peaked at 350 on July 18. As Israel expanded the scope of targets in Lebanon, so Hezbollah's rockets marched ever deeper inside Israel—Haifa on July 14, Tiberias on July 15, and Nazareth and Afula on July 16. The rate of fire and incremental increase in range were consistent with Hezbollah's defensive posture during the war. Every time Israel escalated its attacks, Hezbollah reciprocated. The calculated and coordinated rocket fire also demonstrated that Hezbollah's command and control remained intact despite punishing air raids.

The deepest penetration into Israel came on August 3 when a 302 mm rocket impacted near Hadera. Curiously, almost none of the Iranian Fajr family of rockets was fired into Israel during the war. The feared Zelzal-2s, with their eleven-hundred-pound warheads and range that brought nearly all Israel's major population centers within reach, were not used, possibly because they were being held in reserve in case Israel escalated its attacks even further. One suspected Zelzal was spotted tumbling out of the sky on July 17 moments after an Israeli air strike on a suburb of Beirut. The target was a Zelzal launcher inside a shipping container. A motor on one of the rockets apparently ignited in the blast, causing it to shoot into the sky.

One medium-range launch site was located in a dense orange orchard on the northern edge of Tyre, and it was reportedly from here that Hezbollah fired the 302 mm rocket that struck Hadera on August 3. In the early hours of August 5, I awoke with a start to the appalling din of multiple machine gun fire and the clatter of helicopters that seemed to be hovering a few feet above the hotel. The inky night sky was lit with brilliant white and orange flashes coming from the northern entrance of Tyre. A team of Israeli Shayetet 13 naval commandos was raiding a building where the operators of the nearby rocket launcher were based.

The gun battle, which lasted perhaps ten minutes, left an Israeli officer and one soldier severely wounded and another six soldiers with slight wounds. At least one Hezbollah fighter was reported dead. The following afternoon, an Israeli jet bombed the building into rubble. Yet within hours, the rocket launcher was back in action in the orange orchard as if nothing had happened.

Hezbollah also launched at least three of its Mirsad-1 UAVs. One was shot down on August 7 off the coast of northern Israel. It was reportedly carrying twenty pounds of explosive packed with ball bearings. Another was intercepted by Israeli helicopters on the night of August 13 off the Tyre headland. From the Al-Fanar hotel, we watched the helicopter finish off the drone, blasting it with machine gun fire and missiles after it fell into the sea. A third UAV was launched the same night but crashed near Tyre.

Hezbollah also claimed to have hit two more vessels with its antiship missiles, one on August 1 and another on August 12. All shipping, whether Israeli navy or commercial vessels, gave the Lebanese coastline a wide berth after the attack on the INS *Hanit*. However, minutes after Hezbollah aired a claim to have hit a ship off the Tyre coast on August 12, I saw from the town's promontory a large plume of white smoke on the horizon to the southwest that lasted for about twenty minutes. I could see no vessel, even with my binoculars, and have no explanation for the smoke. The Israelis denied that any more ships were struck by missiles.

Hezbollah fighters in the frontline area moved on foot at night and generally under cover of thick undergrowth. To travel farther distances, fighters rode off-road rally bikes and all-terrain vehicles with the lights switched off. Inside some villages, fighters disguised themselves as old men and women to move around. Rather than using tunnels dug between houses, holes were knocked through the walls of adjacent buildings so that fighters could traverse the village quickly without exposing themselves on the street.

The advanced Russian antitank missile systems were usually reserved for Israeli armored vehicles. The Hezbollah tank hunter-killer teams demonstrated impressive accuracy, hitting targets at distances of three miles at the outer edges of the missile's range. Missiles were often fired in volleys of up to a dozen at a time, a relatively high expenditure. The purpose was to "swarm" armored vehicles with missiles to blast off outer layers of reactive armor and expose the vulnerable steel skin, a continuation of a tactic developed in the mid-1990s. They made effective use of the older wire-guided Sagger systems by firing them against buildings housing IDF troops. In one instance, nine paratroopers were killed and eleven wounded when Sagger missiles smashed through the cinder block walls of the building in which they were sheltering.

Despite the invisible Hezbollah air defense during the war, one anti-armor team showed some initiative in shooting down an Israeli helicopter with an antitank missile. A CH-53 Yasur troop transport helicopter momentarily touched down on a hillside near Yater village to drop off a platoon of soldiers. A quick-thinking Hezbollah team fired a missile at the CH-53 as it took off, knocking it out of the sky and killing all five crew members.

Abu Khalil, who had deployed to the Marjayoun area in the opening hours of the war, spent the first fifteen days assisting antitank units. He and two colleagues carried missiles packed inside wooden crates to pre-selected locations where they could be collected by the antitank teams. One fighter would walk a few paces ahead to reconnoiter the route through the thick undergrowth while the other two carried the case containing the missiles on their shoulders. Abu Khalil was told nothing about the systems he was carrying, and he concluded that they must be antitank missiles from the length of the wooden boxes (much too short to be 120 mm Katyusha rockets) and the Russian lettering on the sides. He and his comrades labored throughout the day, pausing every few hours to glug down orange energy tablets dissolved in canteens of water. Despite the heat, they were careful not to drink too much liquid. They had been warned that if they urinated, their scent could be detected by Israeli trackers with sniffer dogs. Such was the level of caution they adopted.

There were no significant reinforcements dispatched to the south to bolster Hezbollah's numbers, simply because they were not needed. Other than the south-based fighters like Abu Khalil, who were deployed immediately after the kidnapping operation on July 12, Hezbollah had sufficient numbers of *tabbiyya* reservists to defend the villages against IDF encroachments. They were supported by some of the regular forces who could plug gaps where needed. Other regular units north of the Litani River or *tabbiyya* reservist fighters in villages just outside the combat areas stayed where they were, ready to confront IDF troops should they move farther north.

"Victory Is Coming, Coming, Coming"

Two of those reservists patiently awaiting their turn to fight were Abu Mohammed and Hajj Rabieh, the Hezbollah veterans from Srifa village whom I encountered two weeks into the fighting.

More than a mile to the east, the neighboring village of Froun was shrouded in a haze of dust and smoke. High above the village, a pair of Israeli jets glinted like silver specks in the deep blue sky as they wheeled and swooped, releasing bombs that exploded in great bursts of dirty brown dust and gray smoke among the houses. Above us, invisible in the brilliant blue sky, whined a reconnaissance drone, an unnerving presence as we paced through the empty village. Srifa's deserted streets and bombed homes reminded me of one of those dummy towns the U.S. army built in the 1950s in the deserts of New Mexico to test weapons and atomic bombs. A twisted sheet of metal banged occasionally in the hot breeze, adding to the sense of apocalyptic desolation. Two scrawny horses stood in the shade of a gas station while a pack of mangy dogs padded silently down the road. Inside one lightly damaged single-story home, the front door left wide open by its fleeing owners, were several family pictures showing happier times. One portrayed a smiling little girl dressed in traditional Lebanese costume.

My two colleagues—Charles Levinson, then a correspondent for Agence France Presse, and Rania Abouzeid, a Lebanese journalist—and I had been in Srifa for about twenty minutes when we were approached by a thin, wiry man with a scraggly beard. He wore plain clothes and his trousers were tucked into socks. But the walkie-talkie he held in his right hand identified him as a Hezbollah man. He was clearly surprised to see foreigners in the village, but we told him we were there to have a look around. The Hezbollah man thought for a moment, then spoke into his walkie-talkie. Making up his mind, he beckoned us to follow him. He said we could call him Abu Mohammed, and he offered to give us a tour of the bombed quarters of the village. We were joined minutes later by a short, stocky Hezbollah fighter with a thick beard and a baseball cap. He called himself Hajj Rabieh. The two men kept to the shadows on the side of the street but otherwise seemed unperturbed by the drone that continued to linger overhead and was making me feel distinctly uneasy. "We take our chances, and we take our precautions, too," Abu Mohammed said with a grin.

We followed them along a twisting alleyway. Part of the alley was strewn with delicate white jasmine petals blown from an overhanging tree by the force of the explosions. For a brief moment the air was filled with the fragrant scent of the flower. At the end of the alley was a small stone house, and inside, seated on thin mattresses on the floor, were four old women. One of them grabbed a white sheet and pulled it over her head in a gesture of Islamic modesty at the sudden presence of men. The women were among the handful of residents who had not left the village and were being cared for by the Hezbollah men and a young woman. "We are trying our best to help the local people. This is the directive of the secretary general," Abu Mohammed said, referring to Nasrallah.

Mariam Faeen, who we were told was a hundred years old, sat upright, long, bony fingers clasped over her thin knees. Her cheeks were sunken and her face furrowed with age. She was deaf, but her bright eyes darted from face to face, following the conversation. Mariam had narrowly survived the second night of bombing in Srifa. One bomb destroyed her house, but she had crawled out of the rubble unharmed. She took shelter in another house, only to have that one blown up over her head less than an hour later. "She came out of the building black with dust and we brought her here," Hajj Rabieh said.

The two Hezbollah men were schoolteachers, but they were also veteran fighters in the Islamic Resistance. Hajj Rabieh was forty years old and had joined the resistance in 1982. His colleague, five years older, had fought with Hezbollah since 1985. They both seemed remarkably re-laxed, exuded self-confidence, and appeared to enjoy our unexpected company. We sat on the floor as they showed us how they communi-cated by walkie-talkie using their ad hoc verbal codes, as described in the previous chapter.

When asked how many fighters were present in the area, Abu Mo-hammed answered rhetorically, "How many angels are there? We are present in the same numbers."

Neither of them felt a need to rush into combat in the villages a little farther south. They knew their mission was to defend Srifa should the Israelis advance deeper into Lebanon.

"We are anxiously waiting for it. We are ready to do whatever we are asked to do," Hajj Rabieh said. "Their [the Israelis] experience in Ma-roun er-Ras and Bint Jbeil show they paid a high price. They will be paying the same price in every town and village they try to invade. Now they are beginning to admit that they can't achieve their objective of destroying us."

Abu Mohammed smiled and said, "Victory is coming, coming, com-ing."

"The New Middle East"

The Israelis were running out of targets. Each day, the jets returned over Lebanon, but by the end of the second week of fighting they were attack-ing targets that already had been pounded into dust during earlier strikes. The momentum was being lost. Ground forces were engaged in a series of limited incursions along the length of the border, but they were making little progress, and Hezbollah's rockets kept slamming into Israel.

By now it was dawning on the Bush administration that Israel was badly bungling the job of crushing Hezbollah. The IDF was supposed to be the most powerful military force in the Middle East. Had it not bull-dozed its way to Beirut in just nine days in June 1982? Why was it strug-gling to crush a few hundred Hezbollah "terrorists" in south Lebanon?

When the war broke out on July 12, it had appeared an opportune moment to deliver a mortal blow to Hezbollah's military capabilities. With leading Lebanese figures in the March 14 parliamentary bloc quietly urging the Americans to finish off Hezbollah, no wonder Condoleezza Rice, the secretary of state, saw little urgency in heading to the Middle East to begin cease-fire talks. On July 21, the same day that the government hospital in Tyre was preparing to bury the decomposing victims of Israeli attacks packed inside the refrigerator truck, Rice glibly described the war in Lebanon as "the birth pangs of the new Middle East."

Three days later, Rice flew to Beirut to begin assessing proposals for an end to the conflict, one that would ensure that Hezbollah could no longer threaten Israel or the Lebanese government. Fouad Siniora had drawn up a seven-point plan to end the fighting, which included recommendations for a beefed-up UNIFIL, the deployment of Lebanese troops up to the border with Israel, the restoration of the 1949 Armistice Agreement, and the transfer of the Shebaa Farms to UN custody.

Olmert categorically rejected handing the Shebaa Farms over to the UN, but the Israelis, Americans, and Siniora government were in tacit agreement that Hezbollah had to emerge from the war weakened.

On July 26, key Middle East actors and UN officials gathered in Rome to hammer out an agreement to end the war. But the meeting failed to reach consensus on a cease-fire proposal. Most countries attending, including those of the European Union and Russia as well as the UN, sought an immediate cease-fire before finding a lasting political settlement. But the United States insisted that a cessation of hostilities was inadequate—"We cannot," Rice said, "return to the status quo ante."

"They Suffocated Under the Dirt"

I woke slowly, tired, craving more sleep, and irritated at the beep of an incoming SMS on my mobile phone. For a moment, I stared stupidly at the message. It told me there had been a massacre in Qana with more than two dozen dead. Qana? Again? Surely not.

Yet the terse message was correct. Just over ten years since the slaughter of more than a hundred civilians in the UNIFIL Fijian battalion headquarters in Qana, violent death had visited this hill village once again. Two families, the Hashems and Shalhoubs, numbering around sixty people, were sheltering in the basement of a three-story home on the edge of Qana when it was struck in the early hours of July 30 by a precision-guided bomb. Five minutes later, the other side of the home was hit by a second bomb. Twenty-seven people died, sixteen of them under the age of twenty.

It was with a sobering sense of déjà vu and a hollow, sick feeling in my stomach that I drove along the winding road from Tyre to Qana. Had I not taken this same route ten years earlier, back then a novice war reporter, mentally preparing myself to see bodies torn apart by artillery shells? That I could be repeating this same trip a decade later seemed inconceivable, yet also oddly typical of the callous coincidences one finds in war and of the bitter twists of fate that seem to blight south Lebanon with merciless regularity.

The Hashem home lay among a cluster of buildings at the end of a road on the edge of a small steep valley filled with olive trees and patches of tobacco. The house, a typical Lebanese construction of reinforced concrete frame and cinder block walls, leaned at a drunken angle, threatening to topple at any moment. Civil defense workers gingerly stooped beneath a collapsed floor to access the bowels of the home where the dead lay. The bomb had buried itself deep underground before exploding. The blast had lifted a huge pile of dirt that had smothered the sleeping families in the basement. It was soon apparent that most of the victims were children.

The bodies emerged into daylight one by one, all gray-skinned with dust, one small boy's mouth stuffed with dirt, a stiff arm pointing accusingly at the sky. Wasps and flies buzzed with greedy excitement around his face and blood-sodden hair. "It's Ali Shalhoub," whispered an onlooker as the child was placed on a stretcher and carried away.

The 1996 Qana massacre was a Goyaesque spectacle of visceral horror, of dismembered and carbonized bodies and the reek of freshly spilled blood. But the victims of this second Qana massacre looked almost as though they could still be sleeping, as each limp body was carried in the arms of the rescue workers from the house. The dead were coated in dust, some with their mouths, ears, and noses clogged with dirt; yet few showed any signs of physical injury.

"They suffocated under the dirt," muttered Sami Yazbek, Tyre's Red Cross chief.

Most of the residents of Qana had escaped the village earlier in the war, but the Hashem and Shalhoub families had been trapped in their homes. "We couldn't get out of our neighborhood because there are only two roads leading out and the Israelis bombed them both several days ago," said Mohammed Shalhoub, a disabled forty-one-year-old who was recovering in a hospital in Tyre. As he was unable to walk, his wife, Rabab, had hauled him from beneath the rubble and dirt and had also rescued their son, Hassan, four. But their six-year-old daughter, Zeinab, had died.

Mohammed's mobile phone rang continually as friends and family asked after him and his relatives. One woman, her voice tinny but audible over the phone's speaker, introduced herself to Mohammed as a friend of Tayseer.

"I am his brother," Mohammed told her.

"How is he?" she asked.

"May God have mercy on him," Mohammed replied gently.

The woman began to sob. "No, no!"

Another phone call, and Shalhoub reeled off a list of names of people who died or survived. "Najwa was injured, Zeinab was martyred," he said. On mentioning his daughter's name, he choked and began weeping. A woman placed a comforting arm across his shoulder.

In a neighboring bed, Noor Hashem, thirteen, told us in a shy, trembling voice that her mother had pulled her free of the rubble along with her older sister and taken them to a neighboring house. Her mother returned to the bombed house to look for Noor's three brothers. "They haven't come to the hospital yet, and my mother hasn't returned," she said, and began crying.

Her three brothers were among the dead, the youngest only nine months old, but no one at the hospital had the heart to break the news to Noor.

This latest massacre in Qana marked a turning point in the war, just as the slaughter at the Fijian headquarters ten years earlier had changed the direction of Grapes of Wrath. U.S. diplomatic efforts to achieve a favorable cease-fire were left in tatters as international opinion began to weigh against Israel. Even Fouad Siniora, responding to the angry mood in Lebanon, snubbed Rice, forcing her to cancel a scheduled return trip to Beirut, just as Hafez al-Assad a decade earlier had refused to meet then secretary of state Warren Christopher during the Grapes of Wrath campaign. Yielding to U.S. pressure, Ehud Olmert agreed to a 48-hour halt in air operations.

The cease-fire provided an opportunity for reporters to visit the front lines where the main fighting had taken place. I knew Bint Jbeil had been bombed heavily during the fighting, but the level of destruction inflicted upon the center of the town was astonishing. The main street, where the weekly market was held, was gone, submerged beneath a carpet of rubble, chunks of concrete, asphalt, and stone, and pitted with pond-sized bomb craters. One unexploded bomb with Hebrew markings sat ominously in the middle of the street. Broken medicine bottles, pills, and diapers were scattered over the debris beside a gutted pharmacy. Several buildings had caught fire, and the smell of stale smoke and explosives hung heavy in the still air. Dozens of cars had been crushed by collapsing buildings. Almost all the small traditional stone houses of the old quarter were damaged or had collapsed into sad piles of stone and timber. Cheap plastic furniture, pictures, books, toys, clothing—the mundane detritus of people's lives—were strewn across the rubble, coated in the ubiquitous gray dust.

Slowly, frail elderly men and women emerged, wraithlike, from the bombed buildings, blinking in the sunlight, stumbling over the rubble and gazing in confusion at what had become of their town.

Mohammed Bazzi, a white-haired and wizened seventy-year-old, said he and his sister, Mariam, had been trapped since the beginning of the war in the basement of their building after it was bombed. They had survived on instant coffee, powdered milk, and water. "It has been a nightmare," he said.

Mariam was too frail to walk or even speak. Reporters briefly set aside notebooks and cameras to carry the seventy-six-year-old woman across the rubble in a wool blanket. Her long white hair fluffed around her face as she sipped from a bottle of water.

"All We Can Do Is Pray"

By the end of July, the IDF had begun calling up some fifteen thousand reservists to help the floundering regular forces. Once the cease-fire was over on August 2, the IDF dispatched larger numbers of troops into Lebanon in an attempt to seize the territory that comprised the old occupation zone. By August 5, there were around ten thousand IDF soldiers operating inside Lebanon. But progress was slow and hesitant. The reservists were ill-trained and poorly equipped, were often reluctant to fight, and suffered a shortage of basic supplies in the field such as food, water, and ammunition because of a badly coordinated logistics chain. Most reservists had spent the previous six years policing the West Bank and Gaza, where the enemy consisted of undisciplined street fighters, suicide bombers, and stone-throwing children. They were not trained for fighting Hezbollah. In fact, only a handful of elite soldiers, such as those belonging to the Egoz commando unit or the Paratroop Reconnaissance Battalion, had ever fought Hezbollah at close range in south Lebanon. Most IDF soldiers in the 1990s had pulled garrison duty in the hilltop compounds, dodging mortar shells and trying to avoid IEDs on foot patrols. Not only were the reservist units ill-prepared to wage a more conventional conflict, the enemy they faced in Lebanon in 2006 was qualitatively different from the guerrillas the IDF had confronted six years earlier. No wonder some soldiers were reluctant to tangle with the missile-wielding Hezbollah men lurking in the villages and valleys ahead of them. The commander of a battalion marching on Aitta Shaab ordered a "tactical retreat" after suffering just one casualty. A reservist engineering officer point-blank refused orders to clear a road into Bint

Jbeil, protesting that "ten soldiers had already been killed there." The brigade commander had the entire platoon arrested and jailed.[4]

The poor quality of the troops and the lack or morale did not go unnoticed. "Israeli troops looked unprepared, sloppy, and demoralized," one former senior U.S. commander noted. "This wasn't the vaunted IDF that we saw in previous wars."[5]

When I joined a UNIFIL relief convoy on August 5 to Dibil, the Christian village where the late SLA commander Aql Hashem lived, not a single Israeli soldier could be seen, even though we were traveling behind the IDF's lines. But there was ample evidence of their passing from the churned earth of tank tracks meandering through small fields of green tobacco on valley floors. There was evidence, too, of fierce fighting in the neighborhood. A burned-out Merkava tank lay on the side of the road a mile west of Aitta Shaab, its sleek lines blackened and blistered, a victim of Hezbollah's antitank missiles. The twin machine guns mounted on the turret were still in place. Beside the tank were broken stretchers and a green canvas military sack stuffed with food and covered in dried blood.

Shelling and air strikes continued uninterrupted, punctuated by the sharp report of outgoing rounds from border gun emplacements and the metallic crack of exploding shells on the hillsides. The barrages had turned swaths of the normally green hillsides around Dibil into black wastelands of carbonized bushes and scorched rock.

Unlike their Shia neighbors, many villagers in Dibil had opted to remain in their homes, a risky decision rooted in a belief that their Christian village would be spared the worst of the onslaught directed against Hezbollah. Most of the villagers had gathered in the center of the village, instinctively drawing closer to the stone church with its bright red-tiled roof. They had run out of flour, milk, and fuel for the cars. There was no electricity, the landline telephone was down, and the cellular network was jammed. "All we can do is pray," said Father Yussef Nadaf, the village priest, with a hopeless shrug. He looked exhausted, and his dog collar hung loosely from his black shirt.

The artillery shells were howling over our heads and exploding in a nearby valley when we reached Jibbayn, a Sunni-populated border village just west of Dibil. The sharp report of each round fired from an emplacement just over the border felt like a physical slap in the face. There were only a few panic-stricken elderly people remaining in the village. They flocked around the UNIFIL armored personnel carriers begging for rescue.

"Are you going to Tyre? Please take us with you," pleaded one woman clutching two plastic bags filled with clothing and personal effects. Another old man leaning on a walking stick insisted to the French soldiers that he must ride with them in an APC. He was told that it was impossible, that there was no room. "But I'm the mayor," he said with helpless indignation.

Israeli troops were present two hundred yards up the road in the northern half of the village, which prevented the UNIFIL convoy from proceeding to Teir Harfa, the last village on the itinerary lying just beyond Jibbayn.

Warrant Officer Martin Lionel, the French convoy commander, studied his map spread out on the hood of a car, looking for alternative routes. There was only one: a narrow stone track that dropped in a series of hairpin bends into a steep valley just to the west of Jibbayn. Lionel pursed his lips as he pondered whether the trucks could make the journey. But there were other perils in the valley besides bad roads. I was familiar with the valley from before the war. It was a Hezbollah "security pocket" and bound to be crawling with fighters firing rockets into Israel and preparing to confront IDF troops. Lionel absorbed this information and then decided against the trip.

"We don't even know if there's anyone left in Teir Harfa," he said, and ordered the convoy back to Naqoura.

"My Tanks Are Getting Mauled!"

In early August, the IDF began firing cluster munitions into south Lebanon, blanketing huge swaths of terrain with millions of bomblets. Although the Israelis claimed to be attempting to neutralize Hezbollah's rocket-firing positions, the submunitions saturated remote valleys, farmland, villages, and towns alike. Human Rights Watch subsequently estimated that 4.6 million submunitions were fired into Lebanon, the bulk of them in the last sixty hours of the war. UN ordnance officers told me that the figure was probably lower, but as the IDF refused to hand over its targeting data to deminers, it was impossible to determine. Many of the bomblets scattered over south Lebanon dated from the Vietnam War and should have been destroyed at the end of the 1970s. One air-dropped container carrying tennis-ball-sized U.S.-made BLU-63 cluster munitions failed to open properly in the air and struck the ground near Nabatiyah with its full consignment of dozens of unexploded munitions. The stamp on the side of the container registered the expiration date for the cluster bomb as July 1974.[6] The UN estimated that 40 percent of the bomblets failed to explode and were left strewn in gardens, houses, and streets and hanging from the branches of trees. On the first day of the cease-fire, I saw unexploded U.S.-made M-77 bomblets lying on the main road outside Tibnine hospital. Hezbollah men had placed plastic crates over each one and directed traffic around them. The UN subsequently pinpointed more than a thousand separate cluster bomb strikes in south Lebanon. Chris Clark, a former British army officer who headed UN mine-clearing efforts in south Lebanon, told me the cluster bomb situation was "unprecedented and unbelievable" and the worst he had ever seen.

On August 7, the IDF announced that plans had been finalized for a ground invasion up to the Litani River and that the operation could proceed in two days time. The diplomatic clock was ticking, however. The UN Security Council was drawing close to reaching an agreement on a cease-fire, which suggested there would be only a small window for a final military move.

Olmert hesitated for two days, torn between ordering the invasion to go ahead and awaiting the outcome of the cease-fire negotiations. The Americans were promising him that a deal favorable to Israel was within reach. But IDF commanders grew increasingly exasperated with each postponement. "The men are fed up, they're asking if this is or isn't a war. Either [we fight] or we leave," Major General Udi Adam, the head of the Northern Command, told Halutz.[7]

On August 11, Olmert studied the draft of UN Security Council Resolution 1701 outlining a cease-fire, which in part called for the deployment of a strengthened UNIFIL numbering fifteen thousand troops and an arms embargo on Lebanon intended to prevent weapons from being smuggled to Hezbollah. There was no demand for the release of the two kidnapped Israeli soldiers, and the international force fell far short of Israeli expectations. The proposal was a disappointment for the Israeli government, and even though it was formally accepted the next day, Olmert finally ordered the ground invasion to proceed.

The dash to the Litani River focused on the villages of Ghandouriyah and Froun on the western lip of Wadi Hojeir, a deep valley lying at the northern end of Wadi Salouqi. Paratroops from the Nahal Brigade were air-dropped into Ghandouriyah, which they took unopposed. An armored assault followed, with two dozen tanks descending westbound into the depths of Wadi Hojeir intending to join the paratroops holding the high ground in Ghandouriyah. But the valley, with its steep, brush-covered slopes, was a natural tank trap. And Hezbollah's tank hunter-killer teams were waiting for the approaching Israelis. As the column began climbing up the western side of the valley it came under a withering fusillade of Kornet missiles. The missiles slammed into the tanks, setting several ablaze as the desperate crews scrambled out the hatches. The company commander cried over the radio, "My tanks are getting mauled," then the radio went dead.[8]

The beleaguered column received little support from the Nahal soldiers on the heights above. The paratroopers, discovering to their surprise that Ghandouriyah was not secured after all, found themselves pinned down by missile and mortar fire from Hezbollah men who had been hiding in the bombed ruins.

By the time the fighting in Wadi Hojeir was over, eleven Israeli officers and soldiers were dead and more than fifty were wounded. Eleven of the twenty-four Merkava Mark 4 tanks had been hit. In all, thirty-three soldiers were killed, about a quarter of the war's total IDF fatalities, in the final sixty-hour push to the Litani before the 8:00 A.M. cease-fire took effect on August 14.

In a final gesture of its undiminished resolve, Hezbollah fired a total of 217 rockets into Israel on the last full day of the war.

"We Brought the Israelis to Their Knees"

The black Toyota Land Cruiser, its windows blown out, a rear tire flat, lurched to a halt beside the Saleh Ghandour hospital at the entrance to Bint Jbeil. Five Hezbollah men tumbled out. They said they were from Aitta Shaab a few miles to the west and had been in the thick of the fighting in the village for the past thirty-four days. Bint Jbeil and Aitta Shaab were in the middle of the area that was supposed to be under Israeli control. Had they not seen any Israeli soldiers on the drive from Aitta Shaab?

"If you want to find Israeli soldiers in Aitta Shaab, look under the rubble," said one of them with a grin. The fighters were bubbling with triumph and exhausted emotion. The fighter, who called himself "the Hajj" wore a grubby sweatshirt and khaki-colored trousers. Some of his companions wore combat trousers and boots, lending them a paramilitary appearance. One man's head and upper left arm were bandaged. "Israel used all kinds of weapons against the resistance men," the Hajj said. "Despite this, Hezbollah stood strong. I fired my weapon for the last time at eight A.M."

The southern half of Aitta Shaab facing the Israeli border was heavily damaged. Small houses of two or three floors each had pancaked into pathetic heaps of rubble. Walls were scored by bullets or punctured by tank rounds and missiles. Jagged shards of steel shrapnel and twisted sheets of missile casings littered the rubble-strewn street. Exhausted fighters, some in uniform, sat on the side of the road in contemplative silence. Two Hezbollah men walked out of a small shell-scarred mosque just as a loudspeaker in the minaret began blaring out a Koranic verse. "That's the first time we have heard the Koran from the mosque in fifteen days," one of the men said.

Most of the residents had fled the village in the early days of the war, seeking refuge with their Christian neighbors in Rmeish a couple of miles away. Now they were returning, small groups of women, elderly men, and children walking along the shell-pocked road and gaping in awe at what had become of their village. It was evident that rebuilding the village would take months, if not years. But for the stoic residents, the massive destruction was a badge of honor for having confronted and triumphed against the vaunted Israeli army.

"Yes, it looks like Leningrad," conceded Sameeh Srour, a fifty-three-year-old policeman, "but we brought the Israelis to their knees."

The thirty-four-day war between Hezbollah and Israel is one of the most closely studied conflicts in recent history. The ability of a relatively small group of nonstate combatants to fight to a standstill the most powerful army in the Middle East has lessons applicable to future theaters of conflict. One influential study concluded that Hezbollah more closely resembled a conventional army in 2006 than a traditional guerrilla force through its emphasis on holding ground, using terrain rather than the population for concealment, and by concentrating its forces.[9]

"Hezbollah's position on the guerrilla-conventional continuum in 2006 was much closer to the conventional end of the scale than non-state actors are normally expected to be. In fact, Hezbollah was in many ways as 'conventional' as some state actors have been in major interstate warfare," the study said.

Nasrallah himself recognized this critical distinction in the evolution of the Islamic Resistance, saying days after the end of the war, "I never made the commitment that we could prevent an invasion, but we managed to do so. The resistance withstood the attack and it fought back. It did not wage a guerrilla war, either. I want to clarify this point: it was not a regular army, but [it] was not a guerrilla [army] in the traditional sense, either. It was something in between."

With the help of its state sponsors, principally Iran, but also to an extent Syria, the Islamic Resistance was transformed in the six years between the Israeli withdrawal in 2000 and the outbreak of the thirty-four-day war into what military analysts today describe as a "hybrid" force—a nonstate militant group employing both irregular and conventional weapons and tactics in a single battlespace. The United States, in particular, has shown great interest in the 2006 war, suspecting that Hezbollah-style hybrid forces will provide a persistent threat to its military in the years ahead, requiring deep thought on future defense planning and force structure.

"The conflict . . . that intrigues me most, and I think speaks more toward what we can expect in the decades ahead, is the one that happened in Lebanon in the summer of 2006," said General George Casey, the U.S. army chief of staff, in May 2009. Referring to Hezbollah's exploitation of rockets, antiship and antiarmor missiles, and sophisticated communications capabilities, Casey added that hybrid warfare opponents offer a conventional force like the U.S. military "a fundamentally more complex and difficult challenge than the challenges of fighting large tank armies on the plains of Europe."

Nonetheless, Hezbollah's stalwart performance against the IDF in 2006 owes much to Israel's poor handling of the war—from the unrealistic expectations and ill-considered decisions of the Israeli civilian and military leadership to the tactical shortcomings and lack of preparedness and coordination among the ground forces. In response to the public outcry over the humiliating outcome of the war, the Olmert government convened a commission of inquiry to examine what had happened and issue recommendations to prevent a recurrence. The commission, headed by retired judge Eliyahu Winograd, issued its final report in January 2008. Olmert, Peretz, and Halutz were harshly criticized, and the latter two subsequently resigned.

There was no Winograd-style commission of inquiry in Lebanon, although Hezbollah's critics, who had remained quiet during the war, certainly felt the party should be held accountable for triggering a conflict that had left around twelve hundred Lebanese dead and caused several billion dollars' worth of damage.

Nasrallah acknowledged that sentiment with an unusual mea culpa in a television interview two weeks after the cease-fire. He said that if Hezbollah's leadership had thought there was a "one percent" chance that Israel would respond in the fashion it did following the abduction of the two soldiers, they would not have approved the operation in the first place.

But Nasrallah also began a carefully constructed narrative that turned Hezbollah's mistake in triggering the war into a stroke of luck in that it had prematurely forced Israel into a conflict it planned to wage anyway. If not in July, then September or October. Israel, he said, had made plans for a massive strike on Lebanon involving a ground invasion of the south, amphibious landings at the mouth of the Litani River, and bombing campaigns against southern Beirut and the Bekaa Valley. "This was the plan. What took place on July 12 cost the Israelis the element of surprise after the capturing, and after there were deaths and injuries.... We were ready for the war when it started. The element of surprise was therefore lost," he said.

It was natural that the IDF would have devised a series of war plans to take into account future contingencies, yet there was no public evidence to suggest that Israel was planning to unilaterally launch a massive strike against Hezbollah in the fall of 2006. Since 2000, Israel had followed a policy of containment along its northern border. Though unhappy with Hezbollah's arms buildup, Israel had little desire to risk upsetting what was proving to be the longest period of calm along its northern border since the late 1960s.

But Nasrallah's explanation was accepted by the Hezbollah support base. Furthermore, Nasrallah asserted that it was "divine will" that had forced the Israelis into a war prematurely. The war, Hezbollah proclaimed, was nothing less than a "victory from God," which, by happy coincidence, was also the meaning of the Hezbollah leader's family name.

"Hezbollah Is Stronger Than the State"

Divine or not, Hezbollah's "victory" was certainly Pyrrhic. It had exposed the bunker networks so painstakingly constructed in the previous six years, and prematurely revealed tactics, electronic warfare capabilities, and weapons systems. Furthermore, the war inflicted devastating punishment on Hezbollah's core Shia support base. Iran had channeled millions of dollars into upgrading Hezbollah's military capabilities from 2000, which were squandered in a war that should never have been started in the first place. No wonder Nasrallah admitted that Hezbollah would not have ordered the kidnapping if the leadership had known what the consequences would be.

The level of destruction in the southern suburbs of Beirut and some villages in south Lebanon was staggering. The government estimated that 125,000 houses and apartments throughout Lebanon were destroyed. As much as 80 percent of some villages in the south were reduced to rubble. Ninety-one bridges were blown up, and highways, roads, and lanes were cratered and rendered impassable from the south all the way up to the remote Akkar district in the far north of Lebanon. The government estimated direct damages from the 2006 war at $2.8 billion and lost output and income at $2.2 billion. Losses to the economy over the following three years were estimated at $15 billion.

The Shias of southern Lebanon are a stoical breed and remarkably resilient in the face of hardship and adversity, a trait rooted in Shia traditions of suffering and sacrifice as well as the bitter experience of living in an area plagued by conflict for four decades. Most of them displayed a fatalistic acceptance of this latest calamity. But it was possible also to detect the first rumblings of disquiet from a community that had been solidly behind Hezbollah. One man I met in Siddiqine, one of the most badly damaged villages in the south, gave a phlegmatic reaction to the near destruction of his simple single-story home.

"We are used to this. God and Nasrallah will provide," he said. I spent about an hour with him as he stumbled over the rubble collecting personal belongings that lay scattered around the ruins. After a while, he relaxed his guard slightly in talking to a foreign journalist and began questioning the point of the war. This was the third time his house had been blown up in the past ten years, he said. All he wanted to do was to cultivate his tobacco and watch his children grow up in peace.

"We thought all this had ended in 2000," he muttered, referring to Israel's withdrawal from Lebanon. "Why must my house be blown up again, six years after the Israelis left?"

But his voice trailed off when two unsmiling men approached and hovered nearby at an indiscreet distance.

Hezbollah was acutely sensitive to signs of unhappiness among the Shia constituency, whose continued goodwill was critical to the party's survival. Not for the first time, nor the last, Hezbollah was caught in the paradox of trying to fulfill its obligations to Iran while trying to satisfy the interests of Lebanese Shias.

In tandem with the propaganda campaign defining the war as a historic and divinely ordained victory, Hezbollah, on a more prosaic level, attempted to win the peace and mollify aggrieved Lebanese Shias by launching a program of financial benefits for those whose homes had been damaged or destroyed. With impressive speed, Hezbollah took over schools and community centers and began handing out $12,000 in cash to homeowners in Beirut and $10,000 to those living in the rural areas. In June 2007, Hezbollah said that it had spent so far $300 million on compensation and reconstruction.

Hezbollah guards, discreetly carrying their AK-47 rifles in soft sheepskin-lined holsters, surrounded the Mahdi high school in Beirut's southern suburbs, where hundreds of claimants filed through the doors to collect their cash handouts. The high security was not without good reason. There must have been millions of dollars stacked on tables and in cardboard boxes. Posters on the walls urged claimants to be patient, remain organized, and follow instructions. Hezbollah workers, equipped with walkie-talkies and earphones, almost outnumbered the claimants. Hezbollah marching songs blared from loudspeakers.

Abdel-Hussein Hodroj did not even bother to count the inch-thick wad of crisp hundred-dollar bills to make sure all $12,000 was there. The grizzled seventy-two-year-old with a stubbly beard and crew cut thanked the bearded young Hezbollah man seated behind the desk. Three of Hodroj's sons were killed fighting the Israelis in the 1980s, and he proudly told me that his ancestral village in the south was the birthplace of Nasrallah. "We have been with them since the beginning," he said.

Hezbollah also launched a massive reconstruction effort dubbed Al-Waad, "The Promise," to rebuild the southern suburbs. It was a daunting task. The heart of Haret Hreik, the former Hezbollah "security quarter" where the leadership lived, had disappeared, reduced to a stormy sea of shattered concrete, twisted metal, smashed furniture, and gaping bomb craters. The lopsided, pancaked upper floors of half-demolished apartment blocks threatened to slide into the rubble below at any moment. The air reeked of rotting garbage and the thick dust tickled the back of the throat. Hezbollah's press office, where I had interviewed Sheikh Nabil Qawq just a month before the outbreak of the war, was gone, transformed into a sad pile of rubble thirty feet high. Red banners stuck in the debris proclaimed "The New Middle Beast," a pun on Condoleezza Rice's ill-advised reference to the war's representing the "birth pangs of a new Middle East."

The speed and organization with which Hezbollah turned to the relief and reconstruction effort underlined just how powerful it had grown in Lebanon. Its construction wing, Jihad al-Bina, had leaped ahead while the government remained mired in spats over which ministry or agency would handle the process and which companies—usually owned by politicians—would win the lucrative contracts to clean up the mess.

"Hezbollah is stronger than the state. This is a fact. This is not Hezbollah's problem, this is the government's problem," Bilal Naim, the head of Hezbollah's Al-Mahdi Scouts, told me as he directed the work of volunteers in the southern suburbs.

"Fighting a Political War"

Hezbollah knew as soon as the fighting with the Israelis ended that a new struggle would be waged on the political front in Lebanon. The battle lines were drawn up in the weeks following the cease-fire, with Hezbollah going on the offensive against its critics, whom the party decried as "traitors," accusing them of urging the United States and Israel to finish off the "resistance" once and for all.

The March 14 political group accused Hezbollah of dragging Lebanon into a ruinous war and insisted that it dismantle its military wing. Ali Ammar, a Hezbollah military policeman, responded in a rally by declaring that "the weapons of the resistance will remain, will remain, will remain."

By the end of October, Lebanon was locked into a deepening political crisis. Hezbollah and its opposition allies were demanding the formation of a new government of national unity in which it would possess a one-third share, allowing Hezbollah to block any legislation of which it did not approve. The March 14 parliamentary majority suspected that Hezbollah's main motivation was to thwart cabinet moves sanctioning the creation of an international tribunal to handle the investigation and future trials of those indicted for the murder of Rafik Hariri.

The UN investigation into the murder had been under way since June 2005. Its first progress report was released that October and made for sensational reading. It said there was "converging evidence" pointing toward the involvement of senior Lebanese and Syrian officials in Hariri's death.

In early November, the political crisis came to a head when all five Shia members of the government abruptly resigned after a week of failed talks on forming a new cabinet. The walkout came on the eve of a cabinet vote on a draft agreement with the UN to establish the Hariri tribunal. March 14 supporters hollered that Hezbollah had engineered the cabinet resignations in a desperate attempt to avoid having to vote for a tribunal that could end up prosecuting the party's allies in Damascus. The government met as scheduled and voted in favor of the tribunal agreement, a move that the opposition decried as unconstitutional because the Shia ministers had not been present.

Still, there was much more at stake than a tussle over the fate of the Hariri investigation. Lebanon was the pivotal battlefield in a regional "cold war" pitting Israel, the United States, and its mainly Sunni Arab allies such as Jordan, Egypt, and Saudi Arabia against a so-called "resistance front" grouping Iran, Syria, Hezbollah, Hamas, and other small pro-Damascus Palestinian factions. For the United States, bringing Lebanon within the Western orbit would weaken Syria's influence and thwart Iranian efforts to influence the Arab-Israeli conflict via Hezbollah, thus helping to preserve Israel's security.

The "resistance front" sought to deny Washington its Levantine toehold and bring the tiny country back once more into the Syrian fold. Isolated internationally since 2005, Syria had dug in its heels and strengthened its alliance with Iran, refusing to buckle to Western pressure. Syria's relations with its Arab neighbors also were fragile. Bashar al-Assad caused deep offense to the Saudi leadership by describing them as "half men" for failing to support Hezbollah in the war. To the ossified Saudi royals, such insults from the feckless young Syrian president were as intolerable as Damascus's deepening ties to Iran.

The political deadlock between the government and the opposition intensified in early December when Hezbollah and its allies staged a mass sit-in in downtown Beirut, blocking streets, erecting tents, and bringing the commercial hub of the city to a standstill.

"We are continuing the war through political means," said Wissam Srour from Aitta Shaab, who lounged in a canvas tent with other Hezbollah supporters one Saturday morning. "First we fought a military war against Israel and now we are fighting a political war against America and its [Lebanese] pupils."

A barricade of coiled razor wire, armored vehicles, and red-bereted Lebanese special forces troops separated the protesters from the imposing façade of the Grand Serail, the Ottoman-era army barracks that today houses the government's offices on a hill overlooking downtown Beirut. Siniora and most of his cabinet colleagues had been working and sleeping in the building as a security measure since Pierre Gemayel, the industry minister and son of Amine Gemayel, the former president, was gunned down in his car a few weeks earlier. Gemayel was the latest victim in a spate of killings following the Hariri assassination that had claimed the lives of prominent politicians, security personnel, and journalists known for their anti-Syrian views.

But Siniora and his colleagues proved more tenacious than Hezbollah had expected. A political paralysis developed as 2006 turned into 2007, with both sides refusing to yield and tensions steadily building between Lebanon's Shia and Sunni communities.

ELEVEN

The "Last War with Israel"

I assure you that we fear no war . . . in all our previous wars we relied on God and we won . . . we will continue to do so. We will defeat the enemy and change the face of the region.

—Sayyed Hassan Nasrallah,
January 15, 2010

Hezbollah will not surprise us again.

—Israeli defense minister Ehud Barak,
September 16, 2010

SEPTEMBER 3, 2006

TYRE, south Lebanon—Shaven-headed Italian naval commandos clad in black neoprene wet suits beached their black Zodiac inflatable speedboats on the pristine sand beside the Rest House hotel. A gray Sea King helicopter shuttled between a battleship riding the swell off the coast and the hotel's parking lot, depositing stern-faced blue-helmeted Italian marine commandos. As the spinning rotor blades whipped up clouds of stinging dust, the soldiers took up a defensive perimeter around the parking lot as if expecting to come under immediate attack by Hezbollah. The soldiers muttered curses as enthusiastic Lebanese photographers tripped over their rifles and stacked knapsacks. A handful of bemused Lebanese looked on. These troops looked very different from the congenial peacekeepers they had grown accustomed to in south Lebanon.

"We have to forget the previous UNIFIL. The previous UNIFIL is dead," observed Major General Alain Pellegrini, the peacekeepers' French commander. UNIFIL was undergoing its most fundamental transformation since it had first arrived on Lebanese shores twenty-eight years earlier. Before the war, UNIFIL's strength had consisted of some two thousand armed observers, composed mainly of contingents from Ghana and India. The Ghanaians had been in Lebanon since 1978 and were easygoing peacekeepers. The Indian troops brought with them military traditions redolent of the British empire, with bagpipes and drummers and shelves groaning with regimental silver in the officers' mess.

UNIFIL had long ago grown accustomed to the realities of peace-keeping in south Lebanon and had an acute understanding of the parameters within which it could function. Other than providing an international window onto the perennially tense Lebanon-Israel border, UNIFIL's most important role in the 2000–2006 period was to serve as interlocutor between Hezbollah and Israel. This discreet channel of communication allowed messages to be passed that helped allay misunderstandings about each other's moves along the border and defuse the occasional outbreaks of violence between the two sides. It was in some respects a cozy existence for the small peacekeeping force. But all that came to an end following the cease-fire. UNIFIL 2, as it was initially dubbed, was to be a more robust force composed of up to fifteen thousand troops, spearheaded by contingents from leading European nations—France, Italy, and Spain. The UN also sanctioned a Maritime Task Force to patrol some five thousand nautical square miles off the Lebanese coast, the first naval force built by the UN to support peace-keeping operations.

The first Spanish troops to arrive in south Lebanon were drawn from the elite Spanish Legion, the equivalent of the French Foreign Legion, tough commandos who sported goatees and had seen combat in Bosnia, Afghanistan, and Iraq. The Spanish were deployed in the eastern sector, facing the Shebaa Farms hills. A huge sprawling military compound was built over a hillside north of Marjayoun, dwarfing the old Indian battalion headquarters on a nearby hilltop. The new camp was ringed with twelve-foot-high security fences and coils of razor wire. The entrances were heavily guarded, with concrete blast walls and chicanes to slow traffic.

"The UN of 2006 is not the UN of ten years ago," Jean-Marie Guehenno, the UN undersecretary for peacekeeping operations, told me as we watched the Italians disembark at Tyre. "We have drawn lessons from past experience. We have robust rules of engagement so that we can defend ourselves and not be humiliated anymore."

Those were bold words, given Lebanon's grim reputation as a graveyard for well-intentioned international peacekeeping missions. There was little appetite among European nations for seeing their troops caught in armed confrontations with Hezbollah and the Israelis; the initial deployment of the French peacekeepers was delayed until Paris was satisfied with the rules of engagement. Like UNIFIL's previous incarnation, the success of the newly reinforced mission would remain dependent on maintaining the goodwill of the local population. If Hezbollah and the residents of the south turned against the peacekeepers, no number of battle-hardened European troops would save UNIFIL.

Yet the first wave of European troops to arrive in Lebanon were mainly drawn from rapid reaction forces used to deploying quickly to hot spots around the world. These were elite soldiers trained to fight rather than to wave civilian traffic through checkpoints, hand out soccer balls to children, or spend hours gazing from an observation post at a tranquil frontier. Furthermore, having fought the Taliban in Afghanistan or Shia and Sunni insurgents in Iraq, many of these incoming soldiers were instinctively predisposed to regard Hezbollah as an enemy and a potential threat.

"So, What Do You Think of Our Bunkers?"

While tolerating UNIFIL's expanded presence, Hezbollah kept a wary eye on the activities of the peacekeepers. One internal UNIFIL intelligence report from early 2007 claimed that Hezbollah in Bint Jbeil had issued instructions to the residents to avoid talking to the peacekeepers, to speak only Arabic in their presence, not to accept food or handouts from foreign NGOs, to report on UNIFIL's movements, and to constantly display the party's symbols, such as flags and posters.

Hezbollah had reduced its profile in the border district in grudging deference to Resolution 1701. The rural security pockets were abandoned in the days after the August cease-fire, with trucks packed with equipment spotted heading north. Most of the bunker networks and camouflaged rocket firing positions were no longer of use to Hezbollah now that their locations were compromised. But that did not mean Hezbollah welcomed UNIFIL troops rummaging through its former security pockets. Difficulties between Hezbollah and UNIFIL grew increasingly apparent when the Spanish battalion began staking out these abandoned military zones, spending days at a time monitoring movements and hunting for old weapons caches and bunker networks. Shepherds roaming the rural districts with their flocks were handed mobile phones and instructed to contact local Hezbollah officials if UNIFIL or strangers were seen tramping around near their facilities.

Indeed, while Ghaith Abdul-Ahad and I were wandering through the small Hezbollah bunker near Alma Shaab in March 2007, we both thought we heard the sound of whispered voices coming from above. Ghaith was shooting pictures, so I said I would climb up the vertical steel-lined access shaft and check. In deference to Ghaith's claustrophobia, I refrained from voicing my paranoid thought that someone might replace the steel cover over the shaft and weigh it down with a large rock, leaving us entombed below. However, there was no one to be seen or heard once I had scrambled up the ladder.

I suspected Hezbollah would not be happy if they had known that I was prowling their former security pockets, obsessively hunting for one of their bunkers. A few weeks after the article about the bunker appeared on *Time* magazine's website, I had an interview with Nawaf Mussawi, then the head of Hezbollah's international relations department. We had not met before, but I knew that he closely followed foreign media coverage of Hezbollah. We met at a café in the southern suburbs of Beirut. Looking slightly disheveled in a tracksuit with dark, tousled hair and carrying a plastic shopping bag, he shook my hand and sat down opposite me. Then he leaned across the table and said, "So, what do you think of our bunkers?"

Taken aback, I replied that I had found them impressive. Mussawi chuckled and, turning to his assistant, said, "This guy went to the south, found one of our bunkers, and wrote this beautiful story about it in *Time.*"

It occurred to me then that if a foreign journalist could write an article about the ingenuity of the Islamic Resistance in building elaborate bunkers in south Lebanon without anyone's ever having noticed, then why should Hezbollah complain?

But special forces units from European countries reconnoitering old Hezbollah security pockets was a different proposition. In early December 2006, Spanish troops accompanied by Lebanese soldiers spent a night encamped near Kfar Shuba village. The next morning they discovered, three hundred yards from where they had slept, that someone overnight had planted several trip-wire-connected IEDs consisting of Claymore antipersonnel mines and an old 81mm mortar shell. An internal UNIFIL memo noted that the IEDs were laid by "experts with a lot of technical experience" and that "this situation suggests a change in the threat that UNIFIL may have to face."

It was later learned that the bombs were planted on the orders of a local Hezbollah commander who had grown irritated at the Spanish activities in his area. Hezbollah subsequently informed UNIFIL that the planting of IEDs was unauthorized and that the commander had been replaced.

"Watching Out for Al-Qaeda"

The main focus of UNIFIL's force protection efforts was on the threat posed by al-Qaeda, not Hezbollah. UNIFIL headquarters in Naqoura and the various contingents each day received raw and unverified intelligence data warning of possible attacks against the peacekeepers. Ayman al-Zawahiri, al-Qaeda's deputy leader, several times had called on Lebanese to ignore Resolution 1701 and encouraged attacks on the peacekeeping force.

The threats against UNIFIL led to a paradoxical cooperation between some European contingents and Hezbollah, both viewing Sunni jihadists as a threat. In April 2007, Italian, French, and Spanish intelligence officers secretly met with Hezbollah representatives in Sidon to enlist the organization's assistance in helping protect the peacekeepers. Afterward, Hezbollah men in civilian clothes occasionally "escorted" Spanish UNIFIL patrols.

The long-feared attack came on June 24, 2007. Six soldiers from the Spanish battalion, three of them Colombian nationals, were killed when their patrol of two armored personnel carriers was struck by a powerful car bomb between Marjayoun and Khiam. It was the deadliest single attack against UNIFIL since the force first arrived in Lebanon in 1978. Investigators later discovered that the bomb was "extraordinarily sophisticated," and the attack must have taken months to prepare. According to UNIFIL's internal investigation, the bomb consisted of an estimated 132 pounds of PETN military-grade explosive packed with aluminum powder to augment the fireball effect and hidden inside a Renault Rapide van parked on the side of the road. The bomb was detonated by an infrared beam and had a shaped-charge configuration directing the blast laterally against the targeted vehicle. The fourteen-ton six-wheeled APC was spun 180 degrees and knocked off the road. Two soldiers standing in the rear hatches were blown clear and survived. There was no claim of responsibility for the attack, although Zawahiri days later released a taped video message in which he praised the bombing as a "blessed operation."

Initial suspicions fell on Sunni jihadists, possibly from one of the Palestinian camps. There were a handful of other isolated attacks against UNIFIL in the weeks that followed, all of them by al-Qaeda sympathizers based in the Palestinian camps or in Sunni-populated areas of south Lebanon. But they were amateurish affairs, involving sticks of dynamite and faulty detonators, claiming no victims. They did not even come close to the deadly proficiency of the Spanish bombing.

The culprit has never been identified, and the separate Lebanese, Spanish, and UNIFIL investigations officially remain open. But I later learned that the Spanish legionnaires were engaged in activities far more sensitive than staking out Hezbollah's old security pockets in the UNI-FIL area of operations. They were also monitoring the hilly terrain north of the Litani River outside the UNIFIL area where Hezbollah was building a new line of defense. According to conversations with numerous UNIFIL officers, the Spaniards had conducted reconnaissance missions from camouflaged observation points on the southern bank of the Litani. They may even have slipped across the narrow, shallow river to infiltrate Hezbollah's new domain. Several UNIFIL officers said they had seen video footage and still photographs shot by the Spanish soldiers showing the movement of vehicles and Hezbollah personnel and newly built positions north of the Litani. "We are already watching out for al-Qaeda, and the last thing we need is some gung-ho soldiers stirring up problems with Hezbollah," one UNIFIL officer grumbled to me at the time.

Did Hezbollah detect the Spanish surveillance and choose to inflict a sharp, painful slap? The potentially provocative reconnaissance of the area north of the Litani, the absence of further sophisticated bomb attacks against the peacekeepers, and the amateurish attacks carried out by known al-Qaeda-inspired jihadists have left more than one observer concluding that they did. If it was a blunt message from Hezbollah, it was received and understood by the Spanish, for the surveillance of the north bank of the Litani came to a halt after the bombing.

The Shia "Bridge"

In the immediate months after the war, with Hezbollah having abandoned its old security pockets in the border district, I began hearing vague rumors of unusual activity occurring in the mountains between the Litani River—UNIFIL's northern perimeter—and Jezzine. The area approximated the northern sector of Israel's former occupation zone, a region of sharp limestone mountains and thick undergrowth, dotted with tiny villages and farms. It was a strategic location, affording sweeping views to the Mediterranean in the west and across the lower reaches of the Bekaa Valley to the east—both traditional axes of advance for armies invading from the south.

Local residents told me in hushed tones that "the boys" had increased their presence in the area, sealing off remote hills and valleys and preventing anyone from entering, mimicking the security pockets Hezbollah established in the border area starting in 2000. Mysterious new dirt tracks materialized, snaking across hillsides before abruptly terminating in thickets of oak and umbrella pines. As the months passed, some of the tracks were hardened with asphalt. An Iran-funded NGO, the Iranian Organization for Sharing the Building of Lebanon, which was contracted to repair war-damaged roads in the south, turned a little-used, potholed lane that crossed the mountains between Jezzine and the southern Bekaa Valley into a gleaming asphalt highway. I began hearing stories of vast tracts of land in the area being snapped up by Ali Tajieddine, a Shia businessman who had made a fortune in Africa and whose alleged connections to Hezbollah in December 2010 earned him a designation on the U.S. Treasury Department's list of terrorist financiers. In the tiny Druze hamlet of Sraireh, squeezed onto the side of a narrow valley above the Litani, a resident told me that Tajieddine was paying between $2 and $4 per square meter of land, often accepting the seller's initial asking price and paying in cash.

Houses and shops decorated with posters of Nasrallah and yellow Hezbollah flags were built beside the "Iranian road" at the southern end of Qotrani, a Christian-populated hamlet just west of Sraireh. On a barren, windswept hillside overlooking the Litani River, a new village was constructed from scratch on land purchased by Tajieddine from Druze owners. The new village was called Ahmadiyah, and laborers there told me that it would be populated by Shias from the Tyre area as well as neighboring Shia villages in the southern Bekaa.

Inevitably, the land purchases aroused the sectarian suspicions of local Christian and Druze politicians, especially Walid Jumblatt, the paramount leader of the Druze and in 2007, the archcritic of Hezbollah. The area in which Hezbollah was consolidating its presence lay at the confluence of several Shia, Christian, and Druze villages, hamlets, and farms. Tajieddine's land purchases appeared to Hezbollah's opponents to be a blatant attempt to build a demographic bridge to connect Shia-populated Nabatiyah in the west to the Shia villages of the southern Bekaa Valley in the east. Such a belt, inhabited by Hezbollah supporters, would improve communications between the two strongholds and allow the Islamic Resistance to consolidate its new front line in a more secure environment.

When a hill near the mixed Shia-Christian village of Kfar Houne caught Tajieddine's attention, Jumblatt tried to enlist the financial support of Carlos Slim, the Mexican business tycoon listed by *Forbes* magazine in 2010 as the richest man in the world. Slim, whose father was born in Kfar Houne, told the Druze leader he was uninterested in outbidding Tajieddine and purchasing the hill. "I may have to fly to Mexico and persuade him face-to-face," Jumblatt mused.

Sheikh Naim Qassem dismissed Jumblatt's allegations that Hezbollah was building a Shia state in the south as unfounded, saying that the Druze leader "likes to stir calm waters."

I interviewed Ali Tajieddine one Saturday morning in his bustling office on the outskirts of Tyre. A short, dapper man, Tajieddine calmly explained that he was simply a businessman who had sensed that money could be made quarrying the limestone mountains for construction material and cement production. The houses in Ahmadiyah were intended to mask the quarry and "enhance the appearance of the area." The homes would be inhabited by his employees, he said. "I have employees who are Shias, Druze, Sunnis, and Christians," he told me. "The people who are making these allegations know better. They are just spreading rumors."

"Access to This Area Is Forbidden"

I wanted to see for myself if there were Hezbollah fighters operating in the hills and valleys north of the Litani. But hiking up a mountainside with a notebook and camera in search of the Islamic Resistance was not advisable. However, a clue to their possible whereabouts lay in the maps produced after 2000 by the UN demining agency showing the mined areas of south Lebanon. The maps had been updated since the 2006 war with the locations of cluster bomb strikes, which were marked with a rash of red circles across much of the UNIFIL-patrolled border district. There were fewer cluster bomb strikes north of the Litani River, but one valley in the heart of Hezbollah's new frontline area had been hit by as many as nine separate bombardments. The concentration of hits suggested it had been a source of Hezbollah rocket fire during the war. Perhaps Hezbollah's fighters were still there.

I attempted to reach the valley by following a potholed lane that wound past a ruined stone farmhouse that before 2000 was used for target practice by Israeli tank gunners. The lane petered out and turned into a rough track that disappeared into a small olive grove. As I was hesitating about proceeding farther, two men in camouflage uniforms, wearing floppy bush hats and carrying AK-47 rifles, silently emerged from behind the trees and walked up to my car. They were polite and seemed more bemused than suspicious at meeting a foreigner in this remote corner of Lebanon. They told me I was in a military zone and jotted down my license plate number before letting me go.

Later the same day, I followed another track that curved around the top of the valley. On turning a corner, I noticed the track was blocked by a chain suspended between two concrete posts. Hanging from the chain was a metal sign with the stenciled Arabic words "Warning. Access to this area is forbidden. Hezbollah." Beside the entrance to this security pocket stood a small sentry box. A burly Hezbollah man in a camouflage uniform and wearing an incongruous pair of green rubber boots emerged from the sentry box and inquired what I was doing. I explained I was working on a story on cluster bombs and knew that the valley had been hit heavily. Could I pass through and have a look? Taken aback by my sudden appearance and unexpected request, he hurried into his sentry hut and spoke into a field telephone. For a fleeting moment, I wondered if they would actually let me enter the security pocket. I could see more uniformed Hezbollah fighters moving around on a nearby hill studded with pine trees. The green-rubber-booted fighter returned. Access was denied. I had to leave at once.

Over the following months, Hezbollah increased its presence in these hills, placing further tracts of land off-limits. Demining and cluster bomb removal teams contracted by the UN were required to coordinate with Hezbollah all clearance operations north of the Litani River. When a demining team requested to enter a certain sector, Hezbollah typically either gave permission immediately, granted it after a few days, or denied access outright. The restricted areas were dubbed "orange" zones by the deminers. As the months progressed, access was increasingly tightened until by early 2008, the entire area was classified as an orange zone. One deminer told me that the hills were "crawling with armed and uniformed Hezbollah fighters" and the sound of explosions and automatic weapons fire was a near-daily occurrence.

Steep, wooded valleys west of the Jezzine salient were also placed off-limits, even on the edges of Christian-populated villages. The number of sealed-off areas expanded farther northward along the sharp mountain peaks until nudging the Druze-populated Chouf Mountains. In April 2010, I learned that a group of hikers had stumbled across a Hezbollah outpost on a windswept ridge at the southern end of the Chouf. The outpost had been inadvertently positioned alongside the Lebanon Mountain Trail, a newly established 275-mile hiker's path from the forested mountains of north Lebanon to Marjayoun in the south. I decided to see the outpost for myself and clambered up the mountain with two friends on a damp, cloudy day. The Hezbollah position was in a small depression surrounded by limestone outcrops and had been used by the Israelis before 1985, judging from the old bulldozed emplacements where Israeli tanks and armored personnel carriers once rested. A fire-blackened cooking pot and a plastic bag of potatoes lay beside a fireplace containing cold, rain-dampened ashes. We could see the concrete entrance of a bunker sunk into the side of the valley. One of my companions said she saw a head momentarily bob out of the entrance before disappearing inside again. But there was no one else to be seen. As we were about to move on, there came a startled shout from the rocks above us. A lithe young man with greasy, lanky hair wearing a camouflage jacket and jeans and carrying an AK-47 rifle bounded down the side of the valley. As he approached, he cocked the rifle with a dramatic flourish. "What are you doing here?" he asked, his face a mix of anger and astonishment. "This is a military zone. You should not be here."

We explained to him that we were hiking across the mountain and that we were following an established trail. I showed him the map marking the path running through his position. He stared at it without comment, then checked the contents of our backpacks before instructing us to move off the mountain. We headed north on the old Israeli dirt track running along the crest. The outpost behind us swiftly disappeared in the mist shrouding the mountaintop. Minutes later, the fighter came running up behind us clutching a walkie-talkie along with his rifle. We had to get off the mountain at once, he said. We were not permitted to continue following the trail. Clearly, he had received instructions from his superiors. There was no sense arguing. We headed east down the mountainside, the fighter watching us from a rocky outcrop until we were swallowed up by the dense thickets of scrub oak.

By summer 2007, it was common knowledge that Hezbollah was operating in the mountains north of the Litani River, but as with its previous security pockets in the border district, it remained unclear exactly what Hezbollah was up to. Perhaps new bunkers were under construction; one Hezbollah fighter told me that the bunkers built after the war are larger and more sophisticated than those from before 2006, with electrical wiring and water pipes embedded in cement-lined walls rather than strung along the ceiling in plastic tubes.

One intelligence source told me that parked UAVs had been spotted in these hills. The UK-based *Jane's Intelligence Review* obtained commercially available satellite imagery of the area dated January and February 2008 and discovered a series of peculiar markings on the side of a sealed-off hill. *Jane's* concluded that the configuration suggested possible use for training or rocket activity. Still, given Hezbollah's custom of operating in strict secrecy inside its security pockets and the near-daily reconnaissance sorties by Israeli jets, UAVs, and AWACS aircraft, it would have been unusual for the organization to construct a site of significant military value in the open, thus raising the possibility that it was simply a decoy to keep Israeli imagery analysts baffled.

In 2008, I learned that similar unusual ground markings had been detected in the area of Hezbollah's original training camp near Janta on the border with Syria. The site included what appeared to be an IED range, a building assault course, a small arms firing range, a driver training track, and bunkers and tunnels dug into the sides of hills. *Jane's* acquired satellite images of the area dated July 2008 and September 2009. When compared, they confirmed substantial construction activity during the fourteen-month period. If the site was genuine and not a decoy, the facilities suggested it was intended for specialist training rather than instruction in regular guerrilla warfare techniques taught at conventional training camps in wooded areas of the Bekaa Valley. The lack of ground cover at the Janta camp made it vulnerable to Israeli aerial observance, and therefore it was probably used on an intermittent basis and for short durations only.

"Man, We Really Did It This Time"

I gained a sharp understanding of Hezbollah's sensitivity toward the Janta area in July 2007 while reporting a story on cross-border smuggling of commercial goods from Syria to Lebanon. I planned to visit a remote village called Tufayl, which lies at the tip of a fingerlike extension of Lebanese territory poking into Syria. To reach Tufayl requires following a rutted dirt track for about sixteen miles over barren mountain ridges before dropping into the arid approaches to the Syrian desert. For the trip, I took along my usual notebook and camera, but also a GPS device, compass, maps, and satellite phone as a contingency in case our vehicle broke down en route and we had to walk out. My colleague, Dergham Dergham, and I had been told that we needed permission from the army to visit Tufayl and had to apply at the military barracks in Ablah in the Bekaa Valley. But the military intelligence officers in Ablah said they could not help us and that we would need to visit the defense ministry in Beirut. It was midmorning Saturday, and the defense ministry would be closed. Dergham and I decided to forget Tufayl and instead report the smuggling story from another border village. We selected Yahfoufah, a pretty little hamlet tucked into a steep valley of craggy limestone about half a mile beyond Janta. A shallow river flanked by walnut and poplar trees splashed along the valley floor. We found a group of diesel smugglers pumping Syrian fuel from a tank on the back of a truck. They told us how the illegal border trade worked and allowed me to snap a few pictures.

As we were leaving the village, a white van swerved in front of us, blocking the road, and three unsmiling bearded men climbed out. They were obviously Hezbollah. They asked us who we were and what we were doing in Yahfoufah and then instructed us to follow them. We arrived at a small house beside the river. Instead of asking questions as I expected, the Hezbollah men invited us to sit down while a demure young headscarfed girl served us tiny cups of coffee. It soon became evident from our taciturn hosts that this was not a gesture of Bekaa hospitality. After half an hour, several more unsmiling Hezbollah men arrived in a fleet of SUVs. Dergham and I were split up for the drive to the nearby village of Nabi Sheet. We parked beside a mosque and were marched up a flight of stairs into an office at the back of the building. The moment I had dreaded came when they inspected the contents of my backpack. Out came the camera, GPS, compass, maps, and satellite phone. It really did not look very good. I was made to wait in a conference room while Dergham was grilled separately. He later told me that the Hezbollah men had insisted to him that I was a spy. A slim middle-aged man with a broad, friendly smile beaming through his thick black beard wandered into the conference room and shook my hand.

"Hello. It is good to see you again," he said in English.

Had I met him before? It was possible, although I did not recognize him.

"You were here last year in Nabi Sheet with some Australian journalists," he explained.

Clearly a case of mistaken identity. I assured him I had not stopped in Nabi Sheet for at least five or six years. No, no, he insisted, he remembered me well.

He placed a notepad on the table and began asking me questions about my background, such as where I was raised in England. He even threw in a couple of questions about English soccer teams. Each answer was carefully written down. Dergham joined me and we were served strong sweet tea in tiny glasses—"to help you stay awake," one of the Hezbollah men joked.

I gave them a list of Hezbollah officials they could contact who would verify my identity. Dergham, a Shia who lived in Beirut's southern suburbs, had his own contacts within Hezbollah. But our captors did not bother to make a single phone call. Instead, one of them politely asked us whether we would mind being handed over to military intelligence. We said that was fine, but I groaned inwardly. It meant that we would be entering a nightmare of slow-paced bureaucracy, ensuring that there would be no swift return to Beirut for either of us. In retrospect, Dergham and I concluded that the Hezbollah men probably did not believe we were spies but calculated that interrogating and temporarily detaining us would send a message that foreigners, especially journalists, were not welcome in this corner of the Bekaa.

We were bundled out of the mosque and driven in two separate vehicles at high speed through Nabi Sheet's narrow, winding streets and out into the open countryside. We rendezvoused with two cars full of plainclothes military intelligence agents who were waiting for us at a farm in the middle of the valley. The officers took custody of us and we continued our journey in their vehicles, arriving minutes later at the Ablah military barracks.

For the next eight hours Dergham and I were questioned repeatedly on who we were and where we had been, while a muscled officer with a shaved head and wearing a grubby white vest slowly wrote down our answers, his face frowning with concentration. Writing, it seemed, did not come easily to our interrogator, who looked as though he would have been much happier extracting answers from us with the aid of a car battery and crocodile clips. They probably believed we were innocent as well, but as we'd been handed to them by Hezbollah, they could not let us slip out the back door immediately. It is no secret that Lebanese military intelligence cooperates closely with Hezbollah, especially in sensitive areas like the Bekaa. One of the officers even had a clip from a Nasrallah speech as the ringtone on his cell phone.

An agent handed me my camera and asked me to run through the pictures. I scrolled through the shots I had taken of the diesel fuel smugglers that morning, which elicited no interest from the officer. Suddenly, a picture flicked up on the small screen showing me firing a 9 mm automatic pistol. It was from a couple of weeks earlier, when Dergham and I and another friend had lunched at a restaurant in the Bekaa frequented by Hezbollah men and then fired a few potshots at a watermelon with a pistol. I had foolishly forgotten to erase the pictures.

"This is you?" asked the astonished agent.

I nodded guiltily, and Dergham closed his eyes in resignation. It was going to be a long night.

Firing weapons is illegal in Lebanon, although it must be the most violated of all Lebanese laws. When Nasrallah begins his speeches, the crackle of celebratory gunfire is heard all over Beirut, despite frequent pleas by the Hezbollah leader for his followers to desist. During the height of the sectarian tensions in Lebanon in 2007 and 2008, the Shia residents of the southern suburbs would aim their celebratory fire toward the neighboring Sunni quarter of Tarikh Jdeide, the spent rounds tumbling out of the sky onto the roofs and streets of their political rivals. One enterprising individual even rented out his rocket-propelled grenade launcher so that people could fire grenades into the air for $30 a pop.

If the intelligence officers were looking for an excuse to detain us longer, now they had one. They refused to allow us to make any phone calls. Dergham suspected that they were deliberately stalling, knowing that our first call would set in motion the process of getting us released. In Lebanon, if you want to get something done, it helps to have *wasta*, connections with powerful people who can pull strings on your behalf. Both Dergham and I had sufficient *wasta*, if only we could contact them.

At midnight, we were handcuffed and driven to the cell block at one end of the barracks. Our cell stank of stale sweat and urine. The lights were switched off, plunging the prison block into darkness. I lay on a smelly wool blanket, using my boots as a pillow, and breathed in the fetid stink from the cell's latrines. Dergham, lying on another reeking blanket, stirred in the darkness.

"Man, we really did it this time," he muttered.

We later learned that we had been tracked down and that the phone lines were burning overnight with generals in the security services, cabinet ministers, prominent businessmen, politicians, and diplomats working to secure our release. The breakthrough came at nine o'clock the next morning when we were told we could leave military custody. The Lebanese military prosecutor presumably had concluded that it was not worth the trouble to charge a foreign journalist with brutally gunning down a defenseless watermelon.

An "Organized and Official Transfer"

Even before Hezbollah began constructing its new lines of defense north of the Litani River after the war, it was steadily restocking its depleted arsenal. Such was the apparent flow of weaponry into Lebanon that Nasrallah was able to declare just five weeks after the end of the war that Hezbollah had already restored its entire military organizational structure and its armaments. "Today, 22 September, 2006, the resistance is stronger than at any time since 1982," he said.

Nasrallah's boast may have been rooted more in propaganda and reinforcing Hezbollah's deterrence against Israel than in reality. But there was little doubt that Hezbollah's arsenals were rapidly filling up with all manner of weaponry.

After a truck loaded with 122 mm Katyusha rockets and mortar shells was stopped by Lebanese customs police on the edge of Beirut in February 2007, Nasrallah candidly admitted that weapons were being transferred to Hezbollah's bases in the south. "The resistance declares now that it is transporting weapons to the front [south]," he said; "we have weapons of all kinds and quantities, as many as you want . . . we don't fight our enemies with swords of wood."

In addition to the air corridor between Iran and Syria, the traditional conduit for the transfer of Iranian arms to Hezbollah, the Iranians may have taken advantage of the sea route to smuggle even larger quantities of basic weapons and ammunition. In 2009 alone, three suspected Iranian arms shipments were intercepted en route. The largest shipment was discovered in November when Israeli commandos stormed the Antigua-flagged *Francop* sailing between Egypt and Syria and found five hundred tons of Iranian-supplied weapons hidden in the hold. The armaments included twenty-nine-hundred 107 mm and 122 mm Katyusha rockets, three thousand antitank rounds for 106 mm recoilless rifles, and twenty thousand hand grenades.

"This could supply Hezbollah for a whole month of fighting," said Rear Admiral Rani Ben-Yehuda, the Israeli navy chief of staff.

In May 2010, Israel leaked to *The Times* of London satellite photographs of a military base eighteen miles east of Damascus near the town of Adra with tunnels sunk into the flanks of the valley where rockets and missiles were stored. Hezbollah militants allegedly had their own living quarters on site and access to a fleet of trucks to ferry the weapons across the border. Western and Lebanese intelligence sources say Hezbollah usually transfers weapons at night and in adverse weather conditions to hinder aerial and satellite reconnaissance. Following the 2006 war, some of the dirt tracks traditionally used by Hezbollah in the Janta area were graded and hardened and in some cases asphalted, according to commercially available satellite imagery.

As an additional security measure, Hezbollah switches off the local electricity supply and jams communications during the transfer of weapons across the border. When local residents suddenly lose the picture on their televisions and their phone lines go dead, they know that the arms convoys are on the move.

Yossi Baidatz, a top Israeli military intelligence officer, told Israel's Knesset in early May 2010 that the huge quantity of arms being sent to Hezbollah by Iran and Syria could no longer be described as smuggling, but was an "organized and official transfer" of weapons.

Hezbollah was also seeking specific weapons systems to burnish the Islamic Resistance with a new qualitative edge against Israel in the next war. Like Israel, top Hezbollah military officials and the leadership of the IRGC's Quds Force undertook a comprehensive after-action review to assess which weapons and tactics worked, discover where shortcomings lay, and prepare fresh battle plans for the next encounter. The main findings appear to have placed a priority on acquiring improved air defense systems and new rockets of increased range and fitted with guidance systems enabling Hezbollah to strike specific strategic targets in Israel such as government, industrial, and military facilities.

"We Will Destroy Buildings in Tel Aviv"

The Zelzal-2 was the largest rocket in Hezbollah's arsenal during the 2006 war, but by 2010 the organization was thought to have acquired the Syrian-manufactured M-600 short-range ballistic missile. Little is known about the M-600. Some analysts believe it is an indigenous Syrian-designed system, others that it is a version of the Iranian Fateh-110 rocket upgraded by the Syrian Scientific Research Council, the state-run weapons development authority. The solid-propellant rocket can carry an eleven-hundred-pound warhead, has a range of around 150 miles, and, according to some analysts, is fitted with an inertial guidance system allowing the weapon to strike within five hundred yards of its target at maximum range. Israel believes the M-600 was transferred to Lebanon in the latter half of 2009. The range of the M-600 allows Hezbollah to deploy the rocket well to the north of the UNIFIL-patrolled southern border district. To strike the oil refinery at Ashkelon, for example, the rocket could be launched from just south of Beirut. To hit targets in Tel Aviv, Hezbollah can deploy M-600 batteries in its hidden strongholds in the central and northern Bekaa Valley.

At almost 27 feet in length, the M-600 is harder to camouflage than smaller rockets systems. To overcome the problem, the rockets are fired from the same specially adapted shipping containers used to launch the Zelzals. The container is fitted on the back of a flatbed truck and the hinged top flips open to reveal a launch rail that can be elevated to the angle necessary for firing.

In April 2010, reports surfaced that Syria had transferred Scud ballistic missiles to Hezbollah. Unlike the relatively unknown M-600s, Scuds evoke among Israelis grim memories of the 1991 Gulf War, when Saddam Hussein fired several of the missiles at Tel Aviv. The notion that Hezbollah was now deploying these weapons along Israel's northern border caused a storm of controversy and recrimination in Washington, Damascus, Beirut, and Jerusalem.

The allegations threatened to undermine the cautious attempts by President Barack Obama's administration to reengage Damascus after the policy of isolation under President George W. Bush. The State Department summoned a Syrian diplomat for the fourth dressing-down in as many months, warning Syria against its "provocative behavior" and that Scuds in Hezbollah's hands "can only have a destabilizing effect on the region."

Sheikh Naim Qassem gave a typically noncommittal response, telling Ash-Sharq al-Awsat newspaper that the fuss "passes over us like a drizzle of light rain."

Possession of the high signature Scud presents significant logistical challenges. Unlike the solid-fueled M-600, the Scud uses liquid propellant, a mixture of two highly toxic substances that must be stored and handled by trained operators and entail a lengthier launch preparation time. Smuggling the forty-foot missiles into Lebanon would be a formidable undertaking given the intelligence scrutiny of the Lebanon-Syria border. The dedicated transporter-erector-launcher required to fire the missiles is even larger, and presumably more difficult to sneak into Lebanon, than the missiles themselves.

Given that the Scud and M-600 carry warheads of similar size, the only real advantage for Hezbollah is the former's extended range—three times the distance of the latter. However, there are few targets that would elicit Hezbollah's interest south of the Tel Aviv area lying beyond the reach of the M-600. Perhaps the only target worthy of the Scud's logistical complications is the nuclear reactor at Dimona in southern Israel, 140 miles south of the Lebanese border. How much damage would be caused by a direct hit by a Scud on the nuclear facility is uncertain, but it would have enormous propaganda value, especially if the strike came in retaliation to an Israeli attack on Iran's nuclear sites.

The concept of reciprocity against Israel is a cornerstone of Hezbollah's strategy. In a speech in February 2010, Nasrallah warned that if Israel hit Hezbollah's stronghold in the southern suburbs of Beirut, known as Dahiyah, the Islamic Resistance had the appropriate weapons to accurately target and destroy buildings in Tel Aviv:

> They [Israel] think they can demolish Dahiyah's buildings as we barely "puncture their walls." But I tell them today: You destroy a Dahiyah building and we will destroy buildings in Tel Aviv.... If you [Israel] target Beirut's Rafik Hariri International Airport, we will strike Tel Aviv's Ben Gurion International Airport. If you target our electricity stations, we will target yours. If you target our plants, we will target yours.

The strategy of reciprocity is not confined to the land theater, but has expanded to the Mediterranean front. In May 2010, Nasrallah indicated that Hezbollah now has the ability to target shipping along Israel's entire coastline. "If you blockade our coastline, shores, and ports, all military and commercial ships heading toward Palestine throughout the Mediterranean Sea will be targeted by the rockets of the Islamic Resistance," he said.

Hezbollah fighters have hinted to me that they have acquired longer-range antiship missiles beyond the C-802/Noor system used in the 2006 war. Iran fields several reverse-engineered antiship missiles other than the Noor. The largest is the Raad, based on the Chinese HY-2 Silkworm, which can carry a seven-hundred-pound shaped-charge warhead a distance of 225 miles. If Hezbollah has received the Raad, it could theoretically target Israeli shipping off the coast of southern Israel from launch sites as far north from the border as Beirut.

"We Are After Quality, Not Quantity"

As for new air defense weapons, another key priority for the Islamic Resistance, news reports in mid-2009 claimed that Hezbollah's cadres were receiving training in Syria on the SA-8 Gecko radar-guided mobile antiaircraft system. At the time, the SA-8 units were not thought to be deployed inside Lebanon, possibly due to Israeli warnings that the transfer of improved air defense systems to Hezbollah would constitute a "red line."

Other reports claimed that Hezbollah had received the SA-24 Grinch shoulder-fired antiaircraft missile system, a more advanced version of the SA-18 Grouse on which it is based. Hezbollah also may have acquired the Misagh-2 shoulder-fired missile produced by Iran and based on Chinese technology.

As usual, Hezbollah refuses to confirm such allegations, and the truth of the claims will probably only become clear in the next war with Israel. But the acquisition of the SA-8 and SA-24 systems would raise the threat profile to Israeli aircraft operating in Lebanese skies, especially to low-flying helicopters and UAVs, necessitating a change in operational procedure.

In 2007, some Israeli media outlets claimed that Hezbollah had installed radars and antiaircraft missiles on top of Mount Sannine, at almost eight thousand feet Lebanon's third highest mountain. DEBKA*file*, an Israeli "intelligence" website that is suspected of being used sometimes to propagate disinformation, said that Hezbollah had "commandeered" the summit at the behest of Iran and Syria. Its radar and air defense systems on the mountaintop "are capable of monitoring and threatening U.S. Sixth Fleet movements in the eastern Mediterranean and Israeli Air Force flights," it said.[1]

The top of Sannine is completely exposed. There is no vegetation, only sheets of frost-shattered limestone and rocky outcrops, so any permanent radar structure erected on Sannine would be vulnerable to attack. Indeed, anyone attempting to erect anything larger than a sand castle would soon be spotted by shepherds, hikers, hunters, and not least by Israeli aerial reconnaissance patrols, which frequently fly over the summit. I climbed up the mountain shortly after the DEBKA*file* story was published in order to confirm my doubts. As expected, the summit of Sannine had changed not one bit since I was last there a year earlier.

Beyond my fellow hikers and the odd lone eagle riding the thermals, nothing stirred within sight of the peak.

However, it was true that there was a Hezbollah presence in the Sannine foothills to the east, which rise up behind a string of Shia villages along the western flank of the Bekaa Valley. These rugged and forested hills had constituted Hezbollah's training areas since the early 1990s. From 2006, the level of activity in these hills increased significantly as Hezbollah launched a massive recruitment and training drive unprecedented in scope since the organization emerged in the early 1980s. Hundreds, perhaps thousands, of young Shias were recruited into the ranks of the Islamic Resistance in the few years after the war. For the first time, I began to hear of new recruits or seasoned veterans who had disappeared from their homes to attend courses in Iran, underlining how large the recruitment and training process had become. Driving up the Bekaa Valley, it was possible sometimes to hear the distant sound of machine gun fire and see puffs of smoke from explosions in wooded hills where the new recruits were drilled.

Hezbollah also resurrected the multifaith volunteer force, the Saraya Muqawama al-Lubnaniyya, or Lebanese Resistance Brigades, which originally was formed in 1997 and then disbanded in 2000 when Israel withdrew from Lebanon. Depending on past military experience, the Saraya volunteers could attend monthlong courses in the Bekaa split into three ten-day phases in which recruits were taught basic weapons-handling skills, communications, deploying IEDs, and first aid. Reviving the Saraya served several purposes for Hezbollah. The inclusion of non-Shia partisans into a reservist "resistance" force helped strengthen the impression of a national resistance rather than one rooted solely in the Shia sect. And giving training to Hezbollah's political allies—Christians, Sunnis, Druze, and Shias alike—helped build esprit de corps within the parliamentary opposition to Fouad Siniora's government between 2006 and 2008. The Saraya militants were not expected to play a significant combat role in the event of another war with Israel; one Hezbollah fighter told me sniffily that the Saraya would "look after the refugees from the south." But the basic weapons training with AK-47s and rocket-propelled grenades meant Hezbollah had a useful army of street fighters under its control if the rising sectarian tensions in Lebanon from 2006 should flare into violence.

Despite the enormous expansion of the Islamic Resistance and the revival of the Saraya in 2006, Hezbollah fighters insist to me that the same strict standards still apply to all recruits. "We are after quality, not quantity," said one Hezbollah unit commander. "There are many new recruits since 2006, but not all of them succeed. Some cannot endure the training, others do not have the right frame of mind. They leave or are expelled or some choose to work in the party's bureaucracy instead."

Nevertheless, since 2006, Hezbollah's ranks have swelled with untested raw recruits, well-trained and motivated, perhaps, but none of whom have experienced the rigors and uncertainties of combat.

Paying Lip Service to Resolution 1701

The consolidation of Hezbollah's new front line north of the Litani River and the extensive training in the Bekaa overshadowed suspected covert military preparations in the UNIFIL-patrolled border district. Resolution 1701 expressly forbade the presence of weapons and armed personnel between the Blue Line and the Litani other than those of the Lebanese government and UNIFIL.

Hezbollah paid lip service to Resolution 1701 publicly, but it was inconceivable that the organization would jeopardize its efforts to plan for the next war because of the edicts of a UN Security Council resolution. Nonetheless, Hezbollah was careful to mask its activities in the border district, partly to disguise what preparations were being made, but also so as not to embarrass the Lebanese army, which has primary responsibility for ensuring the implementation of Resolution 1701. While the focus of Hezbollah's war preparations before 2006 was on the remote valleys and hills of the border district, since then it appears to have centered on the villages and towns of the area. It is more than probable that new bunkers and tunnels have been constructed in the villages to connect buildings and arms storage points. In 2007, one of my sources

in south Lebanon told me that Hezbollah men had been spotted returning to their homes at dawn "covered in dirt," suggestive of digging activity. Weapons and ammunition are believed to have been smuggled into
the border district and dispersed in the villages. There may have been
some new underground construction in the rural areas as well. In summer 2009, a UNIFIL officer told me that Hezbollah had spread a large
canvas screen over part of a valley floor beneath which small tracked
earth excavators were spotted removing rock and soil. UNIFIL and Lebanese army liaison officers were denied entry to the valley by Hezbollah
men, who claimed that it was private property and therefore outside
UNIFIL's jurisdiction. The digging lasted for about two months. Was it
another decoy?

Sometimes Hezbollah's clandestine activities in the UNIFIL area
were accidentally exposed. In March 2008, Italian UNIFIL soldiers on a
night patrol in armored vehicles spotted a truck towing a trailer in the
opposite direction. As the patrol turned to follow the truck, two Mercedes cars raced past. Once between the truck and the patrol, the cars
turned and stopped, headlights on full beam at the approaching Italians.
Five men climbed out of the cars and retrieved automatic rifles from the
trunks. A tense standoff occurred until Lebanese troops arrived fifteen
minutes later, by which time the gunmen and the truck and trailer had
disappeared.

In December 2009, another UNIFIL night patrol came upon several
men behaving suspiciously on a hill overlooking the border south of
Khiam. On seeing the patrol, the men escaped by car, leaving behind 550
pounds of explosive inside twelve boxes. The size of the explosives suggested that the men were Hezbollah operatives preparing to mine a border road with an antitank belly charge.

In July 2009, a half-constructed building on the outskirts of Khirbet
Silm village was destroyed by as many as sixty separate blasts when
stored ammunition exploded early one morning. The munitions were
generally old and consisted mainly of mortar rounds and short-range
Katyusha rockets. UNIFIL found evidence that it was an actively maintained depot, and the UN condemned the incident as a breach of Resolution 1701. Three months later, there was a report of another mysterious

explosion in a garage in the center of Teir Filsay village. Israel released UAV footage purporting to show Hezbollah men removing munitions, including a suspected Katyusha rocket, from the building and transporting them to a lockup in a neighboring village. Hezbollah produced its own video footage showing the "Katyusha" was just a roller garage door. When UNIFIL investigators inspected the site in Teir Filsay, they discovered that Hezbollah had torched the inside of the garage to remove any remaining evidence. But evidence of what? UNIFIL was never able to determine exactly what had happened, nor how the Israelis were able to deploy a UAV over the site quickly enough to film the aftermath.

Israeli civilian and military officials regularly grumbled that Hezbollah was flouting Resolution 1701 by bringing arms into Lebanon and storing them in the border district. Ehud Barak, who was appointed Israeli defense minister in 2008 in Benjamin Netanyahu's government, complained in August that Resolution 1701 "did not work, doesn't work, and is a failure."

But Israel's complaints were undermined by its own breaches of Resolution 1701, such as the near-daily aerial reconnaissance flights and the continued occupation of the northern (Lebanese) part of Ghajar, which had been patrolled by Israeli troops since the 2006 war.

In July 2010, Israeli military intelligence took the unusual step of releasing video footage, maps, 3-D animated graphics, and aerial photographs of what it said were Hezbollah's arms depots in Khiam. The Israelis said that Khiam was just one of a hundred villages in the border district that had been transformed into "military bases." "Every day, they are collecting significant intelligence on our forces along the border, and every day they are engaged in digging, building, and laying communications infrastructure to prepare themselves for war," said Colonel Ronen Marley, commander of the IDF's Western Division on the border.

In publicizing the sensitive intelligence data, the Israelis hoped to bolster its deterrence by warning Hezbollah that it had detailed information on its military disposition in the border area. Furthermore, it hoped to catalyze resentment toward Hezbollah from the local population, who might take exception to living next to a building packed with ammunition and weapons, the existence of which the Israelis were aware and which they would assuredly flatten in the next war.

A Giant Leap in Technology

In tandem with the acquisition of new and improved weapons and the expansion of the Islamic Resistance, Hezbollah, with the assistance of Iranian technology, made further advances starting in 2006 in its communications and electronic warfare capabilities.

After the war Iranian technicians installed a highly sophisticated secure cellular telephone network restricted to Hezbollah military commanders and intelligence personnel using frequency-hopping encrypted cell phones. Hezbollah's network allows top cadres to communicate in complete security and cannot be accessed by normal civilian networks.

The fiber optic telecommunications network was expanded in the south, particularly in Hezbollah's new frontline areas north of the Litani River, connecting bases, training areas, and local headquarters. UN deminers saw Hezbollah men digging trenches alongside roads, including those constructed by the Iranian company, and burying the inch-thick fiber optic cables. The network also extended into new areas, covering the northern Bekaa and allegedly crossing the mountainous backbone of Lebanon to link up with the handful of Shia villages tucked into the mainly Christian-populated mountains overlooking the Mediterranean north of Beirut. The high-speed broadband data connections for the first time allowed Hezbollah commanders to hold video conferences via computer screens. In southern Beirut, Hezbollah technicians installed a WiMAX system allowing long-range wi-fi coverage of a mile or more.[2]

Fiber optic cables cannot be intercepted electronically, only by a physical tap, which presents a challenge for those looking to eavesdrop on Hezbollah's communications. However, in October 2009, Hezbollah personnel discovered in a valley a mile and a half from the border with Israel a highly complex tapping device hooked into one of its fiber optic cables. The bulky device, which UNIFIL suspected was planted during the 2006 war when Israeli troops briefly controlled the area, was buried a couple of feet underground. It had three main components: an interceptor attached to the fiber optic cable, a transmitter buried about ten yards away and connected to the interceptor by a cable, and a battery pack containing 360 individual batteries. The three units were booby-trapped with explosives. There were no identifying marks except for a small metal label inscribed "Omnetics," the name of a Minneapolis-based company specializing in the manufacture of commercial and military-spec cables and connectors.

UNIFIL electronic experts said that the device was highly advanced. The transmitter had no antenna aboveground and may have used a VLF (very low frequency) system to send radio signals through solid rock. The UNIFIL technicians even thought that the batteries could be recharged wirelessly. "The unit could have carried on working for twenty-five years," one UNIFIL officer told me.

It appears that Hezbollah had discovered that there was a tap somewhere on its fiber optic cable, possibly due to the reduced flow in data between two nodes on either side of the interception. A Hezbollah team slowly walked the line, stopping every few yards to check the cable. An Israeli UAV steadily tailed the Hezbollah team. When the tapping device was discovered, the Hezbollah men backed away, and the Israelis attempted to destroy the evidence by remote control. But only the transmitter blew up. When UNIFIL and Lebanese troops arrived to investigate the cause of the explosion, the Israelis were obliged to contact the peacekeepers and warn them to stay away. The second device and battery pack were successfully blown up the next day, but only after UNIFIL and the Lebanese army had photographed and inspected the machine in situ.

The secret electronic intelligence war between Hezbollah and Israel has steadily intensified since 2006, as each side uses ever more sophisticated technology to outwit the other, similar to the tit-for-tat advances in the IED war of the 1990s.

In December 2010, the Lebanese army announced that it had discovered two Israeli reconnaissance systems hidden inside hollow fiberglass rocks, similar to those used by Hezbollah to disguise IEDs, on the Sannine and Barouk mountains. The device on Sannine consisted of five separate components, including a laser designator, a long-range camera, a transmitter, and a battery pack. Both devices were planted overlooking the Bekaa Valley to the east and apparently transmitted collected data to a mountaintop IDF outpost in the Shebaa Farms in direct line of sight.

Two more Israeli camera systems were uncovered in March 2011, this time in south Lebanon. One of them was hidden close to the UNI-FIL headquarters in Naqoura and had views of the coastline south of Tyre. This device apparently transmitted its data to passing Israeli UAVs.

The sudden discovery of sophisticated Israeli surveillance systems was not a coincidence but due to the persistence and expertise of Hezbollah's counterintelligence technicians. Equipped with spectrum analyzers, the technicians constantly sweep the country looking for anomalous radio signals that could indicate the presence of an Israeli surveillance device. The technique takes patience and skill, especially as the Israeli devices presumably convey data using short-burst transmissions of a second or less. Once a suspicious signal is detected, it can be monitored and analyzed for a period of time and then its location determined. Hezbollah passes on the information to the Lebanese army, which recovers the devices from the field.

By summer 2010, the ether in the southern Lebanon border district was awash with rival electronic signals that constantly disrupted civilian and military communications and radar coverage. In early 2010, some UNIFIL battalions were picking up rocket launch signals on their ground radars. The radars showed the source of fire inside Lebanon, tracked the trajectory, and marked the impact point in Israel. Only there were no rocket launches. UNIFIL investigators initially pondered whether Hezbollah had found a way to trick radars by transmitting false launch signals to disguise its real rocket launches. Then UNIFIL thought it might be due to Israeli interference; but the peacekeepers were unable to come to a firm conclusion.

On at least one occasion, Israel deliberately jammed radar in Lebanon, including the air traffic control tower at Beirut airport, possibly using a system similar to the U.S. Air Force's Suter program, which can infiltrate and manipulate enemy radars like a computer virus. The Israelis may have used the same technology in September 2007 to neutralize the Syrian air defense network, allowing Israeli jets to bomb a suspected nuclear reactor under construction on the bank of the Euphrates River near Deir ez-Zor in northern Syria. For two days after the air raid, the entire coastline from Sidon in Lebanon to Ashdod in Israel found itself under an intense radar-jamming blanket. The Israelis blamed a Dutch naval ship then serving with UNIFIL's maritime component. But the peacekeepers denied they were responsible, and the source of the jamming remains unknown.

The Israelis also regularly jam the areas facing their outposts in the Shebaa Farms, a source of continual annoyance to the Lebanese living opposite who cannot use their cell phones. The Lebanese cell phone network was also hampered by UNIFIL's own radio frequency jammers fitted onto their vehicles. The number of jammers increased significantly after the 2007 bomb attack against the Spanish UNIFIL battalion. In late 2009, UNIFIL discovered that a large area east of Khiam was completely jammed. Even the Israelis were having communications difficulties along the border opposite Khiam. Each side blamed the other. But it turned out that the fault lay with UNIFIL. The peacekeepers discovered that when a large number of their vehicles were parked close together, their individual jammers, when switched on, merged electronically to create a single "superjammer" that blocked all communications in the surrounding area.

Other than intercepting and jamming Israeli communications, Hezbollah's SIGINT teams are rumored to be working on a means of cracking the encrypted data feeds from Israeli UAVs. The Israelis reportedly began encrypting the video data from drones following the Ansariyah ambush in 1997. But by 2010, Hezbollah may actually have succeeded in breaking the code after acquiring the computer program to an Israeli UAV that had been sold to another country. It is unclear which country and which drone, but several states are recipients of Israeli-manufactured drones, including Turkey, which operates the Heron UAV built by Israel Aerospace Industries, and Georgia, which possesses Elbit Systems's Hermes 450. Both drones plow the skies above Lebanon.

Additionally, Hezbollah is exploring measures to neutralize UAVs by jamming the communications link between a UAV and its ground control base, or by electronically interfering with drones that are on autonomous preprogrammed flight missions.

The extent of Hezbollah's acquisition of advanced communications and SIGINT systems is uncertain, although Israeli intelligence reportedly operates on the principle that whatever Iran possesses—both weapons and communications technology—could potentially be in Hezbollah's hands, too. Certainly, Hezbollah does not appear to be lagging very far behind the IDF's own advances in SIGINT and communications, thanks to the assistance of Iran.

The secrecy surrounding Hezbollah's communications and electronic warfare capabilities is indicative of the critical importance technology plays in the organization's ability to wage war against Israel. Hezbollah has advanced enormously in terms of weapons, training, organization, and tactics since its formative stages in the early 1980s, but it is the giant leap in technology that perhaps best illustrates the extent of Hezbollah's military evolution, underlining the essential role that state sponsorship plays in permitting an armed group to possess capabilities normally only found in a conventional national army.

"They Ran Away Like Rabbits"

In May 2008, Nasrallah acknowledged that Hezbollah's communications network was "the most important weapon in the resistance." His statement came at a climactic moment in the confrontation between the Hezbollah-led parliamentary opposition and Fouad Siniora's government. For more than sixteen months, the country had remained in political gridlock. The opposition was still encamped in downtown Beirut, although most of the tents were empty, with skeleton crews of activists rotated in and out to maintain the semblance of a sit-in. Sunni-Shia tensions had worsened amid street skirmishes in mixed neighborhoods and endless mutual accusations that political factions were arming themselves and forming private militias. The price of weapons soared on the black market—always the best indicator of the level of tensions in Lebanon. A good quality AK-47 rifle was worth around $1,000 by early 2008, double the price in 2006.

In early May 2008, the government concluded an official inquiry into Hezbollah's telecoms system, finding that "hundreds of thousands" of lines had been installed linking all Shia areas of the country and connecting with Syrian telecommunications lines. The inquiry also found that Hezbollah had built solar-powered communications towers in the mountains flanking the border with Syria. Marwan Hamadeh, the minister of telecommunications, said that Hezbollah's phone network was "no longer an issue concerning the security of the resistance, but rather the security of Lebanon and the toppling of its regime."

Following a lengthy cabinet meeting on May 5, the government announced it intended to shut down Hezbollah's communications network, to launch an inquiry into Hezbollah's alleged surveillance of Beirut's Rafik Hariri Airport, and to dismiss a security chief at the airport who was deemed too close to the party.

The Hezbollah-led opposition immediately took to the streets under the guise of a national union strike, blocking main roads with barriers of dumped earth and burning tires. Three days after the cabinet decision, in a news conference in Beirut's southern suburbs, Nasrallah warned that the government decision was "tantamount to a declaration of war . . . on the resistance and its weapons in the interests of America and Israel."

"We have a right to defend our existence from whoever declares and begins a war on us, even if they are our brothers," he said. "Whoever is going to target us will be targeted by us. Whoever is going to shoot at us will be shot by us."

At the end of the news conference, I approached Ibrahim al-Amine, the chairman of the *Al-Akhbar* newspaper, who has unrivaled access to Hezbollah among journalists. I asked him what he thought was going to happen next.

"You may find out tonight," he said with a knowing smile.

The crackle of small arms fire and the pop of rocket-propelled grenades had begun even before I had reached home. That night fighters from numerous opposition factions—Amal, the Syrian Social Nationalists, Baathists—under Hezbollah's direction overran the western half of Beirut in a preplanned and coordinated assault. The homes of top March 14 leaders, including Saad Hariri, the son and political heir of the slain Rafik, and Walid Jumblatt, were surrounded; the offices of the Hariri-owned Future TV and *Al-Mustaqbal* newspaper were ransacked and burned. Sunni gunmen loosed a few rocket-propelled grenades, then fled. The Lebanese army stood on the sidelines, unwilling to challenge Hezbollah on the streets.

By dawn the next morning, Hezbollah and its allies controlled the western half of the city. I found one Hezbollah unit commander, a short, stocky former Amal militiaman, resting with his squad in a Sunni quarter not far from Hariri's home. He leaned against a doorway, his olive-green webbing stuffed with hand grenades, ammunition clips, and a walkie-talkie. "The people here went to sleep last night with Omar and woke up this morning with Ali," he joked, referring to typical Sunni and Shia names respectively.

Tired but clearly triumphant, he gave a dismissive wave of the hand when asked about the opposition he had faced from Sunni gunmen the previous night. "They ran away like rabbits," he said.

I found Walid Jumblatt at his home in the Clemenceau district. Tired and unshaven, he sat quietly in a garden chair in the courtyard, his frame hunched, his legs crossed, staring pensively at the ground. The Druze leader had been the driving force behind persuading the government to crack down on Hezbollah's communications network. He had gambled and lost, and now he had to ponder his next move. "We wanted the army to provide security for us, but what can the army do when this militia, called Hezbollah, is stronger than the army?" Jumblatt grumbled.

Under Hezbollah's orders, the opposition gunmen melted away after a few hours, allowing the army to take control of the streets. But fighting continued over the next few days, with bloody clashes in north Lebanon and particularly in the Chouf Mountains, where Jumblatt's Druze loyalists fought fiercely against the Shia interlopers of Hezbollah. But Jumb-latt knew this was a battle he could not win, and he sued for peace after Hezbollah fighters deployed onto the windswept heights of the Barouk Mountains and aimed Katyusha rockets at the Druze leader's ancestral home in Mukhtara in the shadowed valleys far below.

Lebanon's bickering leaders were flown to Doha in Qatar, where a reconciliation agreement was hammered out. The agreement led to the election as president of Michel Suleiman, the commander of the Leba-nese army, and ushered in a period of relative political stability. As part of the deal, the government canceled its decision to shut down Hez-bollah's telecommunications network.

The outcome of the May 2008 "events," as they are euphemistically referred to by the Lebanese, broke the back of the political deadlock that had paralyzed Lebanon since the 2006 war and confirmed Hez-bollah as the dominant force on the Lebanese "street." But it came at a price. For Hezbollah, in dispatching its fighters against the Sunni sup-porters of Saad Hariri and the Druze partisans of Walid Jumblatt, had broken an until-then sacred taboo. How many times had Nasrallah and other Hezbollah leaders insisted that the arms of the Islamic Resistance were aimed only at Israel and would never be used against fellow Leba-nese? Hezbollah justified its takeover of west Beirut as an act of defense against an American-Israeli plot to rob the "resistance" of its vital com-munications weapon. But it was an excuse that rang hollow in the ears of those Lebanese who had previously given Hezbollah the benefit of the doubt over its relentless determination to keep its weapons. Fur-thermore, Hezbollah and its allies had humiliated Beirut's Sunnis in their own neighborhoods, streets, and homes. The Sunnis may have acknowledged that there was little they could do to challenge Hez-bollah's seizure of the western half of the city, but that failed to dampen their sense of humiliation and deep resentment toward their Shia antagonists. Hezbollah, which has always championed unity be-tween the two main sects of Islam, now faced the question of how to reconcile with the Sunnis and prevent the intra-Muslim schism from deepening.

"Hezbollah Was Quite a Surprise"

Hezbollah was not alone in readying itself for a new war with Israel. Since the trauma of Israel's poor performance in the 2006 war, the IDF switched its attention from the asymmetrical confrontation with the Palestinians to the conventional threat on the northern front posed by Hezbollah and Syria.

"The military had adopted [before 2006] a training and operational concept related to the Palestinian theater," said Gabriel Siboni, a reservist IDF colonel and a military strategist at the Institute for National Security Studies in Tel Aviv. "The war against the [Palestinian] suicide bombers worked. We won that war in 2005. Then Hezbollah came in and that was quite a surprise."

Since 2006, Israel has improved its military preparedness by increasing the quality of training for reservist brigades and the frequency of drills and exercises, improving operational planning, bringing new weapons systems online, and tightening coordination between the IDF, the Israeli Air Force, and the intelligence community.

At the Elyakim training base at the southern end of Mount Carmel near Haifa, a terrain of woods and hills that resemble south Lebanon, the IDF built a series of Hezbollah-style bunkers and rocket-firing positions and littered the area with fake roadside bombs.[3] Troops practice maneuvering through the rugged terrain, learning how to seek out and destroy rocket positions. Given the expectation that much of the next war will be fought in villages and towns in south Lebanon, the IDF plans to increase the number of urban warfare training centers from around fifteen in summer 2010 to about twenty-two by the end of 2011.[4] Two of the centers were expected to include tunnel-and-bunker complexes similar to those constructed by Hezbollah.

Barely a week passes without a new defensive system being unveiled in the Israeli media, most of them connected to the asymmetrical conflict with Hezbollah in Lebanon and Hamas in the Gaza Strip. By summer 2010, Israel was close to fielding a multitier antirocket umbrella. It includes the Iron Dome interceptor to counter rockets with ranges of between three and forty-three miles, the David's Sling weapons system to defeat cruise missiles and large-caliber rockets such as the M-600, and the Arrow system, under development since the mid-1990s, which is intended to intercept ballistic missiles such as Iran's Shahab-3.

On the ground, Israel has developed armor defense systems to neutralize the advanced antitank missiles wielded by Hezbollah. They include the Trophy system, which fires a projectile from a targeted tank toward the incoming missile, destroying it in the air. From 2010, Trophy was fitted as standard to all new tanks coming off the production line.

The antirocket shield has been trumpeted as a major technological breakthrough, the culmination of a decade and a half searching for a solution to the threat posed by Hezbollah's rockets. According to the Israeli media, the Iron Dome system "aced" its field tests, successfully shooting down numerous calibers of rocket and even mortar rounds. But it is uncertain how it will fare in a wartime scenario against multiple rocket barrages from Lebanon. Critics claim the concept is prohibitively expensive, noting the exorbitant cost of the interceptor missiles (estimated at $300,000 to $400,000 each for David's Sling and $35,000 to $50,000 each for Iron Dome) compared with the few hundred dollars each for Hezbollah's Katyusha and Hamas's Qassam rockets they are meant to defeat. Iron Dome's manufacturer, the state-owned Rafael Advanced Defense Systems—the same company that developed the Spike antitank missile in the 1990s—says that the system is intended to target only those rockets that are heading toward towns and villages. The rockets falling toward unpopulated areas will be left alone.

The real flaw, however, is that the antirocket systems are a tactical solution to a strategic problem. The threat posed by the rockets of Hamas and particularly Hezbollah is not in the number of casualties nor the amount of direct damage they inflict, but in the disruption they cause to normal life in Israel. When fighting flares along the border, the residents of northern Israel are instructed to enter the bunkers or leave their homes for safer areas farther south regardless of whether Hezbollah actually launches rockets. During the flare-up in fighting in February 2000, Hezbollah paralyzed life in northern Israel for 48 hours at a cost of $2.4 million a day in lost business without firing a single rocket across the border.

No matter how effective the Iron Dome and David's Sling systems, they cannot neutralize the strategic dilemma caused by Hezbollah's rockets. For example, if Hezbollah fires ten thousand rockets into northern Israel in the next war and 80 percent of them are knocked out of the sky by interceptor missiles, that still leaves two thousand rockets falling on the heads of Israeli citizens. Does the Israeli army tell the residents of the north not to bother heading to the bunkers or moving south because only two thousand rockets are coming their way instead of ten thousand?

The Israeli public may discover that in the next war the costly antirocket batteries will not be deployed to defend their homes and businesses but will be installed around key strategic sites in Israel such as industrial and infrastructure centers and army and air force bases, which are expected to be the focus of Hezbollah's newly acquired guided missiles.

Even the antimissile defenses for Israel's fleet of Merkava Mark 4 tanks may struggle against the "swarming" tactics being further developed by Hezbollah's antitank units. From the mid-1990s, Hezbollah practiced firing multiple missiles at a single Israeli tank or APC with the aim of detonating the panels of reactive armor, thereby exposing the steel skin and making it vulnerable to a follow-up missile. The tactic was used extensively during the 2006 war, although it involved the expenditure of large numbers of relatively expensive advanced antitank missiles such as the AT-14 Kornet for each target. To overcome the new defensive measures being installed on Israeli Merkava tanks, Hezbollah fighters have hinted to me that they will double up the swarming tactic by firing large numbers of relatively unsophisticated and cheap rockets and missiles, such as recoilless rifles, RPGs, and older antitank missile systems. That could explain the inclusion of three thousand antitank rounds for 106 mm recoilless rifles found by Israeli naval commandos when they stormed the cargo vessel *Francop* in 2009. The 106 mm recoilless rifle is considered obsolete by most armies and is incapable of piercing the armor of modern tanks, especially those as well protected as the Merkava Mark 4. But it is accurate to a thousand yards and would be an effective, and economical, swarming weapon in tandem with RPGs and

the smaller man-portable SPG-9 73 mm recoilless rifles with which
Hezbollah is also equipped to overwhelm Israeli armor defenses. Once
the panels of reactive armor have been destroyed, the killing blow could
then be delivered by a more advanced missile such as the Kornet AT-14.

"We Cannot Defeat Hezbollah"

In October 2008, Major General Gadi Eisenkot, the head of the IDF's
Northern Command, unveiled the so-called "Dahiyah doctrine," named
after Beirut's southern suburbs where Hezbollah's leadership resides.
The doctrine states that in a future war, Hezbollah areas would be flattened, similar to the destruction inflicted on Dahiyah in the 2006 conflict. "We will wield disproportionate power against every village from
which shots are fired on Israel, and cause damage and destruction," he
said in an interview with Israel's *Yedioth Ahronoth* newspaper. "From
our perspective, these are military bases. This isn't a suggestion. This is
a plan that has already been authorized."

The idea was expanded upon by Gabriel Siboni, the Israeli military
strategist, who recommended swift strikes that prioritized infrastructure assets over rocket launchers.[5] In Syria, Siboni added, punishment
should be aimed at the leadership, the military, and the state infrastructure. In Lebanon, Hezbollah targets should be hit simultaneously with
economic interests and the centers of civilian power that support the
organization. "Moreover, the closer the relationship between Hezbollah
and the Lebanese government, the more the elements of the Lebanese
state infrastructure should be targeted," he wrote. Siboni's article was
written a year before two Hezbollah ministers joined the coalition government headed by Saad Hariri. "Such a response will create a lasting
memory among Syrian and Lebanese decision makers, thereby increasing Israeli deterrence and reducing the likelihood of hostilities against
Israel for an extended period," Siboni added.

The public threats and articulation of a massive and disproportionate bombing campaign against Lebanon is intended, first and foremost,
to deter Hezbollah from launching a war. If a conflict does break out,

however, Israeli strategists believe that attempting to crush Hezbollah with militarily force cannot succeed. Hunting for camouflaged and mobile rocket launchers and flushing Hezbollah fighters from their underground lairs is labor-intensive and will incur heavy troop casualties without any guarantee of success.

"For practical reasons, we cannot defeat Hezbollah," Giora Eiland, a former Israeli national security advisor during the governments of Ariel Sharon, told me. "We have to define Lebanon as our enemy. The Lebanese government must know that it has only two possibilities: one, to let the relative calm continue, and two, that a war will devastate Lebanon."

A foretaste of what the Lebanese can expect in the next war came at the end of December 2008, when Israel launched a three-week ground and air offensive against Gaza. Dubbed by Israel as Operation Cast Lead, the purpose was to inflict massive damage on Hamas, which not only retained a military wing but also had administered Gaza since winning legislative elections in January 2006. Israeli military engineers neutralized many of Hamas's IEDs by jamming radio frequencies and using brute force, with armored D-9 bulldozers clearing paths for troops. Coordination among separate military units—ground troops, artillery, air force, and navy—was greatly improved. Frontline commanders for the first time were allocated direct control over air support operations, including UAVs, without the need to pass requests through the Israeli Air Force. Many new technological systems were fielded for the first time, including remote control surveillance vehicles and handheld tennis-ball-shaped reconnaissance cameras that could be thrown inside buildings for 360-degree coverage of the interior.

Hamas's military performance was poor. The Palestinian group had borrowed some of Hezbollah's tactics—including the construction of bunkers and tunnels and extensive use of IEDs and antiarmor missiles—while firing rockets into Israel. But the qualitative differences between Hamas's capabilities and those of Hezbollah, as well as their respective operational environments, were enormous.

By the time fighting ended on January 17, Israel had achieved a tactical victory over Hamas, helping restore some confidence within the IDF and the Israeli public after the debacle of the 2006 war against Hezbollah.

But Israel's use of overwhelming force against Gaza and the high number of Palestinian casualties (around thirteen hundred, mostly civilians) and widespread destruction to property drew international reproach and led to a precedent-setting UN inquiry, the results of which could have legal ramifications for Israel's future conduct in war. The inquiry headed by Richard Goldstone, a South African judge, found that both Israel and Hamas had committed war crimes, but the bulk of the final report's criticism was directed at the Jewish state. The Goldstone report could complicate Israel's plans to implement the Dahiyah doctrine in Lebanon. The promised destruction of Lebanese infrastructure in the next war has already garnered the attention of international human rights groups.

In some respects, the Dahiyah doctrine is a throwback to the air and artillery offensives the IDF waged against Hezbollah in the 1990s—the seven-day Operation Accountability in July 1993 and the sixteen-day Grapes of Wrath in April 1996. Both operations were intended to inflict punishment on Lebanese civilians and government for supporting Hezbollah's resistance campaign against the IDF in south Lebanon. They both failed because Israel misunderstood the dynamics between Hezbollah and the civilian population and the realities of the Lebanon-Syria relationship in which Beirut was subordinate to Damascus and could not have blocked Hezbollah even if it had wanted to. Furthermore, Israel's excessive use of firepower (in which a total of 280 Lebanese died in the two operations) cost the sympathy of the international community.

The difference between the 1990s operations and the Dahiyah doctrine is that the former campaigns were tactical knee-jerk responses to deteriorating situations in south Lebanon rather than a component of a long-term strategy. The Dahiyah doctrine has been conceived in a different political environment to that of the mid-1990s. Hezbollah's popularity has declined since 2000, with the Lebanese today evenly split over Hezbollah's armed status. Israel anticipates that if the Dahiyah doctrine were implemented against Lebanon, the backlash in the aftermath would further erode Hezbollah's domestic standing.

Yet the real utility of the doctrine lies in its powers of deterrence rather than its application. Israel regularly promotes the doctrine to scare the Lebanese and to discourage Hezbollah from creating mischief out of fear of the repercussions on its core Shia constituency. On this level, the Dahiyah doctrine has some purpose. The flaw in the doctrine will emerge, however, if a conflict arises and Israel chooses to launch an overwhelming assault on Lebanese infrastructure. In such an event, Hezbollah will not play by Israel's rules and merely retire chastened when the IDF decides after a few days that sufficient punishment has been inflicted on Lebanon. On the contrary, Hezbollah will press on with its attack and Israel will be forced to respond and get dragged into an inevitable ground campaign with the resulting high casualties and uncertain outcome.

"The Last War with Israel"

Hezbollah's unprecedented military buildup since 2006 in arms, technology, and manpower, coupled with the IDF's reconfiguration to fight a war on its northern front and the creation of the Dahiyah doctrine, suggests that the next conflict will be fought with few restraints.

Hezbollah believes that the scale of the next war will be of such magnitude that the result will change the political shape of the Middle East and will even mark the beginning of the end of Israel. Since 2006, the notion that Israel faces imminent destruction has become a cornerstone of Nasrallah's speeches. In August 2007, he addressed the Israelis, saying, "If you Zionists think of launching a war on Lebanon, I will not promise you surprises like the ones that happened [in 2006], but I promise you a big surprise that could change the course of the war and the fate of the region." Nasrallah elaborated on this theme in February 2008, saying that the "elimination of Israel from existence is inevitable because this is a historical and divine law from which there is no escape. This is definite."

Other than heavenly decree, Nasrallah listed several more prosaic reasons why he believes Israel is doomed in the long term. Among them were the fact that Israel was an "alien entity" in a region of mainly Arabs and Muslims; the continued determination of the Palestinian people to return to their homeland despite six decades of exile; declining international support for Israel; the higher Palestinian birthrate (the so-called "demographic weapon"); the moral decay he sees within Israeli society; and the waning reputation of the Israeli army.

Nasrallah argues that if one accepts that the IDF is the backbone of Israel, then its defeat will presage the downfall of the Jewish state. In February 2008, Nasrallah warned Israel it would experience in the next war "a fight that you have never witnessed throughout your history."

"Your army, your tanks, the remainder of your standing, and the remainder of your deterrence will be destroyed in the south, and Israel will remain without an army," he said. "When Israel becomes without an army, it will no longer exist."

Such thunderous and apocalyptic predictions are part of Hezbollah's skillful information operations, a tool of psychological warfare to help bolster Hezbollah's deterrence posture against Israel and preserve the "balance of terror." But for the grassroots cadres of the Islamic Resistance, Nasrallah's promises of Israel's imminent destruction are not dismissed as mere rhetorical flourishes but are absorbed and accepted, becoming an article of faith that is further sustained by the intense training programs and exhaustive battle plans for the next war. In numerous conversations with Hezbollah fighters since 2006, I hear the same rigid, unassailable confidence that Israel will be defeated and destroyed in the next war.

"The next war will be the last war with Israel. We will liberate Palestine. We truly believe that," said Khodr, the stocky, muscular young combatant we met in chapter 3, who by 2011 had attended multiple training sessions in Iran and was a fully qualified member of Hezbollah's antitank unit. He fixed me with an unflinching gaze to emphasize the import of what he had just said. "The mujahideen are completely focused on the next war, even ignoring families and friends," he continued. "They are just waiting for the next war."

But Khodr was a university student, an educated young man. How could he relish the prospect of another war with Israel, one that promises to be the most destructive ever inflicted upon Lebanon?

Khodr took a sip from a can of cola and thought for a moment before replying slowly in English.

"I have two lives going in parallel. I have my studies at university and my family, but I also have the life of jihad and preparations for the coming war," he said. "I consider my jihad duties as something joyful. You cannot understand the joy of jihad unless you are in Hezbollah. The atmosphere within Hezbollah is very spiritual. Jihad is a very pleasant state of mind."

Sentiments such as these underline the yawning gulf that separates the Hezbollah combatant from most other Lebanese. Khodr yearns for the next war because he will be fulfilling his jihadist obligations and he believes that it will lead to the destruction of Israel. But Khodr's youthful non-Hezbollah contemporaries in Lebanon are more interested in finding decent jobs and homes and raising families as well as enjoying the sybaritic pleasures that the country offers with its golden beaches, snow-capped mountains, and frenetic nightlife. Did Khodr have any empathy with those Lebanese who are horrified at the prospect of another war with Israel?

"These people don't know what they are talking about," he said with a dismissive wave of his hand. "They think all they have to do is work and enjoy life. Well, we work and enjoy life too, but they don't realize that Israel can do what it wants to the country unless we resist."

This cold-blooded detachment from the prevailing sentiment in Lebanon is chilling and hard to fathom, but it underlines the single-minded dedication of the Hezbollah fighter. The "Chief," the tall, gregarious unit commander we also encountered in chapter 3, took a car ride with me in early 2010, and as we passed through Beirut's southern suburbs with their bland concrete high-rises, he said nonchalantly, "Take a good look around you, because next time all this will be gone."

This was his neighborhood, home to his family and friends. Was he not worried about the prospect of the area's being flattened by Israeli bombs in the next war?

"We can always rebuild," he replied. "Our dignity is more important than roofs over our heads."

"We Will Go into Palestine Next"

Only Hezbollah's top level military commanders have a clear picture of how the organization will fight the next war. On the broader level, the strategy probably will remain much the same as in 2006: striking targets in Israel with accurate and sustained rocket fire while robustly confronting any ground invasion by the IDF. The chief difference is that Hezbollah will probably go on the offensive next time, rather than wage the defensive war it fought in 2006. Instead of reacting to Israeli actions, Hezbollah will attempt to seize the initiative and dictate the pace of the conflict.

Hezbollah officials and fighters repeatedly allude to "surprises" that they say will give the organization an edge in the next war, leaving analysts to ponder exactly what they have in mind. The obvious possible "surprises" are related to new weapons systems—guided surface-to-surface rockets capable of hitting specific military and infrastructure targets the length of Israel, extended-range antiship missiles, new air defense systems to dent Israel's aerial superiority.

But Hezbollah may be planning to "surprise" Israel not only with new weapons but also with innovative tactics. Since 2006, Hezbollah fighters have repeatedly hinted to me that they are being trained to launch commando raids into northern Israel.

"God willing, we will go into Palestine next. No more south Lebanon. That's why training is so intense and there is so much of it," said one fighter. He added that the training included learning how to seize and hold ground, a tactic not normally found within the canon of traditional guerrilla warfare, which tends to emphasize hit-and-run operations.

Another fighter told me that the next war "will be fought more in Israel than in Lebanon." Abu Khalil, the shaven-headed veteran unit commander from the 1990s, once quipped, "You will see that next time maybe the UN will ask us to withdraw from northern Israel rather than Israel withdraw from south Lebanon."

Even Nasrallah eventually referred to a cross-border campaign by Hezbollah as a highlight of one of his periodic "deterrence" speeches. "I tell the resistance fighters to be prepared for the day when war is imposed on Lebanon. Then the resistance leadership might ask you to lead the resistance to liberate Galilee," he said in February 2011.

Taking the fight across Lebanon's southern border into Israel in some respects is the next logical step in Hezbollah's military evolution. Hezbollah would be forcing the Israelis to fight on their own territory, reversing the established Israeli doctrine of fighting its wars on the soil of its neighbors. The number of targets available to small squads of well-armed Hezbollah fighters is limited only by the imagination. Bridges and roads could be dynamited or booby-trapped with IEDs, ambushes conducted against military convoys, electricity and telephone pylons toppled, gas stations blown up. Israel's air control base atop Mount Meron lies only nine miles south of the border, separated by a rugged terrain of wooded valleys that could provide ample cover for infiltrating commando units. Other military facilities, such as the Israeli Air Force base at Kiryat Shemona, are within easy reach of the border. The Israeli frontier settlements are even more vulnerable, especially those such as Manara and Misgav Am that abut the boundary fence. Imagine the reaction in the Israeli defense ministry when senior IDF officers following the progress of their armored columns charging into Lebanon suddenly learn that Hezbollah has stormed a settlement and taken hostage a dozen or more households. Imagine, too, the electrifying effect on public opinion in the Arab and Muslim worlds if combat cameramen accompany the commando squads and beam out images of Hezbollah fighters brandishing yellow party flags surging through Israeli towns and villages.

Dispatching commando units into Israel will not win the war for Hezbollah—most, if not all, of the fighters slipping across the border will surely not make it back. But the tactic is more than justified from Hezbollah's perspective as an element of psychological warfare—causing

chaos and panic in northern Israel and rallying popular support for
Hezbollah throughout the region.

This tactic, in fact, may not be that new. I first heard about it from
sources in south Lebanon as long ago as 2002 and wrote in *The Daily
Star* that Hezbollah might be planning to storm border settlements and
seize hostages in the event of a full-scale war with Israel. The revelation
raised some eyebrows at the time, but not anymore.

As for the feasibility of infiltrating Israel, Hezbollah secretly built a
network of tunnels between 2000 and 2006 along the border from east
to west. Who is to say that they did not also dig some tunnels running
south, beneath the fence? Taking the idea a step further, could Hezbollah
have borrowed a terrifying and destructive tactic of trench warfare from
World War I and tunneled beneath Israeli positions in order to blow
them up at a later date with a large quantity of explosives? The former
battlefields of northern France are still scarred by massive craters left
over from the detonation of trench mines, some resulting from as much
as forty thousand pounds of dynamite packed beneath the German
front line. There is a precedent for such a tactic in the Middle East. In
December 2004, five Israeli soldiers were killed when part of an IDF
outpost near Rafah in the Gaza Strip was blown up after Palestinian
militants tunneled beneath the position and planted an explosive charge.

The IDF may have discovered one such Hezbollah tunnel during the
2006 war. An Israeli TV news crew reportedly caught on microphone a
conversation between an IDF officer and a wounded soldier. The soldier
told the officer that a tunnel discovered north of the border in Lebanon
ran south to beneath an IDF outpost. Nothing more was heard about
the revelation.[6]

Other than ground infiltrations of Israel, Hezbollah's amphibious
warfare unit could launch seaborne incursions along the coast of northern Israel. According to a private briefing paper I obtained, compiled by
the IDF's Operational Theory Research Institute, Hezbollah's amphibious warfare unit includes a "divers unit" of combat frogmen and a "vessels unit" responsible for "attack craft" and training on the systems. It is
unclear what sea vessels, if any, have been transferred to Hezbollah beyond Zodiac inflatable boats. However, Iran and North Korea operate

midget submarines and a number of torpedo-armed semisubmersible and submersible fast attack craft. Iran also manufactures a Swimmer Delivery Vehicle (SDV), a twenty-four-foot torpedo-shaped submersible that is operated by a crew of two and can carry up to seven additional divers. Small fast attack craft, mini-submarines, and SDVs would suit Hezbollah's operational needs for sabotage operations in Israeli harbors or for infiltrating commando teams onto the beaches of northern Israel.

A retired Israeli intelligence officer once told me that at least one attempted operation inside Israel had been mounted by Hezbollah's amphibious warfare unit. This incident, the details of which are still classified, occurred sometime between 2000 and 2006 and involved an underwater sabotage operation against Israeli shipping in Haifa's port. According to the Israeli officer, Hezbollah frogmen planned to attach limpet mines to the hulls of docked ships. Evidently, the mission was unsuccessful, as no ships were blown up. The fate of the frogmen was not revealed, although it can be assumed that they went to a watery grave.

"None of Us Knew It Was Him"

Despite the feverish war preparations undertaken by both sides beginning in 2006, the residents of southern Lebanon and northern Israel were enjoying their most prolonged period of calm in more than four decades. There were a handful of isolated cross-border Katyusha rocket attacks, believed to be the work of Islamist radicals or Palestinian renegades. But Hezbollah had not fired a shot across the border since August 2006. Even the Shebaa Farms remained quiet, despite Israel's continued occupation of the area. Sheikh Naim Qassem explained that the reality of Resolution 1701 precluded a resumption of the Shebaa Farms campaign. Instead, Hezbollah was using the time to prepare "in case Israel decides to launch an aggression against us."

"This is the shape of the resistance at this stage," he told me in July 2009.

But there was no letup in the shadowy covert intelligence war waged between Israel and Hezbollah. Since 2006, the Lebanese security services have had an unprecedented success in breaking up Israeli-run spy rings, arresting more than a hundred people, some of whom have been collaborating with the Israelis for decades. They included retired generals, several active-duty colonels in the army, a deputy mayor of a town in the Bekaa Valley, a butcher from south Lebanon, telecoms engineers, and former SLA militiamen. Their diverse social and sectarian backgrounds—Shia, Sunni, Christian, Druze, and Palestinian—testify to the extent of Israel's intelligence penetration of Lebanon.

One of the most potentially damaging cases was that of Marwan Faqih, a Shia from the southern town of Nabatiyah who owned a car dealership and garage. Faqih was close to Hezbollah and a major supplier of vehicles to the organization. But on each new vehicle for Hezbollah, he installed a GPS tracking device and voice recorder. The GPS device recorded the route taken by each vehicle, and the information was sent via satellite. Over time, the recorded GPS "tracks" presumably allowed the Israelis to construct a computerized map not only of homes and offices inhabited by Hezbollah men, but possibly military positions and arms depots and other sensitive locations scattered around the country.

According to Hezbollah's official account, Faqih was unmasked when a garage assistant noticed some unusual wiring sticking out from the bottom of a vehicle he was servicing. When he informed the owner of the car, a Hezbollah member, the party launched an investigation. Another version, however, suggests that the GPS trackers were discovered after the Iranians handed Hezbollah powerful surveillance monitors and it was discovered that their vehicles were beaming a stream of data to satellites.[7]

The spate of arrests and the collapse of several spy networks were due in large part to the serendipitous provision by France and the United States of sophisticated phone-tapping equipment and data-processing programs to the intelligence bureau of the Lebanese police, according to Lebanese security sources. The equipment was supposed to assist the police in tracing the killers of Rafik Hariri by analyzing phone records of suspects, but the police discovered that it was equally useful in finding and disrupting Israeli spy rings.

But Hezbollah's enemies also had their successes, most notably on the evening of February 12, 2008, when a heavy-set bearded man climbed into his Mitsubishi Pajero in a narrow street in a Damascus suburb seconds before a bomb exploded inside the vehicle.

I was told the news early the next morning by a friend who called me as I sipped my first cup of coffee of the day and asked, "Have you heard? Imad Mughniyah's been killed."

My immediate response was skepticism. But that changed when I switched on Hezbollah's Al-Manar television channel. On the screen was a photograph of a chubby-faced man with a full beard streaked with gray, wearing wire-rimmed spectacles, a dark green baseball cap, and a camouflage uniform. A slight smile played around his lips. It had taken the death of Imad Mughniyah for the world to finally get a glimpse of what this most elusive and cunning of Islamic militants actually looked like. Throughout the ranks of Hezbollah, astonished fighters realized that the military commander many of them knew only as "Hajj Radwan" was in fact none other than the fabled Imad Mughniyah.

"I saw him not so long ago at a meeting and I had no idea he was Mughniyah," a grizzled Hezbollah veteran called Abu Hussein told me days later in Mughniyah's natal village of Teir Dibna in south Lebanon. "He used Hajj Radwan as his name. None of us knew it was him."

Mughniyah had attended a reception in the Kfar Susa neighborhood of Damascus to mark the anniversary of the Islamic revolution in Iran. The party was a who's who of radical Palestinians, Hezbollah officials, top Syrian officers, and Iranian diplomats. Mughniyah left the party before midnight and crossed the road to his car. A suspected remote control bomb blew up his vehicle as he started the car, killing him instantly.

Mughniyah had artfully evaded his pursuers for nearly three decades. But his enemies had caught up with him in, of all places, Damascus, where one would have thought he could enjoy a degree of security.

Israel, of course, was the chief suspect, despite its denials. Danny Yatom, the former head of Mossad, described Mughniyah's death as "a great achievement for the free world in its fight on terror."

"There are numerous intelligence agencies and countries that have been pursuing him, and the one that was successful in reaching him [has proven itself] to have a high intelligence and operational capability," Yatom said, with perhaps just a hint of self-congratulation.

Israel had operated in Damascus before, assassinating a top Hamas military commander in 2004, also in a car bomb explosion. Anis Naqqash, Mughniyah's old friend, who only on the death of his onetime student began publicly admitting their long-standing association, believes that Mughniyah simply made a fatal mistake.

"He stayed in one home in Damascus for more than six months and was receiving important people," he told me, adding that Ramadan Shalah, the head of Palestinian Islamic Jihad, and Khaled Meshaal, the leader of Hamas, were regular visitors to his home.

"Even if they didn't know he was Imad, they knew it was an important Hezbollah person meeting with top Palestinians, Syrians, and Iranians. Maybe they were able to obtain a photograph and begin finding out who he was."

But surely a man with such a high sense of personal security, who had eluded his enemies for so long, would not make such a fundamental error?

Naqqash nodded in agreement.

"I told him this was a big mistake he was making. He never made such mistakes before. He didn't make such mistakes when he was living in Tehran. I didn't even know his home in Tehran. He kept it a secret. But it was not a secret in Damascus, and Damascus is not a safe city."

Naqqash believes that Mughniyah had burned himself out in the wake of the 2006 war and had grown weary of a life of secrecy. "The actual strategy of Hezbollah for the next war was planned by Imad immediately after the 2006 war," he said. "He immediately understood what he needed to do. It took him, according to his friends, six months to make the picture complete, and then he said 'go implement this.' I think after 2006, he achieved something very big and became tired of the constant secrecy."

The veil of silence that had shrouded Mughniyah for more than two decades was ripped open upon his death as Hezbollah elevated him to the pantheon of the movement's greatest martyrs, forming a trinity alongside Sheikh Ragheb Harb and Sayyed Abbas Mussawi. Two days after his death, tens of thousands of Hezbollah supporters crammed into a vast hall in the southern suburbs of Beirut or stood in the pouring rain outside for Mughniyah's funeral. It was an occasion typical of Hezbollah's sense of pomp and ceremony, with banners, brass bands, flags, politicians in dark suits and open-necked shirts, and clerics in robes and turbans. Black-suited security officers clutching walkie-talkies connected to earpieces marshaled the mourners through a row of metal detectors at the entrance of the auditorium and guided them to the thousands of white plastic chairs. Sitting in a line below the stage and facing the crowd were some of Hezbollah's top leaders, including Sheikh Naim Qassem, Sheikh Nabil Qawq, and Hussein Khalil, Nasrallah's senior adviser, there to receive the flow of delegations and individuals coming to pay condolences.

Mughniyah's refrigerated coffin lay in state on the stage, draped in a yellow Hezbollah flag, four black-uniformed and bereted fighters standing at attention alongside it. Mughniyah's plump face gazed out at the throng from several large portraits mounted around the stage.

Addressing the audience from a giant video screen, Nasrallah vowed to wage "open war" against Israel in response to Mughniyah's assassination, adding that the slain military commander had left behind him "tens of thousands" of well-trained combatants "ready for martyrdom." "Hajj Imad's blood will mark the beginning of the downfall of the state of Israel," he vowed.

The commemorations continued a week later when Hezbollah marked the annual "Day of the Resistance" with another huge ceremony in the southern suburbs. The brother of Sheikh Ragheb Harb sat next to Mughniyah's father. Yasser Mussawi, the thickly bearded son of Sayyed Abbas Mussawi, was there as well. Then onto the stage strode a young man, ramrod straight, a grim expression on his clean-shaven face. He was dressed in a neat camouflage uniform and forage cap. This was Jihad Mughniyah, Imad's seventeen-year-old son. He launched into a passionate oration, lauding his late father and vowing his continued commitment to the cause.

"We are here today on the path of Imam Hussein . . . and we are going to stay on this path, the way of resistance and with Nasrallah," he thundered to a deafening chorus of "Yes to Nasrallah!" from the crowd.

His fervor, self-confidence, and rhetoric stirred much of the audience to tears. Even the tough security officers in their black suits and earphones were openly sobbing into their handkerchiefs. It was an extraordinary performance from a teenager, and I could not help but wonder whether we were looking at a future leader of the Islamic Resistance.

A Circle of Hell

Even before Lebanese security services began unmasking cells of Israeli-paid agents, the police's technical department was painstakingly connecting together another secret network of individuals, this one allegedly linked to the assassination of Rafik Hariri. The network was discovered early in the investigation. The UN investigation's initial progress report in October 2005 detailed the discovery of a network of six prepaid telephone cards. The people using these cards had been in proximity to Hariri for several weeks, suggesting they were monitoring his movements, and had also lined the route taken by the former premier's motorcade on the day of his assassination. The persons using the cell phone cards called only one another, and the last calls occurred a few minutes before the explosion that killed Hariri and twenty-one others. The technical department had teased out a network of conspirators from all the other millions of phone calls made each day in Lebanon, but their identities remained unknown.

Then, in the spring of 2009, rumors began to circulate that the Hariri investigation was heading in a dramatic new direction—toward Hezbollah. I first heard the rumor during a visit to Washington and New York in April, where the news was conveyed in whispers and sly, knowing nods and winks. The speculation exploded into the open a month later when the German news magazine *Der Spiegel* revealed that the investigation had found another cell phone network that had led them to Hezbollah. The breakthrough reportedly came when Abed al-Majid

THE "LAST WAR WITH ISRAEL"

Ghamloush, apparently a Hezbollah operative from the southern Lebanese village of Roumin, used one of the "hot" cell phones to call his girlfriend, enabling investigators to identify him. From Ghamloush, who vanished and has not been seen since, investigators were able to pinpoint who they believe is the mastermind of the operation: a man known only as Hajj Salim, a top Hezbollah intelligence officer from the Nabatiyah area.

The *Der Spiegel* story was greeted with shock, dismay, skepticism, and denials in Lebanon. The notion that Hezbollah might have been involved in the Hariri assassination was a near-taboo subject, too awful to contemplate, and one that threatened to disrupt the relative political harmony that had existed in Lebanon since the Doha accord ended the May 2008 fighting.

Four people were subsequently named in the first set of indictments connected to the Hariri murder case, which were submitted to the Lebanese authorities in June 2011. Among the four was Mustafa Badreddine, a top Hezbollah security officer who had spent the latter half of the 1980s languishing in a Kuwaiti prison; his brother-in-law, Imad Mughniyah, had allegedly abducted Westerners in Lebanon in an attempt to secure his release. According to the charge, Badreddine was responsible for planning Hariri's assassination, while another Hezbollah operative, Salim Ayyache, also named on the indictment, oversaw the operation on the ground.

The missing ingredient in this latest sensational twist was a motive. There was no obvious reason why Hezbollah would want Hariri dead. Even as Hariri's relations with the Syrian leadership and its Lebanese allies were steadily worsening during the fall of 2004, Nasrallah must have realized that Hariri posed no real threat to Syria's status in Lebanon, nor to Hezbollah itself. Hariri was a pragmatist and a compromiser whose primary interest was to secure a free hand to implement his economic and reconstruction policies without obstruction from President Lahoud. He was not on a moral crusade to oust Syria from Lebanon and to disarm Hezbollah. On the contrary, right up until the end he was signaling a desire for a rapprochement with Damascus.

More important, while Hezbollah may have had the technical and logistical expertise to kill Hariri, it did not have the political latitude to independently undertake an assassination of such strategic import. If, on the other hand, the Syrians decided that Hariri must be eliminated and persuaded the Iranians to tap Hezbollah for the job, one can only wonder what was passing through Nasrallah's mind those many late nights sitting opposite the doomed Hariri, sipping coffee and munching on fruit, chuckling at each other's jokes and discussing the woes of Lebanon and the region, knowing all the time that his guest was to die in a matter of weeks.

However, there is a view that Nasrallah in fact knew nothing of the plot until after Hariri's death. The assassination, so the theory goes, was subcontracted to a special intelligence unit inside Hezbollah that acted independently from the organization as a whole. Rumors have linked Imad Mughniyah's name to such a unit, which raises intriguing questions over the circumstances of his car bomb immolation in Damascus. Did the Syrians engineer Mughniyah's death, thereby severing in one sharp blow the link connecting the team that carried out the Hariri assassination to those who gave the order? Some Hezbollah people have privately muttered dark thoughts about Syrian culpability in Hajj Radwan's demise. Mughniyah's death even provoked a rare public disagreement between Syria and Iran when an anonymous Syrian official described as "categorically baseless" an announcement by an Iranian official two days earlier that the two countries had decided to form a joint investigation into Mughniyah's death. Damascus said that the investigation would be conducted by the "competent Syrian authorities alone," although no results have ever been released, assuming there was a probe in the first place.

Hezbollah has spent years carefully crafting its image as a champion of anti-Israel resistance, expelling the Israelis from occupied Lebanese land in 2000, defeating them six years later, and lending support to the Palestinian cause. Therefore, accusations of Hezbollah complicity in Hariri's assassination threatened to undermine Nasrallah's leadership and discredit his organization as a gang of Shia assassins who had murdered not only a prominent Sunni leader but presumably some of the other Lebanese journalists, politicians, and security officers killed over the following three years.

In 2010, as the first set of indictments drew closer to being issued, Hezbollah sought to mitigate the damage to its reputation by mounting a carefully planned and skillfully implemented public relations campaign that chiefly attempted to discredit the Special Tribunal for Lebanon, the Netherlands-based judicial body established by the UN to try suspects in the Hariri case. In tandem with the campaign, Saad Hariri, the prime minister, came under increasing pressure to endorse Hezbollah's view that the tribunal was politically tainted and to announce publicly that Lebanon would cease all cooperation with it. Since being appointed prime minister in 2009, Hariri had already undertaken the difficult step of reconciling with Bashar al-Assad, whom he continued to believe ordered the assassination of his father. But disavowing the tribunal was a demand he could not accept.

In January 2011, just as the tribunal's prosecutor was completing his first set of indictments, which media reports said would name Hezbollah operatives, Hezbollah and its allies in Hariri's coalition government resigned en masse, toppling the cabinet. Within days, Najib Mikati, a billionaire businessman from Tripoli, a close friend of Assad and a political moderate, was appointed prime minister. As Lebanon steadily slid back into Syria's political orbit, Hariri and the tattered remnants of the March 14 parliamentary coalition suddenly found themselves on the opposition benches for the first time since the tumultuous Beirut Spring six years earlier.

The Narrowing Corridor

The dilemma facing Hezbollah over the investigation into the Hariri assassination is but one component of a broader paradox that has dogged the organization since its inception in the 1980s. For all the progress Hezbollah has made in its three decades of existence, it remains beholden to two potentially conflicting dynamics: its military and ideological submission to Iran and its social and political obligations to its Shia constituency in Lebanon. The two are not necessarily mutually compatible, but Hezbollah needs both if it wishes to survive in its current form.

Iran provided the critical state support in terms of weapons, logistics, training, and funds that allowed Hezbollah to become arguably the most powerful nonstate military organization in the world. Such comprehensive and sustained backing comes with a hefty price tag: total obedience.

On the other hand, Hezbollah could not have survived for three decades in as fractious, complex, and pluralistic an environment as Lebanon if it had failed to maintain the support of the Shia community. That explains why Hezbollah has invested so much effort over the years in building and sustaining its popular base, primarily through the provision of social services to satisfy material needs but also by unifying the community through the tireless promotion of a "society of resistance."

While Hezbollah confronted Israel in south Lebanon and serviced the needs of its Shia constituents, its two commitments lived comfortably with each other. Yet a glance at Hezbollah's history since the early 1980s suggests that meeting its obligations to both Iran and the Lebanese Shias is a paradox that is growing ever more difficult to reconcile.

In the beginning, when Hezbollah burst upon the scene, Lebanon was mired in civil war, Israel was occupying the southern half of the country, and there was little or no state control. Lebanon was a broad canvas upon which the nascent organization could do much as it pleased under the stewardship of the Iranians. This was the era of suicide bombings against Western targets, kidnapping foreigners, and hijacking airliners. The idealistic Islamic revolutionaries scorned, rejected, and vowed to overturn the Lebanese political system with its sectarian checks and balances, nepotistic feudal leaders, and corrupt patronage networks. Even Syria was treated as an enemy, its officers and soldiers attacked, the decrees of Damascus ignored.

But with the end of the civil war in 1990 and the dawn of the Pax Syriana in Lebanon, the corridor began to narrow, necessitating a change of attitude and conduct, if not ideology and agenda. Syria was no longer an enemy but a newfound ally and protector. Hezbollah astutely chose to embrace parliamentary politics, despite its earlier public disavowal of the political system, winning seats in the 1992 election and performing credibly in the years ahead as an opposition to the governments of Rafik Hariri. It had no desire to join the government but was content with its parliamentary toehold, where it could generally remain aloof from the sordid bargaining and compromises inherent in Lebanese politics. Hezbollah's pragmatism and recognition of Syrian hegemony were rewarded by Damascus in the preservation of its resistance priority. These were Hezbollah's "golden years," in which it waged an increasingly successful resistance campaign against Israel and enjoyed a broad consensus across Lebanese society. Analysts spoke of Hezbollah's "Lebanonization" and pointed to the party's behavior in the 1990s as a potential model for the accommodation of Islamist groups within pluralistic societies.

Inevitably, the national consensus over Hezbollah's right to bear arms ended with the successful conclusion of the resistance campaign when Israel unilaterally withdrew in 2000. The corridor had narrowed a little further as Hezbollah faced the quandary of justifying resistance when there was nothing left to justifiably resist. However, the Shebaa Farms loophole provided the excuse, and Syria's continued domination of Lebanon provided the cover. Hezbollah also began articulating the argument of a national defense strategy incorporating its arms to counter the growing number of dissenters.

Then, in 2005, following Hariri's assassination and the subsequent disengagement of Syria from Lebanon, Hezbollah found itself hemmed in even more. It allied with onetime rival Amal, reached out to the Christian supporters of Michel Aoun, and entered the government for the first time, taking a previously unwanted step deeper into the morass of Lebanese politics to better defend its resistance priority now that the Syrian umbrella had been removed. The fate of Hezbollah's weapons became the single most divisive issue in Lebanon, splitting the country roughly in two. Hezbollah played for time, bogging down the question of its arms in a series of fruitless national dialogue sessions beginning in early 2006 in which Lebanon's top leaders discussed weighty national issues.

In July 2006, Hezbollah's weapons inadvertently plunged the country into a destructive war followed by successive political crises and deadlock that soured communal tensions even further and sparked bouts of street violence, mainly between Shias and Sunnis. Even some Shia sympathizers were beginning to rue the alienation of the community from other Lebanese sects and to privately question the cost of unlimited support for Hezbollah. Some southern Shias began to wonder aloud how many more wars they would have to endure under the rubric of Hezbollah's defense of the nation.

By early 2008, the sheen of nobility and sacrifice that had given luster to the "resistance" in the 1990s was looking badly tarnished as Hezbollah squirmed within its ever-narrowing corridor to face down the increasing hostility and impatience of its Lebanese critics. Under pressure, it began making errors in judgment. The mass sit-in in downtown Beirut in December 2006 was supposed to last for no more than two or three weeks; but when the Siniora government refused to buckle, Hezbollah found it could not back down first. The protest grew increasingly banal and apathetic, each passing month of continued stalemate simply underlining its failure.

Even those who had given Hezbollah the benefit of the doubt watched aghast as the party's fighters stormed west Beirut in May 2008 and fought furious battles with the Druze in the Chouf Mountains, smashing a long-standing promise never to turn its weapons against other Lebanese. The rage and humiliation felt by Lebanon's Sunnis further aggravated the already raw wound of intra-Muslim relations, a serious setback to Hezbollah's commitment to unity between the two great Islamic sects.

True, Hezbollah's domestic power grew substantially in the vacuum left by the withdrawal of Syrian forces in 2005 and the consequent reduction in Damascus's influence. But this was a power that was not won through persuasion, compromise, and consensus, but through the weight of its arms and the implicit threat of violence. By 2011, it is fair to say that many Lebanese fear Hezbollah. They fear its obedience to Iran, they fear its determination to keep its arms at all costs, and they fear that its unrelenting hostility toward Israel will inevitably drag Lebanon into yet another destructive conflict.

"A Thing Called Greed"

Even as Hezbollah has struggled to fend off its opponents, it has had to cope with rot from within. Despite its reputation for financial probity, Hezbollah was rocked in 2009 by a serious financial scandal when it emerged that Saleh Ezzieddine, a prominent Shia businessman with close ties to the party, had embezzled an estimated $300 million in a massive Ponzi scheme. As many as ten thousand Shia investors had handed money to Ezzieddine, who promised colossal returns of between 40 and 80 percent. Ezzieddine was trusted because of his close ties to Hezbollah. He owned the Dar al-Hadi publishing house, which handles many of Hezbollah's publications and is named after Nasrallah's son who was killed in 1997. The story broke when Hussein al-Hajj Hassan, a Hezbollah MP, sued Ezzieddine for bouncing a check worth $200,000. Nasrallah denied Hezbollah had anything to do with Ezzieddine, but the scandal left thousands of defrauded investors feeling angry and bitter and many accusing Hezbollah of "moral guilt" because they had entrusted their investments to Ezzieddine on the basis of his ties to the organization.

More significant, however, I began to hear of rumblings of discontent from some of the rank-and-file fighters questioning the investments made by Hezbollah officials. Hezbollah was supposed to be dedicated to the cause of confronting Israel; why were Hezbollah officials involved in the sordid pursuit of profit from investments, which, after all, is forbidden by Islamic law? And where did they find tens or hundreds of thousands of dollars to invest in the first place? Even Jihad Mughniyah, the son of the late Imad, who had given such a rousing speech in the wake of his father's death, was suddenly tainted with corruption rumors. Residents in Beirut's southern suburbs whispered that Jihad had invested half a million dollars in a cell phone business and had been spotted driving an expensive SUV. Where did the son of the great Hajj Radwan find $500,000 to invest?

The scandal represented "the greatest alarm bell" for Hezbollah, wrote Ibrahim al-Amine, the chairman of *Al-Akhbar* newspaper and Hezbollah confidant. He accused Hezbollah of becoming lazy and soft, surrendering its position as "the sacrificers of worldly life" for a "certain pattern of consumption . . . a thing . . . called greed."

According to Hezbollah sources, in the wake of the Ezzieddine scandal, Nasrallah assembled the top leadership, admonished those who had been paying too much attention to filling their bank accounts, and instituted new rules governing personal finances. Nasrallah is surely aware that the festering cancer of corruption poses an even greater menace to the organization in the long term than the military threat posed by Israel. Uri Lubrani, who for many years was Israel's top civilian official overseeing Lebanon, once declared that Hezbollah would be defeated only when it became infected by the PLO "virus"—in other words, lazy, bourgeois, and greedy.

Even as Nasrallah was slapping the wrists of his avaricious lieutenants, Hezbollah was running into problems with its Shia support base, particularly in the Bekaa Valley. Despite Hezbollah's strict adherence to Islamic values, it has learned over the years to grant a relatively wide latitude to the Shia community as a whole and not become too involved in issues of lifestyle or behavior in areas under its control. Hezbollah is wary of roiling social waters by trying to impose its brand of Islamic observance upon such a heterogeneous society. In the Hezbollah stronghold of the southern suburbs of Beirut, for example, it is more common to see young girls dressed in tight jeans and T-shirts with long flowing hair than wearing the full-length black chador worn by more pious women. Alcohol is banned from stores, but so long as decent behavior is maintained, Hezbollah is uninterested in stopping young Shias from enjoying themselves at restaurants, beaches, movie theaters, and fairgrounds.

That laissez-faire attitude even extends into the lawless northern Bekaa, where drug barons retain small private militias to protect their hashish fields, where stolen cars are traded and counterfeit money printed. Hezbollah disapproves of drugs on moral and religious grounds, even though it is not averse to using narcotics as a weapon of war against the West and Israel. But it turns a blind eye to the cultivation of hashish in the flat, dusty plain of the northern Bekaa Valley, unwilling to antagonize the powerful clans that profit from the illicit business.

"They Can't Afford to Mess with the Tribes"

One chilly fall morning in 2008, as the sun crested the barren ridges of the mountains marking the border with Syria to the east, a bleary-eyed bodyguard dressed in military trousers and boots with a gray blanket wrapped around his shoulders shuffled out of a ground-floor dormitory clutching a small metal pot of steaming Turkish coffee. He poured us tiny cups as we sat in the courtyard of a walled compound belonging to Noah Zeaiter, one of the Bekaa's most notorious hashish farmers. His home lay outside Knaysse village, a small cluster of stone houses and narrow, empty streets that looked like the set of a Sergio Leone western. Surrounding Noah's compound were fields of shoulder-high green cannabis plants ready for harvesting. In the distance we could hear the faint staccato thump of machine gun fire carried on the cool morning breeze from the wooded hills to the west, where a Hezbollah training session was under way.

Noah was still asleep upstairs. He and his men had spent the previous night shooting up a house with machine guns and rocket-propelled grenades in Baalbek, a few miles to the south of Knaysse. The house belonged to a building contractor who unwisely had run away with $140,000 of Noah's money. The gunfire had attracted the attention of local Hezbollah men in Baalbek, but when they saw it was Noah and his boys who were the source of the commotion, they left him alone.

The sun had climbed high into the deep blue sky by the time Noah joined us for coffee. At over six feet tall and powerfully built, with a thick ponytail dangling from beneath his baseball cap, Noah was a legendary figure in the Bekaa. There were dozens of outstanding warrants for his arrest, but the police were unwilling to tackle the ferocious bandit and his small private militia comprised of villagers and criminals on the run who had sought his protection. Unusually for the publicity-averse hashish farmers of the Bekaa, Noah did not mind meeting journalists and attempted to cultivate something of a Robin Hood image, the altruistic outlaw growing and selling hashish to feed and clothe his people in the face of government neglect.

Although the annual harvest was about to begin, Noah had more pressing matters to deal with first. It turned out that the brother of the building contractor whose home Noah had riddled with bullets and RPG rounds the night before was a local Hezbollah official. The Hezbollah man repeatedly called Noah on his cell phone during the morning as the two of them tactfully negotiated the fate of the building contractor. "He's telling me I'll get the money back, just don't kill his brother," Noah chuckled.

Noah had little liking for Hezbollah—his face wrinkled with disgust and he pretended to wipe dirt off his shoe when he referred to the party for the first time in the conversation. He boasted that he had chased some Hezbollah men out of Knaysse who had offered to rebuild the village mosque, and that he had told the villagers not to vote for Hezbollah in the municipal elections. "Hezbollah is not allowed to come onto my land," he said. "They are powerful, but they can't afford to mess with the tribes here, so they leave us alone."

Hezbollah doubtless regarded Noah and his kind with equal distaste, but local political realities deterred the organization from tangling with the Bekaa clans. However, in response to rising vehicle thefts, Hezbollah in 2008 gave a quiet nod to the Lebanese authorities to crack down on car thieves operating in the Bekaa Valley. Hezbollah apparently was spurred into green-lighting the operation when thieves were caught trying to steal the car of Jihad Mughniyah, who was hunting with friends in the valley. The tough clansmen apparently were unimpressed with Mughniyah's "Don't you know who I am?" protestations.

But the army and police soon expanded their crackdown from car theft gangs to currency counterfeiters and hashish farmers. In late 2008, the army raided Noah's compound, forcing him to flee with his men into the surrounding hills. In early 2009, Lebanese troops ambushed and shot dead a top member of the powerful Jaafar clan, sparking a reprisal attack in which four soldiers were killed.

Some of the tribes vowed to vote against Hezbollah in the parliamentary elections in June 2009 as punishment for permitting the crackdown in the first place. More broadly, the bitterness revived the old grievance that the modern Hezbollah was dominated by southerners and that the Bekaa warriors, those who had comprised the original cadres and leadership in 1983, were marginalized from decision-making levels.

In an attempt to mollify the angry clans, Nasrallah devoted a speech to the Bekaa fighters at the end of May, a week before the elections, in which he paid tribute to their sacrifices in the resistance and denounced the long-standing neglect of the region by the state.

Even in the more passive rural environment of south Lebanon, Hezbollah sometimes has to tread carefully in order not to upset local sentiment. In the buildup to the municipal elections in 2010, I heard of two Shia-populated Hezbollah-supporting villages in the south—and there may have been more—that rebelled at the imposition of a list of candidates presented by local Hezbollah men as a fait accompli. The village elders refused to accept the lists, compelling apologetic Hezbollah officials to hold a series of meetings to work out a compromise.

This perpetual delicate dance performed by Hezbollah to balance its obligations to Iran and to its Shia constituency in Lebanon was evident in the long-awaited update to its original 1985 Open Letter manifesto. The new manifesto, unveiled in December 2009, was an exercise in pragmatism and tact in which Hezbollah's unyielding worldview was tailored to conform to the prevailing political reality in Lebanon. Much of the thirty-two-page document covered familiar ground in articulating Hezbollah's resistance priority. The United States was cast as a hegemonic global bully, the origin of "every aspect of terrorism" and the "most loathsome nation in the world." Israel was a "usurping fabricated entity" that "represents an eternal threat to Lebanon."

However, the document was perhaps more notable for its omissions than for the topics included. Gone were the fiery rhetoric and zealous language of the 1985 original. Gone, too, was any reference to an Islamic state in Lebanon and to the *wilayat al-faqih,* even though it remains the indissoluble thread that binds the party to Iran. Although Hezbollah's leaders long ago publicly acknowledged that the establishment of an Islamic state in Lebanon is a practical impossibility, given the country's pluralistic identity, it remains among its founding principles. Indeed, as an Islamist, jihadist organization, it would be anathema for Hezbollah to renounce the ambition of living in a state run by Sharia law. The new document even excluded any repetition of the 1985 manifesto's demand for the destruction of Israel as an ideological imperative.

During the presentation of the new manifesto, Nasrallah admitted that it was essentially a "political document" that did not touch on "matters of creed, ideology, or thought." Hezbollah's view on the *wilayat al-faqih,* he added, "is not a political stand that can be subjected to revision."

Hezbollah had been mulling an update to the Open Letter from as long ago as 2002. Sheikh Naim Qassem told me that year that the update was necessary because "much has happened and much has changed between 1985 and now. Our basic principles remain the same because they are at the heart of our movement, but many other positions have changed due to evolving circumstances around us." He said that Hezbollah needed to be "flexible" and to adapt to the prevailing situation, but, he added, "the resistance against Israel has been our core belief and that has never changed."

"Ignite the Whole Region"

The "resistance" is Hezbollah's beating heart, its one immutable defining certainty. All the other components of the organization—the parliamentary presence, the social welfare networks that have helped entrench it within Lebanese society—exist essentially to support and sustain the resistance priority. Paradoxically, however, accommodation with and assimilation into Lebanese society bring new responsibilities and obligations that Hezbollah cannot disregard irrespective of its allegiance to the *wali al-faqih.*

Hezbollah's critics argue that the so-called "Lebanonization" process of the 1990s was nothing more than a chimera, a deceitful fig leaf masking the party's slavish obedience to the *wali al-faqih* and its role as the Lebanese detachment of the Iranian Revolutionary Guards Corps. While there is some validity to the claim, it misses the point. Hezbollah had no choice but to "Lebanonize"—tactically, if not strategically—to accommodate to the post–civil war realities in Lebanon. It could not have survived into the 1990s if it had not done so.

Hezbollah may continue to adhere to its core ideological goals, including living under an Islamic regime in Lebanon, but the party has given considerable thought to a more pragmatic system of governance in keeping with the realities of a multiconfessional Lebanon. In its 2006 memorandum of understanding with Michel Aoun and in the updated manifesto of 2009, Hezbollah states that "consensual democracy" remains the "fundamental basis for governance" in Lebanon until the sectarian system can be abolished. Emphasizing a commitment to the Lebanese "homeland" and support for consensual democracy helps make Hezbollah more palatable to other sects, particularly the Christians, allowing the party to build alliances beyond the narrow confines of its core Shia constituency and thus better protecting its resistance priority. It also represents a potential new platform for Hezbollah if ever there is a region-shaping dynamic that fundamentally alters the Iran-Israel conflict paradigm, such as the conclusion of a comprehensive Middle East peace or the collapse of the Islamic Republic, which would compel the party to reassess its agenda in order to survive.

Still, one should be under no illusions that Hezbollah's public backing of consensual democracy and outreach to other sects represents a moderation of its ideological aspirations and agenda. After all, the legions of raw recruits who attend Hezbollah's religious classes and military training programs are not there to learn about consensual democracy and coexistence.

The seeming contradiction between Hezbollah's increasingly complex Lebanoncentric attitudes and its continued obligation to the Islamic Republic in part explains why there are such differing views held by academics, journalists, policy makers, and others who closely monitor and analyze the party's actions and behavior. Some will lean more toward Hezbollah's evolving integration into the Lebanese milieu; others remain convinced that the party is little more than a ruthless tool of Iranian power projection. Hezbollah's identity today actually lies somewhere in between. Certainly, Hezbollah long ago outgrew the ragtag Iranian proxy militia status of its earliest years and is today the dominant political and military actor in Lebanon, a multi-billion-dollar corporation with commercial interests and pockets of influence spanning much of the globe. Iran has a clear understanding of Hezbollah's domestic realities and grants Nasrallah autonomy in matters related to Lebanese policy.

While Hezbollah usually plays down its logistical and military ties to Iran, it does not disguise its ideological commitment to the Islamic Republic and to the *wali al-faqih* even though such declarations provide grist to those who deride the organization as an Iranian puppet. In May 2008, Nasrallah mocked Hezbollah's opponents "who imagine they insult us when they call us the party of the *wilayat al-faqih*. . . . Absolutely not. Today I declare—and this is nothing new—that I am proud of being a member of the *wilayat al-faqih* party, the wise *faqih*, the scholar *faqih*, the courageous *faqih*, the truthful and sincere *faqih*."

Hezbollah is Iran's only true success in exporting the Islamic revolution, and its continued viability is important to Iran on several levels. It allows the Islamic Republic to project influence directly into the confrontation against the Jewish state; and Hezbollah's martial successes against Israel over the years have helped burnish Iran's standing in the Middle East and ameliorate to some extent the historic suspicions Sunni Arabs hold for the Shia Persians. Most important, however, Hezbollah's military might today serves as a component of deterrence against the possibility of an attack by the West or Israel against Tehran's nascent nuclear facilities. After all—and there should be no misunderstanding here—the billions of dollars Iran has spent on Hezbollah since 2000 was not an altruistic gift to help Lebanon defend itself against the possibility of future Israeli aggression. If Iran was so concerned about Lebanon's territorial integrity, it could have directed its philanthropy into upgrading the Lebanese army on a transparent state-to-state basis. Instead, through Hezbollah, Iran has established a bridgehead on Israel's northern border, enhancing its deterrence posture and expanding its retaliatory options in the event of an attack on the Islamic Republic.

Yet here again Hezbollah faces the quandary of balancing its obligations to Iran and meeting the needs of its Shia constituency in Lebanon. The Shias of Lebanon generally support Hezbollah as a resistance to regain Israeli-occupied Lebanese territory and to defend against the possibility of future Israeli aggression. But they would have little sympathy for Hezbollah if the organization were to plunge Lebanon into another war with Israel for the sake of protecting the nuclear ambitions of a country lying 650 miles to the east.

Hezbollah officials, in keeping with their customary ambiguity on such matters, decline to respond to specific questions on their expected course of action if Iran was attacked. Sheikh Naim Qassem once waved his hand dismissively and told me that Iran has plenty of retaliatory options without requiring Hezbollah's assistance. But he added that much depended on the circumstances of an attack on Iran—the identity of the attacking force, the scale of the assault, and whether it was limited just to the Islamic Republic. "We don't know what shape the Israeli aggression would take at that time and what areas it would include," he said. "Would it be restricted to a limited strike on Iran or a large-scale one involving several countries? I can say that if it takes place from Israel, it is liable to ignite the whole region."

Pondering Hezbollah's likely response is dependent on too many variables. But Iran must appreciate that Hezbollah is essentially a one-shot retaliatory option and therefore must be utilized wisely. If Iran is subjected to a limited attack, designed to set back the nuclear program a few months or years, that leaves the regime intact, would Iran really direct Hezbollah to respond by launching a cross-border offensive into Israel from Lebanon? Such a move would trigger the long-feared destructive war, the outcome of which is uncertain. Furthermore, there are no guarantees that Hezbollah would be in a position to rearm once more, as it did after the 2006 war, in readiness to counter a more ambitious attack on Iran.

On the other hand, if the United States and its allies launch a massive, wide-ranging, and prolonged strike that is intended to destroy the nuclear program and cripple the regime in Tehran, then Iran may consider it has little left to lose by activating Hezbollah, rallying its allies in the region, and launching the apocalyptic "last war" with Israel.

"The Story of Resistance"

To mark the tenth anniversary of Israel's withdrawal from south Lebanon, Hezbollah opened in May 2010 its old military base in the oak-tree-shrouded hillside at Mlita on the edge of what used to be the northern sector of the Israeli occupation zone. It was by far the most ambitious of Hezbollah's many exhibitions and events held to laud the resistance and promote the struggle against Israel. Thousands of visitors descended on the site in the first few weeks to gawp at symbolic displays of smashed tanks, armored vehicles, and jeeps and piles of old military helmets. One Merkava tank had its barrel twisted into a knot. Another tank had run up against a giant concrete wall inscribed with Imad Mughniyah's signature. A sandbagged walkway beneath trees led past numerous tableaux of dummy Hezbollah fighters in camouflage uniforms carrying Katyusha rockets or creeping through the undergrowth with rifles. One could even visit the alcove in the rocks where Sayyed Abbas Mussawi once prayed. His prayer mat, rifle, and copy of the Koran rested alongside a photograph of the slain Hezbollah leader. A recording of his gravelly voice reciting prayers wafted through the trees.

"Those of us who used to be based here in the 1980s when Sayyed Abbas was here begin to weep when they hear his voice in this place," said Abu Hadi, the Hezbollah fighter who first met Mussawi at Mlita so many years earlier (as recounted in chapter 2) and today gives guided tours of the site.

Perhaps the highlight of the display is the tunnel-and-bunker system built in the 1980s, the prototype of those I explored in the border district after the 2006 war. A glassed-in "operations room" deep inside the bunker had military maps pinned to a wall and an old computer on the desk. Recordings of fighters communicating by radio were played over loudspeakers.

A small landscaped garden on top of the hill was lined with tools of Hezbollah's trade: antitank missiles, including an AT-14 Kornet that had so bedeviled Israeli armor in 2006, and a variety of recoilless rifles and antiaircraft cannons, including the 57 mm gun that Hezbollah once fired across the border to alarm the residents of Galilee in response to the daily Israeli overflights in Lebanese airspace. From Mlita, one could gaze across a steep valley to the old Sojod compound just visible on the opposite side, once the most heavily hit outpost in the occupation zone.

The Mlita project was undeniably slick—the organizers even hired a marketing consultant to design a logo and "corporate identity" for the facility.

"As the main center of the resistance from the 1980s, this place talks to the souls of the visitors," said Sheikh Ali Daher, the head of Hezbollah's publicity department. "The whole project is to tell the story of resistance to the new generation." He said that there were plans to expand the facility with a cable car and to open additional theme parks in the south. But Daher also cheerfully admitted that the Israelis were certain to bomb Mlita into dust in the next war.

The landscape of the south has changed little in the ten years since those tumultuous few days in May 2000 when the SLA collapsed and the last Israeli troops dashed for the border with Hezbollah fighters and Lebanese civilians at their heels. The hardy little hill villages remain the same, largely bereft of the young, who migrate to Beirut or travel overseas to find work, leaving the dusty streets to the ruminations of the elderly and the watchful eyes of the resistance. Most of those who remain follow the same ineluctable agrarian cycle as their ancestors, tilling the stony chocolate-colored soil for tobacco and wheat and picking citrus fruit in the coastal orchards and olives and apples on the cooler mountain slopes farther east.

The mementos of occupation fade a little more with each passing year. The Israeli and SLA outposts, those menacing volcano cones silhouetted on the ridges and hills of the old front line, have gradually vanished, the overgrown earthen ramparts subsiding beneath eleven years of winter rains or leveled by the bulldozers of construction workers. One still remains relatively intact—the old SLA compound near the village of Talloussa, where I was once briefly detained by militants after stumbling across their antiaircraft gun hidden inside. The position was bombed by Israeli jets in 2006, leaving a gaping crater on one side and a sagging roof of reinforced concrete. It is still possible to walk up the cramped staircases and corridors that lead to the cinder-block-lined parapets and machine gun posts with their wide horizontal window slits and views over the old Wadi Salouqi front line. Here SLA militiamen once shivered in winter and baked in summer, doubtless mulling their ultimate fate while sheltering from Hezbollah's near-daily mortar bombardments. What ghosts must still linger in these darkened corridors and weed-ridden ramparts?

What ghosts, too, flit through the thickly wooded slopes of Wadi Salouqi, the scene of so many bloody clashes between Hezbollah fighters and Israeli troops? Once inaccessible, it is reachable today by a gleaming black asphalt road that winds along the valley floor, and if one knows where to look deep into the shadowed foliage on either side, there are fleeting glimpses to be obtained of ruined and abandoned Hezbollah facilities—the entrance to a bunker here, smashed cinder block huts and sandbagged steps there.

There are ghosts in the unsmiling faces of bygone martyrs whose portraits adorn electricity pylons and telephone poles, an ever-present reminder of past sacrifices and an inspiration for new generations of mujahideen. The sun-faded and rust-speckled tin-panel portraits of Mohammed Saad, with his scraggly beard and sharp eyes, still hang in the villages where this early resistance leader once lived, fought, and died.

There are ghosts here for me, too, having spent a third of my life chasing Hezbollah and watching the occupations, battles, massacres, victories, and defeats of war in the valleys and hills of the south.

I see them in the golden beams of sunlight that pierce the brooding purple rain clouds of winter and spotlight tracts of gray stony hillside beneath Beaufort Castle. I see them in the hot, dry wind that blows up from Galilee in the heavy heat of August and buffets the Shebaa Farms mountains rising above the cool, limpid waters of the Wazzani springs. I see them in the poppies, cornflowers, and buttercups of spring in the meadows of the Litani River below Marjayoun, like some vast Impressionist canvas suffused with the scent of wild thyme and sage.

There are ghosts in the forest of umbrella pines and the forbidding mountains overlooking Jezzine where I once spent an evening with Johnny, the whisky-swigging SLA militiaman, his old wartime comrade Nimr, and Manny, the terrified teenager.

There are ghosts in Tyre at what was once UNIFIL's logistics base— and is today a parking lot—where I would sip morning coffee and chat with my friend Hassan Siklawi and his colleagues Rula and Joumana in their portacabin office before heading for a tour of "the area," the volatile frontline district.

There are ghosts where the border road takes a sharp left turn near the village of Meiss al-Jabal, where Abed Taqqoush was murdered by an Israeli tank gunner. The rusted skeleton of his burned-out car was towed away for scrap many years ago, and for a long time the only physical reminder of what happened there was the melted patch of asphalt where Abed's car was engulfed in flames. Even that ugly cicatrix eventually disappeared beneath a fresh layer of asphalt, but the memory lingers and dampens my mood every time I pass by.

I see ghosts, too, in the faces of the southern Lebanese, whose stoicism and unbreakable sense of humor helped sustain them through decades of sacrifice, violence, and bloodshed. Scarcely a village along the old front line or in the border district does not hold some memory for me. Mansouri, to give one of many examples, where in August 1999 I met with the family of Mahmoud Zabad a few hours after an Israeli tank had fired antipersonnel rounds filled with thousands of steel darts into his home, knocking holes in a wall and nearly killing his children. As we sat chatting over tiny cups of coffee, Mahmoud reduced his family to hysterical laughter with a graphic account of how his seven-year-old son, Hassan, had urgently needed to visit the bathroom even as the tank shells were exploding outside. Dozens of the vicious steel darts were still embedded in his ruined kitchen wall as Mahmoud clutched his behind and staggered in front of his family in imitation of the incontinent Hassan, to hoots of laughter that even a flare-trailing Israeli jet swooping over the village failed to diminish.

There are ghosts—too many ghosts—in Qana, once famous in Lebanon for being the place where the Lebanese believe Christ performed the wedding miracle of turning water into wine, but today synonymous with bloody massacre.

It was this village that Mahmoud Ahmadinejad, the diminutive, narrow-eyed Iranian president who seems to take puckish delight in pricking Western sensibilities, chose to visit in October 2010 on his inaugural trip to Lebanon as president. He had held a triumphal rally in Beirut the evening before, attended by the Hezbollah faithful. Nasrallah, who since 2006 has delivered nearly all his speeches by video screen for security reasons, disappointed his supporters by not standing in person beside Ahmadinejad at the Beirut rally. But the Hezbollah leader doubtless anticipated that his rare appearance in the flesh would completely overshadow the presence of his Iranian guest.

There was another huge crowd awaiting Ahmadinejad in Bint Jbeil the next day. Hezbollah security men clutching the ubiquitous walkie-talkies marshaled the throng along the streets to the sports stadium, which was bedecked with Lebanese and Iranian flags. A giant banner reading "Welcome" in Arabic and Farsi hung by the stage. The sun had dropped below the stadium walls by the time Ahmadinejad arrived on the floodlit stage. To one side of him stood Sheikh Nabil Qawq, Hezbollah's tall southern commander, who was dressed in his customary brown cloak and white turban. The crowd roared their greeting and Ahmadinejad smiled, waved his hand, and gave V for Victory signs. He stood less than two miles from the border with archenemy Israel, a country he has insisted must be destroyed—an ambition that Hezbollah's faithful hope to fulfill.

Thousands of balloons in red, white, and green—by happy coincidence, the colors of both the Iranian and the Lebanese flags—were released in the town center. The cloud of balloons drifted southward on

the gentle evening breeze, toward the Israeli border. Some Israeli activists also released balloons of their own, inscribed with anti-Iranian messages; the wind, however, seemed to be in Lebanon's favor, blowing those
messages back at their senders.

In his address, Ahmadinejad praised the resolve of the southern Lebanese and heaped extravagantly phrased plaudits on the Islamic Resistance. "You are a solid mountain," he said, speaking in Farsi, his words
translated into Arabic for the audience. "We are proud of you and will
remain forever by your side. . . . You have proved that your jihad is
stronger than armadas and tanks."

After ten minutes I had to leave. My story was due and I had yet to
write and file it. The audience, too, seemed to have heard enough. They
were streaming out of the stadium and hurrying home even as Ahmadinejad continued to deliver praise for their steadfastness. The good folk
of Bint Jbeil had done their duty, waved a flag, and cheered the visiting
head of state, and now it was time to go home.

It was dark by the time Ahmadinejad's entourage raced out of Bint
Jbeil toward his next engagement in Qana, sirens blaring and police on
motorcycles furiously waving traffic aside. Dergham drove in hot pursuit as I wrote my story in the passenger seat, the laptop computer
bouncing on my knees. By the time we arrived at Qana, the village had
been sealed off and there was nowhere close enough to the center to
park. Lights flashed and police and soldiers directed the clogged traffic,
yelling at the impatient and laughing with passing friends. I could not
obtain an Internet connection, so for the first time in years I had to dictate my story by phone to the *Times* copytaker, just as I had done a decade earlier before reliable Internet service arrived in Lebanon.
Ahmadinejad's voice boomed over loudspeakers from the center of the
village as I read my story into the phone.

By the time I had finished, Ahmadinejad was gone. We drove into
Qana and parked beside the newly constructed mausoleum where the
victims of the April 1996 massacre lie. Qana was strangely subdued now
that the Ahmadinejad cavalcade had passed through. A few locals loi-
tered on the street, others stacked chairs where the ceremony had been
held. I stepped into the hushed hall of the mausoleum. Flowers had been

placed on the tombs in the cordoned-off center of the hall. Red roses lay on the ground, thrown by Ahmadinejad and his entourage minutes before when they had entered to say a prayer for the dead. The only sound breaking the quiet was the gentle helicopter-like thwack of the ceiling fans. I thought of Saadallah Balhas, who had joined his deceased family here upon his death two years earlier, of Fatmeh Balhas, who had seen her children blown to pieces in front of her eyes, of Ibrahim Taqi, whose near-decapitated corpse is forever seared into my memory.

"From Karbala to Qana, the blood meets," read a banner strung along one wall. Another banner featured the kindly face of Imam Musa Sadr, the gentle cleric whose tireless efforts half a century earlier had helped lift the Shias of Lebanon from their communal torpor.

A man with jangling keys stepped into the hall and closed one of two heavy steel doors, bolting it in place.

"You're closing?" I asked.

"Yes," he replied with a smile. "We're closing."

I walked out into the cool evening air as the caretaker flicked off the lights, swung shut the second door, and locked it carefully behind him.

And inside, darkness fell over the cold silent tombs.

Notes

CHAPTER ONE: The "Sleeping Giant"

1. *Mitwali* is a term of obscure origin formerly used to describe the Shia. Today, it has derogatory overtones.
2. Constantin-François Volney, *Travels Through Egypt and Syria* (New York: John Tiobout, 1978), originally published in 1787.
3. Baron de Tott, *The Memoirs of Baron de Tott* (London: G. G. J. and J. Robinson, 1785).
4. Volney, *Travels Through Egypt and Syria.*
5. Amnon Cohen, *Palestine in the 18th Century: Patterns of Government and Administration* (Jerusalem: Magnes Press, Hebrew University, 1973).
6. De Tott, *The Memoirs of Baron de Tott.*
7. David Urquhart, *The Lebanon (Mount Souria): A History and a Diary* (London: Thomas Cautley Newby, 1860).
8. Cunningham Geikie, *The Holy Land and the Bible: A Book of Scripture Illustrations Gathered in Palestine* (London: Cassell and Company, Limited, 1887).
9. "Sayyed" is a term used to denote direct descendants of the Prophet Mohammed. Clerical sayyeds are distinguished by their black turbans, compared to the white turbans worn by nondescendants of Mohammed.
10. *Nida al-Watan,* August 31, 1993, in *Voice of Hezbollah: The Statements of Sayyed Hassan Nasrallah,* edited by Nicholas Noe (London: Verso, 2007).
11. Ibid.
12. *New York Times,* February 25, 1977.
13. Yezid Sayigh, "Palestinian Military Performance in the 1982 War," *Journal of Palestine Studies,* vol. XII, no. 4, Summer 1983.
14. Ibid.
15. Avi Shlaim, *The Iron Wall: Israel and the Arab World* (London: Penguin, 2001).

CHAPTER TWO: The "Shia Genie"

1. Author interview with Sheikh Sobhi Tufayli, September 10, 2003.
2. John Yemma, "Can the UN peace-keeping forces in southern Lebanon keep the peace?" *Christian Science Monitor,* June 9, 1982.
3. Sheikh Naim Qassem, *Hezbollah: The Story from Within* (London: Saqi Books, 2005).
4. *Christian Science Monitor,* August 13, 1982.
5. *Nass al-risala al-maftuha allati wajjaha hizb allah ila al-mustadafin fi lubnan wa al-alam* (Open Letter Addressed by Hezbollah to the Downtrodden in Lebanon and the World), February 16, 1985. In *Amal and the Shia,* Augustus Richard Norton, ed. (Austin: University of Texas Press, 1987).
6. Avner Yaniv, *Dilemma of Security Politics, Strategy, and the Israeli Experience in Lebanon* (New York: Oxford University Press, 1987).
7. Sevag Kechichian, *The Many Faces of Violence and the Social Foundations of Suicide Bombings, Lebanon 1981–2000* (February 2007). Unpublished paper.
8. *As-Safir,* April 30, 1996, in Noe, *Voice of Hezbollah,* p. 157.
9. *New York Times,* February 20, 1985.
10. *Middle East International,* March 8, 1985.
11. S/17093, "Report of the Secretary General on the United Nations Interim Force in Lebanon," April 11, 1985 & S/17557, "Report of the Secretary General on the United Nations Interim Force in Lebanon," October 10, 1985.
12. Author interviews with residents of Marakeh, March 7, 2010.
13. *New York Times,* February 18, 1985.
14. Author interviews with former CIA field officers and analysts, 2001–2010.
15. *South Lebanon, Facts & Figures, 1948–1986* (Beirut: Lebanese Ministry of Information, 1986).
16. The Sannine listening post was destroyed in 1990 during fighting between rival Christian factions.
17. Robert Baer, *See No Evil: The True Story of a Ground Soldier in the CIA's War on Terrorism* (New York: Crown, 2002).
18. *Nida al-Watan,* August 31, 1993, in Noe, *Voice of Hezbollah,* p. 139.
19. Information based on multiple author interviews and conversations with Hezbollah fighters.
20. *Al-Khaleej,* March 11, 1986, translated in Noe, *Voice of Hezbollah,* p. 29.
21. *An-Nahar,* June 8, 2007.
22. *As-Safir,* August 24, 2009.
23. *Al-Wahda al-Islamiya,* February 3, 1989, in Noe, *Voice of Hezbollah,* p. 39.

CHAPTER THREE: The "Gate of the Mujahideen"

1. The Mercedes was later transported to Mussawi's home village of Nabi Sheet in the Bekaa Valley, where it remains on public view today on a

tractor-trailer outside the mausoleum where the slain Hezbollah leader is buried.

2. *As-Safir,* February 27, 1992, in Noe, *Voice of Hezbollah,* p. 61.

3. Ibid., p. 62.

4. *Al-Watan al-Arabi,* September 11, 1992, in Noe, *Voice of Hezbollah,* p. 88.

5. Qassem, *Hezbollah: The Story from Within,* p. 35.

6. Agence France Presse, June 11, 1994.

7. *Al-Nahar al-arabi wal-duwali* (newspaper), July 21, 1986.

8. *Tishreen,* June 21, 1999, Translated in Noe, *Voice of Hezbollah,* p. 201.

9. Free Arab Voice, July 3, 2000.

10. "Hizballah: 13 Principles of Warfare," *Jerusalem Report,* March 21, 1996.

11. *Foreign Report,* December 5, 1991; *Jane's Intelligence Review,* February 1, 1995.

12. Ron Schleifer, "Psychological Operations: A New Variation on an Age-Old Art: Hezbollah Versus Israel," *Studies in Conflict & Terrorism* 29: 1–19, 2006.

13. Ibid.

14. "When David Became Goliath," Major Christopher E. Whitting, U.S. Army Command and General Staff College, Fort Leavenworth, Kansas, 2001.

15. *The Independent,* May 18, 1995.

CHAPTER FOUR: The Scent of Orange Blossom in the Spring

1. Based on several author interviews with Irish UNIFIL officers and other UNIFIL personnel, 1999–2001.

2. "Baseless US and Israeli Calls for 'Anti-Terrorism' War Against Hezbollah and Iran," op-ed submitted by Neil Sammonds to *Al-Quds al-Arabi* newspaper, 2002.

3. "Israel Defends Record on 'Grapes of Wrath,' " *Jane's Defence Weekly,* June 5, 1996.

4. *As-Safir,* April 30, 1996, in Noe, *Voice of Hezbollah.*

5. Author interview, April 3, 1997.

6. Report dated May 1, 1996, of the Secretary General's Military Adviser concerning the shelling of the United Nations compound at Qana on April 18, 1996.

7. "Boutros-Ghali bites back," *The Nation,* June 14, 1999.

8. *Middle East Mirror,* June 11, 1996.

9. *Yedioth Ahronoth,* February 5, 1997.

CHAPTER FIVE: The "Deluxe Laboratory Without Settlers"

1. *Al-Ahad* weekly, September 6, 1997.

2. Ibid.

3. Nasrallah interview on Future Television, September 16, 1998.

4. The Turkish government subsequently opted for the Leopard tank of

Germany, although Israel's Military Industries won a contract to upgrade Turkey's fleet of M-60 tanks with the Merkava's 120 mm barrel.

5. Gal Luft, "Israel's Security Zone in Lebanon—a Tragedy?" *Middle East Quarterly,* September 2000.

6. Nasrallah interview on Future Television, September 16, 1998.

7. According to casualty lists compiled by the author at the time.

8. *Maariv,* November 25, 1998.

9. *Haaretz,* March 6, 1999.

10. Ibid.

11. Ibid.

12. *Yedioth Ahronoth,* March 2, 1999.

CHAPTER SIX: "The Lebanese Valley of the Dead"

1. *Jerusalem Post,* April 16, 2000.

2. See Nicholas Blanford, *Killing Mr. Lebanon: The Assassination of Rafik Hariri and Its Impact on the Middle East* (London: I. B. Tauris, 2006), and Dennis Ross, *The Missing Peace* (New York: Farrar, Straus and Giroux, 2004).

3. See the interview with Uri Saguy, a former head of IDF military intelligence and a member of Barak's negotiating team with the Syrians, in *Yedioth Friday Political Supplement,* June 11, 2010. Saguy said that the peace deal with the Syrians would have occurred if "we had done what we promised ourselves, the Americans, and the Syrians." He blamed Barak for reneging on his earlier promise to discuss water and borders with the Syrians at Shepherdstown.

4. Bill Clinton, *My Life* (New York: Knopf, 2004).

5. *Al-Hayat,* March 2, 2000.

6. *Al-Quds al-Arabi,* March 3, 2000.

CHAPTER SEVEN: The "Spider's Web"

1. *The Daily Star,* June 3, 2000.

2. Israeli army statement, June 16, 2000.

3. *Haaretz,* May 21, 2010.

4. Al-Manar, October 7, 2000.

5. Told to the author by a UN source, April 29, 2001.

6. The story was subsequently confirmed to me by several sources in south Lebanon, including a confederate of Ramzi Nohra and former Lebanese military intelligence agents who had intimate knowledge of the background to the kidnapping.

7. Israeli Channel 2 television, October 16, 2005.

CHAPTER EIGHT: "The Fence Around the Homeland"

1. Al-Manar, September 4, 2004.

2. The seven outposts, from south to north, are at Moghr Shebaa, Fashkoul,

Maazrat Zebdine, Ramta, Jabal Summaqa, Roweisat Allam, and "Radar." Although Radar lay outside the geographical area of the Shebaa Farms, it was included in Hezbollah's list of targeted outposts.

3. *Foreign Report,* April 18, 2002.
4. *Haaretz,* April 12, 2002.
5. *Maariv,* October 24, 2002.
6. Ibid.
7. Radio France International, October 14, 2002.
8. Interview with Hezbollah spokesman Hassan Ezzieddine on LBC International, January 19, 2004.
9. *Hatzofe,* July 22, 2004.

CHAPTER NINE: Spoonfuls of Cement

1. *Jane's Defence Weekly,* July 13, 2006.
2. *Yedioth Ahronoth,* November 12, 2009.
3. *Al-Rai al-Aam,* November 16, 2001.
4. Joseph Felter and Brian Fishman, redacted interrogation report 013, Appendix A, "Iranian Strategy in Iraq: Policy and 'Other Means,'" Combating Terrorism Center, October 13, 2008.
5. *Yedioth Ahronoth,* September 26, 2001.
6. *Zaim* (plural *zuama*) is an Arabic term for a feudal leader or chieftain.
7. *The Daily Star,* March 5, 2004.
8. *Jerusalem Post,* May 30, 2006.

CHAPTER TEN: "Birth Pangs"

1. *Al-Hayat,* May 17, 2007.
2. Matt Matthews, We Were Caught Unprepared: The 2006 Hezbollah-Israeli War, The Long War Series Occasional Papers 26, 2008.
3. Ibid.
4. Ibid.
5. Alistair Crooke and Mark Perry, "How Hezbollah Defeated Israel, Part Two: Winning the Ground War," *Asia Times,* October 13, 2006.
6. "Mine Action Structure in the Republic of Lebanon," Lebanon Mine Action Center (lebmac.org/files/publications/Mine_Action_in_the_Republic_of_Lebanon.pdf).
7. Amos Harel and Avi Issacharoff, *34 days: Israel, Hezbollah and the War in Lebanon* (New York and Hampshire: Palgrave Macmillan, 2008).
8. Ibid.
9. Stephen Biddle and Jeffrey A. Friedman, "The 2006 Lebanon Campaign and the Future of Warfare: Implications for Army and Defense Policy," Strategic Studies Institute, September 2008.

Chapter Eleven: The "Last War with Israel"

1. *DEBKAfile,* July 12, 2007.
2. See the diplomatic cable from the U.S. embassy in Beirut titled 08BEIRUT523 in which Marwan Hamadeh, then minister of telecommunications, discusses with U.S. diplomats Hezbollah's fiber optic network. The cable was among the 250,000 diplomatic dispatches that WikiLeaks began re-leasing in late 2010.
3. *Haaretz,* July 2, 2010.
4. *Jerusalem Post,* July 5, 2010.
5. Gabi Siboni, "Disproportionate Force: Israel's Concept of Response in Light of the Second Lebanon War," *INSS Insight,* No. 74, October 2, 2008.
6. *Jerusalem Post,* October 29, 2007.
7. *The National,* February 23, 2009.

Acknowledgments

It would not have been possible to write *Warriors of God* without the kindness and good-humored hospitality of the people I have encountered during seventeen years of reporting the travails of south Lebanon. Despite the hardships of occupation and war and the many tragedies suffered by families that inevitably draw correspondents, vulturelike, to their door, I was always greeted with warmth and understanding and plied with the inevitable glasses of tea, cups of coffee, and often plates of food. To all of them I am deeply grateful.

I must thank my former colleagues at *The Daily Star,* the newspaper where I worked between 1996 and 2002, both my editors for granting me wide latitude to cover the Israeli occupation of south Lebanon and my fellow correspondents, some of whom patiently acted as translators on my trips to the south.

When I began planning this book, I assumed that I would need the formal assistance of Hezbollah in arranging interviews or helping to fill gaps in my research. But as the writing process got under way, I quickly realized that my problem was not obtaining more information, but choosing what to exclude from an ever-expanding manuscript. Consequently, I neither asked for, nor was given, formal help from Hezbollah in writing this book. However, I would like to thank Hezbollah's media department, which has arranged almost all of my newspaper interviews with officials and fighters since 1994, which I drew upon for *Warriors of God.* In particular I would like to thank Ibrahim Moussawi, Hussein

Rahhal, Hassan Ezzedine, Haidar Diqmaq, Wafa Hoteit, and Hussein Naboulsi.

Very special thanks also goes to all those Hezbollah combatants who gave unauthorized interviews for this book.

I would like to express my gratitude to all who agreed to be interviewed for *Warriors of God,* Lebanese and Israeli alike. In particular I would like to thank the following for their assistance, advice, and insights: Noam Ben-Zvi, Christopher Clark, Andrew Exum (who had the misfortune of reading most of the considerably longer original manuscript), Timur Goksel, Amos Harel, Ahmad Husseini, Hassan Husseini, Avi Issacharoff, Clive Jones, Colin King, Meris Lutz, Mahmoud Manaa, Hassan Saad, Hassan Siklawi, James Spencer, and Boutros Wanna. Most of all I would like to thank Dergham Dergham, fixer, friend, and briefly cell mate.

Special thanks to Gail Ross and her team, who took an idea that had been germinating in my mind for almost a decade and helped me shape it into a coherent product. Also grateful thanks to Random House and my editor, Jonathan Jao, for his patience and guidance; to his assistant Samuel Nicholson; and to Loren Noveck, the production editor.

Finally, I would like to thank my family, Reem, Yasmine, and Alexander, for their tolerance and understanding while I wrote this book.

Index

About the Type

This book was set in Minion, a 1990 Adobe Originals typeface by Robert Slimbach. Minion is inspired by classical, old-style typefaces of the late Renaissance, a period of elegant, beautiful, and highly readable type designs. Created primarily for text setting, Minion combines the aesthetic and functional qualities that make text type highly readable with the versatility of digital technology.